The Design and Analysis of Spatial Data Structures

The Design and Analysis of Spatial Data Structures

Hanan Samet

UNIVERSITY OF MARYLAND

ADDISON - WESLEY PUBLISHING COMPANY, INC.
Reading, Massachusetts • Menlo Park, California • New York
Don Mills, Ontario • Wokingham, England • Amsterdam
Bonn • Sydney • Singapore • Tokyo • Madrid • San Juan

This book is in the Addison-Wesley Series in Computer Science
Michael A. Harrison: Consulting Editor

Many of the designations used by manufacturers and sellers to distinguish their products are claimed as trademarks. Where those designations appear in this book, and Addison-Wesley was aware of a trademark claim, the designations have been printed in initial caps or all caps.

The programs and applications presented in this book have been included for their instructional value. They have been tested with care, but are not guaranteed for any particular purpose. The publisher does not offer any warranties or representations, nor does it accept any liabilities with respect to the programs or applications.

Library of Congress Cataloging-in-Publication Data

Samet, Hanan.
    The Design and analysis of spatial data structures/by Hanan Samet.
      p.   cm.
    Bibliography: p.
    Includes index.
    ISBN 0-201-50255-0
    1. Data structures (Computer science)   2. Computer graphics.
I. Title.
QA76.9.D35S26   1989   89-30382
005.7'3 — dc19   CIP

Reprinted with corrections April, 1990

Credits:
Thor Bestul created the cover art.
    Gyuri Fekete generated Figure 1.16; Daniel DeMenthon, Figures 1.20, 1.21, and 1.23; Jiang-Hsing Chu, Figures 2.48 and 2.52; and Walid Aref, Figures 4.38 through 4.40.
    Figures 1.1, 4.9, and 4.10 are from H. Samet and R. E. Webber, On encoding boundaries with quadtrees, *IEEE Transactions on Pattern Analysis and Machine Intelligence 6*, 3 (May 1984), 365–369. © 1984 IEEE. Reprinted by permission of IEEE.
    Figures 1.2, 1.3, 1.5 through 1.10, 1.12, 1.14, 1.25, 1.26, 2.3, 2.4, 2.18, 2.20, 2.30, 2.32, 2.53, 2.54, 2.57, 2.58, 3.20, 3.21, 4.1 through 4.5, 4.7, 4.8, 4.11, and 5.2 are from H. Samet, The quadtree and related hierarchical data structures, *ACM Computing Surveys 16*, 2 (June 1984), 187–260. Reprinted by permission of ACM.
    Figures 1.4 and 5.6 are from H. Samet and R. E. Webber, Hierarchical data structures and algorithms for computer graphics. Part I. Fundamentals, *IEEE Computer Graphics and Applications 8*, 3 (May 1988), 48–68. © 1988 IEEE. Reprinted by permission of IEEE.
    Figure 1.30 is from M. Li, W. I. Grosky, and R. Jain, Normalized quadtrees with respect to translations, *Computer Graphics and Image Processing 20*, 1 (September 1982), 72–81. Reprinted by permission of Academic Press.
    Figures 2.7 and 2.10 through 2.15 are from H. Samet, Deletion in two-dimensional quad trees, *Communications of the ACM 23*, 12 (December 1980), 703–710. Reprinted by permission of ACM.
    Figures 2.26 and 2.27 are from D. T. Lee and C. K. Wong, Worst-case analysis for region and partial region searches in multidimensional binary search trees and quad trees, *Acta Informatica 9*, 1 (1977), 23–29. Reprinted by permission of Springer-Verlag.
Continued on p. 493

To my parents, Julius and Lotte

PREFACE

Spatial data consist of points, lines, rectangles, regions, surfaces, and volumes. The representation of such data is becoming increasingly important in applications in computer graphics, computer vision, database management systems, computer-aided design, solid modeling, robotics, geographic information systems (GIS), image processing, computational geometry, pattern recognition, and other areas. Once an application has been specified, it is common for the spatial data types to be more precise. For example, consider a geographic information system (GIS). In such a case, line data are differentiated on the basis of whether the lines are isolated (e.g., earthquake faults), elements of tree-like structures (e.g., rivers and their tributaries), or elements of networks (e.g., rail and highway systems). Similarly region data are often in the form of polygons that are isolated (e.g., lakes), adjacent (e.g., nations), or nested (e.g., contours). Clearly the variations are large.

Many of the data structures currently used to represent spatial data are hierarchical. They are based on the principle of recursive decomposition (similar to *divide and conquer* methods [Aho74]). One such data structure is the quadtree (octree in three dimensions). As we shall see, the term *quadtree* has taken on a generic meaning. In this book, it is my goal to show how a number of hierarchical data structures used in different domains are related to each other and to quadtrees. My presentation concentrates on these different representations and illustrates how a number of basic operations that use them are performed.

Hierarchical data structures are useful because of their ability to focus on the interesting subsets of the data. This focusing results in an efficient representation and in improved execution times. Thus they are particularly convenient for performing set operations. Many of the operations described can often be performed as efficiently, or more so, with other data structures. Nevertheless hierarchical data structures are attractive because of their conceptual clarity and ease of implementation. In addition, the use of some of them provides a spatial index. This is very useful in applications involving spatial databases.

As an example of the type of problems to which the techniques described in this book are applicable, consider a cartographic database consisting of a number of maps and some typical queries. The database contains a contour map, say at 50-foot elevation intervals, and a land use map classifying areas according to crop growth. Our goal is to determine all regions between 400- and 600-foot elevation levels where wheat is grown. This will require an intersection operation on the two maps. Such an analysis could be rather costly, depending on the way the maps are represented. For example, since areas where corn is grown are of no interest, we wish to spend a minimal amount of effort searching such regions. Yet traditional region representations such as the boundary code [Free74] are very local in application, making it difficult to avoid examining a corn-growing area that meets the desired elevation criterion. In contrast, hierarchical representations such as the region quadtree are more global in nature and enable the elimination of larger areas from consideration.

Another query might be to determine whether two roads intersect within a given area. We could check them point by point; however, a more efficient method of analysis would be to represent them by a hierarchical sequence of enclosing rectangles and to discover whether in fact the rectangles do overlap. If they do not, the search is terminated. If an intersection is possible, more work may have to be done, depending on which method of representation is used.

A similar query can be constructed for point data — for example, to determine all cities within 50 miles of St. Louis that have a population in excess of 20,000. Again we could check each city individually. However, using a representation that decomposes the United States into square areas having sides of length 100 miles would mean that at most four squares need to be examined. Thus California and its adjacent states can be safely ignored.

Finally, suppose we wish to integrate our queries over a database containing many different types of data (e.g., points, lines, areas). A typical query might be, "Find all cities with a population in excess of 5,000 people in wheat-growing regions within 20 miles of the Mississippi River." In this book we will present a number of different ways of representing data so that such queries and other operations can be efficiently processed.

This book is organized as follows. There is one chapter for each spatial data type, in which I present a number of different data structures. The aim is to gain the ability to evaluate them and to determine their applicability. Two problems are treated in great detail: the rectangle intersection problem, discussed in the context of the representation of collections of small rectangles (Chapter 3), and the point location problem, discussed in the context of the representation of curvilinear data (Chapter 4). A comprehensive treatment of the use of quadtrees and octrees in other applications in computer graphics, image processing, and geographic information systems (GIS) can be found in [Same90b].

Chapter 1 gives a general introduction to the principle of recursive decomposition with a concentration on two-dimensional regions. Key properties, as well as a historical overview, are presented.

Chapter 2 discusses hierarchical representations of multidimensional point data. These data structures are particularly useful in applications in database management systems because they are designed to facilitate responses to search queries.

Chapter 3 examines the hierarchical representation of collections of small rectangles. Such data arise in applications in computational geometry, very large-scale integrations (VLSI), cartography, and database management. Examples from these fields (e.g., the rectangle intersection problem) are used to illustrate their differences. Many of the representations are closely related to those used for point data. This chapter is an expansion of [Same88a].

Chapter 4 treats the hierarchical representation of curvilinear data. The primary focus is on the representation of polygonal maps. The goal is to be able to solve the point location problem. Quadtree-like solutions are compared with those from computational geometry such as the K-structure [Kirk83] and the layered dag [Edel86a].

Chapter 5 looks at the representation of three-dimensional region data. In this case, a number of octree variants are examined, as well as constructive solid geometry (CSG) and the boundary model (BRep). Algorithms are discussed for converting between some of these representations. The representation of surfaces (i.e., 2.5-dimensional data) is also briefly discussed in this chapter.

There are a number of topics for which justice requires a considerably more detailed treatment. However, due to space limitations, I have omitted a detailed discussion of them and instead refer interested readers to the appropriate literature. For example, surface representations are discussed briefly with three-dimensional data in Chapter 5 (also see Chapter 7 of [Same90b]). The notion of a pyramid is presented only at a cursory level in Chapter 1 so that it can be contrasted with the quadtree. In particular, the pyramid is a multiresolution representation, whereas the quadtree is a variable resolution representation. Readers are referred to Tanimoto and Klinger [Tani80] and the collection of papers edited by Rosenfeld [Rose83a] for a more comprehensive exposition on pyramids.

Results from computational geometry, although related to many of the topics covered in this book, are discussed only in the context of representations for collections of small rectangles (Chapter 3) and curvilinear data (Chapter 4). For more details on early work involving some of these and related topics, interested readers should consult the surveys by Bentley and Friedman [Bent79b], Overmars [Over88a], Edelsbrunner [Edel84], Nagy and Wagle [Nagy79], Peuquet [Peuq84], Requicha [Requ80], Srihari [Srih81], Samet and Rosenfeld [Same80d], Samet [Same84b, Same88a], Samet and Webber [Same88c, Same88d], and Toussaint [Tous80].

There are also a number of excellent texts containing material related to the topics that I cover. Rosenfeld and Kak [Rose82a] should be consulted for an encyclopedic treatment of image processing. Mäntylä [Mänt87] has written a comprehensive introduction to solid modeling. Burrough [Burr86] provides a survey of geographic information systems (GIS). Overmars [Over83] has produced a particularly good treatment of multidimensional point data. In a similar vein, see Mehlhorn's [Mehl84] unified treatment of multidimensional searching and computational geometry. For thorough introductions to computational geometry, see Preparata and

Shamos [Prep85] and Edelsbrunner [Edel87] (also see [Prep83, ORou88]). A broader view of the literature can be found in related bibliographies such as the ongoing collective effort coordinated by Edelsbrunner [Edel83c, Edel88], and Rosenfeld's annual collection of references in the journal *Computer Vision, Graphics, and Image Processing* (e.g., [Rose88]).

Nevertheless, given the broad and rapidly expanding nature of the field, I am bound to have omitted significant concepts and references. In addition at times I devote a disproportionate amount of attention to some concepts at the expense of others. This is principally for expository purposes; I feel that it is better to understand some structures well rather than to give readers a quick runthrough of buzzwords. For these indiscretions, I beg your pardon and hope you nevertheless bear with me.

My approach is an algorithmic one. Whenever possible, I have tried to motivate critical steps in the algorithms by a liberal use of examples. I feel that it is of paramount importance for readers to see the ease with which the representations can be implemented and used. In each chapter, except for the introduction (Chapter 1), I give at least one detailed algorithm using pseudo-code so that readers can see how the ideas can be applied. The pseudo-code is a variant of the ALGOL [Naur60] programming language that has a data structuring facility incorporating pointers and record structures. Recursion is used heavily. This language has similarities to C [Kern78], PASCAL [Jens74], SAIL [Reis76], and ALGOL W [Baue68]. Its basic features are described in the Appendix. However, the actual code is not crucial to understanding the techniques, and it may be skipped on a first reading. The index indicates the page numbers where the code for each algorithm is found.

In many cases I also give an analysis of the space and time requirements of different data structures and algorithms. The analysis is usually of an asymptotic nature and is in terms of *big O* and Ω notation [Knut76]. The *big O* notation denotes an upper bound. For example, if an algorithm takes $O(\log_2 N)$ time, then its worst-case behavior is never any worse than $\log_2 N$. The Ω notation denotes a lower bound. As an example of its use, consider the problem of sorting N numbers. When we say that sorting is $\Omega(N \cdot \log_2 N)$ we mean that given any algorithm for sorting, there is some set of N input values for which the algorithm will require at least this much time.

At times I also describe implementations of some of the data structures for the purpose of comparison. In such cases counts, such as the number of fields in a record, are often given. These numbers are meant only to amplify the discussion. They are not to be taken literally, as improvements are always possible once a specific application is analyzed more carefully.

Each chapter contains a substantial number of exercises. Many of the exercises develop further the material in the text as a means of testing the reader's understanding, as well as suggesting future directions. When the exercise or its solution is not my own, I have preceded it with the name of its originator. The exercises have not been graded by difficulty. They rarely require any mathematical skills beyond the undergraduate level for their solution. However, while some of the exercises are quite straightforward, others require some ingenuity. Solutions, or references to papers that contain the solution, are provided for a substantial number of the exercises that do not require programming. Readers are cautioned to try to solve the exercises before turning to the solutions. It is my belief that much can be learned this way (for the student and, even more so, for the author). The motivation for undertaking this task was my wonderful experience on my first encounter with the rich work on data structures by Knuth [Knut73a, Knut73b].

An extensive bibliography is provided. It contains entries for both this book and the companion text [Same90b]. Not all of the references that appear in the bibliography are cited in the two texts. They are retained for the purpose of giving readers the ability to access the entire body of literature relevant to the topics discussed in them. Each reference is annotated with a key word(s) and a list of the numbers of the sections in which it is cited in either of the texts (including exercises and solutions). In addition, a name and credit index is provided that indicates the page numbers in this book on which each author's work is cited or a credit is made.

ACKNOWLEDGMENTS

Over the years I have received help from many people, and I am extremely grateful to them. In particular Robert E. Webber, Markku Tamminen, and Michael B. Dillencourt have generously given me much of their time and have gone over critical parts of the book. I have drawn heavily on their knowledge of some of the topics covered here. I have also been extremely fortunate to work with Azriel Rosenfeld over the past ten years. His dedication and scholarship have been a true inspiration to me. I deeply cherish our association.

I was introduced to the field of spatial data structures by Gary D. Knott who asked "how to delete in point quadtrees." Azriel Rosenfeld and Charles R. Dyer provided much interaction in the initial phase of my research. Those discussions led to the discovery of the neighbor-finding principle. It is during that time that many of the basic conversion algorithms between quadtrees and other image representations were developed as well. I learned much about image processing and computer vision from them. Robert E. Webber taught me computer graphics, Markku Tamminen taught me solid modeling and representations for multiattribute data, and Michael B. Dillencourt taught me about computational geometry.

During the time that this book was written, my research was supported, in part, by the National Science Foundation, the Defense Mapping Agency, the Harry Diamond Laboratory, and the Bureau of the Census. In particular I would like to thank Richard Antony, Y. T. Chien, Su-shing Chen, Hank Cook, Phil Emmerman, Joe Rastatter, Alan Saalfeld, and Larry Tokarcik. I am appreciative of their support.

Many people helped me in the process of preparing the book for publication. Acknowledgments are due to Rene McDonald for coordinating the day-to-day matters of getting the book out and copyediting; to Scott Carson, Emery Jou, and Jim Purtilo for TROFF assistance beyond the call of duty; to Marisa Antoy and Sergio Antoy for designing and implementing the algorithm formatter used to typeset the algorithms; to Barbara Burnett, Michael B. Dillencourt, and Sandra German for help with the index; to Jay Weber for setting up the TROFF macro files so that I can keep track of symbolic names and thus be able to move text around without worrying about the numbering of exercises, sections, and chapters; to Liz Allen for early TROFF help; to Nono Kusuma, Mark Stanley, and Joan Wright Hamilton for drawing the figures; to Richard Muntz and Gerald Estrin for providing temporary office space and computer access at UCLA; to Sandy German, Gwen Nelson, and Janet Salzman for help in initial typing of the manuscript; to S. S. Iyengar, Duane Marble, George Nagy, and Terry Smith who reviewed the book; and to Peter Gordon, John Remington, and Keith Wollman at Addison-Wesley Publishing Company for their encouragement and confidence in this project.

Aside from the individuals named above, I have also benefited from discussions with many other people over the past years. They have commented on various parts of the book and include Chuan-Heng Ang, Walid Aref, James Arvo, Thor Bestul, Sharat Chandran, Chiun-Hong Chien, Jiang-Hsing Chu, Leila De Floriani, Daniel DeMenthon, Roger Eastman, Herbert Edelsbrunner, Christos Faloutsos, George (Gyuri) Fekete, Kikuo Fujimura, John Gannon, John Goldak, Erik Hoel, Liuqing Huang, Frederik W. Jansen, Ajay Kela, David Kirk, Per Åke Larson, Dani Lischinski, Don Meagher, David Mount, Randal C. Nelson, Glenn Pearson, Ron Sacks-Davis, Timos Sellis, Clifford A. Shaffer, Deepak Sherlekar, Li Tong, Brian Von Herzen, Peter Widmayer, and David Wise. I deeply appreciate their help.

A GUIDE TO THE INSTRUCTOR

This book can be used in a second data structures course, one with emphasis on the representation of spatial data. The focus is on the use of the principle of divide-and-conquer for which hierarchical data structures provide a good demonstration. Throughout the book both worst-case optimal methods and methods that work well in practice are emphasized in conformance with my view that the well-rounded computer scientist should be conversant with both types of algorithms. This material is more than can be covered in one semester; but the instructor can reduce it as necessary. For example, the detailed examples can be skipped or used as a basis of a term project or programming assignments.

The book can also be used to organize a course to be prerequisite to courses in computer graphics and solid modeling, computational geometry, database management systems, multidimensional searching, image processing, and VLSI design. The discussions of the representations of two-dimensional regions in Chapter 1, polygonal representations in Chapter 4, and most of Chapter 5 are relevant to computer graphics and solid modeling. The discussions of plane-sweep methods and their associated data structures such as segment trees, interval trees, and priority search trees in Sections 3.2 and 3.3 and point location and associated data structures such as the

K-structure and the layered dag in Section 4.3 are relevant to computational geometry. Bucket methods such as linear hashing, spiral hashing, grid file, and EXCELL, in Section 2.8, and R-trees in Section 3.5.3 are important in the study of database management systems. Methods for multidimensional searching that are discussed include k–d trees in Section 2.4, range trees and priority search trees in Section 2.5, and point-based rectangle representations in Section 3.4. The discussions of the representation of two-dimensional regions in Chapter 1, polygonal representations in Chapter 4, and use of point methods for focussing the Hough Transform are relevant to image processing. Finally the rectangle-representation methods and plane-sweep methods of Chapter 3 are important in the field of VLSI design.

The natural home for courses that use this book is in a computer science department, but the book could also be used in a curriculum in geographic information systems (GIS). Such a course is offered in geography departments. The emphasis for a course in this area would be on the use of quadtree-like methods for representing spatial data.

CONTENTS

INTRODUCTION 1

There are numerous hierarchical data structuring techniques in use for representing spatial data. One commonly used technique is the quadtree, which has evolved from work in different fields. Thus it is natural that a number of adaptations of it exist for each spatial data type. Its development has been motivated to a large extent by a desire to save storage by aggregating data having identical or similar values. We will see, however, that this is not always the case. In fact, the savings in execution time that arise from this aggregation are often of equal or greater importance.

In this chapter we start with a historical overview of quadtrees, including definitions. Since the primary focus in this book is on the representation of regions, what follows is a discussion of region representation in the context of different space decomposition methods. This is done by examining polygonal and nonpolygonal tilings of the plane. The emphasis is on justifying the use of a decomposition into squares. We conclude with a detailed analysis of the space requirements of the quadtree representation.

Most of the presentation in this chapter is in the context of two-dimensional regions. The extension of the topics in this chapter, and remaining chapters, to three-dimensional region data, and higher, is straightforward and, aside from definitions, is often left to the exercises. Nevertheless, the concept of an octree, a quadtree-like representation of three-dimensional regions, is defined and a brief explanation is given of how some of the results described here are applicable to higher-dimensional data.

1.1 BASIC DEFINITIONS

First, we define a few terms with respect to two-dimensional data. Assume the existence of an array of picture elements (termed *pixels*) in two dimensions. We use the term *image* to refer to the original array of pixels. If its elements are black or white, then it is said to be *binary*. If shades of gray are possible (i.e., gray levels), the image is said to be a *gray–scale* image. In the discussion, we are primarily concerned with binary images. Assume that the image is on an infinite background of white pixels. The *border* of the image is the outer boundary of the square corresponding to the array.

Two pixels are said to be 4-*adjacent* if they are adjacent to each other in the horizontal or vertical direction. If the concept of adjacency also includes adjacency at a corner (i.e., diagonal adjacencies), then the pixels are said to be 8-*adjacent*. A set S is said to be *four–connected* (*eight–connected*) if for any pixels p, q in S there exists a sequence of pixels $p = p_0, p_1, \cdots, p_n = q$ in S, such that p_{i+1} is 4-adjacent (8-adjacent) to p_i, $0 \le i < n$.

A black *region*, or black four-connected *component*, is a maximal four-connected set of black pixels. The process of assigning the same label to all 4-adjacent black pixels is called *connected component labeling* (see Chapter 5 of [Same90b]). A white *region* is a maximal *eight–connected* set of white pixels defined analogously. The complement of a black region consists of a union of eight-connected white regions. Exactly one of these white regions contains the infinite background of white pixels. All the other white regions, if any, are called *holes* in the black region. The black region, say R, is surrounded by the infinite white region and R surrounds the other white regions, if any.

A pixel is said to have four edges, each of which is of unit length. The *boundary* of a black region consists of the set of edges of its constituent pixels that also serve as edges of white pixels. Similar definitions can be formulated in terms of rectangular blocks, all of whose pixels are identically colored. For example, two disjoint blocks, P and Q, are said to be 4-*adjacent* if there exists a pixel p in P and a pixel q in Q such that p and q are 4-adjacent. Eight-adjacency for blocks (as well as connected component labeling) is defined analogously.

1.2 OVERVIEW OF QUADTREES AND OCTREES

The term *quadtree* is used to describe a class of hierarchical data structures whose common property is that they are based on the principle of recursive decomposition of space. They can be differentiated on the following bases:

1. The type of data they are used to represent
2. The principle guiding the decomposition process
3. The resolution (variable or not)

Currently they are used for point data, areas, curves, surfaces, and volumes. The decomposition may be into equal parts on each level (i.e., regular polygons and termed a *regular decomposition*), or it may be governed by the input. In computer graphics this distinction is often phrased in terms of image-space hierarchies versus object-space hierarchies, respectively [Suth74]. The resolution of the decomposition

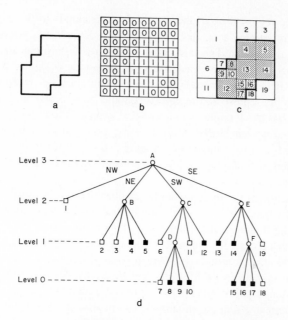

Figure 1.1   An example of (a) a region, (b) its binary array,
(c) its maximal blocks (blocks in the region are shaded), and
(d) the corresponding quadtree

(i.e., the number of times that the decomposition process is applied) may be fixed beforehand, or it may be governed by properties of the input data. For some applications we can also differentiate the data structures on the basis of whether they specify the boundaries of regions (e.g., curves and surfaces) or organize their interiors (e.g., areas and volumes).

The first example of a quadtree representation of data is concerned with the representation of two-dimensional binary region data. The most studied quadtree approach to region representation, called a *region quadtree* (but often termed a *quadtree* in the rest of this chapter), is based on the successive subdivision of a bounded image array into four equal-sized quadrants. If the array does not consist entirely of 1s or entirely of 0s (i.e., the region does not cover the entire array), then it is subdivided into quadrants, subquadrants, and so on, until blocks are obtained that consist entirely of 1s or entirely of 0s; that is, each block is entirely contained in the region or entirely disjoint from it. The region quadtree can be characterized as a variable resolution data structure.

As an example of the region quadtree, consider the region shown in Figure 1.1a represented by the $2^3 \times 2^3$ binary array in Figure 1.1b. Observe that the 1s correspond to picture elements (i.e., pixels) in the region, and the 0s correspond to picture elements outside the region. The resulting blocks for the array of Figure 1.1b are shown in Figure 1.1c. This process is represented by a tree of degree 4 (i.e., each nonleaf node has four sons).

In the tree representation, the root node corresponds to the entire array. Each son of a node represents a quadrant (labeled in order NW, NE, SW, SE) of the region represented by that node. The leaf nodes of the tree correspond to those blocks for which no further subdivision is necessary. A leaf node is said to be black or white depending on whether its corresponding block is entirely inside (it contains only 1s) or entirely outside the represented region (it contains no 1s). All nonleaf nodes are said to be gray (i.e., its block contains 0s and 1s). Given a $2^n \times 2^n$ image, the root node is said to be at level n while a node at level 0 corresponds to a single pixel in the image.[1] The region quadtree representation for Figure 1.1c is shown in Figure 1.1d. The leaf nodes are labeled with numbers, while the nonleaf nodes are labeled with letters. The levels of the tree are also marked.

Our definition of the region quadtree implies that it is constructed by a top-down process. In practice, the process is bottom-up, and one usually uses one of two approaches. The first approach [Same80b] is applicable when the image array is not too large. In such a case, the elements of the array are inspected in the order given by the labels on the array in Figure 1.2 (which corresponds to the image of Figure 1.1a). This order is also known as a Morton order [Mort66] (discussed in Section 1.3). By using such a method, a leaf node is never created until it is known to be maximal. An equivalent statement is that the situation does not arise in which four leaf nodes of the same color necessitate the changing of the color of their parent from gray to black or white as is appropriate. (For more details, see Section 4.1 of [Same90b].)

The second approach [Same81a] is applicable to large images. In this case, the elements of the image are processed one row at a time—for example, in the order given by the labels on the array in Figure 1.3 (which corresponds to the image of Figure 1.1a). This order is also known as a row or raster-scan order (discussed in Section 1.3). A quadtree is built by adding pixel-sized nodes one by one in the order in which they appear in the file. (For more details, see Section 4.2.1 of [Same90b].) This process can be time-consuming due to the many merging and node insertion operations that need to take place.

The above method has been improved by using a predictive method [Shaf86a, Shaf87a], which only makes a single insertion for each node in the final quadtree and performs no merge operations. It is based on processing the image in row order (top to bottom, left to right), always inserting the largest node (i.e., block) for which the current pixel is the first (upper leftmost) pixel. Such a policy avoids the necessity of merging since the upper leftmost pixel of any block is inserted before any other pixel of that block. Therefore it is impossible for four sibling nodes to be of the same color. This method makes use of an auxiliary array of size $O(2^n)$ for a $2^n \times 2^n$ image. (For more details, see Section 4.2.3 of [Same90b].)

The region quadtree is easily extended to represent three-dimensional binary region data and the resulting data structure is called a *region octree* (termed an *octree*

---

[1] Alternatively we can say that the root node is at depth 0 while a node at depth n corresponds to a single pixel in the image. In this book both concepts of level and depth are used to describe the relative position of nodes. The one that is chosen is context dependent.

1	2	5	6	17	18	21	22
3	4	7	8	19	20	23	24
9	10	13	14	25	26	29	30
11	12	15	16	27	28	31	32
33	34	37	38	49	50	53	54
35	36	39	40	51	52	55	56
41	42	45	46	57	58	61	62
43	44	47	48	59	60	63	64

Figure 1.2   Morton order for the pixels of Figure 1.1

in the rest of this chapter). We start with a $2^n \times 2^n \times 2^n$ object array of unit cubes (termed *voxels* or *obels*). The octree is based on the successive subdivision of an object array into octants. If the array does not consist entirely of 1s or entirely of 0s, it is subdivided into octants, suboctants, and so on until cubes (possibly single voxels) are obtained that consist of 1s or of 0s; that is, they are entirely contained in the region or entirely disjoint from it.

This subdivision process is represented by a tree of degree 8 in which the root node represents the entire object and the leaf nodes correspond to those cubes of the array for which no further subdivision is necessary. Leaf nodes are said to be black or white (alternatively, full or void) depending on whether their corresponding cubes are entirely within or outside the object, respectively. All nonleaf nodes are said to be gray. Figure 1.4a is an example of a simple three-dimensional object, in the form of a staircase, whose octree block decomposition is given in Figure 1.4b and whose tree representation is given in Figure 1.4c.

The region quadtree is a member of a class of representations characterized as being a collection of maximal (according to an appropriate definition) blocks, each of which is contained in a given region and whose union is the entire region. The simplest such representation is the runlength code, where the blocks are restricted to $1 \times m$ rectangles [Ruto68]. A more general representation treats the region as a union of maximal square blocks (or blocks of any other desired shape) that may possibly overlap. Usually the blocks are specified by their centers and radii. This representation is called the *medial axis transformation* (*MAT*) [Blum67, Rose66]. Of course, other approaches are also possible (e.g., rectangular coding [Kim83, Kim86], TID [Scot85, Scot86]).

1	2	3	4	5	6	7	8
9	10	11	12	13	14	15	16
17	18	19	20	21	22	23	24
25	26	27	28	29	30	31	32
33	34	35	36	37	38	39	40
41	42	43	44	45	46	47	48
49	50	51	52	53	54	55	56
57	58	59	60	61	62	63	64

Figure 1.3   Raster-scan order for the pixels of Figure 1.1

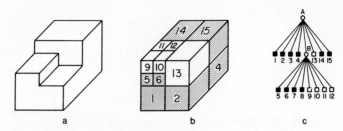

Figure 1.4 (a) Example three-dimensional object; (b) its octree block decomposition; (c) its tree representation

The region quadtree is a variant on the maximal block representation. It requires the blocks to be disjoint and to have standard sizes (i.e., sides of lengths that are powers of two) and standard locations. The motivation for its development is a desire to obtain a systematic way to represent homogeneous parts of an image. Thus to transform the data into a region quadtree, a criterion must be chosen for deciding that an image is homogeneous (i.e., uniform).

One such criterion is that the standard deviation of its gray levels is below a given threshold t. Using this criterion, the image array is successively subdivided into quadrants, subquadrants, and so on until homogeneous blocks are obtained. This process leads to a regular decomposition. If one associates with each leaf node the mean gray level of its block, the resulting region quadtree will then completely specify a piecewise approximation to the image where each homogeneous block is represented by its mean. The case where $t = 0$ (i.e., a block is not homogeneous unless its gray level is constant) is of particular interest since it permits an exact reconstruction of the image from its quadtree.

Note that the blocks of the region quadtree do not necessarily correspond to maximal homogeneous regions in the image. Most likely there exist unions of the blocks that are still homogeneous. To obtain a segmentation of the image into maximal homogeneous regions, we must allow merging of adjacent blocks (or unions of blocks) as long as the resulting region remains homogeneous. This is achieved by a 'split-and-merge' algorithm [Horo76]. However, the resulting partition will no longer be represented by a quadtree; instead the final representation is in the form of an adjacency graph. Thus the region quadtree is used as an initial step in the segmentation process.

For example, Figure 1.5b–d demonstrates the results of the application, in sequence, of merging, splitting, and grouping to the initial image decomposition of Figure 1.5a. In this case, the image is initially decomposed into 16 equal-sized square blocks. Next the 'merge' step attempts to form larger blocks by recursively merging groups of four homogeneous 'brothers' (the four blocks in the NW and SE quadrants of Figure 1.5b). The 'split' step recursively decomposes blocks that are not homogeneous (the NE and SW quadrants of Figure 1.5c) until a particular homogeneity criterion is satisfied or a given level is encountered. Finally the 'grouping' step aggregates all homogeneous 4-adjacent black blocks into one region apiece;

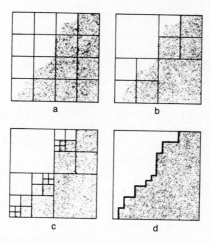

Figure 1.5 Example illustrating the 'split-and-merge' segmentation procedure: (a) start, (b) merge, (c) split, (d) grouping

the 8-adjacent white blocks are similarly aggregated into white regions (Figure 1.5d).

An alternative to the region quadtree representation is to use a decomposition method that is not regular (i.e., rectangles of arbitrary size rather than squares). This alternative has the potential of requiring less space. Its drawback is that the determination of optimal partition points may be computationally expensive (see Exercise 1.10). A closely related problem, decomposing a region into a minimum number of rectangles, is known to be NP-complete[2] [Gare79] if the region is permitted to contain holes [Ling82].

The homogeneity criterion ultimately chosen to guide the subdivision process depends on the type of region data represented. In the remainder of this chapter we shall assume that the domain is a $2^n \times 2^n$ binary image with 1, or black, corresponding to foreground and 0, or white, corresponding to background (e.g., Figure 1.1).

---

[2] A problem is in NP if it can be solved nondeterministically in polynomial time. A nondeterministic solution process proceeds by 'guessing' a solution and then verifying that the solution is correct. Assume that n is the size of the problem (e.g., for sorting, n is the number of records to be sorted). Intuitively, then, a problem is in NP if there is a polynomial $P(n)$ such that if one guesses a solution, it can be verified in $O(P(n))$ time, whether the guess is indeed a correct solution. Thus the verification process is the key to determining whether a problem is in NP, not the actual solution of the problem.

A problem is NP-complete if it is 'at least as hard' as any other problem in NP. Somewhat more formally, a problem P_1 in NP is NP-complete if the following property holds: for all other problems P_i in NP, if P_1 can be solved deterministically in $O(f(n))$ time, then P_i can be solved in $O(P(f(n)))$ time for some polynomial P. It has been conjectured that no NP-complete problem can be solved deterministically in polynomial time, but this is not known for sure. The theory of NP-completeness is discussed in detail in [Gare79].

Nevertheless the quadtree and octree can be used to represent multicolored data (e.g., a landuse class map associating colors with crops [Same87a]).

It is interesting to note that Kawaguchi, Endo, and Matsunaga [Kawa83] use a sequence of m binary-valued quadtrees to encode image data of 2^m gray levels, where the various gray levels are encoded by use of Gray codes (see, e.g., [McCl65]). This should lead to compaction (i.e., larger-sized blocks) since the Gray code guarantees that the binary representation of the codes of adjacent gray level values differ by only one binary digit.[3] Note, though, that if the primary interest is in image compression, there exist even better methods (see, e.g., [Prat78]); however, they are beyond the scope of this book (but see Chapter 8 of [Same90b]). In another context, Kawaguchi, Endo, and Yokota [Kawa80b] point out that a sequence of related images (e.g., in an animation application) can be stored compactly as a sequence of quadtrees such that the ith element is the result of exclusive oring the first i images (see Exercise 1.7).

Unfortunately the term *quadtree* has taken on more than one meaning. The region quadtree, as described earlier, is a partition of space into a set of squares whose sides are all a power of two long. This formulation is due to Klinger [Klin71] and Klinger and Dyer, who used the term *Q-tree* [Klin76], whereas Hunter [Hunt78] was the first to use the term *quadtree* in such a context. Actually a more precise term would be *quadtrie*, as it is really a trie structure [Fred60] in two dimensions.[4] A similar partition of space into rectangular quadrants, also termed a *quadtree*, was used by Finkel and Bentley [Fink74]. It is an adaptation of the binary search tree [Knut73b] to two dimensions (which can be easily extended to an arbitrary number of dimensions). It is primarily used to represent multidimensional point data, and we shall refer to it as a *point quadtree* where confusion with a region quadtree is possible.

As an example of a point quadtree, consider Figure 1.6, which is built for the sequence Chicago, Mobile, Toronto, Buffalo, Denver, Omaha, Atlanta, and Miami[5]

---

[3] The Gray code is motivated by a desire to reduce errors in transitions between successive gray level values. Its one bit difference guarantee is achieved by the following encoding. Consider the binary representation of the integers from 0 to $2^m - 1$. This representation can be obtained by constructing a binary tree, say T, of height m where each left branch is labeled 0 while each right branch is labeled 1. Each leaf node, say P, is given the label formed by concatenating the labels of the branches taken by the path from the root to P. Enumerating the leaf nodes from left to right yields the binary integers 0 to $2^m - 1$. The Gray codes of the integers are obtained by constructing a new binary tree, say T', such that the labels of some of the branches in T' are the reverse of what they were in T. The algorithm is as follows. Initially, T' is a copy of T. Next, traverse T in preorder (i.e., visit the root node, followed by the left and right subtrees). For each branch in T labeled 1, exchange the labels of the two descendant branches of its corresponding branch in T'. No action is taken for descendants of branches in T labeled 0. Enumerating the leaf nodes in T' from left to right yields the Gray codes of the integers 0 to $2^m - 1$. For example, for 8 gray levels (i.e., $m = 3$), we have 000, 001, 011, 010, 110, 111, 101, 100.

[4] In a one-dimensional *trie* structure, each data item or key is treated as a sequence of characters where each character has M possible values. A node at depth i in the trie represents an M-way branch depending on the ith character. The data are stored in the leaf nodes, and the shape of the trie is independent of the order in which the data are processed. Such a structure is also known as a *digital tree* [Knut73b].

[5] The correspondence between coordinate values and city names is not geographically correct. This liberty has been taken so that the same example can be used throughout the text to illustrate a variety of concepts.

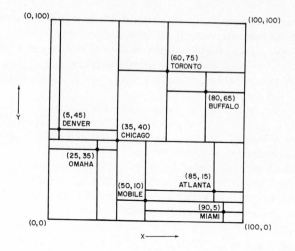

Figure 1.6   A point quadtree and the records it represents

in the order in which they are listed here.[6] Its shape is highly dependent on the order in which the points are added to it. Of course, trie-based point representations also exist (see Sections 2.6.1 and 2.6.2).

Exercises

1.1. The region quadtree is an alternative to an image representation that is based on the use of an array or even a list. Each of these image representations may be biased in favor of the computation of a particular adjacency relation. Discuss these biases for the array, list, and quadtree representations.

1.2. Given the array representation of a binary image, write an algorithm to construct the corresponding region quadtree.

---

[6] Refer to Figure 2.5 to see how the point quadtree is constructed in an incremental fashion for Chicago, Mobile, Toronto, and Buffalo.

1.3. Given an image represented by a region quadtree with B black and W white nodes, how many additional nodes are necessary for the nonleaf nodes?

1.4. Given an image represented by a region octree with B black and W white nodes, how many additional nodes are necessary for the nonleaf nodes?

1.5. Suppose that an octree is used to represent a collection of disjoint spheres. What would you use as a leaf criterion?

1.6. The quadtree can be generalized to represent data in arbitrary dimensions. As we saw, the octree is its three-dimensional analog. The renowned artist Escher [Coxe86] is noted for etchings of unusual interpretations of geometric objects such as staircases. How would you represent one of Escher's staircases?

1.7. Let $\oplus$ denote an exclusive or operation. Given a sequence of related images, $<P_n, P_{n-1}, \cdots, P_0>$, define another sequence $<Q_n, Q_{n-1}, \cdots, Q_0>$ such that $Q_0 = P_0$ and $Q_i = P_i \oplus Q_{i-1}$ for $i > 0$. Show that when the sequences P and Q are represented as quadtrees, replacing sequence P by sequence Q results in fewer nodes.

1.8. Prove that in Exercise 1.7 the sequence P can be reconstructed from the sequence Q. In particular, given Q_i and Q_{i-1}, determine P_i.

1.9. Write an algorithm to construct the Gray codes of the integers 0 to $2^m - 1$.

1.10. Find a polynomial-time algorithm to decompose a region optimally so that its quadtree representation uses a minimum amount of space (i.e., a minimum number of nodes). In this case, you can assume that the decomposition lines can be placed in arbitrary positions so that the space requirement is reduced. In other words, the decomposition lines need not split the space into four squares of equal size. Thus the decomposition is similar to that induced by a point quadtree.

1.3 HISTORY OF THE USE OF QUADTREES AND OCTREES

The origin of the principle of recursive decomposition, upon which all quadtrees are based, is difficult to ascertain. Below, to give some indication of the uses of the region quadtree, some of its applications to geometric data are traced briefly. Most likely it was first seen as a way of aggregating blocks of zeros in sparse matrices. Indeed Hoare [Hoar72] attributes a one-level decomposition of a matrix into square blocks to Dijkstra. Morton [Mort66] used it as a means of indexing into a geographic database (i.e., it acts as a spatial index).

Warnock, in a pair of reports that serve as landmarks in computer graphics [Warn68, Warn69b], described the implementation of hidden-line and hidden-surface elimination algorithms using a recursive decomposition of the picture area. The picture area is repeatedly subdivided into rectangles that are successively smaller while searching for areas that are sufficiently simple to be displayed. Klinger [Klin71] and Klinger and Dyer [Klin76] applied these ideas to pattern recognition and image processing, while Hunter [Hunt78] used them for an animation application.

The SRI robot project [Nils69] used a three-level decomposition of space to represent a map of the robot's world. Eastman [East70] observes that recursive decomposition might be used for space planning in an architectural context and presents a simplified version of the SRI robot representation. A quadtree-like representation in the form of production rules called DF-expressions (denoting 'depth-first') is discussed by Kawaguchi and Endo [Kawa80a] and Kawaguchi, Endo, and Yokota

[Kawa80b] (see also Section 1.5). Tucker [Tuck84a] uses quadtree refinement as a control strategy for an expert vision system.

The three-dimensional variant of the region quadtree—the octree—was developed independently by a number of researchers. Hunter [Hunt78] mentioned it as a natural extension of the quadtree. Reddy and Rubin [Redd78] proposed the octree as one of three representations for solid objects. The second is a three-dimensional generalization of the point quadtree of Finkel and Bentley [Fink74]—that is, a decomposition into rectangular parallelepipeds (as opposed to cubes) with planes perpendicular to the x, y, and z axes. The third breaks the object into rectangular parallelepipeds that are not necessarily aligned with an axis. The parallelepipeds are of arbitrary sizes and orientations. Each parallelepiped is recursively subdivided into parallelepipeds in the coordinate space of the enclosing parallelepiped. Reddy and Rubin prefer the third approach for its ease of display.

Situated somewhere between the second and third approaches of Reddy and Rubin is the method of Brooks and Lozano-Perez [Broo83] (see also [Loza81]), who use a recursive decomposition of space into an arbitrary number of rectangular parallelepipeds, with planes perpendicular to the x, y, and z axes, to model space in solving the *findpath* or *piano movers* problem [Schw88] in robotics. This problem arises when planning the motion of a robot in an environment containing known obstacles and the desired solution is a collision-free path obtained by use of a search. Faverjon [Fave84] discusses an approach to this problem that uses an octree, as do Samet and Tamminen [Same85g] and Fujimura and Samet [Fuji89].

Jackins and Tanimoto [Jack80] adapted Hunter and Steiglitz's quadtree translation algorithm [Hunt78, Hunt79b] to objects represented by octrees. Meagher [Meag82a] developed numerous algorithms for performing solid modeling operations in an environment where the octree is the underlying representation. Yau and Srihari [Yau83] extended the octree to arbitrary dimensions in the process of developing algorithms to handle medical images.

Both quadtrees and octrees are frequently used in the construction of meshes for finite element analysis. The use of recursive decomposition for meshes was initially suggested by Rheinboldt and Mesztenyi [Rhei80]. Yerry and Shephard [Yerr83] adapted the quadtree and octree to generate meshes automatically for three-dimensional solids represented by a superquadric surface-based modeler. This has been extended by Kela, Voelcker, and Goldak [Kela84b] (see also [Kela86]) to mesh boundary regions directly, rather than through discrete approximations, and to facilitate incremental adaptive analysis by exploiting the spatial index nature of the quadtree and octree.

Parallel to the development of the quadtree and octree data structures, there has been related work by researchers in the field of image understanding. Kelly [Kell71] introduced the concept of a *plan*, which is a small picture whose pixels represent gray-scale averages over 8×8 blocks of a larger picture. Needless effort in edge detection is avoided by first determining edges in the plan and then using these edges to search selectively for edges in the larger picture. Generalizations of this idea motivated the development of multiresolution image representations—for example,

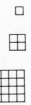

Figure 1.7   Structure of a pyramid having three levels

the recognition cone of Uhr [Uhr72], the preprocessing cone of Riseman and Arbib [Rise77], and the pyramid of Tanimoto and Pavlidis [Tani75]. Of these representations, the pyramid is the closest relative of the region quadtree.

Given a $2^n \times 2^n$ image array, say $A(n)$, a *pyramid* is a sequence of arrays $\{A(i)\}$ such that $A(i-1)$ is a version of $A(i)$ at half the scale of $A(i)$. $A(0)$ is a single pixel. Figure 1.7 shows the structure of a pyramid having three levels. It should be clear that a pyramid can also be defined in a more general way by permitting finer scales of resolution than the power of two scale.

At times, it is more convenient to define a pyramid in the form of a tree. Again, assuming a $2^n \times 2^n$ image, a recursive decomposition into quadrants is performed, just as in quadtree construction, except that we keep subdividing until we reach the individual pixels. The leaf nodes of the resulting tree represent the pixels, while the nodes immediately above the leaf nodes correspond to the array $A(n-1)$, which is of size $2^{n-1} \times 2^{n-1}$. The nonleaf nodes are assigned a value that is a function of the nodes below them (i.e., their sons) such as the average gray level. Thus we see that a pyramid is a multiresolution representation, whereas the region quadtree is a variable

1	2	3	4	5	6	7	8
9	10	11	12	13	14	15	16
17	18	19	20	21	22	23	24
25	26	27	28	29	30	31	32
33	34	35	36	37	38	39	40
41	42	43	44	45	46	47	48
49	50	51	52	53	54	55	56
57	58	59	60	61	62	63	64

Figure 1.8   Example pyramid A(3)

A	B	C	D
E	F	G	H
I	J	K	L
M	N	O	P

Figure 1.9   A(2) corresponding to Figure 1.8

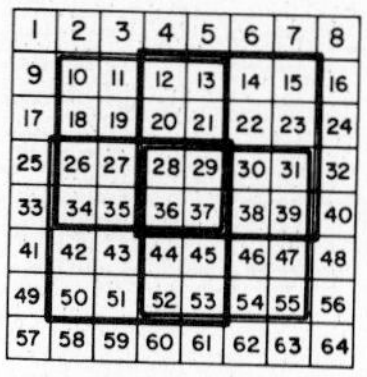

1	2	3	4	5	6	7	8
9	10	11	12	13	14	15	16
17	18	19	20	21	22	23	24
25	26	27	28	29	30	31	32
33	34	35	36	37	38	39	40
41	42	43	44	45	46	47	48
49	50	51	52	53	54	55	56
57	58	59	60	61	62	63	64

Figure 1.10   The overlapping blocks in which pixel 28
participates

resolution representation. Another analogy is that the pyramid is a complete quadtree
[Knut73a].

The above definition of a pyramid is based on nonoverlapping 2×2 blocks of
pixels. An alternative definition, termed an *overlapping pyramid*, uses overlapping
blocks of pixels. One of the simplest schemes makes use of 4×4 blocks that overlap
by 50% in both the horizontal and vertical directions [Burt81]. For example, Figure
1.8 is a $2^3 \times 2^3$ array, say $A(3)$, whose pixels are labeled 1-64. Figure 1.9 is $A(2)$
corresponding to Figure 1.8 with elements labeled A-P. The 4×4 neighborhood
corresponding to element F in Figure 1.9 consists of pixels 10–13, 18–21, 26–29, and
34–37. This method implies that each block at a given level participates in four
blocks at the immediately higher level. Thus the containment relations between
blocks no longer form a tree. For example, pixel 28 participates in blocks F, G, J, and K
in the next higher level (see Figure 1.10 where the four neighborhoods corresponding
to F, G, J, and K are drawn as squares).

To avoid treating border cases differently, each level in the overlapped pyramid
is assumed to be cyclically closed (i.e., the top row at each level is adjacent to the bottom row and similarly for the columns at the extreme left and right of each level).
Once again we say that the value of a node is the average of the values of the nodes in
its block on the immediately lower level. The overlapped pyramid may be compared
with the Quadtree Medial Axis Transform (see Section 9.3.1 of [Same90b]) in the
sense that both may result in nondisjoint decompositions of space.

Pyramids have been applied to the problems of feature detection and extraction
since they can be used to limit the scope of the search. Once a piece of information of
interest is found at a coarse level, the finer resolution levels can be searched. This
approach was followed by Davis and Roussopoulos [Davi80] in approximate pattern
matching. Pyramids can also be used for encoding information about edges, lines, and
curves in an image [Shne81c, Krop86]. One note of caution: the reduction of resolution has an effect on the visual appearance of edges and small objects [Tani76]. In
particular, at a coarser level of resolution, edges tend to get smeared, and region
separation may disappear. Pyramids have also been used as the starting point for a
'split-and-merge' segmentation algorithm [Piet82].

Quadtree-like decompositions are useful as space-ordering methods. The purpose is to optimize the storage and processing sequences for two-dimensional data by
mapping them into one dimension (i.e., linearizing them). This mapping should pre-

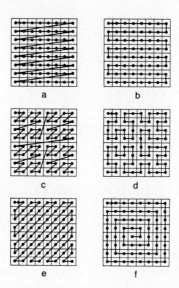

Figure 1.11 The result of applying a number of different space-ordering methods to an 8 × 8 image whose first element is in the upper left corner of the image: (a) row order, (b) row-prime order, (c) Morton order, (d) Peano-Hilbert order, (e) Cantor-diagonal order, (f) spiral order

serve the spatial locality of the original two-dimensional image in one dimension. The result of the mapping is also known as a *space-filling curve* [Gold81, Witt83] because it passes through every point in the image.

Goodchild and Grandfield [Good83] discuss a number of space-ordering methods, some of which are illustrated in Figure 1.11. Each has different characteristics. The row (Figure 1.11a), also known as raster-scan, and row-prime orders (Figure 1.11b) are similar in the same way as are the Morton [Mort66, Pean90] (Figure 1.11c) and the Peano-Hilbert [Hilb91] (Figure 1.11d) orders. The primary difference is that in both the row-prime and Peano-Hilbert orders every element is a 4-adjacent neighbor of the previous element in the sequence, and thus they have a slightly higher degree of locality than the row and Morton orders, respectively. Both the Morton and Peano-Hilbert orders exhaust a quadrant or subquadrant of a square image before exiting it. They are both related to quadtrees; however, as we saw above, the Morton order does not traverse the image in a spatially contiguous manner (the result has the shape of the letter 'N' or 'Z' and is also known as N order [Whit82] and Z order [Oren84]).

For both the Morton and Peano-Hilbert orders, there is no need to know the maximum values of the coordinates. The Morton order is symmetric, while the Peano-Hilbert order is not. One advantage of the Morton order is that the position of each element in the ordering (termed its *key*) can be determined by interleaving the bits of the x and y coordinates of the element; this is not easy for the Peano-Hilbert order. Another advantage of the Morton order is that the recursion necessary for its generation is quite easy to specify.

Other orders are the Cantor-diagonal order (Figure 1.11e) and the spiral order (Figure 1.11f). The Cantor-diagonal order proceeds outward from the origin and visits the elements in an order similar to row-prime with the difference that elements are visited in order of their increasing 'Manhattan' (or 'city block') distance.[7] Thus it is good for ordering a space that is unbounded in the two directions emanating from the origin. On the other hand, the spiral order is attractive when ordering a space that is unbounded in the four directions emanating from the origin.

The most interesting orders, as far as we are concerned, are the Morton and Peano-Hilbert orders since they can also be used to order a space that has been aggregated into squares. Of these two orderings, the Morton order is by far the more frequently used as a result of the simplicity of the conversion process between the key and its corresponding element in the multidimensional space. In this book we are primarily interested in Morton orderings. (For further discussion of some of the properties of these two orderings, see [Patr68, Butz71, Alex79, Alex80, Laur85].)

Exercises

1.11. Write an algorithm to extract the x and y coordinates from a Peano-Hilbert order key.

1.12. Write an algorithm to construct the Peano-Hilbert key for a given point (x,y). Try to make it optimal.

1.13. Suppose that you are given a $2^n \times 2^n$ array of points such that the horizontal and vertical distances between 4-adjacent points are 1. What is the average distance between successive points when the points are ordered according to the orders illustrated in Figure 1.11? What about a random order?

1.14. Suppose that you are given a $2^n \times 2^n$ image. Assume that the image is stored on disk in pages of size $2^m \times 2^m$ where n is much larger than m. What is the average cost of retrieving a pixel and its 4-adjacent neighbors when the image is ordered according to the orders illustrated in Figure 1.11?

1.15. The traveling salesman problem [Lawl85] is one where a set of points is given and it is desired to find the path of minimum distance such that each point is visited only once. This is an NP-complete problem [Gare79] and thus there is a considerable amount of work in formulating approximate solutions to it [Bent82]. For example, consider the following approximate solution. Assume that the points are uniformly distributed in the unit square. Let d be the expected Euclidean distance between two independent points. Now, sort the points using the row order and the Morton order. Laurini [Laur85] simulated the average Euclidean distance between successive points in these orders and found it to be $d/2$ for the row order and $d/3$ for the Morton order. Can you derive these averages analytically? What are the average values for the other orders illustrated in Figure 1.11? What about a random order?

---

[7] The Manhattan distance between points (x_1, y_1) and (x_2, y_2) is $|x_1 - x_2| + |y_1 - y_2|$ (for more details, see Section 9.1 of [Same90b]).

1.16. Suppose that the traveling salesman problem is solved using a traversal of the points in Morton order as discussed in Exercise 1.15. In particular, assume that the set of points is decomposed in such a way that each square block contains just one point. This yields a point representation that is analogous to the region quadtree (termed a PR quadtree and discussed in Section 2.6.2). How close does such a solution come to optimality?

1.4 SPACE DECOMPOSITION METHODS

In general, any planar decomposition used as a basis for an image representation should possess the following two properties:

1. The partition should be an infinitely repetitive pattern so that it can be used for images of any size.
2. The partition should be infinitely decomposable into increasingly finer patterns (i.e., higher resolution).

In this section, the discussion is restricted to two-dimensional data. Thus we are dealing with planar space decompositions. Space decompositions can be classified into two categories, depending on the nature of the pattern. The pattern can consist of polygonal shapes or nonpolygonal shapes. The polygonal shapes are generally computationally simpler since their sides can be expressed in terms of linear relations (e.g., equations of lines). They are good for approximating the interior of a region. The nonpolygonal shapes are more flexible since they provide good approximations, in terms of measures, of the boundaries (e.g., perimeter) of regions as well as their interiors (e.g., area).[8]

Moreover, the normals to the boundaries of nonpolygonal shapes are not restricted to a fixed set of directions. For example, in the case of rectangular tiles, there is a 90 degree discontinuity between the normals to boundaries of adjacent tiles. This lack of continuity is a drawback in applications in fields such as computer graphics where such tasks as shading make use of the directions of the surface. However, working with nonpolygonal shapes generally requires use of floating point arithmetic, and hence it is usually more complex.

The remainder of this section expands on a number of polygonal decompositions and compares them. It also contains a brief discussion of one nonpolygonal decomposition that consists of a collection of sector-like objects whose arcs are not necessarily part of a circle. This method is based on polar coordinates where the arc joining two distinct points is formed by linear interpolation. The term *sector tree* is used to describe it. This discussion is of an advanced nature and can be skipped on an initial reading.

---

[8] Recall the statement in Section 1.2 that hierarchical data structures are often differentiated on the basis of whether they specify the boundaries of regions or organize their interiors.

1.4.1   Polygonal Tilings

Bell, Diaz, Holroyd, and Jackson [Bell83] discuss a number of polygonal tilings of the plane (i.e., tessellations) that satisfy property 1. Figure 1.12 illustrates some of these tessellations. They also present a taxonomy of criteria to distinguish between the various tilings. The tilings, consisting of polygonal tiles, are described by use of a notation based on the degree of each vertex as the edges (i.e., sides) of the 'atomic' tile are visited in order, forming a cycle. For example, the tiling described by $[4.8^2]$ (Figure 1.12c) has the shape of a triangle where the first vertex has degree four while the remaining two vertices have degree eight apiece.

A tiling is said to be *regular* if the atomic tiles are composed of regular polygons (i.e., all sides are of equal length as are the interior angles). A *molecular tile* is an aggregation of atomic tiles to form a hierarchy. It is not necessarily constrained to have the same shape as the atomic tile. When a tile at level k (for all $k > 0$) has the same shape as a tile at level 0 (i.e., it is a scaled image of a tile at level 0), then the tiling is said to be *similar*.

Bell et al. focus on the isohedral tilings where a tiling is said to be *isohedral* if all the tiles are equivalent under the symmetry group of the tiling. A more intuitive

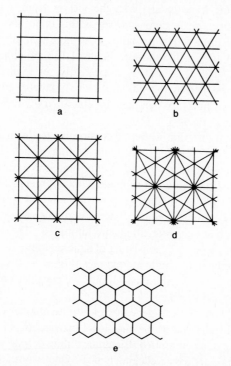

Figure   1.12   Sample   tessellations: (a) $[4^4]$ square;
(b) $[6^3]$ equilateral   triangle;   (c) $[4.8^2]$ isoceles   triangle;
(d) $[4.6.12]$ 30–60 right triangle; (e) $[3^6]$ hexagon

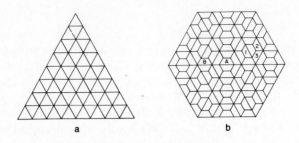

*Figure 1.13   Examples of (a) isohedral and
(b) nonisohedral tilings*

way to conceptualize this definition is to assume the position of an observer who stands in the center of a tile having a given orientation and scans the surroundings. If the view is independent of the tile, the tiling is isohedral. For example, consider the two tilings in Figure 1.13 consisting of triangles (Figure 1.13a) and trapezoids (Figure 1.13b). The triangles are isohedral, whereas the trapezoids are not, as can be seen by the view from tiles A and B.

In the case of the trapezoidal tiling, the viewer from A is surrounded by an infinite number of concentric hexagons, whereas this is not the case for B. In other words, the trapezoidal tiling is not periodic. Also note that all of the tiles in Figure 1.13a are described by $[6^3]$, while those in Figure 1.13b are either $[3^2.4^2]$, $[3^2.6^2]$, or $[3.4.6^2]$ (i.e., tiles labeled 1, 2, and 3, respectively, in Figure 1.13b). When the isohedral tilings are classified by the action of their symmetry group, there are 81 different types [Grün77, Grün87]. When they are classified by their adjacency structure, as done here, there are 11 types.

The most relevant criterion to the discussion is the distinction between limited and unlimited hierarchies of tilings. A *limited* tiling is not similar. A tiling that satisfies property 2 is said to be *unlimited*. Equivalently, in a limited tiling, no change of scale lower than the limit tiling can be made without great difficulty. An alternative characterization of an unlimited tiling is that each edge of a tile lies on an infinite straight line composed entirely of edges. Interestingly the hexagonal tiling $[3^6]$ is limited. Bell et al. claim that only four tilings are unlimited. These are the tilings given in Figure 1.12a–d. Of these, $[4^4]$, consisting of square atomic tiles (Figure 1.12a), and $[6^3]$, consisting of equilateral triangle atomic tiles (Figure 1.12b), are well-known regular tessellations [Ahuj83]. For these two tilings we consider only the molecular tiles given in Figures 1.14a and 1.14b.

The tilings $[4^4]$ and $[6^3]$ can generate an infinite number of different molecular tiles where each molecular tile at the first level consists of n^2 atomic tiles ($n > 1$). The remaining nonregular unlimited triangular tilings, $[4.8^2]$ (Figure 1.12c) and $[4.6.12]$ (Figure 1.12d), are less well understood. One way of generating $[4.8^2]$ and $[4.6.12]$ is to join the centroids of the tiles of $[4^4]$ and $[6^3]$, respectively, to both their vertices and midpoints of their edges. Each of the tilings $[4.8^2]$ and $[4.6.12]$ has two

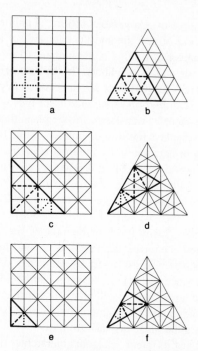

Figure 1.14   Examples illustrating unlimited tilings: (a) [4⁴]
hierarchy, (b) [6³] hierarchy, (c) ordinary [4.8²] hierarchy,
(d) ordinary [4.6.12] hierarchy, (e) rotation [4.8²] hierarchy,
(f) reflection [4.6.12] hierarchy

types of hierarchy. $[4.8^2]$ has an ordinary (Figure 1.14c) and a rotation hierarchy
(Figure 1.14e) requiring a rotation of 135 degrees between levels. $[4.6.12]$ has an
ordinary (Figure 1.14d) and a reflection hierarchy (Figure 1.14f), which requires a
reflection of the basic tile between levels.

The distinction between the two types of hierarchies for $[4.8^2]$ and $[4.6.12]$ is
necessary because the tiling is not similar without a rotation or a reflection when the
hierarchy is not ordinary. This can be seen by observing the use of dots in Figure 1.14
to delimit the atomic tiles in the first molecular tile. Similarly broken lines are used to
delimit the components of tiles at the second level (assuming atomic tiles are at level
0). For the ordinary $[4.8^2]$ and $[4.6.12]$ hierarchies, each molecular tile at the first
level consists of n^2 $(n > 1)$ atomic tiles. In the reflection hierarchy of $[4.6.12]$, each
molecular tile at the first level consists of $3 \cdot n^2$ $(n > 1)$ atomic tiles, while for the
rotation hierarchy of $[4.8^2]$, $2 \cdot n^2$ $(n > 1)$ atomic tiles comprise a molecular tile at the
first level.

To represent data in the Euclidean plane, any of the unlimited tilings could have
been chosen. For a regular decomposition, the tilings $[4.8^2]$ and $[4.6.12]$ are ruled out.
Comparing 'square' $[4^4]$ and 'triangular' $[6^3]$ quadtrees, we find that they differ in
terms of adjacency and orientation. Let us say that two tiles are *neighbors* if they are

adjacent either along an edge or at a vertex. A tiling is *uniformly adjacent* if the distances between the centroid of one tile and the centroids of all its neighbors are the same. The adjacency number of a tiling is the number of different intercentroid distances between any one tile and its neighbors. In the case of $[4^4]$, there are only two adjacency distances, whereas for $[6^3]$ there are three adjacency distances.

A tiling is said to have *uniform orientation* if all tiles with the same orientation can be mapped into each other by translations of the plane that do not involve rotation or reflection. Tiling $[4^4]$ displays uniform orientation, while $[6^3]$ does not. Under the assumption that uniform orientation and a minimal adjacency distance is preferable, we say that $[4^4]$ is more useful than $[6^3]$. It is also very easy to implement. Nevertheless, $[6^3]$ has its uses. For example, Yamaguchi, Kunii, Fujimura, and Toriya [Yama84] use a triangular quadtree to generate an isometric view from an octree representation of an object (see Section 7.1.4 of [Same90b]).

Of the *limited* tilings, many types of hierarchies may be generated [Bell83]; however, in general, they cannot be decomposed beyond the atomic tiling without changing the basic tile shape. This is a serious deficiency of the hexagonal tessellation $[3^6]$ (Figure 1.12e) since the atomic hexagon can be decomposed only into triangles. Nevertheless the hexagonal tessellation is of considerable interest. It is regular, has a uniform orientation, and, most important, displays a uniform adjacency (i.e., each neighbor of a tile is at the same distance from it).

There are a number of different hexagonal hierarchies distinguished by classifying the shape of the first-level molecular tile on the basis of the number of hexagons that it contains. Three of these tiling hierarchies are given in Figure 1.15 and are called *n-shapes* where *n* denotes the number of atomic tiles in the first-level molecular tile. Of course, these n-shapes are not unique.

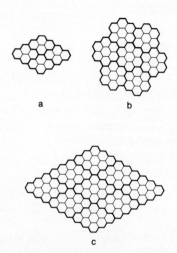

a   b

c

Figure 1.15   Three different hexagonal tiling hierarchies:
(a) 4-shape, (b) 7-shape, (c) 9-shape

The 4-shape and the 9-shape have an unusual adjacency property in the sense that no matter how large the molecular tile becomes, contact with two of the tiles (i.e., the one above and the one below) is along only one edge of a hexagonal atomic tile, while contact with the remaining four molecular tiles is along nearly one-quarter of the perimeter of the corresponding molecular tile. The hexagonal pattern of the 4-shape and 9-shape molecular tiles has the shape of a rhombus. In contrast, a 7-shape molecular tile has a uniform contact with its six neighboring molecular tiles.

The type of quadtree used often depends on the grid formed by the image sampling process. Square quadtrees are appropriate for square grids and triangular quadtrees for triangular grids. In the case of a hexagonal grid [Burt80], the 7-shape hierarchy is frequently used since the shape of its molecular tile is more like a hexagon. It is usually described as *rosette*−like (i.e., a *septree*). Note that septrees have jagged edges as they are merged to form larger units (e.g., Figure 1.15b). The septree is used by Gibson and Lucas [Gibs82] (who call it a *generalized balanced ternary* or *GBT* for short) in the development of algorithms analogous to those existing for quadtrees.

Although the septree can be built up to yield large septrees, the smallest resolution in the septree must be decided upon in advance since its primitive components (i.e., hexagons) cannot later be decomposed into septrees. Therefore the septree yields only a partial hierarchical decomposition in the sense that the components can always be merged into larger units, but they cannot always be broken down. For region data, a pixel is generally an indivisible unit, and thus unlimited decomposition is not absolutely necessary. However, in the case of other data types such as points (see Chapter 2) and lines (see Chapter 4), we will see that the decomposition rules of some representations require that two entities be separated, which may lead to a level of decomposition not known in advance (e.g., a decomposition rule that restricts each square to contain at most one point). In this book the discussion is limited to square quadtrees and their variants.

When the data are spherical, a number of researchers have proposed the use of a representation based on an icosahedron (a 20-faced polyhedron whose faces are regular triangles) [Dutt84, Feke84]. The icosahedron is attractive because, in terms of the number of faces, it is the largest possible regular polyhedron. Each of the triangular faces can be further decomposed in a recursive manner into n^2 ($n > 1$) spherical triangles (the $[6^3]$ tiling).

Fekete and Davis [Feke84] let $n = 2$, which means that at each level of decomposition, three new vertices are generated by halving each side of the triangle; connecting them together yields four triangles. They use the term *property sphere* to describe their representation. The property sphere has been used in object recognition; it is also of potential use in mapping the globe because it can enable accurate modeling of regions around the poles. For example, see Figure 1.16, which is a property sphere representation of some spherical data. In contrast, planar quadtrees are less attractive the farther we get from the equator due to distortions in planarity caused by the earth's curvature. Of course, for true applicability for mapping, we need a closer approximation to a sphere than is provided by the 20 triangles of the icosahedron. Moreover, we want a way to distinguish between different elevations.

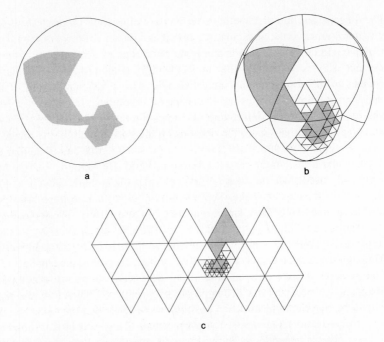

Figure 1.16 Property sphere representation of some spherical data: (a) data, (b) decomposition on a sphere, (c) decomposition on a plane

Dutton [Dutt84] lets $n = \sqrt{3}$, which means that at each level of decomposition, one new vertex is created by connecting the centroid of the triangle to its vertices. The result is an alternating sequence of triangles so that each level is fully contained in the level that was created two steps previously and has nine times as many triangles as that level. Dutton uses the term *triacon* to describe the resulting hierarchy. As an example, consider Figure 1.17, which illustrates four levels of a triacon decomposition. The initial and odd-numbered decompositions are shown with heavy lines, and the even-numbered decompositions are shown with broken and thin lines.

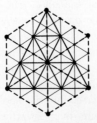

Figure 1.17   Example of a triacon hierarchy

The icosahedron is not the only regular polyhedron that can be used to model spherical data. Others include the tetrahedron, hexahedron, octahedron, and dodeca-hedron, which have 4, 6, 8, and 12 faces, respectively. Collectively these five polyhedra are known as the *Platonic solids* [Peuq84]. The faces of the tetrahedron and octahedron are equilateral triangles, while the faces of the hexahedron and do-decahedron are squares and regular pentagons, respectively.

The dodecahedron is not an appropriate primitive because the pentagonal faces cannot be further decomposed into pentagons or other similar shapes. The tetrahedron and hexahedron (the basis of the octree) have internal angles that are too small to model a sphere properly, thereby leading to shape distortions.

Dutton [Dutt84] points out that the octahedron is attractive for modeling spheri-cal data such as the globe because it can be aligned so that the poles are at opposite vertices and the prime meridian and the equator intersect at another vertex. In addi-tion, one subdivision line of each face is parallel to the equator. Of course, for all of the Platonic solids, only the vertices of the solids touch the sphere; the facets of the solids are interior to the sphere.

Other decompositions for spherical data are also possible. Tobler and Chen [Tobl86] point out the desirability of a close relationship to the commonly used sys-tem of latitude and longitude coordinates. In particular, any decomposition that is chosen should enable the use of meridians and parallels to refer to the data. An addi-tional important goal is for the partition to be into units of equal area, which rules out the use of equally spaced lines of latitude (of course, the lines of longitude are equally spaced). In this case, the sphere is projected into a plane using Lambert's cylindrical projection [Adam49], which is locally area preserving. Authalic coordinates [Adam49], which partition the projection into rectangles of equal area, are then derived. (For more details, see [Tobl86].)

The quadtree decomposition has the property that at each subdivision stage, the image is subdivided into four equal-sized parts. When the original image is a square, the result is a collection of squares, each of which has a side whose length is a power of 2. The binary image tree (termed *bintree*) [Know80, Tamm84a, Same88b] is an alternative decomposition defined in a manner analogous to the region quadtree except that at each subdivision stage we subdivide the image into two equal-sized parts. In two dimensions, at odd stages, we partition along the x coordinate, and at even stages, along the y coordinate. The bintree is equivalent to the region quadtree if we replace all leaf nodes at odd stages of subdivision by two identically colored sons.

The bintree is related to the region quadtree in the same way as the k-d tree [Bent75b] (see Section 2.4) is related to the point quadtree [Fink74]. The difference is that region quadtrees and bintrees are used to represent region data with fixed subdivi-sion points, while point quadtrees and k-d trees are used to represent point data where the values of the points determine the subdivision. For example, Figure 1.18 is the bintree representation corresponding to the image of Figure 1.1. We assume that for the x (y) partition, the left subtree corresponds to the west (south) half of the image and the right subtree corresponds to the east (north) half. Once again, as in Figure 1.1, all leaf nodes are labeled with numbers, and the nonleaf nodes are labeled with letters.

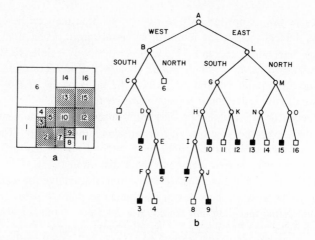

Figure 1.18   Bintree representation corresponding to Figure 1.1: (a) block decomposition, (b) bintree representation of blocks in (a)

The quadtree and bintree decompose a region into equal-sized parts. Kanatani [Kana85] suggests using splitting rules based on the Fibonacci sequence of numbers. The Fibonacci numbers consist of the sequence of numbers f_i that satisfy the relation $f_i = f_{i-1} + f_{i-2}$, with $f_0 = 1$ and $f_1 = 1$. We can try to devise both quadtree and bintree splitting rules based on such a sequence. Generally for a decomposition scheme to be useful in geometric applications, it must have pixel-sized squares (i.e., 1×1) as the primitive tiles. At first glance, it appears that the Fibonacci sequence gives quite a bit of leeway in deciding on a splitting sequence and on the sizes of the regions corresponding to the subtrees and the primitive tiles.

One possible quadtree splitting rule is to restrict all shapes to squares with sides whose lengths are Fibonacci numbers. Clearly not all the shapes can be squares since we cannot aggregate these squares into larger squares that obey this rule. Another possibility is to restrict the shapes to rectangles the length of whose sides are either equal Fibonacci numbers or are successive Fibonacci numbers (see Exercise 1.26). We term this condition the *2-d Fibonacci condition*.

In this discussion, we have assumed splitting rules that ensure that vertical subdivision lines at the same level are colinear as well as for horizontal lines at the same level. For example, when using a quadtree splitting rule, the vertical lines that subdivide the NW and SW quadrants are colinear, as well as for the horizontal lines that subdivide the NW and NE quadrants. An alternative is to relax the colinearity restriction; however, the sides of the shapes must still satisfy the 2-d Fibonacci condition (see Exercise 1.27).

As can be seen in Exercises 1.26 and 1.27, neither a quadtree nor a bintree can

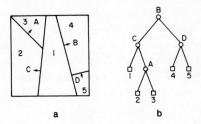

Figure 1.19   (a) An arbitrary space decomposition and (b) its BSP tree. The arrows indicate the direction of the positive halfspaces.

be used by itself as a basis for Fibonacci-based space decomposition; however, a combination of the two structures could be used. When the lengths of the sides of a rectangle are equal, the rectangle is split into four rectangles such that the lengths of the sides satisfy the 2-d Fibonacci condition. When the lengths of the sides of a rectangle are not equal, the rectangle is split into two rectangles with the split along a line (an axis) parallel to the shorter (longer) of the two sides. Interestingly the dimensions of the A-series of European paper are based on a Fibonacci sequence—that is, the elements of the series are of dimension $f_i \times f_{i-1}$ multiplied by an appropriate scale factor.

Another variation on the bintree idea, termed *adaptive hierarchical coding* (*AHC*), is proposed by Cohen, Landy, and Pavel [Cohe85b]. In this case, the image is again split into two equal-sized parts at each stage, but there is no need to alternate between the x and y coordinates. The decision as to the coordinate on which to partition depends on the image. This technique may require some work to get the optimal partition from the point of view of a minimum number of nodes (see Exercise 1.29).

An even more general variation on the bintree is the BSP tree of Fuchs, Kedem, and Naylor [Fuch80, Fuch83]. Its variants are used in some hidden-surface elimination algorithms (see Section 7.1.5 of [Same90b]) and in some implementations of beam tracing (see Section 7.3 of [Same90b]). It is applicable to data of arbitrary dimension, although here it is explained in the context of two-dimensional data. At each subdivision stage, the image is subdivided into two parts of arbitrary size. Note that successive subdivision lines need be neither orthogonal nor parallel. Therefore the resulting decomposition consists of arbitrarily shaped convex polygons.

The BSP tree is a binary tree. To be able to assign regions to the left and right subtrees, we associate a direction with each subdivision line. In particular, the subdivision lines are treated as separators between two halfspaces.[9] Let the line have the

---

[9] A (linear) *halfspace* in d-space is defined by the inequality $\sum_{i=0}^{d} a_i \cdot x_i \geq 0$ on the $d + 1$ homogeneous coordinates ($x_0 = 1$). The halfspace is represented by a column vector a. In vector notation, the inequality is written as $a \cdot x \geq 0$. In the case of equality, it defines a hyperplane with a as its normal. It is important to note that halfspaces are volume, not boundary, elements.

equation $a \cdot x + b \cdot y + c = 0$. We say that the right subtree is the 'positive' side and contains all subdivision lines formed by separators that satisfy $a \cdot x + b \cdot y + c \geq 0$. Similarly we say that the left subtree is 'negative' and contains all subdivision lines formed by separators that satisfy $a \cdot x + b \cdot y + c < 0$. As an example, consider Figure 1.19a, which is an arbitrary space decomposition whose BSP tree is given in Figure 1.19b. Notice the use of arrows to indicate the direction of the positive halfspaces.

Exercises

1.17. Given a $[6^3]$ tiling such that each side of an atomic tile has a unit length, compute the three adjacency distances from the centroid of an atomic tile.

1.18. Repeat Exercise 1.17 for $[3^6]$ and $[4^4]$, again assuming that each side of an atomic tile has a unit length.

1.19. Suppose that you are given an image in the form of a binary array of pixels. The result is a square grid. How can you view this grid as a hexagonal grid?

1.20. Show how the property sphere data structure can be used to model the earth. In particular, discuss how to represent landmass features, such as mountain ranges and crevices.

1.21 Suppose that you use an icosahedron to model spherical data. Initially there are 20 faces. How many faces are there after the first level of decomposition when $n = 2$? $n = \sqrt{3}$?

1.22. What is the ratio of leaf nodes to nonleaf nodes in a bintree for a d-dimensional image?

1.23. What is a lower bound on the ratio of leaf nodes in a bintree to that in a quadtree for a d-dimensional image? What is an upper bound? What is the average?

1.24. Is it true that the total number of nodes in a bintree is always less than that in the corresponding quadtree?

1.25. The Fibonacci numbers are defined by the relation $f_n = f_{n-1} + f_{n-2}$. Devise a two-dimensional analog of this relation to correspond to a splitting rule that would have to be satisfied in a Fibonacci-based space decomposition that yields four parts. Generalize this result to n dimensions.

1.26. Give a counterexample to the use of a quadtree splitting rule in a Fibonacci-based space decomposition.

1.27. Give a counterexample to the use of a bintree splitting rule in a Fibonacci-based space decomposition.

1.28. Suppose that you use the combination quadtree-bintree approach to a Fibonacci-based space decomposition. Prove that any image such that the lengths of its sides satisfy the 2-d Fibonacci condition can be decomposed into subimages whose sides obey this property and with a primitive tile of size 1×1.

1.29. Suppose that you use the AHC method. How many different rectangles and positions must be examined in building such a structure for a $2^n \times 2^n$ image?

1.4.2 Nonpolygonal Tilings

In the previous section we focused on space decompositions based on polygonal tiles. This is the prevalent method in use today. For certain applications, however, the use of polygonal tiles can lead to problems. For example, suppose that we have a decomposition based on square tiles. In this case, as the resolution is increased, the area of the approximated region approaches the true value of the area; however, this is not true for a boundary measure such as the perimeter. To see this, consider a quadtree approximation of an isosceles right triangle where the ratio of the approximated perimeter to the true perimeter is $4/(2 + \sqrt{2})$ (see Exercise 1.30). Other problems include the discontinuity of the normals to the boundaries of adjacent tiles.

There are a number of ways of attempting to overcome these problems. The *hierarchical probe model* of Chen [Chen85b] is an approach based on treating space as a polar plane and recursively decomposing it into sectors. We say that each sector consists of an origin, two sides (labeled 1 and 2 corresponding to the order in which they are encountered when proceeding in a counterclockwise direction), and an arc. The points at which the sides of the sector intersect (or touch) the object are called *contact points*. (ρ,θ) denotes a point in the polar plane. Let (ρ_i, θ_i) be the contact point with the maximum value of ρ in direction θ_i. Each sector represents a region bounded by the points $(0,0)$, (ρ_1,θ_1), and (ρ_2,θ_2), where $\theta_1 = 2k\pi/2^n$ and $\theta_2 = \theta_1 + 2\pi/2^n$ such that k and n are nonnegative integers ($k < 2^n$). The arc between the two nonorigin contact points (ρ_1, θ_1) and (ρ_2, θ_2) of a sector is approximated by the linear parametric equations ($0 \le t \le 1$):

$$\rho(t) = \rho_1 + (\rho_2 - \rho_1) \cdot t \quad \theta(t) = \theta_1 + (\theta_2 - \theta_1) \cdot t.$$

Note that the interpolation curves are arcs of spirals due to the linear relation between ρ and θ.

The *sector tree* is a binary tree that represents the result of recursively subdividing sectors in the polar plane into two sectors of equal angular intervals. Thus the recursive decomposition is only with respect to θ, not ρ. The decomposition stops whenever the approximation of a part of an object by a sector is deemed to be adequate. The computation of the stopping condition is implementation dependent. For example, it can be the maximum deviation in the value of ρ between a point on the boundary and the corresponding point (i.e., at the same value of θ) on the approximating arc. Initially the universe is the interval $[0,2\pi)$.

In the presentation, we assume that the origin of the polar plane is contained within the object. See Exercise 1.36 for a discussion of how to represent an object that does not contain the origin of the polar plane. The simplest case arises when the object is convex. The result is a binary tree where each leaf node represents a sector and contains the contact points of its corresponding arc. For example, consider the object in Figure 1.20. The construction of its sector tree approximation is shown in

Figure 1.20   Example convex object

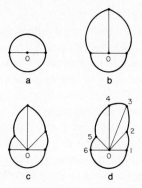

a   b

c   d

Figure 1.21   Successive sector tree approximations for the object of Figure 1.20: (a) π intervals, (b) π/2 intervals, (c) π/4 intervals, (d) π/8 intervals

Figures 1.21a–d. The final binary tree is given in Figure 1.22 with interval endpoints labeled according to Figure 1.21d.

The situation is more complex when the object is not convex. This means that each side of a sector may intersect the boundary of the object at an arbitrary, and possibly different, number of contact points. In the following, each sector will be seen to consist of a set of alternating regions within and outside the object. These regions are three-sided or four-sided and have at least one side that is colinear with a side of the sector. The discussion is illustrated with the object of Figure 1.23a whose sector tree decomposition is given in Figure 1.23b. The final binary tree is given in Figure 1.24. A better indication of the quality of the approximation can be seen by examining Figure 1.23c, which contains an overlay of Figures 1.23a and 1.23b.

When the boundary of the object intersects a sector at two successive contact points, say P and Q, that lie on the same side, say S, of the sector, then the region

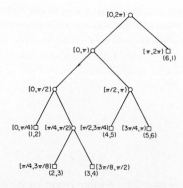

Figure 1.22   Binary tree representation of the sector tree of Figure 1.20

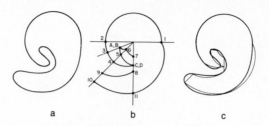

a   b   c

Figure 1.23   (a) Example object, (b) its sector tree description, and (c) a comparison of the sector tree approximation
(thin lines) with the original object (thick lines). Note the
creation of a hole corresponding to the region formed by
points 5, 6, 7, and C

bounded by S and PQ must be approximated. Without loss of generality, assume that the region is inside the object. There are two choices. An inner approximation ignores the region by treating the segment of S between P and Q as part of the approximated boundary (e.g., the region between points 9 and 10 in sector $[9\pi/8, 5\pi/4)$ in Figure 1.23b).

An outer approximation inserts two identical contact points, say R and T, on the other side of the sector and then approximates the region by the three-sided region formed by the segment of S between P and Q and the spiral arc approximations of PR and QT. The value of R (and hence T) is equal to the average of the value of ρ at P and Q. For example, the region between points 4 and 5 in sector $[5\pi/4, 3\pi/2)$ in Figure 1.23b is approximated by the region formed with points C and D.

Of course, the same approximation process is applied to the part of the region outside the object. In Figure 1.23b, we have an inner approximation for the region between points 7 and 8 in sector $[3\pi/2, 2\pi)$, and an outer approximation for the region between points 5 and 6 in sector $[9\pi/8, 5\pi/4)$, by virtue of the introduction of points A and B.

One of the problems with the sector tree is that its use can lead to the creation of holes that do not exist in the original object. This situation arises when the decomposition is not carried out to a level of sufficient depth. For example, consider Figure 1.23b, which has a hole bounded by the arcs formed by points A, B, 6, 7, C, D, and 5. This is a result of the inner approximation for the region between points 7 and 8 in sector $[3\pi/2, 2\pi)$ and an outer approximation for the region between points 4 and 5 in sector $[5\pi/4, 3\pi/2)$. This situation can be resolved by further decomposition in either or both of sectors $[3\pi/2, 2\pi)$ and $[5\pi/4, 3\pi/2)$.

The result of the approximation process is that each sector consists of a collection of three-sided and four-sided regions that approximate the part of the object contained in the sector. This collection is stored in the leaf node of the sector tree as a list of pairs of points in the polar plane. It is interesting to observe that the boundaries of the interpolated regions are not stored explicitly in the tree. Instead each pair of points corresponds to the boundary of a region. Since the origin of the polar plane is within the object, an odd number of pairs of points is associated with each leaf node. For

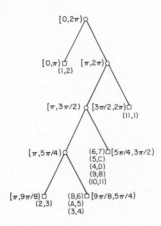

Figure 1.24 Binary tree representation of the sector tree of Figure 1.23

example, consider the leaf node in Figure 1.24 corresponding to the sector $[5\pi/4, 3\pi/2)$. The first pair, together with the origin, defines the first region (e.g., (6,7)). The next two pairs of points define the second region (e.g., (5,C) and (4,D)), with each successive two pairs of points defining the remaining regions.

The sector tree is a partial polar decomposition, as the subdivision process is based only on the value of θ. A total polar decomposition would partition the polar plane on the basis of both ρ and θ. The result is analogous to a quadtree, and it is termed a *polar quadtree*. There are a number of possible rules for the decomposition process (see Exercise 1.42). For example, consider a decomposition that recursively halves both ρ and θ at each level. In general, the polar quadtree is a variant of a maximal block representation. As in the sector tree, the blocks are disjoint. Unlike the sector tree, blocks in the polar quadtree do have standard sizes. In particular, all blocks in the polar quadtree are either three sided (i.e., sectors) or four sided (i.e., quadrilaterals, two of whose sides are arcs). Thus the sides of polar quadtree blocks are not based on interpolation.

The primary motivation for presenting the sector tree is to show that space decompositions could also be based on nonpolygonal tiles. In the rest of this book the primary concern is with space decompositions based on rectangles (especially squares) and showing how a number of operations can be performed when they serve as the underlying representation. The techniques are quite general and can be applied to most space decomposition methods. Thus the sector tree is not discussed further except in the context of its adaptation to the representation of three-dimensional data (see Section 5.6). Nevertheless, the following contains a brief mention of some of the operations to which the sector tree lends itself.

Set operations such as union and intersection are straightforward. Scaling is trivial as the sector tree need not be modified; all values of ρ are interpreted as scaled by the appropriate scale factor. The number of nodes in a sector tree is dependent on its orientation—that is, on the points chosen as the origin and the contact point chosen to serve as (ρ,0). Rotation is not so simple; it cannot be implemented by simply rearranging pointers (but see Exercise 1.40). Translation is computationally expensive since the change in the relative position of the object with respect to the origin means that the entire sector tree must be reconstructed.

Exercises

1.30. Prove that for an isosceles right triangle represented by a region quadtree, the ratio of the approximated perimeter to the true perimeter is $4/(2 + \sqrt{2})$.

1.31. Repeat Exercise 1.30 for a circle (i.e., find the ratio).

1.32. When the objects have linear sides, polygonal tiles are superior. How would you use the sector tree decomposition method with polygonal tiles?

1.33. In the discussion of the situation arising when the boundary of the object intersects a sector at two successive contact points, say P and Q, that lie on the same side, say S, of the sector, we assumed that the region bounded by S and PQ was inside the object. Suppose that this region is outside the object. How does this affect the inner and outer approximations?

1.34. Can you traverse the boundary of an object represented by a sector tree by visiting each leaf node just once?

1.35. When using a sector tree, how would you handle the situation that the boundary of the object just touches the side of a sector without crossing it (i.e., a tangent if the boundary is differentiable)?

1.36. How would you use a sector tree to represent an object that does not contain the origin of the polar plane?

1.37. The outer approximation used in building a sector tree always yields a three-sided region. Two of the sides are arcs of spirals with respect to a common origin. This implies a sharp discontinuity of the derivative at the point at which they meet. Can you devise a way to smoothe this discontinuity?

1.38. Does the inner approximation used in building a sector tree always underestimate the area? Similarly does the outer approximation always overestimate the area?

1.39. Compare the inner and outer approximations used in building a sector tree. Is there ever a reason for the outer approximation to be preferred over the inner approximations (or vice-versa)?

1.40. Define a complete sector tree in an analogous manner to a complete binary tree—that is, all leaf nodes are at the same level, say n. Prove that a complete sector tree is invariant under rotation in multiples of $2\pi/2^n$.

1.41. Write an algorithm to trace the boundary of an object represented by a sector tree.

1.42. Suppose that it is desired to decompose space into nonpolygonal shapes. Develop a quadtree-like data structure based on polar coordinates (i.e., ρ and θ). Investigate different splitting rules for polar quadtrees. In particular, you do not need to alternate the splits—that is, you could split on ρ several times in a row, and so on. This technique is used in the adaptive k–d tree [Frie77] (see Section 2.4.1) by decomposing the quartering process into two splitting operations—one for the x coordinate and one for the y coordinate. What are the possible shapes for the quadrants of such trees (e.g., a torus, doughnut, wheels with spokes)?

1.5   SPACE REQUIREMENTS

The primary motivation for the development of the quadtree was the desire to reduce the amount of space necessary to store data through the use of aggregation of homogeneous blocks. As we will see in subsequent chapters, an important by-product of this aggregation is the reduction of the execution time of a number of operations (e.g., connected component labeling, component counting). However, a quadtree implementation does have overhead in terms of the nonleaf nodes. For an image with B and W black and white blocks, respectively, $4 \cdot (B + W)/3$ nodes are required. In contrast, a binary array representation of a $2^n \times 2^n$ image requires only 2^{2n} bits; however, this quantity grows quite quickly. Furthermore, if the amount of aggregation is minimal (e.g., a checkerboard image), the quadtree is not very efficient.

The overhead for the nonleaf nodes can be reduced at times by using a pointerless representation. Pointer-less representations can be grouped into two categories. The first, termed a *DF-expression*, represents the quadtree as a traversal of its constituent nodes [Kawa80a]. For example, letting 'B', 'W', and 'G' correspond to black, white, and gray nodes, respectively, and assuming a traversal in the order NW, NE, SW, and SE, the quadtree of Figure 1.1 would be represented by GWGWWBBGWGW BBBWBGBBGBBBWW.

The second approach treats the quadtree as a collection of the leaf nodes comprising it. Each node is represented by a pair of numbers [Garg82c]. The first number is the level of the tree at which the node is located. The second number is termed a *locational code*. It is formed by a concatenation of base 4 digits corresponding to directional codes that locate the node along a path from the root of the quadtree. The directional codes take on the values 0, 1, 2, 3 corresponding to quadrants NW, NE, SW, SE, respectively. For example, node 15 in Figure 1.1 is represented by the pair of numbers (0,320), which is decoded as follows. The base 4 locational code is 320. The pair denotes a node at level 0 that is reached by a sequence of transitions, SE, SW, and NW, starting at the root. A quadtree representation based on the use of locational codes is called *linear quadtree* by Gargantini [Garg82a, Garg82c] (because the addresses are keys in a linear list of nodes). Pointer-less representations are discussed in greater detail in Chapter 2 of [Same90b].

The worst case for a quadtree of a given depth in terms of storage requirements occurs when the region corresponds to a checkerboard pattern as in Figure 1.25. The amount of space required is obviously a function of the resolution (i.e., the number of levels in the quadtree), the size of the image (i.e., its perimeter), and its positioning in the grid within which it is embedded. As a simple example, Dyer [Dyer82] has shown that arbitrarily placing a square of size $2^m \times 2^m$ at any position in a $2^n \times 2^n$ image requires an average of $O(2^{m+2} + n - m)$ quadtree nodes. An alternative characterization of this result is that the average amount of space necessary is $O(p + n)$ where p is the perimeter (in pixel widths) of the block.

Dyer's $O(p + n)$ result for a square image is merely an instance of the earlier work of Hunter and Steiglitz [Hunt78, Hunt79a] who proved some fundamental theorems on the space requirements of images represented by quadtrees. In their

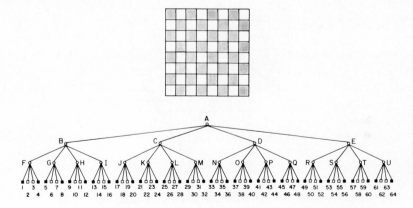

Figure 1.25   A checkerboard and its quadtree

studies, Hunter and Steiglitz used simple polygons (polygons with nonintersecting edges and without holes); however, these theorems have been observed to hold in arbitrary images (see [Rose82b] for empirical results in a cartographic environment).

In Hunter and Steiglitz's formulation, a polygon is represented by a three-color variant of the quadtree. In essence, there are three types of nodes: interior, boundary, and exterior. A node is said to be of type *boundary* if an edge of the polygon passes through it. *Interior* and *exterior* nodes correspond to areas within, and outside, respectively, the polygon and can be merged to yield larger nodes. The resulting quadtree is analogous to the MX quadtree representation of point data described below (for more details, see Section 2.6.1), and this term will be used to describe it. In particular, boundary nodes are analogous to black nodes, while interior and exterior nodes are analogous to white nodes.

Figure 1.26 illustrates a sample polygon and its MX quadtree. One disadvantage of the MX quadtree representation for polygonal lines is that a width is associated with them, whereas in a purely technical sense these lines have a width of zero. Also shifting operations may result in information loss. (For more appropriate representations of polygonal lines, see Chapter 4.)

An upper bound on the number of nodes in such a representation of a polygon can be obtained in the following manner. First, we observe that a curve of length $d + \varepsilon \, (\varepsilon > 0)$ can intersect at most six squares of side width d. Now consider a polygon, say G, having perimeter p, that is embedded in a grid of squares each of side width d. Mark the points at which G enters and exits each square. Choose one of these points, say P, as a starting point for a decomposition of G into a sequence of curves. Define the first curve in G to be the one extending from P until six squares have been intersected and a crossing is made into a different seventh square. This is the starting point for another curve in G that intersects six new squares, not counting those intersected by any previous curve.

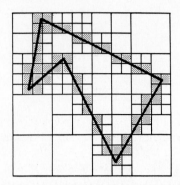

Figure 1.26   Hunter and Steiglitz's quadtree representation of a polygon

We now decompose G into a series of such curves. Since each curve adds at most six new squares and has length of at least d, we see that a polygon with perimeter p cannot intersect more than $6 \cdot \lceil p/d \rceil$ squares. Given a quadtree with a root at level n (i.e., the grid of squares is of width 2^n), at level i each square is of width 2^i. Therefore polygon G cannot intersect more than $B(i) = 6 \cdot \lceil p/2^i \rceil$ quadrants at level i. Recall that our goal is to derive an upper bound on the total number of nodes. This bound is attained when each boundary node at level i has three brother nodes that are not intersected. Of course, only boundary nodes can have sons, and thus no more than $B(i)$ nodes at level i have sons. Since each node at level i is a son of a node at level $i+1$, there are at most $4 \cdot B(i+1)$ nodes at level i. Summing up over n levels (accounting for a root node at level n and four sons), we find that the total number of nodes in the tree is bounded by

$$1 + 4 + \sum_{i=0}^{n-2} 4 \cdot B(i+1)$$

$$\leq 5 + 24 \cdot \sum_{i=0}^{n-2} \left\lceil \frac{p}{2^{i+1}} \right\rceil$$

$$\leq 5 + 24 \cdot \sum_{i=0}^{n-2} \left(1 + \frac{p}{2^{i+1}}\right)$$

$$\leq 5 + 24 \cdot (n-1) + 24 \cdot p \cdot \sum_{i=0}^{n-2} \frac{1}{2^{i+1}}$$

$$\leq 24 \cdot n - 19 + 24 \cdot p.$$

Therefore, we have proved:

> **Theorem 1.1** The quadtree corresponding to a polygon with perimeter p embedded in a $2^n \times 2^n$ image has a maximum of $24 \cdot n - 19 + 24 \cdot p$ (i.e., $O(p+n)$) nodes. ☐

The proof of Theorem 1.1 is based on a decomposition of the polygon into a sequence of curves, each of which intersects at most six squares. This bound can be tightened by examining patterns of squares to obtain minimum lengths and corresponding ratios of possible squares per unit length. For example, observe that once a curve intersects six squares, the next curve of length d in the sequence can intersect at most two new squares. In contrast, it is easy to construct a sequence of curves of length $d + \varepsilon$ ($\varepsilon > 0$) such that almost each curve intersects two squares of side length d. Such a construction leads to an upper bound of the form $a \cdot n + b + 8 \cdot p$ where a and b are constants (see Exercise 1.48). Hunter and Steiglitz use a slightly different construction to obtain a bound of $16 \cdot n - 11 + 16 \cdot p$ (see Exercise 1.49).

Nevertheless, the bound of Theorem 1.1 is attainable as demonstrated by the following examples. First, consider a square of side width 2 that consists of the central four squares in a $2^n \times 2^n$ image (see Figure 1.27). Its quadtree has $16 \cdot n - 11$ nodes (see Exercise 1.50). Second, consider a curve that follows a vertical line through the center of a $2^n \times 2^n$ image. Now, make it a bit longer by making it intersect all of the pixels on either side of the vertical line (see Figure 1.28). As n increases, the total number of nodes in the quadtree approaches $8 \cdot p$ where $p = 2^n$ (see Exercise 1.51). A polygon having a number of nodes approaching $8 \cdot p$ can be constructed in a similar manner by approximating a square in the center of the image whose side is one-fourth the side of the image (see Exercise 1.52). In fact, it has been shown by Hunter [Hunt78] that $O(p+n)$ is a least upper bound on the number of nodes in a quadtree corresponding to a polygon (see Exercise 1.53).

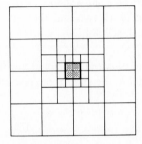

Figure 1.27   Example quadtree with $16 \cdot n - 11$ nodes

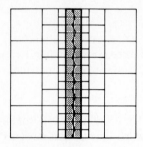

Figure 1.28 Example quadtree with approximately 8 · p nodes

Theorem 1.1 can be recast by measuring the perimeter p in terms of the length of a side of the image in which the polygon is embedded—i.e., for a $2^n \times 2^n$ image $p = p' \cdot 2^n$. Thus the value of the perimeter no longer depends on the resolution of the image. Restating Theorem 1.1 in terms of p' results in a quadtree having $O(p' \cdot 2^n + n)$ nodes. This leads to the following important corollary:

Corollary 1.1 The maximum number of nodes in a quadtree corresponding to an image is directly proportional to the resolution of the image. □

The significance of Corollary 1.1 is that when using quadtrees, increasing the image resolution leads to a linear growth in the number of nodes. This is in contrast to the binary array representation where doubling the resolution leads to a quadrupling of the number of pixels.

Since in most practical cases the perimeter, p, dominates the resolution, n, the results of Theorem 1.1 are usually interpreted as stating that the number of nodes in a quadtree is proportional to the perimeter of the regions contained therein.[10] Meagher [Meag80] has shown that this theorem also holds for three-dimensional data (i.e., for polyhedra represented by octrees) when the perimeter is replaced by the surface area. The perimeter and the surface area correspond to the size of the boundary of the polygon and polyhedron—that is, in two and three dimensions, respectively. In d dimensions this result can be stated as follows:

Theorem 1.2: The size of a d-dimensional quadtree of a d-dimensional polyhedron is proportional to the sum of the resolution and the size of the boundary of the object. □

---

[10] Of course, the storage used by runlength codes is also proportional to the perimeter of the regions. However, runlength codes do not facilitate access to different parts of the regions (i.e., they have poor spatial indexing properties).

Aside from their implications on the storage requirements, Theorems 1.1 and 1.2 also directly affect the analysis of the execution time of algorithms. In particular, most algorithms that execute on a quadtree representation of an image instead of an array representation have an execution time proportional to the number of blocks in the image rather than the number of pixels. In its most general case, this means that the application of a quadtree algorithm to a problem in d-dimensional space executes in time proportional to the analogous array-based algorithm in the $(d-1)$-dimensional space of the surface of the original d-dimensional image. Thus quadtrees are somewhat like dimension-reducing devices.

Theorem 1.2 assumes that the image consists of a polyhedron. Walsh [Wals85] lifts this restriction and obtains a weaker complexity bound. Assuming an image of resolution n and measuring the perimeter, say p, in terms of the number of border pixels, he proves that the total number of nodes in a d-dimensional quadtree is less than or equal to $4 \cdot n \cdot p$. Furthermore he shows that the number of black nodes is less than or equal to $(2^d - 1) \cdot n \cdot p / d$.

The complexity measures discussed above do not explicitly reflect the fact that the amount of space occupied by a quadtree corresponding to a region is extremely sensitive to its orientation (i.e., where it is partitioned). For example, in Dyer's experiment, the number of nodes required for the arbitrary placement of a square of size $2^m \times 2^m$ at any position in a $2^n \times 2^n$ image ranged between $4 \cdot (n-m) + 1$ and $4 \cdot p + 16 \cdot (n-m) - 27$, with the average being $O(p+n-m)$. Clearly shifting the image within the space in which it is embedded can reduce the total number of nodes. The problem of finding the optimal position for a quadtree can be decomposed into two parts. First, we must determine the optimal grid resolution and, second, the partition points.

Grosky and Jain [Gros83] have shown that for a region such that w is the maximum of its horizontal and vertical extent (measured in pixel widths) and $2^{n-1} < w \le 2^n$, the optimal grid resolution is either n or $n+1$. In other words embedding the region in a larger area than $2^{n+1} \times 2^{n+1}$ and shifting it around will not result in fewer nodes. Using similar reasoning, it can be shown that translating a region by 2^k pixels in any direction does not change the number of black or white blocks of size less than $2^k \times 2^k$ [Li82].

Armed with the above results, Li, Grosky, and Jain [Li82] developed the following algorithm that treats the image as a binary array and finds the configuration of the region in the image so that its quadtree requires a minimum number of nodes. First, enlarge the image to be $2^{n+1} \times 2^{n+1}$, and place the region within it so that the region's northernmost and westernmost pixels are adjacent to the northern and western borders, respectively, of the image. Next apply successive translations to the image of magnitude power of two in the vertical, horizontal, and corner directions and keep count of the number of leaf nodes required. Initially 2^{2n+2} leaf nodes are necessary. The following is a more precise statement of the algorithm:

1. Attempt to translate the image by (x,y) where x and y correspond to unit translations in the horizontal and vertical directions, respectively. Each of x and y takes on the values 0 or 1.

2. For the result of each translation in step 1, construct a new array at one-half the resolution. Each entry in the new array corresponds to a 2×2 block in the translated array. For each entry in the new array that corresponds to a single color (not gray) 2×2 block in the translated array, decrement the leaf node count by 3.

3. Recursively apply steps 1 and 2 to each result of steps 1 and 2. This process stops when no single-color 2×2 block is found in step 2 (i.e., they are all gray) or if the new array is a 1×1 block. Record the total translation and the minimum leaf node count.

Step 2 makes use of the property that for a translation of 2^k, there is a need to check only if single-color blocks of size $2^k \times 2^k$ or more are formed. In fact, because of the recursion, at each step we check only for the formation of blocks of size $2^{k+1} \times 2^{k+1}$. Note that the algorithm tries every possible translation since any integer can be decomposed into a summation of powers of two (i.e., use its binary representation). In fact this is why a translation of (0,0) is part of step 1. Although the algorithm computes the positioning of the quadtree with the minimum number of leaf nodes, it is also the positioning of the quadtree with the minimum total number of nodes since the number of nonleaf nodes in a quadtree of T leaf nodes is $(T-1)/3$.

As an example of the algorithm, consider the region given in Figure 1.29a whose block decomposition is shown in Figure 1.29b. Its quadtree requires 52 leaf nodes. The first step is to enlarge the image, place the region in the upper left corner, and form the array (Figure 1.30). The optimal positioning is such that Figure 1.30 is shifted 7 units in the horizontal direction and 3 units in the vertical direction. This corresponds to a sequence of translations (1,1), (1,1), and (1,0). The intermediate translated arrays are shown in Figure 1.31. All gray nodes in the translated arrays are labeled with a 'G' while black nodes are shaded. The optimal quadtree contains 46 leaf nodes and is given in Figure 1.32.

Now let us trace the algorithm as it applies the optimal sequence of translations, in more detail. Initially the leaf node count is 256. A translation of (1,1) leads to Figure 1.31a where 58 of the array entries correspond to single-color 2×2 blocks in the translated array. The leaf node count is decremented by $58 \cdot 3 = 174$, resulting in

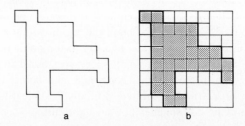

a   b

Figure 1.29   Example (a) image and (b) its block decomposition used to demonstrate the optimal positioning process

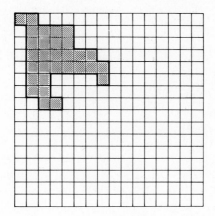

Figure 1.30   The array corresponding to the image in Figure 1.29 prior to the start of the optimal positioning process

82. The next translation of (1,1) leads to Figure 1.31b, where 11 of the array entries correspond to single-color 2×2 blocks. Therefore $11 \cdot 3 = 33$ is subtracted from 82, and the leaf node count is now 49. The final translation of (1,0) leads to Figure 1.31c, where only one of the array entries corresponds to a single-color 2×2 block in the translated array. Decrementing the leaf node count results in 46 nodes, and the process terminates. Of course, we have failed to describe the remaining $4^n - 3$ translations that were also attempted.

Despite trying all possible translations, the algorithm is quite efficient. The key is that for each translation, only the blocks whose motion can lead to space saving need to be considered. This is a direct consequence of the property that a translation of 2^k does not change the number of blocks of size less than $2^k \times 2^k$. For an image that has been enlarged to fit in a $2^{n+1} \times 2^{n+1}$ array, the algorithm will have a maximum depth of recursion of n. Since at each level of recursion we need an array at half the resolution of the previous level, the total amount of space required is $(4/3) \cdot 2^{2n+2}$.

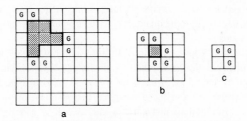

Figure 1.31   The successive translated arrays at half-resolution after application of (a) (1,1) and (b) (1,1), and (c) (1,0) to the original image array of Figure 1.30

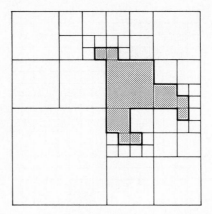

Figure 1.32   Optimal positioning of the quadtree of Figure 1.29

The basic computational task of the algorithm is to count 2×2 blocks of a single color. It can be shown that $4 \cdot n \cdot 2^{2n+2}$ array elements are examined in this process (see Exercise 1.63). Thus the algorithm uses $O(2^{2n})$ space and takes $O(n \cdot 2^{2n})$ time. Nevertheless experiments with typical images show that the algorithm has little effect (e.g., [Same84c]).

Exercises

1.43. Consider the arbitrary placement of a square of size $2^m \times 2^m$ at any position in a $2^n \times 2^n$ image. Prove that in the best case $4 \cdot (n-m) + 1$ nodes are required, while the worst case requires $4 \cdot p + 16 \cdot (n-m) - 27$ nodes. How many of these nodes are black and white, assuming that the square is black? Prove that on the average, the number of nodes that is required is $O(p+n-m)$.

1.44. What are the worst-case storage requirements of storing an arbitrary rectangle in a quadtree corresponding to a $2^n \times 2^n$ image? Give an example of the worst case and the number of nodes it requires.

1.45 Assume that the probability of a particular pixel's being black is one-half and likewise for being white. Given a $2^n \times 2^n$ image represented by a quadtree, what is the expected number of nodes, say $E(n)$, in the quadtree? Also compute the expected number of black, white, and gray nodes.

1.46 Suppose that instead of knowing the probability a particular pixel is black or white, we know the percentage of the total pixels in the image that are black. Given a $2^n \times 2^n$ image represented by a quadtree, what is the expected number of nodes in the quadtree?

1.47. The proof of Theorem 1.1 and the subsequent discussion raise the question of how N squares should be arranged so that each is intersected by a curve of minimum length extending to the outside of the squares on each end. Such a configuration leads to a minimal curve in the sense that it has a maximal ratio of squares to length. For which value of N is this ratio the smallest?

1.48. Try to prove that the upper bound of Theorem 1.1 can be tightened to be $a \cdot n + b + 8 \cdot p$ where a and b are constants.

1.49. Decompose the polygon used in the proof of Theorem 1.1 into a sequence of curves in the following manner. Mark the points where G enters and exits each square of side width d. Choose one of these points, say P, and define the first curve in G as extending from P until four squares have been intersected and a crossing is made into a different fifth square. This is the starting point for another curve in G that intersects four new squares, not counting those intersected by any previous curve. Prove that all of the curves, except for the last one, must be at least of length d. Using this result, prove that the upper bound on the number of nodes in the quadtree is $16 \cdot n - 11 + 16 \cdot p$.

1.50. Prove that the quadtree corresponding to a square of side width 2 consisting of the central four squares in a $2^n \times 2^n$ image has $16 \cdot n - 11$ nodes (see Figure 1.27).

1.51. Take a curve that follows a vertical line through the center of a $2^n \times 2^n$ image and lengthen it slightly by making it intersect all of the pixels on either side of the vertical line (see Figure 1.28). Prove that as n increases, the total number of nodes in the quadtree approaches $8 \cdot p$ where $p = 2^n$.

1.52. Using a technique analogous to that used in Exercise 1.51, construct a polygon of perimeter p by approximating a square in the center of the image whose side is one-fourth the side of the image. Prove that its quadtree has approximately $8 \cdot p$ nodes.

1.53. Prove that $O(p+n)$ is a least upper bound on the number of nodes in a quadtree corresponding to a polygon. Assume that $p \le 2^{2n}$ (i.e., the number of pixels in the image). Equivalently the polygon boundary can touch all of the pixels in the most trivial way but can be no longer. Decompose your proof into two parts depending on whether p is greater than $4 \cdot n$.

1.54. Can you prove that for an arbitrary quadtree (not necessarily a polygon), the number of nodes doubles as the resolution is doubled?

1.55. Derive a result analogous to Theorem 1.1 for a three-dimensional polyhedron represented as an octree. In this case the perimeter corresponds to the surface area.

1.56. Prove Theorem 1.2.

1.57. Assuming an image of resolution n and measuring the perimeter, say p, in terms of the number of border pixels, prove that the total number of nodes in a d-dimensional quadtree is less than or equal to $4 \cdot n \cdot p$.

1.58. Assuming an image of resolution n and measuring the perimeter, say p, in terms of the number of border pixels, prove that the total number of black nodes in a d-dimensional quadtree is less than or equal to $(2^d - 1) \cdot n \cdot p/d$.

1.59. How tight are the bounds obtained in Exercises 1.57 and 1.58 for the number of nodes in a d-dimensional quadtree for an arbitrary region? Are they realizable?

1.60. Prove that for a region such that w is the maximum of its horizontal and vertical extent (measured in pixel widths) and $2^{n-1} < w \le 2^n$, the optimal grid resolution is either n or $n+1$.

1.61. Prove that translating a region by 2^k pixels in any direction does not change the number of black or white blocks of size less than $2^k \times 2^k$.

1.62. Can you formally prove that the method described in the text does indeed yield the optimal quadtree?

1.63. Prove that $4 \cdot n \cdot 2^{2n+2}$ array elements are examined in the process of constructing the optimal quadtree.

1.64. How would you find the optimal bintree?

POINT DATA 2

Multidimensional point data can be represented in a variety of ways. The representation ultimately chosen for a specific task is heavily influenced by the type of operations to be performed on the data. As our discussion unfolds, the following issues will be seen to dominate, and thus it is useful to set them forth briefly. Should we organize the data or the embedding space from which the data are drawn? Is the database static or dynamic (i.e., can the number of data points grow and shrink at will)? Can we assume that the volume of data is sufficiently small so that it can all fit in core, or should we make provisions for accessing disk-resident data?

For data represented in core using trees, are the data restricted to the leaf nodes, or can they appear in nonleaf nodes as well? Disk-resident data implies grouping the data into physical units, termed *buckets*, and leads to questions about their size and how they are to be accessed. Do we require a constant time to retrieve a record from a file, or is a logarithmic function of the number of records in the file adequate? This is equivalent to asking if the access is via a directory in the form of an array (i.e., direct access) or by a tree. How large can the directories be allowed to grow? Also should ordering play a role in determining how individual records are grouped in storage?

The field of multidimensional point data structures is developing rapidly. There are no definitive ways to deal with these issues. In this chapter, our focus is on dynamic files and applications involving search. The presentation is limited to methods that can be viewed as direct applications of a quadtree-like recursive subdivision approach. These considerations will be seen to have a strong influence on the scope of the discussion of the above issues. However, whenever possible, references are given to alternative methods.

2.1 INTRODUCTION

Our database is a collection of records, termed a *file*. There is one record per data point. Each record contains several attributes or keys. A *query* is a request for all records that satisfy a predicate or have specific values or ranges of values for specified keys. Assume that a file contains N records with k keys apiece. Knuth [Knut73b] lists three typical queries:

1. A *point query*, which determines if a given data point is in the database and, if so, yields the address corresponding to the record in which it is stored.
2. A *range query* (i.e., region search), which asks for a set of data points whose specified keys have specific values or values within given ranges (this category includes the partially specified queries, also known as partial match and partial range, in which case unspecified keys take on the range of the key as their domain).
3. A *Boolean query*, which consists of combinations of types 1 and 2 with the Boolean operations AND, OR, NOT, and so on.

Another common query seeks the n nearest neighbors of a given point [Bent75a].

Nievergelt, Hinterberger, and Sevcik [Niev84] group searching techniques into two categories: those that organize the data to be stored and those that organize the embedding space from which the data are drawn. In computer graphics, this distinction is often phrased in terms of object-space hierarchies versus image-space hierarchies, respectively [Suth74]. In a more formal sense, the distinction is between *trees* and *tries* [Fred60], respectively. The binary search tree [Knut73b] is an example of the former since the boundaries of different regions in the search space are determined by the data being stored. Address computation methods such as radix searching [Knut73b] (also known as digital searching) are examples of the latter, since region boundaries are chosen from among locations that are fixed regardless of the content of the file.

An alternative way of viewing the distinction between trees and tries is by comparing the region quadtree with the point quadtree [Fink74]. The region quadtree is based on a regular decomposition, while the point quadtree is not. Nevertheless, as we shall later see, this categorization is not as clear-cut as the discussion seems to imply. In particular, some of the methods that are discussed will be characterized as hybrid in the sense that some attributes are organized in one way and the remaining attributes in another way. Still other methods will be described as organizing the embedding space, although the organization will be dictated by the data being stored.

There are a number of approaches to the problem of designing a representation for a file of multidimensional point data. The feasibility of these approaches depends, in part, on the number of attributes and their domains. At one extreme is a pure bit-map representation of the attribute space with one bit reserved for each possible record in the multidimensional point space whether or not it is present in the file. This representation may be of some value when the domains of the attributes are discrete and small (e.g., binary).

For a large set of attributes, as well as attributes with a continuous domain, the pure bitmap representation is not feasible for reasons that include the requirement of an impractical amount of storage. Instead we concentrate on files with records that have a finite number of attributes with large, but linearly ordered, domains. It will become clear that although the bitmap representation in its pure form is inappropriate, the grouping of bits into n-dimensional ($n \leq k$) cells (rectangles in two dimensions) is the key to a large number of solutions. The result of applying these methods is analogous to a compressed bitmap representation.

In this chapter, our attention is focused primarily on hierarchical data structures such as the quadtree and its variants, as well as the k-d tree. We also examine some data structures (such as the range tree) designed especially for optimal execution of range queries, albeit with significantly higher storage requirements. These hierarchical structures are compared with nonhierarchical data structures that include those based on grid methods. Actually they also exhibit hierarchical behavior but in a very limited sense. The discussion is primarily in the context of in-core applications. It is followed by a presentation of *bucket* methods aimed at ensuring efficient access to disk data. These are differentiated by the ways in which the buckets are accessed (e.g., directly or via trees). At the end we compare the various methods and show how closely related they really are. (Readers who are interested are urged to consult the surveys of Bentley and Friedman [Bent79b] and Overmars [Over88a], and the monograph of Overmars [Over83].)

All of the examples in this chapter are limited to two dimensions, although they can be easily generalized to an arbitrary number of dimensions. Multidimensional data arise in two ways. The domain may be intrinsically multidimensional, as in a multiattribute database. Alternatively such data may result from the application of a mapping from another domain. For example, in a two-dimensional space, rectangular objects with sides parallel to the coordinate axes can be represented as points in a four-dimensional space (see Section 3.4). As another example, Arvo and Kirk [Arvo87] make use of such a mapping in a ray tracing application (see Section 7.3 of [Same90b]). They represent a ray in a three-dimensional space as a point in a five-dimensional space by specifying the ray in terms of the x, y, and z coordinate values of its origin and the θ and ϕ parameters of its direction.

This chapter stresses techniques for building hierarchical data structures, to the extent that detailed algorithms are given for some of them (i.e., insertion and deletion of records), and on how they facilitate search queries, in particular, a range query. At times we also evaluate storage requirements of the various representations. For the purposes of the discussion, we shall assume that each field in a record occupies one computer word.

NAME	X	Y
CHICAGO	35	40
MOBILE	50	10
TORONTO	60	75
BUFFALO	80	65
DENVER	5	45
OMAHA	25	35
ATLANTA	85	15
MIAMI	90	5

Figure 2.1   Sequential list

2.2 NONHIERARCHICAL DATA STRUCTURES

The simplest way to store point data is in a sequential list. Given N records and k attributes to search on, searching such a data structure is an $O(N \cdot k)$ process since each record must be examined. As an example, consider the set of eight cities and their x and y coordinates as shown in Figure 2.1.[1] Another common technique is the inverted list method [Knut73b], in which for each key a sorted list is maintained of the records in the file.

Figure 2.2 is the inverted list representation of the data in Figure 2.1. There are two sorted lists, one for the x coordinate and one for the y coordinate. Note that the data stored in the lists are pointers into Figure 2.1. This enables pruning the search with respect to one key. In essence, the endpoints of the desired range for one key can be located efficiently by using its corresponding sorted list (e.g., by use of binary search). This resulting list is then searched by brute force. The average search has been shown in [Frie75] to be of $O(N^{1-1/k})$, under certain assumptions.

A popular method used by cartographers is called the *fixed-grid* (or *cell*) method [Knut73b, p. 554; Bent79b]. It divides the space into equal-sized cells (i.e., squares and cubes for two- and three-dimensional data, respectively) having width equal to the

X	Y
DENVER	MIAMI
OMAHA	MOBILE
CHICAGO	ATLANTA
MOBILE	OMAHA
TORONTO	CHICAGO
BUFFALO	DENVER
ATLANTA	BUFFALO
MIAMI	TORONTO

Figure 2.2   Inverted lists corresponding to Figure 2.1

---

[1] Recall from Section 1.2 that the correspondence between coordinates and city names is not geographically correct. This liberty has been taken so that the same example could be used throughout the text to illustrate a variety of concepts.

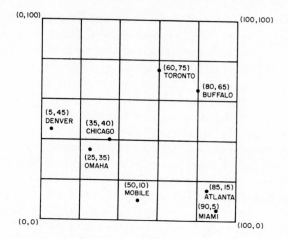

Figure 2.3 *Fixed-grid representation corresponding to Figure 2.1 with a search radius of 20*

search radius for a range query.[2] These cells are often referred to as *buckets*. The data structure is essentially a directory in the form of a k-dimensional array with one entry per cell. Each cell may be implemented as a linked list to represent the points within it.

Figure 2.3 is a fixed-grid representation for the data in Figure 2.1 for a search radius consisting of a square of size 20×20. Assuming a 100×100 coordinate space, we have 25 squares of equal size. We adopt the convention that each square is open with respect to its upper and right boundaries and closed with respect to its lower and left boundaries. Therefore Toronto, located at (60,75), is found in the square centered at (70,70). Also all data points located at grid intersection points are said to be contained in the cell for which they serve as the SW corner (e.g., the point (20,20) is contained in the square centered at (30,30)).

The average search time for a range query using the fixed-grid method has been shown by Bentley, Stanat, and Williams [Bent77b] to be $O(F \cdot 2^k)$ where F is the number of records found. The factor 2^k is the maximum number of cells that must be accessed when the search rectangle is permitted to overlap more than one cell. For example, to locate all cities within a 20×20 square centered at (32,37) we must examine the cells centered at (30,30), (50,30), (30,50), and (50,50). Thus, four cells are examined and, for our example database, the query returns Chicago and Omaha.

If range queries are made using only a fixed search radius, the fixed grid is an efficient representation. It is also efficient when the data points are known a priori to be uniformly distributed over space (it is analogous to hashing [Knut73b]). For a non-

---

[2] This method can also be described as yielding an *adaptive uniform grid* to emphasize that the cell size is a function of some property of the points (e.g., [Fran84, Fran88]).

uniform distribution, it is less efficient because buckets may be unevenly filled, leading to nearly empty pages as well as to long overflow chains.

A number of deficiencies are associated with the inverted list and the fixed-grid method. Both techniques can be characterized as organizing the embedding space of the data into regions (i.e., buckets) that contain records. In the inverted list, the values of the primary key determine the region boundaries so that the bucket occupancies are uniform. The domain of the secondary keys is partitioned independently of the data to be stored. This is not optimal in an environment where several attributes are equally significant since range searching may require an excessive number of records to be retrieved. The fixed-grid method is satisfactory for independent, uniformly distributed attributes. However, when the domains of the attributes are not uniformly distributed, some buckets will overflow, and others will be underutilized.

The problem with bucket overflow is that it leads to a large number of disk accesses for all subsequent queries involving the bucket that overflowed. These problems and some solutions based on hashing are discussed in Section 2.8. It should be clear that a properly chosen hashing function, by virtue of its randomizing nature, could be used to overcome the nonuniform distribution. However, the property of randomization may destroy the order that is crucial to the efficient implementation of range queries. Thus the hashing function chosen should be order preserving (see Section 2.8.2.1).

Exercises

2.1. Given a file containing N records with k keys apiece, implemented as an inverted list, prove that the average search for a particular record is $O(N^{1-1/k})$.

2.2. Given a file containing records with k keys apiece, implemented using the fixed-grid method such that each cell has a width equal to the search radius of a range query, prove that the average time for the range query is $O(F \cdot 2^k)$ where F is the number of records found and 2^k is the number of cells that must be accessed.

2.3 POINT QUADTREES

The point quadtree, invented by Finkel and Bentley [Fink74], is a marriage of the fixed-grid method and the binary search tree that results in a tree-like directory with nonuniform-sized cells containing one element apiece. The k-d tree, invented by Bentley [Bent75b] (and discussed in Section 2.4), is an improvement over the point quadtree because it reduces the branching factor at each node and the storage requirements. (Other data structures, which are primarily of theoretical rather than practical interest, have been described by Lueker [Luek78], Lee and Wong [Lee77b], Willard [Will82], Bentley [Bent79a], and Bentley and Maurer [Bent80d].)

The point quadtree is implemented as a multidimensional generalization of a binary search tree. In two dimensions each data point is represented as a node in a quadtree in the form of a record of type *node* containing seven fields. The first four fields contain pointers to the node's four sons corresponding to the directions (i.e.,

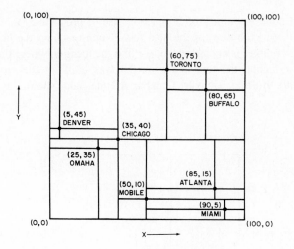

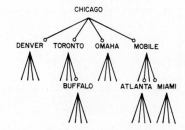

Figure 2.4   A point quadtree and the records it represents

quadrants) NW, NE, SW, and SE. If P is a pointer to a node and I is a quadrant, then these fields are referenced as SON(P, I). XCOORD and YCOORD contain the x and y coordinates, respectively, of the data point. The NAME field contains descriptive information about the node (e.g., city name). For example, see Figure 2.4, which is the point quadtree corresponding to the data of Figure 2.1.

We assume that each data point is unique. Should an application permit collisions (i.e., several data points with the same coordinates), then the data structure could contain an additional field in which a pointer to an overflow collision list would be stored. It could be argued that devoting an extra field to a rare event such as a collision wastes storage; however, without it, we would require a considerably more complicated node insertion procedure.

2.3.1 Insertion

Records are inserted into point quadtrees in a manner similar to that done for binary search trees. In essence, we search for the desired record based on its x and y coordinates. At each node a comparison is made by use of procedure PT_COMPARE and the appropriate subtree is chosen for the next test. Upon reaching the bottom of the tree (i.e., when a NIL pointer is encountered), we find the location where the record is to be inserted. For example, the tree in Figure 2.4 was built for the sequence Chicago, Mobile, Toronto, Buffalo, Denver, Omaha, Atlanta, and Miami. Figure 2.5 shows

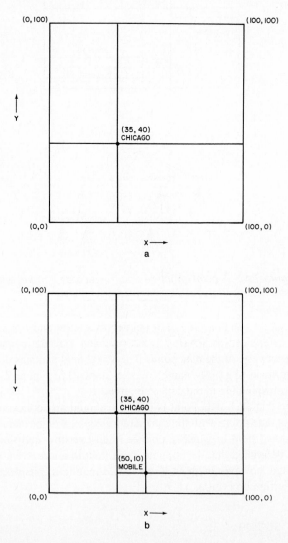

Figure 2.5   Sequence of partial quadtrees demonstrating the addition of (a) Chicago, (b) Mobile, (c) Toronto, and (d) Buffalo

how the tree was constructed in an incremental fashion for Chicago, Mobile, Toronto, and Buffalo. The actual insertion is achieved by use of procedure PT_INSERT.

To cope with data points that lie directly on one of the quadrant lines emanating from a data point, say P, we adopt the same conventions used for the grid method; the lower and left boundaries of each block are closed, while the upper and right boundaries of each block are open. For example, in Figure 2.4, insertion of Memphis with coordinates (35,20) would lead to its placement somewhere in quadrant SE of the tree rooted at Chicago (i.e., at (35,40)).

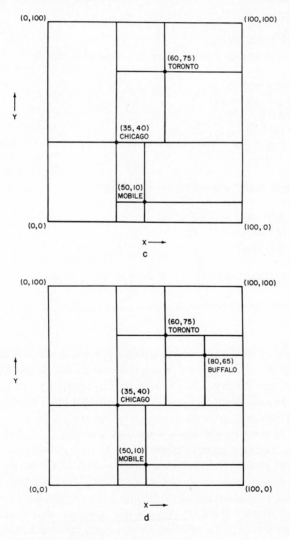

```
quadrant procedure PT_COMPARE(P,R);
/* Return the quadrant of the point quadtree rooted at node R in which node P belongs. */
begin
  value pointer node P,R;
  return(if XCOORD(P) < XCOORD(R) then
            if YCOORD(P) < YCOORD(R) then 'SW'
            else 'NW'
          else if YCOORD(P) < YCOORD(R) then 'SE'
          else 'NE');
end;


procedure PT_INSERT(P,R);
/* Attempt to insert node P in the point quadtree rooted at node R. */
begin
  value pointer node P;
  reference pointer node R;
  pointer node F;
  quadrant Q;
  if null(R) then R ← P  /* The tree at R is initially empty */
  else
    begin
      while not(null(R)) and not(EQUAL_COORD(P,R)) do
        begin
        F ← R; /* Remember the father */
        Q ← PT_COMPARE(P,R);
        R ← SON(R,Q);
        end;
      if null(R) then SON(F,Q) ← P; /* P is not already in the tree */
    end;
end;
```

The amount of work expended in building a point quadtree is equal to the total path length (TPL) [Knut73a] of the tree as it reflects the cost of searching for all of the elements. Finkel and Bentley [Fink74] have shown empirically that the TPL of a point quadtree under random insertion is roughly proportional to $N \cdot \log_4 N$, which yields an average cost of inserting, as well as searching for (i.e., a point query), a node of $O(\log_4 N)$. The extreme case is much worse (see Exercise 2.10) and is a function of the shape of the resulting point quadtree. This is dependent on the order in which nodes are inserted into it. The worst case arises when each successive node is the son of the currently deepest node in the tree. Consequently there has been some interest in reducing the TPL. Two techniques for achieving this reduction are described.

Finkel and Bentley [Fink74] propose one approach that assumes that all the nodes are known a priori. They define an optimized point quadtree so that given a node A, no subtree of A accounts for more than one-half of the nodes in the tree rooted at A. Building an optimized point quadtree from a file requires that the records in the file be sorted primarily by one key and secondarily by the other key. The root of the tree is set to the median value of the sorted file, and the remaining records are regrouped into four subcollections that will form the four subtrees of A. The process is recursively applied to the four subtrees.

The reason that this technique works is that all records preceding A in the sorted list will lie in the NW and SW quadrants (assuming that the x coordinate serves as the primary key) and all records following A will lie in the NE and SE quadrants. Thus the requirement that no subtree can contain more than half the total number of nodes is fulfilled. Of course, this construction method still does not guarantee that the resulting tree will be complete[3] (see Exercise 2.4).

The optimized point quadtree requires that all of the data points are known a priori. Overmars and van Leeuwen [Over82] discuss an alternative approach that is a dynamic formulation of the above method—that is, the optimized point quadtree is built as the data points are inserted into it. The algorithm is similar to the one used to construct Finkel and Bentley's optimized point quadtree, except that every time the tree fails to meet a predefined balance criterion, the tree is partially rebalanced. For more details, see Exercise 2.7.

Exercises

2.3. Suppose that a point quadtree node is implemented as a record with a FATHER field containing a pointer to its father. Modify procedure PT_INSERT to take advantage of this addition.

2.4. Suppose that you could construct the optimized point quadtree (i.e., minimal depth) for N nodes. What is the worst-case depth of an optimized point quadtree?

2.5. What is the maximum TPL in an optimized point quadtree?

2.6. Analyze the running time of the algorithm for constructing an optimized point quadtree.

2.7. In the text, we intimated that the optimized point quadtree can also be constructed dynamically. Given δ ($0 < \delta < 1$), we stipulate that every nonleaf node with a total of m nodes in its subtrees has at most $\lceil m/(2 - \delta) \rceil$ nodes in each subtree. Give an algorithm to construct such a point quadtree.

2.8. Prove that the depth of the optimized point quadtree constructed in Exercise 2.7 is always at most $\log_{2-\delta} n + O(1)$ and that the average insertion time in an initially empty data structure is $O(\frac{1}{\delta}\log_2^2 N)$. n denotes the number of nodes currently in the tree and N is the total number of nodes that have been inserted.

2.9. The TPL can also be reduced by applying balancing operators analogous to those used to balance binary search trees. Give the point quadtree analogs of the single and double rotation operators [Knut73b, p.454].

2.10. What is the worst-case cost of building a point quadtree of N nodes?

---

[3] A t-ary tree containing N nodes is *complete* if we can map it onto a one-dimensional array so that the first element consists of the root, the next t elements are the roots of its t subtrees ordered from left to right, the next t^2 elements are the roots of all of the subtrees of the previous t elements again ordered from left to right, and so on. This process stops once N is exhausted. Thus all but the deepest level of the tree contain a maximum number of nodes. The deepest level is partially full but has no empty positions when using this array mapping. For more details, see Knuth [Knut73a, pp. 400–401].

Figure 2.6   Idealized quadtree deletion situation

2.3.2 Deletion

Deletion of nodes in two-dimensional point quadtrees is rather complex. Finkel and Bentley [Fink74] suggest that all nodes of the tree rooted at the deleted node must be reinserted—usually an expensive process. In the rest of this section we describe a more efficient process developed by Samet [Same80c]. It may be skipped on an initial reading.

Ideally we want to replace the deleted node (say A at (x_A, y_A)) with a node (say B at (x_B, y_B)), such that the region between the lines $x = x_A$ and $x = x_B$ and the region between the lines $y = y_A$ and $y = y_B$ are empty. The shaded area in Figure 2.6 illustrates this concept for nodes A and B in that A is deleted and replaced by B. The term *hatched* is used to describe the region that we would like to be empty. Unfortunately finding a node that will lead to an empty hatched region requires a considerable amount of search. In fact, it is not uncommon that such a node fails to exist, as when deleting node A in Figure 2.7.

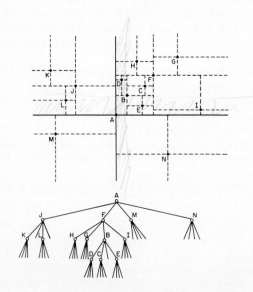

Figure 2.7   A quadtree and the records it represents

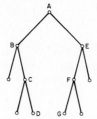

Figure 2.8   Example binary search tree

The algorithm we describe proceeds in a manner analogous to the method for binary search trees. For example, for the binary search tree of Figure 2.8, when node A is to be deleted, it can be replaced by one of nodes D or G—the two 'closest' nodes in value. In the case of a quadtree (e.g., Figure 2.7), it is not clear which of the remaining nodes should replace A because no node is simultaneously the closest in both the *x* and *y* directions. No matter which of the nodes is chosen, some of the nodes will assume different positions in the new tree. For example, in Figure 2.7, if L replaced A, then J would no longer occupy the NW quadrant with respect to L and, thus, J would need to be reinserted, along with some of its subtrees, in the quadrant rooted at F. Similarly E and I would have to be reinserted, along with some of their subtrees, in the quadrant rooted at N.

In a point quadtree there are four candidate nodes for the replacement node— one for each quadrant. They are located by procedure FIND_CANDIDATE, given below. FIND_CANDIDATE is invoked once for every son of the node to be deleted. This process is facilitated by the primitive OPQUAD(Q), which yields the quadrant that is 180 degrees apart from quadrant Q (e.g., OPQUAD('NW') = 'SE'). For example, Figure 2.9 shows how node D is selected as the candidate node from the NE quadrant of node A.

pointer node procedure FIND_CANDIDATE(P,Q);
/* P is a pointer to the son in quadrant Q of the node to be deleted. Starting at P, repeatedly follow the branch corresponding to OPQUAD(Q) until a node having no subtree along this branch is encountered. If P is initially NIL, then use INF to return a pointer to a fictitious point in the quadrant that is farthest from the deleted node (e.g., ($-\infty$, $-\infty$) in the SW quadrant). */

Figure 2.9   Application of the FIND_CANDIDATE procedure in the NE quadrant of node A

```
begin
  value pointer node P;
  value quadrant Q;
  if null(P) then return(INF(Q));
  while not(null(SON(P,OPQUAD(Q)))) do P ← SON(P,OPQUAD(Q));
  return(P);
end;
```

Once the set of candidate nodes is found, an attempt is made to find the 'best' candidate, which becomes the replacement node. There are two criteria for choosing the best candidate. Criterion 1 stipulates the choice of the candidate that is closer to each of its bordering axes than any other candidate on the same side of these axes, if such a candidate exists. For example, in Figure 2.7 the candidates are B, J, M, and N, with B being the best candidate according to this criterion. Note that the situation may arise that no candidate satisfies criterion 1 (e.g., Figure 2.10) or that several candidates satisfy it (e.g., B and D in Figure 2.11). In such a case, the candidate with the minimum L_1 metric value is chosen. This is called criterion 2. It is also known as the *city block metric* (or the *Manhattan metric*).

The L_1 metric is the sum of the displacements from the bordering x and y axes. To justify its use, we assume that the nodes are uniformly distributed in the two-dimensional space. Our goal is to minimize the area obtained by removing from the hatched region the rectangle whose opposite vertices are the root node and the candidate node (e.g., nodes A and B in Figure 2.6).

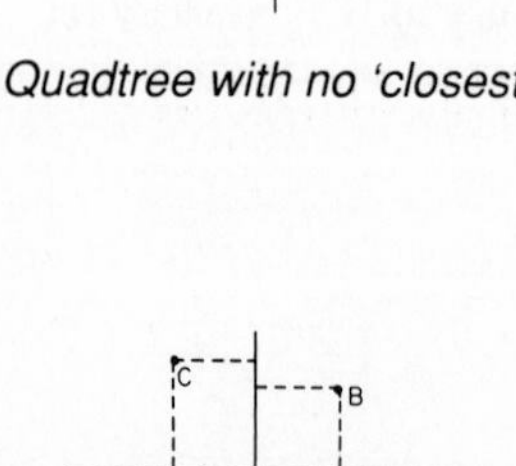

Figure 2.10   Quadtree with no 'closest' terminal node

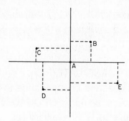

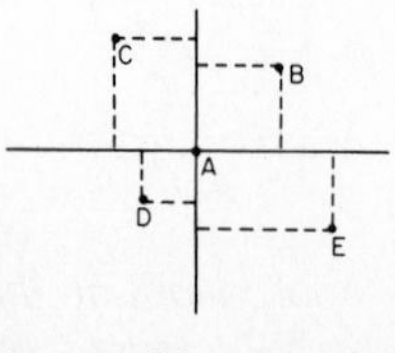

Figure 2.11   Quadtree with two nodes being closest to their bordering axes

Figure 2.12   Example of a two-dimensional space

Assume that the two-dimensional space is finite, having sides of length L_x and L_y parallel to the x and y axes, respectively. Let this space be centered at the node to be deleted. Assume further that the candidate node is at a distance of d_y and d_x from the x and y axes, respectively. Under these assumptions, the remaining area is $L_x \cdot d_y + L_y \cdot d_x - 2 \cdot d_x \cdot d_y$ (Figure 2.12). We can ignore the area of the rectangle with sides d_x and d_y because the candidate selection process guarantees that it is empty. As L_x and L_y increase, as occurs in the general problem domain, the contribution of the $2 \cdot d_x \cdot d_y$ term becomes negligible, and the area is proportional to the sum of d_x and d_y.[4]

Criterion 2 is not sufficient by itself to ensure that the selected candidate partitions the space so the hatched region contains no other candidate. For example, see Figure 2.13, in which O has been deleted and A satisfies criterion 2 but only C satisfies criterion 1. A pair of axes through C leaves all other candidates outside the hatched region, while a pair of axes through A results in B's being in the hatched region.

If no candidate is found to satisfy criterion 1, then criterion 2 guarantees that at least one of the candidates, say X, has the property that no more than one of the remaining candidates occupies the hatched region between the original axes and the axes passing through X. To see this, we examine Figure 2.10 and note that whichever candidate is selected to be the new root (say C in the NW quadrant), then the candidate in the opposite quadrant (i.e., SE) lies outside the hatched region. In addition, the candidate in a quadrant on the same side of an axis as is C, and to which axis C is closer (i.e., B), lies outside the hatched region.

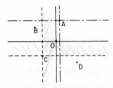

Figure 2.13   Example of the insufficiency of criterion 2 for an empty hatched region

---

[4] Actually this statement holds only for $L_x = L_y$. However, this approximation is adequate for the purpose of this discussion.

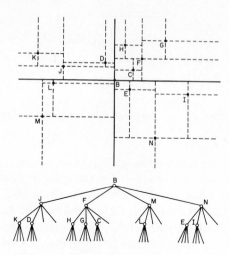

Figure 2.14   Result of deleting node A from the quadtree
of Figure 2.4 and replacing it with node B

We are now ready to examine the deletion algorithm. It makes use of the properties of the space obtained by the new partition to reduce the number of nodes
requiring reinsertion. The algorithm consists of two procedures ADJQUAD and NEW-
ROOT. Let A be the node to be deleted, and let I be the quadrant of the tree containing
B, the replacement node for A. Note that no nodes in quadrant OPQUAD(I) need to be
reinserted. Separately process the two quadrants adjacent to quadrant I using procedure ADJQUAD described informally below.

> Procedure ADJQUAD   Examine the root of the quadrant, say R. If R
> lies outside the hatched region, then two subquadrants can automatically
> remain in the quadrant and need no further processing while the remaining
> subquadrants are separately processed by a recursive invocation of ADJ-
> QUAD. Otherwise the entire quadrant must be reinserted in the quadtree,
> which was formerly rooted at A.   □

For example, consider Figure 2.7 where node A is deleted and replaced by node
B in the NE quadrant. The subquadrant rooted at J and the subquadrant rooted at K
remain in the NW quadrant, while the subquadrant rooted at L is recursively processed.
Eventually L must be reinserted in the tree rooted at M. The SE quadrant of A (rooted at
N) does not require reinsertion. Figure 2.14 shows the result of the deletion.

Once the nodes in the quadrants adjacent to quadrant I have been processed, we
must process the nodes in I. Clearly all of the nodes in subquadrant I of I will retain
their position. Bearing this in mind, we apply procedure NEWROOT, described informally below, to the remaining subquadrants of I.

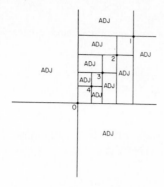

Figure 2.15   Subquadrants processed by ADJ when node
0 is deleted and replaced by node 4

Procedure NEWROOT   Apply procedure ADJQUAD to the subquadrants adjacent to subquadrant *I* and iteratively reapply NEWROOT to
subquadrant OPQUAD(*I*). This is done until an empty link in direction OP-
QUAD(*I*) is encountered (i.e., at this point we are at *B*, the node replacing
the deleted node). Insert the nodes in the subquadrants adjacent to
subquadrant *I* of the tree rooted at *B* in the quadrants adjacent to quadrant *I*
of the tree rooted at *A*. Recall that by virtue of the candidate selection process, subquadrant OPQUAD(*I*) of the tree rooted at *B* is empty. Also
subquadrant *I* of the tree rooted at *B* replaces subquadrant OPQUAD(*I*) of
the previous father node of *B*.   □

Figure 2.15 illustrates the subquadrants that are processed by ADJQUAD when
node 0 is deleted and the resulting tree is rooted at node 4. For the example of Figure
2.7, the tree rooted at G is left alone. Trees rooted at H and I are processed by ADJ-
QUAD. Trees rooted at D and E are reinserted in quadrants NW and SE, respectively.
The tree rooted at C replaces B as the son of F in subquadrant SW. Figure 2.14 shows
the result of deleting A from Figure 2.7.

A more formal specification of the deletion algorithm is given below using procedures PT_DELETE, ADJQUAD, and NEWROOT. PT_DELETE controls the deletion process
by first finding a replacement node for the deleted node and then invoking ADJQUAD
and NEWROOT to rearrange the quadtree to be consistent with the new root node. In
the process, we make use of CQUAD(*Q*) and CCQUAD(*Q*), which yield the adjacent quadrants in the clockwise and counterclockwise directions, respectively, from *Q*. Procedure INSERT_QUADRANT(*P*, *R*) inserts the nodes of the subtree rooted at *P* in the subtree rooted at *R*.

```
procedure PT_DELETE(P,R);
/* Delete node P from the point quadtree rooted at node R. If the root of the tree was
   deleted, then reset R. */
begin
 value pointer node P;
 reference pointer node R;
 pointer node J;
 quadrant Q;
 if HAS_NO_SONS(P) or HAS_ONLY_ONE_SON(P) then
   /* Set P's father to the son of P if one exists; otherwise, return NIL */
   begin
    J ← FIND_FATHER(P);
    if null(J) then R ← NON_EMPTY_SON(P)
    else SON(J,SONTYPE(P)) ← NON_EMPTY_SON(P);
    returntoavail(P);
    return;
   end
 else /* Find the 'best' replacement node for P and rearrange the tree */
   begin
    J ← 'best' replacement node for P;
    Q ← quadrant of P containing J;
    /* Copy the coordinate values of node J to node P */
    XCOORD(P) ← XCOORD(J);
    YCOORD(P) ← YCOORD(J);
    /* Rearrange the remaining quadrants */
    ADJQUAD(CQUAD(Q),OPQUAD(Q),CQUAD(Q),P,P);
    ADJQUAD(CCQUAD(Q),OPQUAD(Q),CCQUAD(Q),P,P);
    NEWROOT(Q,SON(P,Q),P,P); /* Rearrange quadrant Q */
    /* Return node J to AVAIL since it is no longer needed */
    returntoavail(J);
   end;
end;



recursive procedure ADJQUAD(Q,D,S,F,R);
/* Rearrange subquadrant SON(F,S) of quadrant Q of the tree rooted at R. R is the node
   that has been deleted. D is the quadrant in which nodes in the subquadrant rooted at
   SON(F,S) may have to be reinserted. Otherwise, they remain in quadrant Q. */
begin
 value quadrant Q,D,S;
 value pointer node F,R;
 pointer node T;
 T ← SON(F,S);
 if null(T) then return /* An empty link */
 else if PT_COMPARE(T,R)=Q then
   /* Node T and subquadrants SON(T,Q) and SON(T,OPQUAD(D)) need no reinser-
      tion */
```

```
 begin
   /* Rearrange subquadrant SON(T,OPQUAD(Q)) */
   ADJQUAD(Q,D,OPQUAD(Q),T,R);
   /* Rearrange subquadrant SON(T,D) */
   ADJQUAD(Q,D,D,T,R);
 end
else
   /* Unlink subquadrant S from F so that it will not be found upon reinsertion should it
      belong to the same quadrant */
 begin
   SON(F,S) ← NIL;
   INSERT_QUADRANT(T,R);
 end;
end;
```

```
recursive procedure NEWROOT(Q,S,R,F);
/* Rearrange the quadrant containing the replacement node for the deleted node—i.e.,
   quadrant Q of node R. R is the node that has been deleted. S is the root of the
   subquadrant currently being processed and is the son of F. */
begin
 value quadrant Q;
 value pointer node S,R,F;
 if null(SON(S,OPQUAD(Q))) then
   /* S is the replacement node. Insert its subquadrants and reset the father of the
      replacement node. */
   begin
     INSERT_QUADRANT(SON(S,CQUAD(Q)),R);
     INSERT_QUADRANT(SON(S,CCQUAD(Q)),R);
     if R ≠ F then  /* Reset the father of the replacement node */
       SON(F,OPQUAD(Q)) ← SON(S,Q)
     else SON(F,Q) ← SON(S,Q);
   end
 else
   /* Rearrange the quadrants adjacent to quadrant Q of the tree rooted at S and reapply
      NEWROOT to SON(S,OPQUAD(Q)) */
   begin
     /* Rearrange subquadrant SON(S,CQUAD(Q)) */
     ADJQUAD(Q,CQUAD(Q),CQUAD(Q),S,R);
     /* Rearrange subquadrant SON(S,CCQUAD(Q)) */
     ADJQUAD(Q,CCQUAD(Q),CCQUAD(Q),S,R);
     /* Rearrange subquadrant SON(S,OPQUAD(Q)) */
     NEWROOT(Q,SON(S,OPQUAD(Q)),R,S);
   end;
end;
```

Theoretical and empirical results for the above deletion method are described by Samet [Same80c]. It is shown theoretically that for data that are uniformly distributed, the average number of nodes requiring reinsertion is reduced by a factor of

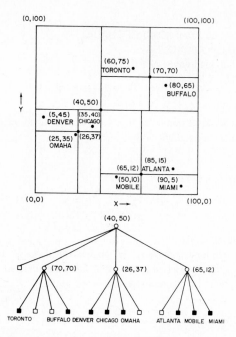

Figure 2.16   A pseudo quadtree and the records it represents

five-sixths (i.e., 83%) when the replacement node satisfies criteria 1 and 2. The relaxation of the requirement that the replacement node must satisfy both criteria, and its substitution by a selection at random of one of the candidates as the replacement node, caused the factor by which the average number of nodes required reinsertion to decrease to two-thirds (i.e., 67%). Of course, the candidate selection process becomes considerably simpler in this case.

The empirical tests led to the following interesting observations. First, the number of comparison operations is proportional to $\log_4 N$ versus a considerably larger factor when using the deletion method of Finkel and Bentley [Fink74]. Second, the total path length of the tree after deletion using Samet's method [Same80c] decreases slightly, whereas when Finkel and Bentley's method [Fink74] is used, the total path length increases significantly. These data are important because they correlate with the effective search time (see also [Bent77b, Lee77b]). In other words, the smaller the total path length, the faster a node can be accessed.

Deletion in point quadtrees is complex because the data points also serve to partition the space from which they are drawn. The pseudo quadtree of Overmars and van Leeuwen [Over82] simplifies deletion by using arbitrary points, not in the set of data points being represented, for the partitioning process. The pseudo quadtree is constructed by repeatedly partitioning the space into quadrants, subquadrants, and so on, until each subquadrant contains at most one data point of the original set. This means that the data points occur as leaf nodes of the pseudo quadtree. The partition points are chosen in a manner that splits the remaining set in the most balanced way.

Overmars and van Leeuwen show that for any N data points in a k-dimensional space, there exists a partitioning point such that every quadrant contains at most $\lceil N/(k+1) \rceil$ data points. They also demonstrate that the resulting pseudo quadtree has a depth of at most $\lceil \log_{k+1} N \rceil$ and can be built in $O(N \cdot \log_{k+1} N)$ time. For example, Figure 2.16 is the pseudo quadtree corresponding to the data of Figure 2.1. Efficient deletion and insertion in a pseudo quadtree requires that the bound on the depth be weakened slightly (see Exercise 2.23).

Exercises

2.11. Suppose that a point quadtree node is implemented as a record with a FATHER field containing a pointer to its father. Modify procedure PT_DELETE to take advantage of this addition.

2.12. Let T be a tree containing N nodes with TPL(T) denoting its total path length. Prove that the sum of the sizes of its subtrees is TPL(T) + N. Show that this result holds for binary trees and quadtrees as well.

2.13. Define a *nontrivial* subtree to be a subtree with two or more nonempty subtrees. Let $Q(N)$ be the expected nontrivial subtree size in a complete point quadtree of N nodes. Prove that as N gets large, $Q(N)$ is $4 \cdot \log_4(\frac{3}{4} \cdot N) - 4/3$. Do not take the root of the subtree into account. Note that $Q(N)$ is the cost of deletion when the method of Finkel and Bentley [Fink74] is used. A complete point quadtree is used because such a configuration minimizes the average cost of deletion in this case since, recalling Exercise 2.12, the sum of the subtree sizes for a given tree T containing N nodes is TPL(T) + N. This quantity is at a minimum when T is a complete tree.

2.14. Assuming a complete point quadtree of N nodes, let $r(N)$ denote the proportion of nodes that do not require reinsertion when using the deletion method of Samet [Same80c]. Let A and B be the deleted and replacement node, respectively, where B is a node returned by FIND_CANDIDATE. Assume that the nodes are partitioned uniformly throughout the partition of the two-dimensional space rooted at A. Use values of one-half for the probability that a node needs to be reinserted. Show that when B satisfies criteria 1 and 2, $r(N)$ is five-sixths or three-quarters depending on whether none of the adjacent quadrants has its candidate replacement node in the hatched region. Similarly show that $r(N)$ is two-thirds when the replacement node is chosen at random from the set of nodes returned by procedure FIND_CANDIDATE.

2.15. Can you prove that the point quadtree deletion algorithm encoded by procedure PT_DELETE is $O(\log_4 N)$?

2.16. Why do the resulting trees get bushier when the point quadtree node deletion algorithm given in procedure PT_DELETE is used?

2.17. Extend the deletion method of Samet [Same80c] to handle k-dimensional point quadtrees and compute $r(N)$.

2.18. Write an algorithm, BUILD_PSEUDO_QUADTREE, to construct a pseudo quadtree for two-dimensional data.

2.19. Given a set of N points in k-dimensional space, prove that there exists a partitioning point such that every quadrant contains $\lceil N/(k+1) \rceil$ points.

2.20. Given a set of N points in k-dimensional space, prove that there exists a pseudo quadtree for it with a depth of at most $\lceil \log_{k+1} N \rceil$.

2.21. Show that the upper bound obtained in Exercise 2.20 is a strict upper bound in that there exists a configuration of N points such that there is no corresponding pseudo quadtree with depth less than $\lceil \log_{k+1} N \rceil$.

2.22. Prove that the pseudo quadtree of Exercise 2.20 can be built in $O(N \cdot \log_{k+1} N)$ time.

2.23. Prove that for any fixed δ $(0 < \delta < 1)$ there is an algorithm to perform N insertions and deletions in an initially empty k-dimensional pseudo quadtree such that its depth is always at most $\log_{k+1-\delta} n + O(1)$ and that the average transaction time is bounded by $O(\frac{1}{\delta} \log_2^2 N)$. n denotes the number of nodes currently in the tree.

2.3.3   Search

The point quadtree is suited for applications that involve proximity search. A typical query is one that requests the determination of all nodes within a specified distance of a given data point—such as all cities within 50 miles of Washington, D.C. The efficiency of the point quadtree data structure lies in its role as a pruning device on the amount of search required. Thus many records will not need to be examined.

For example, suppose that in the hypothetical database of Figure 2.1 we wish to find all cities within eight units of a data point with coordinates (83,10). In such a case, there is no need to search the NW, NE, and SW quadrants of the root (i.e., Chicago with coordinates (35,40)). Thus we can restrict the search to the SE quadrant of the tree rooted at Chicago. Similarly there is no need to search the NW and SW quadrants of the tree rooted at Mobile (i.e., coordinates (50,10)).

As a further illustration of the amount of pruning of the search space achievable by use of the point quadtree, we make use of Figure 2.17. In particular, given the

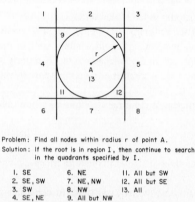

Problem: Find all nodes within radius r of point A.
Solution: If the root is in region I, then continue to search in the quadrants specified by I.

1. SE	6. NE	11. All but SW
2. SE, SW	7. NE, NW	12. All but SE
3. SW	8. NW	13. All
4. SE, NE	9. All but NW	
5. SW, NW	10. All but NE	

Figure 2.17   Relationship between a circular search space and the regions in which a root of a quadtree may reside

problem of finding all nodes within radius r of point A, use of the figure indicates which quadrants need not be examined when the root of the search space, say R, is in one of the numbered regions. For example, if R is in region 9, all but its NW quadrants must be searched. If R is in region 7, the search can be restricted to the NW and NE quadrants of R.

Similar techniques can be used to search for data points in any connected figure. For example, Finkel and Bentley [Fink74] give algorithms for searching within a rectangular window of arbitrary size. To handle more complex search regions such as halfspaces and convex polygons, Willard [Will82] defines a *polygon tree* where the $x - y$ plane is subdivided by J lines that need not be orthogonal, although there are other restrictions on these lines (see Exercise 2.29). When $J = 2$, the result is a point quadtree with nonorthogonal axes.

Thus we see that quadtrees can be used to handle all three types of queries specified by Knuth [Knut73b]. Range and Boolean queries are described immediately above while simple queries (e.g., what city is located at a given pair of coordinate values) are a by-product of the point quadtree insertion process already described.

The cost of search in a point quadtree has been studied by Bentley, Stanat, and Williams [Bent77b] (see Exercise 2.25) and Lee and Wong [Lee77b]. In particular, Lee and Wong show that in the worst case, range searching in a complete two-dimensional point quadtree takes $O(2 \cdot N^{1/2})$ time. This result can be extended to k dimensions to yield $O(k \cdot N^{1-1/k})$ and is derived in a manner analogous to that for k-d trees as discussed in Section 2.46. Note that complete point quadtrees are not always achievable as seen in Exercise 2.4. Partial range queries can be handled in the same way as range searching. Lee and Wong [Lee77b] show that when ranges for s out of k keys are specified, the algorithm has a worst-case running time of $O(s \cdot N^{1-1/k})$.

Exercises

2.24. Write a procedure PT_REGION_SEARCH that performs a region search for a circular region. Repeat for a rectangular region.

2.25. Bentley and Stanat [Bent75c] define a *perfect point quadtree* of height m as a point quadtree that (1) has 4^i nodes at level $m-i$ where the root is at level m, $0 \le i \le m-1$, and (2) every node is at the centroid of the finite space spanned by its subtrees. Assume a search space of $[0,1]^2$ and a rectangular search region of sides of length x and y where x and y are in $[0,1]$. Find the expected number of nodes visited in a perfect point quadtree of height m when a region search procedure is applied to the above search region.

2.26. Bentley and Stanat [Bent75c] also define the concept of overwork of a search algorithm as the difference between the number of records visited and the number of records in the search region. Assume a search space of $[0,1]^2$ with N records and a square search region of side length x where x is in $[0,1]$. Compare the amount of overwork for an inverted file and a perfect point quadtree.

2.27. Prove that the worst-case running time for a partial range query such that ranges for s out of k keys are specified is $O(s \cdot N^{1-1/k})$.

2.28. Perform an average-case analysis for a region query in a point quadtree.

2.29. What are the restrictions on the choice of subdivision lines in Willard's polygon tree [Will82]?

2.4 K-D TREES

Point quadtrees have several deficiencies. First, at each node a test (i.e., a PT_COM-PARE operation) requires testing all k keys for a k-dimensional quadtree. Second, each leaf node is rather costly in terms of the amount of space required due to a multitude of NIL links.[5] Third, the node size gets rather large for a k-dimensional tree since $k + 2^k + 1$ words are required for each node. Also the same data structure cannot be used to represent a node for all values of k. The k-d tree of Bentley [Bent75b] and its variants is an improvement that serves to alleviate some of these deficiencies.

In the term *k-d tree*, k denotes the dimensionality of the space being represented. In principle, it is a binary search tree with the distinction that at each depth a different attribute (or key) value is tested when determining the direction in which a branch is to be made. In two dimensions (i.e., a 2-d tree), we compare x coordinate values at the root and at even depths (assuming that the root is at depth 0) and y coordinate values at odd depths.

Each data point is represented as a node in the k-d tree in the form of a record of type *node* containing six fields. The first two fields contain pointers to the node's two sons corresponding to the directions 'LEFT' and 'RIGHT'. If P is a pointer to a node and I is a direction, then these fields are referenced as SON(P, I). At times, these two fields are also referred to as LOSON(P) and HISON(P), corresponding to the left and right sons, respectively. XCOORD and YCOORD contain the values of the x and y coordinates, respectively, of the data point. The NAME field contains descriptive information about the node (e.g., city name). The DISC field indicates the name of the coordinate that the node discriminates (i.e., tests).

We adopt the convention that when node P is an x-discriminator, then all nodes having an x coordinate value less than that of P are in the left son of P and all those with x coordinate values greater than or equal to that of P are in the right son of P. A similar convention holds for a node that is a y-discriminator. Actually the DISC field is not necessary since it is easy to keep track of the type of node being visited as the tree is descended. Figure 2.18 illustrates the 2-d tree corresponding to the same eight nodes as in Figure 2.1. Note that it is assumed that each data point is unique, although this assumption can be overridden by using collision lists.

In the definition of a discriminator, the problem of equality of keys is resolved by stipulating that equal keys are in the right subtree (i.e., HISON). As an alternative, Bentley [Bent75b] defines a node in terms of a *superkey*. Given a node P, let $K_0(P)$, $K_1(P)$, etc., refer to its k keys. Assuming a value of j for DISC(P), then for any node Q in LOSON(P), $K_j(Q) < K_j(P)$, and likewise for any node R in HISON(P), $K_j(R) > K_j(P)$. In the case of equality, a superkey, $S_j(P)$, is defined by forming a cyclical concatenation of all keys starting with $K_j(P)$. In other words, $S_j(P) = K_j(P) \, K_{j+1}(P) \, \cdots \, K_{k-1}(P) \, K_0(P) \, \cdots \, K_{j-1}(P)$. Now, when comparing two keys P and Q we turn to the

---

[5] Of course, these NIL pointers can be avoided in an efficient implementation (e.g., see Section 2.1.2 of [Same90b]).

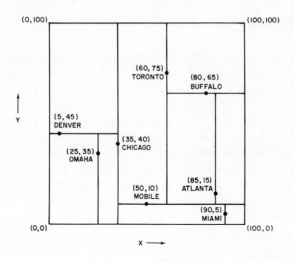

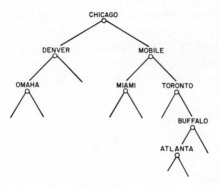

Figure 2.18   A k-d tree and the records it represents

left when $s_j(Q) < s_j(P)$ and to the right when $s_j(Q) > s_j(P)$. If $s_j(Q) = s_j(P)$, then all k keys are equal, and a special value is returned to so indicate. The algorithms presented below do not make use of a superkey.

The subdivision lines of the k-d tree as defined here are constrained to be orthogonal. The BSP tree of Fuchs, Kedem, and Naylor [Fuch80], discussed in Section 1.4.1, is an example of a k-d tree where the subdivision lines are not necessarily orthogonal. In the BSP tree, each node is represented by its linear halfspace equation, which is a line in two dimensions and a plane in three dimensions. Similarly in two dimensions each node's block is a convex polygon, while in three dimensions it is a convex polyhedron.

2.4.1 Insertion

Records are inserted into k-d trees in a manner analogous to binary search trees. In essence, we search for the desired record based on the values of its x and y coordinates, comparing x coordinate values at even depths of the tree and y coordinate values at odd depths. The comparisons are made by use of procedure KD_COMPARE. When we reach the bottom of the tree (i.e., when a NIL pointer is encountered), we find the location where the node is to be inserted. As in the case of point quadtrees, the shape of the resulting k-d tree depends on the order in which the nodes are inserted into it. Bentley [Bent75b] shows that given N points, the average cost of inserting, as well as searching for (i.e., a point query), a node is $O(\log_2 N)$.

Figure 2.18 is the k-d tree for the sequence Chicago, Mobile, Toronto, Buffalo, Denver, Omaha, Atlanta, and Miami. Figure 2.19a–d shows how the tree was constructed in an incremental fashion for these four cities. The actual insertion is achieved by use of procedure KD_INSERT.

It should be clear that in the insertion process described here, each node partitions the portion of the plane in which it resides into two segments. Thus, in Figure 2.18, Chicago divides the plane into all nodes whose x coordinate value is less than 35 and all nodes whose x coordinate value is greater than or equal to 35. In the same figure, Denver divides the set of all nodes whose x coordinate value is less than 35 into those whose y coordinate value is less than 45 and those whose y coordinate value is greater than or equal to 45.

```
direction procedure KD_COMPARE(P,Q);
/* Return the son of the k-d tree rooted at node Q in which node P belongs. */
begin
  value pointer node P,Q;
  return(if DISC(Q)='X' then
           if XCOORD(P) < XCOORD(Q) then 'LEFT'
           else 'RIGHT'
         else if YCOORD(P) < YCOORD(Q) then 'LEFT'
           else 'RIGHT');
end;

procedure KD_INSERT(P,R);
/* Attempt to insert node P in the k-d tree rooted at node R. */
begin
  value pointer node P,R;
  direction Q;
  if null(R) then R ← P  /* The tree at R is initially empty */
  else
    begin
      while not(null(R)) and not(EQUAL_COORD(P,R)) do
        begin
          F ← R; /* Remember the father */
          Q ← KD_COMPARE(P,R);
```

```
      R ← SON(R,Q);
   end;
   if null(R) then /* P is not already in the tree */
   begin
      SON(F,Q) ← P;
      DISC(P) ← NEXT_DISC(F);
   end;
end;
end;
```

As in the case of the point quadtree, the amount of work expended in building a k-d tree is equal to the total path length (TPL) of the tree as it reflects the cost of

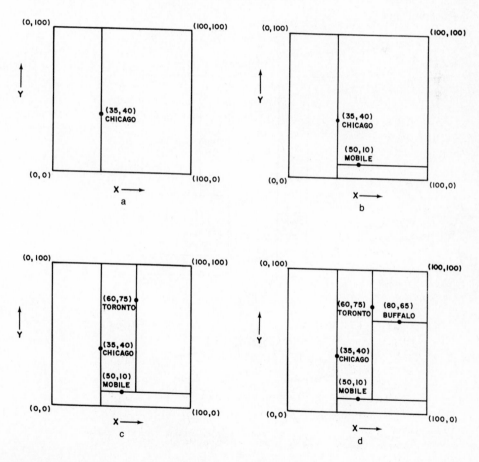

Figure 2.19   *Sequence of partial k-d trees demonstrating the addition of (a) Chicago, (b) Mobile, (c) Toronto, and (d) Buffalo*

searching for all of the elements. Bentley [Bent75b] shows that the total path length of a k-d tree built by inserting N points in random order into an initially empty tree is $O(N \cdot \log_2 N)$ and thus the average cost of inserting a node is $O(\log_2 N)$. The extreme cases are worse since the shape of the k-d tree depends on the order in which the nodes are inserted into it, thereby affecting the TPL. In the following, we examine the static and the dynamic approaches to reducing the TPL.

The static approach assumes that all nodes are known a priori. Bentley [Bent75b] proposes an optimized k-d tree, which is constructed in the same manner as the optimized point quadtree of Section 2.3.1. An alternative static data structure incorporating 'adaptive partitioning' is the 'adaptive k-d tree' of Friedman, Bentley, and Finkel [Frie77]. Unlike the standard k-d tree, and in the spirit of the pseudo quadtree of Overmars and van Leeuwen [Over82] (see Section 2.3.2), data are stored only at the leaf nodes. Each interior node contains the median of the set (along one key) as the discriminator.

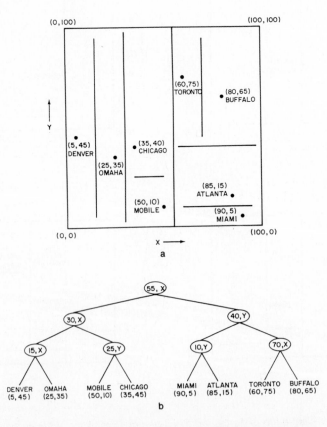

Figure 2.20   Adaptive k-d tree: (a) set of points in 2-space, (b) 2-d tree

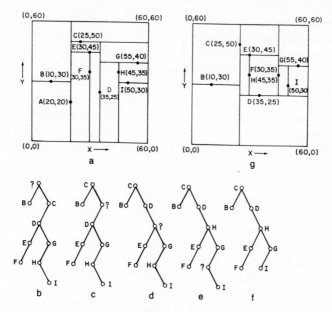

Figure 2.21   Example demonstrating deletion in k-d trees (? indicates the node being deleted): (a) original k-d tree, (b)–(f) successive steps in deleting node A, (g) final k-d tree

The discriminator is chosen to be the key for which the spread of the values of the key is a maximum. This spread can be measured by any convenient statistic, such as the variance or the distance from the minimum to the maximum value (usually normalized with respect to the median value). All records with key values less than the discriminator are added to the left subtree, and all records with key values greater than or equal to the discriminator are added to the right subtree. This process is continued recursively until only a few nodes are left in a set, at which point they are stored as a linked list. Note that we no longer require a cyclical discriminator sequence. In other words, the same key may serve as the discriminator for a node and its father, as well as its son.

Figure 2.20 shows the adaptive k-d tree corresponding to the data of Figure 2.1. Note that although Figure 2.20b leads to the impression that the adaptive k-d tree is balanced, this is not necessarily the case. For example, when several nodes have the same value for one of their attributes (e.g., nodes E and F of Figure 2.21), then a middle value is impossible to obtain. The concept of a superkey is of no use in such a case.

The adaptive k-d tree is a static data structure in the sense that we must know all of the data points a priori before we can build the tree. Thus deletion of nodes is considerably more complex than for conventional k-d trees (see Section 2.4.2) since we must obtain new partitions for the remaining data. Searching in adaptive k-d trees proceeds in an analogous manner to that in conventional k-d trees.

The dynamic approach to reducing the TPL in k-d trees constructs the tree as the data points are inserted into it. The construction algorithm is similar to that used to construct the optimized k-d tree except that every time the tree fails to meet a predefined balance criterion, the tree is partially rebalanced. This approach is discussed by Overmars and van Leeuwen [Over82] (see also Willard [Will78]), who present two variations; the first is analogous to the optimized point quadtree and the second to the pseudo quadtree. Such methods are characterized by Vaishnavi [Vais84] as yielding 'severely' balanced trees in that they are generalizations of complete binary trees for one-dimensional data. As such, they cannot be updated efficiently.

Vaishnavi proposes a relaxation of the balancing criterion by generalizing the height-balancing constraint for height-balanced trees (also known as AVL trees [Adel62, Aho74]). This is done by storing data in a nested sequence of binary trees so that each nonleaf node tests a given attribute, say P with DISC(P)=J. Each nonleaf node P has three sons. The left and right sons point to nodes with smaller and larger, respectively, values for the Jth attribute. The third son is the root of a $(k-1)$-dimensional tree containing all data nodes that have the same value for the Jth attribute as the data point corresponding to P. The 'rotation' and 'double rotation' restructuring operations of height-balanced trees are adapted to the new structure. For N points, their use is shown to yield $O(\log_2 N + k)$ bounds on their search and update times (i.e., node insertion and deletion). This data structure does not appear well-suited to range queries.

Exercises

2.30. Suppose that a k-d tree node is implemented as a record with a FATHER field containing a pointer to its father. Modify procedure KD_INSERT to take advantage of this addition.

2.31. Modify procedures KD_COMPARE and KD_INSERT to handle a k-d tree node implementation that makes use of a superkey in its discriminator field.

2.32. Prove that the TPL of a k-d tree of N nodes built by inserting the N points in a random order is $O(N \cdot \log_2 N)$.

2.33. Write a procedure, BUILD_OPTIMIZED_KDTREE, to construct an optimized k-d tree.

2.34. Write a procedure, BUILD_ADAPTIVE_KDTREE, to construct an adaptive k-d tree.

2.35. Analyze the running time of procedure BUILD_ADAPTIVE_KDTREE.

2.36. Recall from the text that the optimized k-d tree can also be constructed dynamically. Given δ ($0 < \delta < 1$), show that there exists an algorithm to build such a tree so that its depth is always at most $\log_{2-\delta} n + O(1)$ and that the average insertion time in an initially empty data structure is $O(\frac{1}{\delta} \log_2^2 N)$. n denotes the number of nodes currently in the tree, and N is the total number of nodes in the final tree.

2.37. Define a pseudo k-d tree in an analogous manner to that used to define the pseudo-quadtree in Section 2.3.2. Repeat Exercise 2.23 for the pseudo k-d tree. In other words, prove that the same result holds for N insertions and deletions in a k-dimensional pseudo k-d tree.

2.38. Give the k-d tree analogs of the single and double rotation operators [Knut73b, p. 454]. Make sure that you handle equal key values appropriately.

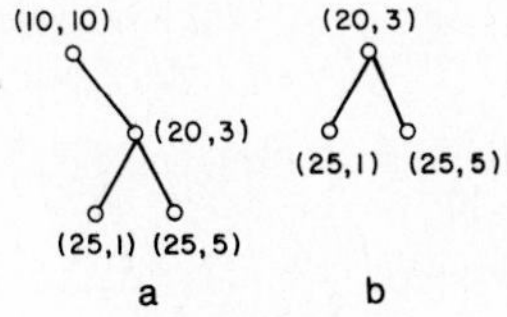

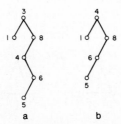

Figure 2.22   Example of a k-d tree in (a) whose right
son (b) is not a k-d tree

2.4.2 Deletion

Deletion of nodes from k-d trees is considerably more complex than for binary search
trees. Observe that, unlike the binary search tree, not every subtree of a k-d tree is
itself a k-d tree. For example, although Figure 2.22a is a k-d tree, its right subtree
(Figure 2.22b) is not. This is because the root node in a 2-d tree discriminates on the
value of the x coordinate, while both children of the root node in Figure 2.22b have x
coordinate values that are larger than that of the root node. Thus we see that special
care must be taken when deleting a node from a k-d tree.

In contrast, when deleting a node from a binary search tree, we simply move a
node and a subtree. For example, deleting node 3 from Figure 2.23a results in replacing node 3 with node 4 and replacing the left subtree of 8 by the right subtree of 4 (see
Figure 2.23b). However, this cannot be done, in general, in a k-d tree because the
nodes with values 5 and 6 might not have the same relative relationship at their new
depths.

Deletion in a k-d tree can be achieved by the following recursive process. Let
us assume that we wish to delete the node (a,b) from the k-d tree. If both subtrees of
(a,b) are empty, replace (a,b) with the empty tree. Otherwise find a suitable replacement node in one of the subtrees of (a,b), say the one rooted at (c,d), and recursively
delete (c,d) from the k-d tree. Once (c,d) has been deleted, replace (a,b) with (c,d).

Figure 2.23   (a) Example of a binary search tree and
(b) the result of deleting its root

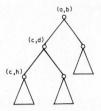

Figure 2.24 Example k-d tree illustrating why the replacement node should be chosen from the right subtree of the
tree containing the deleted node

At this point, it is appropriate to comment on what constitutes a 'suitable'
replacement node. Recall that an x-discriminator is a node that appears at an even
depth, and hence partitions its space based on the value of its x coordinate. A y-
discriminator is defined analogously for nodes at odd depths. Assume that (a,b) is an
x-discriminator. We know that every node in its right subtree has an x coordinate with
value greater than or equal to a. The node that will replace (a,b) must bear the same
relationship to the subtrees of (a,b). Using the analogy with binary search trees, it
would seem that we would have a choice with respect to the replacement node. It
must either be the node in the left subtree of (a,b) with the largest x coordinate value
or the node in the right subtree of (a,b) with the smallest x coordinate value.

Actually we do not really have a choice, as the following comments will make
clear. If we use the node in the left subtree of (a,b) with the maximum x coordinate
value, say (c,d), and there exists another node in the same subtree with the same x
coordinate value, say (c,h), then when (c,d) replaces node (a,b), there will be a node
in the left subtree of (c,d) that does not belong there by virtue of having an x coordinate value of c. Thus, we see that given our definition of a k-d tree, the replacement
node must be chosen from the right subtree. Otherwise a duplicate x coordinate value
will disrupt the proper interaction between each node and its subtrees. Pictorially this
can be seen by examining Figure 2.24. Note that the replacement node need not be a
leaf node.

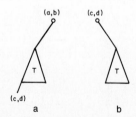

Figure 2.25 (b) The result of deleting (a,b) from the k-d
tree in (a)

The only remaining question is how to handle the case when the right subtree of (a,b) is empty. This is solved by the following recursive process. Find the node in the left subtree of (a,b) that has the smallest value for its x coordinate, say (c,d). Attach the left subtree of (a,b) to the right son of (c,d) and recursively apply the deletion procedure to node (c,d) from its prior position in the tree (i.e., in the left subtree of (a,b)). Pictorially this can be seen by examining Figure 2.25.

The problem of deleting a node (a,b) from a k-d tree is reduced to that of finding the node with the least x coordinate value in a subtree of (a,b). Unfortunately locating the node with the minimum x coordinate value is considerably more complex than the analogous problem for a binary search tree. In particular, although the node with the minimum x coordinate value must be in the left subtree of an x-discriminator, it could be in either subtree of a y-discriminator. Thus search is involved, and care must be taken in coordinating this search so that at each odd depth only one of the two subtrees is searched.

As can be seen from the discussion, deleting a node from a k-d tree can be costly. We can obtain an upper bound on the cost in the following manner. Clearly the cost of deleting the root of a subtree is bounded from above by the number of nodes in the subtree. Letting TPL(T) denote the total path length of tree T, it can be shown that the sum of the subtree sizes of a tree is TPL(T) $+ N$ (see Exercise 2.12).

Bentley [Bent75b] proves that the TPL of a tree built by inserting N points in a random order is $O(N \cdot \log_2 N)$, which means that the average cost of deleting a randomly selected node from a randomly built k-d tree has an upper bound of $O(\log_2 N)$. This relatively low value for the upper bound reflects the fact that most of the nodes in the k-d tree are leaf nodes. The cost of deleting root nodes is considerably higher. Clearly it is bounded by N. Its cost is dominated by the cost of the process of finding a minimum element in a subtree that is $O(N^{1-1/k})$ (see Exercise 2.43) since on every k^{th} level, only one of the two subtrees needs to be searched.

As an example of the deletion process, consider the k-d tree in parts a and b of Figure 2.21. We wish to delete the root node A at (20,20). Assume that A is an x discriminator. The node in the right subtree of A with a minimum value for its x coordinate is C at (25,50). Thus C replaces A (see Figure 2.21c), and we recursively apply the deletion procedure to C's position in the tree. Since C's position was a y-discriminator, we seek the node with a minimum y coordinate value in the right subtree of C. However, C's right subtree was empty, which means that we must replace C with the node in its left subtree that has the minimum y coordinate value.

D at (35,25) is the node in the left subtree that satisfies this minimum value condition. It is moved up in the tree (see Figure 2.21d). Since D was an x-discriminator, we replace it by the node in its right subtree having a minimum x coordinate value. H at (45,35) satisfies this condition, and it is moved up in the tree (see Figure 2.21e). Again, H is a x-discriminator and we replace it by I—the node in its right subtree with a minimum x coordinate value. Since I is a leaf node, our procedure terminates. Figure 2.21f and 2.21g shows the result of the deletion process. Procedures KD_DELETE and KD_DELETE1, given below, are a formal description of the deletion process. Note that KD_DELETE1 is recursive.

```
procedure KD_DELETE(P,R);
/* Delete node P from the k-d tree rooted at node R. If the root·of the tree was deleted,
   then reset R. */
begin
  value pointer node P;
  reference pointer node R;
  pointer node F,N;
  N ← KD_DELETE1(P);
  F ← FIND_FATHER(P);
  if null(F) then R ← N /* Reset the pointer to the root of the tree */
  else SON(F,SONTYPE(P)) ← N;
  returntoavail(P);
end;


recursive pointer node procedure KD_DELETE1(P);
/* Delete node P and return a pointer to the root of the resulting subtree. */
begin
  value pointer node P;
  pointer node F,R;
  direction D;
  if null(LOSON(P)) and null(HISON(P)) then
    return(NIL) /* P is a leaf */
  else D ← DISC(P);
  if null(HISON(P)) then /* Special case when HISON is empty */
    begin
      HISON(P) ← LOSON(P);
      LOSON(P) ← NIL;
    end;
  R ← FIND_D_MINIMUM(HISON(P),D);
  F ← FIND_FATHER(R);
  SON(F,SONTYPE(R)) ← KD_DELETE1(R); /* Reset the father of R */
  LOSON(R) ← LOSON(P);
  HISON(R) ← HISON(P);
  DISC(R) ← DISC(P);
  return(R);
end;
```

The above discussion required a special provision to account for the definition of a k-d tree node as a partition of space into two parts—one less than the key value tested by the node and one greater than or equal to the value tested by the node. Defining a node in terms of a superkey alleviates this problem since we no longer have to choose the replacing node from the right subtree, we now have a choice. The best algorithm is one that 'flip-flops' between the left and right sons, perhaps through the use of a random number generator (see Exercise 2.41). Of course, node insertion and search are slightly more complex since it is possible that more than one key will have to be compared at each level in the tree (see Exercises 2.31 and 2.47).

Exercises

2.39. Suppose that a k-d tree node is implemented as a record with a FATHER field containing a pointer to its father. Modify procedures KD_DELETE and KD_DELETE1 to take advantage of this addition.

2.40. Convince yourself that procedures KD_DELETE and KD_DELETE1 really work by hand tracing their operation on Figure 2.21; that is, delete node A.

2.41. Modify procedures KD_DELETE and KD_DELETE1 to handle a k-d tree node implementation that makes use of a superkey in its discriminator field.

2.42. Given a node P in a k-d tree that discriminates on attribute D, write an algorithm, FIND_D_-MINIMUM, to compute the D-minimum node in its left subtree. Repeat for the right subtree of P. Generalize your algorithm to work for either of the two subtrees.

2.43. Prove that the cost of finding a D-minimum element in a k-d tree is $O(N^{1-1/k})$.

2.44. Modify procedures KD_DELETE and KD_DELETE1 so that they need not recompute the father of the node being deleted.

2.4.3 Search

Like point quadtrees, k-d trees are useful in applications involving search. Again we consider a typical query that seeks all nodes within a specified distance of a given point. The k-d tree data structure serves as a pruning device on the amount of search required; that is, many nodes need not be examined. To see how the pruning is achieved, suppose we are performing a region search of distance d around a node with coordinates (a,b). In essence, we want to determine all nodes (x,y) whose Euclidean distance from (a,b) is less than or equal to d—that is, $d^2 \geq (a - x)^2 + (b - y)^2$.

Clearly this is a circular region. The minimum x and y coordinate values of a node in this circle cannot be less than $a - d$ and $b - d$, respectively. Similarly the maximum x and y coordinate values of a node in this circle cannot be greater than $a + d$ and $b + d$, respectively. Thus if the search reaches a node with coordinate values (e,f) and KD_COMPARE$((a - d, b - d),(e,f)) = $ 'RIGHT', then there is no need to examine any nodes in the left subtree of (e,f). Similarly, the right subtree of (e,f) need not be searched when KD_COMPARE$((a + d, b + d),(e,f)) = $ 'LEFT'.

For example, suppose that in the hypothetical data base of Figure 2.18 we wish to find all cities within three units of a point with coordinates (88,6). In such a case, there is no need to search the left subtree of the root (i.e., Chicago with coordinates (35,40)). Thus we need only examine the right subtree of the tree rooted at Chicago. Similarly there is no need to search the right subtree of the tree rooted at Mobile (coordinates (50,10)). Continuing our search, we find that only Miami, at coordinates (90,5), satisfies our request. Thus we had to examine only three nodes during the search.

In general, the search cost depends on the type of query. Given N points, Lee and Wong [Lee80a] have shown that in the worst case, the cost of a range search of a complete k-d tree is $O(k \cdot N^{1-1/k})$. To see how this bound is obtained we assume that $k = 2$ and, without loss of generality, consider a rectangular search region (see

PW.

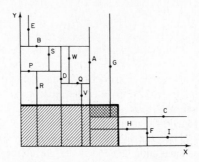

*Figure 2.26   Example k-d tree illustrating the worst case
for the search procedure*

Exercise 2.45), marked hatched, in Figure 2.26. We use the number of nodes visited while searching the tree as a measure of the amount of work that needs to be expended.

Since we are interested in the worst case, we assume that B and C (Figure 2.26) partition the tree rooted at A in such a way that the search region is overlapped by the regions rooted at B and C. If B is within the search region, the tree rooted at D need not be searched further. If B is outside the search region (as is the case here), the tree rooted at E need not be searched further. Similarly if F is within the search region, the tree rooted at H need not be searched further. Finally, when F is outside the search region (as is the case here), the tree rooted at I need not be searched further. G is chosen in such a way that both of its subtrees will have to be searched. Further partitioning of G is analogous to a recursive invocation of this analysis two levels lower than the starting level (see the cross-hatched region in Figure 2.26).

The remaining subtrees of B and F (D and H) are equivalent to each other and enable the elimination of two subtrees from further consideration at every other level. For example, the sons of D are P and Q, with sons R and S, and V and W, respectively. Both S and W need no further processing.

We are now ready to analyze the worst case of the number of nodes that will be visited in performing a range search in a 2-d tree. Let t_i denote the number of nodes visited when dealing with a k-d tree rooted at level i. Let u_j denote that number of nodes visited when dealing with a subtree of the form illustrated by the trees rooted at nodes D and H in Figure 2.26. This leads to the following recurrence relations:

$$t_i = 1 + 1 + 1 + t_{i-2} + u_{i-2} + 1 + u_{i-3}$$
$$u_j = 1 + 1 + 1 + 2 \cdot u_{j-2}$$

with initial conditions $t_0 = u_0 = 0$ and $t_1 = u_1 = 1$.

t_i and u_j can best be understood by referring to Figure 2.27, which is a tree-like representation of the k-d tree of Figure 2.26. The terms in t_i correspond to nodes A, B, C, G, D, F, and H in order, while the terms in u_j correspond to nodes D, P, Q, R, and V in

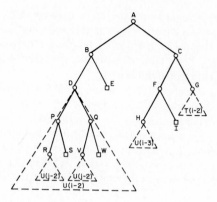

Figure 2.27   Tree representation of Figure 2.26

order. The square nodes in the figure (e.g., E, I, S, and W) correspond to subtrees that have been pruned; they do not have to be searched.

When these relations are solved, we find that, under the assumption of a complete binary tree (i.e., $N = 2^{n-1}$), t_n is $O(2 \cdot N^{1/2})$. Note that, unlike the point quadtree, a complete binary k-d tree can always be constructed (see the optimized k-d tree of Bentley [Bent75b] discussed in Section 2.4.1). In general, for arbitrary k, t_n is $O(k \cdot N^{1-1/k})$.

Partial range queries can be handled in the same way as range searching. Lee and Wong [Lee77b] show that when ranges for s out of k keys are specified, the algorithm has a worst-case running time of $O(s \cdot N^{1-1/k})$. For an alternative derivation, see Exercise 2.50.

As is the case for the point quadtree, the k-d tree can be used to handle all three types of queries specified by Knuth [Knut73b]. The range query is described above. Simple queries are a by-product of the k-d tree insertion process. Boolean queries are straightforward. Range queries can be facilitated by use of a bounds array B[i] of $2 \cdot k$ elements stored at each node. It contains the range of values for all of the coordinates of the points stored in the k-d tree rooted at the node.

Exercises

2.45. Why was the search region in Figure 2.26 chosen in the lower left corner of the space instead of somewhere in the middle?

2.46. Write a procedure KD_REGION_SEARCH to determine all the nodes in a given k-d tree that intersect a given rectangular region in k-dimensional space. Use a bounds array to facilitate your task. KD_REGION_SEARCH should make use of a pair of auxiliary functions—one to determine if a subtree can be pruned and the other to determine if a node is indeed in the search region.

2.47. Modify procedure KD_REGION_SEARCH of Exercise 2.46 to handle a k-d tree node implementation that makes use of a superkey in its discriminator field.

2.48. Solve the recurrence relations for t_i and u_j used to analyze range searching in a k-d tree.

2.49. A partial match query is closely related to the range query. In this case, values are specified for t ($t < k$) of the keys, and a search is made for all records having such values for the specified keys. Show how you would use procedure KD_REGION_SEARCH of Exercise 2.46 to respond to a partial match query.

2.50. Given a complete k-d tree of N nodes where $N = 2^{k \cdot h} - 1$ and all leaf nodes appear at depth $k \cdot h - 1$, prove Bentley's [Bent75b] result that, in the worst case, $O(N^{(k-t)/k})$ nodes are visited in performing a partial match query with t out of k keys specified.

2.51. In Exercise 2.25 a *perfect point quadtree* was defined and used to analyze the expected number of nodes visited in performing a region query for a 2-dimensional point quadtree. Define a *perfect k-d tree* in an analogous manner and repeat this analysis.

2.52. Perform an average-case analysis for region queries and partially specified queries in a k-d tree.

2.4.4 Comparison with Point Quadtrees

From the previous discussion we see that k-d trees alleviate many of the deficiencies of point quadtrees pointed out earlier. Assuming a k-dimensional space, at each node, only one key needs to be compared instead of k, as is the case with point quadtrees. Terminal nodes, as well as other nodes, do not occupy too much space since the number of pointers per node is reduced to 2 for all values of k instead of 2^k.

Nevertheless, the k-d tree node is still not of uniform size for all values of k since the k key values must be stored at each node. Therefore the total space requirement per node is $4 + k$ words: one word each for the NAME and DISC fields, two words for the LOSON and HISON pointers, and k words for the k key values. Actually we can get by with $3 + k$ words per node since the DISC field is not necessary. If the adaptive k-d tree is used, then no data need to be stored in the nonleaf node, except for the partition value of the discriminator key, which requires one word. However, a DISC field must be stored in such a case. Therefore the total space requirement is five words per nonleaf node, and our goal of a uniform node size has been attained.

The point quadtree does have one advantage over the k-d tree. The point quadtree is an inherently parallel data structure, and thus a key comparison operation can be performed in parallel for the k key values. This cannot be done for the k-d tree. Therefore we can characterize the k-d tree as a superior serial data structure and the point quadtree as a superior parallel data structure. For a discussion of the use of point quadtrees in a multiprocessor environment, see Linn [Linn73].

2.5 RANGE TREES AND PRIORITY SEARCH TREES

Finding efficient data structures for range searching has been an area of much interest. The *range tree* of Bentley and Maurer [Bent79a, Bent80d] is an asymptotically faster search structure compared to the point quadtree and the k-d tree; however, it has significantly higher storage requirements. It stores points and is designed to detect all points that lie in a given range.

The range tree is best understood by first examining the one-dimensional range searching problem. A one-dimensional range tree is a balanced binary search tree where the data points are stored in the leaf nodes and the leaf nodes are linked in sorted order by use of a doubly linked list. A range search for $[L : R]$ is performed by searching the tree for the node with the smallest value that is $\geq L$ and then following the links until reaching a leaf node with a value greater than R. For N points, this process takes $O(\log_2 N + F)$ time and uses $O(N)$ storage. F is the number of points found.

A two-dimensional range tree is a binary tree of binary trees. It is formed in the following manner. First, sort all of the points along one of the attributes, say x, and store them in the leaf nodes of a balanced binary search tree, say T. With each nonleaf node of T, say I, associate a one-dimensional range tree, say T_I, of the points in the subtree rooted at I where now these points are sorted along the other attribute, say y.

A range search for $([L_x : R_x], [L_y : R_y])$ is performed by procedure 2D_SEARCH, given below. It makes use of procedure 1D_SEARCH, not given here. Procedure 2D_-SEARCH starts by searching T for both L_x and R_x. Let Q be the common ancestor of L_x and R_x in T that is closest to them (and hence the farthest from the root in terms of node links). Let $\{L_i\}$ and $\{R_i\}$ denote the sequences of nonleaf nodes that form the paths in T from Q to L_x and R_x, respectively. Let LEFT(P) and RIGHT(P) denote the left and right sons, respectively, of nonleaf node P. RANGE_TREE(P) is the one-dimensional range tree for y that is stored at nonleaf node P.

For each P that is an element of $\{L_i\}$ such that LEFT(P) is also in $\{L_i\}$, 2D_-SEARCH performs a one-dimensional range search for $[L_y : R_y]$ in the one-dimensional range tree for y rooted at node RIGHT(P). For each P that is an element of $\{R_i\}$ such that RIGHT(P) is also in $\{R_i\}$, 2D_SEARCH performs a one-dimensional range search for $[L_y : R_y]$ in the one-dimensional range tree for y rooted at node LEFT(P).

```
procedure 2D_SEARCH(LX,RX,LY,RY,T);
/* Perform a range search for the two-dimensional interval ([LX:RX],[LY:RY]) in the two-
   dimensional range tree rooted at T. The interval is defined by the values stored in
   nodes LX, RX, LY, and RY. */
begin
  value pointer node LX,RX,LY,RY,T;
  pointer node P,Q;
  set PATH_TO_LX, PATH_TO_RX;
  Q ← closest common ancestor of LX and RX;
  PATH_TO_LX ← {nonleaf nodes on the path from Q to LX};
  PATH_TO_RX ← {nonleaf nodes on the path from Q to RX};
  foreach P in PATH_TO_LX do
    begin
      if LEFT(P) ∈ PATH_TO_LX then
        1D_SEARCH(LY,RY,RANGE_TREE(RIGHT(P)));
    end;
  foreach P in PATH_TO_RX do
    begin
      if RIGHT(P) ∈ PATH_TO_RX then
```

```
        1D_SEARCH(LY,RY,RANGE_TREE(LEFT(P)));
    end;
end;
```

For example, the desired closest common ancestor of L_x and R_x in Figure 2.28 is Q. One-dimensional range searches would be performed in the one-dimensional range trees rooted at nodes A, B, C, and D since $\{L_i\} = \{L_1, L_2, L_3\}$ and $\{R_i\} = \{R_1, R_2, R_3\}$. For N points, procedure 2D_SEARCH takes $O(\log_2^2 N + F)$ time where F is the number of points found (see Exercise 2.57). The two-dimensional range tree uses $O(N \cdot \log_2 N)$ storage (see Exercise 2.56).

The range tree also can be adapted easily to handle k-dimensional data. In such a case, for N points, a k-dimensional range search takes $O(\log_2^k N + F)$ time where F is the number of points found. The k-dimensional range tree uses $O(N \cdot \log_2^{k-1} N)$ storage (see Exercise 2.58).

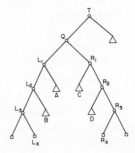

Figure 2.28   Example 2-d range tree to illustrate 2-d range searching

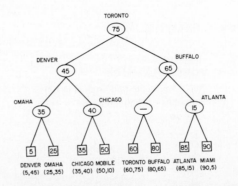

Figure 2.29   Priority search tree for the data of Figure 2.1. Each leaf node contains the value of its x coordinate. Each marked nonleaf node contains the value of its y coordinate

Edelsbrunner [Edel81a] has reduced the order of execution time for the two-dimensional range searching query to $O(\log_2 N + F)$ time (but still using $O(N \cdot \log_2 N)$ storage) by making use of McCreight's priority search tree [McCr85]. The *priority search tree* is a data structure designed for solving queries involving semi-infinite ranges in two-dimensional space. A typical query has a range of the form ($[L_x : R_x]$, $[L_y : \infty]$).

A priority search tree is built in the following manner. Assume that no two data points have the same x coordinate value (see Exercise 2.63). Sort all the points along the x coordinate, and store them in the leaf nodes of a balanced binary search tree, say T. We proceed from the root node toward the leaf nodes. With each nonleaf node of T, say I, associate the point in the subtree rooted at I with the maximum value for its y coordinate that has not already been stored at a shallower depth in the tree. If such a point does not exist, leave the node empty. For example, Figure 2.29 is the priority search tree for the data of Figure 2.1. For N points, this structure uses $O(N)$ storage (see Exercise 2.61).

It is not easy to perform a two-dimensional range query of the form ($[L_x : R_x]$, $[L_y : R_y]$) with a priority search tree. The problem is that only the values of the x coordinates are sorted. In other words, given a node I that stores point (x_I, y_I), we know that the values of the x coordinates of all nodes to the left of I are smaller than x_I and all those to the right of I are greater than x_I. On the other hand, with respect to the values of the y coordinates, we know only that all nodes below nonleaf node I with value y_I have smaller values; the y coordinate values associated with the remaining nodes in the tree may be larger or smaller than that of I.

This is not surprising because a priority search tree is really a variant of a range tree in x (see Exercise 2.53) and a heap (i.e., priority queue) [Knut73b] in y. A heap enables finding the maximum (minimum) value in $O(1)$ time. More generally the largest (smallest) F out of N values can be determined in $O(F)$ time, but the F values are not sorted. Whether the heap is used to find the largest or smallest values depends on how it is constructed. The way in which we specify the priority search tree enables finding the largest values.

However, priority search trees make it very easy to perform a semi-infinite range query of the form ($[L_x : R_x]$, $[L_y : \infty]$). The control structure is quite similar to that of 2D_SEARCH. Descend the tree looking for the nearest common ancestor of L_x and R_x, say Q. Recursively, apply the following search procedure to the subtree rooted at Q. Let T denote the root of the subtree currently being processed, and let P be the point associated with it. If no such P exists, we are finished with the entire subtree rooted at T because all points in its subtrees have already been examined and/or reported. Examine the y coordinate value of P, say P_y. If $P_y < L_y$, we are finished with the entire subtree rooted at T since P is the point with the maximum y coordinate value in the subtree. Otherwise perform the following two steps:

1. Check if the x coordinate value of P is in the range $[L_x : R_x]$. If yes, then output P as satisfying the query.
2. Determine where the search is to be continued. If both T and its right son are on the path from Q to L_x, continue in the right son of T. If both T and its

left son are on the path from Q to R_x, continue in the left son of T; otherwise continue in the two sons of T.

For N points, performing a semi-infinite range query in this way takes $O(\log_2 N + F)$ time. F is the number of points found (see Exercise 2.62). To answer the two-dimensional range query $([L_x : R_x], [L_y : R_y])$, perform the semi-infinite range query $([L_x : R_x], [L_y : \infty])$ and discard all points (x, y) such that $y > R_y$.

Edelsbrunner [Edel81a] introduces a variation on the priority search tree, which we term a *range priority tree*, to obtain an $O(\log_2 N + F)$ algorithm for range searching in a two-dimensional space. Define an *inverse priority search tree* to be a priority search tree S such that with each nonleaf node of S, say I, we associate the point in the subtree rooted at I with the minimum (instead of the maximum) value for its y coordinate that has not already been stored at a shallower depth in the tree. The range priority tree is a balanced binary search tree, say T, where all the data points are stored in the leaf nodes and are sorted by their y coordinate values. With each nonleaf node of T, say I, which is a left son of its father, we store a priority search tree of the points in the subtree rooted at I. With each nonleaf node of T, say I, which is a right son of its father we store an inverse priority search tree of the points in the subtree rooted at I. For N points, the range priority tree uses $O(N \cdot \log_2 N)$ storage (see Exercise 2.69).

Performing a range query for $([L_x : R_x], [L_y : R_y])$ using a range priority tree is done in the following manner. We descend the tree looking for the nearest common ancestor of L_y and R_y, say Q. The values of the y coordinates of all points in the left son of Q are less than R_y. We can obtain them with the semi-infinite range query $([L_x : R_x], [L_y : \infty])$. This can be done by using the priority tree associated with the left son of Q. Similarly, the values of the y coordinates of all points in the right son of Q are greater than L_y. We can obtain them with the semi-infinite range query $([L_x : R_x], [-\infty : R_y])$. This can be done by using the inverse priority search tree associated with the right son of Q. Thus for N points the range query takes $O(\log_2 N + F)$ time where F is the number of points found (see Exercise 2.71).

Exercises

2.53. Is there a difference between a balanced binary search tree where all the data are stored in the leaf nodes and a one-dimensional range tree?

2.54. Why does procedure 2D_SEARCH provide the desired result?

2.55. Prove that no point is reported more than once by the algorithm for executing a range query in a two-dimensional range tree.

2.56. Show that $O(N \cdot \log_2 N)$ storage suffices for a two-dimensional range tree for N points.

2.57. Given a two-dimensional range tree containing N points, prove that a two-dimensional range query takes $O(\log_2^2 N + F)$ time, where F is the number of points found.

2.58. Given a k-dimensional range tree containing N points, prove that a k-dimensional range query takes $O(\log_2^k N + F)$ time, where F is the number of points found. Also show that $O(N \cdot \log_2^{k-1} N)$ storage is sufficient.

2.59. Write a procedure to construct a two-dimensional range tree.

2.60. Write a procedure to search a two-dimensional range tree for a rectangular search region.

2.61. Prove that a priority search tree for N points uses $O(N)$ space.

2.62. Prove that for a priority search tree with N points, a semi-infinite range query can be performed in $O(\log_2 N + F)$ time, where F is the number of points found.

2.63. Why can't two data points in a priority search tree have the same x coordinate value?

2.64. How can you get around the restriction that no two data points in a priority search tree have the same x coordinate value?

2.65. Prove that the construction of a priority search tree takes $O(N \cdot \log_2 N)$ time for N rectangles.

2.66. Write a procedure to construct a priority search tree.

2.67. Write a procedure to search a priority search tree for a semi-infinite range query.

2.68. Can you extend the priority search tree to handle k-dimensional data? If so, show how you would do it.

2.69. Prove that a range priority tree for N points uses $O(N \cdot \log_2 N)$ space.

2.70. Prove that the construction of a range priority tree takes $O(N \cdot \log_2 N)$ time for N rectangles.

2.71. Prove that for a range priority tree with N points, a two-dimensional range query can be performed in $O(\log_2 N + F)$ time, where F is the number of points found.

2.72. Can you extend the range priority tree to handle k-dimensional range queries? What is the order of the execution time of the query? How much space does it use?

2.73. Write a procedure to construct a range priority tree.

2.74. Write a procedure to search a range priority tree for a rectangular search region.

2.6   REGION-BASED QUADTREES

The quadtree is a member of a class of hierarchical data structures based on the principle of recursive decomposition. For the point quadtree and the k-d tree, the points of decomposition are the data points themselves (e.g., in Figure 2.4, Chicago at location (35,40) subdivides the two-dimensional space into four rectangular regions). Requiring that the regions resulting from the subdivision process be of equal size leads to the region quadtree. In this section we show how the region quadtree can be adapted to handle point data.

Although conceivably there are many ways of adapting the region quadtree to represent point data, our presentation focuses on two methods, the MX and the PR quadtrees, and outlines in detail how they are created and updated, as well as a brief review of some of their applications. We omit a discussion of search operations because they are performed in the same manner as in point quadtrees and k-d trees. We conclude with a comparison of these methods with the point quadtree.

Since the bintree is related to the region quadtree in the same way as the k-d tree is related to the point quadtree, the bintree can be adapted in an analogous manner to handle point data. This is left as an exercise. Note that the type of structure described in this section is also known as a *trie* [Fred60]. A trie is a branching structure in which a data item or key is treated as a sequence of characters where each character has M possible values. A node at level i in the trie represents an M-way branch depending on the value of the ith character.

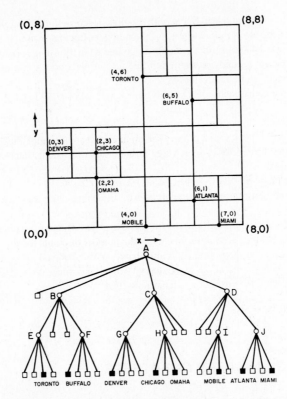

Figure 2.30   MX quadtree and the records it represents

2.6.1   MX Quadtrees

There are a number of ways of adapting the region quadtree to represent point data. If the domain of data points is discrete, we can treat data points as if they were black pixels in a region quadtree. An alternative characterization is to treat the data points as nonzero elements in a square matrix. This characterization will be used in the subsequent discussion. To avoid confusion with the point and region quadtrees, the resulting data structure is termed an *MX quadtree* (MX for matrix), although the term *MX quadtrie* would probably be more appropriate.

The MX quadtree is organized in a similar way to the region quadtree. The difference is that leaf nodes are black or empty (i.e., white) corresponding to the presence or absence, respectively, of a data point in the appropriate position in the matrix. For example, Figure 2.30 is the $2^3 \times 2^3$ MX quadtree corresponding to the data of Figure 2.1. It is obtained by applying the mapping f such that $f(z) = z$ div 12.5 to both x and y coordinates. The result of the mapping is reflected in the coordinate values in the figure.

Each data point in an MX quadtree corresponds to a 1×1 square. For ease of notation and operation using modulo and integer division operations, the data point is associated with the lower left corner of the square. This adheres to the general convention followed throughout this presentation that the lower and left boundaries of each block are closed, while the upper and right boundaries of each block are open. We also assume that the lower left corner of the matrix is located at (0,0). Note that, unlike the region quadtree, when a nonleaf node has four black sons, they are not merged. This is natural since a merger of such nodes would lead to a loss of the identifying information about the data points, as each data point is different. On the other hand, the empty leaf nodes have the absence of information as their common property, so four white sons of a nonleaf node can be safely merged.

Each node in an MX quadtree is stored as a record of type *node* containing six fields. The first four fields contain pointers to the node's four sons corresponding to the four quadrants. If P is a pointer to a node and I is a quadrant, these fields are referenced as SON(P, I). The fifth field, NODETYPE, indicates whether the node contains a data point (BLACK), is empty (WHITE), or is a nonleaf node (GRAY). The NAME field contains descriptive information about the data point stored at a node (e.g., city name). There is no need to store information about the coordinates of the data point since this is derivable from the path to the node from the root of the MX quadtree.

We assume that each data point is unique. If more than one data point were permitted to have the same coordinates, an overflow list would be required at each data point node. In such a case, we have a hierarchical variant of the fixed-grid (or cell) method discussed in Section 2.2. The difference from the fixed-grid method is that empty sibling cells are merged. The minimum size of the space spanned by an MX quadtree is a square 1×1 matrix. The empty MX quadtree is represented by NIL. Using these conventions, the function MX_COMPARE, given below, determines the quadrant in which a given data point lies relative to a grid subdivision point.

```
quadrant procedure MX_COMPARE(X,Y,W);
/* Return the quadrant of the MX quadtree of width 2 · W centered at (W,W) in which data
   point (X,Y) belongs. */
begin
  value integer X,Y,W;
  return(if X < W then
           if Y < W then 'SW'
           else 'NW'
         else if Y < W then 'SE'
         else 'NE');
end;
```

Data points are inserted into an MX quadtree by searching for them. This search is based on the location of the data point in the matrix (e.g., the discretized values of its x and y coordinates in our city data base example) and is guided by the function MX_COMPARE. If the search is unsuccessful, we end up at a leaf node. If this leaf node is occupied by another record, it is replaced by a record corresponding to the

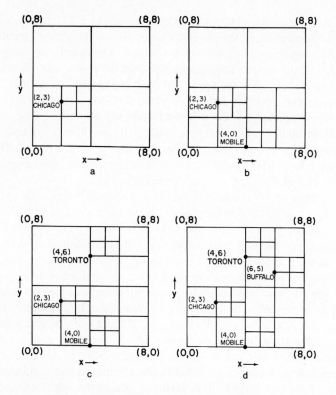

Figure 2.31   Sequence of partial MX quadtrees demonstrating the addition of (a) Chicago, (b) Mobile, (c) Toronto,
and (d) Buffalo

data point being inserted (although the location is the same, some of the attribute information may have changed). If the leaf node is NIL, then we may have to subdivide the space spanned by it repeatedly until it is a 1 × 1 square. This will result in the creation of nonleaf nodes. This operation is termed *splitting*. For a $2^n \times 2^n$ MX quadtree, splitting will have to be performed at most n times.

The shape of the resulting MX quadtree is independent of the order in which data points are inserted into it. However, the shapes of the intermediate trees do depend on the order. For example, Figure 2.31a–d shows how the tree was constructed in incremental fashion for Chicago, Mobile, Toronto, and Buffalo. The actual insertion is achieved by procedure MX_INSERT given below.

procedure MX_INSERT(P,X,Y,R,W);
/* Attempt to insert node P corresponding to data point (X,Y) in the MX quadtree rooted at node R of width W. If the tree is empty, then R is set to point to the new root. Nodes are created by use of CREATE_PNODE. GRAY is used to specify nonleaf nodes. */

```
begin
  value pointer node P;
  reference pointer node R;
  value integer X,Y,W;
  pointer node T;
  quadrant Q;
  if W = 1 then
    begin /* The tree corresponds to a one element data set */
      R ← P;
      return;
    end
  else if null(R) then
    R ← CREATE_PNODE('GRAY'); /* The tree at R is initially empty */
  T ← R;
  W ← W/2;
  Q ← MX_COMPARE(X,Y,W);
  while W>1 do
    begin
      if null(SON(T,Q)) then SON(T,Q)) ← CREATE_PNODE('GRAY');
      T ← SON(T,Q);
      X ← X mod W;
      Y ← Y mod W;
      W ← W/2;
      Q ← MX_COMPARE(X,Y,W);
    end;
  SON(T,Q) ← P;
end;


pointer node procedure CREATE_PNODE(C);
/* Create a node with color C and return a pointer to it. */
begin
  value color C;
  pointer node P;
  quadrant I;
  P ← create(node);
  NODETYPE(P) ← C;
  for I in {'NW', 'NE', 'SW', 'SE'} do SON(P,I) ← NIL;
  return(P);
end;
```

Deletion of nodes from MX quadtrees is considerably simpler than for point quadtrees since all records are stored in the leaf nodes. This means that we do not have to be concerned with rearranging the tree as is necessary when a record stored in a nonleaf node is being deleted from a point quadtree. For example, to delete Omaha from the MX quadtree of Figure 2.30 we simply set the SW son of its father node, H, to NIL. Deleting Toronto is slightly more complicated. Setting the SW son of its father node, E, to NIL is not enough. We must also perform merging because all four sons of

E are NIL. This leads to replacing the NW son of E's father, B, by NIL and returning nonleaf node E to the free storage list. This process is termed *collapsing* and is the counterpart of the splitting operation that was necessary when inserting a record in an MX quadtree.

Collapsing may take place over several levels. In essence, we apply the collapsing process repeatedly until encountering a nearest common ancestor with an additional non-NIL son. As collapsing takes place, the affected nonleaf nodes are returned to the free storage list. For example, suppose that after deleting Toronto from Figure 2.30 we also delete Buffalo. The subsequent deletion of Buffalo means that nodes F and B are subjected to the collapsing process, with the result that the NE son of node A is set to NIL and nonleaf nodes B and F are returned to the free storage list.

The actual deletion is achieved by procedure MX_DELETE, which follows. The execution time of MX_DELETE is bounded by two times the depth of the quadtree. This upper bound is achieved when the nearest common ancestor for the collapsing process is the root node.

```
procedure MX_DELETE(X,Y,R,W);
/* Delete the node corresponding to data point (X,Y) from the MX quadtree rooted at node
   R of width W. If (X,Y) is the only data point in the tree, then the root will be set to NIL. If
   all of (X,Y)'s brothers are NIL, then the nearest ancestor of (X,Y) that has more than
   one non-NIL son is set to point to NIL in the direction of (X,Y). The nonleaf nodes that
   are bypassed as a result of this collapsing process are returned to the free storage
   list. */
begin
  reference pointer node R;
  value integer X,Y,W;
  pointer node F,T,TEMP;
  quadrant Q,QF;
  if null(R) then return /* The tree is empty */
  else if W = 1 then
    begin /* The resulting tree is empty */
      returntoavail(R);
      R ← NIL;
      return;
    end;
  T ← R;
  F ← NIL;
  do
    begin /* Locate the quadrant in which (X,Y) belongs */
      W ← W/2;
      Q ← MX_COMPARE(X,Y,W);
      if not(null(SON(T,CQUAD(Q)))) and
          null(SON(T,OPQUAD(Q))
          null(SON(T,CCQUAD(Q))) then
        begin   /* As the tree is descended, F and QF keep track of the */
          F ← T; /* nearest ancestor of (X,Y) with more than one son */
```

```
        QF ← Q;
      end;
    T ← SON(T,Q);
    X ← X mod W;
    Y ← Y mod W;
  end;
  until W = 1 or null(T);
if null(T) then return /* Data point (X,Y) is not in the tree */
else
  begin /* Collapse as much as possible */
    T ← if null(F) then R /* The entire tree will be collapsed */
        else SON(F,QF);
    Q ← 'NW';
    while GRAY(T) do
      begin /* Collapse one level at a time */
        while null(SON(T,Q)) do
          Q ← CQUAD(Q); /* Find non-NIL son */
        TEMP ← SON(T,Q);
        SON(T,Q) ← NIL;
        returntoavail(T);
        T ← TEMP;
      end;
    returntoavail(T);
    if null(F) then R ← NIL /* The tree contained just one node */
    else SON(F,QF) ← NIL; /* Reset the link of the nearest ancestor */
  end;
end;
```

Performing a range search in an MX quadtree is done in the same way as in the point quadtree. The worst-case cost of searching for all points that lie in a rectangle whose sides are parallel to the quadrant lines is $O(F + 2^n)$ where F is the number of points found and n is the maximum depth (see Exercise 2.80).

The MX quadtree is used in a number of varied applications. It can serve as the basis of a quadtree matrix manipulation system (see Exercises 2.81–2.85). The goal is to take advantage of the sparseness of matrices to achieve space and execution time efficiencies (e.g., [Abda88, Wise87a, Wise87b]). Algorithms for matrix transposition and matrix multiplication that take advantage of the recursive decomposition are easy to develop. Letelier [Lete83] makes use of the MX quadtree to represent silhouettes of hand motions to aid in the telephonic transmission of sign language for the hearing impaired. The region quadtree formulation of Hunter and Steiglitz [Hunt78, Hunt79a] (see Sections 1.5 and 4.2) utilizes a three-color variant of the MX quadtree to represent digitized simple polygons. De Coulon and Johnsen [DeCo76] describe the use of the MX quadtree in the coding of black and white facsimiles for efficient transmission of images.

Exercises

2.75. Suppose that an MX quadtree node is implemented as a record with a FATHER field containing a pointer to its father. Modify procedures MX_INSERT and MX_DELETE to take advantage of this addition.

2.76. Convince yourself that procedure MX_DELETE really works by hand tracing its operation on Figure 2.30; that is, delete nodes Atlanta, Miami, and Mobile in sequence.

2.77. In the implementation of an MX quadtree node, there is no need to store a NAME field with nonleaf nodes. Modify the definition of an MX quadtree node to make a distinction between leaf and nonleaf nodes and show the changes that must be made to procedures MX_INSERT and MX_DELETE.

2.78. Adapt the bintree to handle point data by defining a data structure called an MX bintree. Give procedures MX_BIN_INSERT and MX_BIN_DELETE to insert and delete data points in an MX bintree.

2.79. Write an algorithm to perform a range search for a rectangular region in an MX quadtree.

2.80. Show that the worst-case cost of performing a range search in an MX quadtree is $O(F + 2^n)$, where F is the number of points found and n is the maximum depth. Assume a rectangular query region.

2.81. The MX quadtree can be used to represent sparse matrices. Give an algorithm to compute the transpose of a matrix represented by an MX quadtree.

2.82. How many interchange operations are necessary when transposing an MX quadtree representation of a $2^n \times 2^n$ matrix such that there is no sparseness (i.e., all blocks are of size 1)?

2.83. Compare the savings in space and time requirements when a matrix is represented as an MX quadtree and as an array. Use the time required to perform a transpose operation as the basis of the comparison. You should assume the worst case, which occurs when there is no sparseness (i.e., all blocks are of size 1).

2.84. Give an algorithm for multiplying two matrices stored as MX quadtrees.

2.85. Why would an MX bintree be a better matrix representation than the MX quadtree?

2.86. Unless there is a large number of square blocks of zeros, the MX quadtree is not a particularly attractive representation for matrix multiplication. The problem is that this is inherently a row and column operation. Thus it would seem that a runlength representation would be better. However, ideally we would like to have both the rows and columns encoded using this technique. Can you see a problem with using such a dual representation?

2.6.2 PR Quadtrees

The MX quadtree is feasible as long as the domain of the data points is discrete and finite. If this is not the case, the data points cannot be represented using it because the minimum separation between the data points is unknown. This observation leads to an alternative adaptation of the region quadtree to point data, which associates data points (which need not be discrete) with quadrants. We call it a *PR quadtree* (P for point and R for region) although the term *PR quadtrie* would probably be more appropriate. The PR quadtree is organized in the same way as the region quadtree. The difference is that leaf nodes are either empty (i.e., white) or contain a data point

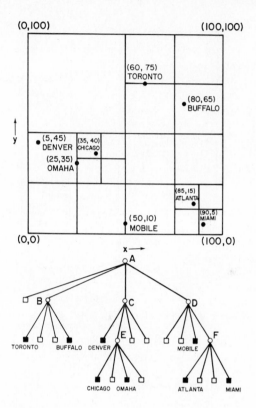

Figure 2.32   PR quadtree and the records it represents

(i.e., black) and its coordinates. A quadrant contains at most one data point. For example, Figure 2.32 is the PR quadtree corresponding to the data of Figure 2.1.

Orenstein [Oren82] describes a *k-d trie*, an analogous data structure that uses binary trees instead of quadtrees. Using our terminology, such a data structure would be called a *PR k-d tree* or a *PR bintree*. Figure 2.33 shows the PR k-d tree corresponding to the data of Figure 2.1.

Each node in a PR quadtree is stored as a record of type *node* containing eight fields. The first four fields contain pointers to the node's four sons corresponding to the four quadrants. If *P* is a pointer to a node and *I* is a quadrant, these fields are referenced as SON(*P*, *I*). The fifth field, NODETYPE, indicates whether the node contains a data point (BLACK), is empty (WHITE), or is a nonleaf node (GRAY). The NAME field contains descriptive information about the data point stored at a node (e.g., city name). XCOORD and YCOORD contain the *x* and *y* coordinates, respectively, of the data point. We assume that each data point is unique. If more than one data point were permitted to have the same coordinates, an overflow list would be required at each data point node. The empty PR quadtree is represented by NIL.

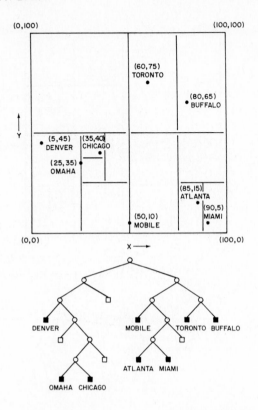

Figure 2.33   PR k-d tree and the records it represents

To cope with data points that lie directly on one of the quadrant lines emanating from a subdivision point, we adopt the convention that the lower and left boundaries of each block are closed, while the upper and right boundaries of each block are open. For example, in Figure 2.32, Mobile with coordinates (50,10) lies in quadrant SE of the tree rooted at (50,50). Using this convention, the function PR_COMPARE, given below, determines the quadrant in which a data point lies relative to a grid subdivision point.

```
quadrant procedure PR_COMPARE(P,X,Y);
/* Return the quadrant of the PR quadtree rooted at position (X,Y) in which node P
   belongs. */
begin
  value pointer node P;
  value real X,Y;
  return(if XCOORD(P) < X then
        if YCOORD(P) < Y then 'SW'
        else 'NW'
```

        else if YCOORD(P) < Y **then** 'SE'
        else 'NE');
end;

    Data points are inserted into PR quadtrees in a manner analogous to that used to insert in a point quadtree. First, an appropriate record is formed for the data point. Next, we search for the desired record based on its x and y coordinates, using the function PR_COMPARE to guide the search. If a record with the same x and y coordinates already exists, we replace it with the new record.

    Actually we do not search for the record. Instead we search for the quadrant in which the record, say A, belongs (i.e., a leaf node). If the quadrant is already occupied by another record with different x and y coordinates, say B, then we must subdivide the quadrant repeatedly (termed *splitting*) until nodes A and B no longer occupy the same quadrant. This may cause a large number of subdivision operations, especially if the two points are contained in a very small quadtree block. A necessary but not sufficient condition for this situation to arise is that the Euclidean distance between A

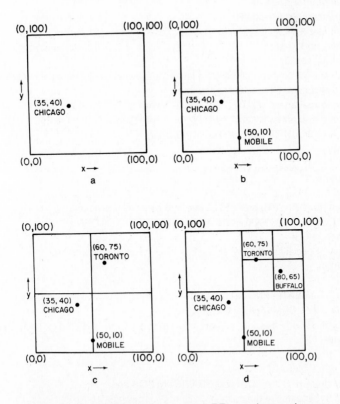

Figure 2.34   Sequence of partial PR quadtrees demonstrating the addition of (a) Chicago, (b) Mobile, (c) Toronto, and (d) Buffalo

and *B* is very small. As a result, we observe that every nonleaf node in a PR quadtree of a data set consisting of more than one data point has at least two descendant leaf nodes that contain data points.

It should be clear that the shape of the resulting PR quadtree is independent of the order in which data points are inserted into it. However, the shapes of the intermediate trees do depend on the order. For example, the tree in Figure 2.32 was built for the sequence Chicago, Mobile, Toronto, Buffalo, Denver, Omaha, Atlanta, and Miami. Figure 2.34a–d shows how the tree was constructed in an incremental fashion for Chicago, Mobile, Toronto, and Buffalo. The actual insertion is achieved by procedure PR_INSERT given below.

```
procedure PR_INSERT(P,R,X,Y,LX,LY);
/* Attempt to insert node P in the PR quadtree rooted at node R which is the center of an
   LX × LY rectangle located at (X,Y). If the tree is empty, then R is set to point to the new
   root. Nodes are created by use of CREATE_PNODE. GRAY is used to specify nonleaf
   nodes. */
begin
  value pointer node P;
  reference pointer node R;
  value real X,Y,LX,LY;
  pointer node T,U;
  quadrant Q,UQ;
  /* XF and YF contain multiplicative factors to aid in the location of the centers of the qua-
     drant sons while descending the tree */
  preload real array XF['NW','NE','SW','SE'] with -0.25,0.25,-0.25,0.25;
  preload real array YF['NW','NE','SW','SE'] with 0.25,0.25,-0.25,-0.25;
  if null(R) then /* The tree at R is initially empty */
    begin
      R ← P;
      return;
    end
  else if not(GRAY(R)) then /* The tree at R contains one node */
    if XCOORD(P) = XCOORD(R) and YCOORD(P) = YCOORD(R)
    then return
    else /* Special handling when the tree initially contains one node */
      begin
        U ← R;
        R ← CREATE_PNODE('GRAY');
        Q ← PR_COMPARE(U,X,Y);
        SON(R,Q) ← U;
      end;
  T ← R;
  Q ← PR_COMPARE(P,X,Y);
  while not(null(SON(T,Q))) and GRAY(SON(T,Q)) do
    begin /* Locate the quadrant in which node P belongs */
      T ← SON(T,Q);
      X ← X+XF[Q]∗LX;
      LX ← LX/2.0;
```

```
    Y ← Y+YF[Q]*LY;
    LY ← LY/2.0;
    Q ← PR_COMPARE(P,X,Y);
  end;
  if null(SON(T,Q)) then SON(T,Q) ← P
  else if XCOORD(P) = XCOORD(SON(T,Q)) and
        YCOORD(P) = YCOORD(SON(T,Q))
  then return /* Node P is already in the tree */
  else
    begin /* Node P's quadrant is already occupied by node U */
    U ← SON(T,Q);
    do      /* Repeatedly subdivide quadrant Q until nodes */
      begin /* P and U no longer occupy the same quadrant */
      SON(T,Q) ← CREATE_PNODE('GRAY');
      T ← SON(T,Q);
      X ← X+XF[Q]*LX;
      LX ← LX/2.0;
      Y ← Y+YF[Q]*LY;
      LY ← LY/2.0;
      Q ← PR_COMPARE(P,X,Y);
      UQ ← PR_COMPARE(U,X,Y);
    end
    until Q
    SON(T,Q) ← P; /* Insert node P */
    SON(T,UQ) ← U; /* Insert node U */
    end;
end;
```

Deletion of nodes in PR quadtrees is considerably simpler than for point quadtrees since all records are stored in the leaf nodes. This means that there is no need to be concerned with rearranging the tree, as is necessary when records stored in nonleaf nodes are being deleted from point quadtrees. For example, to delete Mobile from the PR quadtree in Figure 2.32, we simply set the SW son of its father node, D, to NIL.

Continuing this example, deleting Toronto is slightly more complicated. Setting the NW son of its father node, B, to NIL is not enough since now we violate the property of the PR quadtree that each nonleaf node in a PR quadtree of more than one record has at least two descendant leaf nodes that contain data points. Thus we must also reset the NE son of A to point to Buffalo and return nonleaf node B to the free storage list. This process is termed *collapsing* and is the counterpart of the splitting operation necessary when inserting a record in a PR quadtree.

At this point, it is appropriate to elaborate further on the collapsing process. Collapsing can take place only when the deleted node has exactly one brother that is a leaf node and has no brothers that are nonleaf nodes. When this condition is satisfied, we can perform the collapsing process repeatedly until encountering the nearest common ancestor that has more than one son. As collapsing occurs, the affected nonleaf nodes are returned to the free storage list.

As an example of collapsing, suppose that we delete Mobile and Atlanta in sequence from Figure 2.32. The subsequent deletion of Atlanta results in Miami's meeting the conditions for collapsing to take place. Miami's nearest ancestor with more than one son is A. The result of the collapsing of Miami is that Miami becomes the SE son of A, and nonleaf nodes D and F become superfluous and are returned to the free storage list.

Procedure PR_DELETE, given below, is a formal description of the deletion process. The execution time of PR_DELETE is bounded by two times the depth of the quadtree. This upper bound is achieved when the nearest ancestor for the collapsing process is the root node.

```
procedure PR_DELETE(P,R,X,Y,LX,LY);
/* Delete node P from the PR quadtree rooted at node R which is the center of an LX × LY
   rectangle located at (X,Y). If P is the only node in the tree, then the root will be set to
   NIL. If P has exactly one brother that is a leaf node, say B, and no brothers that are
   nonleaf nodes, then the nearest ancestor of P that has more than one non-NIL son is
   set to point to B. The nonleaf nodes that are bypassed as a result of this collapsing pro-
   cess are returned to the free storage list. */
begin
  value pointer node P;
  reference pointer node R;
  value real X,Y,LX,LY;
  pointer node F,FT,T,TEMP;
  quadrant Q,QF;
  integer S;
  /* XF and YF contain multiplicative factors to aid in the location of the centers of the qua-
     drant sons while descending the tree */
  preload real array XF['NW','NE','SW','SE'] with -0.25,0.25,-0.25,0.25;
  preload real array YF['NW','NE','SW','SE'] with 0.25,0.25,-0.25,-0.25;
  if null(R) then return /* The tree is empty */
  else if not(GRAY(R)) then /* the tree contains exactly one node */
    if not(XCOORD(P) = XCOORD(R) and YCOORD(P) = YCOORD(R))
    then return
    else
      begin
        returntoavail(R);
        R ← NIL;
        return;
      end;
  T ← R;
  F ← NIL;
  do
    begin /* Locate the quadrant in which node P belongs */
      Q ← PR_COMPARE(P,X,Y);
      if GRAY(SON(T,Q)) and
        not(null(SON(T,CQUAD(Q)))) and
          null(SON(T,OPQUAD(Q))) and
          null(SON(T,CCQUAD(Q)))) then
```

```
          begin  /* As the tree is descended, F and QF keep track of the */
             F ← T; /* nearest ancestor of (X,Y) with more than one son */
             QF ← Q;
          end;
        FT ← T;
        T ← SON(T,Q);
        X ← X+XF[Q]*LX;
        LX ← LX/2.0;
        Y ← Y+YF[Q]*LY;
        LY ← LY/2.0;
      end
    until null(T) or not(GRAY(T));
  if null(T) or
    not(XCOORD(P) = XCOORD(T) and
        YCOORD(P) = YCOORD(T)) then
    return /* Node P is not in the tree */
  else
    begin /* Determine if collapsing is possible */
      returntoavail(T);
      SON(FT,Q) ← NIL;
      S ← 0;
      for Q in {'NW', 'NE', 'SW', 'SE'} do
        begin /* Determine the number of brother leaf nodes */
          if GRAY(SON(FT,Q)) then
            return /* No collapsing is possible */
          else if not(null(SON(FT,Q))) then S ← S+1;
        end;
      if S>1 then return /* No collapsing is possible */
      else
        begin
          T ← if null(F) then R
              else SON(F,QF);
          Q ← 'NW';
          while GRAY(T) do
            begin /* Collapse one level at a time */
              while null(SON(T,Q)) do
                Q ← CQUAD(Q); /* Find non-NIL son */
              TEMP ← SON(T,Q);
              SON(T,Q) ← NIL;
              returntoavail(T);
              T ← TEMP;
            end;
          if null(F) then R ← T
          else SON(F,QF) ← T;
        end;
    end;
end;
```

Analyzing the cost of insertion and deletion of nodes in a PR quadtree depends on the data points already in the tree. In particular, this cost is proportional to the maximum depth of the tree. For example, given a square region of side length s, such that the minimum Euclidean distance separating two points is d, the maximum depth of the quadtree can be as high as $\lceil \log_2((s/d) \cdot \sqrt{2}) \rceil$. Assuming that the data points are drawn from a grid of size $2^n \times 2^n$, for N data points the storage requirements can be as high as $O(N \cdot n)$. This analysis is somewhat misleading as N and n do not necessarily grow in an independent manner. Often the storage requirements are proportional to N (see Exercises 2.93 and 2.94).

Performing a range search in a PR quadtree is done in basically the same way as in the MX and point quadtrees. The worst-case cost of searching for all points that lie in a rectangle whose sides are parallel to the quadrant lines is $O(F + 2^n)$, where F is the number of points found and n is the maximum depth (see Exercise 2.96).

Anderson [Ande83] makes use of a PR quadtree (termed a *uniform* quadtree) to store endpoints of line segments to be drawn by a plotter. The goal is to reduce pen plotting time by choosing the line segment to be output next whose endpoint is closest to the current pen position.

Rosenfeld, Samet, Shaffer, and Webber make use of the PR quadtree in a geographic information system [Rose83b]. There the PR quadtree is implemented using a linear quadtree [Garg82a]. This is a pointer-less representation, described briefly in Section 1.5, and in much greater detail in Section 2.1 of [Same90b]. The linear quadtree is a collection of all the leaf nodes in the quadtree. Each leaf node is encoded by a pair of numbers corresponding to its level and a locational code. The latter is a base 4 number corresponding to a sequence of directional codes that locate the leaf along a path from the root of the quadtree. This is equivalent to taking the binary representation of the values of the x and y coordinates of a designated pixel in the block and interleaving them (i.e., alternating the bits for each coordinate value).

Let us look at an example of the linear quadtree representation of the PR quadtree. Let the codes 0, 1, 2, and 3 correspond to quadrants NW, NE, SW, and SE, respectively, and assume that Figure 2.32 is $2^3 \times 2^3$ image. The block containing Atlanta is represented by the numbers 3 and 60 (in base 10) corresponding to the level (the root is at level 0 in this case) and the locational code, respectively. There is also a value field indicating the actual coordinate values of the point associated with each PR quadtree node.

One of the shortcomings of the PR quadtree is that when the data are not uniformly distributed (e.g., when the data are clustered),[6] the tree contains many empty nodes and thereby becomes unbalanced. For example, inserting Amherst at location (79,64) in the PR quadtree given in Figure 2.32 will result in much decomposition to separate it from Buffalo, which is at (80,65). This effect is explicitly shown by the amount of decomposition necessary to separate Omaha and Chicago in the PR k-d tree given in Figure 2.33.

---

[6] See [Tamm85a] for an analysis of this situation.

This shortcoming is overcome by using test compression techniques similar to those devised by Ohsawa and Sakauchi [Ohsa83a, Ohsa83b] in their development of the BD tree (also termed a BANG file by Freeston [Free87]).[7] In essence, the PR quadtree is compressed so that all nonleaf nodes that have just one non-NIL son are eliminated. In particular, these nodes are replaced by one nonleaf node that indicates the results of the comparisons performed in accessing the first node in the path that has more than one non-NIL son. This is similar to the notion of Patrician tries in digital searching [Knut73b, p. 490].

As an example of the use of test compression techniques, let us examine their application to the PR k-d tree given in Figure 2.33. The BD tree as described by Ohsawa and Sakauchi is a bucketing method in the sense that the nodes in the tree correspond to buckets and are split once they overflow. In our example, we assume a bucket capacity of 1. Each nonleaf node in the BD tree contains a variable-length string, say s, consisting of 0s and 1s that indicates the results of the tests that lead to the left son of the node. The right son is accessed by complementing the last binary digit of s. We say that 0 and 1 correspond to '<' and '≥', respectively. This string is termed a *discriminator zone expression* (*DZE*) by Ohsawa and Sakauchi.

Figure 2.35a–h shows how a BD tree is constructed in an incremental fashion for Chicago, Mobile, Toronto, Buffalo, Denver, Omaha, Atlanta, and Miami, in order. All nonleaf nodes are labeled with their DZEs, indicating a sequence of alternating $x, y, x, y, \cdots$, tests starting at the left end of the DZE. For example, in Figure 2.35b, the root has a DZE of 0, which means that the left son corresponds to $x < 50$ (the left half of the space spanned by the quadtree). As a more complicated example, the left son of the root in Figure 2.35e has a DZE of 000, which means that the left son of the left son of the root corresponds to $x < 25$ and $y < 50$.

At this point, let us make a few observations about the BD tree. First, the BD tree is not unique. Rotation operations can be applied to reformulate the tests in the nonleaf nodes so that a greater degree of balancing is achieved. Such transformations are easy to express in terms of the DZEs [Ohsa83b]. Second, when the bucket capacity is greater than 1, say B, we can decide to continue splitting until no region contains more than $x \cdot B$ $(0 < x < 1)$ points. Ohsawa and Sakauchi suggest choosing $x = 2/3$ [Ohsa83a, Ohsa83b]. Third, unlike the PR quadtree and PR k-d tree, a BD tree does not result in the partitioning of space into a collection of hyperrectangles.

It should be clear that the BD tree can be used for data of arbitrary dimensionality. (For more details on how to implement basic operations such as insertion and deletion, as well as answering exact match, partial match, and range queries for BD trees, see Dandamudi and Sorenson [Dand86]. For an empirical performance comparison of the BD tree with some variations of the k-d tree, see Dandamudi and Sorenson [Dand85].)

---

[7] The hB-tree of Lomet and Salzberg [Lome89a, Lome89b, Salz88] is closely related to the BD tree.

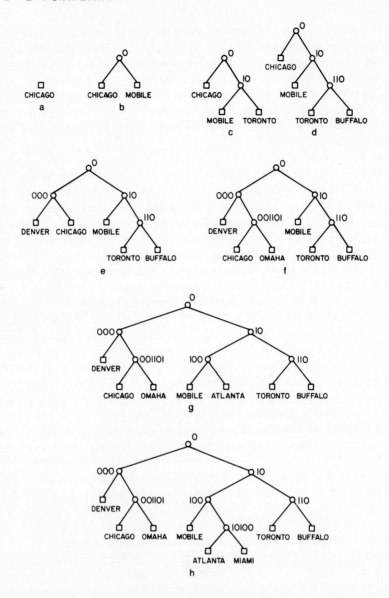

Figure 2.35   Sequence of partial BD trees demonstrating the insertion of (a) Chicago, (b) Mobile, (c) Toronto, (d) Buffalo, (e) Denver, (f) Omaha, (g) Atlanta, and (h) Miami

Exercises

2.87. Suppose that a PR quadtree node is implemented as a record with a FATHER field containing a pointer to its father. Modify procedures PR_INSERT and PR_DELETE to take advantage of this addition.

2.88. Convince yourself that procedure PR_INSERT really works by hand tracing its operation on Figure 2.32. For example, insert Pensacola with coordinates (48,8).

2.89. Convince yourself that procedure PR_DELETE really works by hand tracing its operation on Figure 2.32. For example, delete nodes Mobile and Miami in sequence.

2.90. Write a pair of procedures PR_BIN_INSERT and PR_BIN_DELETE to insert and delete, respectively, data points in a PR bintree.

2.91. Assuming that keys are uniformly distributed real numbers in [0,1) represented in binary, prove that the average depth of a PR bintree is $O(\log_2 N)$. Can you extend this result to PR quadtrees?

2.92. Assume that the minimum Euclidean distance separating two points is d. Given a square region of side length s, show that $\lceil \log_2((s/d) \cdot \sqrt{2}) \rceil$ is the maximum depth of the PR quadtree.

2.93. Suppose that you are given N data points drawn from a grid of size $2^n \times 2^n$. Construct an example PR quadtree that uses $O(N \cdot n)$ storage.

2.94. Under what situation does the PR quadtree use storage proportional to N?

2.95. Write an algorithm to perform a range search for a rectangular region in a PR quadtree.

2.96. Show that the worst-case cost of performing a range search in a PR quadtree is $O(F + 2^n)$, where F is the number of points found and n is the maximum depth. Assume a rectangular query region.

2.97. Exercises 2.97–2.104 are based on an analysis of PR quadtrees performed by Hunter [Hunt81]. Assume that you are given point data that are uniformly distributed in the unit square. What is the probability of a node at level k containing a particular point?

2.98. Continuing the previous exercise, for a collection of v points, what is the probability that none of them lies in a given cell at level k?

2.99. What is the probability that exactly one of the v points lies in a given cell at level k?

2.100. What is the probability that a given cell at level k contains two or more points (i.e., it corresponds to a parent node)?

2.101. Each of the nodes that contains two or more points in it must be a nonleaf node and hence will have four sons. From the probability of the existence of a nonleaf node at level k, derive the expected total number of nodes (i.e., leaf plus nonleaf nodes) at level $k+1$.

2.102. From the expected number of nodes at level $k + 1$, derive the expected number of nodes in the entire PR quadtree, say E. Can you find a closed form solution to it?

2.103. Calculate the ratio of E/v, the expected number of nodes per point. Does it converge?

2.104. Extend these results to data that are uniformly distributed in the m-dimensional unit hypercube.

2.105. In general, the BD tree does not result in the partitioning of space into a collection of hyperrectangles. Under what conditions do some of the subtrees correspond to hyperrectangles?

2.106. Is it necessary to store the entire DZE with each node in the BD tree?

2.107. Write a procedure to insert a point into a two-dimensional BD tree.

2.108. Write a procedure to delete a point from a two-dimensional BD tree.

2.109. Write a procedure to perform a point search in a two-dimensional BD tree.

2.110. Write a procedure to perform a range search for a rectangular region in a two-dimensional BD tree.

2.6.3 Comparison of Point and Region-based Quadtrees

The comparison of the MX, PR, and point quadtrees reduces, in part, to a comparison of their respective decomposition methods. Both the MX and PR quadtrees rely on regular decomposition (i.e., subdivision into four identical rectangular regions). Data points are associated only with leaf nodes in MX and PR quadtrees, whereas for point quadtrees, data points can also be stored at nonleaf nodes. This leads to a considerably simpler node deletion procedure for MX and PR quadtrees since there is no need to be concerned about rearranging the tree as is the case when nonleaf nodes are being deleted from a point quadtree.

A major difference between the three data structures is in the size of the rectangular regions associated with each data point. For both the MX and PR quadtrees, the space spanned by the quadtree is constrained to a maximum width and height. For the point quadtree, the space is rectangular and may at times be of infinite width and height. For the MX quadtree, this region must be a square with a particular size associated with it. This size is fixed at the time the MX quadtree is defined and is the minimum permissible separation between two data points in the domain of the MX quadtree (equivalently it is the maximum number of elements permitted in each row and column of the corresponding matrix). For the PR quadtree, this region is also rectangular, and its size depends on what other data points are currently represented by nodes in the quadtree.

In the case of the MX quadtree, a fixed discrete coordinate system is associated with the space spanned by the quadtree, whereas no such limitation exists for the PR quadtree. The advantage of such a fixed coordinate system is that there is no need to store coordinate information with a data point's leaf node. The disadvantage is that the discreteness of the domain of the data points limits the differentiation between data points.

The size and shape of a quadtree are important from the standpoints of efficiency of storage and search operations. The size and shape of the point quadtree is extremely sensitive to the order in which data points are inserted into it during the process of building it. This means that for a point quadtree of N records, its maximum depth is $N - 1$ (i.e., one record is stored at each level in the tree), while its minimum depth is $\lceil \log_4((3 \cdot N + 1)/4) \rceil$ (i.e., each level in the tree is completely full) where we assume that the root of the tree has a depth of 0.

In contrast, the shape and size of the MX and PR quadtrees are independent of the insertion order. For the MX quadtree all nodes corresponding to data points appear at the same depth in the quadtree. The depth of the MX quadtree depends on the size of the space spanned by the quadtree and the maximum number of elements permitted in each row and column of the corresponding matrix. For example, for a $2^n \times 2^n$ matrix, all data points will appear as leaf nodes at a depth of n.

The size and shape of the PR quadtree depend on the data points currently in the quadtree. The minimum depth of a PR quadtree for $N > 1$ data points is $\lceil \log_4 N \rceil$ (i.e., all the data points are at the same level). There is no upper bound on the depth in terms of the number of data points. Recall from Section 2.6.2 that for a square region of side length s, such that the minimum Euclidean distance separating two points is d, the maximum depth of the quadtree can be as high as $\lceil \log_2((s/d) \cdot \sqrt{2}) \rceil$.

The volume of data also affects the comparison among the three quadtrees. When the volume is very high, the MX quadtree loses some of its advantage since an array representation may be more economical in terms of space, as there is no need for links. While the size of the PR quadtree was seen to be affected by clustering of data points, especially when the number of data points is relatively small, this is not a factor in the size of a point quadtree. However, when the volume of data is large and is uniformly distributed, the effect of clustering is lessened, and there should not be much difference in storage efficiency between the point and PR quadtrees.

Exercises

2.111. Use the uniform distribution over [0,1] to construct two-dimensional point quadtrees, MX quadtrees, and PR quadtrees and compare them using the criteria set forth in this section. For example, compare their total path length and maximum depth.

2.112. Perform an average-case analysis of the cost of a partial match query (a subset of the range query) for a point quadtree and a PR quadtree when the attributes are independent and uniformly distributed.

2.7 BIT INTERLEAVING

Whether using in-core methods or bucket methods, an important factor in the choice of representation of multidimensional point data is that the resulting structure be balanced. This has a critical impact on the performance of operations such as search and update. As we saw in the previous discussions, balancing is not always possible. Since balancing techniques for one-dimensional data are well known (e.g., AVL trees [Adel62, Aho74]), it has been suggested by a number of researchers that multidimensional data points should be first mapped into one-dimensional data points, termed *codes*, and then represented using balanced binary tree methods or some other representations that have a similar effect. For example, Tropf and Herzog [Trop81] propose bit interleaving and bit concatenation as two alternative mappings.

Bit interleaving consists of taking the bit representations of the keys comprising a record and forming a *code* consisting of alternating bits from each key. For example, for $k = 2$, the code corresponding to data point $A = (X, Y) = (x_m x_{m-1} \cdots x_0, y_m y_{m-1} \cdots y_0)$ is $y_m x_m y_{m-1} x_{m-1} \cdots y_0 x_0$, where attribute y is arbitrarily deemed to be the most significant. Figure 2.36 is an example of the bit interleaving mapping when $k = 2$. The codes corresponding to the cities of the example database of Figure 2.1 have been labeled by applying the mapping f defined by $f(z) = z$ div 12.5 to the values of their x and y coordinates. Recall that the same mapping was used to obtain the MX quadtree of Figure 2.30. Bit concatenation consists of concatenating the keys (e.g., for data point A the concatenated code would be $y_m y_{m-1} \cdots y_0 x_m x_{m-1} \cdots x_0$).

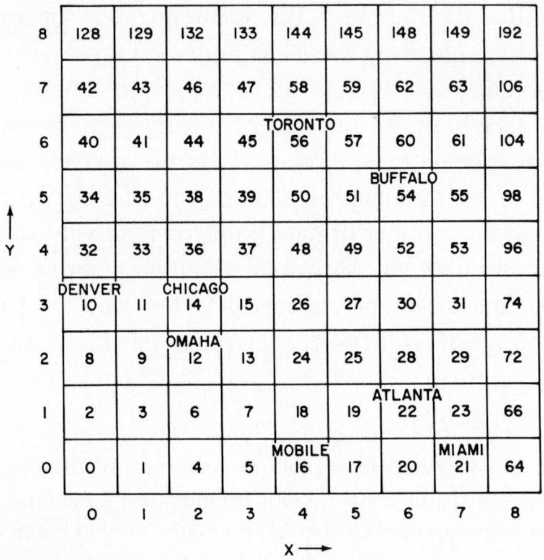

Y \ X	0	1	2	3	4	5	6	7	8
8	128	129	132	133	144	145	148	149	192
7	42	43	46	47	58	59	62	63	106
6	40	41	44	45	TORONTO 56	57	60	61	104
5	34	35	38	39	50	51	BUFFALO 54	55	98
4	32	33	36	37	48	49	52	53	96
3	DENVER 10	11	CHICAGO 14	15	26	27	30	31	74
2	8	9	OMAHA 12	13	24	25	28	29	72
1	2	3	6	7	18	19	ATLANTA 22	23	66
0	0	1	4	5	MOBILE 16	17	20	MIAMI 21	64

Figure 2.36 Example of the bit interleaving mapping as applied to two keys ranging in values from 0 to 8. The city names correspond to the data of Figure 2.1 scaled by a factor of 12.5 to fall in this range.

It should be clear that in the light of our interest in range searching, bit interleaving is superior to the bit concatenation method since the latter results in long, narrow search ranges, whereas the former results in square search ranges. This argument leads to the conclusion that bit concatenation is analogous to the inverted list method, while bit interleaving is analogous to the fixed-grid method. In fact, bit concatenation results in the records being sorted according to a primary key, secondary key, and so on.

It is difficult to determine the origin of the notion of bit interleaving. Orenstein and Merrett [Oren84] term it z order while reviewing its use in a number of data structures in the context of range searching. The first mention of it was by Peano [Pean90]. It was used by Morton [Mort66] as a linear index into a two-dimensional spatial database (see Section 2.1.1 of [Same90b]). It was proposed by Tropf and Herzog [Trop81] to give a linear order on multidimensional data in forming a binary search tree or balanced variant thereof, while White [Whit82] used it to form a B-tree [Come79]. Orenstein and Merrett term the result a *zkd tree*, while cautioning that it differs from the k-d tree of Bentley [Bent75b] since an in-order traversal of a k-d tree does not necessarily yield the nodes in z order.

Bentley [Bent75b] attributes bit interleaving to McCreight as a way to use B-trees [Come79] to represent multidimensional data. The resulting B-tree is called an *N-tree* by White [Whit82], while Orenstein and Merrett term it a *zkd Btree*. Note that the result is different from the k-d-B-tree of Robinson [Robi81] (see Section 2.8.1).

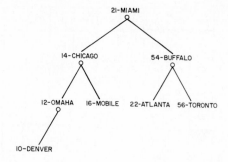

Figure 2.37   The 1-2 tree corresponding to the city database of Figure 2.36

Tamminen [Tamm81b] uses bit interleaving to implement EXCELL (on the basis of EXHASH, the extendible hashing function [Fagi79]). It has been adapted by Burkhard [Burk83] (who terms it *shuffle* order) in an analogous manner to serve as the hashing function in linear hashing [Litw80, Oren83, Ouks83] (see Section 2.8.2.1). It also serves as the cycling order in which individual bits of component keys of a record are tested in the k-d trie (i.e., PR k-d tree) of Orenstein [Oren82]. The difference is that in the case of the PR k-d tree, the discriminating key is part of the data structure. On the other hand, bit interleaving is part of the data representation itself, and there still remains a choice as to how to structure the data.

As an example of the utility of bit interleaving in range searching[8] we examine how it is used by Tropf and Herzog [Trop81]. They chose to structure the data by use of 1-2 brother trees [Ottm80] because of their conceptual simplicity, although the AVL tree [Adel62, Aho74] would also have been an appropriate choice. These trees are height-balanced search trees in which each nonleaf node either has two sons or, if it has one son, then its brother has zero or two sons. Insertion and deletion for 1-2 brother trees have $O(\log_2 N)$ worst-case execution times. Nevertheless, in the example, a binary search tree is used, although the range-searching algorithm described can be applied to balanced trees as well. Figure 2.37 is a binary search tree corresponding to the city data base of Figure 2.1 encoded as in Figure 2.36.

Range searching using the binary search tree is fairly straightforward. The code range is specified by the minimum and maximum codes in the search area. For example, to find all the cities within the rectangular area defined by (25,25), (50,25), (50,63), and (25,63), which is represented by codes 12, 24, 50, and 38 (see Figure 2.38), respectively, we must examine the codes between 12 and 50. The simplest algorithm is recursive and traverses the binary search tree starting at its root. If the

---

[8] This example is very specialized and can be omitted. In such a case, skip this and the following four paragraphs and continue with the discussion of Gray codes.

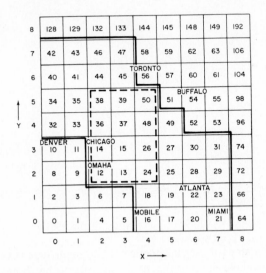

Figure 2.38   Illustration of the range search process when using bit interleaving

root lies between the minimum and maximum codes in the range, both subtrees must be examined (e.g., code 21 in Figure 2.37). Otherwise one subtree needs to be searched (e.g., the left subtree of code 54 in Figure 2.37).

This algorithm is inefficient because many codes lie in the range between the minimum and maximum codes without being within the query rectangle. This is illustrated by the two staircases in Figure 2.38. Codes above the upper staircase are greater than the maximum search range code, while codes below the lower staircase are less than the minimum search range code. All remaining codes are potential candidates, yet most are not in the query rectangle.

To prune the search range when the root lies within the search range (e.g., code 21 in Figure 2.37), Tropf and Herzog define two codes, termed LITMAX and BIGMIN, which correspond to the maximum code in the left son and the minimum code in the right son, respectively, that are in the query rectangle. The subsequent search of the left son uses LITMAX as the maximum code in the range (e.g., 15 in the left subtree of Figure 2.37) while the search of the right son uses BIGMIN as the minimum code in the range (e.g., 24 in the right subtree of Figure 2.37), with the result that many codes are eliminated from consideration (e.g., codes between 16 and 23 in Figure 2.37 after examining the root for the query rectangle between 12 and 50).

Experiments reported by Tropf and Herzog [Trop81] show that given N records, for small hypercube ranges, the average number of records inspected is $O(k \cdot \log_2 N + F)$, where F is the number of records found. White [Whit82] shows how to perform the same task when using a B-tree as the underlying representation with the same order of execution time.

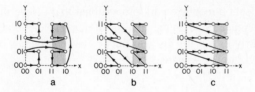

Figure 2.39   Orderings induced on points from {0,1,2,3} and the result of the partial query X ≥ 2 shown shaded: (a) Gray codes prior to interleaving, (b) bit interleaving without Gray codes, (c) bit concatenation with Y being more significant than X

An interesting twist on bit interleaving that improves the efficiency of partial match, and potentially for range queries, is reported by Faloutsos [Falo86]. He suggests that the attributes be encoded by their Gray codes (recall the definition in Section 1.2) prior to the application of bit interleaving. The result is that the transitions between successive points in the ordering are either in the horizontal or vertical directions—not diagonal as is the case for the z order, which characterizes the normal bit interleaving process. Faloutsos feels that diagonal transitions between successive records are undesirable because these records do not have any attribute values in common. This is most visible when performing a partial match query.

As an example of the use of Gray codes, suppose $k = 2$ and the attributes are X and Y with ranges between 0 and 3. The query $X \geq 2$ means that we need to examine only one cluster of points (e.g., Figure 2.39a) when bit interleaving is applied after coding the attributes with their Gray codes (but see Exercise 2.118). In contrast, for the same query, using bit interleaving without a Gray code means that we must examine two clusters of points (e.g., Figure 2.39b). Using bit concatenation such that attribute Y is more significant than X, the same query requires us to examine four clusters of points (e.g., Figure 2.39c).

Depending on how the data are structured, a multiplicity of clusters may have a significant impact on the cost of retrieving the answer. Faloutsos [Falo88] has shown that for a partial match query, using the Gray codes never increases the number of clusters and can reduce the number of clusters by at most 50%. Faloutsos further conjectures that the use of Gray codes has a similar effect on range queries, although at the present this is an open problem. The overhead incurred by using Gray codes is that of conversion from a binary representation, which is linear in the size of the code word [Rein77].

To summarize, bit interleaving makes it possible to balance a data base of multidimensional point data dynamically. It leads to logarithmic insertion, deletion, and search algorithms. It does have drawbacks, however. First, and most serious, is that bit interleaving is not performed efficiently on general computers. Its complexity depends on the total number of bits in the keys. Thus in k dimensions, when the maximum depth is n, the work required is proportional to $k \cdot n$. In contrast, a quadtree or bintree node at depth d requires work proportional to d. Nevertheless bit interleaving is a useful conceptual model in the analysis of quadtree and bintree data structures. Second, it is primarily useful for discrete rather than continuous data. Finally, code words may get rather large as k increases.

Exercises

2.113. Write an algorithm to perform bit interleaving of the x and y coordinates of a point in an efficient manner.

2.114. Write a procedure BI_SEARCH to perform a range search for a rectangular region in a 2-dimensional database implemented as a binary search tree with bit interleaving as the mapping function.

2.115. Assume a k-dimensional database implemented as a B-tree with bit interleaving as the mapping function. Write a procedure BTREE_SEARCH to perform a range search for a k-dimensional rectangular region.

2.116. Given a database of N records, prove that for a small rectangular k-dimensional region, the range search in Exercise 2.115 takes $O(k \cdot \log_2 N + A)$ time where A is the number of records found.

2.117. Give an algorithm for converting between a binary representation and a Gray code and vice-versa.

2.118. Give an example partial match query involving attributes X and Y with ranges between 0 and 3 such that the use of Gray codes prior to interleaving does not result in a decrease in the number of clusters from the number of clusters that result from normal bit interleaving.

2.119. Prove that for partial match queries, using Gray codes prior to bit interleaving never increases the number of clusters and can reduce them by a maximum of 50%.

2.120. Derive a method of enumerating all the possible partial match queries for two attributes. Evaluate the expected number of clusters when using bit concatenation, bit interleaving, and bit interleaving using Gray codes.

2.121. What is the effect on range queries of using Gray codes prior to bit interleaving?

2.122. One of the problems with the Gray code encoding is the existence of long horizontal and vertical transitions between successive elements in the order. Find an ordering that avoids this problem (recall Section 1.2).

2.8 BUCKET METHODS

Most of the data structures discussed in Sections 2.3–2.7 make use of trees. Thus they are primarily designed for in-core applications, although their uses can be extended elsewhere. The problem is that when data are stored in external storage, tree structures often require that pointers be followed. This invariably gives rise to page faults. To overcome this problem, methods have been designed to collect the points into sets (termed *buckets*) corresponding to the storage units (i.e., pages) of the disk. The remaining task is to organize the access to these buckets by use of an appropriate directory to facilitate address computation. We term such techniques *bucket methods*.

The goal of bucket methods is to ensure efficient access to disk data. The simplest bucket method is the fixed-grid (or cell) method (discussed in Section 2.2) whose directory is a k-dimensional array with one entry per cell. The major deficiency of this method is that the fixed size for the blocks results in both overflow and underflow. The methods presented next are examples of attempts to address this deficiency from both hierarchical and nonhierarchical viewpoints (using directories in the form of trees and arrays, respectively).

2.8.1 Hierarchical Bucket Methods

The use of a directory in the form of a tree to access the buckets was first proposed by Knott [Knot71]. Orenstein [Oren82] discusses a *hybrid k-d trie*, a bucket method having a directory in the form of a k-d trie. This is a bucket analog of the PR k-d tree in which regions are split until no subregion contains more data points than the bucket capacity. Matsuyama, Hao, and Nagao [Mats84] define a bucket PR quadtree in an analogous manner.

Figure 2.40 is the bucket PR quadtree corresponding to the data of Figure 2.1 when the bucket capacity is 2. Having buckets of capacity c ($c > 1$) reduces the dependence of the maximum depth of the PR k-d tree on the minimum Euclidean distance separation of two distinct points to that of two sets of c points. The term *bucket PR k-d tree* is used to refer to this structure. The effect of the minimum Euclidean distance separation of two distinct points can be further reduced by using a BD tree with bucket capacity c ($c > 1$), as discussed in Section 2.6.2.

Nelson and Samet [Nels86b, Nels87] analyze the distribution of nodes in a bucket PR quadtree in terms of their occupancies for various values of the bucket capacity. They model a quadtree as a collection of populations in which each population represents the set of nodes in the quadtree that have a particular occupancy. Thus the set of all empty nodes constitutes one population, the set of all nodes containing a single point constitutes another population, and so on. The individual populations contain nodes of different sizes.

As points are added to the bucket PR quadtree, each population grows in a manner that depends on the other populations. For example, when the bucket capacity is c, the probability of producing a new node with occupancy i depends both on the fraction of nodes with occupancy $i - 1$ and on the population of full nodes (occupancy c), since nodes of any occupancy can be produced when a full node splits.

The result of the analysis is the determination of a steady state where the proportions of the various populations are constant under addition of new points according to some data model (e.g., uniform distribution, Gaussian distribution). This steady state is taken as a representative distribution of populations from which expected values for structure parameters such as average node occupancies are calculated.

The population model is an alternative to the use of a statistical analysis to define a 'typical' structure. The statistical analyses are based on the computation, relative to some model of data distribution, of statistical sums over the space of possible data structure configurations. Statistical analyses for uniformly distributed data

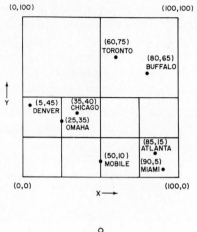

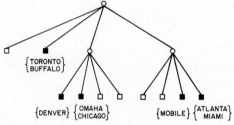

*Figure 2.40   Bucket PR quadtree corresponding to Figure
2.1 for bucket size = 2*

have been applied by Fagin et al. to extendible hashing [Fagi79], Flajolet and Puech
[Flaj83] to tries, Regnier to the grid file (see Section 2.8.2.3) [Regn85], and Tamminen to EXCELL (see Section 2.8.2.4) [Tamm83].

The advantage of the population model is that dependencies between various
populations and the steady state can be determined with relative ease. Moreover, the
method is sufficiently flexible that it can be applied to other data structures in which
the decomposition is determined adaptively by the local concentration of the data.

Nelson and Samet [Nels86b, Nels87] computed the average bucket occupancies
for a number of different bucket capacities when points were generated under a uniform distribution. They found that the theoretical occupancy predictions were consistently slightly higher than the experimental values and that the size of the
discrepancy had a cyclical structure. They use the terms *aging* and *phasing*, respectively, to describe these phenomena.

The population model of bucket splitting assumes that the probability of a
point's falling into a node of type n_i (i.e., occupancy i) is proportional to the fraction
of the total type n_i nodes. This means that the average size of a node is independent

of its occupancy. In actuality nodes with a larger area are formed before the nodes with a smaller area and, hence, the origin of the term *aging*. These larger nodes will tend to have a slightly higher average occupancy than the smaller nodes. Therefore to maintain a steady-state situation, the fraction of high occupancy nodes must be less than predicted by the model, with the result that we have more lower occupancy nodes, thereby yielding a smaller average bucket occupancy.

When nodes are drawn from a uniform distribution, the nodes in the quadtree will tend to split and fill in phase with a logarithmic period repeating every time the number of points increases by a factor of four. In particular, all nodes of the same size tend to fill up and split at the same time. This situation is termed *phasing*. It explains why the average bucket occupancy for a fixed bucket size oscillates with the number of data points. In contrast, when the distribution of points is nonuniform (e.g., Gaussian), then initially there is oscillatory behavior; however, it damps out as node populations in regions of different densities get out of phase.

The nodes in a B-tree can also be used as buckets. A linear ordering on multidimensional point data can be obtained by using bit interleaving, as mentioned in Section 2.7, and then storing the results in a B-tree (recall the zkd B-tree). Unfortunately, in such a case, a B-tree node does not usually correspond to a k-dimensional rectangle. Thus the representation is not particularly conducive to region searching. To overcome this deficiency, Robinson [Robi81] introduces the *k-d-B-tree*, which uses an adaptive k-d tree partition to dictate the contents of each B-tree node. The problem with this technique is that B-tree performance guarantees are no longer valid. For example, pages are not guaranteed to be 50% full without very complicated record insertion and deletion procedures. Nevertheless Robinson [Robi81] reports that empirical tests led to 60% page occupancy for uniformly distributed data.

The nodes of the k-d-B-tree correspond to disjoint regions. The R-tree of Guttman [Gutt84] is another adaptation of the B-tree for representing point data that does not require the regions covered by the nodes to be disjoint. The k-dimensional point data are stored in the leaf nodes, while the nonleaf nodes are the minimum covering k-dimensional rectangles for the area covered by their elements. Using such an approach enables the B-tree performance guarantees to hold. However, search operations are not as efficient since a point may be in the space covered by more than one node. Roussopoulos and Leifker [Rous85] suggest that this shortcoming can be alleviated, in a static environment, either completely by using rotations or partially by using the packed R-tree. The R-tree is more commonly used for two-dimensional spatial data such as rectangles. It is discussed in greater detail in Section 3.5.3.

Matsuyama, Hao, and Nagao [Mats84] use the adaptive k-d tree as a basis for bucket methods in a geographic information system (see also the spatial k-d tree of Ooi, McDonell, and Sacks-Davis [Ooi87], which is discussed in Section 3.4). A bucket is split whenever it overflows its capacity, and in contrast to the bucket PR k-d tree, there is a choice as to the dimension across which to split. For example, consider Figure 2.41, the bucket adaptive k-d tree corresponding to the data of Figure 2.1 when the bucket capacity is 2. The splitting rule is one that uses as a discriminator the attribute that maximizes the spread of the values of the key.

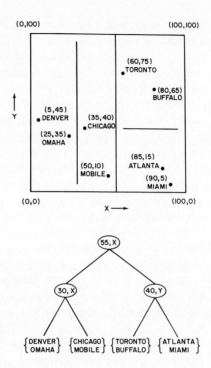

Figure 2.41   Bucket adaptive k-d tree corresponding to
Figure 2.1 for bucket size = 2

O'Rourke [ORou81, ORou84] also uses the bucket version of the adaptive k-d tree, calling it a *Dynamically Quantized Space (DQS)*. It is useful for cluster detection as well as for multidimensional histogramming, in particular, to aid in focusing the Hough Transform. The rest of this section elaborates further on the use of the DQS and its relative, the *Dynamically Quantized Pyramid (DQP)* [Sloa81, ORou84], in conjunction with the Hough Transform. This discussion is very specialized, and thus the rest of this section can be skipped.

The Hough Transform facilitates the detection of arbitrary sparse patterns, such as curves, by mapping them into a space where they give rise to clusters. A DQS has *k* attributes or dimensions corresponding to a set of parameters that can be mapped by an appropriate function to yield image patterns. The buckets correspond to the parameter regions. Associated with each bucket is a count indicating the number of times that an element in its region appears in the data. The goal is to find evidence for the presence of clusters in parameter space.

The DQS is particularly useful in parameter spaces of high dimension (i.e., $\gg 2$). However, for the sake of this discussion, we look at only two-dimensional data. In particular, consider a large collection of short edges and try to determine if many of them are colinear. We do this by examining the values of their slopes and y-intercepts (recall that the equation of a line is $y = m \cdot x + b$). It turns out that a high density of points (i.e., counts per unit volume) in the (m, b) plane is evidence that many colinear edges exist. We want to avoid wasting the space while finding the cluster (most of the space will be empty). To do this, we vary the sizes of the buckets (i.e., their parameter regions) in an attempt to keep the counts equal.

In two dimensions, the Hough Transform for detecting lines is quite messy unless each detected point has an associated slope. The same would be true in three dimensions where we would want not only a position reading (x, y, z) but also the direction cosines of a surface normal (α, β, γ). We can then map each detection into the parameters of a plane, e.g., (ρ, α, β), where ρ is the perpendicular distance from the plane to the origin. If there are many coplanar detectors, this should yield a cluster in the vicinity of some particular (ρ, α, β).

As the buckets overflow, new buckets (and corresponding parameter regions) are created by a splitting process. This splitting process is guided by the two independent goals of an equal count in each bucket and the maintenance of a uniform distribution in each bucket. This is aided by keeping a count and an imbalance vector with each bucket. When the need arises, buckets are split across the dimension of greatest imbalance. There is also a merging rule, which is applied when counts of adjacent neighbors (possibly more than two) are not too large and the merge will not produce any highly unbalanced region. This is especially useful if the data are dynamic.

Sloan [Sloa81, ORou84] addresses the same problem as O'Rourke, albeit with a different data structure which he calls a *Dynamically Quantized Pyramid* (*DQP*). It is based on the pyramid data structure (i.e., a full balanced tree where each nonleaf node has 2^k sons [Tani75]—see Section 1.3 for more details). In this case, the number of buckets (i.e., parameter regions) and the relationship between fathers and sons are fixed. The DQP differs from the conventional pyramid in that the partition points (termed *cross-hairs*) at the various levels are variable rather than fixed. Thus the result is analogous to a complete point quadtree with buckets.

The partition points of a DQP are initialized to the midpoints of the different attributes. They are adjusted as data are entered. This adjustment process occurs at all levels and is termed a *warping process*. One possible technique when inserting a new data point, say P, in a space rooted at Q, is to take a weighted average of the position of P, say α, and of Q, say $(1 - \alpha)$. This changes the boundaries of all nodes in the subtree rooted at Q. P is recursively added to the appropriate bucket (associated with a leaf node), which causes other boundaries to change.

Figure 2.42 is an example of a two-dimensional DQP for three levels. It should be clear that regions grow smaller near inserted points and that the shape of the DQP depends on the insertion history, thereby providing an automatic focusing mechanism. The warping process is analogous to the splitting operation used in conjunction with a DQS. The advantage of a DQP over the DQS is that it is easier to implement, and merging is considerably simpler. On the other hand, the DQP allocates equal resources for each dimension of the parameter space, whereas the DQS can ignore irrelevant dimensions, thereby yielding more precision in its focusing. Also, the DQS takes up less storage than the DQP.

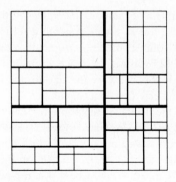

Figure 2.42   Example two-dimensional DQP for three levels

Exercises

2.123. Let the size of a data item be bounded by h (i.e., the maximum total number of bits in the k keys) and let the bucket capacity be c. Suppose that a bucket in a bucket PR k-d tree overflows. Assuming that each bit has an equal probability of being 0 or 1, find the expected number of bits that must be tested to resolve the overflow.

2.124. Assuming a file with N records, can you adapt the B-tree to handle multidimensional point data in a way that guarantees worst-case performance of insertion and deletion of records in $O(\log_2 N)$ time and that pages are always at least 50% full? Searching for k-dimensional rectangular ranges should have performance of $O(\log_2 N + F)$, where F is the number of records found.

2.125. Implement a BD tree with a bucket capacity of c. In particular, write procedures to insert and delete nodes from it. The key issue is how to handle bucket overflow and underflow. Try to use techniques analogous to those used for B-trees—such as rotation of elements between adjacent buckets that are not completely full.

2.126. Implement an R-tree for n points so that there is no overlap—that is, each point appears in just one node at all levels in the tree.

2.127. Can you apply the techniques used to solve Exercise 2.126 to deal with a collection of rectangles rather than points?

2.128. How would you use the Hough Transform to detect if some range data (i.e., x, y, z readings) are coplanar?

2.8.2   Nonhierarchical Bucket Methods

The nonhierarchical bucket methods discussed in this section use a directory in the form of an array. The first method is an adaptation of linear hashing. This is analogous to implicitly using a directory in the form of a one-dimensional array. The advantage of linear hashing is a linear growth of the directory (i.e., one bucket at a time). It breaks up the file into a set of primary and overflow buckets. At most, two hash operations are required to determine the primary bucket to be accessed. A draw-back of linear hashing is that the manner in which the directory grows is unrelated to the probability of the occurrence of an overflow in the bucket that is expanded. The second method, spiral hashing, overcomes this disadvantage by always expanding the bucket that has the highest probability of overflowing.

The remaining methods, the grid file and EXCELL, are closely related. Both organize space into buckets corresponding to k-dimensional rectangles, use a directory in the form of a k-dimensional array, and guarantee the retrieval of a record with two disk accesses. They differ in the nature of the directory and the rate at which it grows. Their similarity to the quadtree lies in the mappings induced by the directories (i.e., EXCELL with the region quadtree and the grid file with the point quadtree).

2.8.2.1 LINEAR HASHING

In the previous sections we examined methods based on comparing a data item with values stored in the data structure (e.g., the point quadtree) and methods that use the digits of the data item as a means of directing the process (e.g., the k-d trie). Hashing [Knut73b] is an alternative. Given a point P, hashing consists of computing a function (termed a *hashing function*) $h(P)$ whose value is the address of a bucket where P and its associated data are stored. Hashing functions are chosen so that they will scramble the data by distributing them equally among all the buckets. Thus they typically de-stroy order. Unfortunately it is rather difficult to discover hashing functions that will map each data point into a unique bucket, and it is not customary to channel too much energy in attempting to do so.

Buckets are usually of finite capacity, although they may be implemented as linked lists. As the amount of data increases, the buckets may get too full and overflow. Since the number of buckets is usually fixed by the hash function, we must modify the hash function to generate more buckets. Ideally this modification should require a minimal amount of rehashing—that is, only a few records should have to be moved to new buckets. Generally most hashing methods do not allow the number of buckets to grow gracefully.

Knott [Knot71] suggests storing the buckets using a trie in the form of a binary tree. In this scheme, bucket overflow is rather trivial since the bucket is split into two parts. The problem with such a scheme is that accessing a bucket at depth l requires l operations. Extendible hashing, as defined by Fagin et al. [Fagi79], is analogous to a trie except that the buckets are at varying levels (trie), while the directory is at a single level. It is usually implemented as a directory of pointers to buckets. This means that accessing a bucket can be done in one operation; however, when a bucket overflows, the size of the directory may have to be doubled.

Linear hashing has been proposed by Litwin [Litw80, Lars88] as a technique providing for linear growth of the file (i.e., one bucket at a time). Its principal innova-tion is the decoupling of the bucket splitting decision from the identity of the bucket that overflowed. There are many variations of linear hashing. The ones explained here are motivated by the desire to represent multidimensional point data in a manner that makes range searching practical. Given a file containing m ($2^n \leq m \leq 2^{n+1} - 1$)

buckets starting at address 0, and a key K, Litwin's method uses the hashing function $h_n(K) = K \bmod 2^n$ to access buckets $m - 2^n$ through $2^n - 1$, and $h_{n+1}(K) = K \bmod 2^{n+1}$ to access buckets 0 through $m - 2^n - 1$ and buckets 2^n through $m-1$. Such a file is said to be of level $n,n+1$ so that the buckets accessed by h_n are at level n while those accessed by h_{n+1} are at level $n+1$. Note that when $m = 2^n$, no buckets are accessed by h_{n+1}.

A file implemented using linear hashing has both primary and overflow buckets. When a record hashes to a full primary bucket, it is inserted into an overflow bucket associated with the primary bucket. Generally the overflow buckets are chained to the primary bucket. When the buckets are addressed from 0 to $m - 1$, there is no need for a directory. The storage utilization factor, τ, is defined to be the ratio of the number of records in the file to the number of positions available in the existing primary and overflow buckets.

When the storage utilization factor exceeds a predetermined value, say α, then one of the buckets is split. When bucket b is split, its records are rehashed using h_{n+1} and distributed into buckets b and $b + 2^n$. The identity of the next bucket to be split is maintained by the pointer s that cycles through the values 0 to $2^n - 1$. When s reaches 2^n, all of the buckets have been split, and thus n is incremented and s is reset to 0. A bucket split does not necessarily occur when a record hashes to a full primary bucket, nor does the split bucket have to be full.

The principle behind linear hashing is that eventually every bucket will be split, and ideally all of the overflow buckets will be emptied and reclaimed. This is similar to the rationale used for analyzing algorithms using the 'amortization' method [Bent80a]. Technically when the storage utilization factor falls below a predetermined value, say β, buckets should be merged (i.e., the bucket splitting process should be reversed). However, this has not been the subject of much research, and we ignore it here (see Exercise 2.130). Note also the similarity to the 'buddy system' [Knut73a] of dynamic storage allocation, although the buddies (i.e., the buckets that are merged) are formed differently.

As an example of linear hashing, consider the database of Figure 2.1. First, apply the mapping f such that $f(z) = z$ div 12.5 to both x and y coordinates. Next, apply bit interleaving to its keys to yield the mapping given in Figure 2.36. Recall that in this case the value of the y coordinate is deemed more significant than that of the x coordinate. Assume that the primary and overflow buckets are both of size 2 and that

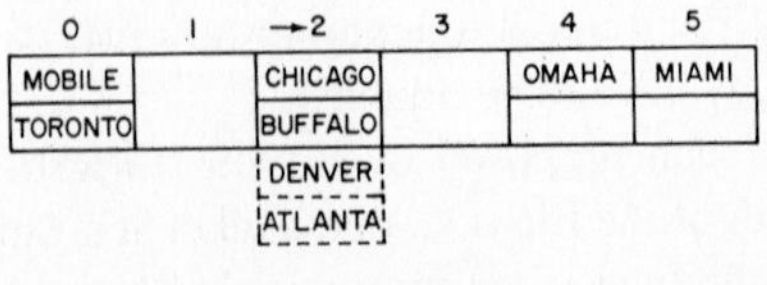

0	1	→2	3	4	5
MOBILE		CHICAGO		OMAHA	MIAMI
TORONTO		BUFFALO			
		DENVER			
		ATLANTA			

Figure 2.43   Result of applying linear hashing to the data
of Figure 2.1 using a hashing function equal to interleaving
the bits

a bucket will be split whenever τ, the storage utilization factor, is greater than or equal to 0.66 (i.e., $\alpha = 0.66$).

Figure 2.43 shows the resulting partition. In the figure, solid lines designate primary buckets, broken lines designate overflow buckets, and a rightward-pointing arrow indicates the next bucket to be split. There are six primary buckets, labeled 0–5, and one overflow bucket. To understand the splitting process, let us examine more closely how linear hashing copes with a sequence of insertion operations. In particular, we observe how Figure 2.43 is constructed for the records of Figure 2.1 in the order in which they appear there: Chicago, Mobile, Toronto, Buffalo, Denver, Omaha, Atlanta, and Miami.

Initially only bucket 0 exists, it is empty, and the file is of level 0,1. The pointer to the next bucket to be split, s, is initialized to 0. The insertion of Chicago and Mobile yields $\tau = 1.00$, causing bucket 0 to be split and bucket 1 to be allocated. s retains its value of 0, and both Chicago and Mobile remain in bucket 0 (Figure 2.44a). Toronto is inserted in bucket 0, but $\tau = 0.75$, which causes bucket 0 to be split, s to be set to 1, bucket 2 to be allocated, and Chicago to be placed in it (Figure 2.44b). Our file is now of level 1,2. Next, we try to insert Buffalo. It belongs in bucket 2. However, now $\tau = 0.67$, causing bucket 1 to be split, s to be reset to 0, and bucket 3 to be allocated (Figure 2.44c).

Attempting to insert Denver causes bucket 2 to overflow and leads to the allocation of an overflow bucket attached to bucket 2 once Denver has been placed in it. Similarly inserting Omaha results in an overflow of bucket 0 and the allocation of an overflow bucket attached to it, once Omaha has been placed in it. Atlanta belongs in bucket 2, and, since it is full, it is placed into its overflow bucket (see Figure 2.44d). Miami is inserted into bucket 1, resulting in $\tau = 0.67$. This causes bucket 0 to be split, s to be set to 1, bucket 4 to be allocated, and Omaha to be moved to bucket 4. Our file is now of level 2,3. Since bucket 0's overflow bucket is now empty, it is deallocated, yielding $\tau = 0.67$. Thus bucket 1 is split, s is set to 2, bucket 5 is allocated, and Miami is moved to it (Figure 2.43).

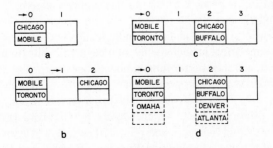

Figure 2.44   Sequence of linear hashing bucket contents demonstrating the insertion of (a) Chicago and Mobile, (b) Toronto, (c) Buffalo, and (d) Denver, Omaha, and Atlanta

Linear hashing as described may require complex searches when many of the records hash to a subset of the buckets. Let S denote this subset. This means that several overflow buckets will be associated with each element of S. On the other hand, there will be few overflow buckets associated with the remaining primary buckets (i.e., not elements of S). Ramamohanarao and Sacks-Davis [Rama84] suggest that the same hashing function be applied to the contents of all of the overflow buckets. This technique is called *recursive linear hashing*, and the result can be viewed as a separate file, termed an *overflow file*. This process is applied as many times as necessary (hence the term *recursive*), each time creating an additional overflow file. However, in practice, it is rare for the hashing function to be applied more than three times [Rama84]. The only difference from the original application of the hashing function is that for the second and subsequent applications of the hashing function, the overflow file is at a lower (i.e., smaller) level from that of the original file.

One problem with recursive linear hashing is that when primary bucket P is split, records in the overflow files that originally hashed to P may have to be moved to a primary bucket or another overflow file. A similar problem arises when two primary buckets are merged. Of course, these problems also arise with conventional linear hashing. Nevertheless recursive linear hashing has the property that all records that originally hashed to P will be stored in a single bucket in each of the overflow files (see Exercise 3.84). Hence the insertion costs for recursive linear hashing and for conventional linear hashing with optimal overflow bucket size [Lars80, Rama82] are similar [Rama84]. (For more details on recursive linear hashing, see [Rama85].)

Linear hashing was proposed initially as a technique for dealing with one-dimensional data. The partitioning imposed by the hash function $h_n(K) = K \bmod 2^n$ has the effect that all of the records in a given bucket agree in the n least significant bits. This is fine for random access; however, it does not support efficient sequential file access since different buckets must be accessed. If the most significant bits of the key were tested instead, then all of the records in a given bucket would be within a given range. Assuming a fixed key length (i.e., the number of bits is fixed), this can be achieved by redefining the hashing function to be $h_n(K) = reverse\ (K) \bmod 2^n$. An implementation of linear hashing satisfying this property is termed *order preserving linear hashing* (OPLH).

In one dimension, OPLH is analogous to a trie. For multidimensional data (e.g., k dimensions), the same effect is obtained by interleaving the bits from the various keys, reversing the result, and then performing a modulo operation. The result is analogous to a k-d trie and was discussed in greater detail under the general heading of bit interleaving in Section 2.7. The combination of reversed bit interleaving with linear hashing seems to have been proposed independently by Burkhard [Burk83], Orenstein [Oren83], and Ouksel and Scheuermann [Ouks83] (see also [Tamm84b]). This combination is applied to range searching by Burkhard [Burk83] and Orenstein and Merrett [Oren84], although different search algorithms are used.

As an example of the partitioning that results when reversed bit interleaving is used with linear hashing, consider again the database of Figure 2.1 after the application of the mapping $f(z) = z$ div 12.5 to the values of both the x and y coordinates.

Table 2.1   Reversed bit interleaving applied to
the result of $f(z) = z$ div 12.5.

Name	x	y	CODE(x)	CODE(y)
Chicago	2	3	44	28
Mobile	4	0	1	2
Toronto	4	6	11	7
Buffalo	6	5	39	27
Denver	0	3	40	20
Omaha	2	2	12	12
Atlanta	6	1	37	26
Miami	7	0	21	42

The result of this mapping is given in columns 2 and 3 of Table 2.1. Next apply bit interleaving to its keys to yield the mappings given in columns 4 and 5 of the same table. Two mappings are possible since we can either take the value of the x coordinate as the most significant (column 4 and labeled CODE(x)) or the y coordinate (column 5 and labeled CODE(y)).

Assuming that the y coordinate is the most significant yields the partition of the database shown in Figure 2.45. Using the same bucket capacities and storage utilization factor as in Figure 2.43, we find that there are six primary buckets, labeled 0–5, and two overflow buckets. To understand the splitting process, we examine

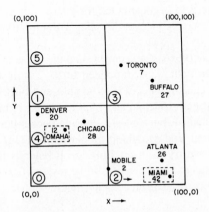

Figure 2.45   Linear hashing using reversed bit interleaving
representation corresponding to Figure 2.1.   Overflow
bucket contents are in boxes whose sides are broken lines.

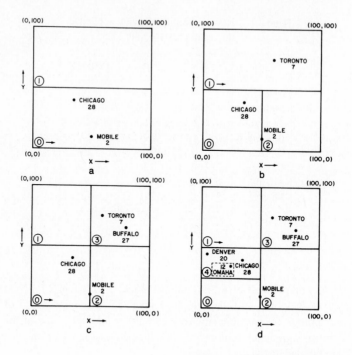

Figure 2.46 Sequence of linear hashing bucket contents using reversed bit interleaving demonstrating the insertion of (a) Chicago and Mobile, (b) Toronto, (c) Buffalo, and (d) Denver and Omaha. Overflow bucket contents are in boxes whose sides are broken lines.

more closely how Figure 2.45 is constructed for the records of Figure 2.1 in the order in which they appear there: Chicago, Mobile, Toronto, Buffalo, Denver, Omaha, Atlanta, and Miami.

Initially only bucket 0 exists, it is empty, and the file is of level 0,1. The pointer to the next bucket to be split, s, is initialized to 0. The insertion of Chicago and Mobile yields $\tau = 1.00$, causing bucket 0 to be split and bucket 1 to be allocated. s retains its value of 0 and both Chicago and Mobile remain in bucket 0 (Figure 2.46a). Toronto is inserted in bucket 1, but $\tau = 0.75$, causing bucket 0 to be split, s to be set to 1, bucket 2 to be allocated, and Mobile to be placed in it (Figure 2.46b). Our file is now of level 1,2. Next we try to insert Buffalo. It belongs in bucket 1. However, now $\tau = 0.67$, causing bucket 1 to be split, s to be reset to 0, bucket 3 to be allocated, and Toronto and Buffalo to be placed in it (Figure 2.46c). Denver is inserted in bucket 0.

Attempting to insert Omaha finds it belonging in bucket 0, but $\tau = 0.75$, causing bucket 0 to be split, s to be set to 1, bucket 4 to be allocated, and Denver and Chicago to be placed in it. Our file is now of level 2,3. Unfortunately Omaha also belongs in bucket 4, and thus an overflow bucket must be allocated, attached to bucket 4, and Omaha is placed in it (see Figure 2.46d). Atlanta is placed in bucket 2. Miami is inserted into bucket 2. However, now $\tau = 0.67$, causing bucket 1 to be split, s to be set to 2, and bucket 5 to be allocated. After the bucket split we still have too many items in bucket 2, and thus an overflow bucket must be allocated, attached to bucket 2; Miami is placed in it (Figure 2.45).

Orenstein [Oren83] discusses a number of problems associated with OPLH. In particular, records may not be well distributed in the buckets when the data are not uniformly distributed. This means that overflow will be more common than with traditional hashing methods. It also has the effect of possibly creating a large number of sparsely filled buckets. Consequently random access is slower since, in the case of overflow, several buckets may have to be examined. Similarly sequential access will also take longer as several buckets will have to be retrieved without finding too many records. The problem is that linear hashing requires that all buckets be stored at one of two levels. This has the advantage that at most two hash operations are required to determine the primary bucket to be accessed (see Exercise 2.129).

Orenstein proposes a technique he terms *multilevel order preserving linear hashing* (MLOPLH). It alleviates the sparseness problem by storing parts of the file in buckets at lower levels than n. Such buckets result from the combination of a sparse bucket with its brother(s). The major problem with the MLOPLH method is that now we may require $n+1$ disk read operations (equal to the number of bucket accesses) to locate a bucket, whereas previously at most two hash operations were necessary.

The reason so many buckets may have to be accessed is that linear hashing methods do not make use of a directory. Thus encountering an empty bucket is the only way to detect that records of one bucket have been merged with those of another bucket at a lower level. Even more buckets will have to be accessed when deletion of a record causes a sparse bucket to be combined with its brother. In contrast, directory-based methods such as the grid file and EXCELL (as described in sections 2.8.2.3 and 2.8.2.4) do not suffer from such a problem to the same extent. The reason is that the sparseness issue can be avoided because the directory consists of grid blocks, and several grid blocks can share a bucket.

Exercises

2.129.   Give an algorithm to look up a record with key K in a file implemented with linear hashing of m buckets. The file is at level $n,n+1$. Do you use h_n first or h_{n+1}? If it makes a difference, explain why.

2.130.   Discuss the issue of merging buckets for linear hashing—that is, when the storage utilization factor falls below a particular threshold, say β.

2.131.   The insertion algorithm for linear hashing described in the text splits bucket s whenever insertion of a record causes the storage utilization factor, τ, to exceed a predetermined value. This is done even if bucket s does not overflow or if no records will move as a result of the bucket splitting operation. Of course, allocating an overflow bucket is also a method of reducing the storage utilization factor. Modify the insertion algorithm so that when the storage utilization factor is too high and there is overflow, a split of bucket s occurs only if it will resolve the overflow; otherwise allocate an overflow bucket. If there is no overflow, bucket s is split as before. Define a measure to compare these two methods, and do so analytically and empirically.

2.132. Exercises 2.132–2.139 are based on an asymptotic analysis of linear hashing described by Larson [Lars88]. Assume that there are no deletions. The implementation is slightly different from the one described in the text. The capacity of the buckets is not restricted, and thus there is no need for overflow buckets. Each bucket is implemented as a linked list (i.e., a chain). In this case, the storage utilization factor τ is the total number of records in the table divided by the number of buckets. Suppose that no bucket splits are ever allowed. Compute $s(\tau)$ and $u(\tau)$, the expected number of key comparisons for a successful and unsuccessful search, respectively. In your answer, for the unsuccessful search case, assume that no key comparison is necessary when the key value is hashed to an empty bucket.

2.133. For this exercise and through Exercise 2.139 assume that a bucket is split each time the storage utilization factor exceeds α. At any instant, let x $(0 \leq x \leq 1)$ denote the fraction of the buckets that have been split and z the expected number of records in an unsplit bucket. The expected number of records in a split or new bucket is $z/2$. Show that $z = \alpha \cdot (1 + x)$.

2.134. Let $s(\alpha, x)$ denote the expected number of key comparisons for a successful search when a fraction x of the buckets have been split. Calculate $s(\alpha, x)$.

2.135. Calculate $U(\alpha, x)$, the expected length of an unsuccessful search.

2.136. When do the minimum expected search lengths occur?

2.137. When do the maximum expected search lengths occur?

2.138. Calculate the average search cost over a cycle (i.e., as x ranges from 0 to 1).

2.139. The cost of each insertion of a record can be decomposed into two parts. The first part is the cost of placing the record at the end of the chain. The second part reflects the situation that a bucket is split and the table is expanded. The cost of the first part is the same as that of an unsuccessful search and the cost of linking the record to the end of the chain. The second part arises with a probability of $1/\alpha$. Here we must rehash each record on the chain and update some pointers. Calculate $A(\alpha, x)$, the expected number of rehashing operations per record that is inserted, and its average over a cycle.

2.140. Repeat the analyses of Exercises 2.132–2.139 when the primary buckets have a finite capacity, say c. This means that overflow buckets will be necessary. Assume an overflow bucket capacity of v.

2.141. Write a procedure LIN_SEARCH to perform a range search for a rectangular region in a 2-dimensional database implemented with linear hashing and reversed bit interleaving as the hashing function.

2.142. Give an algorithm to insert a record with key K in a file implemented with recursive linear hashing of m primary buckets that is at level $n, n+1$.

2.143. Give an algorithm to look up a record with key K in a file implemented with recursive linear hashing of m primary buckets that is at level $n, n+1$.

2.144. Give an algorithm to delete a record with key K from a file implemented with recursive linear hashing of m primary buckets that is at level $n, n+1$.

2.145. Prove that recursive linear hashing has the property that all records that originally hashed to primary bucket P will be stored in a single bucket in each of the overflow files.

2.8.2.2 SPIRAL HASHING

One of the drawbacks of linear hashing is that the order in which the buckets are split is unrelated to the probability of the occurrence of an overflow. In particular, all the buckets that are candidates for a split have the same probability of overflowing. Moreover the expected cost of retrieving a record and updating the table of active buckets varies cyclically in the sense that it depends on the proportion of the buckets split during a bucket expansion cycle (see Exercises 2.132–2.139).

Proposed by Martin [Mart79, Lars88, Mull85], spiral hashing is a technique whose performance (i.e., the expected search length in a bucket) has been observed to be independent of the number (or fraction) of the buckets that have been split. Thus it is said to have uniform performance (see Exercise 2.172). This is achieved by distributing the records in an uneven manner over the active buckets. Moreover it always splits the bucket that has the highest probability of overflowing.

Spiral hashing is similar in spirit to linear hashing. To simplify the explanation, we identify the buckets by their addresses. The central idea behind spiral hashing is that there is an ever-changing (and growing) address space of active bucket addresses that is moving forward (e.g., Figure 2.47). This is in contrast to linear hashing in which the active bucket addresses always range from 0 to $m-1$. Recall that in linear hashing, when the bucket at address s is split, a new bucket is created at location m, and the previous contents of bucket s are rehashed and inserted into buckets s and m, as is appropriate.

In the following discussion, we assume that a bucket can be split into d buckets rather than just 2 as was the case in the presentation of linear hashing. d is called the growth factor. We assume further that d is an integer; however, this restriction can be lifted. Let s and t denote the addresses of the first and last active buckets, respectively, so that each bucket with address i ($s \leq i \leq t$) is active. Define the storage utilization factor, τ, in the same way as for linear hashing—that is, the ratio of the number of records in the file to the number of positions available in the existing primary and overflow buckets. A bucket is split whenever τ exceeds a predetermined value, say α. When τ falls below a predetermined value, say β, buckets should be merged (i.e., the

Figure 2.47 Example of a changing (and growing) address space of active bucket addresses. When a bucket is split, three new buckets are created, and the bucket that has been split is no longer active.

bucket splitting process should be reversed). However, this has not been the subject of much research, and we ignore it here (see Exercise 2.154).

When the bucket at address s is split, say into d buckets, then d new buckets are allocated starting at bucket address $t + 1$, and the contents of bucket s are rehashed into these new buckets. Bucket address s is no longer used (but see Exercise 2.156), and the active bucket addresses now range from $s + 1$ to $t + d$. As we will see, the manner in which the hashing function is chosen guarantees that the expected load (i.e., the expected number of records per bucket) is always at a maximum at bucket s and is at a minimum at bucket t. Moreover, the expected load of bucket $i + 1$ is less than the expected load of bucket i ($s \leq i < t$).

The presentation is simplified considerably if we assume that initially there are $d - 1$ active buckets starting at address 1. For example, when $d = 2$, initially there is one active bucket starting at address 1; after the first split, there are two active buckets starting at address 2; after the second split, there are three active buckets starting at address 3; and so on. When $d = 3$, initially there are two active buckets starting at address 1; after the first split, there are four active buckets starting at address 2; after the second split, there are six active buckets starting at address 3; and so on. This splitting sequence (i.e., for $d = 3$) is illustrated in Figure 2.47. In general, it can be shown that for arbitrary values of d, after the occurrence of s bucket split operations, there are always $(s + 1) \cdot (d - 1)$ active bucket addresses (see Exercise 2.146).

The growth pattern described is obtained by using a combination of two hashing functions. The first function, say $h(K)$, is used to map key K uniformly into a value in $[0,1)$. Next, we map $h(K)$ into its bucket address, denoted by y such that y is in the range $[s + 1, \ s + 1 + (s + 1) \cdot (d - 1))$. This is achieved by the function $y = \lfloor d^x \rfloor$ where $x = \lceil \log_d(s + 1) - h(K) \rceil + h(K)$ (see Figure 2.48 for $d = 2$). This is a result of

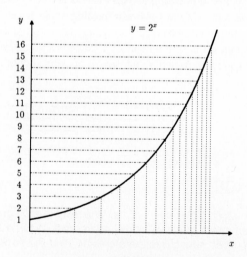

Figure 2.48   The function $y = 2^x$

Table 2.2   Bucket address mapping for $d = 2$

Bucket address	Hash interval	Relative load
1	[0.0000,1.0000)	1.0000
2	[0.0000,0.5849)	0.5849
3	[0.5849,1.0000)	0.4151
4	[0.0000,0.3219)	0.3219
5	[0.3219,0.5849)	0.2630
6	[0.5849,0.8073)	0.2226
7	[0.8073,1.0000)	0.1927
8	[0.0000,0.1699)	0.1699
9	[0.1699,0.3219)	0.1520
10	[0.3219,0.4594)	0.1375
11	[0.4594,0.5849)	0.1255
12	[0.5849,0.7004)	0.1155
13	[0.7004,0.8073)	0.1069
14	[0.8073,0.9068)	0.0995
15	[0.9068,1.0000)	0.0932

the observation that there exists a value of z such that $s + 1 = d^z$ and $s + 1 + (s + 1) \cdot (d - 1) = d^z + 1$. This relation is easy to verify by noting that the addresses of the active buckets range between d^z and $d^{z+1} - 1$. Thus there are $d^{z+1} - d^z = d^z \cdot (d - 1) = (s + 1) \cdot (d - 1)$ active buckets.

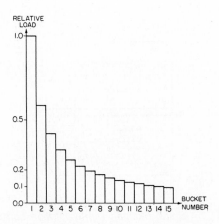

Figure 2.49   *Relative load of buckets 1–15 when d = 2*

Table 2.3   Bit interleaving the result of $f(z) = z$ div 12.5

Name	x	y	CODE(x)	CODE(x)/64	CODE(y)	CODE(y)/64
Chicago	2	3	13	0.203125	14	0.218750
Mobile	4	0	32	0.500000	16	0.250000
Toronto	4	6	52	0.812500	56	0.875000
Buffalo	6	5	59	0.921875	54	0.843750
Denver	0	3	5	0.078125	10	0.156250
Omaha	2	2	12	0.187500	12	0.187500
Atlanta	6	1	41	0.640625	22	0.343750
Miami	7	0	42	0.656250	21	0.328125

Table 2.2 illustrates the use of the second hashing function for $d = 2$. Given a bucket address, it shows its corresponding interval from [0,1) and the proportion of the data that the bucket contains (labeled 'relative load'). Notice that the relative load decreases as the bucket addresses increase (see also Figure 2.49). This verifies the claim that the bucket to be split is the one with the highest probability of overflowing.

Now, let us see the use of spiral hashing by examining its behavior for the database of Figure 2.1. First, apply the mapping f such that $f(z) = z$ div 12.5 to the values of both the x and y coordinates. The result of this mapping is given in columns 2 and 3 of Table 2.3. Next, apply bit interleaving to its keys to yield the mappings given in columns 4 and 6 of the same table. Two mappings are possible since we can either take the x coordinate as the most significant (column 4 and labeled CODE(x)) or the y coordinate (column 6 and labeled CODE(y)). Finally, reduce each interleaved

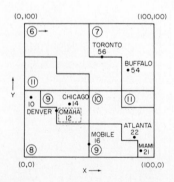

Figure 2.50   Spiral hashing representation corresponding to Figure 2.1. Overflow bucket contents are surrounded by broken lines.

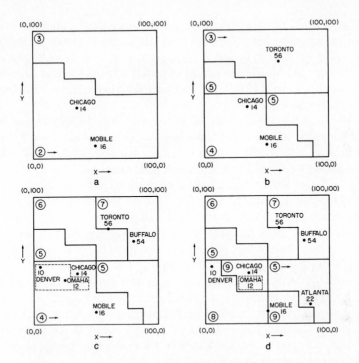

Figure 2.51 Sequence of spiral hashing bucket contents using bit interleaving demonstrating the insertion of (a) Chicago and Mobile, (b) Toronto, (c) Buffalo, Denver, and Omaha, and (d) Atlanta. Overflow bucket contents are surrounded by broken lines.

value to a point in $[0,1)$ by using $h(\kappa) = \kappa/64$ to yield columns 5 and 7 of the same table.

In the following example, we assume that the y coordinate is the most significant, that the primary and overflow buckets are both of size 2, $d = 2$, and that a bucket will be split whenever τ, the storage utilization factor, is greater than or equal to 0.66. Figure 2.50 shows the resulting partition. In the figure, solid lines designate primary buckets, broken lines designate overflow buckets, and a rightward-pointing arrow indicates the next bucket to be split. There are six primary buckets, at addresses 6–11, and one overflow bucket. To understand the splitting process, let us examine more closely how spiral hashing copes with a sequence of insertion operations. In particular, we observe how Figure 2.50 is constructed for the records of Figure 2.1 in the order in which they appear there: Chicago, Mobile, Toronto, Buffalo, Denver, Omaha, Atlanta, and Miami.

Initially only bucket 1 exists, and it is empty. The pointer to the next bucket to be split, s, is initialized to 1. Applying the hashing function to Chicago and Mobile yields the values 0.21875 and 0.25, respectively. Since these values are in the range [0,1), both belong to bucket 1, in which they are inserted. However, this results in $\tau = 1.00$, causing bucket 1 to be split, s to be set to 2, buckets 2 and 3 to be allocated, and both Chicago and Mobile are moved to bucket 2 (Figure 2.51a) since their hash values are both in the range [0,0.5849). Bucket 1 is no longer active. Buckets 2 and 3 are now the active buckets.

Toronto hashes to 0.875. This value is in the range [0.5849,1) and Toronto is inserted in bucket 3. As a result of this action $\tau = 0.75$, causing bucket 2 to be split, s to be set to 3, buckets 4 and 5 to be allocated, and both Chicago and Mobile are moved into bucket 4 (Figure 2.51b) since their hash values fall in the range [0,0.3219). Bucket 2 is no longer active. The active buckets now range from 3 to 5.

Buffalo hashes to 0.84375. This value is in the range [0.5849,1) and Buffalo is inserted in bucket 3. However, now $\tau = 0.67$, causing bucket 3 to be split, s to be set to 4, buckets 6 and 7 to be allocated, and both Toronto and Buffalo are moved into bucket 7 since their hash values fall in the range [0.8073,1). Bucket 3 is no longer active. The active buckets now range from 4 to 7.

Denver hashes to 0.15625. This value is in the range [0,0.3219), which belongs to bucket 4. However, attempting to insert Denver causes bucket 4 to overflow and leads to the allocation of an overflow bucket attached to bucket 4, once Denver has been placed in it. Omaha hashes to 0.1875. This value is in the range [0,0.3219), which belongs to bucket 4. Bucket 4 already has an overflow bucket associated with it, and thus Omaha is placed in it (Figure 2.51c).

Atlanta hashes to 0.34375. This value is in the range [0.3219,0.5849), which belongs to bucket 5. However, now $\tau = 0.70$, causing bucket 4 to be split, s to be set to 5, and buckets 8 and 9 to be allocated. In addition, Denver moves to bucket 8 since its value falls in the range [0,0.1699), while Chicago, Mobile, and Omaha belong in bucket 9 since they fall in the range [0.1699,0.3219). This means that an overflow bucket must be allocated and attached to bucket 9, and Omaha is placed in it (Figure 2.51d). Bucket 4 is no longer active. The active buckets now range from 5 to 9.

Miami hashes to 0.328125. This value is in the range [0.3219,0.5849), which belongs to bucket 5. But $\tau = 0.67$, causing bucket 5 to be split, s to be set to 6, buckets 10 and 11 to be allocated, and both Atlanta and Miami are moved into bucket 10 (see Figure 2.50) since they fall in the range [0.3219,0.4594). Bucket 5 is no longer active. The active buckets now range from 6 to 11.

The example used the hashing function $h(K) = K/2^n$, where n is the total number of bits that make up the interleaved key value. It has the same effect as the function $h'(K) = reverse(K) \bmod 2^n$, where $reverse$ corresponds to reversed bit interleaving, which was used in the discussion of linear hashing (see Section 2.8.2.1). In particular, for linear hashing, $h'(K)$ has the property that all the records in a given bucket agree in the n most significant bits of K, and hence all are within a given range. Unfortunately this property does not hold always when using spiral hashing.

Although the records in each bucket are within disjoint ranges of values of key K, the most significant bits of their keys are not necessarily the same. The problem is the nonuniformity of the relative load of the buckets. This means that there is no analogy to the quadtree-like decomposition that is achieved when using linear hashing; that is, the space is not being split into halves, quarters, and so on. In fact, the spatial regions associated with some of the buckets may even be noncontiguous (e.g., bucket 11 in Figure 2.50). Instead the space is partitioned into contiguous regions according to Z order (recall Section 2.7).

The main advantage of spiral hashing over linear hashing is that the bucket that is split is the one that is most likely to overflow. There are two disadvantages to spiral hashing. The first is that the buckets that have been split are not reused. This problem can be overcome by using one of a number of alternative mappings between logical and physical addresses [Lars88, Mull85] (see Exercises 2.156 and 2.159). The second is that it is computationally expensive to calculate a function such as $y = d^x$—the bucket address. Of course, most programming languages have a runtime library where such functions are available. However, their computation is time-consuming since it usually requires a polynomial approximation.

Martin [Mart79] suggests replacing d^x by another function $f(x)$, which is easier to compute. In particular, $f(x)$ is used to approximate d^x in [0,1] so that d^x is approximated in [n, $n+1$] (n is an integer) by $d^n \cdot f(x-n)$. One such function, according to Martin, is

$$f(x) = a + \frac{b}{c - x} \quad 0 \le x \le 1 .$$

The values of a, b, and c are obtained by calculating the value of f at three points. The most appropriate points are the endpoints—$x = 0$ and $x = 1$—and another point in [0,1] such as $x = 0.5$. We also need the inverse of $f(x)$, which is

$$x = c + \frac{b}{a - y} .$$

Larson [Lars88] reports on some experiments that compare spiral hashing with linear hashing, as well as unbalanced binary search trees and a traditional hashing scheme that makes use of chaining. In each case, the tables and trees are all stored in main memory. Using large files, averaging over many insertions, and different storage utilization factors, he found that linear hashing consistently outperformed spiral hashing in terms of average CPU time per key in both loading the tables and searching them. The differences ranged from 1% to 20%. Larson attributes these differences primarily to the cost of address computation.

Further experiments with binary search trees showed that loading was faster for small key sets than linear hashing; however, in all cases searching was faster when hashing methods were used. A comparison of linear hashing with a traditional hash table implemented using double hashing, so that the costs of a periodic reorganization of the hash table are taken into account, resulted in a definite trend showing that the cost of linear hashing is usually lower (although at times slightly higher).

When the tables and trees are not constrained to be stored in main memory, the results of the comparison may be different. Recall that the number of overflow

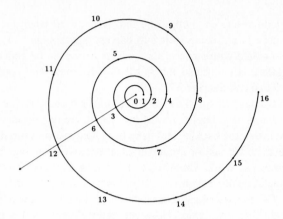

Figure 2.52   Spiral corresponding to $\rho = e^{(\ln 2) \cdot \theta/2\pi} = 2^\theta/2\pi$

records and their distribution over the buckets of the file (table) are different for linear and spiral hashing. In particular, at certain stages of a cycle, linear hashing has more overflow records, clustered on a few pages. The expected search lengths per bucket depend on how these overflow records are handled. For example, some overflow handling methods, such as linear probing [Knut73b], are more sensitive to clustering of overflow records. In such a case, spiral hashing should have better performance than linear hashing. Moreover, since we are dealing with external files, the fact that spiral hashing has a higher address computation cost is not important.

At this point, it is interesting to explain the motivation for the qualifier 'spiral' used to describe this variant of linear hashing. In the earlier discussion, we mapped each key value into a real number x, which was, in turn, mapped into an address y by the function $y = \lfloor d^x \rfloor$. This mapping can be rewritten in terms of polar coordinates—ρ and θ—as $\rho = \lfloor (e^k)^\theta \rfloor = \lfloor e^{k \cdot \theta} \rfloor$ with ρ, e^k, and θ taking on the roles of y, d, and x, respectively. This is the equation of a spiral. For example, Figure 2.52 is the spiral corresponding to $\rho = e^{(\ln 2) \cdot \theta/2\pi}$ and is equivalent to $\rho = 2^{\theta/2\pi}$. Of course, any spiral (i.e., c^θ) can be used, not just the natural spiral.

Using polar coordinates in this way means that the active buckets are always within one complete arc of the spiral. For example, if the first active bucket is at $a = \lfloor e^{k \cdot b} \rfloor$ (i.e., at $\theta = b$), then the last active bucket is at $c = \lceil e^{k \cdot (b + 2\pi)} \rceil - 1$. This is illustrated in Figure 2.52 by the infinite line that emanates from the origin and passes through $\rho = 3, 6, 12, \cdots$. A bucket split has the effect that the active bucket at $\rho = a$ (i.e., at $\theta = b$) is split, and its contents are distributed into buckets $c + 1$ through g where $g = \lfloor e^{k \cdot (b + 2\pi + \phi)} \rfloor$ and $\phi = b - \ln(a + 1)/k$. The value of ϕ is the solution of $a + 1 = e^{k \cdot (b + \phi)}$. Buckets $a + 1$ through g are now the active buckets.

Two items are worthy of further note. First, instead of using the hash function $h(K)$ initially to map key K uniformly into $[0,1)$, we use a different hash function, say $h_\theta(K)$, initially to map key K uniformly into a value in $[0,2\pi)$. Second, the length of the arc of the spiral is also meaningful as it has a constant value between successive integer values of ρ (see Exercise 2.173); however, it has no relation to the capacity of the bucket.

Exercises

2.146. Prove that for arbitrary values of d, after the occurrence of s bucket split operations, there are always $(s + 1) \cdot (d - 1)$ active bucket addresses.

2.147. Suppose that regardless of the value of the growth factor d, initially there is just one active bucket. How does this affect the function that maps $h(\kappa)$ into a bucket address?

2.148. Suppose that spiral hashing is used to store two-dimensional point data, and each point is mapped to a key by use of bit interleaving. Prove that each bucket will span at most two spatially noncontiguous regions.

2.149. Suppose that spiral hashing is used to store point data of arbitrary dimension, and each point is mapped to a key by use of bit interleaving. What is the maximum number of spatially noncontiguous regions that can be spanned by a bucket?

2.150. Can you come up with a mapping for multidimensional point data to a key so that when it is used in conjunction with spiral hashing each bucket will span just one spatially contiguous region?

2.151. Show the result of applying spiral hashing to the database of Figure 2.1 using reversed bit interleaving. Thus instead of using the hashing function $h(\kappa) = \kappa/2^n$ where n is the total number of bits that make up the interleaved key value, use the function $h''(\kappa) = reverse(\kappa)/2^n$, in which *reverse* reverses the value of key κ prior to the application of the hashing function. Is there a difference in this example between using the value of the x coordinate as the more significant or that of the y coordinate?

2.152. Is there any advantage to using reversed bit interleaving with spiral hashing?

2.153. Show the result of applying spiral hashing to the database of Figure 2.1 when the capacity of the buckets is not constrained to be finite. Instead each bucket is implemented as a linked list (i.e., a chain). Thus there is no need for overflow buckets. The storage utilization factor τ is the total number of records in the table divided by the number of buckets.

2.154. Discuss the issue of merging buckets—that is, when the storage utilization factor falls below a particular threshold, say β.

2.155. In the discussion of the use of polar coordinates, we calculated a value of ϕ to determine the buckets into which the contents of the split bucket were to be redistributed. It is given as the solution of $a + 1 = e^{k \cdot (b + \phi)}$. Why did we not use $a + 1 = \lfloor e^{k \cdot (b + \phi)} \rfloor$?

2.156. One of the deficiencies of the implementation of spiral hashing described is that each time a bucket is split, its address is no longer used. This can be wasteful of storage. It would be nice if these locations could be reused. This is facilitated by making a distinction between a bucket's logical and physical address and finding a way to map a bucket's logical address into its physical address. This mapping is necessary for the implementation of all operations (e.g., insert, split, merge, access). Mullin [Mull85] suggests the following approach. Assume again that initially there are $d - 1$ buckets with logical addresses 1 through $d - 1$ occupying physical addresses 1 through $d - 1$. The first bucket split is at logical address 1. This split results in the creation of d new buckets at logical addresses d through $2 \cdot d - 1$. The buckets at logical addresses d through $2 \cdot d - 2$ are stored at physical addresses d through $2 \cdot d - 2$ while physical address 1 is reused to store the bucket at logical address $2 \cdot d - 1$. The second bucket split again results in the creation of d new buckets at logical addresses $2 \cdot d$ through $3 \cdot d - 1$. This time the buckets at logical addresses $2 \cdot d$ through $3 \cdot d - 2$ are stored at physical addresses $2 \cdot d - 1$ through $3 \cdot d - 3$ while physical address 2 is reused to store the bucket at logical address $3 \cdot d - 1$. It should be clear how the rest of the splits are handled. Give an algorithm that takes as its input the logical address of a bucket and returns its physical address.

2.157. The solution to Exercise 2.156 is specified using recursion. However, it is tail recursive, and thus can be rewritten using iteration. Given a growth factor of d and a maximum logical bucket address t, what is the maximum number of iterations?

2.158. Assume that a bucket at physical address s is split. Let t be the maximum logical address that corresponds to physical address p. In such a case, the technique described in Exercise 2.156 creates d new buckets starting at logical addresses $t + 1$ through $t + d$. The buckets at logical addresses $t + 1$ through $t + d - 1$ are stored at physical addresses $p + 1$ through $p + d - 1$. The bucket at logical address $t + d$ is stored in physical address s. Suppose that instead we store the buckets at logical addresses $t + 2$ through $t + d$ in physical addresses $p + 1$ through $p + d - 1$ and store the bucket at logical address $t + 1$ at physical address s. Give an algorithm that takes as its input the logical address of a bucket and returns its physical address.

2.159. Mullin's [Mull85] technique of reusing the space occupied by the buckets that have been split requires the computation of an algorithm that maps a logical address into a physical address. As we saw in Exercise 2.157, its execution time may grow with the size of the logical address space. Can you avoid this growth by using a limited amount of extra space? In other words, devise a data structure that tries to reuse most of the buckets but is not guaranteed to reuse every bucket at each instance.

2.160. Suppose that the addresses corresponding to the buckets that have been split are reused as in Exercise 2.156. Repeat Exercise 2.154 in such an environment, discussing the issue of merging buckets.

2.161. Suppose that the addresses corresponding to the buckets that have been split are reused as in Exercise 2.159. Repeat Exercise 2.154 in such an environment, discussing the issue of merging buckets.

2.162. Suppose that the function $y = d^x$ is approximated by $d^n \cdot f(x - n)$ where $f(x - n) = a + b/(c - x + n)$, such that x is in $[n, n + 1]$. Calculate the values of a, b, and c for $d = 2$ by using $x = 0$, $x = 0.5$, and $x = 1$.

2.163. Suppose that the function $y = d^x$ is approximated by $d^n \cdot f(x - n)$ where $f(x - n) = a + b/(c - x + n)$, such that x is in $[n, n + 1]$. Does use of the approximation affect the bucket split algorithm?

2.164. Suppose that $f(x)$ is approximated by a second-degree polynomial instead of by $a + b/(c - x)$. What is the disadvantage of such an approximation?

2.165. Exercises 2.165–2.170 are based on an asymptotic analysis of spiral hashing described by Larson [Lars88]. Assume that $d = 2$ and that there are no deletions. The implementation is slightly different from the one described in the text. The capacity of the buckets is not restricted, and thus there is no need for overflow buckets. Each bucket is implemented as a linked list (a chain). In this case, the storage utilization factor τ is the total number of records in the table divided by the number of buckets. Assume that the overall value of τ is kept constant at α ($\alpha > 0$). However, the expected value of τ for the different buckets can and does vary over the bucket address space. Assume a normalized address range $[1,2)$ as any address in the range $[2^x, 2^x + 1)$ can be normalized by multiplying it by 2^{-x}. Let $p(y)$ be the probability that a key hashes to a normalized address in $[y, y + dy) \subseteq [1,2)$. Show that $p(y)$ is $dy/(y \cdot \ln2)$, and hence the probability density function is $1/(y \cdot \ln2)$.

2.166. Assume that the expected value of the storage utilization factor of a bucket at address y, say $\tau(y)$, is proportional to the insertion probability at y. Use the result of Exercise 2.165 to show that $\tau(y) = \alpha/(y \cdot \ln2)$.

2.167. Assume that each record is equally likely to be retrieved. Therefore the probability that a successful search lands on a bucket at address y, say $q(y)$, is proportional to the storage utilization factor of the bucket. Show that $q(y) = 1/(y \cdot \ln2)$.

2.168. Noting that each bucket is implemented as a linked list, calculate the expected cost of a successful search.

2.169. Noting that each bucket is implemented as a linked list, calculate the expected cost of an unsuccessful search.

2.170. When a record is inserted, its cost can be decomposed into two parts. The first part is the cost of placing the record at the end of the chain. Its cost is the same as that of an unsuccessful search plus the cost of linking the record to the end of the chain. The second part reflects the situation that a bucket is split and its contents need to be rehashed so that they can be properly distributed in the new buckets. This situation arises only for the first bucket. What is the expected number of extra hashing operations per record that is inserted?

2.171. What is the effect of using an arbitrary value of d in Exercises 2.165–2.170?

2.172. Prove that spiral hashing has uniform performance. In other words, prove that the expected search lengths in the buckets is independent of the table size, which in turn is a function of how many bucket split operations have taken place.

2.173. Prove that the length of the arc of a spiral has a constant value between successive integer values of ρ (i.e., it is directly proportional to ρ).

2.8.2.3   GRID FILE

The *grid file* of Nievergelt, Hinterberger, and Sevcik [Niev84, Hinr85a, Hinr85b] is a variation of the fixed-grid method, which relaxes the requirement that cell division lines be equidistant. Its goal is to retrieve records with at most two disk accesses and to handle range queries efficiently. This is done by using a grid directory consisting of grid blocks that are analogous to the cells of the fixed-grid method. All records in one grid block are stored in the same bucket. However, several grid blocks can share a bucket as long as the union of these grid blocks forms a k-dimensional rectangle in the space of records. Although the regions of the buckets are piecewise disjoint, together they span the space of records.

The purpose of the grid directory is to maintain a dynamic correspondence between the grid blocks in the record space and the data buckets. The grid directory consists of two parts. The first is a dynamic k-dimensional array, containing one entry for each grid block. The values of the elements are pointers to the relevant data buckets. Usually buckets will have a capacity of 10 to 1000 records. Thus the entry in the grid directory is small in comparison to a bucket. We are not concerned with how records are organized within a bucket (e.g., linked list, tree). The grid directory may be kept on disk.

The second part of the grid directory is a set of k one-dimensional arrays called *linear scales*. These scales define a partition of the domain of each attribute. They

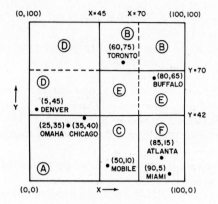

Figure 2.53   Grid file partition for the data of Figure 2.1

enable access to the appropriate grid blocks by aiding the computation of their address based on the value of the relevant attributes. The linear scales are kept in core. It should be noted that the linear scales are useful in guiding a range query by indicating the grid directory elements that overlap the query range.

Thus we see that the two goals of the grid file are met. Any record is retrieved with two disk accesses—one disk access apiece for the grid block and bucket. Range queries are efficient, although since the sizes of the grid blocks (the ranges of their intervals) are not related to the query range, it is difficult to analyze the amount of time necessary to execute a range query.

As an example, consider Figure 2.53, which shows the grid file representation for the data in Figure 2.1. Once again we adopt the convention that a rectangle is open with respect to its upper and right boundaries and closed with respect to its lower and left boundaries. The bucket capacity is 2 records. There are $k = 2$ different attributes. The grid directory consists of 9 grid blocks and 6 buckets labeled A-F. We refer to grid blocks as if they are array elements; grid block (i, j) is the element in column i (starting at the left) and row j (starting at the bottom) of the grid directory.

Grid blocks (1,3), (2,2), and (3,3) are empty; however, they do share buckets with other grid blocks. In particular, grid block (1,3) shares bucket D with grid block

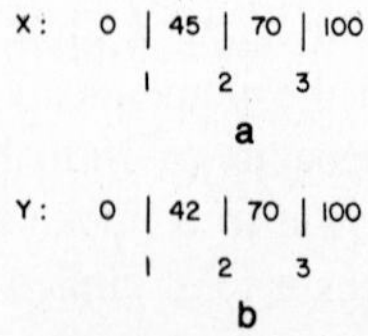

```
X :   0  | 45 | 70 | 100
        I    2    3
             a

Y :   0  | 42 | 70 | 100
        I    2    3
             b
```

Figure 2.54   Linear scales for (a) x and (b) y corresponding to the grid directory of Figure 2.53

(1,2), grid blocks (2,3) and (3,3) share bucket B, and grid blocks (2,2) and (3,2) share bucket E. The sharing is indicated by the broken lines. Figure 2.54 contains the linear scales for the two attributes (i.e., the x and y coordinates). For example, executing a point query with $x = 80$ and $y = 65$ causes the access of the bucket associated with the grid block in row 2 and column 3 of the grid directory of Figure 2.53.

The grid file is attractive, in part, because of its graceful growth as more and more records are inserted. As the buckets overflow, we apply a splitting process, which results in the creation of new buckets and a movement of records. To understand the splitting process, let us examine more closely how the grid file copes with a sequence of insertion operations. Again we assume a bucket capacity of 2 and observe how a grid file is constructed for the records of Figure 2.1 in the order in which they appear there: Chicago, Mobile, Toronto, Buffalo, Denver, Omaha, Atlanta, and Miami.

The insertion of Chicago and Mobile results in bucket A's being full. Insertion of Toronto leads to an overflow of bucket A, causing a split. We arbitrarily split the y coordinate at $y = 70$ and modify the linear scale for attribute y accordingly. Toronto is inserted in B, the newly allocated bucket (Figure 2.55a).

Next we try to insert Buffalo and find that the bucket in which it belongs (A) is full. We split the x coordinate at $x = 45$ and modify the linear scale for attribute x. This results in the insertion of Buffalo in bucket C and the movement of Mobile from bucket A to bucket C (Figure 2.55b). As a result of this split, both grid blocks (1,1) and (1,2) share bucket A, although grid block (1,2) is empty. Alternatively we could have marked grid block (1,2) as empty when the x coordinate was split. This has the disadvantage that should we later wish to insert a record in grid block (1,2), we would have to allocate a new bucket or search for a neighboring bucket that is not full and whose grid blocks form a convex region with grid block (1,2).

The insertion of Denver proceeds smoothly. It is placed in bucket A. Omaha also belongs in bucket A, which means that it must be split again. We split the y coordinate at $y = 42$ and modify the linear scale for attribute y. In addition, we create a new bucket, D, to which Denver is moved while Omaha and Chicago remain in bucket A (Figure 2.55c). By virtue of the requirement that all buckets be convex, we must associate grid block (1,3) with bucket D instead of bucket A. As a result of this split, both grid blocks (2,1) and (2,2) share bucket C, contributing Buffalo and Mobile, respectively.

Attempting to insert Atlanta finds it belonging in bucket C, which is full, yet grid block (2,1) is not full. This leads to splitting bucket C and the creation of bucket E. Bucket C now contains Mobile and Atlanta and corresponds to grid block (2,1), while bucket E now contains Buffalo and corresponds to grid block (2,2) (Figure 2.55d). Note that we did not have to partition the grid in this case. Thus no change needs to be made to the linear scales; however, the grid directory must be updated to reflect the association of grid block (2,2) with bucket E instead of bucket C.

Finally insertion of Miami finds it belonging to bucket C, which is full. We split the x coordinate at $x = 70$ and modify the linear scale for attribute x. A new bucket, F, is created to which Atlanta and Miami are moved (Figure 2.53). Once again

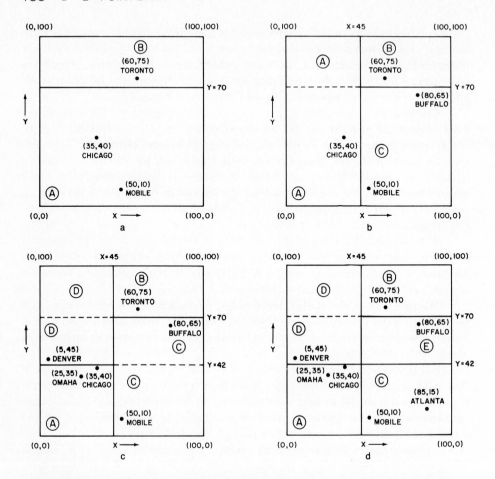

Figure 2.55   Sequence of partial grid partitions demonstrating the addition of (a) Chicago, Mobile, and Toronto, (b) Buffalo, (c) Denver and Omaha, and (d) Atlanta

we observe that as a result of this split, grid blocks (2,3) and (3,3) share bucket B, although grid block (3,3) is empty. Similarly grid blocks (2,2) and (3,2) share bucket E, although grid block (2,2) is empty.

At this point, we are ready to elaborate further on the splitting process. From the discussion, we see that two types of bucket splits are possible. The first, and more common, occurs when several grid blocks share a bucket that has overflowed (e.g., the transition between Figures 2.55c and 2.55d upon the insertion of Atlanta). In this case, we merely need to allocate a new bucket and adjust the mapping between grid blocks and buckets.

The second type of a split arises when we must refine a grid partition. It is triggered by an overflowing bucket, all of whose records lie in a single grid block (e.g., the overflow of bucket A upon insertion of Toronto in Figure 2.55a). In this case we have a choice with respect to the dimension (i.e., axis) and the location of the splitting point (i.e., we do not need to split at the midpoint of an interval). Without any external knowledge or motivation, a reasonable splitting policy is one that cycles through the various attributes (e.g., first split on attribute x, then attribute y, attribute x, etc., as was done in Figure 2.55) and uses interval midpoints. This is the approach used in the grid file implementation [Niev84].

An alternative splitting policy is an adaptive one favoring one attribute over others. This is akin to a favored attribute in an inverted file. It results in an increase in the precision of answers to partially specified queries where the favored attribute is specified. Such a policy is triggered by keeping track of the most frequently queried attribute (in the case of partial match queries) and by monitoring dynamic file content, thereby increasing the granularity of the attribute scales. Splitting at locations other than interval midpoints is also an adaptive policy.

The grid refinement operation is common at the initial stage of constructing a file. However, as the file grows, it becomes relatively rare in comparison with the overflowing bucket that is shared among several grid blocks. Nevertheless the frequency of grid refinement can be reduced by varying the grid directory as follows. Implement the grid directory as a k-dimensional array whose size in each dimension is determined by the shortest interval in each linear scale (i.e., if the linear scale for attribute x spans the range 0–64 and the shortest interval is 4, then the grid directory has 16 entries for dimension x).

This variation is a multidimensional counterpart of the directory used in extendible hashing [Fagi79] and is the basis of EXCELL [Tamm81a] (see Section 2.8.2.4). Its advantage is that a refinement of the grid partition will cause a change in the structure of the directory only if the shortest interval is split, in which case the grid directory will double in size. Such a representation anticipates small structural updates and replaces them by a large one. It is fine as long as the data are uniformly distributed. Otherwise many empty grid blocks will arise.

The counterpart of splitting is merging. There are two possible instances where merging is appropriate: bucket merging and directory merging. Bucket merging, the more common of the two, arises when a bucket is empty or nearly empty. Bucket merging policy is influenced by three factors. First, we must decide which bucket pairs are candidates for merging. This decision can be based on a *buddy system* or a *neighbor system*.

In a *buddy system* [Knut73a], each bucket, say X, can be merged with exactly one bucket, say B_i, in each of the k dimensions. Ideally the chosen bucket, say B_j, should have the property that at some earlier point it was split to yield buckets X and B_j. We call this buddy the 'true' buddy. For example, consider the grid directory of Figure 2.56, which contains buckets A-K and X. Assume that when a bucket is split, it is split into two buckets of equal size. Since $k = 2$, the only potential buddies of bucket X are I and J. We can keep track of the 'true' buddies by representing the splitting process as a binary tree, thereby maintaining the buddy relationships.

In a *neighbor system*, each bucket can be merged with either of its two adjacent neighbors in each of the k dimensions (the resulting bucket region must be convex). For example, in the grid directory of Figure 2.56, bucket X can be merged with any

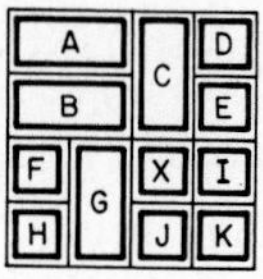

Figure 2.56 Example grid directory illustrating bucket merging

one of its neighbors (buckets C, I, or J). Note that X cannot be merged with neighbor bucket G since the resulting bucket region would not be convex.

The second factor influencing bucket merging policy deals with the ordering among possible choices should there be more than one candidate. In the case of the buddy system, we give priority to the 'true' buddy. Otherwise this factor is relevant only if it is desired to have a varying granularity among attributes. If the splitting policy favors some attributes over others, then the merging policy should not undo it.

The third factor is the merging threshold: when should a candidate pair of buckets actually be merged? It should be clear that the sum of the bucket occupancy percentages for the contents of the merged bucket should not be too large, as otherwise it would soon have to be split. Nievergelt et al. [Niev84] conducted simulation studies showing the average bucket occupancy to be 70% and suggest that this is an appropriate merging threshold for the occupancy of the resulting bucket.

Directory merging arises when all the grid blocks in two adjacent cross-sections (i.e., slices along one axis) in the grid directory are associated with the same bucket. For example, consider the two-dimensional grid directory of Figure 2.57, where all grid blocks in column 2 are in bucket C and all grid blocks in column 3 are in bucket D. In such a case, if the merging threshold is satisfied, buckets C and D can be merged and the linear scales modified to reflect this change.

Generally directory merging is of little practical interest since even if merging is allowed to occur, it is probable that splitting will soon have to take place. Nevertheless there are occasions when directory merging is of use. First, directory merging is necessary in the case of a shrinking file. Second, it is appropriate when the granularity of certain attributes is being changed to comply with the access frequency of the attribute. Third, it is a useful technique when attempting to get rid of inactive attributes. In such a case, the attribute could be set to a 'merge only' state. Eventually the

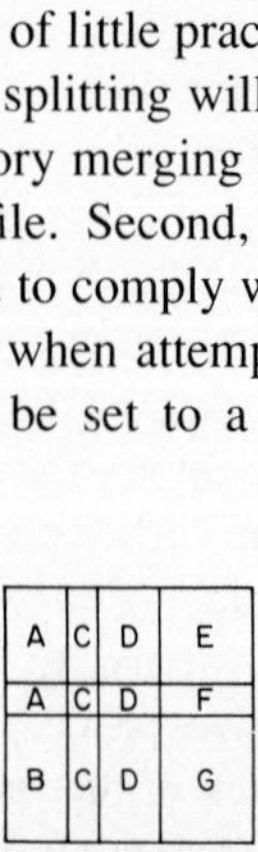

A	C	D	E
A	C	D	F
B	C	D	G

Figure 2.57 Example grid directory illustrating directory merging

partition will be reduced to one interval, and the corresponding dimension in the grid directory can be removed or assigned to another attribute.

Merrett and Otoo describe a technique termed *multipaging* [Merr78, Merr82], which is similar to the grid file. It also uses a directory in the form of linear scales called *axial arrays*. Instead of using a grid directory, however, multipaging accesses a data page and its potential overflow chain using an address computed directly from the linear scales. There are two variants of multipaging. In dynamic multipaging [Merr82], performance is controlled by setting a bound on the probe factor (defined as the average number of pages accessed in a probe). In static multipaging [Merr78], performance is controlled by setting a bound on the load factor, or the average page occupancy.

Comparing the grid file and multipaging, we find that the grid file uses multipaging as an index to the grid directory. Therefore multipaging saves space by not requiring a grid directory, but this is at a cost of requiring bucket overflow areas. This means that multipaging can obtain good average-case performance, but it cannot guarantee record retrieval with two disk accesses. In addition, insertion and deletion in multipaging involves whole rows or columns (in the two-dimensional case) of data pages when splitting or merging buckets, while the grid file can split one page at a time and localize more global operations in the grid directory.

The grid file guarantees that any record can be retrieved with two disk accesses. This is fine for point queries (exact match); however, range queries require considerably more disk accesses. Kriegel [Krie84] reports on an empirical comparison of the grid file and a pair of versions of a multidimensional B-tree termed the *kB-tree* [Güti80, Güti81] and the *MDBT* [Sche82]. Kriegel's data show that when the attributes are correlated and nonuniformly distributed, the grid file is superior with respect to insertions, deletions, and point queries while the B-tree variants are superior with respect to range queries. On the other hand, when the attributes are independent and uniformly distributed, the grid file is superior on all counts. In all cases, the storage requirements of the grid file are always lower than the B-tree variants. The relative performance of the kB-tree and the MDBT was comparable.

Exercises

2.174. Implement a database that uses the grid file to organize two-dimensional data.

2.175. Calculate the expected size of the grid directory for uniformly distributed data.

2.8.2.4   EXCELL

The *EXCELL* method of Tamminen [Tamm81a] is a bintree together with a directory in the form of an array providing access by address computation. It can also be viewed as an adaptation of extendible hashing [Fagi79] to multidimensional point data. It implements EXHASH, the extendible hashing hash function, by interleaving, in principle, the most significant bits of the data (analogous to the locational codes discussed in Section 2.1 of [Same90b]). Similar in spirit to the grid file, it is based on a regular decomposition and also makes use of a grid directory; however, all grid blocks are of the same size.

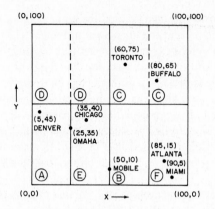

Figure 2.58   EXCELL representation corresponding to Figure 2.1

The principal difference between the grid file and EXCELL is that grid refinement for the grid file splits only one interval in two and results in the insertion of a $(k-1)$-dimensional cross-section. In contrast, a grid refinement for the EXCELL method splits all intervals in two (the partition points are fixed) for the particular dimension and results in doubling the size of the grid directory.

The result is that the grid directory grows more gradually when the grid file is used, whereas use of EXCELL reduces the need for grid refinement operations at the expense of larger directories in general due to a sensitivity to the distribution of the data. However, a large bucket size reduces the effect of nonuniformity unless the data consist entirely of a few clusters. The fact that all grid blocks define equal-sized regions (and convex as well) means that EXCELL does not require a set of linear scales to access the grid directory, as is needed for the grid file. Thus grid directory access operations are considerably faster for EXCELL.

It should be clear that since EXCELL is a regular decomposition of the data space, the partition points are fixed and are not chosen on the basis of the data, as is the case for the grid file. This means that range queries are efficient. Their execution time is proportional to the number of data buckets corresponding to the grid blocks that comprise the range being searched.

An example of the EXCELL method is given in Figure 2.58, which shows the representation for the data in Figure 2.1. Again the convention is adopted that a rectangle is open with respect to its upper and right boundaries and closed with respect to its lower and left boundaries. The capacity of the bucket is 2 records. There are $k = 2$ different attributes. The grid directory is implemented as an array, and in this case it consists of 8 grid blocks (labeled in the same way as for the grid file) and 6 buckets labeled A-F. Note that grid blocks (3,2) and (4,2) share bucket C, while grid blocks (1,2) and (2,2), despite being empty, share bucket D. The sharing is indicated by the broken lines. Furthermore when a bucket size of 1 is used, the partition of space induced by EXCELL equals that of a PR k-d tree [Oren82], although they differ by virtue of the presence of a directory in the case of EXCELL.

As a database represented by the EXCELL method grows, buckets will overflow. This leads to the application of a splitting process, which results in the creation of new buckets and a movement of records. To understand the splitting process, we examine how EXCELL copes with a sequence of insertion operations corresponding to the data of Figure 2.1. Again we assume a bucket capacity of 2 and that the records are inserted in the order in which they appear in Figure 2.1: Chicago, Mobile, Toronto, Buffalo, Denver, Omaha, Atlanta, and Miami.

The insertion of Chicago and Mobile results in bucket A's being full. Insertion of Toronto leads to an overflow of bucket A, which compels us to double the directory by splitting along attribute *x*. We split bucket A and move Mobile and Toronto to B,

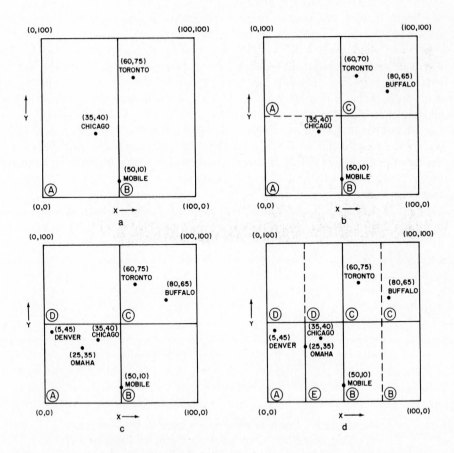

Figure 2.59   Sequence of EXCELL partitions demonstrating the insertion of
(a) Toronto, (b) Buffalo, and (c–d) Omaha

the newly allocated bucket (Figure 2.59a). Next we insert Buffalo and find that the bucket in which it belongs (B) is full. This causes us to double the directory by splitting along attribute y. We now split bucket B and move Toronto and Buffalo to C, the newly allocated bucket (Figure 2.59b). Note that bucket A still contains Chicago and overlaps grid blocks (1,1) and (1,2).

The insertion of Denver proceeds smoothly, and it is placed in bucket A. Omaha also belongs in bucket A, which has now overflowed. Since bucket A overlaps grid blocks (1,1) and (1,2), we split it, thereby allocating a new bucket, D, such that buckets A and D correspond to grid blocks (1,1) and (1,2), respectively (Figure 2.59c). However, neither Denver, Chicago, nor Omaha can be moved to D, thereby necessitating a directory doubling along attribute x. We now split bucket A and move Chicago and Omaha to E, the newly allocated bucket (Figure 2.59d). Note that buckets B, C, and D retain their contents, except that now each bucket overlaps two grid blocks.

Next Atlanta is inserted in bucket B. Insertion of Miami causes bucket B to overflow. Since B overlaps grid blocks (3,1) and (4,1), we split it, thereby allocating a new block, F, such that buckets B and F correspond to grid blocks (3,1) and (4,1), respectively. Atlanta and Miami are moved to F (see Figure 2.58).

From the discussion, we see that two types of bucket splits are possible. The first, and more common, occurs when several grid blocks share a bucket that has overflowed (e.g., the transition between Figures 2.59d and 2.58 caused by the overflow of bucket B as Atlanta and Miami are inserted in sequence). In this case, we allocate a new bucket and adjust the mapping between grid blocks and buckets.

The second type of a split causes a doubling of the directory and arises when we must refine a grid partition. It is triggered by an overflowing bucket that is not shared among several grid blocks (e.g., the overflow of bucket A upon insertion of Toronto in Figure 2.59a). The split occurs along the different attributes in a cyclic fashion (first split along attribute x, then y, then x, etc.).

For both types of bucket splits, the situation may arise that none of the elements in the overflowing bucket belongs to the newly created bucket, with the result that the directory will have to be doubled more than once. This is because the splitting points are fixed for EXCELL. For example, consider bucket A in Figure 2.60a with bucket

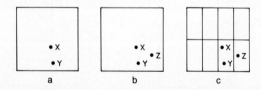

a   b   c

Figure 2.60   Example showing the need for three directory doubling operations when inserting Z (bucket capacity = 2) using EXCELL

capacity 2 and containing points X and Y. Insertion of point Z (Figure 2.60b) leads to overflow of A and causes three directory doublings (Figure 2.60c). In contrast, the fact that the splitting point is not fixed for the grid file means that it can be chosen so that only one grid refinement is necessary. Thus we see that the size of the EXCELL grid directory is sensitive to the distribution of the data. However, a large bucket size reduces the effect of nonuniformity unless the data consist entirely of a few clusters.

Although, for pedagogical purposes, the grid directories of Figures 2.53 and 2.58 were constructed in such a way that EXCELL required fewer grid blocks than the grid file (eight versus nine), this is not generally the case. In fact, splitting points can always be chosen so that the number of grid blocks and buckets required by the grid file is less than or equal to the number required by EXCELL. For example, if the space of Figure 2.53 were split at $x = 55$ and $y = 37$, then only four grid blocks and buckets would be necessary.

The counterpart of splitting is merging; however, it is considerably more limited in scope for EXCELL than for the grid file. Also it is less likely to arise because EXCELL has been designed primarily for use in geometrical applications where deletion of records is not so prevalent. There are two cases where merging is appropriate.

The first, and more common, is bucket merging, which arises when a pair of buckets is empty or nearly empty. The buckets that are candidates for merging, say X and Y, must be buddies in the sense that earlier one of them was split, say X, to yield X and Y (e.g., A and E in Figure 2.58 but not A and C). Once such a bucket pair has been identified, we must see if its elements satisfy the merging threshold. In essence, the sum of the bucket occupancy percentages for the contents of the merged bucket should not be too large, as otherwise it might soon have to be split.

The second instance where merging is possible is directory merging. It arises when each bucket-buddy pair in the grid directory either meets the merging threshold (e.g., B and C, and D and E in Figure 2.61), or the bucket overlaps more than one grid block (e.g., bucket A overlaps grid blocks (1,2) and (2,2), and bucket F overlaps grid blocks (3,1) and (4,1) in Figure 2.61). This is quite rare.

Earlier we observed that EXCELL yields the same partitioning of the space as is obtained by the bucket PR k-d tree (also known as a hybrid k-d trie [Oren82]) discussed in Section 2.8.1. The difference is that the directory of EXCELL corresponds to the deepest level of a complete bucket PR k-d tree. Alternatively EXCELL provides a directory to a database that is implemented as a bucket PR k-d tree. In particular

Figure 2.61 Example demonstrating the possibility of directory merging using EXCELL

EXCELL results in faster access to the buckets since the k-d trie search step (i.e., following pointers in the tree) is avoided. However, if the longest search path in a bucket PR k-d tree has length s, the EXCELL directory has 2^s entries.

EXCELL is also closely related to linear hashing when reversed bit interleaving is used as the hashing function (see Section 2.8.2.1). The key difference is that EXCELL has a directory and a set of buckets. In contrast, linear hashing has an implicit directory in the sense that there is one directory element per primary bucket, and a primary bucket also serves as a directory element.

Other differences are that in EXCELL a bucket overflow may trigger a bucket split or a doubling of the directory, whereas in linear hashing at most two new buckets are allocated (one for a bucket split and one for an overflow bucket—recall the insertion of Omaha in the transition from Figure 2.46c to 2.46d in Section 2.8.2.1). In essence, using linear hashing there is a more gradual growth in the size of the directory at the expense of the loss of the guarantee of record retrieval with two disk accesses. In addition, assuming equal bucket sizes, linear hashing requires more buckets, since the bucket that is split is not necessarily the one that has overflowed.

To facilitate a comparison between EXCELL and linear hashing, suppose that we implement EXCELL by splitting along the y coordinate first. This yields Figure 2.62 as the EXCELL representation corresponding to Figure 2.1. Comparing Figures 2.45 and 2.62 finds that using EXCELL requires 16 directory elements and 7 buckets, whereas linear hashing requires 6 primary buckets and 2 overflow buckets. Note that EXCELL never requires overflow buckets; this is at the expense of a possibly large directory.

The gradual growth of the number of directory elements when using linear hashing can be illustrated by comparing the EXCELL representation of Figure 2.58 with a similarly constructed linear hashing representation. To see this relationship, we need

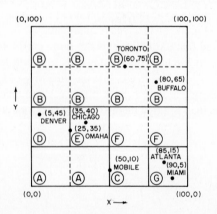

Figure 2.62 EXCELL representation corresponding to Figure 2.1 when the y coordinate is split before the x coordinate

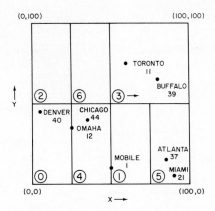

Figure 2.63   Linear hashing using reversed bit interleaving representation corresponding to Figure 2.1 when the x coordinate is taken as the most significant

to revise the bit interleaving hashing function so that the x coordinate is the most significant prior to the reversal of the bits (see Table 2.1 for the result of applying such a mapping to the data of Figure 2.1).

Assuming the same bucket sizes and storage utilization factor used in the construction of Figures 2.43 and 2.44, the application of such a hashing function to the data of Figure 2.1 yields Figure 2.63. Note that linear hashing requires seven buckets whereas EXCELL needs only six buckets since it split only the buckets that were full. Of course, the next bucket to be split by linear hashing will be bucket 3, whereas the next bucket to be split by EXCELL could result in a doubling of the number of directory elements (e.g., the insertion of New Orleans at (45,10)).

Exercises
2.176. Implement a database that uses EXCELL to organize two-dimensional data.
2.177. Compare the rate of growth of directory elements when using linear hashing with reversed bit interleaving, grid file, and EXCELL.
2.178. Why does linear hashing usually require at least as many buckets as EXCELL?
2.179. Given a large set of multidimensional point data, which of the three bucket methods would you use? Take the volume of the data and their distribution into account. Can you support your choice using analytic methods?

2.9   CONCLUSION

The introduction mentioned that searching techniques can be grouped into three primitive categories: those that organize the data to be stored (denoted by D), those that organize the embedding space from which the data are drawn (denoted by E), and

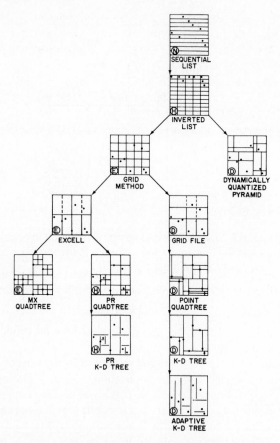

Figure 2.64   Tree representation of the interrelationship among the data structures discussed in Chapter 2

those that require no organization (denoted by N). At this point, it is useful to review the various data structures described in the previous sections and see how they fit into the taxonomy. To understand better their interrelationship, we make use of Figure 2.64, a tree whose nodes are data structures.

For each node we draw an approximation of how it represents the data of Figure 2.1. We make no special distinction between bucket and nonbucket methods; however, when a data structure corresponds to a bucket method, we use a bucket capacity of 2. Also, we assume two-dimensional data ($k = 2$). Each node is labeled with the name of the corresponding data structure. In addition, to each node we attach one of the labels D, E, H, and N corresponding to the category in which it belongs. H denotes a hybrid category and indicates that the data structure exhibits behavior that we associate with at least two of D, E, and N.

The depths of the nodes in the tree also convey important information on the relationship between the various data structures. We assume that the root of the tree is at depth 0. Note that these characterizations are not necessarily unique. Other characterizations are undoubtedly equally valid (see Exercise 2.184), and some characterizations or data structures may have been omitted (see Exercise 2.183). Nevertheless an attempt has been made to place each of the data structures discussed in an appropriate position relative to the other representations.

Depth 0 represents no identifiable organization of the data. The data are maintained in a sequential list that usually corresponds to the order in which it was inserted into the data base.

Depth 1 corresponds to a partition of space that takes only one attribute into consideration. The inverted list appears at this depth and is characterized as being hybrid. The attribute governing the partition exhibits behavior of type D. In contrast, the data values of the remaining attributes have no influence on the way the space is organized and hence exhibit behavior of type N.

At depth 2, all attributes are taken into account resulting in a partition that yields a decomposition into a fixed number of cells. We distinguish between cells of equal size and of varying size. The fixed-grid method, type E, is an example of the former and the Dynamically Quantized Pyramid (DQP), type D, is an example of the latter.

Depth 3 is a generalization of depth 2. It permits the cells of the representations at depth 2 to vary in number. The fixed-grid method is refined to yield the grid file, type D, with varying cell boundaries, and EXCELL, type E, with fixed cell boundaries. Notice that the representations at depths 2 and 3 use directories in the form of arrays to access the data. In addition, the representations at depth 3 enable the retrieval of a record in constant time.

When a cell in one of the representations at depth 4 overflows, only that particular cell is partitioned. In contrast, at depth 3 a partition is made over a $(k-1)$-dimensional cross-section. The partition in the representations at depth 4 results in a cell being decomposed into 2^k cells. At this depth, we find that the grid file is refined to yield the point quadtree of type D. EXCELL is refined to yield an MX quadtree of type E and a PR quadtree of type H. The PR quadtree is of type H because the partition points are fixed; however, the number of partition points depends on the relative position of the data points.

When a cell in one of the representations at depth 5 overflows, it is partitioned but it is only decomposed into two cells in contrast with 2^k for depth 4. The partitions that are made at the different levels in the relevant data structures cycle through the attributes. At this depth, we find that the point quadtree is refined to yield a k-d tree of type D, and the PR quadtree is refined to yield a PR k-d tree of type H.

When a cell in one of the representations at depth 6 overflows, a partition is made using the attribute that has the greatest spread in values across the cell. Thus, we no longer need to cycle through the various attributes as was done for the representations at depth 5. The adaptive k-d tree, as well as the Dynamically Quantized Space (DQS), both of type D, are characteristic of this class of data structure.

At this point, it is appropriate to ask how bit interleaving fits in our taxonomy. One possibility is to look at the shape of the search region corresponding to a range query. All of the data structures examined so far, save for the sequential list, result in each range query having a convex shape in the form of a k-dimensional rectangle. This is not the case for bit interleaving as can be seen by the staircase corresponding to the range query as shown in Figure 2.38.

Thus, it would seem that we should insert the bit interleaving data structure as another son of the sequential list, where the inverted list corresponds to rectangular search regions while the bit interleaving method does not.

Actually, this line of reasoning is erroneous because bit interleaving does not *per se* fit into our taxonomy since it is simply a part of the data representation. Only when we have decided how to structure the data that has been the subject of bit interleaving (e.g., by using a B-tree, binary search tree, etc.), can we place it in our taxonomy.

Exercises

2.180. How does linear hashing using bit interleaving fit into the taxonomy of Figure 2.64?

2.181. How does spiral hashing using bit interleaving fit into the taxonomy of Figure 2.64?

2.182. How does the BD tree fit into the taxonomy of Figure 2.64?

2.183. The taxonomy shown in Figure 2.64 could be formulated differently. First, we qualify the E and D categories as being of type 1 or k depending on whether they take 1 or k dimensions into account. Also, let depth 3 be characterized as a refinement of depth 2 with overflow handling. Add another data structure, termed a *pyramid*, which yields a 2^k growth in the directory upon a bucket overflow. Now, depth 4 can be recast as replacing a directory in the form of an array by a directory in the form of a tree. How would you rebuild depths 3–6 of Figure 2.64 using this new taxonomy? How does linear hashing with reversed bit interleaving fit in?

2.184. [Markku Tamminen] In the opening section of this chapter a number of issues was raised with respect to choosing an appropriate representation for point data. Can you devise a taxonomy in the same spirit as Figure 2.64 using them? For example, let each depth of the tree correspond to a different property. At depth 0, distinguish between an organization of the data and an organization of the embedding space. At depth 1, distinguish between dynamic and static methods. At depth 2, distinguish between the number of sons. At depth 3, distinguish between the presence and absence of a directory. At depth 4, distinguish between bucketing and nonbucketing methods.

2.185. The Euclidean matching problem consists of taking a set of $2 \cdot N$ points in the plane and decomposing it into the set of disjoint pairs of points so that the sum of the Euclidean distances between the components of each pair is a minimum. Would any of the representations discussed in this chapter facilitate the solution of this problem? Can you solve this problem by building a set of pairs, finding the closest pair of points, discarding it, and then applying the same procedure to the remaining set of points? Can you give an example that demonstrates that this solution is not optimal?

2.186. An alternative solution to the one proposed in Exercise 2.185 proceeds in a manner analogous to that used in constructing the adaptive k-d tree in Section 2.4.1. In essence, we sort the points by increasing x and y coordinate values and then split them into two sets by splitting across the coordinate with the largest range. This process is applied recursively. Implement this method and run some experiments to show how close it comes to achieving optimality. Can you construct a simple example where the method of Exercise 2.185 is superior?

2.187. Suppose that you are given N points in a two-dimensional space, and a rectangular window, say R, whose sides are parallel to the coordinate axes. Find a point in the plane at which the window can be centered so that it contains a maximum number of points in its interior. The window is not permitted to be rotated—it can only be translated to the point. Would any of the representations discussed in this chapter facilitate the solution of this problem?

COLLECTIONS
OF SMALL
RECTANGLES

3

The problem of how to represent collections of small rectangles arises in many applications. The most common example occurs when a rectangle is used to approximate other shapes for which it serves as the minimum enclosing object. Of course, the exact boundaries of the object are also stored, but usually they are accessed only if a need for greater precision exists. For example, bounding rectangles can be used in cartographic applications to approximate objects such as lakes, forests, and hills [Mats84]. In such a case, the approximation gives a rough indication of the existence of an object. This is useful in processing spatial queries in a geographic information system. Such queries can involve the detection of overlapping areas, a determination of proximity, and so on. Another application is the detection of cartographic anomalies that require further resolution when a map is printed.

Rectangles are also used for design rule checking in very large-scale integration (VLSI) as a model of chip components for the analysis of their proper placement. Again the rectangles serve as minimum enclosing objects. This process includes such tasks as determining whether components intersect, ensuring the satisfaction of constraints involving factors as minimum separation and width. These tasks have a practical significance in that they can be used to avoid design flaws.

The size of the collection depends on the application; it can vary tremendously. For example, in cartographic applications, the number of elements in the collection is usually small, and frequently the sizes of the rectangles are of the same order of magnitude as the space from which they are drawn. On the other hand, in VLSI applications, the size of the collection is quite large (e.g., millions of components), and the sizes of the rectangles are several orders of magnitude smaller than the space from which they are drawn.

In this chapter, we focus primarily on how to represent a large collection of rectangles common in VLSI applications. The techniques, however, are equally applicable to other domains. We assume that all rectangles are positioned so that their sides are parallel to the x and y coordinate axes. We start with a general introduction to the problem domain and to the tasks whose solutions such representations are intended to facilitate. The issues that arise are reminiscent of earlier discussions on handling point data (see Chapter 2).

Initially representations designed for use with the plane-sweep solution paradigm [Sham76, Prep85] are presented. For many tasks, use of this paradigm yields worst-case optimal solutions in time and space. We examine its use in solving two problems:

1. Reporting all intersections between rectangles (the rectangle intersection problem).
2. Computing the area of a collection of d-dimensional rectangles (the measure problem).

We focus on the segment, interval, and priority search trees. They represent a rectangle by the intervals that form its boundaries. However, these representations are usually for formulations of the tasks in a static environment. This means that the identity of all the rectangles must be known a priori if the worst-case time and space bounds are to hold. Furthermore, for some tasks, the addition of a single object to the database may force the reexecution of the algorithm on the entire database.

The remaining representations are for a dynamic environment. They are differentiated by the way in which each rectangle is represented. The first type of representation reduces each rectangle to a point in a higher (usually) dimensional space and then treats the problem as if it involves a collection of points. The second type is region based in the sense that the subdivision of the space from which the rectangles are drawn depends on the physical extent of the rectangle; it does not represent a rectangle as just one point.

Many of the representations are variants of the quadtree. We will see that these quadtree variants are similar to the segment and interval trees used with the plane-sweep paradigm. Moreover, we will observe that the quadtree serves as a multidimensional sort and the process of traversing it is analogous to a plane sweep in multiple dimensions. Finally, we discuss some representations that are more commonly used in a problem domain that involves a relatively small number of rectangles (e.g., as found in a cartographic application).

3.1 INTRODUCTION

In choosing a representation for a collection of objects,[1] we are faced with two issues: choosing a representation for the objects and then deciding whether (and if so, then how) to organize the objects making up the collection. During the decision process we will be confronted with many of the same issues that arose in the representation of multidimensional point data discussed in Chapter 2.

For example, we must decide between a static and a dynamic representation, between making use of comparative search and address computation, between retrieval on one key, which is a combination of all the keys, and using a subset of the keys. There are many other options and factors, and thus a choice can be made only after a careful consideration of the type of operations (including queries) that we wish to support. Not surprisingly the operations are similar to those considered in Chapter 2.

There are situations in which the representation issue is not as crucial. For example, implementing an operation using plane-sweep methods (see Section 3.2) implies a sequential process in which only a subset of the objects is generally of interest. Thus there is no need to be concerned about how to represent the entire collection of objects.

Hinrichs and Nievergelt [Hinr83, Hinr85a] suggest that the representations of the individual objects can be grouped into three principal categories. First, we can use a representative point (e.g., the centroid). Such an approach is not good for proximity queries if the object's extent (e.g., lengths of the sides for a rectangle) is not stored together with the coordinate values of the representative point.

Second, we can represent an object by its characteristic parts. There are many choices, among them the following:

1. The representation can be based on the interior of the object. For example, we can decompose the object into smaller units (e.g., a decomposition of a rectangle into squares as would be done by a region quadtree). Each unit contains a pointer to the complete description of the object.

2. The representation can be based on the boundary of the object. For example, polygons are often represented as an ordered collection of vertices or, equivalently, by the line segments comprising their boundaries.

3. The representation can be procedural—that is, a combination of choices 1 and 2 according to a well-defined set of rules. The combination can also be based on a decomposition into units of a smaller dimension. For example, a rectangle is often represented as the Cartesian product of two one-dimensional spheres (i.e., intervals).

---

[1] In this section, we assume that the objects have an arbitrary shape, although the subsequent discussion is restricted to rectangles.

There are several difficulties with such approaches. One problem is that updating (e.g., insertion or deletion) will generally require processing several units. A more serious drawback is that at times a query is posed in such a manner that none of the characteristic parts of an object, say O, that satisfies the query will match the query's description, yet O does satisfy the query. The problem is that not all properties are inherited by the parts. For example, suppose that we are dealing with a collection of polygons stored so that each polygon is represented by the line segments that constitute its edges. We wish to determine if a given polygon contains a given rectangle. Clearly no edge of the polygon will contain the rectangle. Hence a solution to this problem requires that with each edge of a polygon (or rectangle) we store an identifier that indicates the polygons or objects associated with each of its sides. (For more details, see the discussion in Section 4.2.3.6.)

Third, we can represent an object by partitioning the space from which it is drawn into cells adapted to the objects. Each cell is like a bucket that contains references to all objects that intersect it. The cells may be disjoint or may be permitted to overlap. In the latter case, if the partition is such that there always exists at least one cell that contains the object in its entirety, then we can avoid the redundancy that is a natural consequence of the multiple references to the object. Of course, the fact that cells may overlap will increase the costs of certain query operations since several cells may cover a specific point.

Once a representation has been selected for the individual objects, we must decide how to represent the collection of the objects. There are numerous ways of doing so. One class of methods consists of variations of linked lists, and one such method, corner stitching, is discussed in Section 3.4. In this book, we are primarily interested in hierarchical representations, so the bulk of the discussion concentrates on hierarchical methods and on operations for which they are useful. As we will see, the method used depends to a large degree on the manner in which the individual objects are represented.

When objects are represented using representative points, then data structures such as those discussed in Chapter 2 are applicable (e.g., grid file, k-d trees, point and PR quadtrees, variations on B-trees). The choice depends on whether we wish to organize the data to be stored (i.e., methods based on comparative search) or the embedding space from which the data are drawn (i.e., methods based on address computation). Similar considerations apply when individual objects are represented by their characteristic parts, as is the case when using variants of the region quadtree.

The principal tasks to be performed are similar to those described in Chapter 2. They range from the basic operations, such as insertion and deletion, to more complex queries that include exact match, partial match, range, partial range, finding all objects (e.g., rectangles) in a given region, finding nearest neighbors with respect to a given metric for the data domain, and even join queries [Ullm82]. The most common of these queries involves proximity relations and is classified into two classes by Hinrichs [Hinr85a]. The first is an intersection query, which seeks to determine if two sets intersect. The second is a subset relation and can be formulated in terms of enclosure (i.e., is A a subset of B?) or of containment (i.e., does A contain B?).

In describing queries involving these relations, we must be careful to distinguish between a point and an object. A *point* is an element in the d-dimensional space from which the objects are drawn. It is not an element of the space into which the objects may be mapped by a particular representation. For example, in the case of a collection of rectangles in two dimensions, a point is an element of the Euclidean plane and not a rectangle, though we may choose to represent each rectangle by a point in some multidimensional space.

In the following sections, the focus is on three types of proximity queries. The first, and most common, is the point query, which finds all the objects that contain a given point. The second type is a point set query, which, given a relation $\oplus$ and a set of points Q (typically a region), finds the set of objects S such that $S \oplus Q$ holds. An example is a query, more commonly known as a window operation, that finds all the rectangles that intersect a given region. In this example, the relation $\oplus$ is defined by $S \oplus Q$ if $S \cap Q \neq \varnothing$, and Q is the query window. The third type of query is a geometric join query which for a relation $\oplus$, and two classes of objects O_1 and O_2 with corresponding subsets S_1 and S_2, finds all pairs (P_1, P_2) with $P_1 \in S_1$, $P_2 \in S_2$, and $P_1 \oplus P_2$. An example is a query that determines all pairs of overlapping rectangles. In such a case both O_1 and O_2 correspond to the set of rectangles, and $\oplus$ is the intersection relation.

Other tasks, less general and more intimately tied to the application domain, are often solved just as efficiently without using hierarchical methods. In the following, we briefly examine them. For example, in a VLSI application it is desired to perform *circuit extraction* (the determination of electrical connectivity). In this case, two rectangles A and B are said to be *electrically connected* if and only if there is a sequence of rectangles $<R_1, R_2, \cdots R_n>$ such that $R_1 = A$, $R_n = B$, and R_i intersects R_{i+1} for $1 \leq i < n$. This is analogous to connected component labeling in images (see Section 5.1 of [Same90b]).

Channel finding [Oust84] is similar to circuit extraction. It finds paths through areas that are not intersected by any of the data rectangles. This is useful for tracing signal paths and is related to performing connected component labeling on the background portion of the image. Once a circuit has been extracted, it is often the case that we wish to view it, and for this purpose it is preferable to eliminate all lines within it so that it can be plotted. This is analogous to hidden line elimination in computer graphics (see Section 7.1 of [Same90b]).

At times, it may be desired to insert a rectangle, but there is no room for it. In such a case, a *plowing* operation [Oust84] is attempted. It tries to move existing rectangles to make room for the new rectangle while still preserving the design rules and topological properties of the circuit, such as connectedness. *Compaction* [Oust84] is a somewhat related operation that tries to eliminate the empty space between nonoverlapping rectangles. Compaction in a single direction can be achieved by plowing a large rectangle across the space from which the rectangles are drawn.

3.2 PLANE-SWEEP METHODS AND THE RECTANGLE INTERSECTION PROBLEM

The term *plane-sweep* is used to characterize a paradigm employed to solve geometric problems by sweeping a line (plane in three dimensions) across the plane (space in three dimensions) and halting at points where the line (plane) makes its first or last intersection with any of the objects being processed. At these points, the solution is partially computed, so that at the end of the sweep, a final solution is available. In this discussion, we are dealing with two-dimensional data. Assume, without loss of generality, that the line is swept in the horizontal direction and from left to right.

To use the plane-sweep technique, we need to organize two sets of data. The first set consists of the *halting points* of the line (i.e., the points of initial or final intersection). It is usually organized as a list of x coordinate values sorted in ascending order. The second set consists of a description of the status of the objects intersected by the current position of the sweep line. This status reflects the information relevant to the problem to be solved, and it must be updated at each halting point.

The data structure used to store the status must be able to handle updates, but it may take advantage of characteristics of the data discovered while the data were sorted. In other words, the data structure may use knowledge about the entire batch of updates. For this reason, these data structures are sometimes called *batched dynamic* [Edel85b]. The characteristics of this data structure will determine, to a large extent, the efficiency of the solution.

The application of plane-sweep methods to rectangle problems is much studied. The solutions to many of these problems require the data to be ordered in a manner that makes use of some variant of multidimensional sorting. In such cases, the execution times of optimal algorithms are often constrained by how fast we can sort, which for N objects usually means a lower bound of $O(N \cdot \log_2 N)$. At times an increase in speed can be obtained by making use of more storage. The text of Preparata and Shamos [Prep85] contains an excellent discussion of a number of problems to which such techniques are applicable.

We assume that each rectangle is specified by four values: the x coordinates of its two vertical sides and the y coordinates of its two horizontal sides (equivalently these are the x and y coordinates of its lower left and upper right corners). We also assume that each rectangle is closed on its left and bottom sides and open on its top and right sides. Applying the same open-closed convention to the boundaries of a rectangle finds that its horizontal (vertical) boundaries are closed on their left (bottom) ends and open on their right (top) ends. Alternatively the boundaries can be described as being *semiclosed*.

In this section, we focus on the efficient solution of the problem of reporting all intersections between rectangles and, to a lesser extent, on some related problems. Note that a naive way to report all intersections is to check each rectangle against every other rectangle. This takes $O(N^2)$ time for N rectangles. The plane-sweep solution of the problem consists of two passes. The first pass sorts the left and right boun-

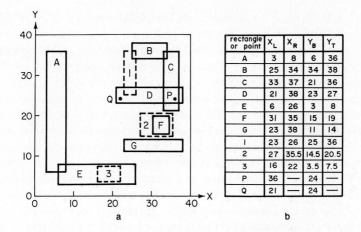

rectangle or point	x_L	x_R	Y_B	Y_T
A	3	8	6	36
B	25	34	34	38
C	33	37	21	36
D	21	38	23	27
E	6	26	3	8
F	31	35	15	19
G	23	38	11	14
I	23	26	25	36
2	27	35.5	14.5	20.5
3	16	22	3.5	7.5
P	36	—	24	—
Q	21	—	24	—

a   b

Figure 3.1   (a) A collection of rectangles. Members of the collection are designated by solid lines and labeled alphabetically (A–G). Query rectangles are designated by broken lines and labeled numerically (1–3). P and Q are query points. (b) The locations of the endpoints of the rectangles and the points in (a). For a rectangle, x_L and x_R correspond to its left and right boundaries, respectively, while Y_B and Y_T correspond to its bottom and top boundaries, respectively. For a point, x_L and y_B are its x and y coordinate values respectively.

daries (i.e., x coordinate values) of the rectangles in ascending order and forms a list. For example, consider the collection of rectangles given in Figure 3.1. Letting R_l and R_r denote the left and right boundaries of rectangle R, the result of the first pass is a list consisting of 3, 6, 8, 21, 23, 25, 26, 31, 33, 34, 35, 37, 38, 38 corresponding to A_l, E_l, A_r, D_l, G_l, B_l, E_r, F_l, C_l, B_r, F_r, C_r, D_r, G_r, respectively.

The second pass sweeps a vertical scan line through the sorted list from left to right, halting at each one of these points. This pass requires solving a quasi-dynamic version of the one-dimensional intersection problem. At any instant, all rectangles that intersect the scan line are considered *active* (e.g., rectangles D, E, and G for a vertical scan line through x = 24 in Figure 3.1). We must report all intersections between a newly activated rectangle and currently active rectangles that lie on the scan line. The sweep process halts every time a rectangle becomes active (causing it to be inserted in the set of active rectangles) or ceases to be active (causing it to be deleted from the set of active rectangles). The key to a good solution is to organize the active rectangles so that intersection detection, insertion, and deletion are executed efficiently.

The first pass involves sorting, and thus it takes $O(N \cdot \log_2 N)$ time. Insofar as the second pass is concerned, each rectangle is nothing more than a vertical line segment (or equivalently a one-dimensional interval). Several data structures can be used to represent line segments. If we care only about reporting the intersections of boundaries (i.e., vertical boundaries with horizontal boundaries), then a balanced binary tree is adequate to represent the bottom and top boundaries (i.e., y coordinate values) of the active rectangles [Bent79d] (see Exercise 3.41). Unfortunately such a representation fails to account for intersections that result when one rectangle is totally contained within another.

In the rest of this section, we focus on solutions to the rectangle intersection problem that use the segment, interval, and priority search trees to represent the active line segments. We first examine the segment tree and then show how the order of the space requirements of the solution can be reduced by using either the interval or priority search trees while still retaining the same order of execution time. Although the interval tree solution for the rectangle intersection problem requires less space than the segment tree solution, the segment tree is important due to its simplicity and finds use in a number of applications. We conclude by briefly examining some alternative solutions and point out related problems that can be solved using the same techniques.

3.2.1 Segment Trees

The segment tree is a representation for a collection of line segments devised by Bentley [Bent77a]. It is useful for detecting all the intervals that contain a given point. It is best understood by first examining a simplified version that we call a *unit-segment tree*, which is used to represent a single line segment. For the moment, assume that the endpoints of the line segments of our collection are drawn from the set of integers $\{i \,|\, 0 \le i \le 2^h\}$. Let s be a line segment with endpoints l and r $(l < r)$. s consists of the set of consecutive unit intervals $[j : j+1)$ $(l \le j < r)$. The unit-segment tree is a complete binary tree of depth h such that the root is at level h and nodes at level 0 (i.e., the bottom) represent the sequence of consecutive intervals $[j : j+1)$ $(0 \le j < 2^h)$. A node at level i in the unit-segment tree represents the interval $[p : p + 2^i)$ (i.e., the sequence of 2^i consecutive unit intervals starting at p, where $p \bmod 2^i$ is 0).

Representing line segment s in a unit-segment tree is easy. We start at the root of the tree and check if its corresponding interval is totally contained in s. If yes, then we *mark* the node with s. In such a case, we say that s *covers* the node's interval. Otherwise we repeat the process for the left and right sons of s. This process visits at most four nodes at each level while marking at most two of them. Thus it is easy to see that inserting a line segment into a unit-segment tree in a top-down manner can be achieved in $O(h)$ time. An equivalent bottom-up description of this process is that a node is marked with s if all (i.e., both) the intervals corresponding to its sons are totally contained in s, in which case the sons are no longer marked with s.

For an example of the unit-segment tree, consider a collection of line segments with integer endpoints that are in the range [0:16). In this case, there are 16 possible intervals, each of unit length. The unit-segment tree for a line segment, named A, of length 8 whose endpoints are at 3 and 11, is given in Figure 3.2. Note that the interval $[i : i+1)$ is represented by the node labeled i. From the figure, it is easy to observe the

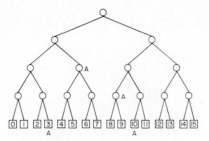

Figure 3.2   The unit-segment tree for the segment [3:11) labeled A in the range [0:16)

close analogy between the unit-segment tree and a one-dimensional region quadtree [Rose82a] where the unit intervals are the one-dimensional analog of pixels. The analogy is completed by letting black (white) correspond to the labeled (unlabeled) nodes, and merging brother nodes of the same color.

The unit-segment tree is inadequate for two reasons: it can represent only one line segment, and it is defined only for line segments with integer endpoints. The segment tree is an adaptation of the unit-segment tree that enables the use of one data structure to represent a collection of line segments with arbitrary endpoints by removing the restriction that the intervals be of uniform length, and by replacing the mark at each node by a linked list of the names of the line segments that contain that node.

This adaptation is achieved in the following manner. Given a set of N line segments, we first sort their endpoints and remove duplicates to obtain $y_0, y_1, \cdots, y_m$ ($m < 2 \cdot N$). Next we form the segment tree in the same way as the unit-segment tree with the exception that interval $[j : j+1)$ is replaced by the interval $[y_j : y_{j+1})$ ($0 \le j < 2^h$ and $2^{h-1} \le m < 2^h$). Each line segment s with endpoints y_l and y_r consists of the sequence of consecutive intervals $[y_j : y_{j+1})$ ($l \le j < r$).

A node at level i in the segment tree represents the interval $[y_p : y_{p+2^i})$ (i.e., the sequence of 2^i consecutive intervals starting at y_p where p mod 2^i is 0). Each node is marked with the names of all the line segments that cover the node's corresponding interval and do not cover the corresponding interval of the parent node. As in the case of the unit-segment tree, both a node and its brother cannot be marked with the same line segment. The set of line segments associated with each node is represented as a doubly linked list. This will be seen to facilitate deletion of line segments.

For example, Figure 3.3 is the segment tree for the set of line segments that correspond to the vertical boundaries of the rectangles in Figure 3.1. Although there are seven line segments, the segment tree contains twelve intervals as there are only thirteen different endpoints. Since the segment tree is a complete binary tree, in this case it has four unused intervals. Each leaf node is labeled with its corresponding interval number and the leftmost endpoint of the interval—node i corresponds to the interval $[y_i : y_{i+1})$. Nodes are also labeled with the sets of names of the line segments

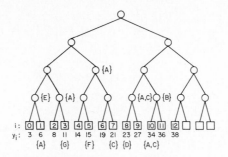

Figure 3.3   The segment tree for the set of line segments
corresponding to the vertical boundaries of the rectangles in
Figure 3.1. Terminal node i corresponds to the interval
$[y_i : y_{i+1}]$.

that cover their corresponding intervals. For example, the interval [23:34) is labeled
with {A,C} because it is covered by these line segments.

Inserting a line segment in the segment tree is analogous to inserting it in the
unit-segment tree. The only difference is that the line segment must also be inserted
in the list of line segments associated with the node. It can be placed anywhere in the
list, and thus we usually attach it to the front of the list. In a domain of N line segments, insertion (into the tree and list) takes $O(\log_2 N)$ time per line segment.

Deleting a line segment from a segment tree is somewhat more complex. We
must remove the line segment from the doubly linked list associated with each node
that contains it. This could be expensive since, in the worst case, it requires the
traversal of $O(\log_2 N)$ linked lists, each containing $O(N)$ entries. This difficulty is
avoided by maintaining an auxiliary table with one entry for each of the N line segments. Each table entry points to a list of pointers. Each pointer points to a list entry
for the line segment in a node, say P, of the segment tree such that P's interval is
covered by the line segment (see Exercise 3.3).

This table is built as the line segments are entered into the segment tree. It contains at most N entries and can be accessed or updated in $O(\log_2 N)$ time when implemented as a balanced binary tree (or even in constant time if implemented as an array,
in which case each line segment must be represented by a unique integer in the range
$1 \cdots N$). We can use an array instead of a dictionary because we know the identities
of the rectangles in advance (i.e., a static environment).

A segment tree for N line segments has a maximum of $2 \cdot N$ leaf nodes. Each
line segment covers the intervals of at most $2 \cdot \lceil \log_2 N \rceil$ nodes of the segment tree. At
each of these nodes, deletion of the line segment can be done in constant time since
the segment lists that are associated with these nodes are implemented as doubly
linked lists. Thus the total cost of deleting a line segment is $O(\log_2 N)$. The segment
tree has a total of $O(N)$ nodes, and, since each line segment can appear in (i.e., cover)

$O(\log_2 N)$ nodes, the total space required (including the auxiliary table) in the worst case is $O(N \cdot \log_2 N)$. Interestingly, Bucher and Edelsbrunner [Buch83] have shown that the average space requirement for a segment tree is also $O(N \cdot \log_2 N)$.

Given F rectangle intersections, using a segment tree to determine the set of rectangles that intersect each other is somewhat complex [Bent80f] if we want to do it in $O(N \cdot \log_2 N + F)$ time. In particular, it involves considerably more work than just inserting a line segment and reporting the rectangles associated with the line segments encountered during the insertion process. We will see by means of an example why this is so, once the algorithm has been described.

Conceptually the problem is quite straightforward. For each line segment S, with starting and ending points l and r, respectively, we want the set of line segments A such that $A_i \cap S$ is nonempty for each $A_i \in A$. Recalling that the segment tree is good for detecting all intervals that contain a given point, we formulate the problem as an infinite set of point queries: for each point p_i in line segment S, find all line segments that contain it. This process takes $O(\log_2 N)$ time for each point queried. To avoid looking at every point in S (an infinite number!), we can restrict the search to the endpoints of the line segments that are overlapped by S. An obvious, but unacceptable, solution is to store with each line segment the set of segments that intersect it, at a total storage cost of $O(N^2)$.

A more reasonable solution, which makes use of the above restriction on the search, is given by Six and Wood [Six80, Six82], who decompose the search into two disjoint problems. They make use of the obvious fact that any line segment with a starting point greater than r or with an ending point less than l does not intersect the line segment S. The first problem consists of determining all line segments with starting points less than l that have a nonempty intersection with S. The second problem consists of determining all line segments with starting points that lie between l and r. Thus there is a need to be concerned only with an ordering based on the starting points.

One way to solve the first problem is to use a balanced binary tree to store the starting points of the line segments. We search for all line segments with starting points that are less than l and check if the ending points are greater than l. Unfortunately this could require us to examine every node in the tree (if l is large). An alternative solution is to perform a point query for point l on the segment tree representation of the line segments. To determine all the line segments that contain l, we simply locate the smallest interval containing it. Since a segment tree for N line segments has a maximum of $2 \cdot N$ leaf nodes, this search visits at most $\lceil \log_2 N \rceil + 1$ nodes, and for each node visited, we traverse its associated list of line segments and report them as containing l. This process takes $O(\log_2 N + F_l)$ time, where F_l is the number of line segments that contain l. Since a segment tree is used, the solution uses $O(N \cdot \log_2 N)$ space.

The second problem is solved by performing a range query for range $[l : r]$ on the set of starting points of the line segments. This query is one for which a range tree that stores the starting points of the line segments is ideal. Recall from Section 2.5 that a range tree is a balanced binary tree where the data points are stored in sorted order in the leaf nodes that are linked in this order by use of a doubly linked list. Therefore both insertion and deletion are $O(\log_2 N)$ processes.

A range query consists of locating the node corresponding to the start of the range, say L, and the closest node to the end of the range, say R, and then reporting the line segments corresponding to the nodes that lie between them by traversing the linked list of nodes. This process takes $O(\log_2 N + F_{lr})$ time, where F_{lr} is the number of line segments with starting points in $[l : r)$. Since a balanced binary tree is used, it needs $O(N)$ space.

The combination of the point and range query solution uses $O(N \cdot \log_2 N)$ space and takes $O(N \cdot \log_2 N + F)$ time, where F is the number of rectangle intersections. At this point, let us see if we can improve on these bounds. Since the first pass also takes $O(N \cdot \log_2 N)$ time, the only room for improvement is in the space requirement, which is bounded from below by $O(N)$ as a result of using the range tree (i.e., a balanced binary search tree with double links between adjacent elements) for the range query.

Suppose that instead of using a segment tree, we use an additional range tree for the ending points (as well as a range tree for the starting points). We perform a range query for range $[l : r)$ on the set of ending points of the line segments. Unfortunately the results of the two range queries are not disjoint, so we will have to remove duplicates. The number of duplicate entries per range query can be as large as N, and we will have to sort them prior to removal. This means that the algorithm has a total worst-case execution time that can be as high as $O(N^2 \cdot \log_2 N)$.

Alternatively we could try to determine the set of rectangles that intersect each other by using just a segment tree. The problem with this approach is that upon insertion of a line segment, say S, in a segment tree, we cannot find all of the existing line segments in the tree that are totally contained in S, or partially overlap S, without examining every node in each subtree containing S. For example, consider the segment tree of Figure 3.3 without line segment A (for segments B, C, D, E, F, and G). Upon inserting line segment A in the node corresponding to interval [14:23), the only way to determine the existence of line segment F (corresponding to the interval [15:19)) that is totally contained in A is to descend to the bottom of the subtree rooted at [14:23).

The problem is not restricted to the situation of total containment; it also arises in the case of partial overlap. For example, consider the segment tree of Figure 3.3 without line segment B (for segments A, C, D, E, F, and G). Upon inserting line segment B in the node corresponding to interval [34:38), the only way to detect the partial overlap of B with line segments A and C in the interval [34:36) is to descend to the bottom of the subtree rooted at [34:38). Checking for total containment or partial overlap in this way takes $O(N)$ time for each line segment or $O(N^2)$ for all the line segments. Thus we must find a more satisfactory solution since we wish to perform this task in $O(N \cdot \log_2 N + F)$ time. This is achieved by using the interval tree, the subject of the next section.

Exercises

3.1. Under what restriction is a segment tree equivalent to a unit-segment tree?

3.2. Is it true that whenever two line segments overlap, at least one node in the segment tree will have more than one line segment associated with it?

3.3. The implementation of the segment tree described in the text makes use of an auxiliary table that contains an entry for each line segment. This entry points to a list of pointers, each of which points to a list entry for the line segment in a node of the segment tree whose intervals are covered by the line segment. Why is this a better solution than merely pointing to the node whose intervals are covered by the line segment?

3.4. Why can't you formulate the sweep pass of the rectangle intersection problem as locating all line segments that start within a given line segment and those that end within the line segment? In this case, there is no need for the segment tree. Instead use two range trees: one for the starting points and one for the ending points.

3.5. Given a point P on a line, devise an algorithm to find all intervals that contain P. This is known as a *stabbing query*. Assume that the intervals are represented using a segment tree. What is the order of the execution time of the algorithm when there are N intervals?

3.6. Suppose that we are interested only in the number of intervals that contain P. This is known as the *stabbing counting* query. Assume that the intervals are represented using a segment tree. Given N intervals, how fast can you determine a solution to this query, and how much space does it require?

3.7. Write an algorithm to insert a line segment in a segment tree.

3.8. Write an algorithm to delete a line segment from a segment tree.

3.9. Write an algorithm to determine if a line segment intersects an existing line segment in a segment tree.

3.10. How would you use a segment tree to determine all the one-dimensional intervals totally contained within a given one-dimensional interval? Given N intervals, and F contained intervals, does your algorithm run in $O(\log_2 N + F)$ time? If not, explain why, and give an alternative solution.

3.11. How would you use a segment tree to determine all the one-dimensional intervals that contain a given one-dimensional interval? Given N intervals, and F containing intervals, does your algorithm run in $O(\log_2 N + F)$ time? If not, explain why.

3.12. Write an algorithm to determine all the intersecting rectangles using a segment tree.

3.2.2 Interval Trees

The problem discussed at the end of Section 3.2.1 with using the segment tree as the basis of the solution to the rectangle intersection problem can be overcome, in part, by making the following modifications. Link each marked node (i.e., a node whose corresponding interval overlaps at least one line segment), say P, to some of the nodes in P's subtrees that are marked. This could be implemented by an auxiliary binary tree with elements that are the marked nodes. Since each line segment can be associated with more than one node in the segment tree, the number of intersections that can be detected is bounded by $2 \cdot N^2 \cdot \log_2 N$ (see Exercise 3.13), while the number of different intersections is bounded by N^2. Removing duplicates will require sorting, and even use of the bin method [Weid78], which is linear, still leaves us with an $O(N^2 \cdot \log_2 N)$ process.

However, duplicate entries can be avoided by redefining the segment tree so that a line segment is associated only with one node: the nearest common ancestor[2] of all the intervals contained in the line segment (e.g., the node corresponding to the interval [3:38) for line segments A and C in Figure 3.3). The absence of duplicate entries also means that the space requirements can be reduced to $O(N)$.

The above modifications serve as the foundation for the development of the *interval tree* of Edelsbrunner [Edel80a, Edel83a, Edel83b] and the *tile tree* of McCreight [McCr80]. The difference between them is that the tile tree is based on a regular decomposition, while the interval tree is not. In the rest of this section, we discuss only the interval tree.

The interval tree is designed specifically to detect all intervals that intersect a given interval. It is motivated by the dual goals of reducing the space requirement to $O(N)$ and maintaining an execution time of $O(N \cdot \log_2 N + F)$. The interval tree solution also makes use of the decomposition of the search into two disjoint tasks:

1. Determining all line segments that overlap the starting point of the query line segment.
2. Determining all line segments with starting points that lie within the query line segment.

Once again, assume that we are given a set of N line segments such that line segment s_i corresponds to the interval $[l_i : r_i)$; l_i and r_i are its left and right endpoints, respectively. The endpoints of the N line segments are sorted (with duplicates removed) to obtain the sequence $y_0, y_1, \cdots, y_m$ ($m < 2 \cdot N$ and $2^{h-1} \le m < 2^h$). The interval tree is a three-level structure in which the first (and principal) level is termed the *primary* structure, the second level is termed the *secondary* structure, and the third level is termed the *tertiary* structure. Figure 3.4 illustrates the discussion. It is the interval tree for the set of line segments corresponding to the vertical boundaries of the rectangles in Figure 3.1.

The primary structure is a complete binary tree with $m + 1$ external (i.e., leaf) nodes such that when the tree is flattened and the nonleaf nodes are removed, external node i corresponds to y_i. In Figure 3.4, the primary structure is denoted by solid lines. In the example, although there are seven line segments, the primary structure contains only 13 external nodes as there are only 13 different endpoints. Each leaf node is labeled with its corresponding endpoint (i.e., y_i for leaf node i ($0 \le i < 2 \cdot N$). Each nonleaf node is assigned an arbitrary value, stored in the field VAL, that lies between the maximum value in its left subtree and the minimum value in its right subtree (usually their average). For example, the root node in Figure 3.4 is labeled 22.

---

[2] The principle of associating key information with the nearest common ancestor is similar to Chazelle and Guibas's *fractional cascading* [Chaz86a, Chaz86b]. It is also used as the basis of an efficient solution of the point location problem by Edelsbrunner, Guibas, and Stolfi [Edel86a] (see Section 4.3.2).

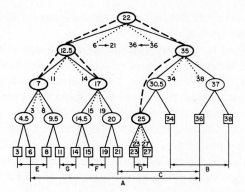

Figure 3.4   The interval tree for the set of line segments corresponding to the vertical boundaries of the rectangles in Figure 3.1. The primary structure is shown by solid lines. The secondary structure is shown by dotted lines. The tertiary structure is shown by broken lines with the active nodes circled with thick lines. The interrelationships between the endpoints of the line segments are also shown.

Given a line segment corresponding to the interval $[l : r)$, we say that its *nearest common ancestor* in the interval tree is the nonleaf node containing l and r in its left and right subtrees, respectively. For example, in Figure 3.4, node 22 is the nearest common ancestor of line segment A, which corresponds to the interval [6,36].

Each nonleaf node in the primary structure, say v, serves as the key to a pair of secondary structures LS and RS that represent the sets of left and right endpoints, respectively, of the line segments for which v is the nearest common ancestor (i.e., they contain v's value). Elements of the sets LS and RS are linked in ascending and descending order, respectively. In Figure 3.4, the secondary structure is denoted by dotted lines emanating from each nonleaf node with a nonempty secondary structure. The sets LS and RS are distinguished by dotted lines emanating from the nonleaf node to its left and right sides, respectively.

When the sets LS and RS contain more than one entry, we show them linked in increasing and decreasing order, respectively (e.g., LS of the root node shows 6 pointing to 21 since the corresponding intervals are [6:36) and [21:36)). Each starting (ending) point appears in LS (RS) as many times as there are line segments that have it as a starting (ending) point. For example, 36 appears twice in RS of the root node in Figure 3.4 as it is the ending point of line segments A and C. To support rapid insertion and deletion, the sets LS and RS are implemented as balanced binary trees (as well as doubly linked lists).

Each nonleaf node in the primary structure has eight pointers: two to its left and right subtrees in the primary structure (LP and RP), two to the roots of LS and RS in the secondary structure, one to the minimum value in LS, one to the maximum value in RS, and two (LT and RT) to its left and right subtrees in the tertiary structure. The LT and RT pointers are discussed below.

A nonleaf node in the primary structure is marked *active* if its corresponding secondary structure is nonempty or both of its sons have active descendants; otherwise it is marked *inactive*. The active nodes of the primary structure form the tertiary structure, which is a binary tree. It is rooted at the root of the primary structure and is linked via the LT and RT fields of the nonleaf nodes of the primary structure. If node v of the primary structure is inactive, then LT(v) and RT(v) are Ω (i.e., pointers to NIL). If v is active, then LT(v) points to the closest active node in the left subtree of v (i.e., in LP(v)), and RT(v) points to the closest active node in the right subtree of v (i.e., in RP(v)). If there are no closest active nodes in the left and right subtrees of v, then LT(v) and RT(v), respectively, are Ω.

In Figure 3.4, the tertiary structure is denoted by broken lines linking all of the active nodes (e.g., nodes 22, 12.5, 7, 17, 35, and 25), also enclosed by thick ellipses. The tertiary structure is useful in collecting the line segments that intersect a given line segment. It enables us to avoid examining primary nodes with no line segments. Note that more than half of the elements of the tertiary structure (i.e., active nodes) have nonempty secondary structures (see Exercise 3.15).

Inserting the line segment [$l : r$) in the interval tree is very simple. We start at the root and locate the first node v such that $l <$ VAL(v) $< r$. In this case, we insert l into LS(v) and r into RS(v). Both of these processes can be achieved in $O(\log_2 N)$ time. Updating the tertiary structure requires us to traverse it in parallel with the primary structure and takes $O(\log_2 N)$ time. Deletion of a line segment is performed in a similar manner and with the same complexity.

Reporting the rectangle intersections in an interval tree is straightforward, although there are a number of cases to consider. Again this task is performed while inserting a vertical line segment, say s corresponding to the interval [$l : r$). During this process we search for and report the line segments that overlap s. Assume that the interval tree is rooted at T_1. The search has three stages:

1. Start at T_1 and find the first node v such that $l <$ VAL(v) $< r$.
2. Start at v and locate l in the left subtree of v.
3. Start at v and locate r in the right subtree of v.

This search involves the secondary structures of the nodes in the primary structure. The tertiary structure reduces the number of nodes in the primary structure with empty secondary structures that must be examined. Note that all of the overlapping line segments will be reported, and each will be reported only once as it is associated with the secondary structure of just one node in the primary structure.

The following contains the main ideas of the three stages. Figure 3.5 aids the visualization of the symbols used in the explanation for [$l : r$). All secondary and tertiary structures that are visited are marked with dotted and broken lines, respectively.

Let us start with stage 1. $\{T_i\}$ denotes the set of nodes encountered during the search for v. I use the insertion of line segment [6:20) into the interval tree of

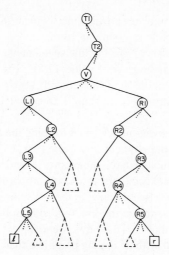

Figure 3.5   Example of an interval tree search for the inter-
val [l:r]. All secondary structures that are visited are
marked with dotted lines. All tertiary structures that are
visited are marked with broken lines.

Figure 3.4 as the example. The secondary structures associated with each T_i must be checked for a possible overlap with s. This is quite simple. Either $l < r < \text{VAL}(T_i)$ or $\text{VAL}(T_i) < l < r$.

If $r < \text{VAL}(T_i)$, then we need only report the line segments in the secondary structure of T_i with starting points less than r (e.g., line segment A upon examining the non-leaf node with value 22). To achieve this, we visit $\text{LS}(T_i)$ in ascending order until we encounter a line segment with a starting point exceeding r. We then search the left subtree of T_i (i.e., $\text{LP}(T_i)$).

Similarly if $\text{VAL}(T_i) < l$, then we need only report the elements of the secondary structure of T_i with ending points greater than l. To do this, we visit $\text{RS}(T_i)$ in descending order until encountering a line segment with an ending point less than l. The search is then continued in the right subtree of T_i (i.e., $\text{RP}(T_i)$).

Both cases are executed in time proportional to the number of intersections reported. Once node v has been located, we report all elements of its secondary structure as intersecting s. In the example, we would report line segment G, since v is the nonleaf node with value 12.5.

Now let us understand stages 2 and 3. Since they are very similar, we look at just stage 2 and use the insertion of line segment [6:34) into the interval tree of Figure 3.4 as the example. In this case, v is the root of the tree (the nonleaf node with value 22). Let $\{L_i\}$ denote the set of nodes encountered during the search for l in this stage. Recall that $l < \text{VAL}(v)$. Either $l < \text{VAL}(L_i)$ or $\text{VAL}(L_i) < l$.

If $l <$ VAL(L$_i$), then s intersects every line segment in the secondary structure of L$_i$. s also intersects all the line segments in the secondary structures in the right sub-tree of L$_i$. The first set consists of just the line segments in RS(L$_i$) (e.g., line segment G upon examining the nonleaf node with value 12.5). The second set is obtained by visiting all the active nodes in the right subtree of L$_i$, RP(L$_i$) (e.g., line segment F during the processing of the nonleaf node with value 12.5 since F is associated with the active nonleaf node with value 17).

To avoid visiting irrelevant nodes when forming the second set, we make use of the tertiary structure using the pointers LT(L$_i$) and RT(L$_i$). Since more than half of the elements of the tertiary structure have nonempty secondary structures (see Exercise 3.15), the time necessary to execute this process is proportional to the number of inter-sections reported. The search is continued in the left subtree of L$_i$, i.e., LP(L$_i$).

If VAL(L$_i$) $< l$, then we report the line segments in the secondary structure of L$_i$ with ending points greater than l. To do this, we visit RS(L$_i$) in descending order until encountering a line segment with an ending point less than l. This process is executed in time proportional to the number of intersections reported. The search is continued in the right subtree of L$_i$, i.e., RP(L$_i$).

Solving the rectangle intersection problem using an interval tree uses $O(N)$ space and takes $O(N \cdot \log_2 N + F)$ time, where F is the number of rectangle intersec-tions.[3] The space requirements are obtained by observing that for N line segments we need at most $2 \cdot N$ leaf nodes in the primary structure; the same is true for the secon-dary structures. The tertiary structure is constructed from nodes in the primary struc-ture, and thus it requires no additional space except for the pointer fields. Making use of the fact that the interval tree is a complete binary tree, the number of nonleaf nodes in the primary and secondary structures is bounded by $2 \cdot N - 1$.

The execution time requirements are obtained by noting that searching the pri-mary structure for the starting and ending points of a line segment takes $O(\log_2 N)$ time. The number of nodes visited in the secondary structure is of the same order as the number of rectangle intersections that are found. Since at least half of the active nodes have nonempty secondary structures, the number of nodes visited in the tertiary structure is no more than twice the number of nodes visited in the secondary structure. Constructing the interval tree takes $O(N \cdot \log_2 N)$ time since the endpoints of the line segments forming the sides of the rectangles must be sorted.

Exercises

3.13. Suppose that you modify the definition of the segment tree so that each marked node, say P, is linked (i.e., a node with a corresponding interval that overlaps at least one line seg-ment) to the nodes in P's subtrees that are marked. Show that the number of intersections that can be detected is bounded by $2 \cdot N^2 \cdot \log_2 N$.

---

[3] For the tile tree, the execution time is $O(N \cdot \log_2(\max(N, K)) + F)$, where the horizontal boundaries of the rectangles are integers between 0 and $K - 1$. The execution time becomes $O(N \cdot \log_2 N + F)$ if the $2 \cdot N$ y coordinate values are first sorted and then mapped into the integers from 0 to $2 \cdot N - 1$.

3.14. Can you implement the segment tree as a complete binary tree with $m + 1$ external nodes as was done for the interval tree—that is, merge the leaf nodes corresponding to the unused intervals? If so, the segment tree would have the same node configuration as the primary structure of the interval tree. If yes, show how the nodes would be marked.

3.15. Why do more than half the elements of the tertiary structure (i.e., active nodes) of the interval tree have nonempty secondary structures?

3.16. Assume that a set of intervals is stored using an interval tree. Given a point P on a line, devise an algorithm to find all intervals that contain P (i.e., a stabbing query). What is the order of the execution time of the algorithm when there are N intervals?

3.17. Can you use the interval tree to determine the number of intervals containing P (i.e., a stabbing counting query) without storing the identities of the intervals? In other words, just store the number of intervals with each nonleaf node.

3.18. Prove that solution of the rectangle intersection problem based on its decomposition into a point and region query does not report an intersection more than once.

3.19. Write an algorithm to insert a line segment in an interval tree. Remember that you must also update the secondary and tertiary structures.

3.20. Write an algorithm to delete a line segment from an interval tree. Remember that you must also update the secondary and tertiary structures.

3.21. How would you use an interval tree to determine all the one-dimensional intervals that are totally contained within a given one-dimensional interval? Given N intervals and F contained intervals, does your algorithm run in $O(\log_2 N + F)$ time? If not, explain why.

3.22. How would you use an interval tree to determine all the one-dimensional intervals that contain a given one-dimensional interval? Given N intervals, and F containing intervals, does your algorithm run in $O(\log_2 N + F)$ time? If not, explain why.

3.23. Write an algorithm to determine all the intersecting rectangles using an interval tree. Remember that during this process you must also simultaneously traverse the tertiary structure.

3.2.3 Priority Search Trees

Using an interval tree, as described in Section 3.2.2, yields an optimal worst-case space and time solution to the rectangle intersection problem. The interval tree solution requires that we know in advance the endpoints of all of the vertical intervals as they must be sorted and stored in a complete binary tree. Thus given N rectangles, the storage requirement is always $O(N)$. The solution can be slightly improved by adapting the priority search tree of McCreight [McCr85] to keep track of the active vertical intervals.

In this case, the storage requirements for the sweep pass depend only on the maximum number of vertical intervals that can be active at any one time, say M. Moreover, there is no need to know their endpoints in advance and thus there is no need to sort them. This also has an effect on the execution time of the algorithm since the data structure used to keep track of the endpoints of the vertical intervals is the determinative factor in the amount of time necessary to do a search. Therefore when using the priority search tree, the sweep pass of the solution to the rectangle intersection problem can be performed in $O(N \cdot \log_2 M + F)$ time rather than in

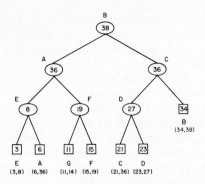

*Figure 3.6   The priority search tree for the set of line seg-
ments corresponding to the vertical boundaries [y$_B$, y$_T$) of
the rectangles in Figure 3.1. Each vertical boundary [y$_B$, y$_T$)
is treated as a point (x, y) in a two-dimensional space. The
leaf nodes contain the y$_B$ values, while the internal nodes
contain the maximum y$_T$ values.*

$O(N \cdot \log_2 N + F)$ time. However, sorting the endpoints of the horizontal intervals, which is the first pass of the plane sweep, still takes $O(N \cdot \log_2 N)$ time.

The priority search tree has been described in Section 2.5. It keeps track of points in a two-dimensional space. Briefly, it is designed for solving queries involving semi-infinite ranges in such a space. A typical query has a range of the form $([L_x : R_x], [L_y : \infty])$. A priority search tree is built in the following manner. Assume that no two data points have the same x coordinate value (see Exercise 2.63). Sort all the points along the x coordinate and store them in the leaf nodes of a balanced binary search tree, say T. We proceed from the root node toward the leaf nodes. With each nonleaf node of T, say I, associate the point in the subtree rooted at I with the maximum value for its y coordinate that has not already been stored at a shallower depth in the tree.

Figure 3.6 is an example of the priority search tree. It is based on treating the vertical boundaries $[y_B, y_T)$ of the rectangles in Figure 3.1 as points (x, y). For N points, the priority search tree uses $O(N)$ storage (see Exercise 2.61). The priority search tree is good for performing a semi-infinite range query $([L_x : R_x], [L_y : \infty])$. For N points, this process takes $O(\log_2 N + F)$ time, where F is the number of points found (see Exercise 2.62).

There are two keys to understanding the use of the priority search tree in solving the rectangle intersection problem. Assume, again, that all intervals are semiclosed (i.e., they are closed on their left ends and open on their right ends). First, each one-dimensional interval, say $[a : b)$, is represented by the point (a, b) in two-dimensional space. This two-dimensional space is represented by a priority search tree.

Second, we observe that the one-dimensional interval $[a : b)$ intersects the interval $[c : d)$ if and only if $a < d$ and $c < b$ (see Exercise 3.24). An equivalent observation is that the point (c,d) lies in the range $([-\infty : b),(a : \infty])$. This equivalence means that to find all one-dimensional intervals that intersect the interval $[a : b)$, we need only perform the semi-infinite range query $([-\infty : b),(a : \infty])$ in the priority search tree. If the priority search tree contains M one-dimensional intervals, then this operation takes $O(\log_2 M + F)$ time, where F is the number of intersecting intervals found.

For the space and time bounds to be comparable with the interval tree, we must also show that a one-dimensional interval can be inserted and deleted from a priority search tree in $O(\log_2 M)$ time. This is achieved by implementing the priority search tree as a 'red-black' balanced binary tree [Guib78]. The red-black balanced binary tree has the property that, for M items, insertions and deletions take $O(\log_2 M)$ time with $O(1)$ rotations [Tarj83]. McCreight [McCr85] shows that the priority search tree adaptation of the red-black balanced binary tree can be maintained at a cost of $O(\log_2 M)$ per rotation (see Exercise 3.29). The use of a red-black balanced binary tree does not affect the $O(M)$ storage requirements of the priority search tree. Hence, the desired time and space bounds are achieved.

When the priority search tree is implemented as a red-black balanced binary tree, its node structure differs from the way it was defined in Section 2.5. In particular, the nonleaf nodes now also contain intervals. The interval associated with a nonleaf node, say I, is the one whose left endpoint, say L, is the median value of the left endpoints of the intervals in I's subtrees. All intervals in I's left subtree have left endpoints less than L while the intervals in I's right subtree have left endpoints greater than L.

Comparing the interval and priority search tree solutions to the rectangle intersection problem, we find that the priority search tree is considerably simpler from a conceptual standpoint than the interval tree. The execution time requirements of the priority search tree are lower when the sort pass is ignored. Also the priority search tree enables a more dynamic solution than the interval tree because, for the priority search tree, only the endpoints of the horizontal intervals need to be known in advance. On the other hand, for the interval tree, the endpoints of both the horizontal and vertical intervals must be known in advance.

Exercises

3.24. Prove that the one-dimensional interval $[a : b)$ intersects the interval $[c : d)$ if and only if $a < d$ and $c < b$.

3.25. The adaptation of the priority search tree as a red-black balanced binary tree differs from the version of the priority search tree described in Section 2.5 in that the data items appear in both leaf and nonleaf nodes. Show that this does not cause any problems in executing the semi-infinite range query.

3.26. Write an algorithm to insert the interval $[a : b)$ in a priority search tree.

3.27. Write an algorithm to delete the interval $[a : b)$ from a priority search tree.

3.28. Prove that a point can be deleted from a red-black balanced binary tree of M items in $O(\log_2 M)$ time with $O(1)$ rotations.

3.29. Prove that the priority search tree adaptation of the red-black balanced binary tree can be maintained at a cost of $O(\log_2 M)$ per rotation.

3.30. Assume that a set of intervals is stored using a priority search tree. Given a point P on a line, devise an algorithm to find all intervals that contain P (i.e., a stabbing query). What is the order of the execution time of the algorithm when there are M intervals?

3.31. Write an algorithm that uses a priority search tree to find all one-dimensional intervals that partially overlap or are contained in a given one-dimensional interval.

3.32. Write an algorithm that uses a priority search tree to find all one-dimensional intervals [x : y] that completely contain the one-dimensional interval [a : b].

3.33. In Section 2.5, an inverse priority search tree was defined to be a priority search tree in which with each nonleaf node of T, say I, we associate the point in the subtree rooted at I with the minimum (instead of the maximum!) value for its y coordinate that has not already been stored at a shallower depth in the tree. Write an algorithm that uses an inverse priority search tree to find all one-dimensional intervals [x : y] completely contained in the one-dimensional interval [a : b].

3.34. Repeat Exercise 3.33 by using a priority search tree instead of an inverse priority search tree.

3.35. Write an algorithm to determine all the intersecting rectangles using a priority search tree.

3.2.4 Alternative Solutions and Related Problems [4]

The time requirements of the interval and priority search tree solutions of the rectangle intersection problem can be reduced further if we can make use of knowledge about the distribution of the data. Such an approach is reported by Bentley, Haken, and Hon [Bent80c]. They performed an empirical study on the distribution of components in VLSI design and determined that the rectangles are uniformly distributed. This distribution was used to organize the segments for the second pass so that the entire plane-sweep algorithm has a linear expected-time behavior.

Bentley et al. obtained expected linear performance in the following manner. The sorting operation of the first pass takes expected linear time by use of the bin method [Weid78]. For the second pass, instead of using an interval tree to store the vertical segments that intersect the sweep line, bins of equal width are used. They are accessed by an array of pointers. Each bin contains a linked list of all the vertical segments that overlap it. The observed data were used to choose a bin width equal to the average width of a rectangle. This implies that each vertical segment is contained in two bins on the average.

The linear expected-time depends on an assumption that the expected number of rectangles per bin is a constant (i.e., independent of the number of rectangles N). This assumption means that the total number of bins is some multiple of $\sqrt{N}$, which is true as long as the data are not highly clustered (e.g., under a uniform distribution).[5] Under these hypotheses, initialization of the bins is an $O(\sqrt{N})$ process. Inserting and deleting

---

[4] The exercises in this section are quite difficult.

[5] When the data are not uniformly distributed, the hierarchical methods described in Section 3.5 may prove more attractive since the bins are of different sizes. Such methods make use of a tree traversal in the order of a space-filling curve (see Section 1.3) instead of sweeping a line across one dimension.

a vertical segment merely involves traversing a linked list of constant expected size. Checking a vertical segment, say S, for intersection with existing vertical segments is achieved by visiting the bins containing S and comparing S with the vertical segments stored within them. This is also achieved in constant time.

A related problem is finding the containment set (also known as the inclusion or enclosure set) of a collection of rectangles. The *containment set* is the set of all pairs of rectangles A and B such that A contains B. Variants of the segment tree are used by Vaishnavi and Wood [Vais80] to solve this problem in $O(N \cdot \log_2^2 N + F)$ time and $O(N \cdot \log_2^2 N)$ space (see Exercise 3.43). The space requirement is reduced to $O(N)$ by Lee and Preparata [Lee82a] who map each rectangle into a point in four-dimensional space and solve a point dominance problem.

As described in Section 3.1, the rectangle intersection problem is closely related to the following problems:

1. Determining all rectangles contained in a given rectangle.
2. Determining all the rectangles that enclose a given rectangle.
3. Determining all rectangles that partially overlap or are contained in a given rectangle (a window query).

The plane-sweep approach is not appropriate for these problems since, regardless of the data structures employed (e.g., segment, interval, or priority search trees), sorting is a prerequisite, and thus any algorithm requires at least $O(N \cdot \log_2 N)$ time for N rectangles. In contrast, the naive solution of intersecting each rectangle with the query rectangle is an $O(N)$ process.

The problems described can be solved by segment trees and interval trees without making use of a plane sweep (e.g., Exercises 3.50 and 3.59) [Over88a]. The key is to adapt these representations to store two-dimensional intervals (see Exercises 3.44 and 3.55) in a manner similar to that in which the two-dimensional range tree was developed from the one-dimensional range tree (see Section 2.5) [Edel81b, Edel82].

For example, for N rectangles, the execution time of the solution to the window query is $O(\log_2^2 N + F)$, where F is the number of rectangles that satisfy the query. The difference is in their storage requirements; the segment tree solution uses $O(N \cdot \log_2^2 N)$ space, while the interval tree solution uses $O(N \cdot \log_2 N)$ space. For both of these structures, judicious use of doubly linked lists ensures that rectangles can be inserted and deleted in $O(\log_2^2 N)$ time (see Exercises 3.45 and 3.56). Of course, these structures must still be built, which takes $O(N \cdot \log_2^2 N)$ time in both cases (see Exercises 3.46 and 3.57). It is not clear how to adapt the priority search tree to store two-dimensional intervals.

The plane-sweep paradigm for solving the geometric problems discussed earlier in this section (e.g., the rectangle intersection problem) assumes that the set of rectangles is processed once. It can be shown that for many of these problems, plane-sweep methods yield a theoretically optimal solution. A disadvantage is that such solutions assume a static environment.

In contrast, in a dynamic environment where update operations occur frequently (i.e., rectangles are added and deleted), the plane-sweep approach is less attractive. Plane-sweep methods require that the endpoints of all rectangles are known a priori, and that the endpoints are sorted prior to the sweep pass. This is not a major problem; as it is easy to maintain a dynamically changing set of points in sorted order. A more serious problem is that in a dynamic environment, the sweep pass of a plane-sweep algorithm will usually have to be reexecuted because there is no data structure corresponding to it. Methods based on persistent search trees [Sarn86, Dris89] may be useful in avoiding the reexecution of the sweep pass.

Exercises

3.36. The rectangle intersection problem is a special case of the problem of determining if any two of a set of N lines in the plane intersect. Give an $O(N \cdot \log_2 N)$ algorithm to solve the line intersection problem.

3.37. Suppose that you are given a set of N vertical line segments in the plane, say V, and a horizontal line segment, say H. Representing V as a segment tree, give an $O(\log_2^2 N + F)$ algorithm to find all elements of V that intersect H that uses $O(N \cdot \log_2 N)$ space. F is the number of intersecting elements.

3.38. Suppose that you are given a set of N arbitrary line segments in the plane, say L, and a rectilinear rectangle, say R. Using range trees and segment trees, give an $O(\log_2^2 N + F)$ algorithm to find all elements of L that intersect R that uses $O(N \cdot \log_2 N)$ space. F is the number of intersecting elements.

3.39. Suppose that instead of reporting all intersecting rectangles, you only want to report if there is at least one pair of intersecting rectangles (including the case that a rectangle is totally enclosed in another rectangle). Once again, a plane-sweep method can be used with a scan from left to right. However, Bentley and Ottman [Bent81] suggest the use of a balanced binary search tree instead of a segment tree to organize the sorted list of bottom and top boundaries of the currently active rectangles during the sweep pass. Show how this technique can be used to yield a simpler $O(N \cdot \log_2 N)$ algorithm to detect the existence of an intersection. Assume that the boundaries are stored in both leaf and non-leaf nodes in the tree.

3.40. Why can't you use the balanced binary search tree method of Exercise 3.39 instead of the segment tree to report all intersections between rectangles? Give an example in which it fails to detect an intersection.

3.41. Given a collection of N rectangles with F intersections between their vertical and horizontal boundaries, how would you use the balanced binary search tree method of Exercise 3.39 to find all the intersections in $O(N \cdot \log_2 N + F)$ time and $O(N)$ space? In this problem, if rectangle A is totally contained in rectangle B, then A and B do not intersect.

3.42. Assume that the result of Exercise 3.41 is used to detect all rectangles that have intersections between their horizontal and vertical boundaries. Add another pass using a segment tree to report all pairs of rectangles in which one rectangle is totally enclosed by the other in $O(N \cdot \log_2 N + F)$ time. F is the number of pairs of rectangles that satisfy the query.

3.43. Using a segment tree, devise a plane-sweep algorithm to report all rectangles contained in other rectangles. In other words, for each rectangle in a collection of rectangles, report all the rectangles contained in it.

3.44. The segment tree can be adapted to represent rectilinear rectangles in a manner analogous to the way in which the one-dimensional range tree was extended to solve two-dimensional range queries in Section 2.5. In particular, project the rectangles on the x axis and store these intervals in a segment tree, say T. Let I be a nonleaf node in T and let R_I denote the rectangles whose horizontal sides are associated with I. For each I, build a segment tree for the projections of R_I on the y axis. Show that this structure uses $O(N \cdot \log_2^2 N)$ storage for N rectangles.

3.45. Assuming N rectangles, prove that a rectangle can be inserted and deleted in $O(\log_2^2 N)$ time in the two-dimensional extension of the segment tree described in Exercise 3.44.

3.46. Prove that the construction of the two-dimensional extension of the segment tree described in Exercise 3.44 takes $O(N \cdot \log_2^2 N)$ time for N rectangles.

3.47. Using the two-dimensional extension of the segment tree described in Exercise 3.44, show that the two-dimensional stabbing query (i.e., find all rectilinear rectangles that contain a given point P) can be determined in $O(\log_2^2 N + F)$ time. N is the total number of rectangles, and F is the number of rectangles that contain P.

3.48. How would you generalize the solution to the two-dimensional stabbing query to k dimensions? How much storage is required, and what is the order of the execution time of the query?

3.49. Can you modify the two-dimensional extension of the segment tree so that the execution time of the two-dimensional stabbing query is reduced to $O(\log_2 N + F)$ with the same space and preprocessing costs? Assume that there are N rectangles, and that F is the number of rectangles that satisfy the query.

3.50. Suppose that you are given a set of N rectangles, say V, and a rectangle, say R. All rectangles are rectilinear. Using range trees and the two-dimensional extension of the segment tree described in Exercise 3.44, give an $O(\log_2^2 N + F)$ algorithm to find all elements of V that intersect R that uses $O(N \cdot \log_2^2 N)$ space. F is the number of intersecting elements.

3.51. How do you avoid reporting some intersections more than once in the solution to Exercise 3.50?

3.52. Suppose that you are given a set of N rectangles, say V, and a rectangle, say R. All rectangles are rectilinear. Using range trees and the two-dimensional extension of the segment tree described in Exercise 3.44, give an algorithm to find all elements of V contained in R.

3.53. Suppose that you are given a set of N rectangles, say V, and a rectangle, say R. All rectangles are rectilinear. Using range trees and the two-dimensional extension of the segment tree described in Exercise 3.44, give an algorithm to find all elements of V that enclose R.

3.54. Repeat Exercise 3.43 with an interval tree.

3.55. How would you use the interval tree to represent N rectilinear rectangles in a manner similar to the adaptation of the segment tree described in Exercise 3.44? Show that the storage requirement is reduced from $O(N \cdot \log_2^2 N)$ to $O(N \cdot \log_2 N)$.

3.56. Assuming N rectangles, prove that a rectangle can be inserted and deleted in $O(\log_2^2 N)$ time in the two-dimensional extension of the interval tree described in Exercise 3.55.

3.57. Prove that the construction of the two-dimensional extension of the interval tree described in Exercise 3.55 takes $O(N \cdot \log_2^2 N)$ time for N rectangles.

3.58. Using the two-dimensional extension of the interval tree described in Exercise 3.55, show that all rectilinear rectangles that contain a given point P can be determined in $O(\log_2 N + F)$ time. N is the total number of rectangles and F is the number of rectangles that contain P.

3.59. Suppose that you are given a set of N rectangles, say V, and a rectangle, say R. All rectangles are rectilinear. Using range trees and the two-dimensional extension of the interval tree described in Exercise 3.55, show that all elements of V that intersect R can be determined in $O(\log_2^2 N + F)$ time. F is the number of intersecting elements.

3.60. Repeat Exercise 3.52 with an interval tree.

3.61. Repeat Exercise 3.53 with an interval tree.

3.62. Repeat Exercise 3.43 with a priority search tree.

3.63. How would you adapt the priority search tree to store two-dimensional intervals? If this is not possible, explain why. If you are successful, use this data structure instead of the two-dimensional extension of the segment tree to solve Exercises 3.50, 3.52, and 3.53.

3.64. Consider a collection of N right triangles so that two of the sides are always parallel to the x and y axes and the third side has a negative slope. Devise an algorithm to report all the intersections between triangles. Can you get its execution time and space requirements to be $O(N \cdot \log_2 N)$ and $O(N)$, respectively?

3.65. Repeat Exercise 3.64 by permitting the third side of the right triangle to have an arbitrary slope.

3.66. Consider a collection of N arbitrary triangles. Devise an algorithm to report all the intersections between triangles. Can you get its execution time and space requirements to be $O(N \cdot \log_2 N)$ and $O(N)$, respectively?

3.3 PLANE-SWEEP METHODS AND THE MEASURE PROBLEM[6]

Data structures such as the segment tree can be used with the plane-sweep paradigm to solve a number of problems other than rectangle intersection. In fact, the segment tree was originally developed by Bentley [Bent77a] as part of a plane-sweep solution to compute the area (also termed a *measure* problem [Klee77]) of a collection of rectangles where overlapping regions are only counted once. It can also be used to compute the perimeter, although it is not discussed here (but see Exercise 3.72).

The central idea behind the use of the segment tree to compute the area is to keep track of the total length of the parts of the vertical scan line, say L_i at halting point X_i, that overlap the vertical boundaries of rectangles that are active just to the left of X_i. This quantity is adjusted at each halting point. The total area is obtained by accumulating the product of this quantity with the difference between the current halting point and the next halting point—that is, $L_i \cdot (X_i - X_{i-1})$.

To facilitate the computation of the area, each node P in the segment tree contains three fields, called INT, LEN, and COUNT. INT(P) is the interval consisting of the union of the intervals corresponding to the subtrees of P. COUNT(P) is the number of active rectangles whose vertical boundaries contain INT(P). LEN(P) contains the length of the overlap of the marked[7] components of P's corresponding interval with the vertical scan line.

---

[6] This section contains some difficult material. It may be skipped on an initial reading.

[7] Recall from Section 3.2.1 that given a line segment 2s, a node P in the segment tree is *marked* with s if P's interval is totally contained in s.

As an example of the computation of the area, consider the collection of rectangles in Figure 3.1. When the scan line passes over $x = 7$, the lengths of its overlaps with the nodes corresponding to intervals [6:8], [3:8], [8:14], [3:14], [14:23], [3:23], [23:34], [34:36], [34:38], [23:38], [23:∞), and [3:∞) (i.e., the values of their LEN fields) are 2, 5, 6, 11, 9, 20, 11, 2, 2, 13, 13, and 33, respectively.

In our example, when $x = 7$, the nodes corresponding to the intervals [6:8], [3:8], [8:14], [14:23], [23:34], and [34:36] are marked once (i.e., their COUNT fields have a value of 1). It turns out that in this example no node is ever marked more than once (see Exercise 3.69). In other words, no node's COUNT field value ever exceeds 1. The values of the LEN and COUNT fields are adjusted whenever a vertical boundary of a rectangle is inserted into, or deleted from, the segment tree—that is, at each halting point. For N rectangles, this adjustment process is performed $O(\log_2 N)$ times per halting point for a total of $O(N \cdot \log_2 N)$ for the area of the entire collection. The total space requirement is $O(N)$ (see Exercise 3.70).

The unit-segment tree is analogous to a region quadtree in one dimension. This analogy is exploited by van Leeuwen and Wood [vanL81] in solving measure problems in higher-dimensional spaces (i.e., $d > 2$). A typical problem is the computation of the volume occupied by the union of a collection of three-dimensional rectangular parallelepipeds. In this case, they use a plane-sweep solution that sorts the boundaries of the parallelepipeds along one direction (say z) and then sweeps a plane (instead of a line) parallel to the x–y plane across it. At any instant of time, the plane consists of a collection of cross-sections (i.e., two-dimensional rectangles). This collection is represented using a region quadtree, which is the two-dimensional analog of the segment tree.

The region quadtree in this case is a complete quadtree. It is built as follows. Note that there is a maximum of $2 \cdot N$ boundaries in all directions. First, sort the x and y boundaries of the parallelepipeds (removing duplicates) obtaining $x_0, x_1, \cdots, x_p$ ($p < 2 \cdot N$), $y_0, y_1, \cdots, y_q$ ($q < 2 \cdot N$), and $2^{h-1} \leq \max(p,q) < 2^h$. Assume without loss of generality that the boundaries are distinct. If not, there are fewer subdivisions. Also add enough subdivision lines so that there are 2^h subdivisions in each of x and y. This grid is irregular (i.e., the cells are of varying size). Next, form a fixed (termed *regular*) grid with an origin at the lower left corner. Each cell in the regular grid with lower left corner at (i,j) corresponds to the cell in the irregular grid with (x_i, y_j) as its lower left corner and of size $(x_{i+1} - x_i) \times (y_{j+1} - y_j)$.

A node at level i in the region quadtree represents the two-dimensional interval corresponding to the Cartesian product of the intervals $[x_p : x_{p+2^i})$ and $[y_q : y_{q+2^i})$ where $p \bmod 2^i$ and $q \bmod 2^i$ are 0. The presence of a cross-section of a particular parallelepiped (a rectangle) is represented by *marking* the nodes that overlap it (recall the definition of marking in the discussion of the computation of area). The rectangle (corresponding to the cross-section) is inserted in the quadtree in a top-down manner analogous to the way a line segment is inserted in a segment tree. As in the computation of the area, we need to record only how many active parallelepipeds contain a particular node (i.e., how many times it is marked), not their identity.

The volume is computed in the same way as the area. The difference is that now we keep track of the total area of the parts of the scan plane, say A_i, at halting point z_i, that overlap the cross-sections of the parallelepipeds active just to the left of z_i. This quantity is adjusted at each halting point by inserting or deleting the cross-sections from the quadtree. The total volume is obtained by accumulating the product of this quantity with the difference between the current halting point and the next halting point— $A_i \cdot (z_i - z_{i-1})$.

Insertion and deletion of a rectangle in a region quadtree is an $O(N)$ process, since a rectangle can appear in at most $O(N)$ nodes (see Exercise 1.44). Thus we see that a plane-sweep algorithm employing the region quadtree will execute in time $O(N \cdot \log_2 N + N^2)$ or $O(N^2)$ as there are $O(N)$ halting points. The $O(N \cdot \log_2 N)$ term is contributed by the initial sort of the boundaries of the parallelepipeds.

This is an improvement over a solution of Bentley [Bent77a] that recursively performs a plane sweep across each of the planes (i.e., it reduces the area problem to N one-dimensional subproblems) for an execution time of $O(N^2 \cdot \log_2 N)$. Generalizing van Leeuwen and Wood's algorithm to d dimensions reduces the time requirement of Bentley's solution from $O(N^{d-1} \cdot \log_2 N)$ to $O(N^{d-1})$; however, this increases the space requirement from $O(N)$ to $O(N^2)$. The new bounds are achieved by recursively reducing the d-dimensional problem to N $(d-1)$-dimensional problems until we obtain the three-dimensional case and then solving each three-dimensional problem as discussed.

Lee [Lee83] uses the same technique to develop an algorithm to compute the maximum number of rectangles with a nonempty intersection (also termed a *maximum clique* [Hara69]). Given N rectangles, the two-dimensional problem can be solved using a segment tree in $O(N \cdot \log_2 N)$ time and $O(N)$ space. In d dimensions, an adaptation of the region quadtree is used that solves the problem in $O(N^{d-1})$ time and $O(N^2)$ space. Note that these algorithms only yield the cardinality of the maximum clique; they do not report its members. The algorithm can be modified to report the members of the maximum clique with the same time bound but using $O(N \cdot \log_2 N)$ space when $d = 2$ and $O(N^3)$ space when $d > 2$. Lee points out that the solution to the maximum clique problem can be used to solve a rectangle placement problem (see Exercise 3.79).

Recently Overmars and Yap [Over88b] have shown how to solve the d-dimensional measure problem in $O(N^{d/2} \cdot \log_2 N)$ time with $O(N)$ space. For $d \geq 3$, this is a significant improvement over the solutions of Bentley [Bent77a] and van Leeuwen and Wood [vanL81]. Below we examine Overmars and Yap's construction for three dimensions; the generalization to $d > 3$ is relatively straightforward. They also use a plane-sweep solution that sorts the boundaries of the parallelepipeds along one direction (say z) and then sweeps a plane parallel to the x–y plane across it.

At any instant of time, the plane consists of a collection of cross-sections (i.e., two-dimensional rectangles). Elements of the collection are termed *active rectangles*. This collection is represented as a set of cells (very much like buckets). Each halting point of the sweep pass requires inserting and/or deleting an active rectangle. Overmars and Yap are able to perform each insertion and deletion into the appropriate cells in $O(\sqrt{N} \cdot \log_2 N)$ time. This means that their algorithm runs in $O(N \cdot \sqrt{N} \cdot \log_2 N)$

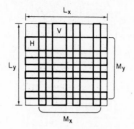

Figure 3.7   A trellis

time. The key to their algorithm is to partition the space into cells of a particular size so that their contents (i.e., rectangles) form a trellis and to use the properties of a trellis in an efficient way.

A *trellis* inside a rectangular cell is a collection of rectangles such that for each rectangle, either its left and right (i.e., vertical) boundaries coincide with the cell boundary, or its top and bottom (i.e., horizontal) boundaries coincide with the cell boundary (Figure 3.7). A *horizontal* rectangle is a rectangle whose left and right boundaries coincide with the cell boundary (e.g., rectangle H), and a *vertical* rectangle is a rectangle whose top and bottom boundaries coincide with the cell boundary (e.g., rectangle V).

Trellises are useful because of the following property. Suppose that the cell is of width L_x and height L_y. Let M_x be the aggregate length of the projections of the union of the vertical rectangles on the x axis, and let M_y be the aggregate length of the projections of the union of the horizontal rectangles on the y axis. The area of the union of the rectangles forming the trellis is $M_x \cdot L_y + M_y \cdot L_x - M_x \cdot M_y$ (see Exercise 3.81).

To keep track of the total area of the union of rectangles in a trellis, it is necessary only to keep track of the lengths of the projections on the axes (the numbers M_x and M_y). This can be done by using two segment trees to store the two sets of projected intervals. It follows that if all the rectangles that are ever active within a cell form a trellis and if there are k such rectangles, the measure of the union of the rectangles can be updated at a cost of $O(\log_2 k)$ per insertion or deletion. Thus the geometry of the trellis enables the exploitation of the fullness of the cell (i.e., bucket).

To exploit the properties of trellises, the plane containing the rectangles is partitioned as follows. First, the horizontal range is split into $\sqrt{N}$ intervals, such that the interior of each interval contains at most $2 \cdot \sqrt{N}$ projections of vertical boundaries of rectangles. This partitions the region into $\sqrt{N}$ vertical *slabs*. Next, each slab is partitioned by horizontal segments into *cells*.

The partitioning within each slab makes use of the concept of a V-rectangle and an H-rectangle. If the interior of a slab contains at least one of the left and right (i.e., vertical) boundaries of a rectangle, we call the rectangle a *V-rectangle* with respect to the slab. If the interior of the slab does not contain either of the left or right

*Figure 3.8   The partition of the collection of rectangles of
Figure 3.1 into slabs and cells*

boundaries of a rectangle but does contain some portion of the rectangle's top or bottom (i.e., horizontal) boundaries, we call the rectangle an *H-rectangle* with respect to
the slab.

The partitioning of slabs into cells is performed as follows. Within each slab, a
horizontal line is drawn through each top and bottom boundary of a V-rectangle, and
through every $\sqrt{N}^{th}$ top or bottom boundary of an H-rectangle. Since there are $\sqrt{N}$
slabs, it can be shown that the partitioning results in a total of $O(N)$ cells. Figure 3.8
is the result of applying this partition to the collection of rectangles in Figure 3.1,
where query rectangles 1 and 3 are treated as members of the collection. The slabs
are labeled S, T, and U. For example, in slab T, rectangles 1, B, D, and G are V-
rectangles, and rectangle D is an H-rectangle.

To see that the partitioning does indeed yield $O(N)$ cells, we observe that there
are at most $2 \cdot \sqrt{N}$ V-rectangles in each slab because of the way the x axis was partitioned. Therefore there are at most $4 \cdot \sqrt{N}$ top and bottom boundaries of V-rectangles
in each slab. Moreover, at most $2 \cdot \sqrt{N}$ top and bottom boundaries of H-rectangles are
chosen to be cell boundaries within a slab. Hence there are at most $6 \cdot \sqrt{N}$ cells in
each slab. Our desired result of $O(N)$ cells follows since there are $\sqrt{N}$ slabs.

It is not hard to show (see Exercise 3.82) that the following properties hold for
the partitioning:

1. The boundary of each rectangle intersects at most $O(\sqrt{N})$ cells.
2. Each cell intersects the boundary of at most $O(\sqrt{N})$ rectangles.
3. For each cell, the intersection of the rectangles with the cell forms a trellis.

To exploit the cell structure efficiently, a tree having these cells as its leaf nodes
is built as follows. Within each slab, vertically adjacent cells are merged (creating a
father node). This process continues until there is one node per slab. Then, neighboring slabs are merged. This tree, called an *orthogonal partition tree*, is a variant of the
k-d tree (see Section 1.3). The x coordinate value serves as the discriminator near the
root of the tree, while the y coordinate value serves as the discriminator at the deeper
nodes.

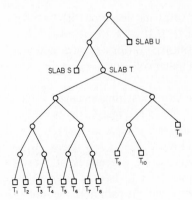

Figure 3.9   The orthogonal partition tree for Figure 3.8. Only slab T is fully expanded.

Since there are $O(\sqrt{N})$ slabs and $O(\sqrt{N})$ cells per slab, the orthogonal partition tree has a maximum depth of $O(\log_2 N)$. Figure 3.9 partially illustrates the orthogonal partition tree for Figure 3.8. In the figure, we expand only the portion corresponding to slab T (containing 11 cells). The cells in each slab are numbered in sequence starting from the top. Thus the cell labeled T_i corresponds to the ith cell from the top of slab T.

As the plane sweep progresses, data rectangles (i.e., two-dimensional cross sections of parallelepipeds) are added to the tree (i.e., become active) and deleted from it (i.e., become inactive). Each node P in the orthogonal partition tree has associated with it five fields, called LEFT, RIGHT, RECT, COUNT, and AREA. LEFT(P) and RIGHT(P) are the left and right sons, respectively, of P.

RECT(P) is the rectangle consisting of the union of the cells descended from P. This rectangle is called the *associated rectangle* of P. COUNT(P) is the number of active data rectangles that contain RECT(P). AREA(P) is the area of the intersection of the union of the active data rectangles with RECT(P). Associated with each leaf node are two segment trees for the trellis of rectangles in the corresponding cell. These segment trees store the projection of the vertical rectangles on the x axis and the projection of the horizontal rectangles on the y axis.

Initially all segment trees associated with leaf nodes are empty, and all AREA and COUNT fields are zero. To insert rectangle R in the tree, we start at the root and proceed recursively as follows. Assume that we are processing node P. There are three cases. If rectangle R contains RECT(P), then we increment COUNT(P). Otherwise there are two cases, depending on whether P is a leaf node. If P is a leaf node, then by property 3, rectangle R is either a vertical or a horizontal rectangle of a trellis, and we insert it in the appropriate segment tree. If P is not a leaf node, we insert rectangle R in the two sons of P.

In all three cases, after the insertion, if COUNT(P) is nonzero, then we set AREA(P) to the area of RECT(P). If COUNT(P) is zero, then we set AREA(P) to the sum of AREA(LEFT(P)) and AREA(RIGHT(P)) (for a nonleaf node) or to the area of the trellis of rectangles in the corresponding cell (for a leaf node). Deleting a rectangle is similar (see Exercise 3.83).

Using the above structure, inserting rectangle R (i.e., making it active) requires at most $O(\sqrt{N} \cdot \log_2 N)$ time. To see that this is true, we observe that two classes of nodes are visited: leaf nodes and nonleaf nodes. By property 1, the boundary of any data rectangle intersects at most $O(\sqrt{N})$ leaf nodes. Updating the two segment trees of each leaf node intersected by R requires at most $O(\log_2 N)$ time. Therefore $O(\sqrt{N} \cdot \log_2 N)$ time is sufficient to update the AREA fields of all leaf nodes that intersect R. For each leaf node visited, the path from the root visits at most $O(\log_2 N)$ nodes for a total of $O(\sqrt{N} \cdot \log_2 N)$ nodes. For each leaf node visited, the sons of at most $O(\log_2 N)$ of the nodes encountered along the path starting from the root have their COUNT field updated. This accounts for all of the nodes that have their COUNT field updated.

The algorithm of Overmars and Yap uses $O(N \cdot \sqrt{N})$ space, as there are $O(N)$ segment trees (one per cell), each using $O(\sqrt{N})$ storage (see Exercise 3.84). Overmars and Yap [Over88b] show that the total storage requirement can be reduced to $O(N)$ by using a technique called *streaming*, due to Edelsbrunner and Overmars [Edel85b]. The basic idea behind streaming is to build only a portion of the tree at a time and to perform all updates to that portion of the tree together. In other words the updates within the structure are grouped sequentially according to location within the structure rather than according to the time at which they occur. (For more details, see [Edel85b].)

Exercises

3.67. Devise an $O(N \cdot \log_2 N)$ algorithm to compute the total length of a collection of N parallel line segments that can overlap. Overlapping parts should be counted only once.

3.68. Compute the total area spanned by the collection of rectangles in Figure 3.1. Letting $(x_{min}, y_{min}, x_{max}, y_{max})$ represent a rectangle, rectangles A, B, C, D, E, F, and G are at (3,6,8,36), (25,34,34,38), (33,21,37,36), (21,23,38,27), (6,3,26,8), (31,15,35,19), and (23,11,38,14), respectively. Overlapping parts should be counted only once.

3.69. Why is no node marked more than once in the computation of the total area spanned by the collection of rectangles in Figure 3.1? In particular, what about the nodes corresponding to intervals [23,34) and [34,36)?

3.70. Prove that an algorithm that uses a segment tree to compute the total area spanned by a collection of N rectangles uses $O(N)$ space.

3.71. Write a procedure SWEEP_AREA to compute the area of a collection of possibly overlapping rectangles. Use the plane-sweep approach with a segment tree. You must code procedures to insert and delete the vertical boundaries of the rectangles from the segment tree.

3.72. Write a procedure SWEEP_PERIMETER to compute the perimeter of a collection of possibly overlapping rectangles. Use the plane-sweep approach with a segment tree. You must code procedures to insert and delete the vertical boundaries of the rectangles from the segment tree.

3.73. Write a procedure MAX_2D_CLIQUE to compute the cardinality of the maximum clique of a collection of possibly overlapping rectangles. Use the plane-sweep approach with a segment tree.

3.74. Modify your solution to Exercise 3.73 so that the identities of the members of the maximum clique, not just the cardinality of the clique, are also reported.

3.75. Write a procedure SWEEP_VOLUME to compute the volume of a collection of possibly overlapping three-dimensional rectangles. Use the plane-sweep approach with a quadtree. You must code procedures to insert and delete the x–y boundaries of the rectangles from the quadtree.

3.76. Write a procedure SWEEP_SURFACE_AREA to compute the surface area of a collection of possibly overlapping three-dimensional rectangles. Use the plane-sweep approach with a quadtree. You must code procedures to insert and delete the x–y boundaries of the rectangles from the quadtree.

3.77. Write a procedure MAX_3D_CLIQUE to compute the cardinality of the maximum clique of a collection of possibly overlapping three-dimensional rectangles. Use the plane-sweep approach with a quadtree.

3.78. Modify your solution to Exercise 3.77 so that the identities of the members of the maximum clique, not just the cardinality of the clique, are also reported.

3.79. Consider the following placement problem. Given n points in a two-dimensional space and a rectangular window, say R, whose sides are parallel to the coordinate axes, find a point in the plane at which the window can be centered so that it contains a maximum number of points in its interior. The window is not permitted to be rotated; it can only be translated.

3.80. Consider a variation of the placement problem of Exercise 3.79 where the points are weighted. Find the location of R in which the sum of the weights of the points in it is maximized.

3.81. Consider a trellis inside a rectangular cell of width L_x and height L_y. Let M_x be the aggregate length of the projections of the union of the vertical rectangles on the horizontal axis, and let M_y be the aggregate length of the projections of the union of the horizontal rectangles on the vertical axis. Show that the area of the union of the rectangles forming the trellis is $M_x \cdot L_y + M_y \cdot L_x - M_x \cdot M_y$.

3.82. Show that properties 1, 2, and 3 used in the construction of Overmars and Yap's solution to the measure problem hold for $d = 3$.

3.83. Give an algorithm to delete a rectangle from an orthogonal partition tree when using Overmars and Yap's solution to the measure problem for $d = 3$.

3.84. Prove that each segment tree in Overmars and Yap's solution to the measure problem in three dimensions for N parallelepipeds uses $O(\sqrt{N})$ space.

3.85. Can you use Overmars and Yap's approach to compute the size of the maximum clique in time $O(N^{d/2} \cdot \log_2 N)$ with $O(N)$ space for N rectangles in a d-dimensional space?

3.86. Suppose that you apply Overmars and Yap's approach to report the members of the maximum clique for N rectangles in a d-dimensional space. What are the time and space requirements? In particular, how much space is needed to store the segment trees in each of the cells?

3.87. Why can't you use a $(d-1)$-dimensional quadtree (e.g., an octree in three dimensions) to compute the measure of a d-dimensional space containing N rectangles in $O(N^2)$ time— that is, represent a $(d-1)$-dimensional cross-section by a $(d-1)$-dimensional quadtree to get the execution time of the algorithm down to $O(N^2)$ and $O(N^{d-1})$ space?

3.88. Consider a collection of N right triangles so that two of the sides are always parallel to the x and y axes and the third side has a negative slope. Devise an algorithm to compute the area of the collection. Can you get its execution time and space requirements to be $O(N \cdot \log_2 N)$ and $O(N)$, respectively?

3.89. Repeat Exercise 3.88 by permitting the third side of the right triangle to have an arbitrary slope.

3.90. [Mark H. Overmars] Consider a collection of N arbitrary triangles. Devise an algorithm to compute the area of the collection. Can you get its execution time and space requirements to be $O(N \cdot \log_2 N)$ and $O(N)$, respectively?

3.4 POINT-BASED METHODS

This section contains a discussion of the representation of rectangles as points followed by an examination of the representation of the collection of points. A common solution to the problem of representing a collection of objects is to approximate elements of the collection by simpler objects. One technique is to represent each object by using one of a number of primitive shapes that contain it. Up to now we have used rectangles, but other shapes, such as triangles, circles, cubes, parallelepipeds, cylinders, and spheres, are also possible.

This approach is motivated, in part, by the fact that it is easier to test the containing objects for intersection than it is to perform the test using the actual objects. For example, it is easier to compute the intersection of two rectangles than of two polygons for which the rectangles serve as approximations. More complex approximations can be created by composing Boolean operations and geometric transformations on instances of the primitive types. In fact, this is the basis of the Constructive Solid Geometry (CSG) technique of representing three-dimensional objects [Voel77, Requ80], discussed further in Section 5.5.

The advantage of using such approximations is that each primitive can be described by a small set of parameters and can in turn represent a large class of objects. In particular, if primitive P is described by k parameters, then each set of parameter values defines a point in a k-dimensional space assigned to the class of objects in which the members are all the possible instances of primitive P. Such a point is termed a *representative point*. Note that a representative point and the class to which it belongs completely define all of the topological and geometric properties of the corresponding object.

Most primitives can be described by more than one set of parameters. For example, using Cartesian coordinates, a circle is described by a representative point in three-dimensional space consisting of the x and y coordinates of its center and the value of its radius. On the other hand, using polar coordinates, a circle can also be described by a representative point in three-dimensional space consisting of the ρ and θ coordinates of its center and the value of its radius. For other primitives, the choices are even more varied. For example, the class of objects formed by a rectangle in two dimensions with sides parallel to the x and y coordinate axes is described by a representative point in four-dimensional space. Some choices for the parameters are as follows:

1. The x and y coordinates of two diagonally opposite corners of the rectangle (e.g., the lower left and upper right).
2. The x and y coordinates of a corner of the rectangle, together with its horizontal and vertical extents.
3. The x and y coordinates of the centroid of the rectangle, together with its horizontal and vertical extents (i.e., the horizontal and vertical distances from the centroid to the relevant sides).

The actual choice depends on the type of operations that we intend to perform on the objects formed by them.

Different parameters have different effects on the queries; thus making the right choice is important. Hinrichs and Nievergelt [Hinr83, Hinr85a] divide the parameters into two classes: location and extension. Location parameters specify the coordinates of a point, such as a corner or a centroid. Extension parameters specify size, for example, the radius of a circle. This distinction is always possible for objects that can be described as Cartesian products of spheres of varying dimension.

Many common objects can be described in this way. For example, a rectangle is the Cartesian product of two one-dimensional spheres, whereas a cylinder is the Cartesian product of a one-dimensional sphere and a two-dimensional sphere. Whenever such a distinction between location and extension parameters can be drawn, the proximity queries that are described in Section 3.1 have cone-shaped search regions. The tip of the cone is usually in the subspace of the location parameters and has the shape of the query point or query object.

The importance of making the right choice can be seen by examining the class of one-dimensional intervals on a straight line. As an example, consider the collection of rectangles given in Figure 3.1. Each rectangle can be represented as the Cartesian product of two one-dimensional spheres corresponding to the sides that are given as horizontal and vertical intervals in Figure 3.10. These intervals can be represented using any of the three representations enumerated above. Representation 1 yields an ordered pair (L,R) where L and R correspond to the left and right, respectively, endpoints of the interval. Figure 3.11 shows how the horizontal intervals would be represented using this method.

In most applications the intervals are small. Therefore for representation 1, L and R are very close in value. L < R means that the representative points are clustered near and above the diagonal. Thus the representative points are not well distributed, and hence any data structure based on organizing the embedding space of the data (e.g., address computation), in contrast to one based on the actual representative points stored (e.g., comparative search), will have to pay a price for the empty half of the embedding space.

On the other hand, Hinrichs and Nievergelt point out that separating the location parameters from the extension parameters results in a smaller embedding space that is

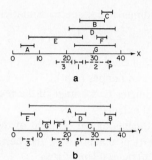

a

b

Figure 3.10   The (a) horizontal (i.e., x) and (b) vertical (i.e., y) intervals corresponding to the sides of the rectangles in Figure 3.1. Solid lines correspond to rectangles in the collection, and broken lines correspond to the query rectangles.

filled more uniformly. For example, representation 3 is used in Figure 3.12, where the horizontal intervals are represented as an ordered pair (CX,DX) such that CX is the centroid of the interval and DX is the distance from the centroid to the end of the interval. Representation 2 is similar to representation 3 (see Exercise 3.97).

Bearing the above considerations in mind, representation 3 seems to be the most appropriate. In such a case, a rectangle is represented by the four-tuple (c_x, d_x, c_y, d_y), interpreted as the Cartesian product of a horizontal and a vertical one-dimensional interval—(c_x, d_x) and (c_y, d_y), respectively.[8] This representation is used by Hinrichs

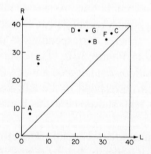

Figure 3.11   Representation of the horizontal intervals of Figure 3.1 as ordered pairs (L, R) where L and R are the left and right endpoints, respectively, of the interval

---

[8] The notation (c_x, d_x) corresponds to a point in a two-dimensional space. It is *not* the open one-dimensional interval whose left and right endpoints are at c_x and d_x, respectively.

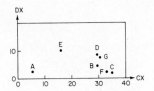

Figure 3.12   Representation of the horizontal intervals of
Figure 3.1 as ordered pairs (CX, DX) where CX and DX are
the centers and half-lengths, respectively, of the interval

and Nievergelt [Hinr83, Hinr85a]; the following examples of its utility are due to
them.

Proximity queries involving point and rectangular query objects are easy to
implement. Their answers are conic-shaped regions in the four-dimensional space
formed by the Cartesian product of the two-interval query regions. This is equivalent
to computing the intersection of the two query regions but is much more efficient. It
also enables us to visualize our examples since the horizontal and vertical intervals
correspond to the projections of the query responses on the c_x-d_x and c_y-d_y planes,
respectively.

The discussion is illustrated with the collection of rectangles given in Figure 3.1
along with query point P and query rectangles 1, 2, and 3. When the query objects are
not individual points or rectangles, the representation of a rectangle as the Cartesian

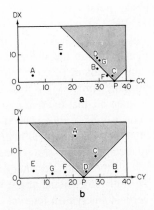

Figure 3.13   Search region for a point query on P for (a)
the horizontal intervals and (b) the vertical intervals of Figure 3.1. All intervals containing P are in the shaded regions.
Intervals appearing in the shaded regions of both (a) and (b)
correspond to rectangles that contain P.

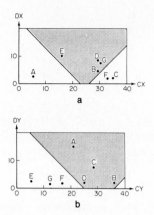

Figure 3.14   Search region for a window query on query rectangle 1 of Figure 3.1 for (a) the horizontal intervals and (b) the vertical intervals of that figure. All intervals that contain points of rectangle I are in the shaded regions. Intervals appearing in the shaded regions of both (a) and (b) correspond to rectangles that intersect rectangle 1.

product of two orthogonal intervals is not that useful (e.g., query regions in the form of an arbitrary line or circle as in Exercises 3.101 and 3.102, respectively).

For a point query, we wish to determine all intervals that contain a given point, say p. These intervals form a cone-shaped region with a tip that is an interval of length zero centered at p.[9] For example, the horizontal and vertical intervals containing P are shown shaded in parts a and b, respectively, of Figure 3.13. To find all the rectangles that contain a given point, we access a specific region in the four-dimensional space defined by the Cartesian product of the horizontal and vertical point-in-interval query regions. For example, P is in the set of rectangles with representative points in the intersection of the shaded portion of parts a and b of Figure 3.13, that is, {C,D} is the intersection of {C,D,G} and {A,C,D}.

A window query is a bit more complex. In this case, the one-dimensional analog of this query is to find all intervals that overlap a given interval, say l. Again the set of overlapping intervals consists of a cone-shaped region with a tip that is the interval l. For example, the horizontal and vertical intervals that overlap the horizontal and vertical sides of query rectangle 1 are shown shaded in parts a and b, respectively, of Figure 3.14. To find all the rectangles that overlap the query window, we access a specific region in the four-dimensional space defined by the Cartesian product of the horizontal and vertical interval-in-interval query regions. For example, query rectangle 1 overlaps the intersection of the shaded portion of parts a and b of Figure 3.14, that is, {B,D} is the intersection of {B,D,E,G} and {A,B,C,D}.

---

[9] McCreight [McCr80] uses the same technique in conjunction with representation 1 to solve this problem.

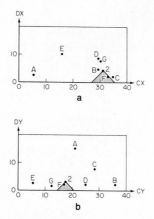

Figure 3.15 Search regions for a containment query on query rectangle 2 of Figure 3.1 for (a) the horizontal intervals and (b) the vertical intervals of that figure. All intervals contained in one of the intervals forming rectangle 2 are in the shaded regions. Intervals appearing in the shaded regions of both (a) and (b) correspond to rectangles contained in rectangle 2.

For a containment query, the one-dimensional analog is to find all the intervals totally contained within a given interval, say *I*. The set of contained intervals consists of a cone-shaped region with a tip at *I* and that opens in the direction of smaller extent values. This makes sense because all intervals within the cone are totally contained in the interval represented by the tip. For example, the horizontal and vertical intervals contained in the horizontal and vertical sides of query rectangle 2 are shown shaded in parts a and b, respectively, of Figure 3.15. To find all the rectangles contained in the query window, we access a specific region in the four-dimensional space defined by the Cartesian product of the horizontal and vertical contained-in-interval query regions. For example, query rectangle 2 contains the intersection of the shaded portion of parts a and b of Figure 3.15, that is, {F}.

For an enclosure query, the one-dimensional analog is to find all the intervals that enclose the given interval, say *I*. The set of enclosing intervals consists of a cone-shaped region with a tip at *I* that opens in the direction of larger extent values. This is logical because the interval represented by the tip is contained (i.e., enclosed) by all intervals within the cone. To find all the rectangles that enclose the query window, we access a specific region in the four-dimensional space defined by the Cartesian product of the horizontal and vertical enclose-interval query regions. For example, the horizontal and vertical intervals that enclose the horizontal and vertical sides of query rectangle 3 are shown shaded in parts a and b, respectively, of Figure 3.16. For example, query rectangle 3 contains the intersection of the shaded portion of parts a and b of Figure 3.16, that is, {E}.

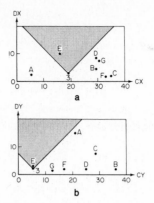

Figure 3.16   Search regions for an enclosure query on query rectangle 3 of Figure 3.1 for (a) the horizontal intervals and (b) the vertical intervals of that figure. All intervals that enclose one of the intervals forming rectangle 3 are in the shaded regions. Intervals appearing in the shaded regions of both (a) and (b) correspond to the rectangles that enclose rectangle 3.

In spite of the relative ease with which the queries are implemented using the representative point method with representation 3, there are queries for which it is ill suited. For example, suppose that we wish to solve the rectangle intersection problem. In fact, no matter which of the three representations we use, to solve this problem we must intersect each rectangle with every other rectangle. The problem is that none of these representations is area oriented; they reduce a spatial object to a single representative point.

Although the extent of the object is reflected in the representative point, the final mapping of the representative point in the four-dimensional space does not result in the preservation of nearness in the two-dimensional space from which the rectangles are drawn. In other words, two rectangles may be very close (and possibly overlap), yet the Euclidean distance between their representative points in four-dimensional space may be quite large, thereby masking the overlapping relationship between them. For example, although rectangles B and D intersect query rectangle 1, we cannot easily tell if they intersect each other except by checking their sizes.

This discussion has emphasized representation 3. Nevertheless, as we will see, the other representations are also commonly used. Interestingly although a rectangle whose sides are parallel to the x and y axes requires four values to be uniquely specified, it is also frequently modeled by a representative point in a two-dimensional space. The representative point corresponds to the centroid of the rectangle or to one of its corners (e.g., lower left).

If rectangles are not permitted to overlap, such a representation is sufficient to ensure that no two rectangles have the same representative point. Of course, since two values do not uniquely specify the rectangle, the remaining values are retained in the record corresponding to the rectangle associated with the representative point. If rectangles are permitted to overlap, then such a representation means that there may be more than one record associated with a specific representative point.

Once a specific representative point method is chosen for the rectangle, we can use the techniques discussed in Chapter 2 to organize the collection of representative points. Again the choice of representation depends to a large extent on the type of operations that we will be performing. Ousterhout [Oust84] uses a nonhierarchical approach where each rectangle, treated as if it were a point, is connected to its neighbors by means of links. This technique is termed *corner stitching*. In particular, for each rectangle, there are two links from the lower left corner to the two neighbors to its left and bottom and two links from the top right corner to the two neighbors to its top and right. This is similar to using representation 1 for the representative point of the rectangle.

The corner stitching representation imposes a partition of the plane that resembles a mosaic consisting of two types of tiles: space and solid. The solid tiles correspond to the rectangles and the space tiles to the void space, if any, between the rectangles. The space tiles are maximal horizontal strips, which means that no space tile is adjacent to a space tile immediately to its left or right. The maximality restriction implies that the decomposition into space and solid tiles is unique.

Links exist between all types of tiles; solid tiles can be linked to both solid and space tiles and likewise for space tiles. It can be shown that for N rectangles, there are at most $3 \cdot N + 1$ space tiles (see Exercise 3.108). Figure 3.17 is an example of the space decomposition imposed by corner stitching for a nonoverlapping subset of the collection of rectangles given in Figure 3.1. The space tiles are delimited by solid and

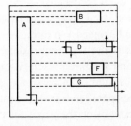

Figure 3.17 Example of the space decomposition imposed by corner stitching for a nonoverlapping subset of the collection of rectangles given in Figure 3.1. The rectangles are delimited by solid lines, while the space tiles are delimited by broken lines. Some of the corner stitches are shown.

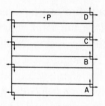

Figure 3.18   An example collection of rectangles A, B, C, D illustrating the worst case when wishing to locate the rectangle associated with point P when the search starts at rectangle A and proceeds in an upward direction.

broken lines, and the rectangles are delimited by solid lines. The corner stitches (i.e., links) are also shown for some of the rectangles and space tiles.

Corner stitching greatly facilitates operations that involve finding nearest neighbors. Overlapping rectangles, however, are not easily handled by it. Moreover, since the only way to move from one rectangle to another is through the links, in the worst case, accessing the rectangle associated with a given point requires that all rectangles be examined (see Exercise 3.110). As an example of this worst case, consider the set of rectangles given in Figure 3.18. A is the first rectangle in the set. We wish to access the rectangle associated with point P and do so by traversing the up links shown in Figure 3.18. The worst case could be overcome by imposing an additional structure in the form of one of the hierarchical organizations described below while still retaining the links. In such a case, however, both the solid and space tiles would have to be represented in the structure. (For a discussion of algorithms using corner stitching see, Shand [Shan87].)

Lauther [Laut78] and Rosenberg [Rose85] make use of a balanced k-d tree (somewhat like the adaptive k-d tree discussed in Section 2.4.1 with the exception that the coordinates are tested in a cyclic order) to organize the rectangles whose representative point uses representation 1. Lauther discusses the solution of the rectangle intersection problem using the balanced k-d tree. The solution is an adaptation of the $O(N^2)$ algorithm. It first builds the tree (equivalent to a sorting process) and then traverses the tree in inorder and intersects each rectangle, say P, with the remaining unprocessed rectangles (i.e., the inorder successors of P).[10]

Two rectangles with sides parallel to the axes intersect if their projections on the x axis intersect and their projections on the y axis intersect. The one-dimensional analog of this condition has been used in the segment and interval tree solutions to the rectangle intersection problem (see Sections 3.2.1 and 3.2.2). More formally, we say that in order for rectangle Q to intersect rectangle P, all four of the following conditions must be satisfied:

---

[10] In this discussion, P is used to refer to both a rectangle and its corresponding node in the tree. The correct meaning should be clear from the context.

1. $x_{\min}(Q) \le x_{\max}(P)$
2. $y_{\min}(Q) \le y_{\max}(P)$
3. $x_{\min}(P) \le x_{\max}(Q)$
4. $y_{\min}(P) \le y_{\max}(Q)$

Armed with this formulation of the problem, we see that there is no need to visit all of the inorder successors of P since, whenever one of these conditions fails to hold at a node Q, the appropriate subtree of Q need not be searched. These conditions can be restated in the following manner, which is more compatible with the way in which the balanced k-d tree is traversed:

1. $x_{\min}(Q) \le x_{\max}(P)$
2. $y_{\min}(Q) \le y_{\max}(P)$
3. $-x_{\max}(Q) \le -x_{\min}(P)$
4. $-y_{\max}(Q) \le -y_{\min}(P)$

Now, we build a balanced k-d tree with discriminators K_0, K_1, K_2, K_3, corresponding to $x_{\min}$, $y_{\min}$, $-x_{\max}$, and $-y_{\max}$, respectively. Whenever we encounter node Q discriminating on K_d such that $K_d(Q) > K_{(d+2) \bmod 4}(P)$, then no nodes in the right subtree of Q need be examined further.

Solving the rectangle intersection problem as described has an upper bound of $O(N^2)$ and a lower bound of $O(N \cdot \log_2 N)$. The lower bound is achieved when pruning is assumed to occur at every right subtree (see Exercise 3.117). When the rectangle intersection problem is posed in terms of conditions 5–8, the relation '$\le$' between Q and P is said to be a *dominance relation* [Prep85]. In such a case, the intersection problem is called the *dominance merge* problem by Preparata and Shamos [Prep85]. Given F rectangle intersections, the algorithm of Preparata and Shamos solves the rectangle intersection problem in $O(N \cdot \log_2^2 N + F)$ time instead of the optimal $O(N \cdot \log_2 N + F)$ time.

A balanced k-d tree takes more time to build than an ordinary k-d tree since medians must be computed to ensure balance. The balanced k-d tree makes point searches and region searches quite efficient. For such operations, the balanced k-d tree is preferable to corner stitching because of the implicit two-dimensional sorting of the rectangles. In addition, overlapping rectangles can be easily handled with the balanced k-d tree, whereas this is quite complicated with corner stitching. However, for operations involving finding nearest neighbors, corner stitching is superior to the balanced k-d tree.

Rosenberg compares the performance of the balanced k-d tree, a point method in his formulation, with linked lists[11] and the area-based quadtree approaches discussed in Section 3.5.1 and concludes that the point methods are superior. However, he takes into account only point and window queries. Comparisons using queries such as finding all intersecting rectangles may lead to a different conclusion.

---

[11] The rectangles are stored in a doubly linked list.

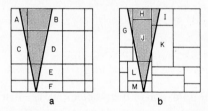

Figure 3.19   Blocks examined when searching for points within a conic region for a collection of intervals represented by (a) a grid file and (b) a k-d tree

Hinrichs and Nievergelt [Hinr83, Hinr85a, Hinr85b] make use of the grid file (see Section 2.8.2.3) to organize the rectangles whose representative point uses representation 3. The result is that proximity queries are answered by examining all grid blocks that intersect the cone-shaped search regions. They prefer this method to one based on a tree (e.g., the k-d tree) because the relevant grid blocks are in contiguous regions, whereas in a tree, contiguous blocks may appear in different subtrees. Hinrichs and Nievergelt are quite concerned with reducing the number of disk access operations necessary to process such queries.

Figure 3.19a is an example of a conic-shaped search region for a grid file organization of rectangles. Figure 3.19b is an example of a conic-shaped search region for a k-d tree organization of rectangles. In the case of a grid file, blocks A, B, C, D, E, and F would be examined, while for a k-d tree blocks G, H, I, J, K, L, and M would be examined. Note that blocks I and K are in a different subtree of the k-d tree than are blocks G, H, J, L, and M. In the worst case, solving the rectangle intersection problem when using a grid file takes $O(N^2)$ time. This is achieved by using the naive method of Section 3.2. However, the expected cost will be lower since it is assumed that the points corresponding to the rectangles are well distributed among the grid blocks. (For an analysis of grid file methods on randomly distributed point data, see Regnier [Regn85].)

The techniques discussed for organizing the collection of representative points assume that the representative point lies in four-dimensional space. Another possibility is to use a representative point in two-dimensional space and to represent the collection by one of the two-dimensional quadtree variants, such as the PR quadtree and the k-d tree. Recall that the PR quadtree is a regular decomposition quadtree that decomposes space until there is only one point per block (for more details, see Section 2.6.2).

As an example of the use of the PR quadtree, suppose that in our application we must perform a point query (i.e., determine the rectangles that contain a given point). In this case, when the representative point is the centroid, a PR quadtree requires that we search the entire data structure because the rectangle centered at a given point can lie in all of the quadrants. Of course, pruning can occur at deeper levels in the tree. In contrast, using the lower left corner as the representative point may permit the pruning of up to three quadrants in the search. For instance, when the query point lies in the SW quadrant of a tree rooted at Q, then no rectangle with a representative point that lies in the NW, NE, or SE quadrants of Q can contain the query point.

Ooi, McDonell, and Sacks-Davis [Ooi87] make use of a variant of a k-d tree that they call a *spatial k-d tree*. Once again the representative point is the centroid of the object. Aside from storing the value and identity of the discriminating key, each nonleaf node, say P discriminating on key K_j, also contains information on the spatial extent of the objects stored in its two subtrees. In particular, it stores the maximum value of the j coordinate for the objects stored in LOSON(P) and the minimum value of the j coordinate for the objects stored in HISON(P). This information aids in reducing the number of nodes that need to be examined when executing a point query. In the worst case, however, the entire tree will still have to be searched.

Exercises

3.91. Suppose that the representative point corresponding to each rectangle is its centroid and that the collection of rectangles is represented using a PR quadtree. Moreover, rectangles are not permitted to overlap. What is the maximum horizontal or vertical separation of two rectangles with representative points that are contained in brother nodes in the PR quadtree (i.e., at level i in a $2^n \times 2^n$ image with a root at level n)?

3.92. Using the same representation and assumption about no overlapping rectangles as in Exercise 3.91, write an algorithm to determine the rectangle associated with a given point. If the representative point is stored in a block at level i, what is the maximum size of the neighborhood that may have to be searched to perform the operation?

3.93. How would you adapt representation 3 to represent a region quadtree for a binary image as a collection of representative points stored as a PR quadtree?

3.94. Prove that storing the region quadtree using a PR quadtree, such that the black nodes are representative points that correspond to the centers of black blocks, never requires more space (i.e., more nodes) than the region quadtree.

3.95. How would you represent a sphere in terms of location and extension parameters?

3.96. How many parameters are necessary to represent a rectangle in a general position in two-dimensional space?

3.97. Discuss the use of representation 2 for the representative points of the horizontal and vertical intervals comprising the sides of a rectangle. Draw a graph such as Figures 3.10 and 3.11 for the horizontal intervals of Figure 3.1 using this representation. What are the advantages and disadvantages in comparison to representations 1 and 3?

3.98. Suppose that you are using representation (1) for the representative point of each interval in a collection of one-dimensional intervals. What is the shape of the search region for a query that seeks all the intervals that contain point P?

3.99. What is the relationship between representations 1 and 3?

3.100. How would you implement a point query for a collection of rectangles with a representative point that uses representation 2? Repeat for a point set query involving intersection (i.e., windowing), as well as the two subset relations (i.e., containment and enclosure).

3.101. Given a line from point (a,b) to point (c,d) and a collection of rectangles with a representative point that uses representation 3, describe the search regions for all the rectangles intersected by the line and all the rectangles that enclose the line. Note that the line need not be horizontal or vertical.

3.102. Given a circle of radius r centered at point (a,b) and a collection of rectangles with a representative point that uses representation 3, describe the search regions for all the rectangles intersected by the circle, the rectangles contained in their entirety in the circle, and the rectangles that enclose the circle.

3.103. Suppose that the representative point for a circle in the x-y plane uses representation 3. Describe the search regions for an object intersection query in which the object is a (a) point, (b) line, (c) circle, or (d) rectangle.

3.104. Suppose that the representative point for a circle, say c, in the x-y plane uses representation 3. Describe the search regions for (a) all circles contained in c and for (b) all circles enclosing c.

3.105. Consider a collection of two-dimensional objects and the implementation of a graphics editor that permits a graphical search and replace operation. Suppose that the objects are represented by their enclosing curves. Moreover, let each curve be approximated by a piecewise linear approximation. Give some possible representative points for the objects. Consider also the issue of translation, rotation, and scale invariance.

3.106. Write an algorithm to insert a rectangle into a corner stitching representation.

3.107. Write an algorithm to delete a rectangle from a corner stitching representation.

3.108. Prove that for N rectangles, the corner stitching representation implies a maximum of $3 \cdot N + 1$ space tiles.

3.109. Under what conditions is the number of space tiles fewer than $3 \cdot N + 1$?

3.110. Write an algorithm to find the rectangle that covers a particular point location when the rectangles are represented using corner stitching.

3.111. Write an algorithm to find all rectangles that intersect a given window when the rectangles are represented using corner stitching.

3.112. Can we say that whenever two rectangles intersect, the corner of one rectangle is contained in the other rectangle?

3.113. By definition, each node in a k-d tree that discriminates on key K_j serves as an upper bound for all the K_j values in the LOSON and as a lower bound for all the K_j values in the HISON. To ensure that point and region searches are efficient in the k-d tree, it is useful to know more about the region below each node. Thus a bounds array is stored with each node to indicate the information necessary to cut off unproductive search. For k-dimensional data, $2 \cdot k$ items are needed to specify completely the k-dimensional volume spanned by the node. Thus for the 4-d trees used for the collection of rectangles, we need eight values at each node. Show that with each node we need to store only three values to specify the two regions (i.e., two-dimensional areas) that comprise the LOSON and HISON of a node. Describe how they would be used to cut off the search. In addition, show that if the only information stored in the bounds array at a node is the region spanned by the node, rather than the regions spanned by LOSON and HISON, then only two values are needed.

3.114. Write an algorithm to find all rectangles that intersect a given point (in two-dimensional space) when each rectangle is represented by a point in four-dimensional space and the collection of rectangles is organized by a balanced k-d tree.

3.115. Repeat Exercise 3.114 for all rectangles that intersect a rectangular window given by P.

3.116. Write an algorithm to determine all the intersecting rectangles using a balanced k-d tree.

3.117. Prove that $O(N \cdot \log_2 N)$ is a lower bound on solving the rectangle intersection problem when using the balanced k-d tree.

3.118.   What is the expected cost of solving the rectangle intersection problem using the grid file?

3.119.   Suppose that you use the spatial k-d tree [Ooi87]. Under what circumstances will a point query require that both sons of a nonleaf node *P* be examined?

3.5   AREA-BASED METHODS

The problem with using trees in conjunction with representative point methods such as those discussed in Section 3.4 is that the placement of the node in the tree (i.e., its depth) does not reflect the size (i.e., the spatial extent) of the rectangle. It primarily depends on the location of the representative point. In this section, we focus on alternative representations provided by area-based methods that associate each rectangle with the blocks containing it or the blocks that it contains. The sizes and positions of these blocks may be predetermined, as is the case in an approach based on the region quadtree; however, this need not be the case, nor must the blocks be disjoint.

As an example of a representation based on the region quadtree, suppose that we represent each rectangle by its minimum enclosing quadtree block (i.e., a square). The rectangle is associated with the center of the quadtree block. Of course, more than one rectangle can be associated with a given enclosing square and a technique must be used to differentiate among them. Observe that in this case we do not explicitly store a representative point. Instead there is a predefined set of representative points with which rectangles can be stored. In some sense this is analogous to hashing where the representative points correspond to buckets. These techniques, which we term CIF quadtrees,[12] have been developed independently by Kedem [Kede82] (called a *quad-CIF tree*) and by Abel and Smith [Abel83].

This section expands on the area-based approaches. We first examine a detailed implementation of one variant of the CIF quadtree that is related to the MX quadtree (see Section 2.6.1). The specific implementation details of the insertion, deletion, and search algorithms may be skipped on an initial reading. Next we look at some quadtree-based alternatives that permit a rectangle to be associated with more than one quadtree block. We conclude by discussing the R-tree [Gutt84] and some of its variants. The R-tree is a hierarchy of rectangular regions containing the data rectangles. The hierarchy is constructed by rules similar to those used to define a B-tree. The regions need not be disjoint. Analyzing the space requirements of these representations, as well as the execution time of algorithms that use them, is quite difficult because they depend heavily on the distribution of the data. In most cases, a limited part of the tree must be traversed, and thus the execution time depends in part on the depth and the shape of the tree.

---

[12] *CIF* stands for Caltech Intermediate Form.

3.5.1 MX-CIF Quadtrees

The *MX-CIF quadtree* associates each rectangle, say R, with the quadtree node corresponding to the smallest block that contains R in its entirety. Rectangles can be associated with both leaf and nonleaf nodes. Subdivision ceases whenever a node's block contains no rectangles. Alternatively subdivision can also cease once a quadtree block is smaller than a predetermined threshold size. This threshold is often chosen to be equal to the expected size of the rectangle [Kede82]. In this section we will assume that rectangles do not overlap, although the techniques can be modified to handle this situation. Figure 3.20 contains a set of rectangles and its corresponding MX-CIF quadtree. Once a rectangle is associated with a quadtree node, say P, it is not considered to be a member of any of the sons of P. For example, in Figure 3.20, rectangle 11 overlaps the space spanned by both nodes D and F but is associated only with node D.

It should be clear that more than one rectangle can be associated with a given enclosing block (i.e., node). There are several ways of organizing these rectangles. Abel and Smith [Abel83] do not apply any ordering. This is equivalent to maintaining a linked list of the rectangles. Another approach, devised by Kedem [Kede82], is described below.

Let P be a quadtree node and S be the set of rectangles associated with P. Members of S are organized into two sets according to their intersection (or the

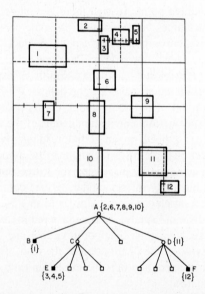

Figure 3.20   An MX-CIF quadtree and the rectangles it represents

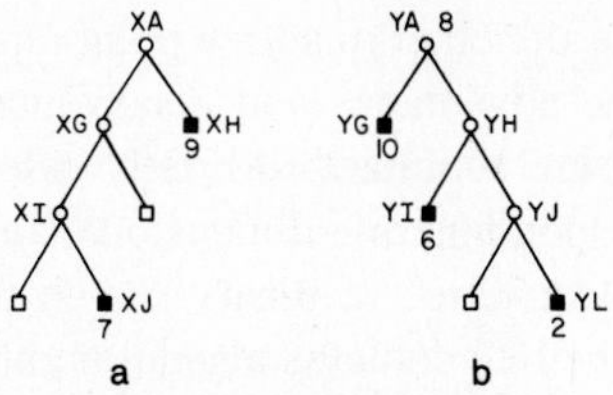

Figure 3.21   Binary trees for the (a) x axis and (b) y axis
passing through node A in Figure 3.20

colinearity of their sides) with the lines passing through the centroid of P's block. The terms *axes* or *axis lines* are used to refer to these lines. For example, consider node P whose block is of size $2 \cdot LX \times 2 \cdot LY$ and is centered at (CX,CY). All members of S that intersect the line $x = CX$ form one set, and all members of S that intersect the line $y = CY$ form the other set. Equivalently these sets correspond to the rectangles intersecting the y and x axes, respectively, passing through (CX,CY). If a rectangle intersects both axes (i.e., it contains the centroid of P's block), then we adopt the convention that it is stored with the set associated with the y axis.

These subsets are implemented as binary trees (really tries), which in actuality are one-dimensional analogs of the MX-CIF quadtree. For example, Figure 3.21 illustrates the binary tree associated with the x and y axes passing through A, the root of the MX-CIF quadtree of Figure 3.20. The subdivision points of the axis lines are shown by the tick marks in Figure 3.20.

The MX-CIF quadtree is related to the region quadtree in the same way as the interval tree is related to the segment tree. It is the two-dimensional analog of the tile tree. The analogy is with the tile tree instead of the interval tree because the MX-CIF quadtree is based on a regular decomposition. In fact, the tile tree and the one-dimensional MX-CIF quadtree are identical when rectangles are not allowed to overlap.

At this point, it is also appropriate to comment on the relationship between the MX-CIF quadtree and the MX quadtree. The similarity is that the MX quadtree is defined for a domain of points with corresponding nodes that are the smallest blocks in which they are contained. Similarly the domain of the MX-CIF quadtree consists of rectangles with corresponding nodes that are the smallest blocks in which they are contained. In both cases, there is a predetermined limit on the level of decomposition. One major difference is that in the MX-CIF quadtree, unlike the MX quadtree, all nodes are of the same type. Thus data are associated with both leaf and nonleaf nodes of the MX-CIF quadtree. Empty nodes in the MX-CIF quadtree are analogous to white nodes in the MX quadtree. In the algorithms described below, an empty node is like an empty son and is represented by a NIL pointer in the direction of a quadrant that contains no rectangles.

Instead of using the one-dimensional analog of the MX quadtrees to organize the set of rectangles covered by a particular quadtree node, we could have adapted the one-dimensional analog of one of the other quadtree point representations discussed in Chapter 2. Not surprisingly, the advantages and disadvantages are similar to those outlined in Section 2.6.3. They are summarized briefly below. In this summary the term *quadtree* refers to the corresponding one-dimensional analog.

An advantage of the point quadtree (a binary search tree in one dimension) is that the depth is reduced when the tree contains a small number of rectangles. This is also an advantage of the PR quadtree, although it is not necessarily true when the rectangles are very close. However, when using a point quadtree, deletion of a rectangle forces us to expend some work in locating a suitable replacement node. The shape of the point quadtree depends on the order in which the rectangles are inserted.

For the PR quadtree, the placement of the rectangle in the tree depends on what other rectangles are present. As rectangles are added to the PR quadtree, existing rectangles may have to be moved to positions farther away from the root (in a node distance sense). On the other hand, once a rectangle is inserted into the MX quadtree, it maintains that position forever since its position is independent of the order of insertion and of the other rectangles present. Another advantage of the MX and PR quadtrees over the point quadtree is that since they are based on a regular decomposition, there is no need to store the subdivision points.

Although the algorithms are defined under the assumption that the rectangles do not overlap, this restriction can be removed quite easily. First, observe that when rectangles are permitted to intersect, there will often be more than one rectangle associated with a node of the one-dimensional MX-CIF quadtree that corresponds to a subdivision point. Thus the issue becomes how to organize these rectangles. The simplest solution is to maintain a linked list of these rectangles. An even more natural solution is to use a tile tree to organize them.

Recall that the tile tree and the one-dimensional MX-CIF quadtree are identical when rectangles are not permitted to overlap. In such a case, the secondary structures of the tile tree consist of, at most, one rectangle. When the tile tree is used in this context, it is not a complete binary tree. Alternatively the tile tree is not necessarily balanced since the subdivision points are fixed by virtue of regular decomposition, rather than being determined by the endpoints of the domain of rectangles as in the definition of the interval tree.

3.5.1.1 INSERTION

The MX-CIF quadtree data structure consists of three types of records, termed *cnode*, *bnode*, and *rectangle*. We use P to denote a pointer to a record. A rectangle is represented by a record of type *rectangle* with five fields that contain the coordinates of its centroid, the distance from the centroid to the borders of the rectangle, and its name. $C(P,A)$ and $L(P,A)$ indicate, respectively, the coordinates of the centroid, and the distance from the centroid to the border of the rectangle. A takes on the values X and Y corresponding to the names of the coordinate axes. The NAME field contains descriptive information about the rectangle stored at a node.

Nodes in the binary trees of the set of rectangles associated with each node of the MX-CIF quadtree are represented by records of type *bnode* with three fields. There

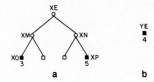

Figure 3.22   Binary trees for the (a) x axis and (b) y axis passing through node E in Figure 3.20

is one node of type *bnode* for each axis subdivision point that is contained in a rectangle or has descendants that contain rectangles. Two of the fields of a *bnode* record are called SON(P,I) and contain pointers to the left and right sons of P, distinguished by I. The third field, called RECT, points to a record of type *rectangle* that contains the axis subdivision point, if such a rectangle exists and is not already included in the binary tree structure associated with an ancestor node in the quadtree structure. Notice that no rectangle is stored in the left (right) subtree of node XN (XM) in Figure 3.22a though rectangle 4 contains it. In this example, rectangle 4 is associated with the *y* axis that passes through node E (i.e., node YE).

Each node in the MX-CIF quadtree is represented by a record of type *cnode* that contains six fields. Four fields are termed SON(P,I), in which I corresponds to one of the four principal quadrant directions. The two remaining fields represent pointers to the binary trees for the rectangles associated with the node. These fields are called BIN(P,I) where I corresponds to one of the two axis names. Note that there is no need to store information about the coordinates of nodes in the MX-CIF quadtree (in records of type *bnode* and *cnode*) since this information can be derived from the path to the node from the root of the MX-CIF quadtree. In the discussion, we assume that each rectangle is unique and does not overlap any other rectangle in the MX-CIF quadtree.

If a rectangle, say R, lies entirely within a block, say B, and one or two sides of R are colinear with axis lines of B, we adopt the convention that R is associated with B. Using this convention, the functions CIF_COMPARE and BIN_COMPARE, given below, determine the quadrant and axis segment, respectively, in which a given rectangle lies relative to a grid or axis subdivision point.

```
quadrant procedure CIF_COMPARE(P,CX,CY);
/* Return the quadrant of the MX-CIF quadtree rooted at position (CX,CY) in which rectan-
   gle P belongs. */
begin
  value pointer rectangle P;
  value real CX,CY;
  return(if C(P,'X') < CX then
            if C(P,'Y') < CY then 'SW'
            else 'NW'
          else if C(P,'Y') < CY then 'SE'
          else 'NE');
end;
```

```
direction procedure BIN_COMPARE(P,CV,V);
/* Determine if the line V=CV lies to the left, right, or passes through rectangle P. */
begin
  value pointer rectangle P;
  value real CV;
  value axis V;
  return(if (C(P,V) – L(P,V)) ≤ CV and CV ≤ (C(P,V) + L(P,V)) then
          'BOTH'
        else if CV < C(P,V) then 'LEFT'
        else 'RIGHT');
end;
```

A rectangle is inserted into an MX-CIF quadtree by a top-down search for the position it is to occupy. We assume that the input rectangle does not overlap any of the existing rectangles. This can be ascertained by preceding the insertion by a call to procedure CIF_SEARCH, described in Section 3.5.1.3. The position to be occupied by a rectangle is determined by a two-step process. First, locate the first quadtree block such that at least one of its axis lines intersects the input rectangle. This search is guided by procedure CIF_COMPARE and controlled by procedure CIF_INSERT. Second, having found such a block and an axis, say V, repeat the subdivision process for the V axis until locating the first subdivision point contained within the rectangle. This search is guided by procedure BIN_COMPARE and controlled by procedure INSERT_-AXIS.

During the process of locating the destination position for the input rectangle we may have to subdivide repreatedly the space spanned by the MX-CIF quadtree (termed *splitting*) and in the process create new nodes. As was the case for the MX quadtree, the shape of the resulting MX-CIF quadtree is independent of the order in which the rectangles are inserted into it, although the shapes of the intermediate trees are dependent on it. Procedures CIF_INSERT and INSERT_AXIS are set forth in greater detail below.

```
procedure CIF_INSERT(P,R,CX,CY,LX,LY);
/* Insert rectangle P in the MX-CIF quadtree rooted at node R. It corresponds to a region
   of size 2 · LX × 2 · LY centered at (CX,CY). If the tree is empty, then R is set to point to
   the new root. Procedure create sets all pointer fields to NIL. */
begin
  value pointer rectangle P;
  reference pointer cnode R;
  value real CX,CY,LX,LY;
  pointer cnode T;
  quadrant Q;
  direction DX,DY;
  /* XF and YF contain multiplicative factors to aid in the location of the centers of the qua-
     drant sons while descending the tree: */
  preload real array XF['NW','NE','SW','SE'] with -1.0,1.0,-1.0,1.0;
  preload real array YF['NW','NE','SW','SE'] with 1.0,1.0,-1.0,-1.0;
  if null(R) then /* The tree at R is initially empty */
```

```
      R ← create(cnode);
      T ← R;
      DX ← BIN_COMPARE(P,CX,'X');
      DY ← BIN_COMPARE(P,CY,'Y');
      while DX ≠ BOTH' and DY ≠ BOTH' do
        begin /* Locate the axis of the quadrant in which P belongs */
          Q ← CIF_COMPARE(P,CX,CY);
          if null(SON(T,Q)) then SON(T,Q) ← create(cnode);
          T ← SON(T,Q);
          LX ← LX/2.0;
          CX ← CX + XF[Q]∗LX;
          LY ← LY/2.0;
          CY ← CY + YF[Q]∗LY;
          DX ← BIN_COMPARE(P,CX,'X');
          DY ← BIN_COMPARE(P,CY,'Y');
        end;
      if DX='BOTH' then /* P belongs on the Y axis */
        INSERT_AXIS(P,T,CY,LY,'Y')
      else INSERT_AXIS(P,T,CX,LX,'X'); /* P belongs on the X axis */
    end;


pointer bnode procedure INSERT_AXIS(P,R,CV,LV,V);
/* Insert rectangle P in the V binary tree rooted at CIF node R. It corresponds to a seg-
     ment of the V axis of length 2 · LV centered at CV. If the V axis is empty, then R is set
     to point to the new root. Procedure create sets all pointer fields to NIL. */
begin
  value pointer rectangle P;
  reference pointer cnode R;
  value real CV,LV;
  value axis V;
  pointer bnode T;
  direction D;
  /* VF contains multiplicative factors to aid in the location of the centers of the segments
     of the axis while descending the tree: */
  preload real array VF['LEFT','RIGHT'] with -1.0,1.0;
  T ← BIN(R,V);
  if null(T) then /* The V axis at T is initially empty */
    T ← BIN(R,V) ← create(bnode);
  D ← BIN_COMPARE(P,CV,V);
  while D ≠ BOTH' do
    begin /* Locate the axis subdivision point that contains P */
      if null(SON(T,D)) then SON(T,D) ← create(bnode);
      T ← SON(T,D);
      LV ← LV/2.0;
      CV ← CV + VF[D]∗LV;
      D ← BIN_COMPARE(P,CV,V);
    end;
  RECT(T) ← P;
end;
```

Building an MX-CIF quadtree of maximum depth n for N rectangles has a worst-case execution time of $O(n \cdot N)$. This situation arises when each rectangle is placed at depth n.[13] Therefore the worst-case storage requirements are also $O(n \cdot N)$. Of course, the expected behavior should be better.

3.5.1.2 DELETION

Deletion of nodes from MX-CIF quadtrees is analogous to the process used for MX quadtrees. The only difference is that collapsing needs to be performed for nodes in the binary trees corresponding to the axes, as well as for the nodes in the MX-CIF quadtree. As an example, to delete rectangle 9 (i.e., node XH in the binary tree for the x axis through node A in Figure 3.21a) from the MX-CIF quadtree of Figure 3.20, we set the RECT field of node XH to NIL and return the space associated with the rectangle record to the free storage list. In addition, since XH has no left or right sons, we can delete it as well. This requires us to set the right son of XH's father node, XA, to NIL.

Deleting rectangle 5 (i.e., node XP in the binary tree for the x axis through E in Figure 3.22a) is slightly more complex. Again we return the space occupied by the RECT field of XP to the free storage list. However, setting the right son of XP's father node, XN, to NIL is not enough. We must also perform merging since both sons of XN are now NIL. This leads to replacing the right son of XN's father, XE, by NIL and returning XN and XP to the free storage list. This process is termed *collapsing* and is the counterpart of the splitting operation that was necessary when inserting a rectangle into an MX-CIF quadtree.

Collapsing can take place over several levels in both the binary tree and in the MX-CIF quadtree. In essence, collapsing is repeatedly applied in the binary tree until encountering the nearest ancestor that has an additional non-NIL son. If the collapsing process brings us to the root of the binary tree (e.g., after deletion of rectangles 3, 4, and 5 from the MX-CIF quadtree of Figure 3.20), then further collapsing of MX-CIF quadtree nodes is possible only if both axes are empty. This process terminates upon encountering a nearest ancestor that has an additional non-NIL son or nonempty axes.

As the collapsing process takes place, the affected nodes are returned to the free storage list. For example, suppose that after deleting rectangle 5 from Figure 3.20 we also delete rectangles 3 and 4. This means that nodes XE, XM, and YE in Figure 3.22 are subjected to the collapsing process, with the result that the axes through E are empty. Since nodes E and E's ancestor, C, have empty axes and no other non-NIL sons, collapsing is applicable with the result that the NE son of A is set to NIL and nodes C, E, XE, XM, XO, and YE are returned to the free storage list.

Procedure CIF_DELETE, given below, is a formal description of the deletion process. The spatial relationships among directions and axes are specified by use of the functions OPDIRECTION and OTHERAXIS. OPDIRECTION(D) yields the direction directly opposite to D (e.g., OPDIRECTION('LEFT') = 'RIGHT' and OPDIRECTION('RIGHT') = 'LEFT' while OPDIRECTION('BOTH') is undefined). Given A as one of two coordinate

---

[13] n is the sum of the maximum depths of the MX-CIF quadtree and of the binary tree.

axes, OTHERAXIS(A) returns the name of the second axis (e.g., OTHERAXIS('X') = 'Y'). The execution time of CIF_DELETE is bounded by two times the maximum depth of the MX-CIF quadtree (including the binary trees for the axes). This upper bound is attained when the nearest ancestor for the collapsing process is the root node.

```
procedure CIF_DELETE(P,R,CX,CY,LX,LY);
/* Delete rectangle P from the MX-CIF quadtree rooted at node R. It corresponds to a
   region of size 2 · LX × 2 · LY centered at (CX,CY). */
begin
  value pointer rectangle P;
  reference pointer cnode R;
  value real CX,CY,LX,LY;
  pointer cnode T,FT,RB,TEMPC;
  pointer bnode B,FB,TEMPB,TB;
  quadrant Q,QF;
  direction D,DF;
  axis V;
  real CV,LV;
  /* XF and YF contain multiplicative factors to aid in the location of the centers of the
     quadrant sons while descending the tree: */
  preload real array XF['NW','NE','SW','SE'] with -1.0,1.0,-1.0,1.0;
  preload real array YF['NW','NE','SW','SE'] with 1.0,1.0,-1.0,-1.0;
  /* VF contains multiplicative factors to aid in the location of the centers of the segments
     of the axis while descending the tree: */
  preload real array VF['LEFT','RIGHT'] with -1.0,1.0;
  if null(R) then return; /* The tree is empty */
  T ← R;
  FT ← NIL;
  while BIN_COMPARE(P,CX,V ← 'X') ≠ 'BOTH' and
        BIN_COMPARE(P,CY,V ← 'Y') ≠ 'BOTH' do
    begin /* Locate the quadrant in which P belongs */
    Q ← CIF_COMPARE(P,CX,CY);
    if null(SON(T,Q)) then return; /* P is not in the tree */
    if not(null(SON(T,CQUAD(Q)))) or
       not(null(SON(T,OPQUAD(Q)))) or
       not(null(SON(T,CCQUAD(Q)))) or
       not(null(BIN(T,'X'))) or
       not(null(BIN(T,'Y'))) then
      begin          /* Reset the common ancestor CIF node with more */
        FT ← T;      /* than one son or at least one nonempty axis. */
        QF ← Q;      /* FT and QF keep track of this information */
      end;
    T ← SON(T,Q);
    LX ← LX/2.0;
    CX ← CX + XF[Q]*LX;
    LY ← LY/2.0;
    CY ← CY + YF[Q]*LY;
    end;
```

```
V ← OTHERAXIS(V); /* Reset the axis since V=CV passes through P */
RB ← T;
FB ← NIL;
B ← BIN(T,V);
CV ← if V='X' then CX
        else CY;
D ← BIN_COMPARE(P,CV,V);
while not(null(B)) and D ≠ 'BOTH' do
  begin /* Locate the point along B's V axis containing P */
    if not(null(SON(B,OPDIRECTION(D)))) or not(null(RECT(B))) then
      begin          /* Reset the nearest ancestor binary tree node which has */
        FB ← B;  /* a rectangle associated with it or more than one */
        DF ← D;  /* son.  FB and DF keep track of this information */
      end;
    B ← SON(B,D);
    LV ← LV/2.0;
    CV ← CV + VF[D]*LV;
    D ← BIN_COMPARE(P,CV,V);
  end;
if null(B) or not(SAMERECTANGLE(P,RECT(B))) then
  return /* P is not in the tree */
else if not(null(SON(B,'X'))) or not(null(SON(B,'Y'))) then
  returntoavail(RECT(B)) /* No collapsing is possible */
else
  begin /* Attempt to perform collapsing */
    TB ← if null(FB) then BIN(RB,V) /* Collapse the entire binary tree */
        else SON(FB,DF);
    D ← 'LEFT';
    while TB ≠ B do
      begin /* Collapse the binary tree one level at a time */
        if null(SON(TB,D)) then D ← OPDIRECTION(D);
        TEMPB ← SON(TB,D);
        SON(TB,D) ← NIL;
        returntoavail(TB);
        TB ← TEMPB;
      end;
    returntoavail(RECT(B));
    returntoavail(B);
    if not(null(FB)) then /* The V axis is not empty */
      SON(FB,DF) ← NIL
    else   /* The V axis is empty */
      begin /* Try to collapse MX-CIF nodes */
        BIN(RB,V) ← NIL;
        if not(null(BIN(RB,OTHERAXIS(V)))) then
          return; /* No further collapsing is possible */
        T ← if null(FT) then R /* Collapse the entire MX-CIF quadtree */
            else SON(FT,QF);
        Q ← 'NW';
```

```
          while not(null(T)) do
            begin /* Collapse one level at a time */
              while null(SON(T,Q)) do Q ← CQUAD(Q);
              TEMPC ← SON(T,Q);
              SON(T,Q) ← NIL;
              returntoavail(T);
              T ← TEMPC;
            end;
            if null(FT) then R ← NIL /* The tree contained just one node */
            else SON(FT,QF) ← NIL; /* Reset the link of the nearest ancestor */
          end;
      end;
  end;
```

3.5.1.3   SEARCH

MX-CIF quadtrees are used to represent small rectangles, and thus one of the most common search queries is to determine if a given rectangle overlaps (i.e., intersects) any of the existing rectangles. This operation is a prerequisite to the successful insertion of a rectangle. It is achieved by use of procedures CIF_SEARCH and CROSS_AXIS, given below. Note the use of Boolean-valued function RECT_INTERSECT to indicate whether two rectangles overlap.

```
Boolean procedure CIF_SEARCH(P,R,CX,CY,LX,LY);
/* Determine if rectangle P intersects any of the rectangles in the MX-CIF quadtree rooted
   at node R.  It corresponds to a region of size 2 · LX × 2 · LY centered at (CX,CY).  */
begin
  value pointer rectangle P;
  value pointer cnode R;
  value real CX,CY,LX,LY;
  quadrant Q;
  /* XF and YF contain multiplicative factors to aid in the location of the centers of the
     quadrant sons while descending the tree: */
  preload real array XF['NW','NE','SW','SE'] with -1.0,1.0,-1.0,1.0;
  preload real array YF['NW','NE','SW','SE'] with 1.0,1.0,-1.0,-1.0;
  if null(R) then return(false)
  else if null(RECT_INTERSECT(P,CX,CY,LX,LY)) then return(false)
  else if CROSS_AXIS(P,BIN(R,'Y'),CY,LY,'Y') or
          CROSS_AXIS(P,BIN(R,'X'),CX,LX,'X') then
    return(true)
  else
    begin
      LX ← LX/2.0;
      LY ← LY/2.0;
      for Q in {'NW', 'NE', 'SW', 'SE'} do
        if CIF_SEARCH(P,SON(R,Q),CX+XF[Q]*LX,CY+YF[Q]*LY,LX,LY) then
          return(true);
      return(false);
```

```
      end;
  end;

  Boolean procedure CROSS_AXIS(P,R,CV,LV,V);
  /* Determine if rectangle P intersects any of the rectangles stored in the binary tree rooted
     at node R which corresponds to a segment of the V axis of length 2 · LV centered at
     CV. */
  begin
    value pointer rectangle P;
    value pointer bnode R;
    value real CV,LV;
    value axis V;
    direction D;
    /* VF contains multiplicative factors to aid in the location of the centers of the segments
       of the axis while descending the tree: */
    preload real array VF['LEFT','RIGHT'] with -1.0,1.0;
    if null(R) then return(false)
    else if not(null(RECT(R))) and
            RECT_INTERSECT(P,C(RECT(R),'X'),C(RECT(R),'Y'),
                                 L(RECT(R),'X'),L(RECT(R),'Y')) then
      return(true)
    else
      begin
        D ← BIN_COMPARE(P,CV,V);
        LV ← LV/2.0;
        return(if D='BOTH' then
                  CROSS_AXIS(P,SON(R,'LEFT'),CV-LV,LV,V) or
                  CROSS_AXIS(P,SON(R,'RIGHT'),CV+LV,LV,V)
               else CROSS_AXIS(P,SON(R,D),CV+VF[D]*LV,LV,V));
      end;
  end;
```

Range queries can also be performed; however, they are more usefully cast in terms of finding all the rectangles in a given area (i.e., a window query). Another popular query is one that seeks to determine if one collection of rectangles can be overlaid on another collection without any of the component rectangles intersecting one another.

These two operations can be implemented by using variants of algorithms developed for handling set operations (i.e., union and intersection) in region-based quadtrees [Hunt78, Hunt79a, Shne81a]. The range query is answered by intersecting the query rectangle with the MX-CIF quadtree. The overlay query is answered by a two-step process. First, intersect the two MX-CIF quadtrees. If the result is empty, they can be safely overlaid, and we merely need to perform a union of the two MX-CIF quadtrees. It should be clear that Boolean queries can be easily handled.

When the rectangles are allowed to intersect, reporting the pairs of rectangles that intersect each other is achieved by traversing the MX-CIF quadtree and for each node examining all neighboring nodes that can contain rectangles intersecting it. In the worst case, for some rectangles we may have to examine the entire MX-CIF quadtree. If this is the case, then the remaining rectangles will not require this much work. Nevertheless, the worst-case execution time of this task is $O(n \cdot N^2)$ for a tree of maximum depth n with N rectangles. The expected behavior should be better.

An alternative solution to the rectangle intersection problem could be formulated by adapting the plane-sweep method described in Section 3.2 to use the MX-CIF quadtree [Same88a]. This is quite straightforward and relies on the observation that a quadtree traversal is analogous to a two-dimensional plane sweep. The effect of the sort phase is obtained by the process of building the MX-CIF quadtree since a quadtree decomposition is equivalent to a multidimensional sort. The effect of the sweep phase is obtained by traversing the quadtree in some order (e.g., Morton order).

The border between the nodes that have been encountered in the traversal and those that have not is the analog of the scan line in the one-dimensional plane sweep. This border is known as the *active border* [Same85f, Same88b] (see Sections 4.2.3 of [Same90b], 5.1.3 of [Same90b], and 6.3.3 of [Same90b]). The adaptation is completed by devising data structures to represent the active border with properties analogous to those of the segment and interval trees (i.e., space and time).

Note that in the plane-sweep solution described in Section 3.2, the sort was performed in one dimension and the sweep in the other direction. In contrast, in the MX-CIF quadtree solution, both the sort and the sweep are performed in the same direction.

The efficiency of operations such as search can be improved by adding a pair of fields, termed CROSS, to the data structure to indicate the size of the minimum enclosing rectangle for the rectangles that intersect each of the two quadrant lines emanating from the subdivision point. However, these additional fields will increase the complexity of the insertion and deletion procedures since these fields must always be updated.

Exercises

3.120. In the following exercises you are to implement functions that may be of use in an information management system for handling a collection of small rectangles based on the MX-CIF quadtree. Assume that the rectangles do not overlap. An MX-CIF quadtree is built by a combination of procedures, CREATE_RECTANGLE, and a variant of CIF_INSERT. A rectangle is created by specifying its centroid and distances to its borders and assigning it a name for subsequent use. You will also want to keep the names in a directory so that rectangles can be retrieved by name without requiring an exhaustive search through the MX-CIF quadtree. This is useful when rectangles have not yet been inserted into the MX-CIF quadtree or after they have been removed. Write a procedure CREATE_-RECTANGLE to do this. It is invoked by a call of the form CREATE_RECT-ANGLE(N,CX,CY,LX,LY) in which N is the name to be associated with the rectangle, CX and CY are the x and y coordinates, respectively, of its centroid, and LX and LY are the horizontal and vertical distances, respectively, to its borders from the centroid.

3.121. Modify procedure CIF_INSERT to take just one argument corresponding to the name of a rectangle and insert it into the MX-CIF quadtree if it does not overlap any of the existing rectangles. To do this, you will need to invoke procedure CIF_SEARCH. If two rectangles only touch along a side or a corner, they are said not to overlap. You are to return *true* if the query rectangle does not overlap any of the intersecting rectangles; otherwise do not insert it, and return the name associated with one of the intersecting rectangles (i.e., if it intersects more than one rectangle).

3.122. Given the x and y coordinates of a point, write a procedure DELETE_POINT to delete the rectangle in which the point is located. Make use of procedure CIF_DELETE.

3.123. Write a procedure DISPLAY to display the block decomposition corresponding to an MX-CIF quadtree on a sheet of line printer output. Assume that the space in which the rectangles are embedded is of size 128×128, with the origin at the lower left corner having coordinates $(0,0)$. Note that the endpoints and widths of the rectangles need not be integers. Each rectangle is displayed by a rectangle with a border consisting of asterisks, while the name of the rectangle appears somewhere inside its boundary. The name is printed horizontally. You may fill the interior of the rectangle with asterisks as long as the name appears as well. All names are restricted in such a way that the number of characters comprising the name of a rectangle never exceeds its length. All rectangles are of size $3+i \times 3+j$, where $0 \le i \le 125$ and $0 \le j \le 125$. In other words, the smallest rectangle is of size 3×3 and the largest is 128×128. The quadrant lines are to be displayed using 'or' symbols (|) and 'hyphens' (-) for vertical and horizontal, respectively. Use a 'plus' symbol (+) at a point where the axes intersect. To facilitate the display of a rectangle, truncate the coordinates of its lower left corner and its side lengths. Do not worry if truncation causes some rectangles to overlap in the display.

3.124. Write a function called LIST_RECTANGLES to list all the elements of a rectangle database in alphanumerical order. This means that letters come before digits in the collating sequence, and shorter identifiers precede longer ones. For example, a sorted list is A, AB, A3D, 3DA, 5. LIST_RECTANGLES yields for each rectangle its name, the x and y coordinates of its centroid, and the horizontal and vertical distances to its borders from the centroid. With this list you are to include the coordinates of its lower left corner and the lengths of its sides. This is of use in interpreting the display since sometimes it is not possible to distinguish the boundaries of the rectangles from the display. The problem is that no asterisks are printed for thin rectangles, and thus several names may run together.

3.125. Write a procedure TOUCH to determine if a given rectangle touches (i.e., is adjacent along a side or a corner) an existing rectangle in the MX-CIF quadtree. It returns a name of a touched rectangle if one is found and NIL otherwise.

3.126. Write a procedure WITHIN to determine if a given rectangle is within a given distance of an existing rectangle in the MX-CIF quadtree. This is the so-called lambda problem. Given a distance d, WITHIN returns the name of a rectangle found to be $\le d$ horizontal or vertical distance units from a side or corner of the query rectangle and NIL otherwise.

3.127. Write a pair of procedures HORIZ_NEIGHBOR and VERT_NEIGHBOR to find the nearest neighbor in the horizontal and vertical directions, respectively, from a given rectangle. HORIZ_NEIGHBOR and VERT_NEIGHBOR return as their value the name of the neighboring rectangle if one exists and NIL otherwise.

3.128. Write a pair of procedures DRAW_HORIZ_NEIGHBOR and DRAW_VERT_NEIGHBOR to draw lines between the two neighbors found in Exercise 3.127.

3.129. Write a procedure LABEL that assigns the same label to all touching rectangles. By touching, it is meant that the rectangles are adjacent along a side or a corner. The collection of rectangles is represented by an MX-CIF quadtree. Display the result of this operation by outputting the MX-CIF quadtree so that all touching rectangles are shown with the same label.

3.130. Write a procedure to find all rectangles that intersect a rectangular window in an MX-CIF quadtree in which rectangles are not permitted to overlap.

3.131. Write a procedure to find all rectangles contained in a rectangular window in an MX-CIF quadtree in which rectangles are not permitted to overlap.

3.132. In Exercises 3.132–3.136, assume that the MX-CIF quadtree allows rectangles to intersect. Use an interval tree to organize the rectangles that cross the axes. Write a procedure to insert a rectangle in an MX-CIF quadtree that permits overlap.

3.133. Write a procedure to delete a rectangle from an MX-CIF quadtree that permits overlap.

3.134. Write a procedure to find all rectangles that intersect a rectangular window in an MX-CIF quadtree that permits overlap.

3.135. Write a procedure to find all rectangles contained in a rectangular window in an MX-CIF quadtree that permits overlap.

3.136. Write a procedure to find all rectangles that enclose a rectangular window in an MX-CIF quadtree that permits overlap.

3.137. Analyze the expected cost of inserting a rectangle into an MX-CIF quadtree.

3.138. What is the expected cost of solving the rectangle intersection problem using the MX-CIF quadtree?

3.139. In the text we saw that the rectangle intersection problem could be solved by using a plane-sweep technique based on a traversal of the MX-CIF quadtree. This requires a data structure with properties similar to the interval tree to represent the active border. Devise such a data structure. What are the space and time requirements of a solution to the rectangle intersection problem that uses it?

3.140. Exercise 2.185 discusses the Euclidean matching problem. Can you use a variant of the MX-CIF quadtree to try to attack this problem? You may wish to represent pairs of points as rectilinear rectangles having the two points as the extreme vertices. In particular, for each point find the closest point, and let them form a rectangle. It should be clear that a point may participate in more than one rectangle. The idea is to obtain a set of rectangles that cover all the points yet have no common points (i.e., they do not touch). Give an example that shows that it is not always possible to find such a set of nontouching rectangles.

3.141. Modify the method proposed in Exercise 3.140 so that it computes a solution without using the greedy-method heuristic (see Exercise 2.185).

3.5.2 Multiple Quadtree Block Representations

Determining how many rectangles intersect a window (e.g., in the form of a rectangle) may be quite costly when using the MX-CIF quadtree and other representations that associate each rectangle with the smallest enclosing quadtree block. The problem is that the quadtree nodes that intersect the query rectangle may contain many rectangles that do not intersect the query rectangle, yet each must be individually compared with the query rectangle to determine the existence of a possible intersection.

For example, consider the MX-CIF quadtree in Figure 3.23, corresponding to the collection of rectangles given in Figure 3.1. Unlike in the examples of the MX-CIF

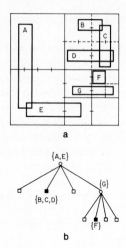

b

Figure 3.23 The MX-CIF quadtree (b) and the block decomposition induced by it (a) for the rectangles in Figure 3.1

quadtree in the previous section, we permit the rectangles to overlap. Although query rectangle 1 (see Figure 3.1) is in the NE quadrant of the root of the MX-CIF quadtree, we still have to check some of the rectangles stored at the root of the entire quadtree since these rectangles could conceivably overlap the query rectangle.

This work could be avoided by using a more compact (in an area sense) representation of each rectangle. Such a representation would use more, and smaller, quadtree blocks to represent each rectangle, but the total area of the blocks would be considerably less than that of the smallest enclosing quadtree block. The result is that more rectangles would be eliminated from consideration by the pruning that occurs during the search of the quadtree. A number of alternatives are available to achieve this effect.

One possibility is to use a region quadtree representation for each rectangle. Such a representation would lead to many nodes since its underlying decomposition rule requires that the block corresponding to each node be homogeneous (i.e., that it be totally contained within one of the rectangles or not be in any of the rectangles). Permitting rectangles to overlap forces a modification of the decomposition rule. In particular, it implies that decomposition ceases when a block is totally contained within one or more rectangles. However, if a block is contained in more than one rectangle, it must be totally contained in all of them.

Abel and Smith [Abel85] present a less radical alternative. They propose that instead of using the minimum enclosing quadtree block, each rectangle is represented by a collection of enclosing quadtree blocks. They suggest that the collection contain a maximum of four blocks, although other amounts are also possible. The four blocks are obtained by determining the minimum enclosing quadtree block, say B, for each

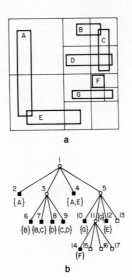

Figure 3.24 *The expanded MX-CIF quadtree (b) and the block decomposition induced by it (a) for the rectangles in Figure 3.1*

rectangle, say R, and then splitting B once to obtain quadtree blocks B_i ($i\in$ {NW, NE, SW, SE}) such that R_i is the portion of R, if any, that is contained in B_i. Next, for each B_i we find the minimum enclosing quadtree block, say D_i, that contains R_i. Now, each rectangle is represented by the set of blocks consisting of D_i. We term such a representation an *expanded MX-CIF quadtree*.

As an example of the expanded MX-CIF quadtree, consider Figure 3.24, corresponding to the collection of rectangles of Figure 3.1. Several items are worthy of note. First, each node appears at least one level lower in the expanded MX-CIF quadtree than it did in the MX-CIF quadtree. Second, some of the D_i may be empty (e.g., rectangle A in Figure 3.24 is covered by blocks 2 and 4; rectangle F in Figure 3.24 is covered by block 14). Third, the covering blocks are not necessarily of equal size (e.g., rectangle E in Figure 3.24 is covered by blocks 4 and 12). It should be clear that the area covered by the collection of blocks D_i is not greater than that of B.

The worst-case execution time for building the expanded MX-CIF quadtree and the space requirements are the same as for the MX-CIF quadtree: $O(n \cdot N)$ for a tree of maximum depth n with N rectangles. The worst-case execution time of the rectangle intersection problem is also the same as that for the MX-CIF quadtree: $O(n \cdot N^2)$. Abel and Smith suggest that the search process can be made more efficient by applying the splitting process again to the blocks D_i. Of course, the more times that we split, the closer we get to the region quadtree representation of the rectangles. Also this increases the space requirement and the insertion and deletion costs.

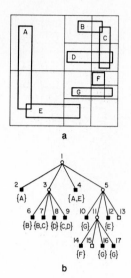

a

b

*Figure 3.25   The RR₁ quadtree (b) and the block decom-
position induced by it (a) for the rectangles in Figure 3.1*

Shaffer [Shaf86a] presents a pair of data structures termed an *RR quadtree* that is somewhat related to the expanded MX-CIF quadtree. Two variants are given. The first, called an *RR₁ quadtree*, makes use of a decomposition rule that splits until each node contains either just one rectangle or all of the rectangles in the node intersect each other (i.e., all the rectangles associated with the node form a clique [Hara69] in the intersection graph). Thus all rectangles are associated with leaf nodes.

When rectangles are not permitted to overlap, this decomposition rule means that no block can contain a part of more than one rectangle. In such a case, the rule is analogous to that used as the basis of the PM quadtree family of line representations described in Section 4.2.3. For example, consider Figure 3.25, which is the RR₁ quadtree corresponding to the collection of rectangles of Figure 3.1. Note that node 3 had to be decomposed further since rectangles B, C, and D do not mutually intersect each other.

The storage requirements of the RR₁ quadtree are much higher than those of the MX-CIF and expanded MX-CIF quadtrees. This is due to the need to decompose the collection when many rectangles are near each other without mutually intersecting each other—such as, a chain formed by intersecting rectangles. This problem is partially resolved by loosening the decomposition criterion of the RR₁ quadtree. In particular, a node, say N, is permitted to contain a pair of rectangles if they intersect or are part of a chain of connected rectangles so that each rectangle in the chain is also in the node. The resulting structure is called an *RR₂ quadtree*. For example, consider Figure 3.26, which is the RR₂ quadtree corresponding to the collection of rectangles of Figure 3.1. Note that now, unlike in the RR₁ quadtree, node 3 need not be further decomposed to

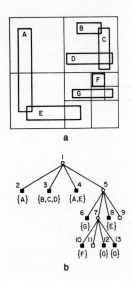

a

b

Figure 3.26   The RR$_2$ quadtree (b) and the block decomposition induced by it (a) for the rectangles in Figure 3.1

deal with rectangles B, C, and D. These three rectangles form a chain but they do not mutually intersect each other.

The RR$_2$ quadtree still requires considerably more storage than the MX-CIF and expanded MX-CIF quadtrees. However, the advantage of the RR quadtree family is that if two rectangles intersect, they must be stored in the same node. This makes window queries quite efficient since fewer rectangles must be examined for intersection. In particular, the number of rectangle comparisons required by a window query in an RR$_2$ quadtree is equal to the number of comparisons that would be made were the query rectangle being inserted into the tree.

Circuit extraction (see Section 3.1) is another operation for which the RR quadtree family is useful since electrical connectedness is easy to detect. Once a circuit has been extracted, it is often desirable to draw it in such a way that all internal lines have been removed (analogous to hidden line elimination in computer graphics). In other words, we want to see only the circuit's outer boundary. This operation is easy to execute in an RR quadtree. For each node, say P, compare each rectangle associated with P with every other rectangle associated with P. Although at first glance this is an $O(N^2)$ operation, in this case, N is the number of rectangles associated with a node which is usually much smaller than the total number of rectangles.

The space requirements of the region quadtree and the RR quadtree family are dependent on the amount of space required to store an individual rectangle. In all three cases, for a tree of maximum depth n, a rectangle uses $O(2^n)$ space. For N rectangles, the time required to build the region quadtree is $O(N \cdot 2^n)$, while for the RR quadtree family it may be as high as $O(N^2 \cdot 2^n)$ since each rectangle must be checked against the rectangles in each node in which it is contained. There are $O(2^n)$ such nodes, and each can contain N rectangles. Solving the rectangle intersection problem is quite easy; it is done by traversing the tree and reporting all nodes that contain more than one rectangle. The execution time and space requirements are of the same order. Each intersection needs to be reported once only (see Exercise 3.160).

Exercises

3.142. Write a procedure called EXPANDED_INSERT to insert a rectangle, R, into an expanded MX-CIF quadtree. Rectangle R may overlap existing rectangles.

3.143. Analyze the expected cost of inserting a rectangle into an expanded MX-CIF quadtree.

3.144. Write a procedure called EXPANDED_WINDOW to find all rectangles that intersect a window in an expanded MX-CIF quadtree.

3.145. Analyze the cost of EXPANDED_WINDOW.

3.146. Prove that the worst-case execution time for building the expanded MX-CIF quadtree, the space requirements, and the worst-case execution time of the rectangle intersection problem are the same as for the MX-CIF quadtree.

3.147. Write a procedure called RR1_INSERT to insert a rectangle, R, into an RR_1 quadtree. Rectangle R may overlap existing rectangles.

3.148. Analyze the expected cost of inserting a rectangle into an RR_1 quadtree.

3.149. Write a procedure called RR1_WINDOW to find all rectangles that intersect a window in an RR_1 quadtree.

3.150. Analyze the cost of RR1_WINDOW.

3.151. What is the expected cost of solving the rectangle intersection problem using an RR_1 quadtree?

3.152. Write a procedure called RR2_INSERT to insert a rectangle, R, into an RR_2 quadtree. Rectangle R may overlap existing rectangles.

3.153. Analyze the expected cost of inserting a rectangle into an RR_2 quadtree.

3.154. Write a procedure called RR2_WINDOW to find all rectangles that intersect a window in an RR_2 quadtree.

3.155. Analyze the cost of RR2_WINDOW.

3.156. Define circuit extraction as a process that finds chains of intersecting rectangles. Write a procedure to perform circuit extraction in an RR_2 quadtree.

3.157. Write a procedure to eliminate the internal lines in a circuit represented by an RR_2 quadtree.

3.158. What is the expected cost of solving the rectangle intersection problem using an RR_2 quadtree?

3.159. A variant of the RR quadtree that stores only one rectangle in each node can be used to represent a binary image. In this case, the image consists of a collection of adjacent but nonoverlapping rectangles. To construct such a quadtree, you merely need to modify the merge routine of the raster-to-quadtree conversion algorithm (see Section 4.2.1 of [Same90b]). In particular, four nodes are merged to form a larger node not if they are leaf nodes with the same value, but, instead, if they are all leaf nodes so that the rectangle descriptions that they store can be merged to form a larger rectangle. For example in Figure 1.1, nodes 2, 3, 4, and 5 can be merged to form a node containing the rectangle formed by black blocks 4 and 5. Write a procedure that builds such a variant of the RR quadtree for a binary image.

3.160. [Clifford A. Shaffer] How would you avoid reporting duplicate intersections when solving the rectangle intersection problem using an RR quadtree (both RR_1 and RR_2)?

3.5.3 R-Trees

The R-tree [Gutt84] is a hierarchical data structure derived from the B-tree [Come79]. In section 2.8.1, its use was mentioned in representing multidimensional point data. In this section I describe its use in the organization of a collection of arbitrary geometric objects by representing them as d-dimensional rectangles. Each node in the tree corresponds to the smallest d-dimensional rectangle that encloses its son nodes. The leaf nodes contain pointers to the actual geometric objects in the database, instead of sons. The objects are represented by the smallest aligned rectangle in which they are contained.

Often the nodes correspond to disk pages, and thus the parameters defining the tree are chosen so that a small number of nodes is visited during a spatial query. Note that rectangles corresponding to different nodes may overlap. Also a rectangle may be spatially contained in several nodes, yet it can be associated with only one node. This means that a spatial query may often require several nodes to be visited before ascertaining the presence or absence of a particular rectangle. This discussion is limited to the representation of rectangles in two dimensions.

The basic rules for the formation of an R-tree are similar to those for a B-tree. All leaf nodes appear at the same level. Each entry in a leaf node is a 2-tuple of the form (R,O) such that R is the smallest rectangle that spatially contains data object O. Each entry in a nonleaf node is a 2-tuple of the form (R,P) such that R is the smallest rectangle that spatially contains the rectangles in the child node pointed at by P. An R-tree of order (m,M) means that each node in the tree, with the exception of the root, contains between $m \leq \lceil M/2 \rceil$ and M entries. The root node has at least two entries unless it is a leaf node.

For example, consider the collection of rectangles given in Figure 3.1, and treat the query rectangles (i.e., 1, 2, and 3) as elements of the collection so that there are 10 rectangles. Let $M = 3$ and $m = 2$. One possible R-tree for this collection is given in Figure 3.27a. Figure 3.27b shows the spatial extent of the rectangles of the nodes in Figure 3.27a, with broken lines denoting the rectangles corresponding to the subtrees rooted at the nonleaf nodes. Note that the R-tree is not unique. Its structure depends heavily on the order in which the individual rectangles were inserted into (and possibly deleted from) the tree.

The algorithm for inserting an object (i.e., a record corresponding to its enclosing rectangle) in an R-tree is analogous to that used for B-trees. New rectangles are added to leaf nodes. The appropriate leaf node is determined by traversing the R-tree starting at its root and at each step choosing the subtree whose corresponding rectangle would have to be enlarged the least. Once the leaf node has been determined, a

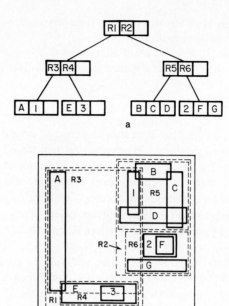

Figure 3.27 (a) R-tree the collection of rectangles in Figure 3.1 and (b) the spatial extents of the enveloping rectangles

check is made to see if insertion of the rectangle will cause the node to overflow. If yes, then the node must be split, and the $M + 1$ records must be distributed in the two nodes. Splits are propagated up the tree.

There are many possible ways to split a node. One possible goal is to distribute the records among the nodes so that the likelihood that the nodes will be visited in subsequent searches will be reduced. This is accomplished by minimizing the total areas of the covering rectangles for the nodes (i.e., coverage). An alternative goal is to reduce the likelihood that both nodes are examined in subsequent searches. This is accomplished by minimizing the area common to both nodes (i.e., overlap). Of course, at times these goals may be contradictory. For example, consider the four rectangles in Figure 3.28a. The first goal is satisfied by the split in Figure 3.28b while the second goal is satisfied by the split in Figure 3.28c.

Guttman [Gutt84] reports on the performance of three node-splitting algorithms based on the minimization of the total area of the covering rectangles (i.e., the first of the goals described). The first is an exhaustive algorithm trying all possibilities. In such a case the number of possible partitions is 2^M-1 (see Exercise 3.169). This is unreasonable for most values of M (e.g., $M = 50$ for a page size of 1024 bytes).

The second is a quadratic cost algorithm that first finds the two rectangles that would waste the most area were they to be in the same node. This is determined by

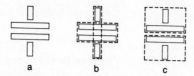

Figure 3.28   (a) Four rectangles and the splits that would
be induced, (b) by minimizing the total area of the covering
rectangles and (c) by minimizing the area common to the
covering rectangles of both nodes

subtracting the sum of the areas of the two rectangles from the area of the covering rectangle. These two rectangles are placed in the separate nodes, say j and k. Next, examine the remaining rectangles and for each rectangle, say i, compute d_{ij} and d_{ik}, which are the increases in the area of the covering rectangles of nodes j and k when i is added to them. Now find rectangle n such that $|d_{nj} - d_{nk}|$ is a maximum, and add n to the node with the smallest increase in area. Repeat this process for the remaining rectangles.

The third is a linear cost algorithm that first finds the two rectangles with the greatest normalized separation along all of the dimensions. For example, assuming that the origin is at the upper left corner of the space, in the vertical dimension these are the rectangles with the maximum lower side and the minimum upper side. The remaining rectangles are processed in arbitrary order and placed in the node whose covering rectangle is increased the least by their addition. Empirical tests showed that there was not much difference between the three splitting algorithms in the performance of search (i.e., in CPU time and in the number of pages accessed). Thus the faster linear splitting algorithm was found preferable even though the quality of the splits was somewhat inferior.

Deletion of a rectangle, say R, from an R-tree proceeds by locating the leaf node, say L, containing R and removing R from L. Next, adjust the covering rectangles on the path from L to the root of the tree while removing all nodes in which underflow occurs and adding them to the set U. Once the root node is reached, if it has just one son, the son becomes the new root. The nodes in which underflow occurred (i.e., members of U) are reinserted at the root. Elements of U that correspond to leaf nodes result in the placement of their constituent rectangles in the leaf nodes, while other nodes are placed at a level so that their leaf nodes are at the same level as those of the whole tree.

The deletion algorithm for an R-tree differs from that for a B-tree in that in the case of underflow, nodes are reinserted instead of being merged with adjacent nodes. The difficulty is that there is no concept of adjacency in an R-tree, although we could merge with the sibling whose area will be increased the least, or alternatively just distribute the elements of the underflowing node among its siblings. Nevertheless, reinsertion is used by Guttman [Gutt84] because of a belief that it enables the tree to reflect dynamically the changing spatial structure of the data rather than the gradual degradation that could arise when a rectangle maintains the same parent throughout its lifetime.

Searching for points or regions in an R-tree is straightforward. The only problem is that a large number of nodes may have to be examined since a rectangle may be contained in the covering rectangles of many nodes while its corresponding record is contained only in one of the leaf nodes (e.g, in Figure 3.27, rectangle 1 is contained in its entirety in R1, R2, R3, and R5). For example, suppose we wish to determine the identity of the rectangle element, in the collection of rectangles given in Figure 3.1, that contains point Q at coordinates (21,24). Since Q can be in either of R1 or R2, we must search both of their subtrees. Searching R1 first, we find that Q could be contained only in R3. Searching R3 does not lead to the rectangle that contains Q even though Q is in a portion of rectangle D that is in R3. Thus we must search R2. We find that Q can be contained only in R5. Searching R5 results in locating D, the desired rectangle.

The insertion algorithm and the accompanying node splitting techniques described above are based on a dynamic database. If the database can be expected to be static and all of the objects are known a priori, then a different technique can be used to build an R-tree. Roussopoulos and Leifker [Rous85] propose the use of a *packed* R-*tree*. This is an R-tree built by successively applying a nearest neighbor relation to group objects in a node after the set of objects has been sorted according to a spatial criterion. Once an entire level of the tree is built, the algorithm is reapplied to add nodes at the next higher level, terminating when a level contains just one node. This is a static method, which fills each node to capacity.

Although the packed R-tree does not necessarily result in a minimum coverage and/or overlap, empirical tests [Rous85] of its performance on point searches in a database of two-dimensional points show its use leads to significant improvements vis-à-vis an R-tree built using the conventional R-tree insertion routine. In these tests each node was constructed by selecting an object from a spatially sorted list and then adding its $M - 1$ nearest neighbors. Once all the nodes at a given level have been constructed, the process is applied recursively, forming nodes at successively higher levels in the tree until just one node remains. A better approach, although far costlier from a combinatorial standpoint, is to choose the M objects simultaneously so that the area of the resulting covering rectangle is minimized.

Another alternative to the R-tree in dealing with rectangles is the R^+-tree [Ston86, Sell87], an extension of the k-d-B-tree [Robi81] (see Section 2.8.1). The motivation for the R^+-tree is to avoid overlap among the bounding rectangles. In particular, all bounding rectangles (i.e., at levels other than the leaf) are nonoverlapping. Thus, each rectangle is associated with all the bounding rectangles that it intersects. The result is that there may be several paths starting at the root to the same rectangle. This will lead to an increase in the height of the tree; however, retrieval time is speeded up.

Figure 3.29 is an example of one possible R^+-tree for the collection of rectangles in Figure 3.1. Once again the query rectangles (i.e., 1, 2, and 3) are treated as elements of the collection, so that there is a total of 10 rectangles. This particular tree is of order (2,3), although in general it is not possible to guarantee always that all nodes

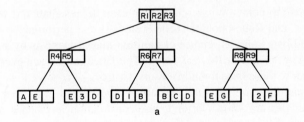

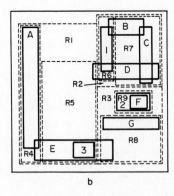

Figure 3.29   *(a) R⁺–tree for the collection of rectangles in Figure 3.1 and (b) the spatial extents of the enclosing rectangles*

will have a minimum of two entries. Notice that rectangles D and E appear in three different nodes, while rectangle B appears in two different nodes. Other variants are possible since the R⁺-tree is not unique.

The *cell tree* of Günther [Günt87, Günt88] is similar to the R⁺-tree. The difference is that the nonleaf nodes of the cell tree are convex polyhedra instead of bounding rectangles. The sons of each node, say *P*, form a binary space partition (BSP) [Fuch80] of *P* (see Section 1.4.1). The cell tree is designed to deal with polyhedral data of arbitrary dimension. As in the R⁺-tree, the polyhedral data being represented may be stored in more than one node.

It is interesting to note that the decomposition into blocks induced by the R⁺-tree is similar to the way a region quadtree would be used to represent a collection of rectangles (see Section 3.5.2). An extension of the k-d-B-tree, the R⁺-tree has a drawback: B-tree performance guarantees are no longer valid. For example, pages are not guaranteed to be half full without very complicated record insertion and deletion procedures. Nevertheless, empirical tests by Faloutsos, Sellis, and Roussopoulos [Falo87] reveal reasonable behavior in comparison to the conventional R-tree.

These tests were coupled with a limited analysis of the behavior of the two data structures when used to represent one-dimensional intervals of equal length by transforming them to points in two dimensions using representation 2 of Section 3.4. Sellis, Faloutsos, and Roussopoulos [Sell87] suggest that performance of the R^+-tree can be improved by a judicious choice of partition lines, as well as by a careful initial grouping of the rectangles at the leaf level. The latter can be achieved by applying heuristics similar to those used to build a packed R-tree.

Assume that the R-tree and the R^+-tree are constructed in a batch manner; that is, all the rectangles are known prior to the construction and hence are arbitrarily grouped together. For N rectangles, the construction time and space requirements of these two data structures are both $O(N)$ and $O(N^2)$, respectively. The reason for the higher costs for the R^+-tree is that a rectangle may appear in N nodes because of its intersection with N other rectangles. This analysis assumes that no optimization is performed when a node overflows. In both cases the worst-case execution time of the rectangle intersection problem is $O(N^2)$ (see Exercises 3.170 and 3.181).

Exercises

3.161. What is the difference between the definition of a node in an R-tree and a node in a B-tree?

3.162. What is the maximum height of an R-tree of order (m,M) with N rectangles (not nodes)?

3.163. What is the maximum number of nodes in an R-tree of order (m,M) with N rectangles?

3.164. Write an algorithm to insert a rectangle into an R-tree. You will have to choose one of the described techniques for splitting a full node with $M + 1$ records.

3.165. Analyze the expected cost of inserting a rectangle into an R-tree.

3.166. Write an algorithm to delete a rectangle from an R-tree.

3.167. Write an algorithm to perform a point query in an R-tree.

3.168. Write an algorithm to perform a window query in an R-tree.

3.169. Prove that there are $2^M - 1$ possible partitions of an R-tree node with $M + 1$ records into two nonempty subsets.

3.170. Prove that the worst-case execution time of the rectangle intersection problem for N rectangles using an R-tree is $O(N^2)$.

3.171. What is the expected cost of the rectangle intersection problem for N rectangles using an R-tree?

3.172. Write an algorithm to build a packed R-tree for a collection of two-dimensional objects. You must decide on a spatial criterion by which to sort the objects prior to inserting them in the tree and for choosing the nearest neighbor. Construct each node by selecting an object from the spatially sorted list and then adding its $M - 1$ nearest neighbors.

3.173. Repeat Exercise 3.172 with a node construction algorithm that chooses the M objects simultaneously so that the area of the resulting covering rectangle is minimized.

3.174. Prove that the packed R-tree construction algorithms of Exercises 3.172 and 3.173 result in reducing coverage and overlap. How close do they come to minimizing them? Perform an empirical study to support your conclusion.

3.175. What are the minimum and maximum heights of an R^+-tree of order (m,M) with N rectangles (not nodes)?

3.176. Write an algorithm to insert a rectangle into an R^+-tree.

3.177. Analyze the expected cost of inserting a rectangle into an R^+-tree.

3.178. Write an algorithm to delete a rectangle from an R^+-tree.

3.179. Write an algorithm to perform a point query in an R^+-tree.

3.180. Write an algorithm to perform a window query in an R^+-tree.

3.181. Prove that the worst-case execution time of the rectangle intersection problem for N rectangles using a R^+-tree is $O(N^2)$.

3.182. What is the expected cost of the rectangle intersection problem for N rectangles using a R^+-tree?

CURVILINEAR DATA

4

The region quadtree is an example of a region representation based on a description of its interior. In this chapter, we focus on hierarchical representations that specify boundaries of regions. This is done in the more general context of hierarchical data structures for curvilinear data. The emphasis is on regions having linear boundaries (i.e., specified by straight lines). The data are usually in the form of a network of adjacent polygons resulting in a subdivision of space termed a *polygonal map*. Vector representations such as chain codes [Free74] or lists of points (e.g., [Nagy79]) are not discussed. For a brief summary of these methods, see the conclusion in Section 4.4.

Curvilinear data can be differentiated on the basis of whether the lines are isolated, are elements of treelike structures, or are elements of networks. In the case of networks, the regions bounded by the network are usually polygons. However, polygons also arise outside the context of a network, as is the case when they are isolated (e.g., lakes) or nested (e.g., contours). It is possible to represent the boundary of each polygon separately (e.g., using a vector or a chain code representation for each curve that bounds two adjacent polygons). However, it is preferable to represent the complete network of boundaries with a single data structure. This is the approach taken in this chapter.

Section 4.1 contains a brief discussion of methods based on rectangular approximations to the data as typified by the strip tree [Ball81]. Section 4.2 presents a number of data structures based on the region quadtree. This presentation includes descriptions of many related data structures and details their interrelationship.

The techniques discussed in Sections 4.1 and 4.2 have been developed primarily because they facilitate set operations. Other data structures for representing curvilinear data have been motivated by other applications. For example, ease of display is a characterization of B-splines and Bezier methods [Cohe80] (see also Chapter 6 of

[Same90b]). Section 4.3 addresses the point location problem by reviewing a couple of solutions that are rooted in computational geometry [Edel84, Tous80]. This problem involves determining the identity of a region that contains a given point. These solutions are compared with one that is based on the region quadtree.

4.1 STRIP TREES, ARC TREES, AND BSPR

Ballard's *strip tree* [Ball81] is a hierarchical representation of a single curve that is obtained by successively approximating segments of it by enclosing rectangles. The data structure consists of a binary tree whose root represents a bounding rectangle for the entire curve. For example, consider Figure 4.1 where the curve between points P and Q, at locations (x_P, y_P) and (x_Q, y_Q), respectively, is modeled by a strip tree. The rectangle associated with the root, A in this example, corresponds to a rectangular strip that encloses the curve, two of whose sides are parallel to the line joining the endpoints of the curve (i.e., P and Q). These sides pass through the points on the curve at a maximum distance from the line joining the curve's endpoints. The resulting rectangle is really a truncated version of what is termed a *band* by Peucker [Peuc76].

Next, this rectangle is decomposed into two parts at one of the points (termed a *splitting point*) on the rectangle that is also part of the curve. There is at least one such splitting point. If there are more, the decomposition is performed using the point at a maximum distance from the line joining the endpoints of the curve. If the curve is both continuous and differentiable at the splitting point, the boundaries of the rectangle that pass through these points are tangents to the curve. This splitting process is recursively applied to the two sons until every strip is of a width less than a predetermined value.

For Figure 4.1, the first splitting operation results in the creation of strips B and C. Strip C is further split, creating strips D and E, at which point the splitting process ceases. Figure 4.2 shows the resulting binary tree. Each node in the strip tree is implemented as a record with eight fields. Four fields contain the x and y coordinates of the endpoints, two fields contain pointers to the two sons of the node, and two

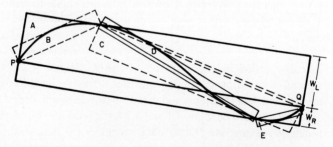

Figure 4.1   A curve and its decomposition into strips

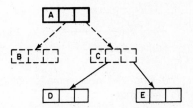

Figure 4.2   Strip tree corresponding to Figure 4.1

fields contain information about the width of the strip (i.e., w_L and w_R of Figure 4.1).

If a closed form representation of the curve is known (i.e., $y = f(x)$), the strip tree is not so useful since many problems (e.g., curve intersection) can be solved directly. However, most often the curve is specified as an ordered sequence of points $t_0, t_1, \cdots, t_n$. Successive pairs of points define line segments, some of which may be colinear. The points are considered to be connected, although this restriction can be relaxed.

Given a curve specified by the sequence $t_0, t_1, \cdots, t_n$, Ballard presents two methods for the construction of its corresponding strip tree. The first method proceeds in a top-down manner and was described above. In this case, each strip, say between points t_a and t_b, is a rectangle that encloses the portion of the curve that lies between t_a and t_b. Note that the result is not the rectangle of minimum bounding area for the strip (see Exercise 4.7). This method requires a search to determine the points on the curve that are at a maximum distance from the line joining t_a and t_b and, thus, takes $O(n \cdot \log_2 n)$ time.

The second method proceeds in a bottom-up manner, as follows. Take successive pairs of points, (t_0, t_1) (t_1, t_2) $\cdots$ (t_{n-1}, t_n), and find their strips, say $s_0, s_1, \cdots, s_{n-1}$. Pair up these strips, that is, (s_0, s_1) (s_2, s_3) $\cdots$, and cover them with larger strips. Continue to apply this process until there is a single strip. This method takes $O(n)$ time; however, the resulting approximations are not as good as those of the first method.

Figure 4.1 is a relatively simple example. To be able to cope with more complex curves, the notion of a strip tree must be extended. In particular, closed curves (e.g., Figure 4.3) and curves that extend past their endpoints (Figure 4.4) require some special treatment. The general idea is that these curves are enclosed by rectangles,

Figure 4.3   The strip tree representation of a closed curve

Figure 4.4   The strip tree representation of a curve that extends past its endpoints

which are split into two rectangular strips. From that point, the strip tree is used as before. To be able to handle curves that consist of disconnected segments, strips are classified as either regular or not, and a flag is associated with each strip to indicate its status. Formally a curve is said to be *regular* if it is connected and its endpoints touch the ends of the strip.

Like point and region quadtrees, strip trees are useful in applications that involve search and set operations. Suppose we wish to determine whether a road crosses a river. Using a strip tree representation for these features, answering this query means basically performing an intersection of the corresponding strip trees. Three cases are possible, as is shown in Figure 4.5. Parts a and b of Figure 4.5 correspond to the answers NO and YES, respectively, while Figure 4.5c requires us to descend further down the strip tree.

The importance of this decomposition into three cases is that we often save a lot of work when an intersection is impossible. The technique is similar to that used by Little and Peucker [Litt79] for bands (see Exercise 4.11). A related operation is determining if a point lies inside an area represented by a strip tree. For closed curves that are well behaved, curve intersection and point membership have an expected execution time of $O(\log_2 n)$ where n is the number of points describing the curve.

Other operations that can be performed efficiently by using the strip tree data structure include the computation of the strip tree corresponding to the union of two curves, length of a curve, areas of closed curves, and intersection of curves with areas [Ball81]. (For more details, see the exercises.) Note that when we compute the strip tree corresponding to the union of two regular curves represented by strip trees, the resulting curve may not necessarily be regular.

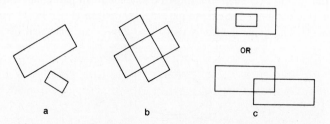

Figure 4.5   Three possible results of intersecting two strip trees: (a) null, (b) clear, (c) possible

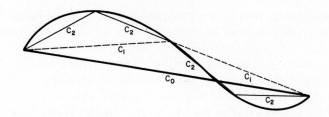

Figure 4.6   The zeroth (C_0), first (C_1) and second (C_2) arc tree approximations of the curve of Figure 4.1

Strip trees are used by Gaston and Lozano-Perez [Gast84] in robotic tactile recognition and localization. The *prism tree* of Faugeras and Ponce [Faug83, Ponc85, Ponc87b] is a variant of the strip tree that hierarchically approximates a surface by using a truncated pyramid as an enclosing box. It is a ternary tree structure and is built from an initial triangulation of an object by using a polyhedral approximation algorithm [Faug84]. (For more details, see Section 5.7.)

The *arc tree* of Günther [Günt87] is a close relative of the strip tree. Its subdivision rule consists of a regular decomposition of a curve based on its length. In particular, the curve is repeatedly approximated by sequences of straight line segments whose endpoints are points on the curve. The curve C of length l is defined parametrically by a function $C(t)$ from the interval [0:1] to the two-dimensional Euclidean space—$x = C_x(t)$ and $y = C_y(t)$, such that the length of the curve from $t = a$ to $t = b$ is $(b - a) \cdot l$.

The kth *approximation of* $C(t)$ is a sequence of 2^k line segments connecting the points $C(i/2^k)$ and $C((i+1)/2^k)$, $0 \le i < 2^k$, where the length of the corresponding arcs is $l/2^k$. For example, Figure 4.6 shows the 0th, 1st, and 2nd approximations of the curve in Figure 4.1. The approximations are labeled with C_0, C_1, and C_2 respectively.

The approximating process for an arc tree is applied in the same manner as the strip tree. The process stops when the straight line approximation of every subarc is within a given tolerance (e.g., the maximum error is less than a predetermined value). The result is a binary tree. The construction of an arc tree requires two passes over the curve. The first pass determines its length. This can be a cumbersome process. If the closed form representation of the curve is known (i.e., $y = f(x)$), this can be done by integration (see Exercise 4.22); however, the result is an elliptic integral, which is not easy to compute. Usually a smoothing step is applied to get rid of noise prior to starting the construction process. The second pass is straightforward.

The arc tree has the interesting property that for each approximation of a segment of the curve, say a subarc, a region can be computed so that the subarc is entirely contained within the region (see Exercise 4.23). This region is an ellipse defined as follows. Consider a subarc, say s, of length of $l/2^k$ between endpoints $C(i/2^k)$ and $C((i+1)/2^k)$, $0 \le i < 2^k$. The ellipse of s has a major axis whose length is $l/2^k$ and its focal points are at $C(i/2^k)$ and $C((i+1)/2^k)$. Using the ellipses as the approximating shapes has an advantage over the use of rectangles in the strip tree because there is no need to make special provisions for closed curves or for curves that extend past their endpoints.

Günther shows how the arc tree can be used to solve a number of problems, such as testing for point inclusion, and set operations, including the detection and computation of the intersection of two curves, a curve with an area, and two areas. However, ellipses are not easy to work with. For example, to determine if two areas intersect, we can first test their bounding areas. This is a complex operation when the bounding areas are ellipses. In fact, often it is preferable to use bounding circles even though they do not provide as tight a fit as does the ellipse. Bounding boxes could also be used.

When the curves consist of straight line segments, it is easier to decompose them at their vertices than to introduce artificial vertices $c(i/2^k)$. Günther uses the term *polygon arc tree* to describe the resulting structure. Given a curve with $n + 1$ vertices labeled $v_1, v_2, \cdots, v_{n+1}$, the first subdivision is at $v_{\lceil n/2 \rceil}$. Unlike the arc tree, however, the length of the curve is no longer implicit from the subdivision point, and hence it must be stored with each node. The maximum depth of the polygon arc tree is $\log_2 n$.

The strip, arc, and polygon arc trees can be characterized as top-down approaches to curve approximation. Burton [Burt77] defines a closely related structure termed *Binary Searchable Polygonal Representation* (*BSPR*), which is a bottom-up approach to curve approximation. The primitive unit of approximation is a rectangle; however, in the case of the BSPR all rectangles are upright (i.e., they have a single orientation).

The curve to be approximated by the BSPR is decomposed into a set of *simple* sections where each simple section corresponds to a segment of the curve that is monotonic in both the x and y coordinate values of the points comprising it. The tree is built by combining pairs of adjacent simple sections to yield *compound* sections. This process is repeatedly applied until the entire curve is approximated by one compound section. Thus we see that leaf nodes correspond to simple sections, and nonleaf nodes correspond to compound sections. For a curve with 2^n simple sections, the corresponding BSPR has n levels.

As an example of a BSPR, consider the regular octagon in Figure 4.7a with vertices A–H. It can be decomposed into four simple sections: ABCD, DEF, FGH, and HA. Figure 4.7b shows a level 1 approximation to the four simple sections consisting of rectangles AIDN, DJFN, HMFK, and AMHL, respectively. Pairing up adjacent simple sections yields compound sections AIJF corresponding to AIDN and DJFN and AFKL corresponding to HMFK and AMHL (Figure 4.7c). More pairing yields the rectangle for compound section IJKL (Figure 4.7d). The resulting BSPR tree is shown in Figure 4.7e. Using the BSPR, Burton shows how to perform point in polygon determination and polygon intersection. These operations are implemented by tree searches and splitting operations.

The strip tree and the arc tree share the property of being independent of the grid system in which they are embedded. The BSPR construction process is similar to

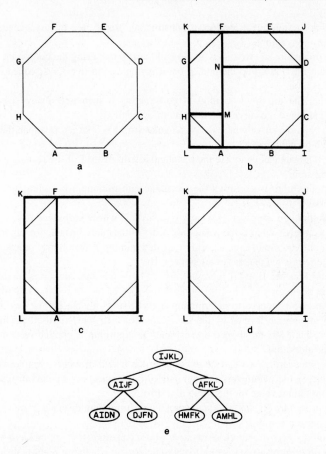

Figure 4.7 (a) A regular octagon and (b)–(d) the three successive approximations resulting from the use of BSPR, (e) the resulting BSPR

the bottom-up strip tree construction process except that in the case of the BSPR the rectangles must be upright. An advantage of the BSPR representation over the strip tree is the absence of a need for special handling of closed curves. However, the BSPR is not as flexible as the strip and arc trees. In particular, the resolution of the approximation is fixed (i.e., once the width of the rectangle is selected, it cannot be varied). In fact, this is similar to the advantage of quadtree-based decomposition methods over hexagon-based systems pointed out in Section 1.4. Recall that for the hexagon, we must decide a priori on the finest resolution.

Exercises

4.1. Write a procedure TOP_DOWN_STRIP to build a strip tree using the top-down method.

4.2. Prove that the top-down method of constructing a strip tree for a sequence of n points takes $O(n \cdot \log_2 n)$ time.

4.3. Write a procedure BOTTOM_UP_STRIP to build a strip tree using the bottom-up method.

4.4. Prove that the bottom-up method of constructing a strip tree for a sequence of n points takes $O(n)$ time.

4.5. Prove that the top-down method of constructing a strip tree always yields a tighter approximation of the curve than the bottom-up method.

4.6. Give an example curve where the rectangular strip has a larger area than the rectangle of minimum bounding area.

4.7. Why is it advantageous to use the rectangular strip instead of the rectangle of minimum bounding area?

4.8. Give an algorithm to construct the rectangle with minimum bounding area for an arbitrary curve.

4.9. Suppose that you are given two curves, C_1 and C_2, whose strip trees have depths d_1 and d_2, respectively. What is the worst-case order of the curve intersection algorithm?

4.10. How would you modify the algorithm for determining if two curves represented by strip trees intersect when the curves are not regular?

4.11. Little and Peucker [Litt79] represent curves by bands that are strips of infinite length. They are analogous to the strip found at the root of the strip tree. Determining if two curves intersect reduces to determining if their bands intersect. The key idea is that if they do, the region formed by the intersection of their bands is used to clip the curves, bands are built for the clipped curves, and the algorithm is applied recursively. Implement this algorithm.

4.12. Write a procedure LENGTH_STRIP to compute the length of a curve represented by a strip tree. One of the parameters to your procedure should be a maximum resolution level (e.g., a minimum value for the width of a strip).

4.13. Write a procedure CLOSEST_STRIP to compute the minimum distance from a given point to a curve represented by a strip tree.

4.14. How would you represent a closed curve whose corresponding region has a hole?

4.15. Write a procedure MEMBER_AREA_STRIP to determine whether a point is inside or outside an area represented by a strip tree.

4.16. Write a procedure AREA_STRIP to compute the area within a closed curve that is represented by a strip tree.

4.17. Write a procedure CURVE_AREA to compute the intersection of a curve represented by a strip tree and an area represented by a strip tree. The result is the portion of the curve that overlaps the area.

4.18. Write a procedure AREA_AREA to compute the intersection of two areas represented by strip trees. The result is an area.

4.19. Write a procedure MEMBER_AREA_BSPR to determine whether a point is inside or outside an area represented by a BSPR.

4.20. Write a procedure INTERSECT_BSPR to determine the points of intersection of two curves represented by a BSPR.

4.21. Is the arc tree unique?

4.22. Suppose you are given a curve specified by $y = f(x)$. What is its length between points a and b?

4.23. Prove that every subarc in an arc tree is completely internal to its approximating ellipse.

4.24. Compare the space requirements of a strip tree and an arc tree.

4.25. How do you determine if a point is inside or outside an ellipse?

4.26. Write a procedure MEMBER_AREA_ARC to determine whether a point is inside or outside an area represented by an arc tree.

4.27. What conditions must be satisfied by the ellipses of two subarcs of an arc tree if the subarcs intersect? Prove that your answer is true.

4.28. Write a procedure to compute the intersection points of two curves represented by arc trees.

4.29. Can you use the result of Exercise 4.28 to determine if two areas represented by arc trees overlap?

4.30. Write a procedure to compute the arc tree corresponding to the intersection of two areas represented by arc trees. How would you handle the situation arising when the two areas have some common edges?

4.2   METHODS BASED ON THE REGION QUADTREE

Strip tree methods approximate curvilinear data with rectangles. Methods based on the use of the region quadtree achieve similar results by use of a collection of disjoint squares having sides of length power of two. A number of variants of quadtrees are in use and can be differentiated by the type of data they are designed to represent. In this section we focus on the edge quadtree, the line quadtree, the PM quadtree, and, to a lesser extent, the MX quadtree (recall Sections 1.5 and 2.6.1).

Each of these data structures is a variant of the region quadtree. All but the PM quadtree are pixel based and yield approximations whose accuracy is constrained, in part, by the resolution of the data that they are representing. Each can be used to represent both linear and nonlinear curves. The latter need not be continuous or differentiable. In contrast, the PM quadtree yields an exact representation of polygons or collections of polygons (e.g., polygonal maps). We conclude by empirically comparing the storage requirements of the various data structures.

4.2.1   Edge Quadtrees

The *edge quadtree* is based on a refinement of the MX quadtree first suggested by Warnock [Warn69b]. Although Warnock did not make use of a tree structure, he observed that the number of squares in the decomposition could be reduced by terminating the subdivision whenever the square contains at most one line of a polygon or the intersection of two polygons. The variant of the edge quadtree formulated by Shneier [Shne81c], and described here, makes use of this observation to store linear feature information (e.g., curves) for an image (binary and gray-scale) in a manner analogous to that used to store region information.

In the edge quadtree, a region containing a linear feature, or part thereof, is subdivided into four squares repeatedly until a square is obtained that contains a single curve that can be approximated by a single straight line. Each leaf node contains the following information about the edge passing through it: magnitude (i.e., 1 in the case

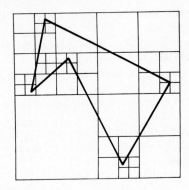

Figure 4.8 The edge quadtree corresponding to the polygon of Figure 1.26

of a binary image or the intensity in the case it is a gray-scale image), direction, intercept, and a directional error term (i.e., the error induced by approximating the curve by a straight line using a measure such as least squares). If an edge terminates within a node, a special flag is set, and the intercept denotes the point at which the edge terminates.

Applying this decomposition process leads to quadtrees in which long edges are represented by large leaf nodes or a sequence of large leaf nodes. Small leaf nodes are required in the vicinity of corners or intersecting edges. Of course, many leaf nodes will contain no edge information at all. As an example of the decomposition imposed by the edge quadtree, consider Figure 4.8, the edge quadtree corresponding to the polygon of Figure 1.26 when represented on a $2^4 \times 2^4$ grid. Note that the edge quadtree in Figure 4.8 requires fewer blocks than the MX quadtree in Figure 1.26, which is the representation of the polygon when using the methods of Hunter and Steiglitz [Hunt78, Hunt79a].

Closely related to the edge quadtree is the *least square quadtree* of Martin [Mart82]. In that representation, leaf nodes correspond to regions that contain a single curve that can be approximated by K (fixed a priori) straight lines within a least square tolerance. This enables handling curved lines with greater precision and uses fewer nodes than the edge quadtree.

A cruder method than the least square quadtree is described by Omolayole and Klinger [Omol80]. They repeatedly decomposed all parts of the image that contain edge data until obtaining a 2×2 quadrant in which they store template-like representations of the edges. This is quite similar to the MX quadtree except that the data are edges rather than points. However, it is too low a level of representation in that it does not take advantage of the hierarchical nature of the data structure (but see [Mano88]).

Exercise

4.31. Write a procedure BUILD_EDGE_QUADTREE to construct an edge quadtree for a given polygonal map.

4.2.2 Line Quadtrees

The *line quadtree* of Samet and Webber [Same82c, Same84f] addresses the issue of hierarchically representing polygonal maps. It encodes both the area of the individual regions and their boundaries in a hierarchical manner. This is in contrast to the region quadtree, which encodes only areas hierarchically, and the strip tree, which encodes only curves hierarchically. The line quadtree requires that all regions be rectilinear and their boundaries lie on the borders of pixels.

The line quadtree partitions the polygonal map (termed a *map*) via a recursive decomposition technique that successively subdivides the map until obtaining blocks (possibly single pixels) with no line segments passing through their interior. With each leaf node, a code is associated that indicates which of its four sides forms a boundary (not a partial boundary) of any single region. Thus instead of distinguishing leaf nodes on the basis of being black or white, boundary adjacency information is used. This boundary information is hierarchical in that it is also associated with non-leaf nodes. In essence, wherever a nonleaf node does not form a T-junction with any of the boundaries of its descendants along a particular side, this side is then marked as being adjacent to a boundary.

As an illustration of a line quadtree, consider the polygonal map of Figure 4.9 whose corresponding line quadtree (i.e., block decomposition) is shown in Figure 4.10. The bold lines indicate the presence of boundaries. Note that the south side of the block corresponding to the root is on a boundary that is also the border of the image. As another example, the western side of the SW son of the root in Figure 4.10 does not indicate the presence of a boundary (i.e., the side is represented by a light line) although it is adjacent to the border of the image. The problem is that the SW son

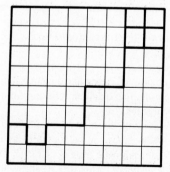

Figure 4.9   Example polygonal map to illustrate line quad-trees

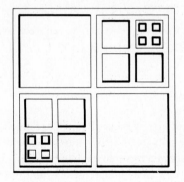

Figure 4.10   Line quadtree corresponding to Figure 4.9

of the root has its NW and SW sons in different regions, as is signaled by the presence of a T-junction along its western side.

Having the boundary information at the nonleaf nodes enables boundary-following algorithms to be performed quickly. This also facilitates the process of superimposing one map on top of another. It is interesting to observe that the line quadtree has the same number of nodes as a region quadtree representation of the image. Boundaries of leaf nodes that are partially on the boundary between two regions can have their boundaries reconstructed by examining their neighbors along the shared boundary. For example, the southern side of the NW son of the SW son of the root in Figure 4.10, say A, represents a partial boundary. The exact nature of the boundary is obtained by examining the NE and NW sons of the southern brother of A.

Exercises

4.32. Prove that the line quadtree of a polygonal map has the same number of nodes as does the region quadtree for the same map when each polygon is treated as a region of another color.

4.33. Write a procedure BUILD_LINE_QUADTREE to construct a line quadtree for a given polygonal map.

4.34. Write a procedure to trace the boundary of the polygonal region that surrounds a given point in a polygonal map represented by a line quadtree.

4.35. Write a procedure to yield the line quadtree resulting from the superposition of the line quadtrees of two polygonal maps.

4.36. The definition of the line quadtree given here stores redundant information with many of the nonleaf nodes. This redundancy can be alleviated by recording the boundary information for just two sides of each node instead of for all four sides. Let us refer to this structure as a *revised line quadtree*. This will affect the merging criteria since now we can merge four nodes only if their corresponding boundaries are identical. For example, suppose that for each node we record the boundary information for only its northern and eastern sides. Use the polygonal map of Figure 4.9 to show that the number of leaf nodes in the revised line quadtree is greater than the number of leaf nodes in the conventional line quadtree.

4.37. What is the maximum increase in the number of nodes in a revised line quadtree over the line quadtree?

4.38. Given a node P in a line quadtree, write an algorithm to find its neighbor of greater than or equal size along side I of P's block.

4.2.3   PM Quadtrees

The PM quadtree is a term used to describe collectively a number of related quadtree-like data structures devised by Samet and Webber [Same85i, Webb84] and Nelson and Samet [Nels86a] to overcome some of the problems associated with the edge quadtree, the line quadtree, and the MX quadtree for representing polygonal maps.

In general, all three of these representations correspond to approximations of a polygonal map. The line quadtree is based on the approximation that results from digitizing the areas of the polygons comprising a polygonal map. For the edge and MX quadtrees, the result is still an approximation because vertices are represented by pixels in the edge quadtree and boundaries are represented by black pixels in the MX quadtree. In other words, the MX quadtree is based on a digitization of the boundaries of the polygons, while the edge quadtree is based on a piecewise linear approximation of the boundaries of the polygons.

Another disadvantage of these three representations is that certain properties of polygonal maps cannot be directly represented by them. For example, it is impossible for five line segments to meet at a vertex. In the case of the edge and MX quadtrees, in such a situation, we would have difficulty in detecting the vertex; for the line quadtree, this situation cannot be handled because all regions comprising the map must be rectilinear, and it is impossible for five rectilinear regions to meet at a point.

Other problems include a sensitivity to shift and rotation, which may result in a loss of accuracy in the original approximation. In addition, due to their approximate nature, these data structures will most likely require a considerable amount of storage since each line is frequently approximated at the pixel level, thereby resulting in fairly deep quadtrees.

In the remainder of this section, a number of variants of the *PM quadtree* are developed. These variants are either vertex based or edge based. Their implementations make use of the same basic data structure. All are built by applying the principle of repeatedly breaking up the collection of vertices and edges (forming the polygonal map) until obtaining a subset that is sufficiently simple that it can be organized by some other data structure. This is achieved by successively weakening the definition of what constitutes a permissible leaf node, thereby enabling more information to be stored at each leaf node.

We also examine how some of the variants can be adapted to deal with fragments that result from set operations such as union and intersection. The goal is to avoid data degradation when fragments of line segments are subsequently recombined. The result is an exact representation of the lines, not an approximation.

These variants are useful in applications that include the determination of the identity of the region in which a point lies (known as the point location problem), the determination of the boundaries of all regions lying within a given distance of a point, and overlaying two maps. We conclude by examining the problem of maintaining region identification information in PM quadtrees. This is relevant to the point location problem.

4.2.3.1   THE PM$_1$ QUADTREE

The PM$_1$ quadtree is organized in a similar way to the region and PR quadtrees. A region is repeatedly subdivided into four equal-sized quadrants until we obtain blocks that do not contain more than one line. To deal with lines that intersect other lines, we say that if a block contains a point, say P, then we permit it to contain more than one line provided that P is an endpoint of each of the lines it contains. A block can never contain more than one endpoint. For example, Figure 4.12 is the block decomposition of the PM$_1$ quadtree corresponding to the polygonal map of Figure 4.11, and Figure 4.13 is its tree representation.

The definition of a PM$_1$ quadtree can be made more rigorous by viewing the polygonal map as a straight-line planar graph consisting of vertices and edges. The term *q-edge* (denoting a quadtree-decomposition edge) is used to refer to a segment of an edge formed by clipping [Roge85] an edge of the polygonal map against the border of the region represented by a quadtree node (e.g., q-edges FG and GH in Figure 4.12). It should be clear that every edge (i.e., line segment) of the map is covered by a set of q-edges that touch only at their endpoints. For example, edge EB in Figure 4.12 consists of the q-edges EF, FG, GH, HI, IJ, JK, and KB. Note that only B and E are vertices; F, G, H, I, J, and K merely serve as reference points. At this point, the definition of a *PM$_1$ quadtree* can be restated as satisfying the following conditions:

1. At most, one vertex can lie in a region represented by a quadtree leaf node.
2. If a quadtree leaf node's region contains a vertex, it can contain no q-edge that does not include that vertex.
3. If a quadtree leaf node's region contains no vertices, it can contain, at most, one q-edge.
4. Each region's quadtree leaf node is maximal.

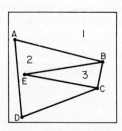

Figure 4.11   Sample polygonal map

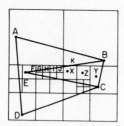

Figure 4.12   PM$_1$ quadtree corresponding to the polygonal map of Figure 4.11

This definition of a PM$_1$ quadtree is similar to that of a PR quadtree. The difference is that we are representing edges here rather than points. This affects the action to be taken when the decomposition induced by the PM$_1$ quadtree results in a vertex that lies on the border of a quadtree node (e.g., vertex A in Figure 4.14). We could move the vertices so that this does not happen, but generally this requires global knowledge about the maximum depth of the quadtree prior to its construction.

Alternatively we could establish the convention that some sides of the region represented by a node are closed and other sides are open (as done for the PR quadtree; that is, the lower and left boundaries of each block are closed while the right and upper boundaries of each block are open). However, this leads to a problem when at least three edges meet at a vertex on the border of a quadtree node such that two of the edges are in the open quadrant (i.e., the one not containing the vertex). These two edges may have to be decomposed to a very deep level in order to separate them (e.g., edges AB and AC in the SW quadrant of Figure 4.14).

Therefore the convention usually adopted is that all quadrants are closed. This means that a vertex that lies on the border between two (or three but never more than

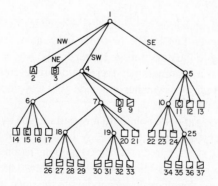

Figure 4.13   Tree representation of the PM$_1$ quadtree corresponding to the polygonal map of Figure 4.11

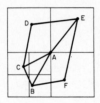

Figure 4.14   Example polygonal map where vertex A lies on the border of a quadtree node. The decomposition lines are those induced by a PM $_1$ quadtree definition in which a vertex is inserted in each of the nodes on whose border it lies.

four) nodes is inserted in each of the nodes on whose border it lies. Such vertices can be treated as edges of zero length.

Since the PM$_1$ quadtree is used to implement isolated points and lines, as well as polygonal maps, its basic entities are vertices and edges. Each vertex is represented as a record of type *point* that has two fields called XCOORD and YCOORD that correspond to the x and y coordinates, respectively, of the point. They can be of type real or integer depending on implementation considerations such as floating point precision.

An edge is implemented as a record of type *line* with four fields, P1, P2, LEFT, and RIGHT. P1 and P2 contain pointers to the records containing the edge's vertices. LEFT and RIGHT are pointers to structures that identify the regions that are on the two sides of the edge. We shall use the convention that LEFT and RIGHT are with respect to a view of the edge that treats the vertex closest to the origin as the start of the edge. For example, for edge DA in the polygonal map of Figure 4.11, its LEFT and RIGHT fields are marked as being associated with regions 1 and 2, respectively. A discussion of how such labels are maintained is orthogonal to the presentation of the development of the PM quadtree and is treated in Section 4.2.3.6. The algorithms given here ignore these two fields.

Each node in a PM$_1$ quadtree is a collection of q-edges represented as a record of type *node* containing seven fields. The first four fields contain pointers to the node's four sons corresponding to the directions (i.e., quadrants) NW, NE, SW, and SE. If P is a pointer to a node and I is a quadrant, then these fields are referenced as SON(P,I). The fifth field, NODETYPE, indicates whether the node is a leaf node (LEAF) or a nonleaf node (GRAY).

The sixth field, SQUARE, is a pointer to a record of type *square* that indicates the size of the block corresponding to the node. It is defined for both leaf and nonleaf nodes. It has two fields, CENTER and LEN. CENTER points to a record of type point that contains the x and y coordinates of the center of the square. LEN contains the length of a side of the square that is the block corresponding to the node in the PM$_1$ quadtree.

DICTIONARY is the last field. It is a pointer to a data structure that represents the set of q-edges associated with the node. Initially the universe is empty and consists of no edges or vertices. It is represented by a tree of one node of type LEAF whose DIC-TIONARY field points to the empty set.

In the implementation given here, the set of q-edges for each LEAF node is a linked list whose elements are records of type *edgelist* containing two fields, DATA and NEXT. DATA points to a record of type line corresponding to the edge of which the q-edge is a member. NEXT points to the record corresponding to the next q-edge in the list of q-edges. Although the set of q-edges is stored as a list here, it should be implemented by a data structure that supports efficient updating and searching, as well as set union and set difference operations.

For example, the set of q-edges could be implemented as a dictionary in the form of a 2-3 tree [Aho74] where the q-edges are ordered by the angle that they form with a ray originating at the vertex and parallel to the positive x axis. Since the number of q-edges passing through a leaf is bounded from above by the number of vertices belonging to the polygonal map, say V, the depth of the dictionary structure is at most $\log_2 V + 1$. However, a linked list is usually sufficient since in the empirical tests for all of the variants of the PM quadtree, described in Section 4.2.4, the list rarely had as many as five items in it. The set of q-edges corresponding to a gray node is said to be empty. Note that all of the q-edges comprising a given edge point to the same line record.

Lines (or edges) are inserted into a PM_1 quadtree by searching for the position they are to occupy. The implementation given below assumes that whenever an edge or an isolated vertex is inserted into the PM_1 quadtree, it is not already there or does not intersect an existing edge. However, an endpoint of an edge may intersect an existing vertex provided it is not an isolated vertex (i.e., an edge with length zero). To insert an edge that intersects an isolated vertex, the isolated vertex should be removed beforehand.

An edge is inserted into a PM_1 quadtree by traversing the tree in preorder and successively clipping it (using CLIP_LINES) against the blocks corresponding to the nodes. Clipping is important because it enables us to avoid looking at areas where the edge cannot be inserted. The insertion process is controlled by procedure PM_INSERT, which actually inserts a list of edges.

If the edge can be inserted into the node (i.e., the conditions of a PM_1 quadtree node are satisfied), say P, then PM_INSERT does so and exits. Otherwise a list, say L, is formed containing the edge and any q-edges already present in the node, P is split using SPLIT_PM_NODE, and PM_INSERT is recursively invoked to attempt to insert the elements of L in the four sons of P. PM_INSERT uses PM1_CHECK and SHARE_PM1_VER-TEX to determine if the conditions of the definition of the PM_1 quadtree are satisfied. Isolated vertices pose no problems and are handled by PM1_CHECK.

Procedure CLIP_SQUARE is a predicate that indicates if an edge crosses a square. Similarly, procedure PT_IN_SQUARE is a predicate that indicates if a vertex lies in a square. They are responsible for enforcing the conventions with respect to vertices and edges that lie on the boundaries of blocks. Their code is not given here. Equality between records corresponding to vertices is tested by use of the '=' symbol, which

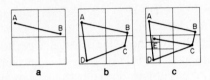

Figure 4.15 Steps in the construction of the PM$_1$ quadtree
for the polygonal map of Figure 4.11 as edges (a) AB, (b)
BC, CD, AD, and (c) CE are processed

requires that its two operands be of the same type (i.e., pointers to records of type
point). For example, Figure 4.15 shows how the PM$_1$ quadtree for the polygonal map
of Figure 4.11 is constructed in incremental fashion for edges AB, BC, CD, AD, and CE.

```
recursive procedure PM_INSERT(P,R);
/* Insert the list of edges pointed at by P in the PM₁ quadtree rooted at R. The same pro-
   cedure is used to insert in PM₂ and PM₃ quadtrees by replacing the calls to PM1_-
   CHECK by calls to PM2_CHECK and PM3_CHECK respectively. */
begin
  value pointer edgelist P;
  value pointer node R;
  pointer edgelist L;
  quadrant I;
  L ← CLIP_LINES(P,SQUARE(R));
  if empty(L) then return; /* No new edges belong in the quadrant */
  if LEAF(R) then /* A leaf node */
    begin
      L ← MERGE_LISTS(L,DICTIONARY(R));
      if PM1_CHECK(L,SQUARE(R)) then
        begin
          DICTIONARY(R) ← L;
          return;
        end
      else SPLIT_PM_NODE(R);
    end;
  for I in {'NW', 'NE', 'SW', 'SE'} do PM_INSERT(L,SON(R,I));
end;

recursive edgelist procedure CLIP_LINES(L,R);
/* Collect all of the edges in the list of edges pointed at by L that intersect the square
   pointed at by R. ADD_TO_LIST(X,S) adds element X to the list S and returns a pointer
   to the resulting list. */
begin
  value pointer edgelist L;
  value pointer square R;
  return(if empty(L) then NIL
```

```
        else if CLIP_SQUARE(DATA(L),R) then
            ADD_TO_LIST(DATA(L),CLIP_LINES(NEXT(L),R))
        else CLIP_LINES(NEXT(L),R));
end;
```

Boolean procedure PM1_CHECK(L,S);
/* Determine if the square pointed at by S and the list of edges pointed at by L form a legal
   PM₁ quadtree node. ONE_ELEMENT(L) is a predicate that indicates if L contains just
   one element. */
begin
  value pointer edgelist L;
  value pointer square S;
  return(**if empty** (L) **then true**
        else if P1(DATA(L))=P2(DATA(L)) **then**
            ONE_ELEMENT(L) /* Isolated vertex */
        else if ONE_ELEMENT(L) **then**
            /* Both vertices can lie outside the square */
            not(PT_IN_SQUARE(P1(DATA(L)),S) **and**
                PT_IN_SQUARE(P2(DATA(L)),S))
        else if PT_IN_SQUARE(P1(DATA(L)),S) **and**
                PT_IN_SQUARE(P2(DATA(L)),S) **then false**
        else if PT_IN_SQUARE(P1(DATA(L)),S) **then**
            SHARE_PM1_VERTEX(P1(DATA(L)),NEXT(L),S)
        else if PT_IN_SQUARE(P2(DATA(L)),S) **then**
            SHARE_PM1_VERTEX(P2(DATA(L)),NEXT(L),S)
        else false);
end;
```

**recursive Boolean procedure** SHARE_PM1_VERTEX(P,L,S);
/* The vertex pointed at by P is in the square pointed at by S.  Determine if all the edges in
   the list of edges pointed at by L share P and do not have their other vertex within S. */
**begin**
  **value pointer point** P;
  **value pointer edgelist** L;
  **value pointer square** S;
  **return**(**if empty**(L) **then true**
        **else if** P=P1(DATA(L)) **then**
            **not**(PT_IN_SQUARE(P2(DATA(L)),S)) **and**
            SHARE_PM1_VERTEX(P,NEXT(L),S)
        **else if** P=P2(DATA(L)) **then**
            **not**(PT_IN_SQUARE(P1(DATA(L)),S)) **and**
            SHARE_PM1_VERTEX(P,NEXT(L),S)
        **else false**);
end;
```

procedure SPLIT_PM_NODE(P);
/* Add four sons to the node pointed at by P and change P to be of type GRAY. */
begin
  value pointer node P;

```
quadrant I,J;
pointer node Q;
pointer square S;
/* XF and YF contain multiplicative factors to aid in the location of the centers of the
   quadrant sons while descending the tree */
preload real array XF['NW', 'NE', 'SW', 'SE'] with -0.25,0.25,-0.25,0.25;
preload real array YF['NW', 'NE', 'SW', 'SE'] with 0.25,0.25,-0.25,-0.25;
for I in {'NW,' 'NE,' 'SW,' 'SE'} do
  begin
    Q ← create(node);
    SON(P,I) ← Q;
    for J in {'NW', 'NE', 'SW', 'SE'} do SON(Q,J) ← NIL;
    NODETYPE(Q) ← 'LEAF';
    S ← create(square);
    CENTER(S) ← create(point);
    XCOORD(CENTER(S)) ← XCOORD(CENTER(SQUARE(P))) +
                        XF[I]*LEN(SQUARE(P));
    YCOORD(CENTER(S)) ← YCOORD(CENTER(SQUARE(P))) +
                        YF[I]*LEN(SQUARE(P));
    LEN(S) ← 0.5*LEN(SQUARE(P));
    SQUARE(Q) ← S;
    DICTIONARY(Q) ← NIL;
  end;
  DICTIONARY(P) ← NIL;
  NODETYPE(P) ← 'GRAY';
end;
```

Deletion of an edge from a PM$_1$ quadtree is analogous to the process used for deletion of points in a PR quadtree (see Section 2.6.2). The control structure is identical to that used in the insertion of an edge. Again the tree is traversed in preorder, and the edge is successively clipped (using CLIP_LINES) against the blocks corresponding to the nodes. This process is controlled by procedure PM_DELETE, which actually deletes a list of edges.

Once a leaf node is encountered in which the edge participates, the node's DICTIONARY field is updated to show the elimination of the edge. After processing the four sons of a gray node, an attempt is made to merge the four sons by use of procedures POSSIBLE_PM1_MERGE and TRY_TO_MERGE_PM1 to check if the conditions of the PM$_1$ quadtree are satisfied. These procedures make use of PM1_CHECK. In the case of a merge, storage is reclaimed by RETURN_TREE_TO_AVAIL.

The check for merging is analogous to the check for collapsing when deleting a point from a PR quadtree. The difference is that for the PM$_1$ quadtree, a check for the possibility of merging is made at each level of the tree in which processing one of the sons of a nonleaf node has resulted in the deletion of a q-edge. In particular, merging can occur if at least one of the sons of a nonleaf node is a leaf node (checked by POSSIBLE_PM1_MERGE). There are two situations where merging must occur.

They are illustrated by the deletion of edge BE from Figure 4.11. The discussion refers to nodes in Figures 4.12 and 4.13.

The first situation arises when the deletion of an edge has resulted in four brother leaf nodes having zero or one edge pass through them. In the example, removal of q-edges FG and GH from nodes 26 and 27 leaves nonleaf node 18 with only one edge (i.e., CE) passing through it. This means that merging can be applied after processing the remaining sons of nonleaf node 18. Similarly removal of q-edges HI and IJ from nodes 30 and 31 leaves node 19 with only one edge (i.e., CE) passing through it. Once again merging is applied after processing the remaining sons of nonleaf node 19. In fact, further merging is possible at this point since nonleaf node 7 now has only one edge (i.e., CE) passing through it.

The second situation is somewhat tricky. It arises when deletion causes all of the remaining edges in the descendants of the nonleaf node, say N, to have a common vertex that lies in one of the sons of N (not a descendant of N, who is not a son). In this case, merging can occur, thereby making N a leaf node. In the example, removal of q-edge JK from node 22 leaves nonleaf node 10 with only two edges (i.e., CE and CD) passing through node 25 and having C as a common vertex. Moreover, removal of q-edge JK also leaves nonleaf node 5 with the three edges BC, CD, and CE passing through it and, again, all having C as a common vertex. Thus merging is applied to the sons of nodes 25, 10, and 5 in succession.

In this example, it is important to note that merging can occur only after processing the sons of nonleaf node 5. The reason it cannot be performed sooner (e.g., in part, after processing the sons of nonleaf nodes 25 or 10) is that the common vertex (i.e., C) is not in the node whose sons are being merged.

```
recursive procedure PM_DELETE(P,R);
/* Delete the list of edges pointed at by P from the PM₁ quadtree rooted at R. The same
   procedure is used to delete from PM₂ and PM₃ quadtrees by replacing the calls to POS-
   SIBLE_PM1_MERGE and TRY_TO_MERGE_PM1 by calls to POSSIBLE_PM23_-
   MERGE and TRY_TO_MERGE_PM23. */
begin
  value pointer edgelist P;
  value pointer node R;
  pointer edgelist L;
  quadrant I;
  L ← CLIP_LINES(P,SQUARE(R));
  if empty(L) then return; /* None of the edges is in the quadrant */
  if GRAY(R) then
    begin
      for I in {'NW', 'NE', 'SW', 'SE'} do PM_DELETE(L,SON(R,I));
      if POSSIBLE_PM1_MERGE(R) then
        begin
          L ← NIL;
          if TRY_TO_MERGE_PM1(R,R,L) then
            begin /* Merge the sons of the gray node */
              RETURN_TREE_TO_AVAIL(R);
```

```
            DICTIONARY(R) ← L;
            NODETYPE(R) ← 'LEAF';
        end;
      end;
    end
  else DICTIONARY(R) ← SET_DIFFERENCE(DICTIONARY(R),L);
end;
```

Boolean procedure POSSIBLE_PM1_MERGE(P);
/* Determine if the subtrees of the four sons of the PM_1 quadtree node pointed at by P
   should be further examined to see if a merger is possible. Such a merger is feasible
   only if at least one of the four sons of P is a LEAF. */
begin
  value pointer node P;
  return(LEAF(SON(P,'NW')) **or** LEAF(SON(P,'NE')) **or**
       LEAF(SON(P,'SW')) **or** LEAF(SON(P,'SE'))));
end;

recursive Boolean procedure TRY_TO_MERGE_PM1(P,R,L);
/* Determine if the four sons of the PM_1 quadtree rooted at node P can be merged.
   Notice that the check for the satisfaction of the PM_1 decomposition conditions is with
   respect to the square associated with the original gray node, rooted at R, whose subtrees are being explored. Variable L is used to collect all of the edges present in the
   subtrees. */
begin
  value pointer node P,R;
  reference pointer edgelist L;
  if LEAF(P) **then**
    begin
      L ← SET_UNION(L,DICTIONARY(P));
      return(true);
    end
  else return(TRY_TO_MERGE_PM1(SON(P,'NW'),R,L) **and**
         TRY_TO_MERGE_PM1(SON(P,'NE'),R,L) **and**
         TRY_TO_MERGE_PM1(SON(P,'SW'),R,L) **and**
         TRY_TO_MERGE_PM1(SON(P,'SE'),R,L) **and**
         PM1_CHECK(L,SQUARE(R))));
end;

recursive procedure RETURN_TREE_TO_AVAIL(P);
/* Return the PM quadtree rooted at P to the free storage list. This process is recursive in
   the case of a PM_1 quadtree. */
begin
  value pointer node P;
  quadrant I;
  if LEAF(P) **then return**
  else
    begin
      for I **in** {'NW', 'NE', 'SW', 'SE'} **do**
        begin

```
        RETURN_TREE_TO_AVAIL(SON(P,I));
        returntoavail(SON(P,I));
        SON(P,I) ← NIL;
      end;
    end;
  end;
```

Analyzing the cost of dynamically inserting or deleting an edge in a PM₁ quadtree is a process that requires us to look at the whole tree, not just at the particular
edge. In the following, the focus is on the cost of insertion. Analyzing the cost of
deletion is somewhat more complex due to the need to check for merging (especially
when merging cannot occur), and thus it is left as an exercise (Exercise 4.54). The
rest of this section contains an analysis of the storage requirements of a PM₁ quadtree.
It is somewhat complex and can be skipped on a first reading.

Initially let us assume that we are given a PM₁ quadtree and that the polygonal
map is embedded in a unit square. Recall that to insert an edge AB, we insert the
appropriate q-edge of AB into each quadrant intersected by AB. In some of these
quadrants, the insertion of a q-edge of AB would cause a violation of one of the conditions of the PM₁ quadtree definition. In such a case, the quadrant in question is subdivided, and insertion is reattempted. This subdivision of a quadrant can cause q-edges
of edges that had been previously inserted to be subdivided further.

For example, consider Figure 4.16. First, we insert the edge AB, which entails
inserting the q-edges: AV, VW, and WB. Now suppose that we insert the edge BC. This

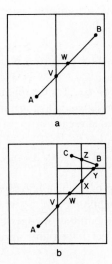

Figure 4.16   Result of inserting line segments into a PM₁
quadtree

entails not only inserting the q-edges CZ and ZB but also the q-edges WX, XY, and YB. Thus the ultimate cost of inserting an edge into a PM_1 quadtree is often paid for over many insertions as q-edges of the edge are further subdivided to accommodate edges that are being subsequently added.

To handle this situation, for our worst-case analysis, we do not consider the total cost of inserting a particular edge in a tree. Instead we consider the ultimate cost of inserting that portion of the map that is currently built. This cost, henceforth known as the *running-sum worst-case cost*, assumes that the map is being built dynamically, that is, information about future edges is not exploited at the time an edge is initially inserted. The running-sum worst-case cost (when summed over the insertions that built the map) is an upper bound on the actual cost of building the map so far.

Implicit in the calculation of the running-sum worst-case cost of building a map is the assumption that we know the ultimate depth to which the tree will be expanded. This approach to cost analysis is related to the 'amortization' method [Bent80a] in that the real difference between the running-sum worst-case cost of the map before and after an insertion is equivalent to the 'amortized' cost of that insertion.

The running-sum worst-case map building cost is the product of the cost of inserting a q-edge and the number of q-edges that would have to be inserted. The cost of inserting a q-edge is the depth of the PM_1 quadtree plus the cost of accessing the dictionary structure of q-edges associated with each leaf node, say A_1. The depth of the PM_1 quadtree is the maximum of the depth required independently by each of the first three conditions in its definition.

The bounds for these depths can be derived easily by making use of the initial assumption that the polygonal map is embedded in a unit square. In such a case, the maximum separation between any two vertices lying in the unit square is $\sqrt{2}$. Vertices that are this far apart require a tree with depth 1 to separate them. Generalizing this result, we have that if $d_{min.vv}$ is the minimum separation between two distinct vertices, then condition 1 implies that the upper bound on the depth of the corresponding PM_1 quadtree is

$$D_1 = 1 + \log_2(\sqrt{2} \, / \, d_{min.vv}).$$

Similarly, for condition 2, if $d_{min.ev}$ is the minimum separation between an edge and a vertex not on that edge (for a given polygonal map), then the upper bound on the depth of the corresponding PM_1 quadtree is

$$D_2 = 1 + \log_2(\sqrt{2} \, / \, d_{min.ev}).$$

Note that a map consisting of a single line segment would have no meaningful value for $d_{min.ev}$. Finally, for condition 3, if $d_{min.ee}$ is the minimum separation between two nonintersecting q-edges (i.e., portions of edges bounded by either a vertex or the boundary of a PM_1 quadtree leaf), then the upper bound on the depth of the corresponding PM_1 quadtree is

$$D_3 = 1 + \log_2(\sqrt{2} \, / \, d_{min.ee}).$$

Now let us turn to the calculation of an upper bound for the number of q-edges that is slightly more complicated. We define L, the length of the perimeter of a polygonal map, to be the sum of the lengths of all the edges that form the map. In the following, the upper bound on the number of q-edges in the representation of the map is shown to be a function of L and the maximum depth, say DMAX, of the quadtree structure (i.e., the maximum of D_1, D_2, and D_3). This is followed by a precise computation of DMAX.

Let us consider the structure of the q-edges that form a single edge. Note that for each edge there are at most two q-edges that have the property of being incident at one of the vertices of the polygonal map. Thus the number of such q-edges is proportional to the number of edges in the polygonal map. Since the factor D_1 is bounded from above by DMAX and requires that no edge is less than 2^{-DMAX} units long, we deduce the following upper bound on the number of edges, denoted by E, in a map.

$$E \cdot 2^{-DMAX} \leq L \qquad \text{or } E \leq L \cdot 2^{DMAX}.$$

Of the remaining P q-edges in the map, all begin and end on the boundary of a square of size 2^{-DMAX} by 2^{-DMAX}. First, we observe that while a line segment that passes through a square may be shorter than the width of that square, a line segment that passes through two congruent squares must be at least as long as the width of one of the squares. For each edge, we group together the maximum number of disjoint pairs of contiguous q-edges.

The result of this pairing process is that for each edge there is at most one unpaired q-edge. Hence the number of unpaired q-edges is bounded from above by E (the number of edges). Let P′ denote the number of q-edges that remain after the elimination of these unpaired q-edges. These P′ q-edges can be grouped into P′/2 pairs of q-edges that pass through two congruent squares. Note that P′ must be even. This leads to the following upper bound on P′:

$$(P'/2) \cdot 2^{-DMAX} \leq L \qquad \text{or } P' \leq L \cdot 2 \cdot 2^{DMAX}.$$

To summarize, the number of q-edges is equal to the number of q-edges incident at a vertex plus the number of q-edges left over after the pairing process plus the number of q-edges that participate in the pairing process. For each of these values, we have an upper bound proportional to the length of the perimeter of the map times 2^{DMAX}. Thus the total number of q-edges is also bounded from above by the length of the perimeter of the map times 2^{DMAX}. Recall that the running-sum worst-case map building cost was proportional to the product of the depth of the entire structure (DMAX plus A_1) and the number of q-edges inserted, for which we have just derived an upper bound. More formally an upper bound on the cost of building a PM_1 quadtree by inserting one edge at a time is given by

$$(E \cdot 3 + L \cdot 2^{\text{DMAX}} + 1) \cdot (\text{DMAX} + A_1),$$

which in turn is bounded from above by

$$(5 \cdot L \cdot 2^{\text{DMAX}}) \cdot (\text{DMAX} + A_1).$$

Samet, Shaffer, and Webber [Same86b, Same87b] show how to compute the maximum depth (i.e., DMAX) of a PM_1 quadtree in a typical, although restricted, environment. The environment from which the vertices are drawn is a $2^d \times 2^d$ grid. Edges are not permitted to intersect at points other than the grid points (i.e., vertices). Thus the locations of all vertices are specified with d bits of precision, and hence there is a minimum separation of 1 between any two vertices.

Of course, DMAX depends on two additional factors: the minimum separation between a vertex and an edge and the minimum separation between two edges ($d_{min.ev}$ and $d_{min.ee}$, respectively). The importance of DMAX should be readily apparent. For example, when implementing a PM_1 quadtree using a pointer-less representation with locational codes such as the linear quadtree (see Section 1.5 and Section 2.1.1 of [Same90b]), it enables a determination of the maximum amount of storage that will be necessary for each node.

The situation that leads to a maximum depth for vertices stored with d bits of precision is derived in the following manner. Initially we determine how close an edge connecting two vertices on the grid can lie to another vertex on the grid without actually touching that vertex. We assume that all vertices lie on the lower left corner of their node's block.

Lemma 4.1   For a $2^d \times 2^d$ grid with all grid points separated by 1, the minimum horizontal (or vertical) separation between a vertex and an edge joining two other vertices satisfying condition 2 is bounded from below by $2^{-(d+1)}$.

Proof   This distance can be attained asymptotically by the following construction. Consider a subset of a $2^d \times 2^d$ grid as shown in Figure 4.17. Let A be at $(0,0)$, B at $(1,0)$, C at $(0,2^d - 1)$, and D at $(0,2^d - 2)$. The distance from A to B and from C to D is 1, and the distance from A to C is $2^d - 1$. This represents a worst-case situation and, in particular, that the closest approach for this grid will be the distance from D to the edge BC. A demonstration that this is indeed the worst-case situation can be found in [Same86b]. $\square$

Incorporation of condition 3 poses a more complex requirement. It stipulates that no block can contain more than one edge unless all the edges meet at a common vertex in the block. Thus the problem reduces to how small a block can be and still fail to satisfy this condition. This situation is at its worst in the nodes immediately adjacent to a node containing a vertex. Note that the width of the smallest block that

Figure 4.17   Example illustrating the worst case decomposition when only conditions 1 and 2 need to be satisfied

fails to separate two edges originating at a vertex within a neighboring block decreases monotonically with the angle between the two edges. Actually we are not looking for the smallest angle between two edges that emanate from the lower left-hand corner of a block of a given size. Instead we are seeking the minimum horizontal (or vertical) separation between these two edges, that is, the edges subtend the smallest portion of a particular side of a block.

Lemma 4.2   Let P be a vertex in a $2^d \times 2^d$ grid with all grid points separated by 1. Let w be the width of P's block. Let l_1 and l_2 be two

Figure 4.18   Example illustrating the minimum separation necessary in a block when attempting to satisfy conditions 1–3 once A's block has been exited

edges that emanate from P and that exit from the same side of P's block. The minimum horizontal or vertical separation between l_1 and l_2 satisfying condition (3) is bounded from below by $w/((2^d - 1) \cdot (2^d - 2))$.

Proof   From Figure 4.18 we observe that the closest approach between two intercepts, say B' and C', of edges with the border of a block of a vertex occurs when the block has its lower left corner A at $(0,0)$ and the edges extend from A to B at $(1, 2^d - 1)$ and C at $(1, 2^d - 2)$. An argument based on similar triangles demonstrating that this is indeed the worst-case situation is given in [Same86b].   ☐

We now turn to the question of what is the worst-case value of DMAX as a function of d when all three conditions are met.

Theorem 4.1   The maximum level DMAX required by a polygonal map whose vertices lie on a $2^d \times 2^d$ grid is bounded from above by $4 \cdot d + 1$.

Proof   The proof develops from an ordered consideration of the impact of the various decomposition conditions for a PM$_1$ quadtree on the worst-case value of DMAX. Condition 1 has the least impact on the value of DMAX. Since all vertices are restricted to lie on the points of a $2^d \times 2^d$ grid, condition 1 will be satisfied by any value DMAX $\geq d+1$. The bound is $d + 1$ instead of d because we assume that each block has a closed boundary; hence at level DMAX $= d$, two neighboring vertices would be corners of a common block.   ☐

As analyzed in Lemma 4.1, condition 2 is independent of, and more restrictive than, condition 1. By 'independent,' it is meant that there is a worst-case map that attains its worst cases with respect to conditions 1 and 2 simultaneously. Thus condition 2 raises the upper bound on DMAX to $2d + 1$.

Condition 3 can be thought of as being applied after the PM$_1$ quadtree decomposition process has proceeded far enough to satisfy conditions 1 and 2. Note that any further decomposition will continue to satisfy conditions 1 and 2. For a given block c, in order for condition 3 to be relevant, at least two edges must intersect block c without intersecting within block c. If the edges do not intersect at all, their closest approach would be between the vertex of one edge and some portion of the other edge. This situation has been analyzed with respect to condition 2. Thus although condition 3 might force further decomposition in the neighborhood of nonintersecting edges, the worst-case situation for nonintersecting edges would be no worse than the condition 2 bound.

Therefore any increase in the upper bound on DMAX due to condition 3 must be the result of the existence of edges with a common vertex that cause a block to contain two edges closer than the closest approach between any vertex and an edge that does not contain that vertex. Let c be the block of smallest width, say w, resulting from conditions 1 and 2, and let T be a vertex on the lower left-hand corner of c. The only way to create a block smaller than the one containing T (i.e., c) is for two or more edges to pass through one of the sides of c. Once these edges exit block c, condition 3 requires that they occupy separate blocks. The analysis of condition 3 performed in Lemma 4.2 did not set an absolute upper bound on DMAX. Instead it indicates a minimum separation, say t, of line segments relative to the width of the block containing the vertex from which the edges emanate.

Now let us apply Lemmas 4.1 and 4.2. From Lemma 4.1 we have that $2^{-(d+1)}$ is a lower bound on w. From Lemma 4.2 we have that the minimum block width, t, is $2^{-(3d+1)}$. Since we assume that all sides of the block are closed, we need to halve this minimum block width to ensure that a block containing a single edge does not contain even a corner point of another edge. Thus the minimum block width is $2^{-(3d+2)}$. This means that $4d+2$ is an upper bound on DMAX (recall that we started with a $2^d \times 2^d$ grid with all grid points separated by 1. Note also that no further interactions are possible between conditions 1–3 that could force t to be smaller.

It is interesting to observe that while the bounds dictated by conditions 2 and 3 are individually attainable (see the proofs of Lemmas 4.1 and 4.2), the constructions used to derive them are mutually incompatible. However, note that the digitization of the lines WK, KZ, and ZL in Figure 4.19 does lead to an asymptotic approach to the bound of Theorem 4.1. In particular, W is at $(1, 2^d - 1)$, K is at $(0,1)$, Z is at $(1, 2^d - 2)$, and L is at $(0,0)$. For a more detailed analysis of this construction, see [Same86b].

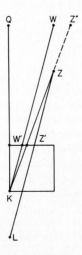

Figure 4.19   Example polygonal map with a value of grid depth that is very close to the worst case

Exercises

4.39. What is the maximum number of entries in the DICTIONARY field of a leaf node in a PM_1 quadtree?

4.40. Prove that the factors D_1 and D_2 are functions of the polygonal map and are independent of the positioning of the underlying digitization grid, while D_3 is dependent on it, and thus it can vary as the polygonal map is shifted.

4.41. Why is condition 4 in the definition of the PM_1 quadtree necessary?

4.42. The PM_1 quadtree is defined in a manner analogous to that of the PR quadtree. Consider the following attempt to tighten the analogy by using a definition of the PM_1 quadtree where conditions 2 and 3 are replaced by $2'$, which requires only that at most one q-edge can lie in a region represented by a PM_1 quadtree leaf. Does condition $2'$ imply condition 1? If not, are conditions 1, $2'$, and 4 sufficient to handle an arbitrary polygonal map?

4.43. Prove that unlike the depth D'_2 in Exercise 4.42, D_3 is bounded.

4.44. The implementation of the PM_1 quadtree does not use the DICTIONARY field of a gray node. Suppose that we use it to record a list of all of the edges that cross its corresponding block or have their endpoints within it. Modify procedures PM_INSERT and PM_DELETE to take advantage of this. Your modification should leave procedures PM1_CHECK and SHARE_PM1_VERTEX unchanged.

4.45. Suppose that, as in Exercise 4.44, you use the DICTIONARY field of a gray node to point to a list of the edges that intersect its corresponding block. Give an upper bound on the number of nodes required to form these lists in a PM_1 quadtree. Assume that for a given polygonal map there are m_i edges stored at level i where the root of the quadtree is at level n. Derive a lower bound by considering how many q-edges of an edge can be present in four nodes that are brothers.

4.46. Prove that when PM_DELETE is invoked to delete one edge from a PM_1 quadtree, merging is impossible if all of the four sons of a gray node are gray.

4.47. Why is it necessary to examine subtrees at several levels of recursion in procedure TRY_-TO_MERGE_PM1 when deleting an edge from a PM_1 subtree?

4.48. One approach to avoid repeatedly invoking procedure PM1_CHECK in TRY_TO_MERGE_PM1 is for PM1_CHECK to use an extra reference parameter to return the name of the vertex that it found to be shared. From now on, all subsequent invocations of PM1_CHECK must share the same vertex or TRY_TO_MERGE_PM1 is false. Modify procedure TRY_TO_MERGE_PM1 to incorporate this change.

4.49. Another approach to avoiding the cost of procedure TRY_TO_MERGE_PM1 is to store a vertex count in each gray node indicating the number of vertices in the subtrees. If this count is 1, merging can be attempted; if it is greater than 1, it cannot. Note that just because the vertex count is less than or equal to 1 does not mean that merging is possible. Modify procedures PM_INSERT and PM_DELETE to incorporate a vertex count.

4.50. Suppose that in addition to keeping a count of the number of vertices in each gray node of a PM_1 quadtree, you also keep track of the number of edges that cross the boundaries of each gray node. Crossing means that the endpoints lie outside the block. When is merging possible? Modify procedures PM_INSERT and PM_DELETE to incorporate vertex and crossing counters.

4.51. The implementation of a node has a field called SQUARE that contains information about the size of the block corresponding to the node. This is not necessary. Instead this information can be calculated as the tree is traversed with the relevant information being passed as parameters to procedures PM_INSERT and PM_DELETE. How many parameters are needed? Modify procedures PM_INSERT and PM_DELETE to accommodate such a representation.

4.52. Procedure PM_INSERT assumes that whenever an edge or an isolated vertex is inserted into the PM_1 quadtree, it is not already there or does not intersect an existing edge. For an isolated vertex, this also means that it is not part of an existing edge. Modify PM_INSERT and the associated procedures to indicate when an isolated vertex or an edge cannot be inserted. There is no need to modify procedures PM1_CHECK or SHARE_PM1_VERTEX.

4.53. Modify procedure PM_INSERT to enable the insertion of edges that intersect existing edges. This means that you may have to perform a node splitting operation and create new edges, as well as delete the edge being intersected and replace it by two edges.

4.54. Analyze the cost of dynamically deleting an edge from a PM_1 quadtree. You may want to use the running-sum worst-case cost approach taken in the analysis of the insertion of a q-edge. Unlike insertion, however, the entire cost of deleting an edge is incurred at the instance at which the edge is deleted. Note that deletion is complicated by the fact that you must check for merging, and this check will often fail.

4.55. Assuming that the x and y coordinates of vertices are represented as integers, how would you detect if two edges are colinear? You want an exact answer, and thus you cannot use real arithmetic.

4.56. Modify procedures PM_INSERT and PM_DELETE to deal with the case that two colinear edges meet at a vertex and no other edge is incident at that vertex. In the case of insertion, you are to handle the situation that the inserted edge is colinear and shares a vertex with an existing edge. Prior to the insertion, the shared vertex has degree 1. In the case of deletion, you are to handle the situation that the deletion of an edge results in a vertex whose two incident edges are colinear. This vertex should be deleted and the two edges replaced by one edge.

4.57. Prove Lemma 4.1.

4.58. Prove Lemma 4.2.

4.59. Consider the problem of mapping a polygonal map onto the digitized plane in a manner analogous to that used in the proof of Theorem 4.1. The digitization is defined in terms of grid cells. The only difference from the definition of the PM_1 quadtree is the inclusion of a fourth condition requiring all grid cells to be of equal size.

    1. At most one vertex lies in each grid cell.

    2. If a grid cell contains a vertex, it can contain no q-edge that does not include that vertex.

    3. If a grid cell contains no vertices, it can contain at most one q-edge.

    4. All grid cells are of equal size.

Let d denote the number of bits used to represent the fixed point coordinates of the vertices of the edges comprising the polygonal map. Let g denote the number of bits required to specify the locations of the grid cells that compose the digitized plane. Thus the digitized plane will consist of $2^g \times 2^g$ grid cells. Prove that it is impossible to find a value of g as a function of d that yields a digitization into grid cells that satisfies the above conditions.

4.2.3.2 The PM_2 Quadtree

Each of D_1, D_2, and D_3 is an upper bound on some aspect of the PM_1 quadtree's construction that can contribute to the depth of the resulting tree. The maximum depth of

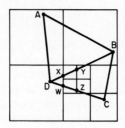

Figure 4.20   Example illustrating $D_3 > D'_2$ in a PM_1 quadtree

the tree is the upper bound of D_1, D_2, and D_3. D_1 and D_2 are functions of the polygonal map and are independent of the positioning of the underlying digitization grid. However, D_3 is dependent on the positioning of the digitization grid, and thus it can vary as the polygonal map is shifted.

Of course, the actual depth of the quadtree that is built could be considerably less than any of these three factors. On the other hand, for maps of the complexity of the one shown in Figure 4.11, D_3 can become arbitrarily large. For example, suppose we shift the polygonal map in Figure 4.11 to the right. As vertex E (see Figure 4.12) moves closer to the quadrant boundary on its right, the minimum separation between the q-edges of BE and CE that are not incident at E becomes smaller and smaller, thereby resulting in the growth of D_3 to unacceptable but bounded values.

To remedy the deficiency associated with condition 3 of the PM_1 quadtree definition, it is necessary to determine when it dominates the cost of storing a polygonal map. In particular, D_3 is greater than D_2 only if $d_{min.ee}$ is smaller than $d_{min.ev}$, which happens only when the two nearest nonintersecting q-edges are segments of edges that intersect at a vertex. For example, Figure 4.20 is the PM_1 quadtree for a polygonal map ABCD such that D_3 is greater than D_2 because $d_{min.ee}$ (the distance between q-edges XY and WZ) is smaller than $d_{min.ev}$ (the distance between C and BD). Note that XY is a q-edge of BD, WZ is a q-edge of CD, and BD intersects CD at vertex D. This analysis leads us to replace condition 3 of the PM_1 quadtree definition with condition 3′ defined below.

> **3′.**   If a quadtree leaf node's region contains no vertices, then it can contain only q-edges that meet at a common vertex exterior to the region.

A quadtree built from conditions 1, 2, 3′, and 4 is termed a *PM_2 quadtree*. For example, the PM_2 quadtree corresponding to the polygonal map of Figure 4.11 is shown in Figure 4.21. Note that q-edges in the same leaf meeting condition 3′ would be ordered angularly in a dictionary as were those q-edges meeting condition 2.

The PM_2 quadtree is represented in the same way as the PM_1 quadtree. Edges are inserted by using procedure PM_INSERT (as for the PM_1 quadtree) with the difference

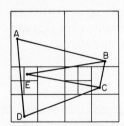

Figure 4.21   PM₂ quadtree corresponding to the polygonal map of Figure 4.11

that PM2_CHECK and SHARE_PM2_VERTEX (given below) are used to determine if the conditions of the definition of the PM₂ quadtree are satisfied. Isolated vertices pose no problems. Note that when a common vertex lies outside the quadtree leaf node, say *N*, none of the vertices of the incident edges may lie in *N*. This situation is correctly handled by PM2_CHECK.

Boolean procedure PM2_CHECK(L,S);
/* Determine if the square pointed at by S and the list of edges pointed at by L form a legal PM₂ quadtree node. SHARE_PM2_VERTEX is invoked with L instead of NEXT(L) because the edge might have one vertex in the square and share the other vertex with the list, which violates the PM₂ quadtree conditions. */
begin
  value pointer edgelist L;
  value pointer square S;
  return(**if empty** (L) **then true**
        else if P1(DATA(L))=P2(DATA(L)) **then**
       ONE_ELEMENT(L) /* Isolated vertex */
        else if PT_IN_SQUARE(P1(DATA(L)),S) **and**
          PT_IN_SQUARE(P2(DATA(L)),S) **then false**
        else if SHARE_PM2_VERTEX(P1(DATA(L)),L,S) **or**
          SHARE_PM2_VERTEX(P2(DATA(L)),L,S) **then true**
        else false);
end;

recursive Boolean procedure SHARE_PM2_VERTEX(P,L,S);
/* The vertex pointed at by P is the shared vertex in a PM₂ quadtree. It can be inside or outside the square pointed at by S. Determine if all the edges in the list of edges pointed at by L share P and do not have their other vertex within S. */
begin
  value pointer point P;
  value pointer edgelist L;
  value pointer square S;
  return(**if** P=P1(DATA(L)) **then**
        not(PT_IN_SQUARE(P2(DATA(L)),S)) **and**
        SHARE_PM2_VERTEX(P,NEXT(L),S)

```
        else if P=P2(DATA(L)) then
            not(PT_IN_SQUARE(P1(DATA(L)),S)) and
            SHARE_PM2_VERTEX(P,NEXT(L),S)
        else false);
end;
```

Edges are deleted by using procedure PM_DELETE (as for the PM₁ quadtree) with the difference that POSSIBLE_PM23_MERGE and TRY_TO_MERGE_PM23 (given below) are used to determine if an attempt should be made to merge the four sons of a gray node after processing them, that is, the conditions of a PM₂ quadtree are satisfied. A merge is feasible only if all four sons of a gray node are leaf nodes. This situation is checked by POSSIBLE_PM23_MERGE. If the merge is feasible, then TRY_TO_MERGE_PM23 is applied to determine if the conditions of the definition of the PM₂ quadtree are satisfied by using PM2_CHECK.

```
Boolean procedure POSSIBLE_PM23_MERGE(P);
/* Determine if an attempt should be made to merge the four sons of the PM₂ or PM₃
   quadtree. Such a merger is feasible only if all four sons of a GRAY node are LEAF
   nodes. */
begin
   value pointer node P;
   return(LEAF(SON(P,'NW')) and LEAF(SON(P,'NE')) and
          LEAF(SON(P,'SW')) and LEAF(SON(P,'SE'))));
end;


Boolean procedure TRY_TO_MERGE_PM23(P,R,L);
/* Determine if the four sons of the PM₂ or PM₃ quadtree rooted at node P can be
   merged. Variable L is used to collect all of the edges present in the subtrees. Note that
   there is no need for parameter R, and the procedure is not recursive. The call to PM2_-
   CHECK is replaced by PM3_CHECK when deleting from a PM₃ quadtree. */
begin
   value pointer node P,R;
   reference pointer edgelist L;
   quadrant I;
   for I in {'NW', 'NE', 'SW', 'SE'} do
      L ← SET_UNION(L,DICTIONARY(SON(P,I)));
   return(PM2_CHECK(L,SQUARE(P)));
end;
```

The cost of dynamically inserting an edge in a PM₂ quadtree is obtained in the same way as for the PM₁ quadtree. The only difference is that now DMAX corresponds to the maximum of D_1 and D_2. Note that the upper bound on the depth contributed by condition 3′ is bounded from above by D_2. The cost of dynamically deleting an edge is obtained in an analogous manner (see Exercise 4.66). Moreover, unlike deletion in a PM₁ quadtree, checking for merging in a PM₂ quadtree can be done in constant time.

Exercises

4.60. What is the maximum number of entries in the DICTIONARY field of a leaf node in a PM_2 quadtree?

4.61. Prove that the upper bound on the depth contributed by condition 3′ is bounded from above by D_2.

4.62. Describe the situation that can lead to $D_1 > D_2$.

4.63. Why is L used as a parameter instead of NEXT(L) when procedure PM2_CHECK invokes SHARE_PM2_VERTEX?

4.64. Prove that when PM_DELETE is invoked to delete one edge from a PM_2 quadtree, merging is possible only if after deletion of the edge from the leaf node containing it, all four sons of a gray node are leaf nodes.

4.65. In the case of a PM_1 quadtree, can you avoid the need to look at subtrees in procedure TRY_TO_MERGE_PM1 by using PM2_CHECK instead of PM1_CHECK? If not, why?

4.66. Analyze the cost of dynamically deleting an edge from a PM_2 quadtree. You may want to use the running-sum worst-case cost approach taken in the analysis of the insertion of a q-edge. However, unlike insertion, the entire cost of deleting an edge is incurred at the instance at which the edge is deleted. Note that unlike the PM_1 quadtree, the check for merging is constant in this case since only the four sons of each gray node must be examined for merging.

4.67. Do Exercise 4.56 for insertion and deletion of colinear edges in a PM_2 quadtree.

4.68. State and prove the analog of Theorem 4.1 of Section 4.2.3.1 for a polygonal map that is represented by a PM_2 quadtree, that is, what is the value of DMAX? Assume that the vertices of the map lie on a $2^d \times 2^d$ grid.

4.2.3.3   THE PM_3 QUADTREE

The PM_2 quadtree is less sensitive to shift and rotation of the polygonal map than the PM_1 quadtree. This is achieved by removing the contribution of condition 3 of the PM_1 quadtree definition. The next step is to remove the contribution of condition 2 as well. This brings us back full circle to the PR quadtree in that only conditions 1 and 4 of the PM_1 quadtree definition must be satisfied. The result is termed a *PM_3 quadtree* and is characterized by having at most one vertex in a region represented by a quadtree leaf node.

For example, Figure 4.22 is the PM_3 quadtree corresponding to the polygonal map of Figure 4.11. It should be clear that the number of quadtree nodes in the PR quadtree for the vertices of a polygonal map is equal to the number of quadtree nodes in the PM_3 quadtree of the polygonal map. Of course, the amount of information stored in the quadtree leaf node of a PM_3 quadtree will be much greater than the amount of information stored in the quadtree leaf node of a PR quadtree.

The q-edges that are in a PM_3 quadtree leaf nodes' block are partitioned into seven classes, each ordered by a dictionary. The most obvious class of q-edges is the class of q-edges that meet at a vertex within the leaf's block. This class is ordered in an angular manner as done for the PM_1 and PM_2 quadtrees. The remaining q-edges that pass through the leaf's block must enter at one side and leave via another. This yields six classes: NE, NS, NW, EW, SW, and SE, where NE denotes q-edges that intersect both the northern and the eastern boundaries of the leaf's block.

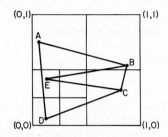

Figure 4.22   PM$_3$ quadtree corresponding to the polygonal map of Figure 4.11

Note that the q-edges are undirected edges. For example, the q-edges in class NE (the other five classes are handled analogously) are ordered according to whether they lie to the left or to the right of each other when viewing them in an easterly direction from the northern boundary of the leaf's block. q-edges that coincide with the border of a leaf's block are placed in either NS or EW as is appropriate. We also observe that in any given leaf, most of the classes will usually be empty. As an example, consider vertex C of Figure 4.22. We find that the only class that is not empty is NW, which contains a q-edge of edge BE. Of course, the class of q-edges passing through vertex C is also not empty; it contains q-edges of edges CB, CD, and CE.

The PM$_3$ quadtree is represented in the same way as the PM$_1$ quadtree. The difference is that the set of q-edges associated with each leaf node is decomposed further into seven subsets, as already described. In the implementation given here, the representation of these subsets is left unspecified. Edges are inserted by using procedure PM_INSERT (as for the PM$_1$ quadtree) with the difference that PM3_CHECK and SHARE_PM3_VERTEX (given below) are used to determine if the conditions of the definition of the PM$_3$ quadtree are satisfied. To allow an isolated vertex to coexist in a leaf node along with the edges that do not intersect it, we use INF to represent a fictitious point at (∞,∞) and invoke SHARE_PM3_VERTEX with it as the shared vertex.

```
recursive Boolean procedure PM3_CHECK(L,S);
/* Determine if the square pointed at by S and the list of edges pointed at by L form a legal
    PM₃ quadtree node. */
begin
  value pointer edgelist L;
  value pointer square S;
  return(if empty(L) then true
        else if P1(DATA(L))=P2(DATA(L)) then /* Isolated vertex */
          SHARE_PM3_VERTEX(INF,NEXT(L),S)
          /* INF ensures that the remaining edges have no vertices in S */
        else if PT_IN_SQUARE(P1(DATA(L)),S) and
            PT_IN_SQUARE(P2(DATA(L)),S) then false
        else if PT_IN_SQUARE(P1(DATA(L)),S) then
```

```
            SHARE_PM3_VERTEX(P1(DATA(L)),NEXT(L),S)
        else if PT_IN_SQUARE(P2(DATA(L)),S) then
            SHARE_PM3_VERTEX(P2(DATA(L)),NEXT(L),S)
        else PM3_CHECK(NEXT(L),S));
end;
```

recursive Boolean procedure SHARE_PM3_VERTEX(P,L,S);
/* The vertex pointed at by P is the shared vertex in a PM_3 quadtree. It is inside the square pointed at by S. Determine if all the edges in the list of edges pointed at by L either share P and do not have their other vertex within S or do not have either of their vertices in S. When P is INF, the rest of the edges have no vertex in S. */
begin
  value pointer point P;
  value pointer edgelist L;
  value pointer square S;
  return(**if empty**(L) **then true**
        else if P=P1(DATA(L)) **then**
            not(PT_IN_SQUARE(P2(DATA(L)),S)) **and**
            SHARE_PM3_VERTEX(P,NEXT(L),S)
        else if P=P2(DATA(L)) **then**
            not(PT_IN_SQUARE(P1(DATA(L)),S)) **and**
            SHARE_PM3_VERTEX(P,NEXT(L),S)
        else not(PT_IN_SQUARE(P1(DATA(L)),S)) **and**
            not(PT_IN_SQUARE(P2(DATA(L)),S)) **and**
            SHARE_PM3_VERTEX(P,NEXT(L),S));
end;

Edges are deleted in the same way, and using the same procedures, as for the PM_2 quadtree. Procedures PM_DELETE, POSSIBLE_PM23_MERGE, and TRY_TO_MERGE_-PM23 are used again with the only difference that PM3_CHECK is used by TRY_TO_-MERGE_PM23 to check if the conditions of a PM_3 quadtree are satisfied.

The cost of dynamically inserting an edge in a PM_3 quadtree is obtained as that for a PM_1 quadtree. There are two differences. First, DMAX corresponds to D_1. Second, the value of A_1, the cost of accessing the dictionary structure of q-edges associated with each leaf node, is now bounded by the number of edges in the polygonal map instead of by the number of vertices (or, more precisely, the maximum degree of a vertex). However, this does not affect the order of magnitude of the worst-case tree depth because, in a planar graph (containing neither multiple edges nor nonlinear edges), the number of edges is bounded from above by six fewer than three times the number of vertices (this is a corollary of Euler's formula [Hara69]). The cost of dynamically deleting an edge is obtained in the same way as that for a PM_2 quadtree.

At this point, the presentation of the development of the vertex-based variants of the PM quadtree is complete, and it is appropriate to compare their storage requirements. Using the polygonal map of Figure 4.11 yields the following comparison. The PM_1 quadtree of Figure 4.12 required 28 quadtree leaf nodes and 31 q-edge nodes (scattered among 24 dictionaries). The PM_2 quadtree of Figure 4.21 required 16 quadtree leaf nodes and 22 q-edge nodes (scattered among 13 dictionaries). The PM$_3$ quad-tree of Figure 4.22 required 7 quadtree leaf nodes and 17 q-edge nodes (scattered among nine dictionaries). Note that many of the dictionaries consist of single data nodes.

Exercises

4.69. Prove that a PM$_3$ quadtree leaf node's boundary can coincide with at most one q-edge.

4.70. Prove that for a given polygonal map, the average depth of a vertex node in a PM$_3$ quad-tree is smaller than in a PM$_2$ (and PM$_1$) quadtree.

4.71. Prove that when PM_DELETE is invoked to delete one edge from a PM$_3$ quadtree, merging is possible only if after deletion of the edge from the leaf node containing it, all four sons of a gray node are leaf nodes.

4.72. Analyze the cost of dynamically deleting an edge from a PM$_3$ quadtree.

4.73. Prove that isolated vertices are correctly handled by procedures PM3_CHECK and SHARE_-PM3_VERTEX.

4.74. Do Exercise 4.56 for insertion and deletion of colinear edges in a PM$_3$ quadtree.

4.2.3.4 PMR QUADTREES

The decomposition conditions of the PM$_1$, PM$_2$, and PM$_3$ quadtrees are formulated in terms of the vertices of the edges of the polygonal map. Thus they are vertex-based representations. In this section we focus on edge-based representations. Of the vertex-based methods, the PM$_3$ quadtree has the least restrictive decomposition rule in that it stipulates that the subdivision ceases whenever no block contains more than one vertex. This decomposition rule is the same as the PR quadtree. Bucket analogs of these three data structures can also be devised, although the most reasonable one is a bucket PM$_3$ quadtree since it is the only one whose decomposition rule is based solely on the number of vertices in the block.

One of the problems with formulating a bucket analog of the PM (i.e., PM$_3$, PM$_1$, or PM$_2$) quadtrees is that it is difficult to determine what it is that the bucket constrains. In the case of the PM$_3$ quadtree, this is not so hard since the most reasonable approach is for the bucket capacity to constrain the number of vertices in the bucket and not the number of edges. The *edge-EXCELL* method of Tamminen [Tamm81a] is an application of the EXCELL method for point data (described in Section 2.8.2.4) to collections of line segments[1] with no restrictions on whether they intersect (polygonal maps are a subset). It addresses this issue by constraining the number of edges in the bucket.

Edge-EXCELL is based on a regular decomposition. The principles guiding the decomposition process and the data structure are identical to those used by EXCELL for representing points. The only difference is that now the data consist of straight line segments that intersect the blocks corresponding to the buckets (i.e., cells or grid

---

[1] In the rest of this section and in the next section, the terms *line segment* and *endpoint* are used instead of *edge* and *vertex*, respectively, in order to emphasize that we are dealing with collections of line segments rather than polygonal maps.

blocks). Blocks are split whenever the number of line segments intersecting them exceeds the bucket capacity. Edge-EXCELL makes use of a grid directory that maps the blocks into storage areas of a finite capacity (i.e., buckets). These buckets often reside on disk. As the buckets overflow (i.e., the number of line segments intersecting them exceeds the capacity of the bucket), they are split into two equal-sized grid blocks, which may also lead to a doubling in the size of the directory.

The primary drawback of edge-EXCELL is that when the collection of line segments corresponds to a polygonal map that contains a vertex of degree m such that m is greater than the bucket capacity, then no matter how many times the bucket is split, it will be impossible to store all the line segments in one bucket. In such a case, edge-EXCELL makes use of overflow buckets. The PMR quadtree of Nelson and Samet [Nels86a] overcomes this problem by permitting all blocks to contain a variable number of line segments, even in excess of the bucket capacity. As in edge-EXCELL, the line segments that occupy a block in a PMR quadtree may intersect although their intersections are not considered vertices. This means that overlapping polygons can be represented (see Exercise 4.76). The PMR quadtree makes use of a probabilistic splitting rule.

A line segment is stored in a PMR quadtree by inserting it into the nodes corresponding to all the blocks that it intersects. During this process, the occupancy of each node intersected by the line segment is checked to see if the insertion causes it to exceed the predetermined bucket capacity. If the bucket capacity is exceeded, the node's block is split *once*, and only once, into four equal quadrants. Thus bucket capacity is really a *splitting threshold*, and in the subsequent discussion this term is used to refer to it.

On the other hand, a line segment is deleted from a PMR quadtree by removing it from the nodes corresponding to all the blocks it intersects. During this process, the occupancy of the node and its siblings is checked to see if the deletion causes the total number of line segments in them to be less than the predetermined splitting threshold. If the splitting threshold exceeds the occupancy of the node and its siblings, they are merged, and the merging process is reapplied to the resulting node and its siblings. Notice the asymmetry between the splitting and merging rules. In particular, the deletion process in a PMR quadtree is handled in the same way as in a bucket PR quadtree.

Figure 4.24 shows the construction of a PMR quadtree with a splitting threshold of two for the collection of line segments in Figure 4.23. The line segments are labeled with numbers corresponding to the order in which they are inserted in the PMR quadtree during its construction. The first block split occurs when line segment 3 is inserted (Figure 4.24a). The insertion of line segment 4 causes the block corresponding to the SE quadrant to be split. The insertion of line segments 5 and 6 does not cause any blocks to be split. Notice that the insertion of line segment 7 (Figure 4.24b) causes two blocks to be split (the ones corresponding to the NW and NE quadrants) since the capacity of each of these blocks is exceeded by the insertion. The insertion of line segment 8 causes three blocks to be split and likewise for the insertion of line segment 9 (Figure 4.24c).

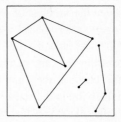

Figure 4.23   Set of line segments

Of course, the splitting rule used does not guarantee that each node will have occupancy less than the bucket capacity as was the case for the bucket PR quadtree for points (but not for line segments for any of the variants of the PM quadtree since an arbitrary number of line segments can intersect at a point). However, empirical tests support the conclusion that except in the unusual case where many line segments share the same endpoint, the node occupancy is unlikely to exceed the splitting threshold by much. For example, when representing a road network, it is unlikely that more than two roads intersect at a given point, and thus a splitting threshold of four is more than adequate.

Observe that the shape of the PMR quadtree for a given set of data is not unique; instead it depends on the order in which the line segments are inserted into the tree. However, since the decomposition is regular and focuses on regions of high density, the effect of this on the average bucket occupancy is small. It is also interesting to observe that the maximum number of line segments that can occur in a node, say P, is the sum of the splitting threshold and the depth of the tree at which P is found (see Exercise 4.75).

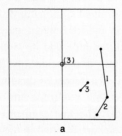
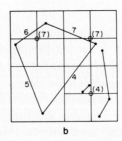
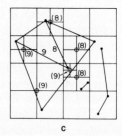

a   b   c

Figure 4.24   The process of building a PMR quadtree for the line seg-
ments of Figure 4.23 with a splitting threshold of 2. (a) The result after the
insertion of line segments 1–3. The plane has been quartered once, as
indicated by the small circle. (b) The result after the insertion of line seg-
ments 4–7. Three blocks have been split. (c) The result after the insertion
of line segments 8–9. Five additional blocks have been split.

Nevertheless, computing the average bucket occupancies for the PMR quadtree is somewhat difficult. Nelson and Samet [Nels86b] do so by using a similar technique to that which they used to compute an average bucket occupancy for the bucket PR quadtree. This requires a determination of the distribution of bucket occupancies that results when splitting a node containing c line segments. Determining the distribution of points is equivalent to determining the distribution of c items into four buckets (see Section 2.8.1). When the items are line segments, the situation is complicated somewhat by the geometry since a line segment can intersect several quadrants of a block, while a point can intersect only one quadrant.

The analysis of Nelson and Samet is simplified by making use of the following assumptions. First, when splitting a block containing a single line segment, they assume that the block does not contain either endpoint. They show that as a result, on the average, the line segment will have to be stored in two of the sons when the node is split (see Exercise 4.77). This means that each quadrant has a probability of 0.5 of being intersected by a line segment contained in its parent block.

Second, unlike the bucket PR quadtree, when adding a line segment to buckets of different occupancies there is no absolute upper bound (i.e., independent of the depth of the tree at which the node is found or the total number of points; see Exercise 4.75) on the node occupancy for a given splitting threshold, say c. Thus, they assume a cut-off occupancy value of $c + 2$ in the sense that they treat the proportion of nodes with occupancy greater than the cutoff as negligible. This is justifiable as the effect of this assumption for $c = 1$ on the analysis is less than 1%, and is even less for higher splitting thresholds.

Nelson and Samet [Nels86b] compared the theoretical predictions of the average bucket occupancies with experimentally generated data for a number of different splitting thresholds. The data were generated by connecting pairs of points, selected at random from a uniform distribution over a square region, to produce a set of line segments that crisscross the plane at random. They found that the theoretical occupancy predictions were generally in good agreement with empirical results (Table 4.1).

In particular, as in the bucket PR quadtree, at higher node capacities aging (Section 2.8.1) was evident in the sense that the theoretical occupancy predictions were higher than the experimental values. Again, as pointed out in Section 2.8.1, this is a result of the implicit assumption in the model that the proportion of nodes of a given occupancy is not correlated with the size of the node. This means that the model tends to underestimate the number of low occupancy nodes while overestimating the number of high occupancy ones.

Unlike the bucket PR quadtree, however, phasing was not significant in this case. The apparent reason seems to be that the local fluctuations in data density are greater for randomly intersecting line segments than for random points. This has the effect of smoothing the transition from one generation of nodes to the next as the tree grows in size.

Table 4.1   Average bucket occupancy for PMR quadtrees

Splitting Threshold	Experimental Occupancy	Theoretical Occupancy	Percentage Difference
1	1.22	1.22	0.0
2	1.62	1.66	2.4
3	2.14	2.20	2.7
4	2.71	2.81	3.6
5	3.31	3.46	4.3
6	3.90	4.14	5.8
7	4.53	4.81	6.0
8	5.10	5.51	7.4

Exercises

4.75. Prove that the maximum number of line segments that can occur in a node in a PMR quadtree, say P, is the sum of the splitting threshold and the depth of the tree at which P is found.

4.76. Suppose that the set of line segments intersect but that their intersections are not considered as vertices (i.e., they are nonplanar). This does not pose a problem for the PMR quadtree. What about the PM_1, PM_2, and PM_3 quadtrees?

4.77. Prove that, on the average, if lines are drawn from a sample distributed uniformly in space and orientation, the average number of quadrants intersected by a line passing through a quartered block is two. This can be done by showing that for lines drawn from a set of parallel lines, say L, passing through the block at angle θ, the average number of blocks intersected by a line is two, independent of θ.

4.78. Assuming that the line segments stored in a node in the PMR quadtree are uncorrelated, use the result of Exercise 4.77 to compute the distribution of occupancies when a node is split into quadrants given a splitting threshold c. Normalize your result so that the expected total number of quadrants is four.

4.79. Using a Gaussian distribution of points over a square region, select points at random and connect them to form a set of line segments that crisscross the plane. Compute the average bucket occupancies for splitting thresholds ranging from one to eight and compare with the theoretical occupancies predicted by using the model described in [Nels86b]. Are aging and phasing evident?

4.80. Prove that the average occupancy of the nodes produced when a node is split is bounded and smaller than the size of the parent.

4.81. Continuing Exercise 4.80, prove that the average size of parent nodes is also bounded by considering the case when the node occupancy i is greater than the splitting threshold c.

4.82. Give an algorithm to insert a line segment into a PMR quadtree.

4.83. Give an algorithm to delete a line segment from a PMR quadtree.

4.84. Discuss the problem of how to effectively generate a collection of random line segments, a set of random polygons, or a polygonal map. How would the results of the analysis of the PMR quadtree be affected by use of random polygonal maps instead of random lines?

4.2.3.5 FRAGMENTS

In many applications, the data are subject to set operations such as union and intersection. For example, consider the result of intersecting a polygonal map with an area map and suppose that the area map is represented by a region quadtree. Since the borders of the area map and the endpoints of the line segments comprising the polygonal map do not necessarily coincide, some line segments may be truncated (i.e., clipped). This may lead to data degradation if subsequently the operation were reversed so that the missing portions of the clipped line segments are reinserted.

Figure 4.25 is an example of such an intersection. Let us call the remaining portion of the line segment a *fragment*, the endpoints created by the intersection *cutpoints*, and the result of the intersection of the fragment with a block a *q-fragment*. In the figures, cutpoints are shown as hollow circles and endpoints as solid circles. Note the analogy between a q-edge and a q-fragment. In this section we are concerned with the representation of fragments.

One possibility is to represent a fragment by introducing new, intermediate endpoints at the cutpoints, thereby creating a new line segment distinct from the one that was clipped. This new line segment is colinear with the original one but has at least one different endpoint. It can be represented exactly in continuous space; however, in discrete space (e.g., as a result of the digitization process), this will not always be possible because the continuous coordinates of the cutpoint do not, in general, correspond exactly to any coordinates in the discrete space. Consequently if the new line segment is represented approximately in the discrete space, then the original information is degraded, and generally it will not be possible to rejoin the clipped portion with the missing portion to reform the original line segment.

Nelson and Samet [Nels86a] devise an alternative solution that retains the description of the original line segment and uses the spatial properties of the quadtree to specify what portions of the line segment are actually present. The descriptor associated with each node is interpreted as implying the presence of just that portion of the line segment that intersects the quadtree block corresponding to the node. Thus a node may contain a reference to a line segment although the entire line segment is not present as a lineal feature in the data set.

The result of an intersection of a line segment with a block is termed a *q-edge* in Section 4.2.3.1; in the context described here, it is termed a *q-fragment*. The original line segment of which the q-fragment is a part is referred to as the *parent segment*.

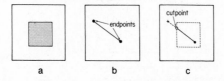

Figure 4.25   Definition of a (c) fragment that results from
the intersection of the segment of (b) with region (a)

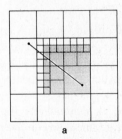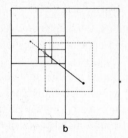

a   b

Figure 4.26   The representation of the fragment of Figure 4.25 using a collection of q-edges: (a) the region quadtree for the area with a line segment superimposed on it; (b) the set of five q-edges comprising the fragment

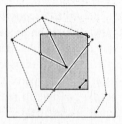

Figure 4.27   The set of five fragments induced by the intersection of a region with the line segments of Figure 4.23

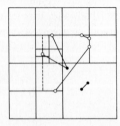

Figure 4.28   The fragment quadtree corresponding to the fragments of Figure 4.27. The cutpoints are shown with hollow circles, while the endpoints are shown with solid circles.

The descriptor of a parent segment is retained as long as there is at least one q-fragment that refers to it. Thus it is clear that a lineal feature can be broken into pieces and rejoined without loss or degradation of information. The use of this principle to represent the lineal features produced by the intersection operation of Figure 4.25 is shown in Figure 4.26.

To represent the fragments properly, we use a decomposition rule that partitions the space until no block contains a cutpoint in its interior. Let us term the result a *fragment quadtree*. For example, Figure 4.28 is the fragment quadtree corresponding to the fragments of Figure 4.27, which in turn results from the intersection of the segments of Figure 4.23 with a rectangular area. The fragment quadtree by itself is not very attractive because the subdivision only localizes the cutpoints. Thus it may result in an unsatisfactory distribution of the q-fragments or the endpoints of the line segments. For example, a block may contain many endpoints or q-fragments. However, the PM quadtree variants discussed in the previous sections can be used to organize the resulting q-fragments and endpoints in the fragment quadtree.

When adapting one of the vertex-based PM quadtrees (PM_1, PM_2, or PM_3), to represent fragments, we must modify its definition to remove condition 4 since the resulting block is maximal only with respect to the initial fragment quadtree decomposition. In addition, the conditions that determine the decomposition should refer only to the q-edges and endpoints that are part of the fragments. For example, when adapting a PM_3 quadtree, condition 1 must be formulated in terms of endpoints of fragments (not cutpoints or endpoints of q-edges that are not members of fragments). Otherwise a situation may arise where a block that does not contain any q-fragments is nevertheless decomposed into four empty nodes (e.g., Figure 4.29). The resulting structure is termed a PM_3-*f quadtree*.

For example, Figure 4.30 is the PM_3–f quadtree corresponding to the fragment quadtree of Figure 4.28. Although the example makes use of an adaptation of the PM_3 quadtree (i.e., PM_3–f), the PM_1 and the PM_2 quadtrees could also have been adapted to form PM_1–f and PM_2–f quadtrees, respectively.

Figure 4.29   Example showing how unattached endpoints (starred) can cause a decomposition of a WHITE block if the decomposition is based on vertices rather than attached endpoints (solid circles) that are not cutpoints (hollow circles)

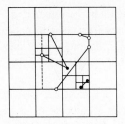

Figure 4.30   The PM$_3$-f quadtree corresponding to the fragment of Figure 4.28. The cutpoints are shown with hollow circles, while the endpoints are shown with solid circles.

Nelson and Samet [Nels86a] use the PMR quadtree, an edge-based PM quadtree. In this case, once the cutpoints have been localized, the remaining fragments are inserted in the structure, and a block is split once if it contains more than c q-fragments where c is the splitting threshold. The result is termed a *PMR-f quadtree*. It should be clear that the shape of the PMR-f quadtree is dependent on the order in which the fragments are inserted into it. For example, Figure 4.31 is the PMR-f quadtree corresponding to the fragment quadtree of Figure 4.28. Notice that the fragments have been labeled with numbers corresponding to the order in which they are inserted into the PMR-f quadtree. Three blocks required splitting (upon the insertion of fragments 3, 4, and 5).

The preceding illustrations of the construction of the PM$_3$-f and PMR-f quadtrees are somewhat misleading. The problem is that in practice the fragments are created by an intersection operation. In this case, a region map serves as a template, which is intersected with a map containing lineal features. Since the cutpoints represent the intersection of the lineal features with the boundary of the template, they are implicitly

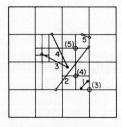

Figure 4.31   The PMR-f quadtree with a splitting threshold of 2 for the fragments of Figure 4.27 inserted in the indicated order. The three circled splits were caused by exceeding the threshold. All other splits are necessary to localize the cutpoints of the fragments.

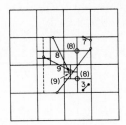

Figure 4.32   The PMR-f quadtree corresponding to the fragment quadtree of Figure 4.28 when the tree is constructed by deleting the q-fragments that do not intersect the region intersected with the PMR quadtree. The q-fragments are numbered in the same way as in Figure 4.24. The three circled splits were caused by exceeding the splitting threshold of 2. The cutpoints are shown as hollow circles while the endpoints are shown as solid circles.

localized.   Thus all that remains is to build the appropriate data structure for the remaining lineal features.

When the lineal features are represented by a member of the PM quadtree family, the resulting structure is constructed by deleting the q-fragments (initially portions of q-edges) that do not intersect the template. Since the shape of the PMR-f quadtree depends on the order in which the fragments are inserted into it, the result is different from that obtained when the structure is built by insertion rather than by deletion. For example, Figure 4.32 is the PMR-f quadtree corresponding to the fragment quadtree of Figure 4.28 instead of Figure 4.31. The difference is that the NW subquadrant of the NW subquadrant of the SE quadrant had to be split. Note that the fragments in Figure 4.32 are numbered in the same way as in Figure 4.24.

The insertion and deletion of a q-fragment is a bit tricky because both operations can cause a merge. In particular, the insertion of a fragment may restore its parent segment. Four sibling blocks are merged whenever there are c (i.e., the splitting threshold) or fewer distinct parent segments in the sibling blocks and the q-fragments are continuous through the block produced by the merge. q-fragments whose blocks can be merged in this manner are said to be *compatible*, while those that do not are said to

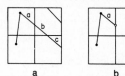

a	b

Figure 4.33   Sibling blocks containing (a) compatible and (b) incompatible sets of q-edges

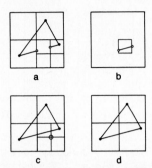

Figure 4.34   Insertion of a q-fragment into a block of equal size in a PMR-f and PM_3-f quadtree: (a) quadtree before insertion; (b) q-fragment being inserted; (c) the insertion produces sibling blocks with compatible q-fragments; (d) the resulting quadtree after merging. The PMR-f and PM_3-f quadtrees are identical. The cutpoints are shown with hollow circles, while the endpoints are shown with solid circles.

be *incompatible*. For example, q-fragments a, b, and c in Figure 4.33a are compatible, while q-fragments a and b in Figure 4.33b are incompatible.

In the following, we examine the process of inserting a q-fragment. Where the type of the quadtree (i.e., PM_3-f or PMR-f) makes a difference, it is noted. The examples assume a splitting threshold of 2, and in each case the initial PM_3-f and the PMR-f quadtrees are the same. Figure 4.34 illustrates the insertion of a q-fragment into a block of equal size. Once the q-fragment has been inserted, merging takes place; the resulting PM_3-f and the PMR-f quadtrees are the same.

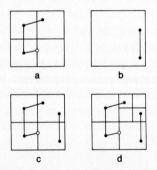

Figure 4.35   Insertion of a line segment into a PMR-f and PM_3-f quadtree: (a) quadtree before insertion; (b) line segment being inserted; (c) the resulting PMR-f quadtree; (d) the resulting PM_3-f quadtree. The cutpoints are shown with hollow circles, while the endpoints are shown with solid circles.

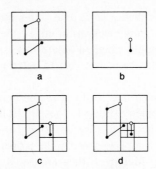

Figure 4.36   Insertion of a q-fragment into a PMR-f and PM₃-f quadtree: (a) quadtree before insertion; (b) q-fragment being inserted; (c) the resulting PMR-f quadtree; (d) the resulting PM₃-f quadtree. The cutpoints are shown with hollow circles, while the endpoints are shown with solid circles.

Figure 4.35 illustrates the insertion of a line segment that must first be decomposed into properly sized q-fragments before the insertion and subsequent check for merging or splitting. The resulting PMR-f quadtree is given in Figure 4.35c, while the resulting PM₃–f quadtree is given in Figure 4.35d. Note that the PM₃–f quadtree requires that the NE quadrant be decomposed in order to separate two endpoints.

Figure 4.36 illustrates the insertion of a q-fragment into a block that must first be decomposed into smaller blocks before the insertion and subsequent check for merging or splitting. The resulting PMR-f quadtree is given in Figure 4.36c, while the resulting PM₃–f quadtree is given in Figure 4.36d. Note that the PM₃–f quadtree requires that the NW subquadrant of the SE quadrant be decomposed in order to separate two endpoints.

Exercises

4.85. Why aren't the blocks in the PM₃-f quadtree maximal?

4.86. Why doesn't it make sense to define a variant of the PM₃ quadtree such that no quadrant contains a cutpoint or an endpoint?

4.87. Give an algorithm to insert a q-fragment into a PMR-f quadtree.

4.88. Give an algorithm to delete a q-fragment from a PMR-f quadtree.

4.89. Give an algorithm to insert a q-fragment into a PM₃-f quadtree.

4.90. Give an algorithm to delete a q-fragment from a PM₃-f quadtree.

4.2.3.6   MAINTAINING LABELS OF REGIONS [2]

The design of the PM quadtree data structure[3] is predicated on the desire to obtain a

---

[2] This section contains material of a specialized nature and can be skipped on an initial reading.

[3] In this section, the term *PM quadtree* is used in a collective sense to include the PM₁, PM₂, and PM₃ quadtrees. The maintenance of labels in a PMR quadtree is dealt with in Exercise 4.91.

dynamic data structure rather than a static one. This means that when updates are made in the form of insertions and deletions of edges, there is no need to reconstruct the entire structure. An example situation where this issue is of importance is the point location problem. In this case, we wish to determine the identity of a region which contains a given point.

The point location problem has received a considerable amount of attention in the field of computational geometry [Edel84, Tous80]. It is discussed in Section 4.3 in the context of a number of hierarchical solutions to it. However, these methods do not lead to a hierarchical decomposition of space in the proper subset sense that is used in the quadtree-based methods. Moreover, they are not dynamic. In this section the focus is on how the PM quadtree can be adapted to support tasks that require the ability to keep track of region information in a dynamic manner. The discussion of the PM quadtree solution to the point location problem is left to Section 4.3.3.

As mentioned in Section 4.2.3.1, in the PM quadtree implementation, the regions of a polygonal map are represented by labeling the borders of the regions with the names of the two regions adjacent to them. These names are recorded in the LEFT and RIGHT fields of each q-edge. The process of recording such information is simple. However, maintaining it so that it remains consistent as edges are inserted and deleted is nontrivial. Figure 4.37 is used to illustrate some of the issues in this task. Of course, we could avoid this issue in its entirety by using the static solution, which is to execute a connected component labeling procedure (see Section 5.1 of [Same90b]) each time an update operation occurs; however, this is too costly.

Figure 4.37 contains a pentagonal region ABCDE with many holes. All the q-edges forming the ABCDE border and those forming the outer border of each of the holes must be labeled with the name of the pentagonal region. Consider what happens if we add an edge between vertices B and E (i.e., BE). The outer border of the pentagonal region has been split in two by the new edge. This results in the formation of two new regions, a triangular region (ABE) and a quadrilateral region (BCDE). Also the holes of the original pentagonal region must have their labels changed to indicate whether they are now in the triangular or the quadrilateral region.

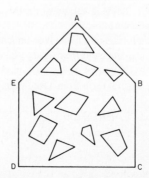

Figure 4.37   Example polygonal map with many holes

If the region labels were stored directly on each q-edge, then updating the region labels requires that every q-edge be visited. The updating process can be simplified greatly if all the q-edges in a particular region are kept in a linked list. However, it will still involve an amount of work proportional to the sum of the number of q-edges in the outer border of the pentagonal region and in the outer border of all the holes inside the pentagonal region. In the following, the q-edges within a region are organized in a more efficient manner than a linked list. Note that the comments about the insertion of the edge BE apply equally to the problem of deleting the edge BE.

The q-edges that border a region can be partitioned into a collection of disconnected chains of q-edges. Elements of this collection correspond to walks along the outer border of the region, to walks along the outer borders of any holes in the region, and miscellaneous q-edges that have the same region on both their left and right sides (and hence are not properly borders of any region). The q-edges of each chain are grouped into a 2-3 tree [Aho74] (termed a *chain* 2-3 tree), and we store only the label information (i.e., an identifier for the chain) in the root of the tree. In fact, each q-edge is linked to the leaf nodes of at most two of these 2-3 trees (one link for the region on each side of the q-edge), and the region information is found by moving up the tree using father links.

The chains of each region are also grouped into a 2-3 tree (termed a *region* 2-3 tree), and again we store only the label information in the root of the tree (this time the label information is the name of the region). The 2-3 tree is chosen because of its algorithmic simplicity (it is a degenerate case of the much-studied B-tree [Come79]). In particular, the 2-3 tree has the property that insertion, deletion, and splitting and concatenation of two 2-3 trees can be performed in $O(\log_2 n)$ time for trees of size n. In addition, two 2-3 trees of size t_1 and t_2, respectively, can be merged into a new 2-3 tree in $O(t_1 + t_2)$ time. However, other balanced tree techniques could have also been used.

To be able to make use of the 2-3 trees, we must be able to define an ordering for q-edges and chains. The q-edges in a given chain can be ordered according to their appearance during a walk along the chain starting at the leftmost of the uppermost vertices incident to the chain. In case of a tie (e.g., a closed chain in which case there are two q-edges meeting this criterion), we choose the q-edge whose other endpoint is uppermost leftmost. We also have to order the collection of chains corresponding to each region, which we do by using their 'extreme' q-edge. By extreme, it is meant that for each chain we choose the q-edge having the uppermost leftmost endpoint. Again in case of a tie (e.g., extreme q-edges that share the same endpoint), we apply the same rule to the second endpoint. This extreme q-edge will provide a unique label for the entire region (with respect to a particular map).

If deletion or insertion of a q-edge does not change the number of regions in the map, then the operation can be performed in $O(\log_2 q)$ time where q is the number of q-edges (i.e., leaf nodes) in the largest chain 2-3 tree associated with a given region. If deletion of a q-edge merges two regions, the region 2-3 trees that order the collection of chains for each region will need to be merged. If the number of leaf nodes (i.e., chains) in the region 2-3 trees representing these two regions is t_1 and t_2, respectively, then the cost of this operation will be $O(t_1 + t_2 + \log_2 q)$ time. This is accomplished by a procedure that merges the two collections of disconnected chains in $O(t_1 + t_2)$ time and creates the border of the new region from the borders of the two merged regions in $O(\log_2 q)$ time.

Note that for cartographic data, the individual chains are typically long (i.e., q can become large), but the number of chains in each region's collection is usually small for a given region (i.e., $t_1 + t_2$ is usually small). Indeed if there are no chains that have the same region on both sides, then the average value of t_1 (and also t_2) could not be larger than 1 (corresponding to the region's outer border) plus the average number of holes. But since each hole is itself a region, the average number of holes cannot exceed 1. Therefore the average value of t_1 (and of t_2) cannot exceed 2.

Similarly, when q-edge insertion causes splitting of a region with a region 2-3 tree of t chains, the cost will be $O(t + \log_2 q)$ time. This is accomplished by a procedure that separates the collection of disconnected chains of q-edges that bounded the old region (i.e., its region 2-3 tree) into a collection for each of the new regions (i.e., new region 2-3 trees) in $O(t)$ time. It also splits the outer border of the old region into the two outer borders of the new regions in $O(\log_2 q)$ time. The new region might be created when the inserted q-edge completes the border of a hole rather than when it connects the outer border in two places. Determining the region to which a q-edge belongs can be done in $O(\log_2 q)$ time.

Exercise

4.91. How would you maintain labels of regions in a PMR quadtree with fragments?

4.2.4 Empirical Comparisons of the Different Representations

Although all of the representations discussed in Sections 4.2.1–4.2.3 are based on a regular decomposition of space, their performance does differ considerably. In this section, we examine the results of empirical comparisons of the four variants of the PM quadtree, the MX quadtree, and the edge quadtree. The data consisted of three maps (Figures 4.38–4.40) chosen from a cartographic database corresponding to a section of the Russian River area in California [Same84d, Same87a, Shaf87c].

The Powerline Map (Figure 4.38) shows the path of the main powerline. The Cityline Map (Figure 4.39) indicates the border of the local municipality. The Roadline Map (Figure 4.40), the most complicated, details part of the local roadway network. Table 4.2 contains the number of vertices and edges in each of these maps. All of these maps consist of edges whose vertices rest on a 512×512 grid offset by half the width of a pixel from the coordinates of the lower left-hand corners of the quadtree nodes at depth 9 (later we will consider the impact of this displacement). In other words, the grid of points from which the vertices are drawn corresponds to the centers of pixels.

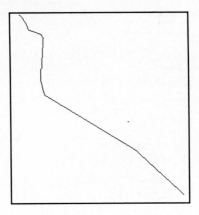

Figure 4.38   Powerline map

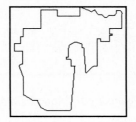

Figure 4.39   Cityline map

Neither the MX quadtree nor the edge quadtree is an appropriate representation for polygonal maps. The problem is that these representations correspond to an approximation (or in the case of the MX quadtree, a digitization) of the map, whereas the variants of the PM quadtree represent the maps exactly. Nevertheless, in practice, for the MX quadtree it is natural to consider the approximation that results from representing edges with the same accuracy as the grid. For the 512×512 images that we are considering, this means that the MX quadtree is built by truncating the decomposition at depth 9. Similarly the edge quadtree is also constructed by truncating the decomposition at depth 9.

Table 4.2   Size of the maps

Map	Number of Vertices	Number of Edges
Powerline	15	14
Cityline	64	64
Roadline	684	763

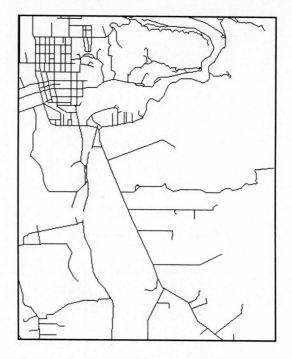

Figure 4.40   Roadline map

Tables 4.3–4.6[4] summarize the storage requirements of the various quadtree methods of representing the maps of Figures 4.38–4.40. As we observed before, the PM₁ quadtree will always be the largest of the PM quadtrees; it will require the most nodes. Therefore let us consider how it compares with two alternative approaches, the MX and edge quadtrees given in Tables 4.3 and 4.4, respectively. Tables 4.5 and 4.6 contain the data for the different PM quadtrees. The PMR quadtree has a splitting threshold value of 4 (labeled PMR₄). Initially the discussion focuses on a comparison of the MX, edge, and vertex-based PM quadtrees (PM₁, PM₂, and PM₃). The PMR quadtree and the effect of varying the value of the splitting threshold are discussed later.

Table 4.6 breaks down the leaf count in terms of the different type of nodes, as well as gives the average number of q-edges for each node type (in parentheses) where relevant. Note that for the PMR quadtree, the concept of a vertex node is irrelevant, and thus only the number of edge nodes is tabulated. In the case of the edge quadtree, the data tabulated are for a variant in which all vertices are represented by single pixel-sized nodes instead of just the ones with degree ≥ 2. This variation is known as the *linear edge quadtree* [Same84c].

---

[4] All the tables in this section were produced by Robert E. Webber.

Table 4.3   Size of the MX quadtrees

Map	Depth	Leaves	Black Nodes	White Nodes
Powerline	9	1597	521	1076
Cityline	9	2347	782	1565
Roadline	9	19,489	7055	12,434

Table 4.4   Size of the edge quadtrees

Map	Depth	Leaves	Vertex Nodes	Edge Nodes	White Nodes
Powerline	9	208	15	66	127
Cityline	9	748	64	214	470
Roadline	9	6733	684	2426	3623

Table 4.5   Size of the PM_1, PM_2, PM_3, and PMR_4 quadtrees

Map	Depth				Leaves			
	PM_1	PM_2	PM_3	PMR_4	PM_1	PM_2	PM_3	PMR_4
Powerline	8	8	8	5	58	58	58	16
Cityline	8	8	8	6	184	181	157	70
Roadline	13	9	9	8	2005	1846	1618	763

Map	Q-edges			
	PM_1	PM_2	PM_3	PMR_4
Powerline	40	40	40	21
Cityline	168	167	159	113
Roadline	2116	2044	1950	1557

Table 4.6   Breakdown of information in Table 4.5
by node type

Map	Vertex Nodes (average q-edges)		
	PM_1	PM_2	PM_3
Powerline	15 (1.9)	15 (1.9)	15 (1.9)
Cityline	64 (2.0)	64 (2.0)	64 (2.1)
Roadline	684 (2.2)	684 (2.2)	684 (2.3)

Map	Edge Nodes (average q-edges)			
	PM_1	PM_2	PM_3	PMR_4
Powerline	12	12 (1.0)	12 (1.0)	8 (2.6)
Cityline	40	38 (1.0)	24 (1.0)	43 (2.6)
Roadline	590	491 (1.1)	336 (1.1)	614 (2.5)

Map	White Nodes			
	PM_1	PM_2	PM_3	PM_4
Powerline	31	31	31	8
Cityline	80	79	69	27
Roadline	731	671	598	149

The MX quadtree (Table 4.3) has the worst performance. In all three examples the MX quadtree is larger than the PM_1 quadtree (Table 4.5) by at least a factor of 9. More generally, we would expect the number of nodes in the MX quadtree for a polygonal map to be roughly as large as the product of the average edge length (in terms of pixel width) and the number of nodes in the corresponding PM_1 quadtree (see Exercise 4.92).

Now, let us compare the edge quadtree with the PM_1 quadtree. The edge quadtree (Table 4.4) is a definite improvement over the MX quadtree. Considering the trivial (but often typical) maps like Powerline and Cityline, we see that the edge quadtree is about three times as large as the PM_1 quadtree. This can be explained by observing that the average depth of a vertex node in the PM_1 quadtree for each of these two maps was between 6 and 7 (not shown in the tables), whereas the corresponding edge quadtree must represent all of the vertex nodes at depth 9.

The Roadline Map, the most complex map in the data, has an edge quadtree that has three times as many nodes as its corresponding PM_1 quadtree. At first this might

Table 4.7   Distribution of node types for PM quadtrees in the roadline map

Depth	Vertex nodes			Edge nodes				White nodes			
	PM_1	PM_2	PM_3	PM_1	PM_2	PM_3	PMR_4	PM_1	PM_2	PM_3	PMR_4
0	0	0	0	0	0	0	0	0	0	0	0
1	0	0	0	0	0	0	0	0	0	0	0
2	0	0	0	0	0	0	4	4	4	4	0
3	1	1	1	0	0	0	8	9	9	9	9
4	15	15	17	6	8	9	49	37	37	37	19
5	78	78	83	39	39	31	111	88	85	83	23
6	182	182	196	109	104	98	243	201	195	187	63
7	242	242	245	194	192	127	183	214	201	181	27
8	131	131	113	181	125	65	20	133	110	76	4
9	35	35	29	31	23	6	0	39	30	21	0
10	0	0	0	7	0	0	0	1	0	0	0
11	0	0	0	10	0	0	0	3	0	0	0
12	0	0	0	10	0	0	0	1	0	0	0
13	0	0	0	3	0	0	0	1	0	0	0

appear surprising since the maximum depth of this quadtree is considerably greater than that required by the digitization grid. In this case, the digitization grid requires a depth of 9, while the PM_1 quadtree requires some nodes to be at a depth of 13.

Although for this map the maximum depth of the PM_1 quadtree is greater (13) than that of the edge quadtree (9), the difference in the number of nodes in the two trees can be explained by examining the distribution of nodes by depth (Table 4.7). In essence, the average depth of a vertex node is again between 6 and 7 for the PM_1 quadtree, and it is 9 for the edge quadtree. The reduction in the average depth of a vertex node in the PM_1 quadtree has a direct effect on the total number of nodes because the decomposition of an edge is identical in the edge and PM_1 quadtrees once the edge has exited the region of the vertex nodes representing its endpoints.

The discussion leads to the conclusion that considering storage, the PM_1 quadtree is an improvement over earlier quadtree-based approaches to handling real data. The PM_1 quadtree has the desirable property of reducing the average depth at which the dominant node type is located. The PM_2 and PM_3 quadtrees are attempts to reduce further the maximum depth of edge and vertex nodes, respectively, in a PM_1 quadtree.

The PM_2 quadtree has the effect of reducing the maximum depth of edge nodes (Table 4.7) by virtue of a more compact treatment of the case when close edges that radiate from the same vertex lie in a different node from the vertex. When comparing the data of the PM_1 quadtree columns with the data of the PM_2 quadtree columns of Table 4.5, we observe no change in the Powerline Map since it consists only of obtuse angles. The Cityline Map has a few acute angles. This creates situations where edge nodes can be formed containing more than one q-edge. This causes some of the edge nodes to be closer to the root and results in a 3% reduction in the number of nodes. This situation is more common in the Roadline Map, which is more complicated, and results in an 8% reduction in the number of nodes. We note that the PM_2 reduction affects only the maximum depth of the edge nodes. Recall that nodes containing a vertex are treated in the same manner in both the PM_1 and PM_2 quadtrees.

Comparing the PM_3 quadtree with the PM_1 and PM_2 quadtrees also shows no change in the number of nodes for the Powerline Map because it contains no edges that pass closely to vertices other than their endpoints. This situation occurs a bit more frequently in the Cityline Map, resulting in a 12% reduction in the number of nodes. Note that the existence of such situations implies that vertex nodes will be slightly closer to the root in the PM_3 quadtree than in the PM_1 and PM_2 quadtrees. For the Roadline Map, the use of the PM_3 quadtree instead of a PM_1 quadtree leads to a 19% reduction in the number of nodes. This is due to the tendency for vertex nodes to occur closer to the root in the PM_3 quadtree than in the PM_1 quadtree and can be seen by examining Table 4.7.

It is also interesting to compare the number of q-edges in the nodes of the different PM quadtrees. In Table 4.5 we find that a reduction in the number of q-edges closely parallels the reduction of the number of quadtree leaf nodes across the different PM quadtrees. Table 4.6 tabulates the average number of q-edges per node of a particular node type. This is placed in parentheses immediately after the count of the number of leaf nodes of that node type. No averages are given for white nodes and PM_1 quadtree edge nodes, as by definition they have zero and one q-edges, respectively.

Investigation of the average number of q-edges per edge node shows that it is rare to have more than one q-edge per edge node. In the case of vertex nodes, we find that the number of q-edges per node is consistently around two, although it does seem to increase slowly with map complexity. These values tend to indicate that a linked list is usually sufficient to organize the q-edges at a given node instead of the 2-3 tree as advocated in Section 4.2.3.6. Implementing the three test maps with PM quadtrees resulted in only one node with as many as five q-edges. Thus not only is the average low, but also there does not seem to be much variance from the average.

From the above, we see that the differences among the various vertex-based PM quadtrees (referred to as PMn here) can be drastic. Nevertheless for typical cartographic data, the difference in the number of nodes in the PMn quadtrees for a particular map has so far proved to be minor. Thus, for cartographic data, the choice of an appropriate PMn quadtree is dictated more by the problems of implementation than by the need to conserve space. However, it should be noted that cartographic data are rather special in that they generally consist of sequences of short edges meeting at obtuse angles. Since the lengths of the edges are often shorter than the distance between the features that the edges are representing, this yields data that tend to bring out the best in each of the PMn quadtrees, with the result that there is little difference between them. For data that are not this simple, the benefits of the PM_2 and PM_3 quadtrees over the PM_1 quadtree should be more pronounced.

Table 4.8   Analysis of splitting threshold values for PMR quadtrees

Splitting Threshold	Depth	Q-edges (Q-edges/edges)	Leaf Nodes	White Nodes
1	10	2584 (3.39)	2902	1205
2	10	2149 (2.82)	1855	632
3	9	1766 (2.31)	1099	277
4	8	1557 (2.04)	763	149
5	8	1452 (1.90)	616	107
6	7	1360 (1.78)	493	73
7	7	1278 (1.67)	388	55
8	7	1228 (1.61)	328	44
16	5	1051 (1.38)	151	13
32	5	947 (1.24)	70	5
64	4	877 (1.15)	34	3
128	3	832 (1.09)	13	0
256	2	797 (1.04)	7	0
512	2	797 (1.04)	7	0
1,024	0	763 (1.00)	1	0

At this point, let us turn to the edge-based PM quadtrees (the PMR quadtree). In this case, the most important issue is the number of q-edges and leaf nodes. As we saw from the tables, there was not a striking difference in these quantities for the vertex-based PM quadtrees. The storage requirements of the PMR quadtree for a given set of line segments will generally vary depending on the choice of the value of the splitting threshold.

Table 4.8 illustrates the behavior of the PMR quadtree as the value of the splitting threshold is varied for the Roadline Map (the most complex map that we tested). The number of leaf nodes in a PMR quadtree seems to halve as the value of the splitting threshold is doubled. The number of q-edges divided by the number of edges in the map (e.g., 763 edges in the Roadline Map) indicates how often a line segment is expected to be split when determining the node that will contain it. From Table 4.8 we see that at worst (i.e., a splitting threshold value of 1), a line segment will be split into 3.4 q-edges on the average. It is interesting to note that for a splitting threshold value of 16, the average number of q-edges is 1.4, which means that for this splitting threshold, at least 60% of the line segments were not split at all.

Let us now reexamine the tables for the vertex-based PM quadtrees. Each of these quadtrees will always split a line segment at least once (since both endpoints of a line segment must be in different nodes). For example, in the case of the Roadline Map, the average number of q-edges per edge for the PM_1, PM_2, and PM_3 quadtrees is 2.8, 2.7, and 2.6, respectively. Thus the average number of q-edges per edge for all of the PMn quadtrees is comparable to that for a PMR quadtree with a splitting threshold value between 2 and 3. Moreover, for each of the PMn quadtrees, the number of leaf nodes is comparable to that obtained when using a PMR quadtree with a splitting threshold value between 2 and 3 (actually the PM$_1$ quadtree has just a few more leaf nodes than a PMR quadtree with a splitting threshold value of 2).

It is also worth noting that the PMR quadtree is less sensitive than the PM$_1$ quadtree with respect to the maximum depth needed to separate data items that are too 'close' (recall Theorem 4.1 and the discussion of the maximum depth of a PM$_1$ quadtree in Section 4.2.3.1). In particular, the maximum depth of the PM$_1$ quadtree for the Roadline Map was 13, whereas even with a splitting threshold value of 1, the maximum depth of the PMR quadtree never exceeded 10.

In conclusion, for maps of the size discussed in this section, it seems that a splitting threshold value of 3 or more will usually yield a PMR quadtree that is more compact than any of the vertex-based PM quadtrees. Nevertheless further empirical and theoretical studies are required before making a decision on the appropriate PM quadtree implementation for a given application.

Exercises
4.92. Show that for a given polygonal map, the expected number of nodes in its MX quadtree is roughly as large as the product of the average edge length (in terms of pixel width) and the number of nodes in the corresponding PM$_1$ quadtree.
4.93. Section 4.2.3 states that one of the motivations for the development of the PM quadtree data structure is that its size is relatively invariant to shifting and rotation. Perform a set of experiments on the effect of minor shifts in positioning the vertices of some test data. Try shifts of 0.0, 0.125, 0.25, 0.5, 0.625, and 0.75.
4.94. In the text it is observed that the number of leaf nodes in the PMR quadtree seems to halve as the value of the splitting threshold is doubled. Can you give a theoretical explanation for this phenomenon?
4.95. Perform a theoretical analysis of the PMR quadtree and derive an optimum value for the splitting threshold.

4.3   METHODS ROOTED IN COMPUTATIONAL GEOMETRY

The hierarchical data structures discussed in the previous sections of this chapter are rooted in computer graphics and image processing. They were designed primarily to represent curves and lines. The field of computational geometry is also relevant [Edel84, Tous80, Prep85, Edel87]. Computational geometry is a changing field having its roots in the work of Shamos and Hoey [Sham75, Sham78]. This work focuses on problems of asymptotical computational complexity of geometric algorithms. Many of the solutions (e.g., [Lipt77]) make heavy use of results from graph theory

[Hara69]. (For a fuller treatment of this subject, see the excellent texts by Preparata and Shamos [Prep85] and Edelsbrunner [Edel87].)

In this section, we look at a small sample of the type of hierarchical representations employed in solutions to problems involving curvilinear data that are based on computational geometry. First, we examine the K-structure of Kirkpatrick [Kirk83]. Next, we look at the separating chain method of Lee and Preparata [Lee77a] and then see what improvements can be made to it that yield the layered dag of Edelsbrunner, Guibas, and Stolfi [Edel86a]. The ideas disussed in this section are of a theoretical nature and may be skipped.

To understand these data structures, it is important to realize the motivation for their development. They were designed primarily to solve the point location problem. In this case, given a query point and a polygonal map, we wish to identify the region in which the point lies. This problem has been much studied. Lipton and Tarjan [Lipt77] have shown that for a planar subdivision of m edges, the optimal solution yields an answer in $O(\log_2 m)$ time using a data structure that uses $O(m)$ space and can be constructed in $O(m)$ time under certain assumptions. Both the K-structure and the layered dag achieve these bounds, although the layered dag is preferable because the constants of proportionality are smaller. The PM quadtree can also be used to do point location. We conclude by briefly discussing how it compares with the K-structure and the layered dag.

4.3.1 The K-Structure

The K-structure is a hierarchical representation based on triangulation rather than a regular decomposition. It is not built directly from the list of line segments in a polygonal map but rather from a triangulation of the map. The notion of hierarchy in the K-structure is radically different from that of a quadtree in that instead of replacing a group of triangles by a single triangle at the next higher level, a group of triangles is replaced by a smaller group of triangles. There is no proper subset relationship between triangles at successive levels. In particular, a triangle at level i can be spanned by more than one triangle at level $i+1$.

Triangles are grouped for replacement because they share a common vertex. The smaller group results from eliminating the common vertex and then retriangulating. At each level of the hierarchy, at least $1/24^{th}$ of the vertices can be eliminated in this manner. Thus the K-structure for a polygonal map of v vertices uses $O(v)$ space and point location can be determined in $O(\log_2 v)$ time. Constructing a K-structure has a worst-case execution time of $O(v)$ for a triangular subdivision and $O(v \cdot \log_2 v)$ for a general one. The latter is dominated by the cost of triangulating the original polygonal map [Hert85]. Below we examine the K-structure in greater detail, as well as illustrate how it is built for the polygonal map of Figure 4.11.

A K-structure is built by first enclosing the map with a bounding triangle anchored at points X, Y, and Z, as shown in Figure 4.41a. Next we perform a planar sweep triangulation by using the method of Hertel and Mehlhorn [Hert85]. To do this, we assume that the vertices have been sorted in increasing order of their x coordinate values. Triangulation is achieved by sweeping (i.e., moving) a vertical line of infinite length from left to right along the x axis. Each time a vertex is encountered, edges are drawn from the vertex to all 'visible' vertices to its left. Vertex V_2 is said to be *visible* from vertex V_1 if an edge can be drawn from V_1 to V_2 without intersecting an existing edge.

For the polygonal map of Figure 4.11, containing regions 1, 2, and 3, the vertices are processed in order X, Y, A, D, E, C, B, and Z. Processing vertex A results in creating edges AX and AY; D in DY; E in EA and ED; C in CY; B in BX; and Z in BZ and CZ. Figure 4.41a contains the outcome of the triangulation. The new edges are represented by broken lines. Region 1 consists of triangles a, b, c, d, i, j, and k; region 2 consists of triangles e, f, and h; region 3 consists of triangle g. These inclusion relationships are shown in Figure 4.41b.

Triangulating a polygonal map of v vertices has a worst-case execution time of $O(v \cdot \log_2 v)$. This is obtained in the following manner. Sorting the x coordinate values of the v vertices is $O(v \cdot \log_2 v)$. Sweeping the vertical line is $O(v)$. In addition, a $\log_2 v$ factor is contributed by the visibility computation at each vertex.

Before proceeding further, we define some terms used in the construction of the K-structure, as well as in the analysis of its space and time requirements. A *K-vertex* is a vertex that has degree of 11 or less. We can establish that at least half of the vertices are K-vertices in the following manner. According to a corollary of Euler's formula [Hara69], any planar graph of v vertices (including a polygonal map) contains at most $3 \cdot v - 6$ edges. Since each edge contributes one edge to the degree of two vertices, the average degree of a vertex is ≤ 6. Therefore at least half the vertices have degree of 11 or less and hence are K-vertices.

Two vertices are said to be *independent* if there is no edge connecting them. Each K-vertex is adjacent to, at most, 11 other K-vertices. Given a triangulated map with v_k K-vertices, at the minimum there is a partition into $v_k/12 \geq v/24$ sets of vertices, each of which has a representative K-vertex. These representative K-vertices are mutually independent.

The *neighborhood* of a K-vertex is defined as the polygon formed by the union of the triangles incident at the K-vertex. Since there are at most 11 such triangles for a given K-vertex, the polygon from the K-vertex's neighborhood has no more than 11 sides.

We are now ready to build the K-structure. Starting at a level corresponding to the result of the initial triangulation step, the next level of the K-structure is built in $O(v)$ time in the following manner. First, find a set S of mutually independent K-vertices. This can be done in $O(v)$ time from an edge-adjacency list of the map. Second, for each of the neighborhoods of an element of the set S, perform the following reduction: remove the K-vertex from the neighborhood and retriangulate its polygon. Thus the triangles of the neighborhood will be linked with a smaller collection of triangles that spans the same region. The remaining levels of the K-structure are formed from an iterative performance of the building procedure until a level is reached that contains a single triangle.

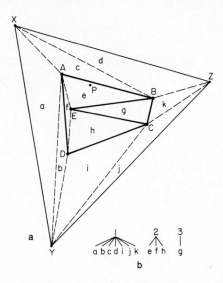

Figure 4.41   The first step in building the K-structure corresponding to Figure 4.11: (a) the result of the initial triangulation. Newly introduced edges are represented by broken lines; (b) the correspondence between the triangles of (a) and the regions of Figure 4.11.

At each level, the cost of building the K-structure is proportional to the number of vertices at that level. Since each level of the K-structure contains at most 23/24*th* of the number of vertices as the previous level, the total number of vertices processed in the construction is at most $24 \cdot v$. Furthermore, as each of the K-vertices is guaranteed to be of degree 11 or less, the cost of retriangulating any polygon is bounded. Thus the K-structure can be built in $O(v)$ time. The number of levels in the K-structure is $O(\log_2 v)$.

Returning to the example, after the initial triangulation, we must identify the maximal subset of mutually independent K-vertices, remove them and their incident edges, and retriangulate. In Figure 4.41a we have a number of choices. We choose vertices B and D. Removing B and D and their incident edges leaves us with polygons XAYX, AECYA, XAECZX, and YCZY, which we label ε, δ, α, and β, respectively. Next, we retriangulate these polygons individually and obtain Figure 4.42a. Polygons ε and β remain unchanged; polygon α consists of triangles α_1, α_2, and α_3; and polygon δ consists of triangles δ_1 and δ_2. These relationships are shown in Figure 4.42b. The edges introduced during the retriangulation are represented by broken lines in Figure 4.42a.

We now have seven triangles and must choose one of vertices A, E, and C as the independent K-vertex. We choose vertex A and after removing it and its incident

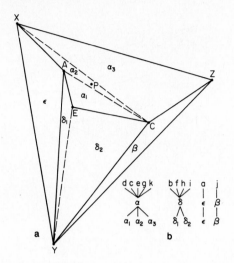

Figure 4.42   The second step in building the K-structure corresponding to Figure 4.11: (a) the result of retriangulating Figure 4.41 once vertices B and D and their incident edges have been removed. Newly introduced edges are shown by broken lines; (b) the relationship between the polygons resulting from (a) and the triangle of Figure 4.41.

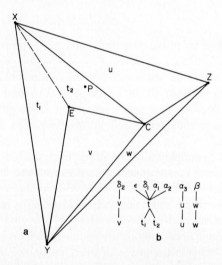

Figure 4.43   The third step in building the K-structure corresponding to Figure 4.11: (a) the result of retriangulating Figure 4.42 once vertex A and its incident edges have been removed. Newly introduced edges are shown by broken lines; (b) the relationship between the polygons resulting from (a) and the triangle of Figure 4.42.

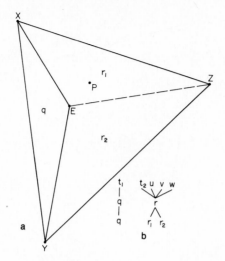

Figure 4.44   *The fourth step in building the K-structure corresponding to Figure 4.11: (a) the result of retriangulating Figure 4.43 once vertex C and its incident edges have been removed. Newly introduced edges are shown by broken lines; (b) the relationship between the polygons resulting from (a) and the triangles of Figure 4.43.*

edges, are left with polygons XYECX, XCZX, ECYE, and YCZY, which we label t, u, v, and w, respectively. After retriangulating the polygons individually, we obtain Figure 4.43a with broken lines corresponding to the added edges. Polygons u, v, and w remain unchanged, while polygon t consists of triangles t_1 and t_2. These relationships are shown in Figure 4.43b.

Reapplying the algorithm to the five remaining triangles, we select vertex C as the independent K-vertex and remove it and its incident edges. The remaining polygons are XEYX and XEYZX which we label q and r, respectively. Only polygon r needs to be retriangulated resulting in triangles r_1 and r_2 as shown in Figure 4.44, with broken lines corresponding to the added edges. We now apply the algorithm for the final time to the three remaining triangles. Removing vertex E and its incident edges leaves a single triangle XYZX, which we label s, as shown in Figure 4.45.

Point location using the K-structure is relatively straightforward. In essence, at each level, the algorithm must determine the relevant triangle that contains the point. The key is that the comparison is made with at most 11 triangles. These 11 triangles form the neighborhood that contains the triangle in which the point was found at the previous level. Thus since the number of levels is $O(\log_2 v)$, point location is solved in $O(\log_2 v)$ time.

As an example, suppose we wish to determine the region in the polygonal map of Figure 4.11 in which point P is located. Rather than give the values of the *x* and *y*

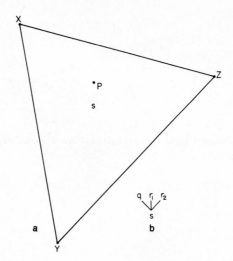

Figure 4.45   The final step in building the K-structure
corresponding to Figure 4.11: (a) the result of retriangulating
Figure 4.44 once vertex E and its incident edges have been
removed; (b) the relationship between the triangle resulting
from (a) and the triangle of Figure 4.44.

coordinates of P, its location is indicated by appropriately marking it in parts a of Figures 4.41–4.45. The explanation is facilitated by making use of part b of these figures.

Initially we start with the triangle of Figure 4.45 and determine that P lies in triangle r_1. Moving down a level we find r_1 in polygon r of Figure 4.44. Searching for P in r we find that it lies in triangle t_2. Moving down a level we find t_2 in polygon t of Figure 4.43. Searching for P in t we find that it lies in triangle α_2. Moving down a level we find α_2 in polygon α of Figure 4.42. Searching for P in α we find that it lies in triangle e. Moving down a level we find e in region 2 of Figure 4.41, and we are done.

Exercises

4.96. Prove that a convex polygon containing v vertices can be triangulated in $O(v)$ time.

4.97. Devise a data structure that enables the 'visibility' computation of Hertel and Mehlhorn's triangulation method [Hert85] to be performed in $O(\log_2 v)$ time.

4.98. There are many triangulation methods in use aside from the plane-sweep method of Hertel and Mehlhorn. These include the 'greedy' method, which triangulates by successively joining the closest two points; the 'minimum-weight' method, which yields a triangulation with the smallest total edge length; and the 'Delaunay' method, which triangulates by maximizing the minimum angle between two edges. Discuss how these methods would be used in conjunction with the K-structure construction algorithm. Is any one of these methods superior to the others? How do they compare with the method of Hertel and Mehlhorn? For a more thorough discussion of triangulation methods, see [Wats84, Saal87].

4.99. Prove that a triangular subdivision on $v \geq 3$ vertices such that each region (including the bounding region) is bounded by three line segments and has exactly $3 \cdot v - 6$ edges and $2 \cdot v - 4$ regions (including the bounding region).

4.100. Give an $O(v)$ time algorithm and $O(v)$ space data structure to find a set s of mutually independent K-vertices.

4.101. Prove that for each independent K-vertex that has been removed in the construction of the K-structure, the number of triangles in the subsequent retriangulation has been reduced by two.

4.102. Write a procedure to do point location in a polygonal map represented by a K-structure.

4.3.2 Separating Chains and Layered Dags

The *layered dag* of Edelsbrunner, Guibas, and Stolfi [Edel86a] is an alternative to the K-structure. It is a refinement of the separating chain method of Lee and Preparata [Lee77a] so that the space requirements and time complexity of point location and structure building are the same as those for the K-structure. The constants of proportionality, however, are smaller for the layered dag than for the K-structure. Like the K-structure, the separating chain method also yields a hierarchical structure; however, this time instead of having a hierarchy of triangulations we have a hierarchy of 'above-and-below' partitions consisting of groups of regions. This hierarchy is based on the existence of a y-monotone subdivision.

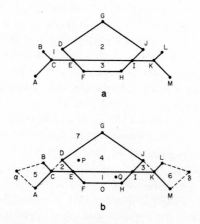

Figure 4.46 (a) Example polygonal map illustrating the use of separating chains and layered dags; (b) the result of regularizing (a) with newly introduced edges represented by broken lines

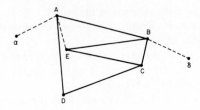

Figure 4.47   The result of regularizing the polygonal map
of Figure 4.11. Newly introduced edges are represented by
broken lines.

The following presentation first outlines the principles underlying the separating chain method and then indicates how it is improved upon by the layered dag. The discussion is illustrated by referring to the polygonal map of Figure 4.46a. Unlike the K-structure, the analyses of the orders of execution times and space requirements are in terms of the number of edges, say m, in the polygonal map instead of the number of vertices, say v. However, by Euler's formula [Hara69], for $v \geq 3$, we have that $m \leq 3 \cdot v - 6$, and thus the two quantities are of the same order of magnitude.

A polygonal map is a *y-monotone subdivision* if no vertical line can intersect a region's boundary more than twice. Alternatively every vertex of the map has at least one edge to its left and one edge to its right (see Exercise 4.103). For example, the polygonal map of Figure 4.46a is not a y-monotone subdivision because vertices J, L, and M have no edges to their right, and vertices A, B, and D have no edges to their left. This map has three regions, labeled 1, 2, and 3. A vertical line through edges CE, DE, and DG crosses the boundary of region 1 three times. A y-monotone subdivision ensures that the 'immediately above' relation is acyclic; that is, region 1 can be either below region 2 or above it, but it cannot be both below and above the same region.

A polygonal map is made into a y-monotone subdivision by a process termed *regularization*, which inserts additional edges as well as two vertices at the extreme left and right of the polygonal map. For example, the broken lines in Figure 4.46b are the result of regularizing the polygonal map of Figure 4.46a. It has eight regions, labeled 0 through 7; two additional vertices, α and δ, at the extreme left and right, respectively, of the map; as well as the new edges αA, αB, CD, JK, Lδ, and Mδ.

Of course, any triangulation can be used as the basis of a y-monotone subdivision; but regularization usually requires considerably fewer edges to be inserted than a triangulation (compare Figures 4.41 and 4.47, which are the results of triangulating and regularizing, respectively, the polygonal map of Figure 4.11). However, like triangulation, regularization of a polygonal map of m edges is performed by a planar sweep algorithm in $O(m \cdot \log_2 m)$ time. These definitions imply that the polygonal map has no vertical edges. However, this restriction is primarily a technical one and can be removed by the adoption of appropriate conventions (see Exercise 4.108).

As the polygonal map is regularized, the identity of each region immediately above and below each edge, say e, is stored with the edge using the fields ABOVE(e)

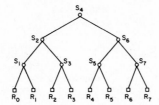

Figure 4.48   The region tree corresponding to the polygo-
nal map of Figure 4.46. Region R_i corresponds to the region
labeled with i.

and BELOW(e). In addition, a list is created of the vertices and edges of the regularized polygonal map in increasing order of x coordinate values. Once the polygonal map has been regularized, the regions are topologically sorted so that they are ordered according to an 'above' relation.

Formally given regions r_1 and r_2, r_1 is *above* r_2 (i.e., $r_1 \geq r_2$) if for every vertically aligned pair of points, (x,y_1) in r_1 and (x,y_2) in r_2, $y_1 \geq y_2$ and there is at least one point where a strict inequality holds. It can be shown that the 'above' relation is acyclic; it yields a partial ordering (see Exercise 4.110). For example, applying topological sort to the polygonal map of Figure 4.46b yields the regions in the order 0, 1, 2, 3, 4, 5, 6, 7. The topological sort is performed by using the contents of the ABOVE field of each edge. Since there are m edges, this process takes $O(m)$ time [Knut73a].

Assuming that there are n regions, let the result of the topological sort be a list of the regions in the order $R_0, R_1, \cdots, R_{n-1}$ such that $R_i \leq R_j$ implies that $i < j$. From this list we construct a complete binary tree for n regions, termed a *region tree*, such that the regions R_i appear as leaf nodes. The nonleaf nodes are labeled $s_1, s_2, \cdots, s_{n-1}$ so that an inorder traversal of the tree yields the nodes in the order $R_0, s_1, R_1, s_2, \cdots, s_{n-1}, R_{n-1}$. For example, Figure 4.48 shows such a tree for the eight regions of Figure 4.46b.

A nonleaf node in the region tree is termed a *separator*. The separators correspond to polygonal lines of infinite length. These lines consist of edges of the y-monotone subdivision such that each polygonal line intersects every vertical line at exactly one point. In particular, each separator s_k serves as the boundary between regions R_i and R_j such that $i < k$ and $j \geq k$. In other words, a vertex or edge e belongs to s_k if, and only if, it is on the border of two regions R_i and R_j with $i < k \leq j$. It can be shown that the regions and separators satisfy the $\leq$ relation in such a way that $R_0 \leq s_1 \leq R_1 \leq s_2 \leq \cdots s_{n-1} \leq R_{n-1}$ (see Exercise 4.112). A consequence of this ordering is that if for a given edge e, $R_i = $ BELOW(e) and $R_j = $ ABOVE(e), then edge e is contained in separators $s_{i+1}, s_{i+2}, \cdots, s_j$ and in no other separators (see Exercise 4.113). This result is referred to as the *edge-ordering* property.

The list of vertices comprising a separator is termed a *separating chain*, and when no confusion is possible, the term *chain* is used to refer to it. For example, Figure 4.49 shows the result of labeling the nonleaf nodes of the region tree of Figure

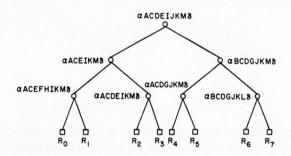

Figure 4.49   The chain tree resulting from labeling the internal nodes of the region tree of Figure 4.48 with their chains

4.48 with their chains. When the region tree is labeled in such a way, it is called a *chain tree*. The tree is rooted at the chain αACDEIJKMδ which separates regions $R_0 - R_3$ (i.e., 0, 1, 2, 3) and $R_4 - R_7$ (i.e., 4, 5, 6, and 7). The left son of the root regions is αACEIKMδ, which separates regions R_0 and R_1 (i.e., 0 and 1) from regions $R_2 - R_7$ (i.e., 2 through 7).

Constructing the separators is a relatively straightforward process. To do this in an efficient manner, let us assume that the n regions are stored in a table, say R, indexed from 0 to $n-1$. Moreover, the ABOVE and BELOW information associated with each edge is the index of the region's entry in R. As an example, for the polygonal map of Figure 4.46b, we have table R such that index 0 corresponds to 0, 1 to 1, $\cdots$, i to i, etc. Therefore for edge EI we find that ABOVE(EI) = 4 and BELOW(EI) = 1.

The construction process makes use of the property that the output of the regularization process is a list of the vertices and edges of the regularized polygonal map in order of increasing x coordinate values. This list is processed in order, and as each edge, say e, is visited, we obtain the values of the indexes of the regions below it, i.e., $i = $ BELOW(e) and $j = $ ABOVE(e), and then append e to each separator s_k such that $i < k \le j$. The correctness of this process follows from the edge-ordering property. Therefore we have shown that for a polygonal map with m edges, the separators can be constructed in $O(m)$ time.

The execution time of the separator construction process described is somewhat misleading because it is heavily influenced by the manner in which the separators are represented. If each separator is represented as an array of all of the vertices and edges contained in it, then the storage requirements are quite high because some of the edges may appear in all but a small number of the separators. In particular, assuming n regions (i.e., $n - 1$ separators), the average length of a separator can be as large as $O(n)$ for some classes of subdivisions (e.g., Figure 4.50). This would result in an $O(n^2)$ storage requirement, and the time to build the structure of separators would also be $O(n^2)$. The same example also shows that the storage requirements can be as high as $O(m^2)$.

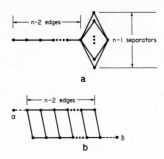

Figure 4.50   Example polygonal maps for which the length of each separator is n

The storage requirements can be reduced in applications such as point location by noting that when an edge is common to several separators, it is sufficient just to store it with the first separator, say s, encountered in a search down the chain tree (i.e., in a preorder traversal).[5] Assume the numbering convention for regions and separators discussed above, and that edge e lies between regions R_a and R_b such that BELOW$(e) =$ a and ABOVE$(e) = b$. In this case, s is the least (or nearest) common ancestor of a and b, and it is denoted by $lca(a,b)$. Using the edge-ordering property, it can be shown that any separator that contains e will be a descendant of the least common ancestor of a and b (see Exercise 4.114).

The result of such a storage scheme for separators is that each edge needs to be stored only once in the chain tree, and thus a separator node need not contain all of the edges in its corresponding separating chain. This leads to the occurrence of breaks in the separating chain. These breaks are called *gaps*. The term *gap tree* is used to describe the variant of the chain tree that results from these economies.

Figure 4.51 shows the gap tree corresponding to Figure 4.49. Each nonleaf node is labeled with the edges that it contains by listing their vertices. A hyphen indicates the absence of an edge between a pair of vertices (i.e., a gap). Note that gaps may also arise at the extreme ends of a chain (e.g., there is a gap at the extreme left and right of the left son of the root in Figure 4.51).

The gap tree uses $O(m)$ space. Building a gap tree for the chain tree is done in the same way as before except that each edge needs to be inserted only once (i.e., in the separator of the least common ancestor). Insertion of an edge requires the ability to compute the index of the region corresponding to the least common ancestor of the regions adjacent to the edge. For a polygonal map of n regions, this process can take as much as $O(\log_2 n)$ time. However, it can be computed in $O(1)$ time by using bit manipulation techniques [Edel86a].

---

[5] The principle of associating key information with the nearest common ancestor is similar to Chazelle and Guibas's *fractional cascading* [Chaz86a, Chaz86b]. It is also used as the basis of an efficient solution of the rectangle intersection problem by Edelsbrunner [Edel80a, Edel83a, Edel83b] (Section 3.2.2).

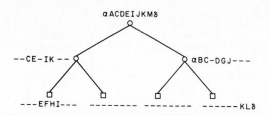

Figure 4.51   The gap tree corresponding to the chain tree
of Figure 4.49

In such a case, a table of n values consisting of the values of the most significant bit in the binary representation of each of the indexes from 0 to $n - 1$ is precomputed and then the least common ancestor is computed by table lookup methods. This technique uses $O(n)$ space for the table (see Exercise 4.115). An alternative technique does not require additional storage but instead uses the reversal of the bit representation of the indexes of the adjacent regions (see Exercise 4.116). This method takes $O(\log_2 n)$ time since the bits are reversed. The reverse function can also be precomputed and then accessed by use of table lookup techniques. This yields an $O(1)$ algorithm.

Point location in the gap tree is achieved by an algorithm that uses two levels of binary search. At each level of the tree, the entire relevant separating chain is searched for an edge or vertex whose projection on the x axis contains the x coordinate value of the query point. The individual separating chains are sorted by the x coordinate value of the leftmost vertices of their constituent edges. The gaps are not stored in the separating chains.

Initially we are searching for an edge that partitions the set of regions bounded by R_0 at the bottom and R_{n-1} at the top. Let a and b designate the indexes of the regions corresponding to the lower and upper boundaries, respectively, of the search space. The search starts at the separating chain stored at the root of the gap tree (i.e., $s_{lca(0,n-1)}$) with $a = 0$ and $b = n - 1$. Having found the appropriate edge, say e, we determine at which node of the gap tree to continue our search by examining the value of the y coordinate of the query point.

If the query point lies below e, the search is resumed in the regions bounded by R_a and $R_{BELOW(e)}$. If it lies above e, the search is resumed in the regions bounded by $R_{ABOVE(e)}$ and R_b. In either case, one of a and b is reset. If the query point lies on the edge, then the search ceases, and we say that the point lies in region $R_{ABOVE(e)}$. The actual node of the gap tree at which the search is resumed is equal to s_l where l is the least common ancestor of a and b (i.e., $s_{lca(a,b)}$). We know that s_l is the separator that will contain the edge separating these regions by virtue of the way in which the gap tree was constructed (and by the edge-ordering property).

For example, to locate point P in the polygonal map of Figure 4.46b, we search for it using Figure 4.51. We first examine the root that corresponds to the separator αACDEIJKMδ and find that it lies above edge EI. The search will continue in the separating chain stored in $s_{lca(\text{ABOVE}(\text{EI}),7)} = s_{lca(4,7)} = s_6$ which is αBC – DGJ – (recall that the hyphens denote gaps). Repeating the search for P, we determine that it lies below edge DG. We are now through since $s_{lca(4,\text{BELOW}(\text{DG}))} = s_{lca(4,4)}$ which is region 4.

Although in this example we performed a test at successive levels of the gap tree, this need not be the case always. Many times, $s_{lca(a,b)}$ may be several levels down in the tree. To see this let us try to locate point Q in the polygonal map of Figure 4.46b. Again, we first examine the separator αACDEIJKMδ in the root of its gap tree in Figure 4.51. We find that Q lies below edge EI and now $s_{lca(0,\text{BELOW}(\text{EI}))} = s_{lca(0,1)} = s_1$, which means that we have skipped a level.

In the worst case, point location in the gap tree requires that we examine each separating chain on the path from the root of the tree to the desired region. Worse, we may also have to search each of these nodes in their entirety. For a regularized polygonal map with n regions and m edges, the binary search of each separating chain can be achieved in $O(\log_2 m)$ time. This assumes that the edges are sorted by the x coordinate value of their left vertex. Since the gap tree has $O(\log_2 n)$ levels, $O(\log_2 n)$ separating chains must be searched. Therefore point location takes $O(\log_2 n \cdot \log_2 m)$ = $O(\log_2^2 m)$ time. This bound is attainable, as can be seen by constructing an example such as Figure 4.52, which has $\sqrt{m}$ separating chains (i.e., $\sqrt{m} + 1$ regions) where each chain contains $\sqrt{m}$ edges.

The main drawback of the algorithm for point location in a gap tree is that for each level of the gap tree, the corresponding separating chain must be searched in its entirety. It is preferable to restart the search in the vicinity of the edge or gap in the appropriate son. Thus what we want is a pointer from each edge or gap on the separating chain, say e, to the edges on the separating chain of each child that overlap e.

The problem is that an edge or gap of a parent may overlap many edges or gaps of the child. For example, in the polygonal map of Figure 4.46b, edge EI in separating chain s_4 (or equivalently gap EI in separating chain s_2) overlaps edges EF, FH, and HI in separating chain s_1. Inserting these additional pointers has a potential of breaking up each separating chain at the x coordinate values of all of the vertices in the subdivision. Consequently this could use quadratic space (i.e., $O(m^2)$).

To solve the problem described, Edelsbrunner, Guibas, and Stolfi [Edel86a] propose a data structure they call a *layered dag*. A layered dag is a separating chain

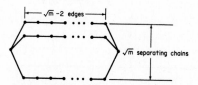

Figure 4.52 *Example polygonal map for which point location using the gap tree requires $O(\log_2^2 m)$ time*

augmented by a set of vertices. In particular, the layered dag, say L_u, corresponding to separating chain, say s_u, is a set of x-*intervals* that cover the entire x axis. Each layered dag is implemented as a set of vertices and a set of edges and gaps. The x-intervals are specified in terms of these vertices, edges, and gaps. Each x-interval of L_u overlaps the x-projection of exactly one edge or gap of s_u and at most two x-intervals of the layered dags corresponding to the left and right sons of s_u. As we shall see later, this condition enables us to keep the storage requirements of the resulting data structure linear.

Let L_u denote the layered dag of node u of a gap tree T whose separating chain is s_u. L_u is constructed by processing the separating chains in T in a bottom-up manner so that the layered dags corresponding to the sons of u are built first. L_u consists of a set of vertices corresponding to union of the endpoints of the edges and gaps in s_u and every other vertex of those present in the layered dags of the left and right sons of u. Duplicate vertices are removed. By convention, we assume that when u is a leaf node of T, the sons of L_u are empty. This process is applied recursively to every node of the gap tree. The result is that as the layered dags are constructed, at each level every other vertex is propagated toward the layered dag that corresponds to the root of the gap tree.

As an example, let us build the layered dags corresponding to the separating chains of the gap tree of Figure 4.51. Let L_i denote the result of applying the construction to s_i. Figure 4.53 shows the result of this construction. For the sake of the current discussion, we examine only how the elements comprising each layered dag are determined. Thus we ignore for the moment, the meaning of the interconnections between elements of the layered dag, as well as how they are formed. In the figure, vertices are depicted by circles, and x-intervals are shown by boxes between circles. In particular, x-intervals corresponding to edges are depicted by solid boxes, and those corresponding to gaps are depicted by broken boxes.

Before describing the correspondence between the layered dags of Figure 4.53 and the separating chains of Figure 4.51, we make the following two observations.

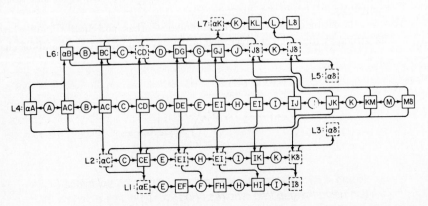

Figure 4.53   Layered dag representation of the gap tree of Figure 4.52

First, the x-interval is labeled with the name of the edge or gap of which it is a subset; it is not necessarily labeled with the vertices to its immediate right and left. This situation arises when the x-interval is part of an edge or gap that extends beyond the endpoints of the x-interval. For example, the x-interval corresponding to vertices A and B in L_4 in Figure 4.53 is labeled AC rather than AB since x-interval AC overlaps edge AB. Second, the layered dags do not include the dummy vertices at the extreme left and right (i.e., α and δ in Figure 4.46b) that are introduced by the regularization process. This means that we ignore them when building the layered dags corresponding to the separating chains. However, the x-intervals in which they participate are included in the layered dag.

In our example, the sets of x-intervals corresponding to L_1, L_3, L_5, and L_7 are identical to the edges and gaps comprising s_1, s_3, s_5, and s_7, respectively. L_1 consists of vertices E, F, H, and I; L_3 and L_5 do not have any vertices; and L_7 consists of vertices K and L.

L_2 is formed by combining vertices C, E, I, and K of s_2; alternating vertices E and H of L_1; while L_3 does not contribute any vertices. The result consists of vertices C, E, H, I, and K and the x-intervals between them — edges CE and IK and gaps αC, EI, EI, and Kδ.

L_6 is formed by combining vertices B, C, D, G, and J of s_6; alternating vertex K of L_7; L_5 does not contribute any vertices. The result consists of vertices B, C, D, G, J, and K and the x-intervals between them — edges αB, BC, DG, and GJ; and gaps CD, Jδ, and Jδ.

L_4 is formed by combining vertices A, C, D, E, I, J, K, and M of s_4; alternating vertices C, H, and K of L_2; and alternating vertices B, D, and J of L_6. The result consists of vertices A, B, C, D, E, H, I, J, K, and M and the x-intervals between them—edges αA, AC, AC, CD, DE, EI, EI, IJ, JK, KM, and Mδ; there are no gaps.

So far we have seen only the correspondence between the information stored in a layered dag and a chain node in the gap tree. We now examine how the information in the layered dag is organized. This organization will be used subsequently in an algorithm to perform point location in $O(\log_2 m)$ time rather than $O(\log_2^2 m)$ time. Figure 4.53 illustrates the presentation. The term *record* refers to the box or circle in the figure associated with an x-interval. The discussion makes heavy use of DOWN, UP, LEFT and RIGHT links, which are all shown with the proper orientation in the figure.

Each x-interval, say I, of layered dag L_u corresponding to separating chain s_u of node u in the gap tree, overlaps at most two x-intervals of the layered dags of the left and right sons of u. We keep track of overlaps by using the two fields DOWN and UP in x-interval I's record. When x-interval I of L_u overlaps only one x-interval of the layered dags of the left (right) son of u, say $L_{\text{LEFT}(u)}$ ($L_{\text{RIGHT}(u)}$), then DOWN(I) (UP(I)) points to the overlapped x-interval's record. For example, x-interval HI in L_4 overlaps x-interval GJ in L_6, and thus its UP link is set to point to GJ's x-interval record. Notice that in this example, x-interval HI is associated with edge EI since it is a subset of this edge.

When x-interval I overlaps two x-intervals of one or both sons, then DOWN(I) (UP(I)) points to the record of the vertex common to the two overlapped x-intervals in $L_{\text{LEFT}(u)}$ ($L_{\text{RIGHT}(u)}$). This situation is facilitated by associating two fields LEFT and RIGHT with each vertex and letting them point to the x-intervals to the left and right of the vertex, respectively. For example, x-interval EH in L_4 overlaps both x-intervals DG and GJ in L_6, and thus its UP link is set to point to G's record in L_6.

Continuing the example, we observe that x-interval EH is associated with edge EI since it is a subset of this edge. Note also that an x-interval can be overlapped by many x-intervals (e.g., CE in L_2 is overlapped by both CD and DE of L_4). Thus it should be clear that the layered dag representation is not a tree. In fact, it resembles the K-structure. Not surprisingly, each vertex can be common to only one x-interval (see Exercise 4.120).

The cost of building the layered dag representation is easy to analyze. As we saw, the process consists of processing the separating chains of the gap tree in a bottom-up manner. The DOWN (UP) links of L_u, corresponding to node u in the gap tree, are set by simultaneously traversing L_u and $L_{\text{LEFT}(u)}$ ($L_{\text{RIGHT}(u)}$) from left to right. Setting the LEFT and RIGHT links of the vertices is accomplished at the same time. The entire building process is linear in the number of edges in the gap tree (i.e., $O(m)$).

We must still show, however, that the amount of space necessary to store the layered dags is $O(m)$. This can be seen by noting that the layered dags corresponding to the gap tree consist of sequences of vertices and then counting them. It can be shown that the total number of vertices in the layered dags is bounded by four times the number of edges in the regularized polygonal map (i.e., $4 \cdot m$).

An intuitive proof of this bound is obtained by observing that if the nodes of the gap tree that correspond to chains have a total of m edges, then there are $2 \cdot m$ vertices that serve as endpoints of these edges. By the construction procedure, only one-half of these vertices are propagated to the father chains, a quarter to the grandfather chains, and so on, and the desired result follows by the properties of an infinite geometric series. For a more formal proof, see Exercise 4.121. Thus the process of building the layered dag representation is $O(m)$ in space and time.

Point location in a layered dag representation is performed in a manner very similar to that in a gap tree. The only difference is that once the initial x-interval is located in the layered dag corresponding to the root of the gap tree, there is no need to search for it in the layered dags at the lower levels. The point is located by simply traversing the appropriate links in the layered dag representation. Let a and b designate the indexes of the regions corresponding to the lower and upper boundaries, respectively, of the search space. They are initialized to 0 and $n - 1$ respectively.

Suppose we want to locate point P. We start at the layered dag, say L, corresponding to the root of the gap tree and search for the x-interval, say I, that contains the x coordinate value of P. Once we have found I, we must decide where to continue the search. Since I must correspond to an edge, say e, after the initial search, we now check the position of the y coordinate value of P relative to e. If P lies below (above) e, then we continue the search at the x-interval pointed at by DOWN(I) (UP(I)) in the regions bounded by R_a and $R_{\text{BELOW}(e)}$ ($R_{\text{ABOVE}(e)}$ and R_b) and reset a and b as is appropriate. If P lies on e, then the search ceases and we say that P lies in region $R_{\text{ABOVE}(e)}$.

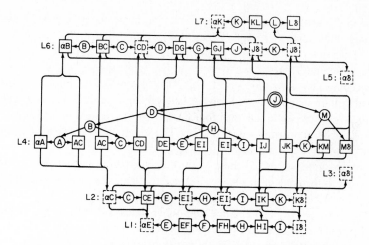

Figure 4.54   Layered dag representation of Figure 4.53 modified to include a binary search tree for the layered dag corresponding to the root of the gap tree

x-interval I in L corresponds to an edge. However, in all subsequent steps of the algorithm, I can correspond to a gap or a vertex as well as an edge. If I corresponds to a gap, there is no test to be performed on P. Nevertheless, we must descend to the appropriate x-interval in the layered dag of the next level. In this case, we have to reconstruct the result of a test at an x-interval at a previous level. This is done by comparing the value of b with the chain number[6] of the layered dag containing I, say c. If b is less than c, we follow link DOWN(I); otherwise we follow link UP(I). If I corresponds to a vertex, then if P's x coordinate value is less than or equal to that of I, we continue the search in x-interval LEFT(I); otherwise we continue in x-interval RIGHT(I).

Note that the way the vertices and x-intervals in the layered dag are organized means that the only time we have to perform a search is when we process L to locate the initial x-interval that contains P. This could be an $O(m)$ process in the worst case. All other searches are achieved by traversing the appropriate links—an $O(1)$ process per level for a total cost of $O(m + \log_2 n)$. The execution time can be reduced further by imposing an additional data structure in the form of a binary search tree on L.

This binary tree is built using the LEFT and RIGHT link fields of the nodes corresponding to the vertices in L. The leaf nodes of this tree consist of the x-intervals (i.e., edges), and the nonleaf nodes consist of the vertices. For example, Figure 4.54 is the modification of the layered dag representation of Figure 4.53 to include the binary search tree. This tree is rooted at vertex J, and thus all point location operations will start at node J. The result is that we have now reduced the cost of the point location

---

[6] Chains are assumed to be numbered from 1 to $n-1$ as illustrated in Figure 4.48.

operation to $O(\log_2 m)$ since m can be larger than n. Comparing point location in a layered dag with point location in a gap tree, we find that the two levels of binary searching have been replaced by a binary search in the root and an $O(1)$ search in the rest of the structure.

Procedure LAYERED_DAG_POINT_LOCATION, given below, implements the point location algorithm using a layered dag. A layered dag is represented as a set of nodes of type *ldnode* where each node has four fields. The TYPE field indicates whether the node corresponds to a vertex, edge, or gap. The remaining three fields depend on the type of data stored in the node.

A vertex node, say P, has three additional fields: LEFT, RIGHT, and X_VAL. LEFT (RIGHT) point to the edge or gap nodes to the left (right) of P, and X_VAL indicates the x coordinate value of P.

An edge node, say E, has three additional fields: DOWN, UP, and EDGE. DOWN (UP) point to the edge, gap, or vertex nodes below (above) E, and EDGE points to a record of type *edge* describing edge E. A record of type *edge* has two fields, called BELOW and ABOVE, that indicate the regions immediately below and above it, respectively, as well as a field specifying the points comprising it—such as an equation of the line corresponding to it.

A gap node, say G, has three additional fields: DOWN, UP, and CHAIN_ID. DOWN (UP) point to the edge, gap, or vertex nodes below (above) G, and CHAIN_ID indicates the chain number of the node in the gap tree corresponding to the layered dag of which G is a member (i.e., u for L_u). A point is implemented using a record of type *point* having two fields XCOORD and YCOORD corresponding to its x coordinate and y coordinate values, respectively. Variables LOW and HIGH represent the lower and upper boundaries, respectively, of the search space.

```
integer procedure LAYERED_DAG_POINT_LOCATION(P,T,N);
/* Search the layered dag representation of a polygonal map rooted at T for the region
   that contains point P and return its value. There are N regions in the polygonal map.
   The regions are numbered from 0 to N–1. */
begin
  value pointer point P;
  value pointer ldnode T;
  value integer N;
  integer LOW,HIGH;
  pointer edge E;
  real Y;
  LOW ← 0;
  HIGH ← N–1;
  while LOW < HIGH do
    begin
      if TYPE(T)='EDGE_TEST' then
        begin
          E ← EDGE(T);
          /* Determine the y coordinate of XCOORD(P) on the edge: */
          Y ← FIND_Y(XCOORD(P),E);
```

```
      if YCOORD(P)=Y then return(ABOVE(E)) /* P is on the edge */
      else if YCOORD(P)>Y then
        begin /* P is above the edge */
          T ← UP(T);
          LOW ← ABOVE(E);
        end
      else
        begin /* P is below the edge */
          T ← DOWN(T);
          HIGH ← BELOW(E);
        end;
      end
    else if TYPE(T)='X_TEST' then
      T ← if XCOORD(P)≤X_VAL(T) then LEFT(T)
          else RIGHT(T)
    else /* A gap test */
      T ← if HIGH<CHAIN_ID(T) then DOWN(T)
          else UP(T);
  end;
  return(LOW);
end;
```

Exercises

4.103. Prove that defining a y-monotone subdivision in terms of not permitting a vertical line to cross a region's boundary more than twice is equivalent to requiring that each vertex have at least one edge to each of its right and left sides.

4.104. Does adding a new edge to a regularized polygonal map always preserve y-monotonicity?

4.105. Is the overlay of two y-monotone subdivisions always a y-monotone subdivision?

4.106. Prove that regularizing a polygonal map of m edges results in a y-monotone subdivision of $\leq 2 \cdot m$ edges.

4.107. Give an algorithm and data structure to regularize a polygonal map.

4.108. Discuss how the separating chain method can be modified to handle polygonal maps with vertical edges.

4.109. Can you devise an algorithm to perform regularization in time faster than $O(m \cdot \log_2 m)$?

4.110. Prove that the 'above' relation is acyclic.

4.111. For each separator in a chain tree, s_k, there exists at least one edge e in s_k such that for a vertical line passing through e at (x_e, y_e), all points (x_e, y) with $y \leq y_e$ are in the regions in the left subtree while those with $y > y_e$ are in the regions in the right subtree. Is this statement correct? If not, give a counterexample.

4.112. Assume a y-monotone subdivision such that $R_0 \leq R_1 \leq \cdots R_{n-1}$. Prove that $R_0 \leq s_1 \leq R_1 \leq s_2 \leq \cdots s_{n-1} \leq R_{n-1}$.

4.113. Assume a y-monotone subdivision such that $R_0 \leq R_1 \leq \cdots R_{n-1}$. Prove the edge-ordering property: that if for a given edge e, $R_i = \text{BELOW}(e)$ and $R_j = \text{ABOVE}(e)$, then edge e is contained in separators $s_{i+1}, s_{i+2}, \cdots, s_j$ and in no other separators.

4.114. Suppose that edge e lies between regions R_a and R_b such that BELOW(e)=a and ABOVE(e)=b. Prove that any separator in a chain tree that contains e will be a descendant of the least common ancestor of a and b.

4.115. Let $lca(i,j)$ denote the least common ancestor of i and j where i and j are between 0 and $n-1$. Let $msb(i)$ denote the most significant bit of the binary representation of i, where i is between 0 and $n-1$ — that is, $msb(i) = lca(0,i)$. Compute $lca(i,j)$ in terms of msb. You should use a combination of Boolean operations such as 'exclusive or,' 'complement,' 'and.'

4.116. Let $rev(k)$ denote a function that reverses the bits in the binary expansion of k. Using the definition of lca in Exercise 4.115, compute $lca(i,j)$ in terms of rev. You should use a combination of Boolean operations such as 'exclusive or,' 'complement,' 'and.'

4.117. In a gap tree, each separating chain is implemented as a list of the x coordinate values of the leftmost vertices of their gaps and edges. How would you cope with a query point that coincides with an endpoint of an edge?

4.118. Write a procedure GAP_TREE_POINT_LOCATION to perform point location in a gap tree.

4.119. In the construction of the layered dag representation of the polygonal map of Figure 4.46b, the alternating vertices were taken in the order first, third, fifth, etc. Repeat this construction by taking them in the order second, fourth, sixth, etc.

4.120. In the layered dag representation of a polygonal map, explain why each vertex can be common to only one x-interval.

4.121. Prove that the total number of vertices in a layered dag representation of a regularized polygonal map of m edges is bounded by $4 \cdot m$. Use induction on the depth of the gap tree that serves as the basis of the construction of the layered dag representation. By letting a_u denote the number of edges in s_u, b_u the number of vertices in L_u, A_u the sum of a_v over all nodes v in the subtree rooted at u, and B_u the sum of b_v over all nodes v in the subtree rooted at u, the problem reduces to showing that $B_r \leq 4 \cdot A_r = 4 \cdot m$ holds for the root node r of the gap tree.

4.122. Is the upper bound derived in Exercise 4.121 a least upper bound? Can you give an example where it is attained? If not, can you obtain a tighter bound?

4.123. The implementation of the layered dag described in the text is somewhat wasteful of space. Discuss how to reduce its space requirements.

4.124. The algorithm described for point location in a layered dag representation will usually visit $\log_2 n$ x-intervals even if all but one of them correspond to gaps. In contrast, the algorithm described for point location in a gap tree made use of the gaps to skip some levels in the tree. Can you modify the structure of the layered dags, and the point location algorithm, to avoid the tests where the x-intervals correspond to gaps?

4.125. How would you adapt the layered dag to deal with the three-dimensional point location problem? If this is not possible, explain why.

4.3.3 Comparison with PM Quadtrees

The PM quadtree can also be used to solve the point location problem. Below, we examine how it is solved with a PM_1 quadtree. Point location in PM_2 and PM_3 quadtrees is done in an analogous manner and is left as an exercise. We conclude by comparing the PM quadtree with the K-structure and the layered dag.

For the PM_1 quadtree, the point location problem has three cases, which are illustrated by queries with respect to the points X, Y, and Z in Figure 4.12. The first case is illustrated by the point labeled X. In this case, the point lies in a leaf containing exactly one q-edge. Since region information is linked to each q-edge indicating the regions associated with the q-edge, the solution consists of determining the side of the q-edge on which the point lies. Note that the cost of determining the region information associated with a q-edge is also, at most, proportional to A_1.

The second case is illustrated by the point labeled Y. In this case, the query point lies in a leaf containing a vertex, C in this example. This situation reduces to finding a q-edge in the dictionary that would neighbor a hypothetical q-edge from C and passing through Y. Such a neighboring q-edge must border the region containing Y. Thus once again the task is reduced to determining on which side of a q-edge a point lies (i.e., Y).

The third case is illustrated by the point labeled Z. In this case, the query point lies in a leaf, say q, containing no q-edges. This means that all the points in the region represented by the leaf q lie in the same region of the polygonal map. It also means that one of q's brothers must be the root of a subtree that contains a q-edge bordering the region containing Z. To find this (not necessarily unique) brother, we visit the brothers in an arbitrary order, say counterclockwise in this example. When considering a brother, one of two cases arises: either q's brother contains a q-edge (the first case), say b, or it does not (the second case).

In the first case, the problem reduces to determining the side of q-edge b on which Z lies. This is accomplished by postulating a hypothetical point Z' in region r that is infinitesimally close to q's region and recursively reapplying the point location procedure to Z'. As an example consider point Z in Figure 4.12. Since q, the leaf containing Z, is empty, we examine its counterclockwise brother, say r, and postulate a point Z' just across the boundary between q and r. Determining the polygon in which Z' lies (in this example) is equivalent to determining the polygon in which X lies.

In the second case, r contains no q-edges, and the algorithm proceeds to examine r's counterclockwise brother. It should be clear that one of the brothers must contain a q-edge; otherwise the brothers would have been merged to yield a larger node.

The worst-case execution time of point location using a PM_1 quadtree is proportional to the depth of the entire structure—that is, the maximum of the depth required independently by each of the first three conditions in its definition plus the maximum depth of the dictionary structure of q-edges associated with each leaf node. This quantity is referred to as $DMAX + A_1$ in the analysis of the cost of inserting an edge into a PM_1 quadtree that was performed in Section 4.2.3.1.

In comparing the PM quadtree to the K-structure and the layered dag, it is important to establish a model of expected data. This is necessary because the DMAX factor of the PM quadtree analysis can grow arbitrarily large without changing the v factor of the K-structure and layered dag analyses. Since $\log_4 v$ is a lower bound on DMAX, the K-structure and the layered dag clearly have a better worst-case performance than the PM quadtree. In practice, however, data seldom exploit this worst-case behavior.

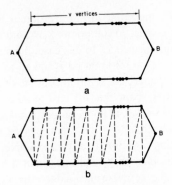

Figure 4.55 (a) A polygonal map and (b) its triangulation (broken lines correspond to the edges added by the triangulation)

Instead we elaborate on the type of data common to cartographic polygonal maps. We observe that such data result from a piecewise linear approximation process. This means that the map will tend to contain only long chains of short line segments. Samet and Webber [Same85i] claim that when the data are digitized to a high level of resolution, the lines that correspond to boundaries of cartographic regions are sufficiently apart that the decomposition is caused primarily by the condition that the endpoints of the line segment must lie in distinct nodes. Thus the number of q-edges per line segment is usually two, as is the degree of a vertex.

If the cartographic data fit this model exactly, the variants of the edge quadtree discussed in Section 4.2.1 would be adequate. The PM quadtree is different from those variants in that while it is most efficient for data that approximate the model closely, there is a smooth degradation of its performance as the data depart from this model. Furthermore the three vertex-based PM quadtrees presented (PM_1, PM_2, and PM_3) degrade at successively slower rates. For data that fit this model closely, the PM quadtree has the following characteristics. Point location is performed in $O(\log_2 v)$ time. This follows from the expectation that half the quadtree leaf nodes are empty and the other half usually contain at most two q-edges (see Exercise 4.134). Dynamic insertion of a line segment can be performed in $O(\log_2 v)$ time (see Exercise 4.135).

In general, the dynamic insertion of an edge into a K-structure takes $O(v)$ time in the worst case. This poor worst-case performance follows from the fact that the triangulation must be updated. The newly inserted edge could intersect $O(v)$ edges in the existing triangulation. For example, if the edge between vertices A and B is inserted into the triangulation of the polygon of Figure 4.55a (shown in Figure 4.55b), which has $2 \cdot v + 2$ vertices, then the new edge will intersect $2 \cdot v - 1$ edges in the triangulation. Updating the triangulation requires, at an absolute minimum, either the addition of a new vertex or the deletion of the old edge for each intersection of the new edge and an old edge. Hence $O(v)$ operations may be required.

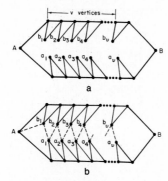

*Figure 4.56   (a) A polygonal map and (b) its regularization
(broken lines correspond to the edges added by the regularization)*

On the other hand, the K-structure can always be updated in $O(v)$ time. To see this, observe that the triangulation can be updated by (1) removing all edges that intersect the new edge, (2) inserting the new edge, and (3) retriangulating the two polygonal regions on either side of the new edge. Step 1 takes $O(v)$ time, and step 2 takes $O(1)$ time. Step 3 can also be done in $O(v)$ time. This is because the two polygons that must be triangulated are *weakly edge visible* from the new edge (i.e., each point in the region is visible from some point on the edge), and polygons with this property can be triangulated in linear time. Once the triangulation is updated, the K-structure can be completely rebuilt in $O(v)$ time, as described in Section 4.3.1.

Now let us consider the insertion of a new edge, say e, in a polygonal map represented by a layered dag. Let E denote the set of the edges introduced by the application of regularization to the original polygonal map. Addition of e may cause $O(v)$ new vertices to be added by virtue of the intersection of e with the set E. This means that the size of the layered dag (i.e., number of regions) will be dominated by the side effects of the regularization process. To avoid this situation, we must reapply the regularization step to the $O(v)$ vertices from which the intersected members of E emanated. In this special case, this process uses $O(v)$ space and time since the vertices are already sorted (see Exercise 4.136).

For example, consider the map of Figure 4.56a, which consists of $4 \cdot v + 4$ vertices and resembles a collection of v toothlike objects. Figure 4.56b is the result of one way of regularizing this map where the added edges ($2 \cdot v$ of them) are shown with broken lines. In particular, we add edges to the left from vertices a_i to b_i ($1 \leq i \leq v$); edges to the right from a_i to b_{i+1} ($1 \leq i < v$); and an edge from b_1 to A. Inserting an edge between vertices A and B into the original map intersects all of the edges added by the regularization. Thus the nature of the $2 \cdot v$ vertices a_i and b_i requires that the map be regularized again since they must have edges to their right and left.

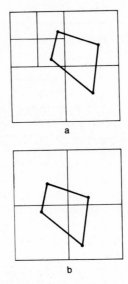

*Figure 4.57   Example demonstrating the sensitivity of the
PR quadtree to shifts*

One difference between these methods and the quadtree approach is that the size of a quadtree is inherently sensitive to the location of the map within the decomposition grid (and hence can change significantly when the map is shifted or rotated). However, the PM quadtree is less prone to suffer from this problem than are other variants of the quadtree. For example, shifting or rotating the region quadtree and the line quadtree can lead to much larger changes in storage requirements.

In contrast, the PM_2 and PM_3 quadtrees can be shifted or rotated without distortion or an unreasonable change in the storage requirements of the structure. Nevertheless the storage requirements are still somewhat dependent on the positioning of the space within which the map is embedded. For example, the polygonal map of Figure 4.57a requires seven PR quadtree leaf nodes. If we shift the map slightly, however, we get Figure 4.57b, which requires only four PR quadtree leaf nodes.

In summary, when the K-structure and the layered dag are compared with the PM quadtree, the qualitative comparison is analogous to that of a point quadtree with a PR quadtree. All of these structures have their uses; the one to use depends on the nature and quantity of the data, the problem to be solved, and the importance of guaranteed worst-case performance. The K-structure and the layered dag organize the data to be stored while the PM quadtree organizes the embedding space from which the data are drawn. The K-structure and the layered dag have better worst-case execution time bounds for point location compared to the PM quadtree. However, considerations such as ease of implementation and integration with representations of other data types must also be taken into account in making an evaluation. In the case of dynamic files, the PM quadtree is preferable over the K-structure and the layered dag since updating it is simpler.

Exercises

4.126. How would you do point location in a PM_2 quadtree?

4.127. How would you do point location in a PM_3 quadtree?

4.128. The map overlay problem is related to the point location problem, and its solution encompasses many of the issues discussed in this and previous sections. In this case, you are given two polygonal maps, and you are to overlay one of them on top of the other. This problem can be viewed as a generalization of the process of dynamic edge insertion in that instead of inserting a single edge, you are now inserting a collection of edges (which happens to be already organized as a polygonal map). The goal is to achieve this in a manner that is more efficient than performing a sequence of dynamic line insertions. Write a set of procedures that will perform map overlay for the PM_3 quadtree. You need not be concerned with region labels in this exercise.

4.129. Modify the algorithms of Exercise 4.128 to handle the generation of labels for the new regions formed by overlaying one map on another.

4.130. Repeat Exercises 4.128 and 4.129 for maps represented by PM_1 and PM_2 quadtrees.

4.131. Prove that two PM quadtrees can be overlaid in $O(v)$ time where v is the number of vertices in the trees.

4.132. How would you compute map overlay using the K-structure and the layered dag?

4.133. Samet and Webber [Same85i] claim that when cartographic data are digitized to a high level of resolution, the lines that correspond to boundaries of cartographic regions are sufficiently apart that the decomposition is caused primarily by the condition that the endpoints of the line segment must lie in distinct nodes. Thus the number of q-edges per line segment in a PM quadtree is usually two as is the degree of a vertex. Verify this observation by examining cartographic data at different levels of resolution.

4.134. Show that for a map containing v vertices, under the model of cartographic data discussed in Exercise 4.133, point location in a PM quadtree is performed in $O(\log_2 v)$ time.

4.135. Show that for a map containing v vertices, under the model of cartographic data discussed in Exercise 4.133, dynamic insertion of a line segment in a PM quadtree is performed in $O(\log_2 v)$ time.

4.136. Suppose that a new edge is inserted into a regularized polygonal map with $O(v)$ vertices represented by a layered dag. Show that applying the regularization process again uses $O(v)$ space and time.

4.137. Let us reexamine the problem of inserting a new edge, say e, in a polygonal map represented by a layered dag. Let E denote the set of the edges introduced by the application of regularization to the original polygonal map. Addition of e may cause new vertices to be added by virtue of the intersection of e with the set E. The text and Exercise 4.136 mention that all edges in E that intersect e must be removed and the regularization process be reapplied. Is this always a better method than simply adding new vertices whenever e intersects one of the elements of E?

4.4 CONCLUSION

At this point, it is appropriate to summarize briefly the key features of the data structures that we have encountered in this chapter. However, we first review briefly some of the more traditional nonhierarchical methods.

The simplest representation for curvilinear data is as a sequence of vectors [Nagy79], which are usually specified in the form of lists (not sets, as they are not unique) of pairs of x and y coordinate values corresponding to their start and end points. When the start and end points are identical, the sequence defines a polygon. This representation is known as a topological model, and an enhancement of it serves as the basis of the GBF/DIME (Geographic Base File/Dual Independent Map Encoding) [Marb84] data structure used by the U.S. Census Bureau for representing address information.

The POLYVRT (POLYgon conVeRTer) model [Peuc75] is a hierarchical refinement of the topological model that stores each topological data type in a separate data structure—for example, a hierarchical relationship between polygons, chains, line segments, nodes, and points. A similar approach serves as the basis of the boundary model for volume data as discussed in Section 5.4. Other popular representations include raster-oriented methods [Merr73, Peuq79], as well as a combination of vectors and rasters (e.g., vasters [Peuq83]).

One of the most common representations for curvilinear data is the chain code [Free74]. It describes a region with a sequence of unit vectors (i.e., one pixel wide) in the principal directions so that the interior of the region is always to the right of the vectors. We can represent the directions by numbers; for example, let i, an integer quantity ranging from 0 to 3, represent a unit vector having a direction of $90 \cdot i$ degrees. For example, the chain code for the boundary of the black region in Figure 1.1a, moving clockwise starting from the midpoint of the extreme right boundary, is

$$3^2 2^2 3^1 2^1 3^1 2^3 1^3 0^1 1^1 0^1 1^2 0^4 3^2 .$$

The above is a four-direction chain code. Generalized chain codes, involving more than four directions, can also be used.

The chain code is the most compact of the representations described. In the case of nonrectilinear data, it is a discrete approximation. Aside from being discrete, it is a very local data structure and is rather cumbersome when attempting to perform set operations such as the intersection of two curves represented using it. In addition, like the strip and arc trees, it is position independent—it is not tied to a particular coordinate system. This is a problem with methods based on the region quadtree, although it is somewhat reduced for the PM quadtree.

Representations based on the region quadtree have a number of advantages over members of the strip tree family. First, more than one curve can be represented with one instance of the data structure, an important feature for maps. Second, they are unique. In contrast, only one curve can be represented by a single instance of any variant of a strip tree. Also members of the strip tree family are not unique when the curve is closed or not regular. However, members of the strip tree family are invariant under shifts and rotations.

The line quadtree is better than the MX quadtree, which represents boundary lines as narrow black regions, for two reasons. First, narrow regions are costly in terms of the number of nodes in the quadtree. Second, the MX quadtree commits the user to a specific boundary line thickness, which may be undesirable (e.g., when regenerating the picture on an output device). Also such arbitrary decisions with respect to the accuracy of the representation are not very appropriate when data are to be stored in a database.

It is also interesting to speculate on some other data structures for curvilinear data. Representations based on the region quadtree are attractive because they enable efficient computation of set operations. Moreover, they make it easy to perform set operations on different kinds of geometric entities (e.g., intersecting curves with areas). They are also more general when compared with hierarchical representations such as the K-structure and the layered dag, as well as exhibiting better dynamic behavior.

Members of the strip tree family are elegant data structures from the standpoint of approximation. Their disadvantage is that the decomposition points are independent of the coordinate system of the image (i.e., they are at points that depend on the data rather than at predetermined positions, as is the case with a data structure based on the region quadtree). Thus, answering a query such as 'Find all wheat-growing regions within 20 miles of the Mississippi River' is not easy to do when the river is represented as a strip tree and the wheat-growing regions are represented by region quadtrees. The problem is that while quadtree methods merely require pointer chasing operations, strip tree methods may lead to complex geometric computations. What is desired is a variant of the strip tree based on the region quadtree.

Exercise

4.138. Devise a variant of the strip tree based on the region quadtree that meets the requirements outlined in this section.

VOLUME DATA 5

When region data are of dimensionality greater than two, we refer to them as volume data. In this case, we are usually dealing with three-dimensional regions. Proper handling of such data is critical in applications in solid modeling. It is also necessary in the fields of computer-aided design/computer-aided manufacturing (CAD/CAM), computer graphics, robotics, computer vision, and medical imaging, among others. In general, the main characteristic of such data is that they are plentiful. Thus it is useful to subject them to some degree of aggregation.

We are primarily interested in aggregation techniques based on using octrees. The basic definition of an octree was given in Section 1.2. However, that presentation was primarily with respect to a variant known as the *region octree*. In this chapter, we focus on the use of variants of the octree and highlight their relationships with more traditional representations. This discussion is in the context of applications in solid modeling.

This chapter is organized as follows. We first examine briefly the representations commonly used in solid modeling with a rationale for their usage. Some of these representations are discussed in greater detail in the subsequent sections. We continue by looking at how region octrees are built. Next the PM octree is presented. This is followed by a more detailed discussion of the boundary model (BRep) and constructive solid geometry (CSG). In particular, the focus is on the conversion between these representations and variants of the octree. We conclude by discussing the representation of objects by their surfaces.[1] This consists of an overview of representations of 2.5-dimensional data, followed by examples of surface-based object representations, such as the prism tree and the cone tree. These methods are somewhat specialized and can be skipped on an initial reading.

---

[1] These methods differ, in part, from the boundary model by being of variable resolution.

5.1 SOLID MODELING

Solid modeling, a branch of geometric modeling, is a rapidly expanding field. The distinction between the two fields is not an easy one to make and is not crucial in this discussion. The goal of solid modeling systems is to be able to answer arbitrary geometric questions algorithmically (i.e., without human intervention) [Mänt87]. The answers often involve performing set operations on solids.

Most existing solid modeling systems are plagued by the fact that manipulation, as well as algorithms for functions such as display, interference detection (i.e., whether two or more objects occupy the same space at the same time), and hidden-surface removal, are time-consuming, in most practical situations. In particular, they usually have polynomial growth (usually quadratic) in the complexity and number of objects that comprise them [Meag82b].

By definition, a solid modeling system must be able to express the entire three-dimensional nature of the object represented. This means that any specified point in space can be unambiguously determined to be part of the object or outside the object. The latter also includes points within an interior void—a cavity. Points that lie on the surface can be classified as interior or exterior or even given a separate classification.

Many existing systems that claim to do solid modeling, however, do not really model the three-dimensional objects that they are supposed to represent. Instead they are usually extensions of drafting systems that make use of edges (i.e., modeling primitives of a two-dimensional drafting system) to represent the projections of solids. The determination of what is solid is usually left to the interpretation (or imagination) of the user. As such, frequently these systems cannot remove all hidden lines, nor can they automatically generate sectional views. This is not surprising because these early systems were often based on a wireframe model of the object. The problem with the wireframe model is that it is ambiguous unless the object is restricted to a convex polyhedron. Moreover this model conveys no information about the shape of the faces of the objects (unless they are restricted to planar faces).

As mentioned in Section 1.2, there are two principal techniques of representing regions: by their boundaries and by their interiors. The same paradigm also holds for three-dimensional objects. The following six representations are the most common bases of solid modelers in existence today. They differ in the way in which they make use of these two principal techniques. Often the result is a hybrid.

1. Boundary Model (BRep): The object is represented by its boundary, which is decomposed into a set of faces, edges, and vertices. The result is an explicit model based on a combined topological and geometric description of the object. The topology is captured by a set of relations that indicate how the faces, edges, and vertices are connected to each other. For example, the object in Figure 5.1a can be decomposed into the set of faces having the topology shown in Figure 5.1b. The geometry of the faces can be specified by use of planes, quadrics, patches, and so on. However, when the equations of the faces are of a degree higher than two, it is difficult or

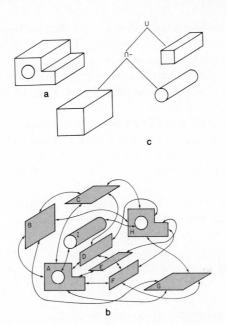

Figure 5.1   (a) A three-dimensional object, (b) its boundary model, and (c) its CSG tree

impossible to determine analytically entities such as the edge of intersection, which are needed in general for set operations.

2. Sweep Methods: A solid is defined as the volume that is swept by a planar or a two-dimensional shape along a curve. There can be both rotational and translational sweep.

3. Primitive Instancing: All of the possible object shapes are known a priori and are defined parametrically. Specific instances of the objects are created by varying the scale and dimension parameters.

4. Constructive Solid Geometry (CSG): Primitive instances of objects are combined to form more complex objects by use of geometric transformations and Boolean set operations. The representation is usually in the form of a tree where the leaf nodes correspond to the primitive instances and the non-leaf nodes correspond to Boolean set operations. For example, the object in Figure 5.1a can be decomposed into three primitive solids with the CSG tree shown in Figure 5.1c (the operation $A \cap - B$ denotes set difference). The key is that this representation is procedural. Thus it indicates how an item can be constructed—that is, what operations are necessary. Often these operations have physical analogs (e.g., drilling). The primitive shapes can be halfspaces (see the definition in Sections 1.4.1 and 5.5.1) or primitive instances (i.e., a predefined combination of halfspaces). A disadvantage of

the CSG representation is that it is not unique. It is impossible to check the identity of two objects represented by it without actually constructing the objects (termed *evaluation*).

5. Spatial Enumeration: This is an approximation of a solid by voxels. It is the three-dimensional analog of a pixel array representation of a two-dimensional region.

6. Cell Decomposition: This yields a decomposition of space into cells, usually of different sizes. It can also be viewed as a hierarchical adaptation of spatial enumeration. The region octree is a regular decomposition variant of this representation.

Let us compare these six representations briefly and see where they are alike. The characterizations presented are not unique; arguments could equally be made to place them in different categories. CSG and sweep methods are similar in the sense that both are procedural. Spatial enumeration and primitive instancing yield representations based purely on the 'interior' of regions. On the other hand, the boundary model and sweep methods usually yield representations based purely on the 'boundary' of regions.

Interestingly although cell decomposition and CSG are usually thought of as being based on the 'interior' of a region, this is not always so. For example, a CSG representation that uses halfspaces as its primitive instances appears to resemble a 'boundary' method. However, this resemblance is false; it is based on the incorrect treatment of the halfspaces as boundaries instead of volumes.

The region octree is an 'interior' method, while the PM octree, an adaptation of the PM quadtree (see Section 4.2.3) to three dimensions, is a 'boundary' method. Actually the most appropriate characterization of the PM octree is that it is a hybrid. In particular, for the PM octree, the octree merely serves as a spatial index into a boundary model. (It should be clear that these characterizations are not the only ones that can be made.)

Exercise

5.1. What are some desirable characteristics of a representation used in a solid modeling system?

5.2 REGION OCTREES

The region octree is the simplest variant of the octree data structure. It is also usually the one that requires the most space. It has the same drawback as the region quadtree in the sense that it is an approximation and thus is not so suitable for some applications. Constructing a region octree from a three-dimensional array representation of an image is quite costly because of the sheer amount of data that must be examined. In particular, the large number of primitive elements that must be inspected means that the conventional raster-scanning approach used to build quadtrees spends much time detecting the mergibility of nodes.

The time and cost of building a region octree from an array can be reduced, in part, by using the predictive technique of Shaffer and Samet [Shaf86a, Shaf87a]. It is described briefly in Section 1.2 and in greater detail in Section 4.2.3 of [Same90b]. This method makes use of an auxiliary array whose storage requirements are as large as a cross-section of the image, which may render the algorithm impractical. However, since this array is often quite sparse, this problem can be overcome by representing it by use of a linked list of blocks in a manner similar to that used by Samet and Tamminen [Same88b] for connected component labeling in images of arbitrary dimension (see Section 5.1.3 of [Same90b]).

The easiest way to speed up the region octree construction process is to reduce the amount of data that need to be processed. Franklin and Akman [Fran85] show how to build a region octree from a set of rectangular parallelepipeds approximating the object. These data can be acquired, for example, by casting parallel rays along the z axis and perpendicular to the x-y plane [Roth82].

In many applications, an even more fundamental problem than building the octree is acquiring the initial boundary data to form the boundary of the object being represented. One approach is to use a three-dimensional pointing device to create a collection of samples from the surface of the object. After the point data are collected, it is necessary to interpolate a reasonable surface to join them.

Interpolation can be achieved by triangulation. A surface triangulation in three-dimensional space is a connected set of disjoint triangles that forms a surface with vertices that are points in the original data set. There are many triangulation methods currently in use, in both two-dimensional [Wats84, Saal87] and three-dimensional spaces [Faug84]. They differ in how they determine which points are to be joined. For example, often it is desired to form compact triangles instead of long, narrow ones. However, the problems of minimizing total edge length or maximizing the minimum angle pose difficult combinatorial problems. Posdamer [Posd82] suggests use of the ordering imposed by an octree on a set of points (e.g., by bit interleaving—see Section 2.7) as the basis for determining which points should be connected to form the triangles.

Posdamer's algorithm uses an octree for which the leaf criterion is that no leaf can contain more than three points (similar to a bucket PR quadtree—see Section 2.8.1). The initial set of triangles is formed by connecting the points in the leaf nodes that contain exactly three points. Whenever a leaf node contains exactly two points, these points are connected to form a line segment associated with the leaf node. This is the starting point for a bottom-up triangulation of the points. It merges disjoint triangulations to form larger triangulations.

The isolated points (i.e., leaf nodes that contain just one point) and isolated line segments are treated as degenerate triangulations. The triangulation associated with a gray node is the result of merging the triangulations associated with each of its sons. By *merging* or *joining* two triangulations, it is meant that a sufficient number of line segments is drawn between vertices of the two triangulations so that we get a new triangulation containing the original two triangulations as subtriangulations.

When merging the triangulations of the eight sibling octants, there are a number of heuristics that can be used to guide the choice of which triangulations are joined first. The order in which we choose the pair of triangulations to be joined is determined, in part, by the following factors. First, and foremost, it is preferred to merge triangulations that are in siblings whose corresponding octree blocks have a common face. If this is impossible, triangulations in nodes that have a common edge are merged. Again, if this is not feasible, triangulations in nodes that have a common vertex are merged. For each preference, the triangulations that are closest, according to some distance measure, are merged first.

There are many other methods of building an octree representation of an object. The simplest is to take quadtrees of cross-sectional images of the object and merge them in sequence. This technique is used in medical applications in which the cross-sections are obtained by computed tomography methods [Yau83]. Yau and Srihari [Yau83] discuss this technique in its full generality by showing how to construct a k-dimensional octree-like representation from multiple $(k-1)$-dimensional cross-sectional images.

Yau and Srihari's algorithm proceeds by processing the cross-sections in sequence. Each pair of consecutive cross-sections is merged into a single cross-section. This pairwise merging process is applied recursively until there is one cross-section left for the entire image. For example, assuming a k-dimensional image of side length 2^n, once the initial 2^n cross-sections have been merged, the resulting 2^{n-1} cross-sections are merged into 2^{n-2} cross-sections. In general, when merging 2^m cross-sections into 2^{m-1} cross-sections, only nonleaf nodes at levels m to n are tested for merging. Thus a cross-section at level m corresponds to a stack of 2^{n-m} volume elements of side length 2^m and is represented by a $(k-1)$-dimensional quadtree whose nodes are at levels m through n.

In other applications, the volume of the available data is not as large. Often a small number of two-dimensional images is used to reconstruct an octree representation of a three-dimensional object or a scene of three-dimensional objects. In this case, projection images (termed *silhouettes*) are taken from different viewpoints. These silhouettes are subsequently swept along the viewing direction, thereby creating a bounding volume, represented by an octree, that serves as an approximation of the object. The octrees of the bounding volumes, corresponding to views from different directions, are intersected to yield successively finer approximations of the object. The rest of this section elaborates on methods based on silhouettes. The discussion is highly specialized for computer vision and can be skipped.

Martin and Aggarwal [Mart83] use this method with volume segments that are parallelepipeds stored in a structure that is not an octree. Chien and Aggarwal [Chie84b, Chie86a] show how to use this method to construct an octree from the quadtrees of the three orthogonal views. Hong and Shneier [Hong85] (see also Chien and Aggarwal [Chie85] and Potmesil [Potm87]) point out that the task of intersecting the octree and the bounding volume can be made more efficient by first projecting the octree onto the image plane of the silhouette and then performing the intersection in the image plane. In contrast, Noborio, Fukuda, and Arimoto [Nobo88] perform the intersection check directly in the three-dimensional space rather than preceding it by a projection. In the rest of this section, it is assumed that the silhouettes result from parallel views, although perspective views have also been used (e.g., [Sriv87]).

Generally three orthogonal views are insufficient to obtain an accurate approximation of the object (see Exercise 5.4), and thus more views are needed. Chien and Aggarwal [Chie86b] overcome this problem by constructing what they term a *generalized octree* from three arbitrary views having the requirement that they are not coplanar. The generalized octree differs from the conventional region octree in that each node represents a parallelepiped with faces parallel to the viewing planes. The approximation is refined by intersecting the projection of each object node, say *P*, in the generalized octree with the image plane of the additional view. *P* is relabeled as a nonobject node or a gray node unless its projection lies entirely within the object region in the additional view. Note the similarity of this method with that of Hong and Shneier [Hong85].

A problem with using additional views from arbitrary viewpoints is that intersection operations must be explicitly performed to determine the relationship between the projections of the octants in the octree space and the silhouette of the new view. In the general case, the silhouette can be approximated by a polygon. The intersection of the polygonal projection of an octant with the polygon approximation of a silhouette is a special case of the polygon clipping problem (for more details see [Roge85]).

Chien and Aggarwal [Chie84b] and Veenstra and Ahuja [Veen85, Veen86, Ahuj89] point out that sweeping the silhouette image of an orthographic parallel projection[2] and restricting the views enable the exploitation of a regular relation between octants in the octree space and quadrants in the image space. This means that the intersection operation can be replaced by a table-lookup operation. The key idea is to represent the image array by a quadtree and to make use of mappings between the quadrants and the octants so that the octree can be constructed directly from the silhouettes of the digitized image. We thereby avoid the need to perform the sweep operation explicitly.

The image array corresponding to the silhouette is processed as if we are constructing its quadtree. Chien and Aggarwal [Chie84b] use three face views, while Veenstra and Ahuja [Veen86, Ahuj89] use 13 views (see Exercise 5.10). The 10 additional views correspond to 6 edge views and 4 vertex views. The face views are taken with the line of sight perpendicular to a different face of the octree space; the faces must be mutually orthogonal. The edge views are taken with the line of sight passing through the center of an edge and the center of the octree space. The vertex views are

---

[2] An *orthographic* parallel projection is a parallel projection in which the direction of the projection and the normal to the projection plane are the same, while in an *oblique* parallel projection they are not [Fole82]. For more details on projections, see Section 7.1.4 of [Same90b].

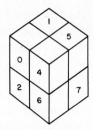

Figure 5.2   Labeling of octants in an octree (octant 3 is not visible)

taken with the line of sight passing through a vertex and the center of the octree space. The vertex views are also known as isometric projections (see Section 7.1.4 of [Same90b]).

At this point, let us see why these 13 particular views are used. Assume the existence of an octree representation of the scene, and consider which projections of the octree are the most natural. The face views enable us to maintain a quadtree representation of the octree's projection. With rectangular-shaped quadtree blocks (having an aspect ratio of $\sqrt{2}:1$), the edge views also enable the projection of the octree to be maintained as a quadtree. Finally, the projection of the octree as seen from the vertex views can be maintained by a quadtree decomposition based on the use of equilateral triangles [Ahuj83, Yama84].

When the views are taken with the line of sight perpendicular to a face, the result is the same as that described by Chien and Aggarwal [Chie86a]. As an example, using the octant labeling convention of Figure 5.2, when the line of sight is perpendicular to the face shared by octants 0, 2, 4, and 6, we find that pairs of octants are mapped into the same quadrant. Figure 5.3a shows the mapping for this particular view; for example, octants 6 and 7 are mapped into the SE quadrant. By reversing this

0 , 1	4 , 5
2 , 3	6 , 7

a

00,01	04,05	40,41	44,45
10,11	14,15	50,51	54,55
02,03	06,07	42,43	46,47
12,13	16,17	52,53	56,57
20,21	24,25	60,61	64,65
30,31	34,35	70,71	74,75
22,23	26,27	62,63	66,67
32,33	36,37	72,73	76,77

b

Figure 5.3   Mapping of octants into quadtrees for a view such that the line of sight is perpendicular to the face shared by octants 0, 2, 4, and 6, using the octant labeling convention of Figure 5.2, at (a) one level of decomposition and (b) two levels of decomposition

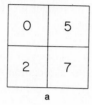 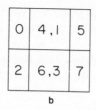

a   b

Figure 5.4   *Mapping of octants into quadrants for a view such that the line of sight passes through the center of the edge formed by octants 4 and 6 and the center of the octree space, using the octant labeling convention of Figure 5.2, depending on whether the parts of the silhouette that correspond to octants 1, 3, 4, and 6 in the octree are (a) all empty or (b) not*

mapping, we construct the octree directly from the silhouette of the digitized image. The process is recursive. We start with an empty quadtree (octree). We check if the image is homogeneous. If yes, no further processing is necessary. Otherwise the image is decomposed into four quadrants, and the process is repeated.

The difference from the conventional quadtree construction process is that each time, instead of adding one node per quadrant into the quadtree, we add a pair of nodes according to the pairing indicated in Figure 5.3a. Each time the level of decomposition increases, there is a doubling of the number of octree nodes mapped into the corresponding quadtree node of the silhouette. For example, Figure 5.3b shows the correspondence of quadtree and octree nodes at depth 2 for the view described in Figure 5.3a. Note the use of concatenation to group the octant labels; for example, 63 denotes suboctant 3 of octant 6.

When the views are taken with the line of sight passing through the center of an edge and the center of the octree space, the situation is more complex [Veen85, Ahuj89]. For such views, the silhouette of a cubelike region is a rectangle such that one of its sides is longer than the other by a factor of $\sqrt{2}$. However, this is not a problem, because we apply a scale transformation that replaces the rectangular pixels by square pixels before constructing the octree. As an example use the view generated by the line of sight perpendicular to the edge formed by octants 4 and 6, according to the octant labeling convention of Figure 5.2.

Depending on its position, each quadrant in the silhouette image can correspond to between one and three octants. There are two possible mappings depending on whether the parts of the silhouette that correspond to octants 1, 3, 4, and 6 in the octree are all empty (e.g., Figure 5.4a) or not (e.g., Figure 5.4b). From Figures 5.4a and 5.4b we see that pixels in the central half (i.e., the area in Figure 5.4b labeled 4, 1, 6, 3) of the silhouette can be part of between one and three octants. The construction process is recursive. We start with an empty quadtree (octree).

We check if the image is homogeneous. If yes, no further processing is necessary. If no, the image is decomposed recursively in two steps:

1. Use the decomposition in Figure 5.4a. For each homogeneous quadrant, add nodes to the octree according to the association indicated in the figure; otherwise recursively apply steps 1 and 2 to the quadrants once step 2 has been completed.

2. Use the decomposition in Figure 5.4b to deal with the central half of the silhouette (i.e., two 'quadrants'). In this case, process the two quadrants in the same way as described above for the case that the line of sight is perpendicular to a face. If the quadrants are homogeneous, add a pair of nodes according to the pairing indicated in the figure; otherwise recursively apply steps 1 and 2 to the two quadrants.

When the views are taken with the line of sight passing through a vertex and the center of the octree space, the silhouette of a cubelike region is a regular hexagon [Veen86, Ahuj89]. The hexagon can be decomposed into six equilateral triangles that are, in turn, treated as triangular quadtrees. The triangular 'quadrants' in the silhouette image can correspond to one, two, or four octants depending on their position. As an example, using the octant labeling convention of Figure 5.2, when the line of sight passes through the exposed vertex of octant 4 and the center of the octree space we have the mapping given in Figure 5.5.

Veenstra and Ahuja [Veen86, Ahuj89] suggest that instead of directly processing the image array of the silhouette, a set of six disjoint triangular quadtrees be built for the silhouette's hexagon. Each octant of the silhouette's octree is constructed by determining if the six triangles that make up the octant's hexagonal silhouette are homogeneous. If they are, the octant is given the appropriate color; otherwise the process is recursively applied to the octant and the corresponding triangles. A similar technique is used by Yamaguchi, Fujimura, and Toriya [Yama84] to display an

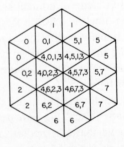

Figure 5.5 Mapping of octants into quadrants of a triangular quadtree for a view such that the line of sight passes through the exposed vertex of octant 4 and the center of the octree space, using the labeling convention of Figure 5.2

isometric view of an object represented by an octree (see Section 7.1.4 of [Same90b]).

In some situations, even 13 views are inadequate to obtain a sufficiently accurate approximation of the object, particularly when the object has a number of concave regions. Here it is best to use a ranging device to obtain range data. The range data can be viewed as partitioning the scene into three parts: the visible surface of the scene, the empty space in front of this surface, and the unknown space behind the surface. Connolly [Conn84] constructs an octree representation of the scene that corresponds to the series of such range images. This octree represents a piecewise linear approximation of the surfaces of the scene. A quadtree is used as an intermediate representation of a piecewise linear surface approximating the data comprising a single-range image prior to its incorporation into the octree. Connolly [Conn85] derives an octree-based heuristic for selecting the positions from which to take subsequent range images. The issue of determining the next 'best' view is still an open problem.

A drawback of Connolly's use of the quadtree as an intermediate representation is that the quadtree must be transformed into the octree coordinate system when the coordinate axes of the quadtree are not aligned with those of the octree. This is a relatively complex process from a computational standpoint (but see Section 6.3.3 of [Same90b]). Chien, Sim, and Aggarwal [Chie88] also represent the views by quadtrees. They point out that Connolly's approach can be simplified by exercising control over the configuration of the range sensor. In particular, much of its complexity can be reduced (and avoided) by assuming that the ranging device is aligned with the cube that corresponds to the scene. This enables them to take advantage of the interrelationship between the quadtree and octree structures. They make use of six views to yield six range images—one for each of three pairs of orthogonal viewing directions.

Chien et al. generate a quadtree for each range image using a decomposition criterion so that each block has a constant range value (i.e., each block contains a square surface patch parallel to the image plane). They assume that the observed object occupies the space extending from the visible surfaces to the rear boundary of the scene cube (with respect to the ranging device being at the front for the particular view in question). Based on this assumption, they use a segment tree (a one-dimensional region quadtree—see Section 3.2.1) to represent the subpart of the object behind the visible surface patch associated with the block. Thus the object corresponding to each view is a quadtree in which each leaf node is, in turn, a segment tree. Whereas the quadtree partitions the two-dimensional image plane into blocks of constant range value, the segment tree decomposes the remaining dimension (i.e., depth) into object and nonobject regions.

The actual octree corresponding to each view (termed a *range octree*) is obtained by recursively merging the segment trees of the quadtree nodes. The rationale for using the combination of quadtrees and segment trees instead of the octree is to reduce the intermediate space requirements. Memory and time can be saved by not merging the six range octrees directly. Instead, once a pair of range octrees corresponding to opposite views (e.g., front and rear) is obtained, they are merged. The final step merges these three range octrees to yield the desired octree.

Exercises

5.2. Write an algorithm to build a region octree of side length 2^n, given the quadtrees corresponding to its 2^n cross-sections.

5.3. Write an algorithm to build a region octree from a set of rectangular parallelepipeds.

5.4. Suppose you are given the three orthogonal views of a three-dimensional object with polygonal faces. What conditions must the object satisfy for you to be able to build its region octree?

5.5. Devise an algorithm that will always be able to build a region octree for an object based on views of the object. In case of ambiguity, your algorithm can ask for more views from different viewpoints.

5.6. Write an algorithm to implement Posdamer's [Posd82] method of interpolating a surface of an object for which point data are given.

5.7. Write an algorithm to detect if two polygons intersect.

5.8. Write an algorithm to compute the geometric intersection of the projection of an octree and a silhouette. You may assume that the silhouette is specified as a polygon.

5.9. Write an algorithm to compute the union and intersection of two polygons. Make sure you account for all the degenerate cases such as coincident edges.

5.10. Why don't Veenstra and Ahuja [Veen86, Ahuj89] use 26 instead of 13 views?

5.11. Write an algorithm to construct the octree corresponding to the silhouette image resulting from a face view—that is, the line of sight is perpendicular to a specific face of the octree space.

5.12. Write an algorithm to construct the octree corresponding to the silhouette image resulting from an edge view—that is, the line of sight passes through the center of a specific edge and the center of the octree space.

5.13. Write an algorithm to construct the octree corresponding to the silhouette image resulting from a vertex view—that is, the line of sight passes through a specific vertex and the center of the octree space.

5.14. Write an algorithm to construct an octree from a range image using the approach of Chien, Sim, and Aggarwal [Chie88]. Build the range octrees first and then the final octree.

5.3 PM OCTREES

One of the deficiencies of the region octree is that if the faces of the object (or objects) represented by it are not rectilinear, the representation is not exact in the sense that it is an approximation. The only exception is if the faces are mutually orthogonal, in which case a suitable rotation operation can be applied to yield rectilinear faces. In many applications this is not a problem. However, in solid modeling it is preferable to have an exact representation. When the object has planar faces, an extension of the PM quadtree, a representation for polygonal maps discussed in Section 4.2.3, can be used; it is the focus of this section. An alternative solution is to store surface normals in the visible surface nodes as discussed by Meager [Meag84] (see Section 7.1.4 of [Same90b]). Chien and Aggarwal [Chie86c] show how to do this directly from boundaries of multiple silhouettes. This approach is not discussed here.

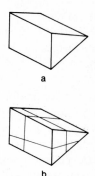

Figure 5.6 (a) Example three-dimensional object and (b) its corresponding PM octree

As we saw in the discussion of the PM quadtree, there are a number of possible variants, largely depending on whether a vertex- or edge-based approach is pursued. In three dimensions, the most logical approach is to adapt the PM$_1$ quadtree. In such a case, the resulting decomposition ensures that each octree leaf node corresponds to a single vertex, a single edge, or a single face. The only exceptions are that a leaf node may contain more than one edge if all the edges are incident at the same vertex. Similarly a leaf node may contain more than one face if all the faces are incident at the same vertex or edge. The result is termed a *PM octree*. The above subdivision criteria can be stated more formally as follows:

1. At most, one vertex can lie in a region represented by an octree leaf node.
2. If an octree leaf node's region contains a vertex, it can contain no edge or face that is not incident at that vertex.
3. If an octree leaf node's region contains no vertices, it can contain at most one edge.
4. If an octree leaf node's region contains no vertices and contains one edge, it can contain no face that is not incident at that edge.
5. If an octree leaf node's region contains no edges, it can contain at most one face.
6. Each region's octree leaf node is maximal.

An implementation of the PM octree consists of leaf nodes of type vertex, edge, and face. For our purposes, it is permissible to have more than two faces meet at a common edge. However, such a situation can not arise when modeling solids bounded by compact, orientable two-manifold surfaces (i.e., only two faces may meet at an edge—see Exercise 5.32).[3] Nevertheless it is plausible when three-dimensional objects are represented by their surfaces.

---

[3] The term *oriented* means two-sided. Thus it is not like a Möbius strip or a Klein bottle.

The space requirements of the PM octree are considerably harder to analyze than those of the region octree [Nava86a] (see Exercise 5.17). Nevertheless it should be clear that the PM octree for a given object is much more compact than the corresponding region octree. For example, Figure 5.6b is a PM octree decomposition of the object in Figure 5.6a.

At this point, it is appropriate to trace briefly the history of the PM octree. Quinlan and Woodwark [Quin82] describe a decomposition rule requiring that a leaf node contain at most one vertex. Otherwise the node can contain either a number of faces or a number of edges and faces. The notion of a 'number' is analogous to the manner in which Tamminen's edge-EXCELL method [Tamm81a, Tamm82b] makes use of a bucket (see Section 4.2.3.4) in the representation of a collection of line segments. The result is somewhat like a three-dimensional adaptation of a combination of EXCELL and a PM$_3$ quadtree. In fact, Tamminen [Tamm81a] does describe an adaptation of EXCELL for three-dimensional data in which faces take the place of line segments.

The PM octree formulation described by criteria 1–6 was reported almost simultaneously by three research groups, who, of course, each gave it a different name [Ayal85, Carl85, Fuji85b]. Ayala, Brunet, Juan, and Navazo [Ayal85] called it an *extended octree*. Carlbom, Chakravarty, and Vanderschel [Carl85] called it a *polytree*. They say that it was initially investigated by Hunter [Hunt81], who termed it a *geometree*. They also state that the geometree is a simplification of a data structure described by Vanderschel [Vand84], who named it a *divided-leaf octal tree*. Fujimura and Kunii [Fuji85b] termed it a *hierarchical space indexing method*. Regardless of its name(s), it is a useful method. The most extensive treatment of this data structure is to be found in the Ph.D. dissertation of Navazo [Nava86a]. This work contains a detailed analysis of the storage requirements of the representation. It also includes algorithms for Boolean operations involving it and conversion between it and a boundary model.

For the proper execution of many operations, the fact that a node is of type vertex, edge, or face is not sufficient to characterize the object properly. At times Carlbom, Chakravarty, and Vanderschel [Carl85] store with each node the polygons determined by the boundary of the object that intersects the node. This is somewhat cumbersome and requires a considerable amount of extra information. Moreover, the vertices of the polygons cannot be specified exactly because most often they are not the vertices of the object. In particular, they are artifacts of the decomposition process. In fact, the edges of the polygons are analogous to the q-edges discussed in Section 4.2.3 in the context of the PM quadtree. Thus using that terminology, the polygons would be more appropriately termed *q-faces*.

Navazo [Nava86a] uses a more efficient representation. In the case of a face node, the equation of the plane of the face associated with the node is recorded with the node. In addition, the direction of the object relative to the face is noted. For nodes of type edge and vertex, the configuration of the faces (i.e., the planes) that make up the edge and vertex must also be recorded. This information is used to classify a point inside the node with respect to the object so that the PM octree can be built.

Figure 5.7   The two possible configurations for the cross-section of an edge node in a PM octree: (a) a convex edge is the result of the intersection of the planes of the two faces that meet at the edge, (b) a concave edge is the result of the union of the planes of the two faces that meet at the edge. The arrows indicate the direction of the object relative to the faces; the broken lines correspond to the parts of the planes that do not form the boundary of the object; the shaded region corresponds to the object.

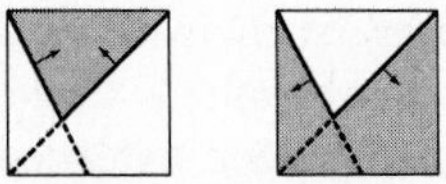

For example, in the case of an edge node, we must know if it is convex or concave. The two possibilities are shown in Figure 5.7. The intersection of the planes of the two faces that meet at the edge results in a convex edge (Figure 5.7a), while the union results in a concave edge (Figure 5.7b). Note the use of arrows to indicate the direction of the object relative to the planes of the faces. In the case of a vertex node, the situation is more complex because the number of possible configurations depends on the number of faces adjacent at the vertex.

In [Nava89], Navazo presents an elegant generalized treatment of vertices with *n* faces that permits the configurations to be classified on the basis of their constituent edge configurations and stores them by their type along with pointers to the plane equations of their faces. This generalized approach is then used as the basis of algorithms to compute Boolean operations involving PM octrees (for another approach, see [Carl87]).

Navazo, Fontdecaba, and Brunet [Nava87] discuss the conversion from a CSG representation to a PM octree. If the objects have planar faces, the conversion process yields an exact representation. The algorithm proceeds in a top-down manner and employs pruning rules similar to those used by Samet and Tamminen [Same85g, Same90c] in the conversion of a CSG tree to a bintree (see Section 5.5.1.2). The principal difference is that Navazo et. al also need to compute the vertex configuration that must be associated with each vertex node in the PM octree. The computational complexity of the algorithm is the same as that of Samet and Tamminen [Same85g, Same90c] when the initial CSG tree is 'well behaved' (i.e., no faces are tangential to each other—see Section 5.5.1.2). The construction of a CSG tree from the PM octree is more complex (see Exercise 5.22).

With the above conversion algorithms at hand, the PM octree can serve as the basis of a hybrid solid modeling system. In such a case, a dual representation could be used, and operations would be performed in the model that most easily supports them. For example, Boolean operations are more easily performed in the PM octree than in the boundary model. Similarly the visualization of objects on a display and the computation of geometric properties, such as the mass, can be performed more easily in the PM octree than in the CSG representation.

PM octree techniques have also been extended to handle curvilinear surfaces. Primitives including cylinders and spheres have been used in conjunction with a decomposition rule limiting the number of distinct primitives that can be associated with a leaf node [Fuji86, Wyvi85] (e.g., the PM-CSG tree as discussed in Section 5.5.2). Another approach [Nava86b] extends the concepts of face node, edge node, and vertex node to handle faces represented by biquadratic patches. The use of biquadratic patches enables a better fit with fewer primitives than can be obtained with planar faces, thereby reducing the size of the octree. The difficulty in organizing curved surface patches by using octrees lies in devising efficient methods of calculating the intersection between a patch and an octree node. Observe that in this approach we are organizing a collection of patches in the image space. This is in contrast to decomposing a single patch in the parametric space by use of quadtree techniques as discussed in Section 7.1.6 of [Same90b].

Fujimura and Samet [Fuji89] treat time as an additional dimension (see also [Gill81, Glas88, Jack83, Same85g, Yau83]) and use a PM octree to represent moving objects in the plane. Their goal is to perform path planning for a robot in an environment that contains moving obstacles. The environment is two-dimensional, and the obstacles are represented using PM_1 quadtrees. The addition of the time dimension yields a PM octree. A safe path is one in which the obstacles do not collide with each other or with the robot. The path is obtained by use of heuristic search.

Exercises

5.15. Suppose that a vertex node is determined by three faces with plane equations h_1, h_2, and h_3. How many different configurations are possible when circular permutations are considered equivalent?

5.16. Suppose that a vertex node is determined by four faces with plane equations h_1, h_2, h_3, and h_4. How many different configurations are possible when circular permutations are considered equivalent?

5.17. In Section 1.5, it was shown that the space requirements of the region octree of a polyhedral object are proportional to the object's surface area. Can you prove that the space requirements of the PM octree for a polyhedral object are proportional to the sum of the lengths of its edges?

5.18. Write an algorithm to compute the intersection of two objects represented by PM octrees.

5.19. Write an algorithm to compute the union of two objects represented by PM octrees.

5.20. Given a position of an observer, write an algorithm to display an object that is represented by a PM octree.

5.21. Write an algorithm to convert from a boundary model to a PM octree.

5.22. Write an algorithm to convert from a CSG representation to a PM octree.

5.23. Write an algorithm to convert from a PM octree to a boundary model.

5.24. Write an algorithm to convert from a PM octree to a CSG representation.

5.25. Section 4.3.3 discusses the solution of the point location problem in two dimensions when a polygonal subdivision is represented by a PM quadtree. How would you adapt this method to three dimensions when a polyhedral subdivision is represented by a PM octree?

5.4   BOUNDARY MODEL (BREP)

In the boundary model (BRep), three-dimensional solids are defined by their enclosing surfaces. A boundary model of an object is a geometric and topological description of its boundary. The object boundary is segmented into a finite number of bounded sub-sets called *faces*. Each face is, in turn, represented by its bounding *edges* and *vertices*. Thus a boundary model consists of three primitive topological entities: faces, edges, and vertices. Faces are contiguous portions of the surface of the volume enclosed by the boundary. Edges are the elements that, when joined together, form the closed face boundaries. Vertices are those points on the surface at which edges intersect.

We are interested in the domain of solid objects bounded by compact, orientable two-manifold surfaces [Mänt87]. In this case, we must also be able to describe objects with multiply connected faces (e.g., holes) or internal cavities (e.g., a cube inside another cube such that the internal cube is hollow). This is achieved by the addition of two higher-level topological entities, termed the *shell* and the *loop*. A *shell* in an object s is defined as any maximal connected set of faces of s. For exam-ple, an object that has an internal cavity, such as that formed by a cube within another cube, has two shells: an internal shell and an external shell. A *loop* on a face f of s is defined as a closed chain of edges bounding f. For example, consider an object such as a nut (e.g., Figure 5.8) in which case the top and bottom faces each have two loops: an internal loop and an external loop.

Both geometric and topological information may be associated with the indivi-dual topological entities. Due to their different characteristics and uses, a clear separation can be made in the boundary model between the topological and geometric descriptions of an object. The topological description consists of the adjacency rela-tions between pairs of individual topological entities (e.g., edges and vertices). There are 25 different adjacency relationships; each consists of a unique ordered pair from the five topological entities described [Weil86].

The geometric description consists of the shape and location in space of each of the primitive topological entities. For example, the geometry of a face may be described by a surface equation. The geometry of an edge may be described by a three-dimensional spline curve. The geometry of a vertex may be described by its Cartesian coordinates. No geometric description is associated with shells and loops since they are collections of primitive topological entities.

Note that the topological and geometric descriptions of an object are not independent. For example, a change in the geometric description of a primitive topo-

Figure 5.8   Example nut illustrating the concept of a loop

logical entity such as an edge from a straight line segment to a piecewise linear approximation will introduce new topological entities (e.g., new edges and vertices).

The boundary model is capable of describing a wide variety of objects at arbitrary levels of detail. It is unambiguous, which means that each boundary model corresponds to a single object. It is also unique when the boundary is partitioned into maximally connected faces [Silv81a]. To understand this concept better, consider an object with planar faces. We achieve a partition into maximally connected faces if we merge all faces that are coplanar (provided that their union is connected). A major drawback of the boundary model is that Boolean operations are costly and tedious to implement.

Regardless of how the geometry and topology are represented, the validity of the resulting object must be guaranteed. A topologically valid boundary model can be constructed by the use of a limited set of primitive functions called Euler operators [Ansa85, Brai80, East79, Mänt82, Mänt87]. Beside the low-level Euler operators, more complex operations (e.g., translational and rotational sweep) are usually available in systems that make use of the boundary model.

The primitive topological entities in a boundary model are faces, edges, and vertices; shells and loops are nonprimitive topological entities. Often the representation is hierarchical in the sense that we first decompose the object into a collection of its constituent shells. Each shell is a collection of faces. Each face is represented by its surface equation and by a collection of its bounding loops. Each loop is a chain of edges. Often a single curved edge is approximated by several linear segments. Each segment is represented by a pair of vertices that correspond to its endpoints.

There are a number of different ways of specifying a boundary model. The most general data structure consists of the set of topological entities that define the boundary of the object, plus a subset of the 25 different adjacency relations between the pairs of individual entities. Recall that the relations are ordered. Thus, for example, there is a difference between an edge-face relation and a face-edge relation. In particular, the edge-face relation associates with each edge the pair of faces that share it, while the face-edge relation associates with each face the edges that bound it.

Many of the data structures proposed in the literature to represent the boundary model (e.g., [Ansa85, Baum72, Weil85, Woo85]) store the edge-vertex and edge-face relations. When the objects have multiple shells and multiply connected faces, then, for example, the edge-face and face-edge relations can be expressed as a combination of the edge-loop and loop-face, and face-loop and loop-edge relations, respectively [Weil86]. The advantage of introducing the combination involving the loop is that, from a hierarchical standpoint, the loop falls somewhere between a face and an edge.

At times, it is desirable to be able to access the information represented by the boundary model by using the identity of a particular face or vertex instead of just an edge. This is the motivation behind the symmetric structure [Woo85] that stores the face-edge and vertex-edge relations, as well as the edge-face and edge-vertex relations. The face adjacency graph [Ansa85] and similar face-based structures are motivated in the same manner. For example, the face adjacency graph differs from Woo's symmetric structure in that it stores a vertex-face relation instead of a vertex-edge relation.

A disadvantage of using relations such as face-edge (e.g., in the symmetric structure) or vertex-face (e.g., in the face adjacency graph) is that the amount of information associated with the first element of the relation is not fixed. For example, each instance of the face-edge relation contains the edges that bound the face, and each instance of the vertex-face relation contains the faces incident at the vertex. On the other hand, for all relations in which the edge appears as the first element, the amount of information associated with an instance of the relation is fixed. This observation forms the basis of the winged-edge data structure of Baumgart [Baum72, Baum74, Baum75]. It is an edge-based specification, and a special case of it is described below.

Assume that the faces of the objects do not have internal loops and are composed of a single shell.[4] Each face is represented as a sequence of the edges comprising it, while the edges are specified as ordered pairs of their constituent vertices. The sequence of edges must be oriented consistently; for example, the edges are listed in a clockwise order as the face is viewed from the outside of the object. The faces of the object are assumed to be compact, orientable two-manifolds [Mänt87] (see Exercise 5.32), which, in essence, means that only two faces are adjacent at each edge. Therefore each edge appears in only two faces—once in each of its orientations.

In other words, given edge $e = (v_1, v_2)$, it appears in one face as (v_1, v_2) and in the other face as (v_2, v_1). This information is captured by recording an orientation (i.e., positive or negative) with each reference to the edge. Using this information, we can make the face data structure have a fixed length by storing with it only the identity of one of its constituent edges and a flag indicating the orientation of the edge. Moreover, with each edge, say e, we keep track of the two edges that follow e (one for each orientation). The result is that the face is represented by a linked list in which the links are stored as part of the edge records.

There are a number of variants of the winged-edge data structure. In its full generality, there is no need for the orientation flag. This is achieved by recording the following eight items of information for each edge: the two constituent vertices (VSTART and VEND), the two adjacent faces (FCW and FCCW), the preceding edges in the two faces (EPCW and EPCCW), and the next edges in the two faces (ENCW and ENCCW).[5] The physical interpretation of these items is illustrated for edge e of the parallelepiped in Figure 5.9. In addition, the identity of one edge is stored with each face and with each vertex.

By keeping track of one of the incident edges with each face, we are able to extract easily the entire set of edges that forms each face (see Exercise 5.29). Similarly by keeping track of one of the incident edges with each vertex, we are able to extract easily the entire set of edges incident at each vertex (see Exercise 5.30).

---

[4] Objects with multiple shells and faces with internal loops require further elaboration in the model (see [Weil85]).

[5] V, E, and F denote vertex, edge, and face, respectively. N and P denote next and preceding, respectively. CW and CCW denote clockwise and counterclockwise, respectively. The direction of the edge is from VSTART to VEND.

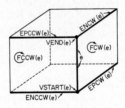

Figure 5.9 The physical interpretation of the fields of a winged-edge data structure for edge e of a parallelepiped

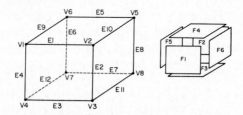

Figure 5.10 Sample parallepiped with vertices (V1–V8), edges (E1–E12), and faces (F1–F6)

Tables 5.1–5.3 illustrate the general winged-edge data structure for the parallelepiped given in Figure 5.10 with the corresponding labels assigned to its vertices, edges, and faces. It should be clear that with this variant of the winged-edge data structure, vertices, edges, and faces are each specified by fixed-length records.

Tamminen and Samet [Tamm84g] show how to convert from a boundary model to a region octree by use of a variant of the connected component labeling algorithm

Table 5.1   Vertex table

VERTEX	X	Y	Z	ESTART
V_1	X_1	Y_1	Z_1	E_1
V_2	X_2	Y_2	Z_2	E_2
V_3	X_3	Y_3	Z_3	E_3
V_4	X_4	Y_4	Z_4	E_4
V_5	X_5	Y_5	Z_5	E_5
V_6	X_6	Y_6	Z_6	E_6
V_7	X_7	Y_7	Z_7	E_7
V_8	X_8	Y_8	Z_8	E_8

Table 5.2   Edge table

EDGE	VSTART	VEND	EPCW	ENCW	EPCCW	ENCCW	FCW	FCCW
E_1	V_1	V_2	E_4	E_2	E_{10}	E_9	F_1	F_4
E_2	V_2	V_3	E_1	E_3	E_{11}	E_{10}	F_1	F_6
E_3	V_3	V_4	E_2	E_4	E_{12}	E_{11}	F_1	F_3
E_4	V_4	V_1	E_3	E_1	E_9	E_{12}	F_1	F_5
E_5	V_5	V_6	E_8	E_6	E_9	E_{10}	F_2	F_4
E_6	V_6	V_7	E_5	E_7	E_{12}	E_9	F_2	F_5
E_7	V_7	V_8	E_6	E_8	E_{11}	E_{12}	F_2	F_3
E_8	V_8	V_5	E_7	E_5	E_{10}	E_{11}	F_2	F_6
E_9	V_1	V_6	E_1	E_5	E_6	E_4	F_4	F_5
E_{10}	V_5	V_2	E_5	E_1	E_2	E_8	F_4	F_6
E_{11}	V_3	V_8	E_3	E_7	E_8	E_2	F_3	F_6
E_{12}	V_7	V_4	E_7	E_3	E_4	E_6	F_3	F_5

(see Section 1.1 for a definition) given in Section 5.1.3 of [Same90b]. Their approach works for collections of three-dimensional objects that do not contain voids (i.e., holes). In their solution, each original object is represented by the collection of its constituent faces, each defined as sequences of coordinate triples (no topological information is required by the algorithm).

They first construct an *MX octree*, a three-dimensional variant of the MX quad-tree, for the objects (see Section 2.6.1). In principle, the MX octree consists of three types of nodes: interior, boundary, and exterior. A node is said to be of type *boundary* if a face of the object passes through it. Boundary nodes are treated as black nodes. It is rare for boundary nodes to be merged, although such merges do arise at times

Table 5.3   Face table

FACE	ESTART
F_1	E_1
F_2	E_5
F_3	E_{11}
F_4	E_9
F_5	E_4
F_6	E_8

(especially when the MX octree is implemented as a bintree). *Interior* and *exterior* nodes correspond to regions within, and outside, respectively, the objects. They are treated as white nodes and can be merged to yield larger nodes. Of course, interior and exterior nodes cannot be merged with each other since they are always separated by boundary nodes.

The MX octree is built by first converting each of the faces individually. The boundary is the union (a set-theoretic operation that is also termed *overlay*) of all of these octrees. To be able to distinguish between a white interior node and a white exterior node, a variant of an algorithm that labels connected components is performed. The variation is that instead of finding the connected black components, we find the connected white components.

The second pass of the algorithm extracts all white components that are not connected to the outside of the image and changes them to black. There are as many such black components as there are distinct objects in the universe being converted. The result of this operation is a region octree where each black node is labeled with the name of the object to which it corresponds. In their implementation, Tamminen and Samet build a region bintree and represent it by its DF-expression (recall Section 1.5).[6]

The MX octree for each face is actually built by projecting it onto one of the coordinate planes (see Exercise 5.38), and then building the corresponding MX quadtree by recursively applying the same algorithm (i.e., a two-dimensional variant of it) to the projections of the original edges of the face. Once the MX quadtree for a projected face is built, the interior of the resulting polygon is colored by using a two-dimensional variant of the connectivity labeling algorithm described above. Next the MX octree for the original face is built by recursively subdividing the universe in order to form the MX octree of the 'infinite' plane corresponding to the face.

During the subdivision, each three-dimensional block, say B, is colored as the corresponding two-dimensional block of the face's projection, say P. This process is facilitated by keeping track of the minimum and maximum values, say L and H, respectively, of the plane equation of the face in each block. If P is white, then B is white. If P is black and is at the voxel level, then B is black. If P is black and is not at the voxel level, then B is white if $L > 0$ or $H < 0$ (i.e., B does not intersect the plane). Otherwise B is gray and is subdivided further.

The execution time complexity of the algorithm depends on the amount of time necessary to perform the tasks of building the MX octrees for the individual faces, overlaying the resulting MX octrees, and labeling connected components. For some of these tasks, the execution time depends on the representation of the resulting octree. In the following, we assume a pointer-based representation.

Building the MX octrees for the individual faces takes time proportional to the sum of the areas of the faces. Building the MX quadtrees for the projections of the

---

[6] A DF-expression represents a bintree as a traversal of its constituent nodes [Kawa80a, Tamm84c]. For example, letting 'B,' 'W,' and 'G' correspond to black, white, and gray nodes, respectively, and assuming a traversal in the order west, east, south, and north, then the bintree of Figure 1.18 would be represented by GGGWGBGGBWBWGGGGBGWBBGWBGGBWGGBW. For more details, see Section 1.5 and Section 2.2 of [Same90b].

individual faces takes time proportional to the sum of the perimeters of their projections. Also the number of nodes in the MX octrees for the faces is proportional to the areas of the faces. The overlay process takes time proportional to the number of nodes in the MX octrees of the polygons that make up the faces. The connected component labeling algorithm is almost linear in the number of nodes of the resulting region octree assuming that the UNION-FIND algorithm (see Section 5.1.1 of [Same90b]) is used to process equivalence classes.

The merits of the approach are best seen by considering the obvious alternative method, which works by block classification (marking a block as inside or outside the object). In particular, the universe is traversed, and each leaf node is explicitly classified by a point-in-polyhedron test. This is a computationally expensive process because for each block, we must determine whether the block intersects the boundary of the object and, if so, if the block is contained within the object. In contrast, the method of Tamminen and Samet does not require a point-in-polyhedron test since the constituent parts of the object (i.e., its faces) are converted directly into MX octrees.

The reverse task of generating a valid boundary model from a region octree is addressed by Kunii, Satoh, and Yamaguchi [Kuni85]. The result is a boundary model where the faces of the object lie in planes perpendicular to a major axis. The heart of the algorithm is the merger of coplanar surfaces of adjacent octree nodes and colinear edges. Veenstra and Ahuja [Veen88] address a similar problem in that they present an algorithm that yields a line drawing of an object represented by a region octree. This means that hidden lines must be eliminated as well. The line drawing uses the parallel projection from any specified viewpoint with hidden lines removed.

Exercises

5.26. Give the boundary representation for the parallelepiped of Figure 5.10 using a (1) face-vertex relation and (2) face-edge and edge-vertex relations.

5.27. Give a representation of the parallelepiped in Figure 5.10 using a variant of the winged-edge data structure that records the orientation.

5.28. How would you extract all of the edges that comprise a face when using the winged-edge data structure that makes use of an orientation flag?

5.29. Give an algorithm to extract the entire set of edges in sequence that makes up a face when using the general winged-edge data structure.

5.30. Give an algorithm to extract the entire set of edges that is incident at each vertex when using the general winged-edge data structure.

5.31. The general winged-edge data structure contains some redundant information in the sense that some of the link fields are unnecessary. In particular, doubly linked lists are used. What is the advantage of this redundancy?

5.32. From the text we see that for the polyhedral objects in which we are interested, each edge belongs to exactly two faces. This is one of three restrictions that lead to a two-manifold. The other two restrictions are (1) that every vertex is surrounded by a single cycle of edges and faces and (2) that faces may not intersect each other, except at common edges or vertices. An alternative definition is that a two-manifold is a connected surface where each point on the surface is topologically equivalent to an open disk [Weil86]. What are some examples of physically realizable objects that are not two-manifolds?

5.33. Using the definition of a two-manifold given in Exercise 5.32, are two-manifold objects closed under Boolean set operations?

5.34. What is the maximum number of loops with which an edge can be associated?

5.35. Give two methods of defining the loop-face relation. Which method is preferable?

5.36. Assuming that a loop-face relation constrains the face to contain all of the edges that comprise the loop, what is the maximum number of faces with which a loop can be associated? Can you give an example?

5.37. Write the algorithm for building an MX octree given its boundary representation.

5.38. How would you choose the projection plane for the construction of the MX quadtree in the algorithm described in this section?

5.39. Can you identify some deficiencies in the algorithm discussed in this section for converting from a boundary representation to a region octree?

5.40. Prove that the algorithm described in this section for converting from a boundary representation to a region octree works—that is, that the process of converting the faces individually into black voxels leaves no 'holes' in the boundary.

5.41. Modify the connected component labeling algorithm given in Section 5.1.3 of [Same90b] to implement the approach of Tamminen and Samet described in this section.

5.42. How would you extend the algorithm for building the region octree from a boundary representation given in this section to permit objects to have holes?

5.43. Why can an MX octree not be built by individually converting the planes of the faces that make up the boundary of the object into region octrees (i.e., using the algorithm described in Section 5.5.1.1) and then taking the intersection of the resulting region octrees?

5.44. Implement an algorithm comparable to the one described in this section to convert a two-dimensional polygon to a region quadtree.

5.45. Can you propose an alternative method to the one described in this section for converting a polyhedron into a region octree?

5.46. How does the use of a DF-expression representation for the MX octree affect the execution time of the algorithm for converting from a boundary representation to a region octree?

5.5 CONSTRUCTIVE SOLID GEOMETRY (CSG)

Constructive solid geometry (CSG) uses trees (CSG trees) of building block primitives (parallelepipeds, spheres, cylinders, . . .), combined by geometric transformations and Boolean set operations as a representation of three-dimensional solid objects [Voel77, Requ80]. At times, it is convenient to decompose each primitive solid further into a subtree whose leaf nodes are halfspaces, each described by an inequality of the form:

$$f(x,y,z) \geq 0. \tag{5.1}$$

Substituting this subtree for every occurrence of that primitive in the original CSG tree gives rise to an expanded tree having only halfspaces as leaf nodes [Wood82b, Okin73]. The CSG approach can be used to describe objects of any dimensionality, and many interesting solid modelers have been based on it [Requ82, Requ83].

When the halfspaces are linear (i.e., planar), the left-hand side of inequality 5.1 is a linear expression of the form $ax + by + cz + d$. (For a description of some recent work in geometric modeling that makes use of linear halfspaces, see the Ph.D. dissertation of Jansen [Jans87a].) Curved halfspaces can also be defined. They are useful for defining objects with nonplanar faces. Such halfspaces are usually specified by nonlinear inequalities. (For a description of geometric modeling with nonlinear halfspaces see Okino et al. [Okin73], and Voelcker and Requicha [Voel77], as well as the survey of Requicha [Requ80] and the systems and articles referenced in [Requ83].)

Most elementary volumes (i.e., solids such as a block, cylinder, sphere, cone) are formed by convex faces. They can be described by a Boolean intersection of halfspaces, some linear and some nonlinear. Volumes formed only of concave faces are rare. It is quite common, however, for volumes to be defined as combinations of convex and concave faces. For example, a sphere with a spherical hole can be decomposed into a Boolean intersection of a solid comprising (1) a Boolean intersection of halfspaces representing the convex face corresponding to the outside sphere and (2) a Boolean union of halfspaces representing the concave face corresponding to the inside sphere.

The CSG representation is primarily of a descriptive nature. It does not lend itself easily to the extraction of information about the underlying object that it represents, such as its mass. Such properties are usually computed by converting a CSG description to a more traditional representation (e.g., boundary model, octree). However, it is not always necessary to perform a complete conversion. For example, to display the CSG representation of an object, several hidden-surface algorithms have been developed that combine the evaluation of the CSG tree with the visibility calculation—that is, the surfaces of the primitives are classified as to whether they make a contribution to the resulting object [Roth82, Athe83, Ross86]. See also [Jans87b] for an overview of CSG classification techniques.

On the other hand, it has been known for some time that octree-like recursive subdivision can facilitate the evaluation of CSG trees, for example, the analysis [Lee82b, Lee82c, Wall84] and display [Wood80, Wood82b, Wood86] of solid objects modeled by them. In particular, the traditional region octree can be used to approximate any shape, and the operations of set union and subtraction are easy to perform. (See [Cohe79] for an earlier reference to a similar method for analyzing convex objects of arbitrary dimensionality.) A hardware processor with such a capability is presented by Meagher [Meag84]. Others (e.g., [Thom83, Jans87b]) also discuss the implementation of quadtree-like image subdivisions in hardware to reduce the complexity of the CSG evaluation and the number of halfspaces to be processed.

In the remainder of this section, two octree approaches to the evaluation of CSG trees are described. The first makes use of the bintree generalization of the octree and assumes that the CSG trees are defined by linear halfspaces. This is based on the work of Samet and Tamminen [Same85g, Same90c]. The second makes use of an adaptation of the PM octree to handle CSG trees. In this case, the definition of CSG trees is not restricted to linear halfspaces. Also, unlike the bintree approach, the result is an exact model, not an approximation. This approach is based on the work of Wyvill and Kunii [Wyvi85].

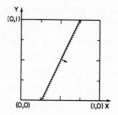

Figure 5.11   Halfspace corresponding to 4x – 2y – 1 ≥ 0

5.5.1   CSG Evaluation by Bintree Conversion

In this section, we examine the evaluation of CSG trees by bintree conversion. The following notation and representations are used. In the interest of simplicity, in the algorithms we use the DF-expression representation of a bintree (see Section 5.4). Although bintrees are size independent—a given tree can define an object in a universe of any size—each bintree is portrayed as embedded in the d-dimensional unit cube.

A (linear) halfspace in d-space is defined by the following inequality on the $d + 1$ homogeneous coordinates ($x_0 = 1$):

$$\sum_{i=0}^{d} a_i \cdot x_i \geq 0. \tag{5.2}$$

The halfspace is represented by a column vector a. In vector notation, inequality 5.2 is written as $a \cdot x \geq 0$. In the case of equality, it defines a hyperplane with a as its normal. For example, Figure 5.11 shows the halfspace represented by $4x - 2y - 1 \geq 0$. The point set satisfying this relation lies to the right of the line (partially shaded). Given a point x, the value of the left side of inequality 5.2 at x is called the *value* of halfspace a at x. Element a_0 corresponds to the scale factor, and it is called the *constant* of a in the subsequent discussion.

The following data structure is used to represent CSG trees. A CSG tree is a binary tree in which nonleaf nodes[7] correspond to geometric transformations[8] and

---

[7] Unfortunately, the terms *tree* and *node* are used in the context of both bintrees and CSG trees. However, in each case their usage is qualified.

[8] The discussion assumes that the transformations have been propagated to the leaf nodes. It also assumes a bounded universe, for simplicity, in the form of the unit cube.

Boolean set operations, while leaf nodes correspond to halfspaces.[9] A node of a CSG tree is described by a record of type *csgnode* with six fields: LEFT, RIGHT, TYP, HSP, H_MIN, and H_MAX. The first two fields, LEFT and RIGHT, contain pointers to the node's left and right sons, respectively. The TYP field indicates the node's type. There are five node types: UNION, INTERSECTION, BLACK, WHITE, and HALFSPACE. Types UNION and INTERSECTION correspond to the Boolean set operations. HALF-SPACE, BLACK, and WHITE correspond to leaf nodes.

The field HSP contains an identifier for the halfspace. It is an index to a table, HS, of $d + 1$ element coefficient vectors of the different halfspaces involved in the CSG tree. The remaining two fields, H_MIN and H_MAX, are used for auxiliary data in the algorithms. They record the minimum and maximum values, respectively, of a halfspace in a given bintree block. These fields are used only in conjunction with nodes of type HALFSPACE. Note that this representation is chosen for its simplicity in describing the algorithms. In an actual implementation, leaf and nonleaf nodes could be implemented as two different record types.

Our definition of a CSG tree allows for leaf nodes that are completely BLACK or WHITE. This is required as an intermediate stage in the conversion algorithm that prunes a CSG tree to a subuniverse corresponding to a bintree block.[10] In addition, in contrast to the conventional use of CSG, we use only the Boolean set operations UNION and INTERSECTION, as the effect of the third one, MINUS, can be achieved by substituting A INTERSECTION COMPLEMENT(B) everywhere for A MINUS B and applying De Morgan's laws to propagate the COMPLEMENT operations to the leaf nodes of the tree.

The regularized complement of a halfspace is obtained by changing the signs of all the coefficients (i.e., the direction of its normal). Therefore regularization means that we consider the point sets $x \cdot a \geq 0$ and $x \cdot a > 0$ to be equivalent. Note that our universe is finite, as required by the bintree representation.

The rest of this section is organized as follows. We first examine the construction of a bintree corresponding to a given halfspace. Next, we see how to convert a CSG tree to a bintree. In both of the constructions, the resulting bintree is represented using a DF-expression. We conclude by discussing how to extend the methods to incorporate the addition of the time dimension. This is useful for solving problems such as interference detection in robotics.

5.5.1.1 ALGORITHM FOR A SINGLE HALFSPACE

The construction of a bintree corresponding to a halfspace as given by inequality 5.2 is achieved by traversing the universe in the DF-order and determining the range of

---

[9] Actually, so-called regularized versions of the set operations must be used [Requ80] to guarantee that the resulting objects correspond to our intuitive notion of solids. In such a case, the result of any set operation involving objects in d-space is always either null or has a nonzero d-dimensional measure. Regularized set operations form a Boolean algebra [Requ80] so that, for instance, De Morgan's laws hold for them. However, the qualification 'regularized' will not be repeated in what follows.

[10] Note that any CSG tree with one or more BLACK or WHITE leaf nodes is equivalent to either the whole universe or the empty set, respectively. Otherwise all the BLACK and WHITE leaf nodes are removed by using the pruning rules described in Section 5.5.1.2. The result is a CSG tree with leaf nodes of type HALFSPACE.

(i.e., the interval of values obtained by) the left side of the inequality in each subuniverse. In essence, we are intersecting the halfspace with a bintree block corresponding to a black subuniverse. Whenever the hyperplane of a halfspace, say H, passes through a subuniverse (i.e., a bintree node), say S, then we say that H is *active* in S (i.e., there exists a point in S such that $a \cdot x = 0$).

Each black node in the bintree in which the halfspace is active is decomposed into two black sons, and the intersection process is recursively applied to them. The process stops when the halfspace is not active in a bintree node or if the bintree node corresponds to a voxel. In the version of the algorithm presented here, all voxels in which the halfspace is active are labeled according to the value of $a \cdot x$ at the centroid of the voxel—that is, if $a \cdot x \geq 0$, then the voxel is labeled black; otherwise it is labeled white.

Determining whether a halfspace is active in a bintree node is facilitated by keeping track of the minimum and maximum values of $a \cdot x$ for each bintree node. Whenever the maximum is ≤ 0, the bintree node is white. Whenever the minimum is ≥ 0, the bintree node is black. Otherwise the halfspace is active, and subdivision is required. Initially for the unit cube, the minimum value of $a \cdot x$ is the constant of a plus the sum of all of the negative coefficients in a. The maximum value is the constant of a plus the sum of all the positive coefficients of a. For example, for Figure 5.11, the initial minimum value is -3 and the initial maximum value is 3.

Whenever a bintree node is subdivided, either the maximum or minimum (never both at the same time) of $a \cdot x$ for each son node changes with respect to that of the father. Let the subdivision be performed on a hyperplane (e.g., a line in two dimensions) perpendicular to the axis corresponding to coordinate i ($1 \leq i \leq d$) and let w_i be the width of the side along coordinate i of the block resulting from the subdivision. The amount of change is $\delta_i = a_i \cdot w_i$. For the left son, if $\delta_i > 0$, then δ_i is subtracted from the maximum; otherwise δ_i is subtracted from the minimum. For the right son, if $\delta_i > 0$, then the minimum is incremented by δ_i; otherwise δ_i is added to the maximum.

As an example, consider the halfspace given by $4x - 2y - 1 \geq 0$ as shown in Figure 5.11. Assume that the universe is the unit square. The maximum and minimum values 3 and -3 are attained, respectively, at $(1,0)$ and at $(0,1)$. Subdividing along the x axis yields two sons. The maximum value of $a \cdot x$ in the left son has decreased by 0.5 times the coefficient of the x coordinate (i.e., 2) to 1 and is attained at $(0.5,0)$, while the minimum value remains the same. The minimum value of $a \cdot x$ in the right son has increased by 0.5 times the coefficient of the x coordinate (i.e., 2) to -1 and is attained at $(0.5,1)$, while the maximum value remains the same.

The conversion of a halfspace to a bintree is performed by procedures HALF-SPACE_TO_BINTREE and H_TRAVERSE given below. In these and all other procedures, we shall use the following global constants: D is the dimensionality of the space, and VOXEL_LEVEL is the level of the bintree corresponding to voxels. Procedure HALF-SPACE_TO_BINTREE serves to initialize the traversal process by computing the minimum and maximum values of the halfspace in the whole universe (i.e., the d-dimensional unit cube).

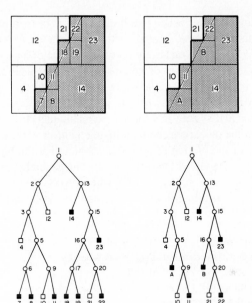

Figure 5.12   Bintree corresponding to the halfspace in Figure 5.11 (a) before collapsing and (b) after collapsing

Procedure H_TRAVERSE traverses the universe by recursively subdividing it, corresponding to the depth-first traversal order of the resulting bintree. Subdivision stops upon encountering a bintree node at level VOXEL_LEVEL, or when the block can be certified as white or black by comparing the minimum or maximum values of the halfspace to zero (note that some tolerance, say epsilon, should actually be used here instead of zero). At level VOXEL_LEVEL the value of a linear halfspace at the centroid of the corresponding geometric cell (i.e., bintree node) is obtained simply as the average of the minimum and maximum values of the halfspace at the node.

The range of the left side of inequality 5.2 is determined in each subuniverse by computing δ, and as a result of the traversal each resulting bintree node either satisfies the inequality completely or not at all (above the voxel level) or contains points satisfying it (at the voxel level). Procedure H_TRAVERSE could avoid recalculating the δ's by precomputing them and storing them in an array indexed by level. In such a case, the traversal can be implemented with only one addition operation for each node whose subuniverse intersects the hyperplane defined by inequality 5.2. Actually, in each nonleaf node, two addition operations must be performed to obtain two son nodes.

Recall that procedures HALFSPACE_TO_BINTREE and H_TRAVERSE do not construct an explicit tree representation of the bintree. Instead they output its nodes in an order corresponding to its depth-first traversal (i.e., a DF-expression representation). The sequence of nodes that is output is not minimal in the sense that collapsing may yet have to be performed (i.e., when two brother leaf nodes are black). For example, Figure 5.12a is the uncollapsed bintree with VOXEL_LEVEL=5 corresponding to the halfspace of Figure 5.11. The nodes are numbered in the order in which they are output. The result of the application of collapsing is shown in Figure 5.12b, in which nodes 7 and 8 are merged into A and nodes 18 and 19 into B.

Collapsing is necessary only when two brother nodes both become black at the voxel level. In an actual system in which these techniques are implemented, collapsing is performed on the DF-expression by utilizing a buffer with size bounded by twice the maximal depth of the bintree [Tamm84f]. Notice that the bintree blocks at level VOXEL_LEVEL are rectangles instead of squares. In general, bintree blocks at level VOXEL_LEVEL are d-dimensional cubes only when (VOXEL_LEVEL mod d) = 0. Otherwise they correspond to d-dimensional rectangles with sides the length of which takes on one of two possible values (e.g., 1/8 and 1/4 in Figure 5.12).

```
procedure HALFSPACE_TO_BINTREE(D,HS);
/* Convert the D-dimensional halfspace HS to a bintree. */
begin
  global value integer D;
  global value real array HS[0:D];
  real MIN,MAX;
  integer I;
  /* Compute the minimum and maximum values of HS in the D-dimensional unit cube */
  MIN ← MAX ← HS[0];
  for I←1 step 1 until D do
    begin
      if HS[I]>0.0 then MAX ← MAX+HS[I]
      else MIN ← MIN+HS[I];
    end;
  H_TRAVERSE(0,1.0,MIN,MAX);
end;

recursive procedure H_TRAVERSE(LEV,W,MIN,MAX);
/* Convert the portion of the halfspace represented by HS that intersects the D-
   dimensional subuniverse of volume 2⁻ᴸᴱⱽ with smallest side of width W. MIN is the
   minimum value of the halfspace in the subuniverse and MAX is its maximum value. */
begin
  value integer LEV;
  value real W,MIN,MAX;
  integer I;
  real DELTA;
  if MAX ≤ 0.0 then output('WHITE')
  else if MIN ≥ 0.0 then output('BLACK')
  else if LEV=VOXEL_LEVEL then
    if ((MAX+MIN)/2 ≥ 0.0) then output('BLACK')
    else output('WHITE')
  else
```

```
begin /* The halfspace is active in the subuniverse (i.e., it intersects it) */
  I ← LEV mod D;
  if I = 0 then W ← W/2;
  DELTA ← HS[I+1]*W; /* Note that DELTA depends only on the level */
  output('GRAY');
  H_TRAVERSE(LEV+1,W,
                  if DELTA ≤ 0.0 then MIN-DELTA
                  else MIN,
                  if DELTA > 0.0 then MAX-DELTA
                  else MAX); /* Process the left son */
  H_TRAVERSE(LEV+1,W,
                  if DELTA > 0.0 then MIN+DELTA
                  else MIN,
                  if DELTA ≤ 0.0 then MAX+DELTA
                  else MAX); /* Process the right son */
end;
end;
```

Our method of checking halfspace inequality 5.2 at each bintree block involves just one addition and one multiplication operation by keeping track of the minimum and maximum values of the left side of the inequality in the parent block. Thus there is no need to check the value of the inequality separately at each of the 2^d vertices of each of the bintree blocks. In fact, the multiplication operation is not necessary if we precompute δ and store it in a table indexed by level.

Exercises

5.47. The determination of the value of halfspace inequality 5.2 at each bintree block is important and should be executed efficiently. Lee and Requicha [Lee82c] make use of a technique that checks the center of each bintree block against two offset halfspaces and hence requires two halfspace evaluations per block. The offset halfspaces are determined so that if the center of a block of this size is contained within one of these halfspaces, the whole block either satisfies the halfspace inequality or fails it. Explain why it works.

5.48. Meagher [Meag82b] was motivated by a desire to eliminate multiplication operations. He evaluates halfspaces by checking the value of inequality 5.2 at two test vertices of a block. This is analogous to our use of the minimum and maximum of the left side of the inequality 5.2 in the parent block. Values at all vertices are obtained from those of the father node by averaging (in the linear case) the value of the left side of the inequality 5.2 at two father vertices for each son vertex. For each son node, 2^d averaging operations are performed. This is clearly more efficient than recomputing the inequality at each of the 2^d vertices. Explain why it works in the case of linear halfspaces.

5.49. How would you apply the technique described for halfspace evaluation in a bintree to octrees?

5.50. Compare the efficiency of halfspace evaluation in an octree as described in Exercise 5.49 with that in a bintree as described in the text.

5.5.1.2 ALGORITHM FOR A CSG TREE

A CSG tree is evaluated, that is, converted, to a bintree by traversing the universe in depth-first order and evaluating each successive subuniverse, S, against the CSG tree. We say that a nonleaf node of a CSG tree with only halfspaces as its leaf nodes is *active* in S if both of its sons are active in S. Leaf nodes (halfspaces) are evaluated using the method described above, and their results are combined by *pruning* the CSG tree to the subuniverse. Pruning means that only that part of the CSG tree that is active within the subuniverse is retained [Wood80, Wood82b, Tilo81, Tilo84]. Once pruning has reduced the CSG tree to a leaf node (i.e., a halfspace), the conversion procedure becomes identical to that described in the previous section for converting a halfspace to a bintree.

An alternative way to conceptualize the conversion process is to note that it is equivalent to intersecting the CSG tree with a bintree corresponding to a black universe. Each node in the bintree, say B, in which the CSG tree is active is decomposed into two black sons, and they, in turn, are intersected with only that part of the CSG tree that is active in B. This process stops when the CSG tree is not active in a bintree node or if the bintree node corresponds to a voxel.

All voxels in which a CSG tree is active are labeled by procedure CLASSIFY_- VOXEL. At its simplest, it treats all such voxels as black (or white). At its most complex, CLASSIFY_VOXEL corresponds to Tilove's NULL-object detection algorithm applied to the active CSG subtree at the voxel [Tilo84]. A compromise that is often good, and is used in the algorithm below, is to have CLASSIFY_VOXEL evaluate the CSG tree at the center of the voxel to obtain a bintree that corresponds to the true object at a certain spatial resolution. Note that the value of each linear halfspace at the center of the voxel is the average of the H_MIN and H_MAX fields of the halfspace node. In such a case, CLASSIFY_VOXEL becomes a version of the pruning algorithm. Other implementors might prefer yet different choices for CLASSIFY_VOXEL, such as one applying Monte Carlo methods.

The conversion of a CSG tree to a bintree is performed by procedures CSG_TO_- BINTREE, INIT_HALFSPACES, CSG_TRAVERSE, PRUNE, and HSP_EVAL, which are given below. They make use of BLACK_CSG_NODE and WHITE_CSG_NODE, constants whose values are pointers to CSG tree nodes of type BLACK and WHITE, respectively. Procedure CSG_TO_BINTREE serves to initialize the traversal process. First, it invokes procedure INIT_HALFSPACES to traverse the CSG tree to compute the minimum and maximum values of each halfspace in the whole universe (i.e., the unit cube). These values are stored in the H_MIN and H_MAX fields of the CSG tree node corresponding to each halfspace. Next it calls on CSG_TRAVERSE to perform the actual conversion.

Procedure CSG_TRAVERSE traverses the universe by recursively subdividing it, corresponding to the depth-first traversal order of the resulting bintree. At each subdivision step, procedure PRUNE is called to attempt to reduce the size of the CSG tree to be evaluated in the bintree block. PRUNE traverses the CSG tree in depth-first order and removes inactive CSG nodes with the aid of HSP_EVAL, which determines if a halfspace is active within a given bintree block. Assuming that T is a CSG node, PRUNE applies the following four rules to the CSG tree:

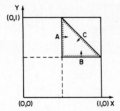

Figure 5.13   Sample triangle image

1. BLACK UNION T = BLACK.
2. WHITE UNION T = T.
3. BLACK INTERSECTION T = T.
4. WHITE INTERSECTION T = WHITE.

As an example, consider the triangle of Figure 5.13 whose CSG tree is given in Figure 5.14. Figure 5.15a is the corresponding bintree, with VOXEL_LEVEL = 6. The nodes are numbered in the order in which they are output. Initially the entire CSG tree (i.e., Figure 5.14) is assumed to be active in the whole universe (i.e., the unit square). Node 1 of the bintree is output as a gray node, and we process its left son next.

First, we attempt to prune the CSG tree with respect to the left half of the universe. Since halfspace A is inactive here (i.e., it is WHITE), we can apply pruning rule 4, and there is no need to process the remainder of the CSG tree in Figure 5.14. Node 2 of the bintree is output as a white node, and we process the right son of node 1 next.

Pruning the CSG tree results in halfspace A's being inactive again but this time it is BLACK. Since both halfspaces B and C are active here, pruning rule 3 leaves us with the CSG tree given by Figure 5.16. We now output node 3 of the bintree as a gray node, and we process its left son next. Pruning the CSG tree results in halfspace B's being inactive (i.e., it is WHITE). Pruning rule 4 means that there is no need to process further the CSG tree of Figure 5.16. Node 4 of the bintree is output as a white node, and we process the right son of node 3 next. This time pruning the CSG tree results in halfspace B's being inactive again but now it is BLACK. Pruning rule 3 leaves us with just halfspace C. Node 5 of the bintree is output as a gray node, and the conversion process is applied to its two sons next.

Figure 5.14   CSG tree corresponding to Figure 5.13

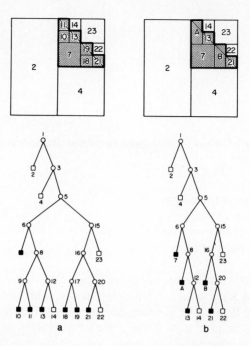

Figure 5.15   Bintree corresponding to the triangle in Figure
5.13 (a) before collapsing and (b) after collapsing

Figure 5.16   Result of pruning the CSG tree of Figure 5.14
in the right half of the root of its bintree

The remainder of the conversion is equivalent to that described in the previous
section for the conversion of a halfspace, as the CSG tree has been reduced to one halfspace. The result is given in Figure 5.15a. Once again we have a DF-expression
representation of the bintree. To get the minimal DF-expression, we must perform collapsing (i.e., merge identically colored leaf nodes that are brothers). The result of the
application of collapsing is shown in Figure 5.15b in which nodes 10 and 11 are
merged into A and nodes 18 and 19 into B.

```
procedure CSG_TO_BINTREE(P,N,HS);
/* Convert the D-dimensional CSG tree P to a bintree. HS contains N halfspaces. */
begin
  value pointer csgnode P;
```

```
  global value integer N;
  global value integer D;
  global value real array HS[1:N,0:D];
  INIT_HALFSPACES(P);
  CSG_TRAVERSE(P,0,1.0);
end;
```

recursive procedure INIT_HALFSPACES(P);
/* Compute the minimum and maximum values of each of the halfspaces in the CSG tree P
   of the D-dimensional unit universe. */
```
begin
  value pointer csgnode P;
  integer I,J;
  if TYP(P)='HALFSPACE' then
    begin
      I ← HSP(P);
      H_MIN(P) ← H_MAX(P) ← HS[I,0];
      for J←1 step 1 until D do
        begin
          if HS[I,J]>0.0 then H_MAX(P) ← H_MAX(P)+HS[I,J]
          else H_MIN(P) ← H_MIN(P)+HS[I,J];
        end;
    end
  else
    begin
      INIT_HALFSPACES(LEFT(P));
      INIT_HALFSPACES(RIGHT(P));
    end;
end;
```

recursive procedure CSG_TRAVERSE(P,LEV,W);
/* Convert the portion of the CSG tree P that overlaps the D-dimensional subuniverse of
   volume 2^{-LEV} with smallest side of width W. The bintree is constructed by evaluating
   the CSG tree in the subuniverse. The evaluation process consists of pruning the nodes
   of the CSG tree that are outside the subuniverse. A new copy of the relevant part of the
   CSG tree is created as each level is descended in the bintree. This storage is reclaimed
   once a subuniverse at a given level has been processed. */
```
begin
  value pointer csgnode P;
  value integer LEV;
  value real W;
  pointer csgnode FS; /* Pointer to stack of free nodes */
  if TYP(P)='BLACK' or TYP(P)='WHITE' then output(TYP(P))
  else if LEV=VOXEL_LEVEL then output(TYP(CLASSIFY_VOXEL(P)))
  else /* Subdivide and prune the CSG trees */
    begin
      FS ← first_free(csgnode); /* Save pointer to free storage stack */
      output('GRAY');
```

```
pointer csgnode Q;
Q ← create_and_copy(P);
J ← HSP(P);
I ← LEV mod D;
DELTA ← HS[J,I+1]*W;
if DIR='LEFT' then
   begin
      if DELTA ≤ 0.0 then H_MIN(Q) ← H_MIN(Q)-DELTA
      else H_MAX(Q) ← H_MAX(Q)-DELTA;
   end
else
   begin
      if DELTA>0.0 then H_MIN(Q) ← H_MIN(Q)+DELTA
      else H_MAX(Q) ← H_MAX(Q)+DELTA;
   end;
   if H_MIN(Q) ≥ 0.0 then return(BLACK_CSG_NODE)
   else if H_MAX(Q) ≤ 0.0 then return(WHITE_CSG_NODE)
   else return(Q); /* The halfspace intersects the subuniverse */
end;
```

At this point, let us analyze the execution time of procedure CSG_TO_BINTREE. A quick perusal of its code reveals that the amount of work performed in the conversion is proportional to the sum of the sizes of the CSG trees active at the bintree nodes (i.e., blocks) that are evaluated. This number can be quite large even though procedure CSG_TRAVERSE attempts to prune the CSG tree each time it descends to a deeper level in the tree. The fact that the unpruned part of the CSG tree is copied at each level of descent does not affect the time complexity, but some of the copying can be avoided by more careful programming (see Exercise 5.54). In a typical case, however, as we descend in the bintree, many of the CSG tree nodes are no longer active, thereby reducing the number of CSG nodes that must be visited.

We are not interested in the absolute worst-case value of the complexity. Instead we focus on the 'practical' efficiency of these algorithms. Very poor cases can be attained by constructing a complicated CSG tree that evaluates to the NULL object in such a way that the whole CSG tree is active in a large number of nodes. For example, consider the intersection of a halfspace with its complement. In fact, a pruned CSG tree may be active in a bintree block even though the CSG tree defines a NULL object in the region corresponding to the block. This can be seen by considering the CSG tree given in Figure 5.17a. It consists of the two circles L1 and R, and the halfspaces A and B, as shown in Figure 5.17b. The CSG tree of Figure 5.17a is active in the bintree block represented by the broken square in Figure 5.17b even though the object defined by it does not extend so far.

First, let us examine the number of halfspaces active at each node of voxel size in a bintree of a polyhedron. This discussion is heuristic in that we speak of voxels as if they were infinitely small. At each vertex of the polyhedron, at least three halfspaces are active. Elsewhere at each edge of the polyhedron, exactly two halfspaces

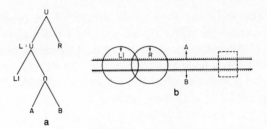

Figure 5.17   (a) A CSG tree and (b) its corresponding object

are active. Elsewhere at each face, only one halfspace is active. We can estimate the total number of active halfspaces by counting the number of voxels that intersect the edges, vertices, and faces of the polyhedron.

The total number of voxels intersecting the faces is proportional to the surface area [Meag80] (see Theorem 1.2 in Section 1.5), while the total number of voxels that intersect the edges is proportional to the sum of the edge lengths at the given resolution [Hunt78, Hunt79a] (see Theorem 1.1 in Section 1.5). The number of voxels containing vertices is always bounded by the number of vertices irrespective of the resolution (i.e., level of decomposition). Assuming a resolution of n, the number of voxels with more than one active halfspace grows only linearly with 2^n, while the total number of voxels grows with 2^{2n}. Thus the average number of halfspaces active in a node of voxel size approaches one asymptotically in a CSG tree that corresponds to a polyhedron. A similar result will hold for polyhedron-like objects of arbitrary dimension.

It should be clear that the amount of work necessary in performing the conversion is at least proportional to the number of nodes in the bintree. Samet and Tamminen [Same90c] show that there exists a class of CSG trees for which the complexity of evaluation is asymptotically of the same order as the number of nodes in the bintree of the corresponding object. Such CSG trees are said to be 'well behaved,' and it is irrelevant whether they are modeled with linear or nonlinear halfspaces. This characterization is determined solely by the way the objects defined by the pair of brother subtrees of the CSG tree intersect each other.

In a well-behaved CSG tree the intersections are not allowed to be 'tangential.' In two dimensions, this means that the boundaries of the objects corresponding to brother subtrees intersect at only a finite number of points. In three dimensions, for polyhedra, the boundaries should not coincide but are permitted to intersect along one-dimensional edges. Similarly, in the general case, for d dimensions, the permitted intersection must be at most $(d-2)$-dimensional (see [Same90c] for more details).

The desired order of complexity is obtained by generalizing Hunter's and Meagher's image complexity results for polygons and polyhedra to d dimensions. In particular, the complexity is $O(2^{n \cdot (d-1)})$ bintree nodes for bintrees of resolution n. This bound is attainable in a manner that does not depend on the number of nodes in the CSG tree. The following theorem (a variant of its proof can be found in [Same90c]) summarizes the above discussion. To avoid 'uninteresting' objects, we limit the objects to those that are *nondegenerate*. This means that the objects are not representable exactly by a finite bintree. Formally, for a given d-dimensional object s, there exists a value A such that when B is the number of nodes in the bintree of s at resolution k, then $B/2^{(d-1)\cdot k} > A$ for all values of k.

> **Theorem 5.1** Let T be a well-behaved CSG tree defining a nondegenerate d-dimensional object. The proportion of bintree nodes in which more than one CSG tree node is active approaches zero asymptotically as the resolution increases. □

Theorem 5.1 leads to the following conclusions about the performance of the above algorithms for the conversion of CSG trees to bintrees when the CSG trees are well-behaved.

1. The 'practical' complexity of CSG tree evaluation is $O(2^{n\cdot(d-1)})$ as resolution n is increased.
2. The average number of active CSG tree nodes in a bintree block approaches one asymptotically as the resolution is increased.
3. The computational complexity of converting a CSG tree approximation of a given object to a bintree is asymptotically independent of the number of halfspaces used in the approximation.

Conclusion 3 means that the linear approximation of curved halfspaces can be computationally practical even though it leads to a great increase in the size of the CSG tree. Of course, the above results are asymptotical and thus are directly relevant only when the number of halfspaces is not large in comparison to the resolution.

The analysis of the execution time of CSG to bintree conversion was based on the definition of well behaved, which eliminated certain objects. If such objects are expected (beside the extensions reported below), then more complicated CSG tree redundancy checking algorithms (e.g., the NULL-object detection algorithms of Tilove [Tilo84]) should be used once the pruned tree has reached a certain (small) size. Note, however, that if we apply as CLASSIFY_VOXEL a CSG evaluation at the center of the voxel, no incorrect 'false positive' bintree nodes result (i.e., nodes that should be completely white but are classified as black).

Exercises
5.51. An alternative approach to the construction of the bintree is to convert the individual halfspaces in sequence and then to perform the Boolean set operations on the results. What is the drawback of this approach?
5.52. Closer examination of procedures CSG_TRAVERSE, PRUNE, and HSP_EVAL reveals that there is much copying of CSG nodes. In particular, each time that CSG_TRAVERSE is invoked to

evaluate a CSG tree in a bintree block, a copy is made of the pruned CSG tree. Why is the copying necessary?

5.53. At worst, how many copies of the CSG tree are created before we can start to release and reclaim storage? When does this situation arise?

5.54. Devise an alternative method of converting a CSG tree to a bintree that does not make repeated copies of the CSG tree. The idea is to use an array of lists (actually stacks) to keep track of the minimum and maximum values of all active halfspaces for each level of the bintree.

5.55. What is the worst case, storage-wise, for the implementation described in Exercise 5.54?

5.56. Compare the worst-case storage requirements of the algorithm described in the text and the implementation described in Exercise 5.54.

5.57. Prove Theorem 5.1.

5.58. The implementation of procedure CSG_TO_BINTREE and the procedures invoked by it does not handle the case that both a halfspace and its complement are leaf nodes of the CSG tree. This case is actually quite common when a CSG tree is composed of a union of convex components (e.g., a pair of adjacent triangles that have a common side). Modify the CSG evaluation in procedure PRUNE to deal with this situation.

5.5.1.3 INCORPORATION OF THE TIME DIMENSION [11]

Time and motion are important elements of advanced solid modeling. In particular, given a moving object we may wish to determine whether it intersects a stationary object (*static interference detection*) or another moving object (*dynamic interference detection*). Although it appears that the time dimension can be added to CSG trees in a conceptually simple fashion, rather little attention has been focused on CSG trees in a dynamic situation. Perhaps this is due to the difficulty of evaluation in the now four-dimensional space. Also the dimensional units of the extra dimension are different (i.e., time instead of distance).

One possible strategy is first to perform boundary evaluation; next to derive the boundary model of the $d+1$-dimensional (space, time)-objects; and finally to check these for intersection. Also standard NULL-object detection algorithms that directly check for an empty boundary of the intersection object could possibly be extended to the $d+1$-dimensional space [Came84]. Note that spatial subdivision is often used to increase the efficiency of such NULL-object detection algorithms.

An alternative solution that is frequently adopted is to transform the object into another representation—one in which the computation is simpler. In this section we show how the time dimension is added to a CSG representation so that motion can be analyzed using the conversion algorithm of the previous section. This approach is different from that of Meagher [Meag82b] and Weng and Ahuja [Weng87]. In particular, Meagher computes the volume swept by an object's (modeled as an octree) motion along a curve specified by its chain code, whereas Weng and Ahuja [Weng87] are concerned with the translation and rotation of objects represented by octrees.

---

[11] This section describes an application of CSG evaluation based on work by Samet and Tamminen [Same85g, Same90c]. It can be skipped on an initial reading.

Let T be a solid model described by a CSG tree and assume that it is defined in some model-specific coordinate system. We describe the motion of T in some common world-coordinate system by a time-varying geometric transformation matrix $A(t)$. Each value of $A(t)$ is a matrix defining a rigid motion from the local coordinates of T to its position and orientation in world coordinates at time t. Note that if our world coordinate system is the unit cube, then we may also have to include a scaling in $A(t)$. We call $A(t)$ the *trajectory* of T. Let $A(t)$ be piecewise linear, meaning that it can be broken down into a series of segments defined by time points $(t_0, t_1, \cdots)$ so that $A_{i+1} = A_i B_i$, where B_i is a transformation matrix corresponding to a translation describing the motion during that time segment. In the following, the motion accomplished in one time segment is discussed in a more concrete setting.

Translating a halfspace, say given by inequality 5.2, along a vector v ($v_0 = 0$) gives rise to the translated halfspace

$$\sum_{i=0}^{d} a_i \cdot x_i - \sum_{i=0}^{d} a_i \cdot v_i \geq 0 . \tag{5.3}$$

If point x satisfies inequality 5.2, then the transformed (translated) point $x+v$ satisfies inequality 5.3. For example, translating the halfspace $4x - 2y - 1 \geq 0$ given in Figure 5.11 by the vector $(0.5, 0.5)$ yields the halfspace $4x - 2y - 2 \geq 0$. To be dimensionally consistent with the d-dimensional unit cube, this discussion always assumes a unit time interval. Motion in a unit time interval, and at a fixed speed defined by vector s with $s_0 = 0$, is described by a vector v such that for all i, $v_i = s_i \cdot t$. Thus, using v to translate halfspace given by inequality 5.2 we find that at each instant, say t, it corresponds to the halfspace given by inequality 5.4. Letting t vary, we obtain a linear halfspace with an additional variable t

$$\sum_{i=0}^{d} a_i \cdot x_i - (\sum_{i=0}^{d} a_i \cdot s_i) \cdot t \geq 0 . \tag{5.4}$$

When we have a CSG tree in motion, transformation 5.4 can be applied to each halfspace separately and the tree of Boolean set operations applied to the resulting $(d+1)$-dimensional halfspaces to define a set of points in (location,time)-space satisfying the CSG tree.

For dynamic interference detection, we must determine whether the intersection of two (location,time) objects is empty. For static interference detection, we must check whether two stationary objects intersect or whether a moving object intersects a stationary one. The intersection of two different (location,time) CSG trees (each derived from a separate motion but with a common 'time axis') is obtained by attaching them as sons to a newly created CSG node of type INTERSECTION. The actual evaluation of the intersection can be performed by applying the bintree conversion algorithm of Section 5.5.1.2 in the $(d+1)$-dimensional space, with time included.

For static interference detection, there is no need to add time as an extra dimension if we can otherwise solve for the swept area of the moving object. Note also that in the case of dynamic interference detection, there is often little motivation for storing the entire resulting tree. Instead a variable can be included in the tree traversal algorithm to indicate the minimal t value of a black node encountered so far in the traversal. Any subtree whose minimum value of t is greater than this value need not be inspected.

Usually primary interest is not in motion along a straight vector but in more complicated trajectories. Assume that such trajectories can be approximated by a sequence of segments, each with motion corresponding to a linear translation at a fixed speed. For example, suppose that we wish to determine whether two motions, defined by piecewise linear trajectories A_{1i} and A_{2i} of objects T_1 and T_2, respectively, intersect in the unit time interval. Let the time intervals defining the n_1 and n_2 linear pieces of the trajectories be $(t_{10}, t_{11}, \cdots)$ and $(t_{20}, t_{21}, \cdots)$, respectively. Now, during the time interval $(0, \min(t_{10}, t_{20}))$ both motions are along a straight line, and their intersection can be determined as discussed—by evaluating the CSG tree resulting from the addition of a node of type INTERSECTION with T_1 and T_2 as sons. This same procedure is applied to the remaining intervals (a maximum of $n_1 + n_2 - 1$ intervals), each preceded by an application of the appropriate transformations A_{ij} to the halfspaces of T_1 and T_2.

If a CSG tree contains nonlinear halfspaces, or the motion itself cannot be described as a series of translations, then the linear methods described are inapplicable. As an example, A_{i+1} is derived from A_i by multiplying it by, say, a rotation matrix with the rotation angle depending on t. In this case, the trajectory is no longer a (piecewise) linear matrix function of t. Nevertheless, we can still use methods similar to the ones described. In particular, each bintree node corresponds to a $(d+1)$-dimensional *interval* such that

$$x_0 \leq x < x_1$$
$$y_0 \leq y < y_1$$
$$\vdots$$
$$t_0 \leq t < t_1.$$

Interval arithmetic is a method of evaluating functions $f(x, y, \cdots)$ in cases where the arguments are not exact values but intervals corresponding to the range of the true value. The result of the interval function corresponding to function f is also an interval. In other words, it is a range of values covering any value that f can take when it is applied to values in the argument intervals. It should be clear that interval arithmetic is appropriate for the CSG tree to bintree conversion process since for an arbitrary function, the value of the corresponding interval function covers the function's possible values in the bintree node. If zero does not belong to this range, the bintree block need not be subdivided.

For example, let us apply the above to determine the (location,time) bintree of a linear halfspace a subjected to general motion defined by the matrix function $A(t)$. Denoting intervals by capital letters, the interval function that must be evaluated at each node of the bintree is $F(X,T) = (A^{-1}(T)a) \cdot X$ where X is an interval in d-dimensional space and T is a time interval. Remember that at each time instant t, $A(t)$ is a linear transformation and the image of a halfspace, say a, is obtained by multiplying a by the inverse of $A(t)$. When $A(t)$ contains a rotation, the interval function will be a linear composition of sine and cosine functions with respect to T. For instance, in the two-dimensional case of motion around the origin with angular speed α the function $A^{-1}(T)$ would be given by the matrix:

$$\begin{bmatrix} \cos(\alpha \cdot T) & \sin(\alpha \cdot T) & 0 \\ -\sin(\alpha \cdot T) & \cos(\alpha \cdot T) & 0 \\ 0 & 0 & 1 \end{bmatrix}.$$

In any subinterval of T, where each component of the composite function is monotonic, interval arithmetic can be applied in such a way that tight bounds are provided for the resulting interval.

Interval arithmetic is easy to incorporate in the CSG tree to bintree conversion algorithm described since the main change is to recast procedure HSP_EVAL in terms of interval evaluations. Procedure INTERVAL_HSP_EVAL, given below, achieves this, and a call to it can be substituted for the call to procedure HSP_EVAL in procedure PRUNE of Section 5.5.1.2. Notice the use of INTERVAL_EVALUATE to determine the range of the function corresponding to the nonlinear halfspace. Its value is a pointer to a record of type *interval* with two fields H_MIN and H_MAX corresponding to an interval covering the function values in the node. Nevertheless, if procedure HSP_EVAL is replaced by INTERVAL_HSP_EVAL, CLASSIFY_VOXEL still has to classify each voxel correctly. CLASSIFY_VOXEL would ordinarily be implemented by computing the value of the active halfspaces at the centroid of the voxel by ordinary arithmetic.

```
pointer csgnode procedure INTERVAL_HSP_EVAL(P,LEV,W,DIR);
/* Use interval arithmetic to determine if the D-dimensional subuniverse of volume 2^-LEV
   intersects nonlinear halfspace P or is BLACK or WHITE. W is its smallest side. The
   subuniverse is the DIR subtree of its father. */
begin
  value pointer csgnode P; /* A leaf of the CSG tree */
  value integer LEV;
  value real W;
  value direction DIR;
  interval I;
  I ← INTERVAL_EVALUATE(P,LEV,W,DIR);
  return(if H_MAX(I)≤0.0 then WHITE_CSG_NODE
         else if H_MIN(I)≥0.0 then BLACK_CSG_NODE
         else 'HALFSPACE');
end;
```

Interval arithmetic has also been applied to the somewhat similar task of evaluating curved surfaces by recursive subdivision [Alan84a, Mudu84]. Nevertheless, this technique should be used with caution. In particular, interval arithmetic does not necessarily yield the minimal range covering the values of the function given the domains of the arguments; instead it may be a wider interval guaranteed to cover the values of the function. This estimate may sometimes be very poor. Clearly the poorer the substitute for the true range of function values, the more unnecessary subdivision must be performed in the bintree conversion. This problem can usually be overcome by use of suitable transformations on functions. Alander et al. [Alan84b] have built a practical system and shown that function transformations greatly enhance and simplify interval arithmetic algorithms for curved surfaces.

A conversion algorithm based on interval arithmetic evaluates an interval function once for each active halfspace at each node. Furthermore, an ordinary function evaluation has to be performed by CLASSIFY_VOXEL for each active halfspace at each voxel. Thus the performance of the conversion algorithm depends on the precision with which interval arithmetic estimates the intervals of halfspace values within nodes. Note that whenever INTERVAL_EVALUATE returns an interval containing 0, when the true interval does not contain 0, then superfluous subdivision will result.

Implementation experience has shown interval arithmetic extensions to be from 5 to 15 times slower than ordinary arithmetic [Cole82, Clem83]. The tightness of the range given by interval arithmetic depends completely on the characteristics of the function within the argument range [Moor79]. The more that is known about the function, the better are the estimates that can be obtained. For instance, Mudur and Koparkar [Mudu84] decompose functions into monotonic parts to enable use of the tighter intervals applicable in such a case.

A general treatment of the characteristics of interval arithmetic is outside the scope of this book. However, from the standpoint of performance, it is generally advisable to consider interval arithmetic more as a conceptual model than as an automatic computational device. Thus efficient custom-tailored methods for obtaining precise range estimates should be developed for each class of halfspaces being used. In particular, maximum utilization should be made of the knowledge of the characteristics of a halfspace within a bintree node. For example, this has been done for quadratic halfspaces [Kois88]. That work reveals that standard techniques for enhancing the efficiency of interval arithmetic, as presented by Ratschek and Rokne [Rats84], lead to computational methods that are identical to the specialized ones described here.

Exercises

5.59. Often time merely serves as an auxiliary variable for describing motion. Show that the process of determining the swept area for static interference detection can be implemented by a projection parallel to the t-axis.

5.60. Can you perform a projection directly in the CSG representation?

5.61. Projection of an object represented by a CSG tree can be implemented by a two-step process. First, evaluate the CSG tree by generating its corresponding bintree and then project it. If the object is d dimensional and time is involved, first generate the $(d+1)$-dimensional bintree and then project it to d dimensions to obtain an evaluation of the projected CSG tree as a d-dimensional bintree. Projection consists of eliminating one coordinate and keeping track of all occupied locations in the resulting d-dimensional space. Give an implementation of this algorithm.

5.62. In general, bintrees of objects in motion tend to become very large when represented in the (location,time)-space. Often when analyzing motion, we are interested only in checking whether an interference exists. Modify the CSG tree conversion algorithm so that it searches only for the first black leaf and outputs a tree where all the rest of the universe is white.

5.5.2 PM-CSG Trees

In the previous section, an algorithm was described to convert a CSG description to a bintree, a variant of the region octree. Unfortunately the traditional region octree is very wasteful of space when the object does not have orthogonal boundaries parallel to the axes of subdivision. Moreover, for such objects, the process of constructing a traditional region octree often results in the loss of some information that may be necessary for some operations. For example, the true surface normal is useful for display purposes, yet it cannot be recovered from the region octree. Of course, this is really a direct result of the fact that the region octree is an approximation. Such shortcomings can be overcome by using a PM octree that provides an exact representation when the objects have planar faces.

Wyvill and Kunii [Wyvi85] are concerned with performing solid modeling operations on objects defined by a CSG tree. They define a variant of the PM octree that we term a *PM-CSG tree*. In essence, they vary the definition of a leaf node so that it refers to a primitive object instead of a vertex, edge, or face as in the case of the PM octree. In particular, the decomposition criterion is such that only one primitive object is allowed to occupy each cell. Furthermore the primitives can be arbitrary; they are not restricted to halfspaces. In general, this decomposition criterion would not be realizable if we were to use a pure CSG representation (see Exercise 5.63).

Wyvill and Kunii do not use the full complement of CSG operations. Instead they use a subset consisting of union and subtraction of sets (i.e., set difference). The set intersection operation is not allowed. Moreover, the set union operation is not general in that it requires that the two operand sets be disjoint. Thus it is more like a set addition operation. This means that no two objects can occupy the same space. If such a situation occurs, it is flagged as an error. An alternative physical analogy is that the operations of set addition and subtraction correspond to gluing and cutting, respectively.

Prior to presenting the PM-CSG tree, we give a more precise description of the subset of CSG in use. It is a variant of the representation of Wyvill and Kunii, termed a *DAG-CSG tree*. The DAG-CSG tree models objects by using combinations of previously defined objects or primitive objects (e.g., cylinders, blocks). The DAG-CSG tree for an object is a binary tree consisting of two types of nodes. The binary set operations (e.g., set addition or set subtraction) comprise the nonleaf nodes. Leaf nodes correspond to objects of which there are two types: primitive and non-primitive.

If the leaf node is a primitive object, the node contains a pointer to a procedure corresponding to the object's functional definition. If the leaf node is a nonprimitive object, then the node contains a pointer to the object's DAG-CSG tree. This is the rationale for using the modifier 'DAG' in the name of the data structure (i.e., directed acyclic graph). To permit the same object descriptions to be used for different instances of the object (primitive and non-primitive), each occurrence of the object in the DAG-CSG tree contains an additional descriptor for the instance. This descriptor includes the following information:

1. A flag that indicates whether the object is being added or subtracted (PLUS or MINUS).
2. Matrices describing the relative spatial location and shape of the instance of this object that is being referred to by this node.

The second part of the descriptor is in the form of a transformation matrix that describes translation, rotation, and scaling. The magnification factors need not be the same for all three directions. This permits one primitive to correspond to parallelepipeds as well as cubes. Similarly the primitive for ellipsoids can also be used to model spheres. Actually each descriptor contains two matrices. The first matrix is used to define the object. The object is properly instantiated by traversing its DAG-CSG tree and performing matrix multiplication operations with respect to an initial position. The second matrix contains an inverse transformation that facilitates detecting if an object occupies a designated portion of the space in which it has been instantiated. This is used in the construction of the object's PM-CSG tree.

Making the PM-CSG tree decomposition criteria compatible with the DAG-CSG tree definition results in the following five types of leaf nodes:

1. A *full* node is completely contained within a single primitive object.
2. An *empty* node is not contained in any of the primitive objects.
3. A *positive boundary* node contains part of one of the primitive objects. The remaining part is empty (i.e., it is not contained in any other primitive object).
4. A *negative boundary* node contains a boundary between a primitive object, say O_1, and another primitive object, say O_2, such that O_1 is being subtracted from O_2. The node contains no other objects or boundaries. Thus the part attributed to O_2 is really empty.
5. A *nasty* node is a node at the lowest level of resolution such that no further decomposition is possible. However, such a node may be occupied by more than one primitive object (aside from a node of type negative boundary).

In many applications (e.g., ray tracing—see Section 7.2 of [Same90b]), when the resolution is sufficiently high, the volume occupied by the nasty cells is so small that it can be safely ignored. As an example, consider the two-dimensional object of

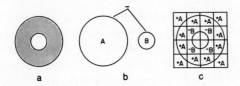

Figure 5.18 *(a) A two-dimensional object, (b) its DAG-CSG tree, and (c) its PM-CSG tree*

Figure 5.18a whose DAG-CSG tree and PM-CSG tree are given in Figures 5.18b and 5.18c, respectively. From the DAG-CSG tree we see that the object is defined by subtracting the smaller circle B from the larger circle A (technically A and B are cylinders). In this example, the leaf nodes of the PM-CSG tree are either positive or negative boundary nodes and are labeled +A or −B, respectively.

Constructing a PM-CSG tree is straightforward but not very easy. In essence, a PM-CSG tree is built for each instance of a primitive object in the DAG-CSG tree. The actual construction proceeds in the following manner. Traverse the DAG-CSG tree and look for primitive instances. Each primitive instance is converted to the appropriate PM-CSG tree with one node, and then subsequent operations, such as addition and subtraction, are performed. During these operations, the leaf nodes in the PM-CSG trees may need to be subdivided. In particular, subdivision must be performed whenever neither node of a pair of corresponding nodes in the two operand PM-CSG trees is full or empty.

The subdivision process makes use of the inverse transformation matrix associated with each object. These matrices enable the projection of the boundaries of each octant back to the original instance of the primitive to determine if the octant corresponds to a full, empty, or boundary node. Node types are also adjusted when PM-CSG tree nodes of equal size are processed by the addition and subtraction processes. Note that since the DAG-CSG tree is not a pure tree, the transformations for each primitive object are obtained in a cumulative manner as the DAG-CSG tree is traversed.

Initially each occurrence of a primitive object in the PM-CSG tree is flagged as being either a result of subtraction (from a full node) or the addition (to an empty node). This flag is used only when the PM-CSG tree consists of just one node. Once other operations have been performed on it, the role of the flag is played by the positive boundary and negative boundary node types.

As an example of the PM-CSG tree construction process, consider the two-dimensional object of Figure 5.18a and its DAG-CSG tree given in Figure 5.18b. We start by building PM-CSG trees for circles A and B (see Figure 5.19). At this point, each tree consists of one node of type boundary. As neither of the nodes is empty or full, they must be subdivided (see Figure 5.20). The result is that the PM-CSG trees of both A and B consist of four nodes, each of which is of type boundary. Again, since none of the nodes is empty or full, applying the subtraction algorithm to

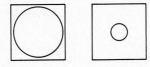

Figure 5.19   First step in the construction of the PM-CSG tree for Figure 5.18

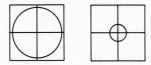

Figure 5.20   Second stage in the construction of the PM-CSG tree for Figure 5.18

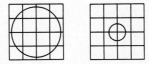

Figure 5.21   Third stage in the construction of the PM-CSG tree for Figure 5.18

the four pairs of corresponding nodes will force all of them to be subdivided (see Figure 5.21).

Now, let us process the four sons of the NW quadrant of the two PM-CSG trees in Figure 5.21. Let $A_{NW,i}$ and $B_{NW,i}$ denote the sons of the NW quadrants of the PM-CSG trees in Figure 5.21. Since $A_{NW,NW}$ is a boundary node and $B_{NW,NW}$ is an empty node, the result of subtraction in this case is a positive boundary node. We get the same result for $A_{NW,NE}$ and $B_{NW,NE}$ and for $A_{NW,SW}$ and $B_{NW,SW}$. On the other hand, since $A_{NW,SE}$ is a full node and $B_{NW,SE}$ is a boundary node, the result of subtraction in this case is a negative boundary node. Repeating this process for the remaining quadrants of A and B yields the PM-CSG tree given in Figure 5.18c, in which the positive and negative boundary nodes are labeled +A and −B, respectively.

The presence of nasty cells at the maximum level of resolution needs some special handling. The problem is that it may correspond to a physically unrealizable situation. There are two easy cases in which such situations can arise. First, a set subtraction operation can lead to the creation of isolated points, lines, and planes of zero measure. Second, a set addition operation on operands with faces that coincide where they meet can result in the creation of nasty cells at every point on the surface. Such situations arise in a natural manner in the course of the application of the PM-CSG tree creation algorithm. They can be eliminated by the application of a process known as *regularization* [Tilo84].

The storage requirements of the PM-CSG tree are proportional to the sum of lengths of the edges where an edge is defined as a line of intersection between the bounding surfaces of two primitive objects [Wyvi85]. This is in contrast to the region octree for which the storage requirement is proportional to the total surface area of all the primitive objects. Nevertheless, the storage requirements of the PM-CSG tree can still be quite large, as they depend on the resolution. In particular, the high resolution is caused by the need for precision in solid modeling applications and the likelihood of occurrence of nasty cells.

Wyvill and Kunii propose two methods to reduce the storage requirements of the PM-CSG tree. The first method attempts to do so by modifying the definition of a nasty cell so that its complexity increases by a limited amount. In particular, it eliminates the dependence of the occurrence of nasty cells, and their number (i.e., reducing it), on the resolution by loosening the decomposition criteria to allow more than one primitive object per cell [Wyvi85]. In particular, they suggest raising it to two primitive objects per cell. This means that an edge would be contained in a normal cell and that nasty cells would be restricted to those instances where more than two edges meet.

Wyvill and Kunii conjecture that the size of such a data structure would grow logarithmically with the resolution. The key to the success of such a decomposition criterion is the relative frequency with which nasty cells arise in real world data. This variation of the decomposition criteria is similar to the bucketing strategy taken by Nelson and Samet [Nels86a, Nels86b] for representing collections of line segments in a geographic information system (see Section 4.2.3.4). In particular, they observe that when the data correspond to a road network, it is very rare for more than two line segments to intersect at one point. Thus when the bucket size is two or more, nasty-like cells disappear.

The second method replaces the *nasty* cell type by a cell type termed *rcsg* corresponding to a reduced version of the DAG-CSG tree [Wyvi86]. It is 'reduced' because it is the result of pruning the original DAG-CSG tree so that it contains only references to the primitive objects that can possibly affect the node. In this case, the data associated with an rcsg node are a tree instead of a DAG because at the time it is built, the position and orientation of each of its primitive blocks has already been determined. The rcsg nodes appear at a predefined level that corresponds to the minimum volume of space we permit in the octree. We term the resultant structure a *PM-RCSG tree*. Generally the PM-RCSG tree will be considerably smaller than the PM-CSG tree because the rcsg cells, unlike the nasty cells, no longer need to be made as small as possible.

Exercises

5.63. In the PM-CSG tree, the decomposition rule is such that only one primitive object is allowed to occupy each cell. Why would this rule not be realizable if we were to use a pure CSG representation?

5.64. Wyvill and Kunii's definition of CSG does not have an intersection operation. Show how you would get the effect of $A \wedge B$ using just set union and set subtraction operations.

5.65. Write an algorithm to instantiate an object whose DAG-CSG tree is pointed at by O and is in position p.

5.66. Write an algorithm to add two PM-CSG octrees pointed at by A and B.

5.67. When subtracting two PM-CSG trees, say $A-B$, what action should be taken when A is a full node and B is a node of type boundary? In particular, what if B is a negative boundary?

5.68. Write an algorithm to subtract two PM-CSG octrees pointed at by A and B.

5.69. Write an algorithm to traverse a DAG-CSG tree and build its corresponding PM-CSG octree. You should make use of procedures ADD and SUBTRACT of Exercises 5.66 and 5.68.

5.70. Design a regularization technique for PM-CSG trees and incorporate it into the PM-CSG tree creation algorithm.

5.71. Prove that the storage requirements of the PM-CSG tree are proportional to the sum of lengths of the edges where an edge is defined as a line of intersection between the bounding surfaces of two primitive objects.

5.72. Wyvill and Kunii [Wyvi85] conjecture that by loosening the decomposition criteria for a boundary node in a PM-CSG tree to allow two primitive objects per cell, the size of the resulting data structure would grow logarithmically with the resolution instead of directly. Test this hypothesis by constructing PM-CSG trees for some real data.

5.73. Formulate a model for solid data for which the conjecture discussed in Exercise 5.72 holds.

5.74. How would you incorporate material properties (e.g., color, reflectance) other than shape into the DAG-CSG and PM-CSG trees?

5.75. Ray tracing is an image rendering technique described in more detail in Section 7.2 of [Same90b]. In essence, it is the process of casting a ray from a viewpoint through a given pixel on the image plane that appears between the viewpoint and the scene. From an implementation standpoint, it requires following a ray through space. How would you follow a ray through a scene modeled by a PM-RCSG tree?

5.76. Using ray tracing to view objects modeled by a PM-RCSG tree requires a determination of whether a point P is inside or outside an object represented by a node of type rcsg in a PM-RCSG octree. Give an algorithm that would work even if the PM-RCSG tree has not been regularized (i.e., isolated points, lines, and planes of zero measure may be present).

5.6 SURFACE-BASED OBJECT REPRESENTATIONS

Often three-dimensional objects can be represented in terms of their surfaces. For some applications the primary interest is in the representation of surfaces as 2.5-dimensional images—that is, for each pair (x,y), there corresponds a unique value of z. In applications in solid modeling the requirement that the value of z be unique is relaxed. This is the subject of the next two sections in which the prism tree and the cone tree are discussed. In this section a brief overview of hierarchical representations of 2.5-dimensional images is given.

Representing surfaces (i.e., 2.5-dimensional images) by hierarchical methods is an interesting area on which, unfortunately, space does not permit us to dwell. They are important in the processing of curved surfaces [Cohe80] (see also Mudur and

Koparkar [Mudu84]). Some of the methods are discussed in Section 7.1.6 of [Same90b] in the context of the display of curved surfaces. For an in-depth overview of this field, see the recent survey of De Floriani [DeFl87]. In the rest of this section, we examine some of the work that has been done in processing topographic data. Naturally our focus is on hierarchical approaches. The problem usually arises as one of reconstructing a surface in a digital environment. It is usually formulated as the interpolation of a function of two variables (say x and y) with values given at points that are either arbitrarily located or drawn from a uniformly spaced grid.

Regardless of how the surface is sampled, the representations should adapt to the changes in the terrain. The most common way of representing topographic data is to record them in a fixed rectangular or triangular grid (known as a gridded digital terrain model). An alternative method, which is more compact, is capable of capturing point and line features (e.g., peaks, pits, passes, ridges, and valleys) in the surface by approximating the surface by a network of planar nonoverlapping triangles. The result is known as a Triangular Irregular Network (TIN) [Peuc75]. Unfortunately an arbitrary triangulation is usually unsatisfactory for the purpose of interpolation due to the high likelihood that the triangles are thin and elongated. In other words, it is desirable that the triangles be as equiangular as possible. The Delaunay triangulation [Dela34, Prep85] is one approach to achieve such a goal.

When the amount of data is large, the triangular network approach becomes unwieldy in terms of storage requirements. In this case, there are two possible solutions. The first is a pyramid-like approach that represents the surface at different predefined levels of precision (i.e., multiple resolution). The second approach, and the one focused on in this section, represents different parts of the surface at different levels of resolution. Representations based on such an approach are usually characterized as being hierarchical. The hierarchical methods commonly used are based on either triangulations or rectangular decompositions.

Hierarchical triangular decomposition methods are differentiated on the basis of whether the decomposition is into three (*ternary*) or four (*quaternary*) parts. Ternary decompositions are formed by taking an internal point of one of the triangles, say T, and joining it to the vertices of T (e.g., Figure 5.22). Quaternary decompositions are formed by joining three points, each on a different side of a given triangle (e.g., Figure 5.23). Hierarchical triangulations are represented by trees where the root corresponds

Figure 5.22   Example ternary decomposition

Figure 5.23   Example quaternary decomposition

to the initial enclosing rectangle; the out degree is three or four depending on the type of decomposition. In the case of a ternary decomposition, each triangle is adjacent to at most one triangle on each side. In contrast, in the case of a quaternary decomposition, each triangle may be adjacent to a number of triangles along a side.

Hierarchical triangulations result in the approximation of a surface, say s, by planar triangular patches whose vertices are a subset of the data points that define s. For each such patch, an approximation error is computed that is usually the maximum error of the data points with projections on the x-y plane overlapping the projection of the patch on the x-y plane. If the approximation error exceeds a predefined tolerance, the patch is subdivided further. The resulting surface depends on the nature of the decomposition.

In the case of a ternary decomposition, the surface described by the triangulation is usually continuous at every level. However, the triangles are often thin and elongated, since the point at which the triangle is decomposed is internal to the triangle. Thus equiangularity is not satisfied (but see the adjustment step in the construction of the prism tree [Faug84, Ponc87b] described in Section 5.7, as well as the triacon hierarchy of Dutton [Dutt84] described in Section 1.4.1). The ternary decomposition is usually used when the surface is defined at points that are randomly located. De Floriani, Falcidieno, Nagy, and Pienovi [DeFl84, DeFl85] discuss its use for surface interpolation, as well as serving as a data compression mechanism.

In the case of a quaternary decomposition, each triangle can be adjacent to a number of triangles on each of its sides. Thus the interpolating surface defined on it is generally not continuous unless all of the triangles are uniformly split—that is, the resulting tree is a complete quadtree. If the initial approximating triangle is equilateral and the triangles are always subdivided by connecting their midpoints, then equiangularity holds and the interpolation is ideal. The quaternary decomposition is especially attractive when the data points are drawn from a uniformly spaced grid.

The quaternary decomposition is used as as surface representation by Gomez and Guzman [Gome79, Soto78] and Barrera and Vazquez [Barr84]. The approach of Barrera and Vazquez uses regular decomposition, while Gomez and Guzman's decomposition is data driven (like a point quadtree). Fekete and Davis [Feke84] use a variant of the quaternary decomposition, which they term a *property sphere* (see Section 1.4.1), to represent the boundary of three-dimensional objects. The result is quite similar to that obtained by looking at the alternating levels of the triacon hierarchy of Dutton [Dutt84] (see Section 1.4.1).

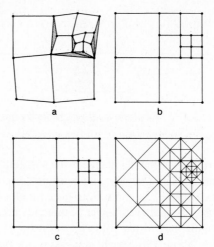

*Figure 5.24   (a) The three-dimensional view of the result-
ing subdivision of a surface using a quadtree-like decomposition rule in parameter space (some of the cracks are
shown shaded); (b) the quadtree of (a) in parameter space;
(c) the restricted quadtree corresponding to (b); (d) the triangulation of (c)*

Hierarchical rectangular decompositions are similar to hierarchical triangulations that are based on a quaternary decomposition. They are used when the data
points are the vertices of a rectangular grid. In this case, a rectangle is split by choosing an internal point and joining it to its projections on the four sides of the rectangle.
When the data are uniformly spaced, the result is analogous to a region quadtree.

For example, Carlson [Carl82] subdivides a surface into rectangular patches
for use in algorithms that perform intersection of sculptured surfaces. Schmitt,
Barsky, and Du [Schm86] use adaptive subdivision for surface fitting in conjunction
with a parametric piecewise bicubic Bernstein-Bezier surface. They start with a
rough approximating surface and recursively refine it where the data are poorly
approximated. Chen and Tobler [Chen86] evaluate the use of different approximations in each rectangular patch in terms of numerical accuracy, execution time, and
storage.

The main drawback of using a rectangular decomposition is the absence of continuity between adjacent patches of unequal width (termed the *alignment problem*).
As an example of the alignment problem, see Figure 5.24a, which is the result of using
a quadtree-like decomposition rule in the parameter space representation of a surface
patch. Notice the presence of cracks along the boundary of the NE quadrant. Barrera
and Hinojosa [Barr87] overcome this problem by using the interpolated point instead
of the true point, while Von Herzen and Barr [VonH87, VonH88] triangulate the
squares.

There are several ways to triangulate a square. It can be split into two, four, or eight triangles, depending on how many lines are drawn through its midpoint (one, two, or four, respectively). The simplest method is to split it into two triangles. Unfortunately, the cracks still remain. Von Herzen and Barr avoid the cracks by converting the rectangular decomposition into a *restricted quadtree*. At this point, a square can be split into either four or eight triangles.

A restricted quadtree is one where all 4-adjacent blocks (i.e., nodes) are either of equal size or of ratio 2:1. Given an arbitrary quadtree decomposition, the restricted quadtree is formed by repeatedly subdividing the larger nodes until the 2:1 ratio holds.[12] It results in the quadtree-like decomposition shown in Figure 5.24c as opposed to the more traditional representation shown in Figure 5.24b. Note that the SE quadrant of Figure 5.24b had to be decomposed once.

Von Herzen and Barr [VonH87, VonH88] overcome the alignment problem by triangulating the quadtree leaf nodes of Figure 5.24c in the manner shown in Figure 5.24d. The rule is that every block is decomposed into eight triangles, or two triangles per edge, unless the edge is shared by a larger block. In that case, only one triangle is formed. Observe that there are no cracks. Cracks can also be avoided by varying the basic decomposition rule so that each block is decomposed into four triangles, or one triangle per edge, unless the edge borders a smaller square. In that case, two triangles are formed along the edge. Von Herzen and Barr prefer the decomposition into eight triangles because it avoids problems when displaying (i.e., shading [Roge85]) the resulting object. (For more details on this approach and on surface representations, see the discussion of the display of curved surfaces in Section 7.1.6 of [Same90b].)

Exercises

5.77. Consider a hierarchical triangulation based on a ternary decomposition. Let t be the number of triangles and v the number of vertices. Prove that $t < 2 \cdot v$.

5.78. Consider a hierarchical triangulation based on a quaternary decomposition. Let t be the number of triangles and v the number of vertices. Prove that $v - 2 \le t < 2 \cdot v$.

5.79. Give an algorithm to perform neighbor finding in the context of the discussion in Chapter 3 of [Same90b] for a hierarchical triangulation that uses a ternary decomposition.

5.80. Does use of the triacon hierarchy of Dutton [Dutt84] (see Section 1.4.1) guarantee that the surface described by the triangulation is continuous at every level of the decomposition?

5.81. Consider a sphere represented by an octree. Compute the ratio of the approximated surface area to the true surface area.

5.82. [David Mount] Prove that the use of the restricted quadtree increases the number of nodes in the quadtree by at most a factor c. What is c?

5.83. Modify Hunter and Steiglitz's quadtree complexity theorem (see Theorem 1.1 of Section 1.5) to deal with the restricted quadtree of Von Herzen and Barr [VonH87, VonH88].

---

[12] This method of subdivision is also used in finite element analysis as part of a technique called *h-refinement* by Kela, Perucchio, and Voelcker [Kela86] to adaptively refine a mesh that has already been analyzed, as well as to achieve element compatibility.

5.84. How would you use the restricted quadtree of Von Herzen and Barr to model terrain elevation data?

5.85. How would you extend the restricted decomposition rule to octrees? Devise a tetrahedralization that would resolve the four-dimensional problem. Can you think of any practical application of this technique?

5.7   PRISM TREES

The *prism tree* is a ternary decomposition devised by Ponce and Faugeras [Ponc87b]. It is a hierarchical representation of an approximation used to model the surfaces of three-dimensional objects that are polyhedra of genus 0 (i.e., they have no holes). The goal is to obtain a reasonable approximation of polyhedra with a large number of faces (e.g., 5000) by polyhedra with a considerably smaller number of faces (e.g., 500). The prism tree is best understood by first examining its predecessor, termed a *polyhedral approximation*, due to Faugeras, Hebert, Mussi, and Boissonnat [Faug84].

To simplify the discussion, let us first consider the construction of a polyhedral approximation of a two-dimensional object as in Figure 5.25a. The object is initially modeled by a triangle with vertices that lie on the object's boundary. Assume for this example that the object is convex. Thus no part of the triangle lies outside the object. For each side of the triangle, say E, find a point on the object's boundary, say M, whose distance from E is a local maximum. If the distance from M to E is greater than a predefined threshold, say ε, then repeat this step for the two new sides of the triangle formed by M and the endpoints of E. This process is repeated for all the new triangles until all of the approximations represented by their sides are within ε or the number of decomposition steps exceeds a predefined value. For example, Figure 5.25b is a possible polyhedral approximation for the object in Figure 5.25a.

The polyhedral approximation provides a hierarchical representation of the boundary. The process of successive subdivision of the boundary yields a tree structure in which, with the exception of the root node, each node represents a straight line and the associated segment of the boundary. For example, Figure 5.25c is the tree structure corresponding to the polyhedral approximation of Figure 5.25b. Notice that the root has three sons, while all remaining nodes have two sons. Often the exact description of the segment of the boundary corresponding to the node is difficult to manipulate (e.g., detecting intersections between boundaries of adjacent objects). Hence, with each node we also associate a quadrilateral approximation of the corresponding boundary segment. The quadrilateral is a trapezoid formed in the following manner.

Let E be a straight line, with endpoints V_1 and V_2, that approximates S, a segment of the object's boundary. Let M be the point on S whose distance from E is a maximum. Let L be the line parallel to E that passes through M. Let B_1 and B_2 be the bisecting lines of E and the visible straight lines that are incident at V_1 and V_2, respectively. The trapezoid for line E is the smallest quadrilateral enclosing S formed by the

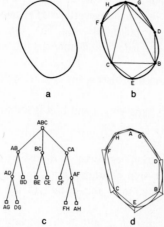

Figure 5.25   A two-dimensional prism tree: (a) object, (b) polyhedral approximation, (c) tree representation, (d) prism tree

intersection of lines E, L, P_1, and P_2, such that P_i is parallel to B_i.[13] The resulting approximation is the two-dimensional version of the prism tree. For example, Figure 5.25d is the two-dimensional prism tree corresponding to the polyhedral approximation given in Figure 5.25b. Notice that the shape of a trapezoid for a given boundary segment, say S, depends on the lines that approximate the segments adjacent to S.

To model three-dimensional objects, the polyhedral approximation uses tetrahedra instead of triangles. Again start by forming a triangle, say T, that splits the surface into two segments, S_1 and S_2. For each segment S_i pick a point, say M_i, on S_i such that the distance from S_i to T is a maximum. The result is a pair of tetrahedra that form a triangular bipyramid (i.e., hexahedron), with T as their common base, that serves as the initial polyhedral approximation. The rest of the approximation procedure consists of repeated application of the following two steps, termed *split* and *adjustment*, respectively:

1.   Split step: For each triangular face, say F, find the point, say M_F, on the surface with a distance to F, say d_F, that is a local maximum. If d_F exceeds a predefined threshold, say ε, then replace F by the tetrahedron formed by the three vertices of F and M_F.

2.   Adjustment step: Whenever the common edge between two adjacent triangles, say T_1 and T_2, is such that the approximation of the surface formed by T_1 and T_2 is not within a predefined tolerance, then an adjustment step is performed that, in effect, removes their common edge, say AB. This is done

[13] P_i and B_i are colinear when the object is convex (see Exercise 5.95).

by replacing edge AB and triangles T_1 and T_2 by four new triangles with vertices that are the two remaining vertices of T_1 and T_2, say M_1 and M_2, respectively, and one new point, say M_n. The four new triangles are M_1AM_n, M_2AM_n, M_1BM_n, and M_2BM_n. M_n satisfies the following three properties:

a. It is on the surface;
b. It is on the plane that bisects the two triangles that are being replaced; and
c. Of all the points satisfying a and b, it is the farthest from the edge being removed.

The three or four new triangles serve as the bases of tetrahedra that are constructed by making use of the split or adjustment steps, respectively. The entire process stops when the approximation of the surface of the object is deemed to be of sufficient accuracy.

The polyhedral approximation results in the modeling of an object by a collection of tetrahedra. The surface of the object is represented by the visible triangular faces of the tetrahedra. The process of successive subdivision of the surface yields a tree structure with the following form. At the initial level, there are two sons. At all remaining levels, there are three sons if the decomposition step did not require an adjustment step; otherwise there are just two sons since a triangle has been replaced by two triangles instead of three.

Each node contains a description of both its corresponding triangle and the associated segment of the surface. In many cases, the exact description of the segment of the surface corresponding to the node is difficult to manipulate (e.g., detecting the intersection of objects by intersecting their surfaces). Thus associated with each node is a polyhedron-like approximation of the corresponding surface segment. This polyhedron is five sided, has the shape of a truncated pyramid, and is formed in the following manner.

Let T be a triangle, with edges E_1, E_2, and E_3, that approximates S, a segment of a surface. Let M be the point on S with the maximum distance from T. Let L be the plane parallel to T that passes through M. Let B_1, B_2, and B_3 be the bisector planes of T and the visible triangles that are incident at E_1, E_2, and E_3, respectively. The truncated pyramid for triangle T is the smallest five-sided polyhedron enclosing S formed by the intersection of planes T, L, P_1, P_2, and P_3 such that P_i is parallel to B_i.[14] The resulting approximation is called a prism tree. The rationale for the use of this term is that the approximating polyhedra look like 'prisms,' although this is wrong from a definitional standpoint. Notice that the shape of a truncated pyramid for a given boundary segment, say S, depends on the triangle that approximates the segments adjacent to S.

The prism tree yields an approximation closely related to the strip tree of Ballard [Ball81] (see Section 4.1). Nevertheless, there are some major differences. First, in the strip tree, boundary (surface) segments are approximated by rectangles

---

[14] P_i and B_i are coplanar when the object is convex (see Exercise 5.95).

(rectangular parallelepipeds), while in the prism tree they are approximated by trapezoids (truncated pyramids). This difference means that when the object is convex (see Exercise 5.95), the interiors of the approximating trapezoids (truncated pyramids) in the prism tree are disjoint and adjacent ones have common edges (faces). Disjointness and common boundaries do not arise frequently in strip trees.

Second, the shape of the approximating trapezoids (truncated pyramids) for a given boundary segment, say s, depends on the line (triangle) that approximates the segments adjacent to s. The shape will also differ depending on the level in the tree at which s's adjacent segments are found. In contrast, the shape of the rectangle (rectangular parallelepiped) used in the strip tree is independent of the approximation of the neighboring segment and of its level in the tree.

Third, in two dimensions, closed curves and curves that extend past their endpoints require no special treatment in the case of the prism tree. This is not true in the case of the strip tree.

Since the prism and strip trees are closely related, they have many of the same advantages. One of the most important is that both make it very easy to detect if it is possible for two solids to intersect without resorting to a possibly complex process to intersect their two surfaces. All that needs to be done is to examine their prism trees. If the prisms do not intersect, it is impossible for the solids to intersect.

Otherwise, depending on the manner in which the prisms intersect, we can either conclusively state that their associated surfaces intersect or that an intersection is possible. The former is the case when the cross-section of one prism is completely contained in the other prism—that is, their intersection forms a cross-like object (compare with Figure 4.5 in Chapter 4). In the latter situation, the trees are descended one level, and the test is repeated. At the leaf nodes, a true intersection test is performed by comparing each of the faces in one object against every face in the other object.

Exercises

5.86. The prism tree is not a true generalization of the strip tree since the approximating shapes are rectangular parallelepipeds for the former while for the latter they are truncated pyramids. Is there an advantage to using trapezoids (truncated pyramids) over rectangles (rectangular parallelepipeds)?

5.87. Define a three-dimensional strip tree so that the approximating shapes are rectangular parallelepipeds.

5.88. What is the motivation for the adjustment step in the construction of the polyhedral approximation?

5.89. In the description of the prism tree approximation, it is stated that the surface of the object is represented by a collection of tetrahedra where for each tetrahedron at most three faces are visible. Why aren't there three visible faces for each tetrahedron?

5.90. It would seem that using a collection of tetrahedra to approximate the surface of a polyhedron is not good for polyhedral-like objects because it may result in an approximating object with many points where the solid angle formed by the three incident faces is less than 90°. How is this situation avoided in the algorithm for obtaining a polyhedral approximation?

5.91. In the adjustment step of the prism tree construction process, it is necessary to find adjacent triangles. How would you achieve this?

5.92. Write an algorithm to build a three-dimensional prism tree.

5.93. What is the space and time complexity of the process of building a three-dimensional prism tree for a polyhedron with n faces?

5.94. Consider a three-dimensional prism tree such that all faces of adjacent approximating truncated pyramids are coplanar. Must these coplanar faces also be identical?

5.95. Define a prism to be *regular* if the three nonparallel faces of the prism lie in the bisecting planes. Prove that if the approximated surface is convex, all prisms at all levels of the prism tree representation of the surface are regular.

5.96. Use the definition of a regular prism given in Exercise 5.95. Suppose that you are approximating an object with a concave surface. Is it possible for all the approximating prisms to be regular?

5.97. Adapt the definition of regularity given in Exercise 5.95 to a strip tree.

5.98. Give an algorithm to find the intersection of two three-dimensional objects represented by prism trees.

5.99. How would you extend the concepts of a polyhedral approximation and a prism tree to more general surfaces than genus 0?

5.8 CONE TREES [15]

As an example of another object representation based on the object's surface, let us examine an extension of the sector tree of Chen [Chen85b] (see Section 1.4.2) to deal with three-dimensional data. In this case, space is treated as a polar sphere, and it is recursively decomposed into cones. The result is termed a *cone tree*. The motivation for its development is the same as that for the sector tree. In particular, we want a representation that provides a good approximation, in terms of a measure, of both the boundary (e.g., surface area) of an object and its interior (e.g., volume). In addition, the normals to the surface should have a minimum amount of discontinuity between adjacent surface elements.

Let (ρ, θ, ϕ) denote a point in the polar sphere. θ and ϕ are called the *polar* and *azimuth* angles, respectively. θ ranges between 0 and π, while ϕ ranges between 0 and 2π. Each cone consists of an origin, four edges (alternatively, pairs of edges form sectors), and a spherical patch. The points at which the edges of the cones intersect (or touch) the object are called *contact points*.

Let $(\rho_{ij}, \theta_i, \phi_j)$ be the contact point with the maximum value of ρ in direction (θ_i, ϕ_j). Each cone (e.g., Figure 5.26) represents a region bounded by the points $(0,0,0)$, $(\rho_{11}, \theta_1, \phi_1)$, $(\rho_{12}, \theta_1, \phi_2)$, $(\rho_{21}, \theta_2, \phi_1)$, and $(\rho_{22}, \theta_2, \phi_2)$. $\theta_1 = k\pi/2^n$ and $\theta_2 = \theta_1 + \pi/2^n$, such that k and n are nonnegative integers ($k < 2^n$). $\phi_1 = 2m\pi/2^n$ and $\phi_2 = \phi_1 + 2\pi/2^n$, such that m and n are nonnegative integers ($m < 2^n$).

The spherical patch having the four nonorigin contact points as its corners is approximated by three parametric equations in s and t such that $0 \le s \le 1$ and $0 \le t \le 1$

---

[15] This section is highly specialized and can be skipped on an initial reading.

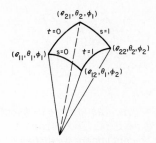

Figure 5.26   Example cone

(see Exercise 5.100). Note that the interpolation curves will be non-linear functions of the parameters s and t. However, at the edges of the patch (e.g., $s = 0$, $s = 1$, $t = 0$, $t = 1$ in Figure 5.26), the approximation is a linear function.

The cone tree is a quadtree that represents the result of recursively subdividing cones in the polar sphere into four cones of square spherical intervals (i.e., $\Delta\theta = \Delta\phi$). The spherical intervals form a two-dimensional space. Since the range of ϕ is twice as large as that of θ, the $\phi-\theta$ space is initially subdivided into two cones at $\phi = \pi$. All subsequent decompositions are into four cones of equal square spherical intervals. The decomposition stops whenever the approximation of a part of an object by the spherical patches represented by the cone is deemed to be adequate. The computation of the stopping condition is implementation dependent. In this presentation the origin of the polar sphere is assumed to be contained within the object.

Assume that the object is convex. Nonconvex objects are beyond the scope of the discussion. The result is a quadtree where each leaf node represents a spherical patch. It contains the contact points of its corresponding patch, which are the corners of the node's block. Unfortunately there exist discontinuities in the approximated surfaces represented by the cone tree. The problem arises when adjacent blocks in the $\phi-\theta$ space are of a different size. For example, consider the block decomposition in Figure 5.27. The approximated surface for block A is computed by using the contact points 1, 2, 3, and 5. The approximated surface for block B is computed by using the contact points 3, 4, 6, and 7. The approximated surface for block C is computed by using the contact points 4, 5, 7, and 8. We now see that the approximated surface of A

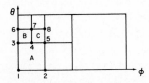

Figure 5.27   Example quadtree decomposition of a surface in $\phi-\theta$ space

Figure 5.28   The cone tree representation of the left half of the surface in Figure 5.27. The shaded area represents a discontinuity in adjacent spherical patches.

does not match the approximated surface of B and C along the common side of their cone tree blocks (see Figure 5.28).

Chen suggests that this situation can be alleviated, in part, by replacing the contact points of the smaller block by points on the approximated surface of the larger adjacent block and subsequently subdividing the larger block if the error is too large. A better solution is to use an approach similar to the restricted quadtree of Von Herzen and Barr [VonH87, VonH88] (described in Section 5.6). In this case, nodes that have a neighbor whose level in the tree is more than one level deeper are subdivided further until the condition holds.

The cone tree can be used to facilitate the same kind of operations as the sector tree. For example, set-theoretic operations, such as union and intersection, are straightforward. Scaling is trivial as the cone tree need not be modified; all values of ρ are interpreted as scaled by the appropriate scale factor. Rotating a cone tree is more complex than rotating a sector tree since two angles must be involved. Translation is expensive as the position of the object relative to the origin changes. Thus the entire cone tree must be reconstructed.

Exercises

5.100. Give the three parametric equations in s and t for a spherical patch at points $(\rho_{11}, \theta_1, \phi_1)$, $(\rho_{12}, \theta_1, \phi_2)$, $(\rho_{21}, \theta_2, \phi_1)$, and $(\rho_{22}, \theta_2, \phi_2)$.

5.101. How would you use a cone tree to represent an object that is not convex?

5.102. How would you use a cone tree to represent an object that does not contain the origin of the polar sphere?

5.103. Write an algorithm to determine if a specific point is inside or outside an object represented by a cone tree.

5.104. How would you adapt the restricted quadtree of Von Herzen and Barr [VonH87, VonH88] (see Section 5.6) to avoid the discontinuities present in the approximated surfaces represented by a cone tree?

SOLUTIONS TO EXERCISES

CHAPTER 1

1.1. The array, not surprisingly, has no such bias. The list is ordered by adjacency in one dimension. The region quadtree is ordered by adjacency in a hierarchical sense (i.e., by use of a parent relation).

1.2. See Section 4.1 of [Same90b].

1.3. $(B + W - 1)/3$.

1.4. $(B + W - 1)/7$.

1.5. No two spheres can occupy the same leaf node. In other words, each leaf node contains a part of just one sphere.

1.6. Since the staircases are usually infinite, a tree is inadequate and a graph is necessary. Use an octgraph.

1.7. Compression is a result of the property of the exclusive or operation that $0 \oplus 0 = 0$ and $1 \oplus 1 = 0$.

1.8. $Q_i \oplus Q_{i-1} = (P_i \oplus Q_{i-1}) \oplus Q_{i-1} = P_i \oplus (Q_{i-1} \oplus Q_{i-1}) = P_i \oplus 0 = P_i$.

1.10. Dillencourt and Mount [Dill87] propose the following solution. An optimal hierarchical decomposition of a binary image can be obtained by using a method based on dynamic programming [Hill67]. Dynamic programming is a general technique in which a problem is solved by storing the solution to all subproblems and combining them appropriately. Assume an $M \times N$ image. The subproblems consist of the possible positions of the rectangles that correspond to the quadrants. There are at most $O(M^2 \cdot N^2)$ subproblems as there are $M \cdot N$ possible positions for the upper leftmost corner of the rectangles, and, for each of these rectangles, there are at most $M \cdot N$ positions for the lower rightmost corner. Thus the total storage is $O(M^2 \cdot N^2)$.

    The algorithm stores with each subproblem (i.e., rectangle) the best decomposition into quadrants, along with the number of rectangles in the decomposition. If the image is a single pixel (i.e., if $M = N = 1$), there is only way to subdivide the image: not to subdivide it at all. Otherwise the image may be subdivided into quadrants in $M \cdot N$ ways, as any grid point splits the image into four quadrants. For an $M \times N$ rectangle, this information is computed by examining all $(M - 1) \cdot (N - 1)$ possibilities, provided the information is known for all smaller rectangles.

The heart of the algorithm is the computation of the solutions of the subproblems. The execution time of the algorithm is $O(M^3 \cdot N^3)$. This is obtained by noting that for each rectangle of size $i \times j$, there are $i \cdot j$ possible partitions, and all must be examined. There are $(M - i + 1) \cdot (N - j + 1)$ rectangles of size $i \times j$. Since i and j vary from 1 to M and 1 to N, respectively, the result follows. Therefore for an $N \times N$ image the optimal quadtree can be computed in $O(N^6)$ time using $O(N^4)$ space.

1.11. See [Good83].

1.13. For the row-prime, Peano-Hilbert, and spiral orders, it is 1. For the Morton order it is:

$$ \frac{1}{2^{2 \cdot n} - 1} \cdot \left[2^{2 \cdot n - 1} + \sqrt{1 + (2^n - 1)^2} + 3 \cdot 2^{2 \cdot n - 1} \cdot \sum_{i=1}^{n-1} \frac{\sqrt{1 + (2^i - 1)^2}}{2^{2 \cdot i}} \right] . $$

1.14. For the Morton and Peano-Hilbert orders, it is $1 + 2^{2-m}$, as each page represents a $2^m \times 2^m$ block. The four corner pixels require that three pages be accessed; the remaining $4 \cdot (2^m - 2)$ pixels along the edges require that two pages be accessed; the neighbors of all other pixels are on the same page, and thus only one page need be accessed. For the row order, it is $3 + 2^{1-2 \cdot m}$, as each page represents a portion of a row of size $2^{2 \cdot m}$. The first and last pixels require that four pages be accessed; the remaining pixels require that three pages be accessed.

1.17. $1/\sqrt{3}$, 1, $2/\sqrt{3}$.

1.18. $\sqrt{3}$ for $[3^6]$; 1 and $\sqrt{2}$ for $[4^4]$.

1.19. Treat every even-numbered row as if it has been shifted to the right (or left) by one-half of the interpixel distance.

1.21. 80 and 60 faces, respectively.

1.22. The same as for a binary tree: one more leaf node than nonleaf nodes. It is independent of d.

1.23. The lower bound is $1/2^{d-1}$ and the upper bound is 1.

1.24. No, since the number of nonleaf nodes in a bintree can be considerably larger than that in the corresponding quadtree.

1.25. In two dimensions, we have $g_{m,n} = g_{m-1,n-1} + g_{m-1,n-2} + g_{m-2,n-1} + g_{m-2,n-2}$ where $g_{m,n}$ corresponds to the area of the rectangle with sides of length f_m and f_n.

1.26. Consider a 3×3 square. It can be split only into two 1×2 rectangles, a 1×1 square, and a 2×2 square. The 1×2 rectangles cannot be further decomposed into 1×1 pixels using a quadtree splitting rule.

1.27. Consider a 3×3 square. It can be split only into 1×3 and 2×3 rectangles. The 1×3 square does not obey the 2-d Fibonacci condition; its sides are not of equal length nor are they successive Fibonacci numbers.

1.29. For a $2^n \times 2^n$ image there are $(n+1) \cdot (n+1)$ different sizes of rectangles. For a given rectangle of size $2^i \times 2^j$ there are $(2^n/2^i) \cdot (2^n/2^j)$ positions where it can be placed when using the AHC method.

1.30. Let r be the length of the perpendicular sides of the triangle. The true perimeter is $2r + r\sqrt{2}$ while the approximated perimeter is $4r$.

1.31. $4/\pi$.

1.32. Use linear interpolation in x and y instead of ρ and θ for the arc of the sector. A combination of polygonal and nonpolygonal tiles could also be implemented by using an additional bit with each sector to indicate the tiling type.

1.33. The inner approximation means that the object is made larger since it is the part outside the object that is truncated. On the other hand, the outer approximation implies the addition of two newly created subregions to the collection represented by the sector.

1.34. No, because the boundary may repeatedly snake through a number of adjacent nodes.

1.35. Let P be the contact point in question and let Q and R be the immediately preceding and following, respectively, contact points on the other side of the sector. Duplicate P in the sector's leaf node and define a three-sided region bounded by the side of the sector between Q and R and the spiral arc approximations of PQ and PR.

1.36. The only difference is that when the origin of the polar plane is outside the object, each leaf node of a sector tree contains an even number of pairs of points instead of an odd number. Each successive two pairs of points define a region within the object.

1.37. Use different origins for the approximating arcs. In particular, the origins are on opposite sides of the arcs. For example, in Figure 1.23b the arc between points 5 and C would have an origin somewhere to the SW of the arc between points 4 and D.

1.38. No, for both approximations, since this depends on the curvature of the boundary where the approximation takes place.

1.40. Rotation requires only rearranging pointers. All interpolations remain the same since each sector corresponds to an angular range of $2\pi/2^n$. Therefore all the approximated arcs remain unchanged.

1.41. Traverse the tree in such a way that nodes corresponding to adjacent boundary segments are visited in sequence. Note that each leaf node may be visited more than once because the boundary may repeatedly snake through a number of adjacent nodes.

1.43. See [Dyer82].

1.44. $O(2^n)$. The worst case is a rectangle of width $2^n \times 2$, that straddles the x axis (i.e., one pixel on on each side). It needs $5 + 16 \cdot 2^{n-2}$ nodes.

1.45. The probability that the entire image is black is $P_b(n) = (1/2)^{2n}$, and similarly the probability that the entire image is white is $P_w(n) = (1/2)^{2n}$. To find $E(n)$, solve the recurrence relation $E(n) = 4 \cdot E(n-1) + 1 - 4 \cdot (P_b(n) + P_w(n))$ with the initial condition $E(0) = 1$. The result is approximately $(29/24) \cdot 2^{2n}$. The expected number of black nodes, $B(n)$, is obtained by solving the recurrence relation $B(n) = 4 \cdot B(n-1) - 3 \cdot P_b(n)$ with the initial condition $B(0) = 1/2$. The result is approximately $(29/64) \cdot 2^{2n}$. The expected number of white nodes is the same as $B(n)$ while the expected number of gray nodes is approximately $(29/96) \cdot 2^{2n} - 1/3$. For more details, see [Chu88a].

1.46. See [Chu88a].

1.49. Let the four squares defining each curve be called A, B, C, and D. If the curve is less than d in length, no two of A, B, C, and D can be d or more apart at their closest points and still permit the curve to enter a fifth different square. The rest of the proof is analogous to that of Theorem 1.1.

1.50. The quadtree contains 1 node at level n (i.e., the root node), 4 nodes at level $n-1$, and 16 nodes at each of levels $n-2$ through 0. Summing up yields the desired result.

1.51. The quadtree contains 1 node at level n (i.e., the root node), 4 nodes at level $n-1$, and $4 \cdot 2^{n-i}$ nodes at level i where i ranges between 0 and $n-2$. Summing up yields $5 + 8 \cdot (2^n - 2)$, equal to $8 \cdot p - 11$.

1.53. When $p \le 4 \cdot n$, use the polygon of Figure 1.27 for the given value of n by extending the perimeter arbitrarily to achieve the desired value of p so that the extended polygon intersects all of the pixels that it intersected prior to the extension. This polygon requires at least $16 \cdot n - 11$ nodes, which is more than $p + n$ but still less than $5 \cdot n$. When $p > 4 \cdot n$, construct a polygon in the form of a concatenated sequence of U patterns of minimal width. The components of the U are reduced in size or perturbed as necessary to yield a polygon of perimeter p. Since each pixel is a leaf, summing up the nodes at all levels yields at least $(4/3) \cdot p$ nodes or $(2/3) \cdot (p+n)$ as $p > n$.

1.55. See [Meag80] for a proof that the size of the octree is bounded by four times the surface area.

1.57. See [Wals85].

1.58. See [Wals85].

1.59. See [Atki85b] for some examples.

1.60. See [Gros83]. Intuitively shifting the region may require fewer nodes as long as the region's maximum extent is such that the region occupies at least one block of side 1 in three horizontally (or vertically) adjacent blocks of size $2^m \times 2^m$. For the given value of w, the value of m is $n-1$ and, hence, the $n+1$ result follows.

1.61. See [Li82]. The proof is analogous to that used to obtain the optimal grid resolution.

1.62. Given a grid of $2^{n+1} \times 2^{n+1}$, the number of elements examined is $4 \cdot (2^{2n+2} + 4 \cdot (2^{2n} + 4 \cdot (2^{2n-2} + \cdots)))$. Summing up over n levels of recursion yields $4 \cdot n \cdot 2^{2n+2}$

CHAPTER 2

2.1. See [Frie75].

2.2. See [Bent77b].

2.4. $\lfloor \log_2 N \rfloor$ when all points are colinear (i.e., they lie on a straight line).

2.5. The maximum path length in an optimized point quadtree of N nodes is $\lfloor \log_2 N \rfloor$. Therefore the maximum TPL is $\sum_{i=1}^{\lfloor \log_2 N \rfloor} i \cdot 2^i$.

2.6. The ordering step on N elements is $O(N \cdot \log_2 N)$. Selecting the median at each level of recursion is $O(N)$. Regrouping the records is also $O(N)$. The depth of the recursion is the maximum path length bounded by $\lfloor \log_2 N \rfloor$. Therefore the running time of the algorithm is $O(N \cdot \log_2 N)$.

2.7. Overmars and van Leeuwen [Over82] use an algorithm similar to that used by Finkel and Bentley [Fink74] to construct their version of an optimized point quadtree. Insert the nodes using the property that for every set of N points a point quadtree can be built in $O(N \cdot \log_2 N)$ time such that for every nonleaf node with M nodes in its subtrees, every subtree contains at most $\lceil M/2 \rceil$ nodes. Each subquadrant is repeatedly subdivided with respect to a point whose coordinate is the median along a chosen axis. If the balance of the tree is destroyed, then rebuild the subtree rooted at the highest nonleaf node at which this is the case as a balanced tree.

2.8. See [Over82].

2.9. See [Fink74, p. 4] who suggest leaf balancing operations they term *single balance* and *double balance*. Kersten and van Emde Boas [Kers79] report on an empirical study of different balancing operations.

2.10. $N \cdot (N - 1)/2$.

2.11. Use induction. Assume that the root is at depth 0. The result is clearly true for $N = 1$. Assume that it is true for $N = i$ and show that it is true for $N = i+1$. Add the $i + 1^{st}$ node at the bottom of the tree—say, to a node at depth m and let T' denote the new tree. TPL(T') increases by m. Also, each of the subtrees rooted at nodes at depths 0 through $m-1$ in which the new node is a member has increased in size by 1 for a total increase of m. Furthermore there is one additional subtree of size 1 corresponding to the $i + 1^{st}$ node. The result follows and holds for trees, as well as binary trees and quadtrees, since empty trees and orientation make no difference.

2.13. See [Same80c].

2.14. See [Same80c].

2.17. See [Same77].

2.19. In the two-dimensional case, first divide the data points into two sets containing $\lceil N/3 \rceil$ and $\lfloor 2 \cdot N/3 \rfloor$ points. Next, divide the larger set into two parts containing $\lceil N/3 \rceil$ points each. This process is applied recursively. Overmars and van Leeuwen [Over82] give more details.

2.20. See [Over82].

2.21. Consider a colinear set of data points (i.e., a straight line). Alternatively the set of points need only have monotonically increasing or monotonically decreasing coordinate values. If the line coincides with one of the axes lines, the axes are rotated slightly.

2.22. See [Over82].

2.23. See [Over82] for a proof similar to that for Exercise 2.8.

2.25. The subtrees at level $m-i$ form a regular checkerboard of 4^i squares. The expected number of squares intersected along the x and y directions is bounded by $x \cdot 2^i + 1$ and $y \cdot 2^i + 1$, respectively. Therefore the number of squares at level i overlapped by the search rectangle is bounded by $(x \cdot 2^i + 1) \cdot (y \cdot 2^i + 1)$. Summing this quantity over all levels $0 \le i \le m-1$ and the fact that N, the number of nodes, is $(4^m - 1)/3$ yields $x \cdot y \cdot N + (x+y) \cdot \sqrt{3 \cdot N} + \log_4(3 \cdot N)$.

2.26. The expected number of records in a square search region is $N \cdot x^2$. The expected number of records visited in such a search in an inverted file is $N \cdot x$, and the expected overwork is $(1-x) \cdot x \cdot N$. From Exercise 2.25 we have that for a square search region in a perfect point quadtree the amount of overwork is approximately $2 \cdot x \cdot \sqrt{3 \cdot N}$. Thus we see that the overwork for square search regions in perfect quadtrees is asymptotically less than that for inverted lists.

2.27. See [Lee77b].

2.29. See [Will82].

2.32. Bentley [Bent75b] shows that the probability of constructing a given k-d tree of N nodes by inserting N nodes in a random order into an initially empty k-d tree is the same as the probability of constructing the same tree by random insertion into a one-dimensional binary search tree. Once this is done, results that have been proved for one-dimensional binary search trees will be applicable to k-d trees. The proof relies on viewing the records as k-tuples of permutations of the integers $1, \ldots, N$. The nodes are considered random if all of the $N!^k$ k-tuples of permutations are permitted to occur. It is assumed that the key values in a given record are independent.

2.35. $N \cdot \log_2 N$ for N points.

2.36. See [Over82].

2.38. See [Vais84] for some hints.

2.43. Assume the worst case: a complete k-d tree and that the D discriminator is found at depth $k-1$. Therefore all nodes at depth 0 through $k-1$ will have to be visited (i.e., $2^k - 1$ nodes) while the right subtrees of nodes at depth $k-1$ are pruned. This pruning occurs repeatedly at depths $h \cdot k - 1$ where $h > 0$. At all other depths, all nodes in nonpruned subtrees must be visited (e.g., all nodes at depth $h \cdot k$ through $h \cdot k - 1$ in the nonpruned subtrees). Summing up yields the desired result.

2.44. Change procedure FIND_D_MINIMUM to return the D-minimum node, its SONTYPE value relative to its father, and its father.

2.45. If the search region had been chosen in the middle of the space, then in the worst case, we would want the root of the k-d tree to partition the region somewhere in the middle. In this case, the subtrees contain identically shaped subregions of the original search region, and the analysis is applied recursively.

2.49. The search region is a $(k-t)$-dimensional hyperplane.

2.50. Assume the most pessimistic case: the first $k-t$ discriminators in the tree correspond to the $k-t$ unspecified keys of the partial match query. Therefore all nodes at depth 0 through $k-t$ must be visited (i.e., $2^{k-t} - 1$ nodes) while pruning occurs at depth $k-t$ through $k-1$, resulting in $t \cdot 2^{k-t-1}$ nodes being visited. This pruning occurs repeatedly at depth $h \cdot k - t$ through $h \cdot k - 1$. At all other depths, all nodes in nonpruned subtrees must be visited (e.g., all nodes at depth $h \cdot k$ through $h \cdot k - t$ in the nonpruned subtrees). Summing up yields the desired result.

2.53. Yes. In the range tree, the leaf nodes are linked in sorted order using a doubly linked list to facilitate retrieval of all elements within a given range in time proportional to the number of elements in the range.

2.54. The reason is that all points in the range trees searched in RIGHT(P) are greater in value than L_x and less than R_x. Similarly all points in the range trees searched in LEFT(P) are less in value than R_x and greater than L_x.

2.55. The points that are found are unique; no point is reported twice since all one-dimensional range trees at a given level are disjoint. The one-dimensional range trees that are examined at the different levels are also disjoint.

2.56. The balanced binary search tree, say T, for the main attribute uses $O(N)$ storage. For each level of T, each data point occurs in exactly one of the one-dimensional range trees for the secondary attribute that are associated with the nonleaf nodes at that level. There are $O(\log_2 N)$ levels, and thus a total of $O(N \cdot \log_2 N)$ storage suffices.

2.57. To perform a range query it takes $\log_2 N$ time to locate the endpoints of the main attribute, plus $O(\log_2 N)$ time to locate the endpoints of the secondary attributes in each of the $O(\log_2 N)$ one-dimensional range trees of the secondary attribute, plus the time to sequence through the answers that are located.

2.58. Overmars [Over88a] suggests using the solution of the following recurrence relation: Let $M(k,N)$ denote the storage necessary for a k-dimensional range tree for N points. At each level of the k-dimensional range tree, at most $M(k-1,N)$ storage is used. Therefore $M(k,N) \le \log_2 N \cdot M(k-1,N)$ and the fact that $M(2,N) = O(N \cdot \log_2 N)$ leads to the desired result. The query time is analyzed in the same manner.

2.61. The balanced binary search tree is equivalent to an extended binary tree. Such a tree with N leaf nodes has $N - 1$ nonleaf nodes.

2.62. Finding the nearest common ancestor requires at most $2 \cdot \log_2 N$ steps. Once the nearest common ancestor has been found, say Q, the search process may visit each point on the path from Q to L_x and R_x, even if it does not satisfy the query. All other nodes visited either cut off or satisfy the search. Of the nodes that cut off the search, at most $2 \cdot F$ are not on the path from Q to L_x and R_x. Empty nodes also cut off the search since their sons have already been reported.

2.63. The key to its performance is that after making $\log_2 N$ comparisons, exactly one point is found in the tree.

2.64. Use a derived pair $(f(x,y),y)$ where $f(x,y) = k \cdot x + y$. f is a mapping such that differences in x are more significant than differences in y.

2.69. The balanced binary search tree is equivalent to an extended binary tree. Such a tree with N leaf nodes has $N - 1$ nonleaf nodes. Each node appears in one priority tree at each level. There are $\log_2 N$ levels.

2.71. Finding the nearest common ancestor requires at most $\log_2 N$ steps, and the remaining work is proportional to the number of points found.

2.80. The worst case arises when the boundaries of the rectangular query region intersect 2^n nodes (i.e., regions).

2.82. $\sum_{i=0}^{n-1} 4^i = (4^n - 1)/3$.

2.83. For a complete MX quadtree (i.e., where no sparseness occurs), the array representation requires one-third less space since the MX quadtree representation needs pointers. However, using the array, one-third more interchange operations must be performed while computing the transpose.

2.84. Wise [Wise85] observes that a quadtree-like decomposition admits a hybrid algorithm that uses *both* Strassen's recurrence [Stra69] and the conventional one (e.g., [Fadd59, Section 1.4]). The conventional recurrence requires eight quadrant multiplications, which is reduced when some of the quadrants correspond to nonleaf nodes that correspond to blocks of zeros. For example, only six quadrant multiplications are necessary when only one of the eight quadrants corresponds to a nonleaf node. The amount of reduction depends on how many such zero quadrants are present, but the improvement is profound with sparse matrices [Abda88]. On larger matrices, use of Strassen's recurrence reduces the count of eight in the conventional recurrence to seven but with a loss of sparseness and a well-known loss of floating-point stability.

2.85. It has a greater potential for saving space.

2.86. Using a runlength representation speeds up the matrix multiplication. However, once the matrices have been multiplied, the dual representation must be built for the resulting matrix. Ironically, in some sense, the quadtree, by being a variant of a two-dimensional runlength representation, addresses this problem in part.

2.91. See Section 6.3 of [Knut73b] for a proof for $k = 1$, which is generalized for arbitrary values of k.

2.92. The $\sqrt{2}$ term arises from the fact that the points may be at opposite corners of the smallest square of side width s/d.

2.93. Overmars [Over88a] suggests that the N points be chosen in such a way that they form $N/2$ clusters of 2 points each. These $N/2$ clusters are the leaf nodes of a complete PR quadtree of depth $\log_4(N/2)$ such that each leaf contains one cluster. At this point, each of the $N/2$ clusters must be further decomposed by use of the PR quadtree. The $N/2$ clusters of points are chosen in such a way that the elements of each cluster appear at the maximum depth in the PR quadtree (i.e., n). The result is that we need $O(N)$ storage for the nodes at depth 0 through $\log_4(N/2)$ and $O((n - \log_4(N/2)) \cdot N)$ for the nodes at the remaining depths up to n. When 2^n is large in comparison to N, this is $O(N \cdot n)$.

2.94. This occurs when 2^n is $O(N)$ or smaller than N.

2.96. The worst case arises when the boundaries of the rectangular query region intersect 2^n nodes (i.e., regions).

2.97. $1/4^k$.

2.98. $(1 - \dfrac{1}{4^k})^v$.

2.99. $\begin{bmatrix} v \\ 1 \end{bmatrix} \cdot \dfrac{1}{4^k} \cdot (1 - \dfrac{1}{4^k})^{v-1}$.

2.100. $1 - (1 - \dfrac{1}{4^k})^v - \begin{bmatrix} v \\ 1 \end{bmatrix} \cdot \dfrac{1}{4^k} \cdot (1 - \dfrac{1}{4^k})^{v-1}$.

2.101. $4^{k+1} \cdot (1 - (1 - \dfrac{1}{4^k})^v - \begin{bmatrix} v \\ 1 \end{bmatrix} \cdot \dfrac{1}{4^k} \cdot (1 - \dfrac{1}{4^k})^{v-1})$. This should be familiar from the proof of Theorem 1.1 in Section 1.5.

2.102. $E = 1 + \displaystyle\sum_{k=0}^{\infty} 4^{k+1} \cdot (1 - (1 - \dfrac{1}{4^k})^v - \begin{bmatrix} v \\ 1 \end{bmatrix} \cdot \dfrac{1}{4^k} \cdot (1 - \dfrac{1}{4^k})^{v-1})$.

2.104. All instances of 2^2 or 4 are replaced by 2^m.

2.105. Left subtrees always correspond to hyperrectangles.

2.106. No. The prefix of each node's DZE can be deduced from the DZE of its parent.

2.112. Flajolet and Puech [Flaj83] perform such an analysis for a k-d tree and a k-d trie (or PR k-d tree) and show that the k-d trie is asymptotically better than the k-d tree.

2.115. See [Whit82].

2.116. See [Whit82].

2.118. The query $X < 2$.

2.119. See Faloutsos [Falo88].

2.122. See the Peano-Hilbert order discussed in Section 1.3 and shown in Figure 1.11d. It has the property that every element is a 4-adjacent neighbor of the previous element in the sequence. Goldschlager [Gold81], Goodchild and Grandfield [Good83], and Witten and Wyvill [Witt83] give algorithms to convert between Peano-Hilbert orders and the corresponding x and y coordinate values of the points.

2.123. The probability that i bit positions of c records are not sufficient to resolve the overflow (i.e., they have identical values) is $p_i = 2^{-ic}$ and the expected number of bits that must be compared is $E = \lim_{h \to \infty} \sum_{i=1}^{h} i \cdot p_{i-1} \cdot (1 - p_i)$. Orenstein [Oren82] shows that E is bounded by 28/9, and as c increases, it approaches 1.

2.125. See [Dand86].

2.126. See [Rous85]. The basic idea is to rotate the n points about the origin until each point has a distinct x coordinate value. This rotation is guaranteed to exist [Rous85]. Now the points are arranged by increasing x coordinate values and grouped in such a way that their bounding rectangles are nonintersecting.

2.127. No. A counterexample can be constructed easily.

2.129. Either one of h_n or h_{n+1} can be used first. The difference is in the mechanics of the lookup operation. Let $2^n \le m \le 2^{n+1} - 1$. Ignore the case where $m = 2^n$ because in this case only h_n is applicable. We apply h_{n+1} first. Let $h_{n+1}(K) = x$. If $x < m$, we have found the location; otherwise $x \ge m$ and we apply $h_n(K)$. Suppose we apply h_n first. Let $h_n(K) = x$. If $x \ge m - 2^n$, we have found the location; otherwise $x < m - 2^n$ and we apply $h_{n+1}(K)$. Suppose that $x < m - 2^n$ and that $h_{n+1}(K) = 2^n + x$. If we had not applied h_{n+1} in this case and instead stored K in bucket x, we would have had a problem in the future. To see this, we observe that since we are now at level $n,n+1$, the next time that bucket x will be split, we will be at level $n+1,n+2$. This means that the records in bucket x will be rehashed using h_{n+2} and distributed into buckets x and $2^{n+1} + x$. However, at this time if we want to look up the record with key K with which we have been dealing, we will have to use hash function h_{n+1}, which will hash to bucket $2^n + x$, and K will not be there.

2.130. There are two possibilities depending on whether s, the next bucket to be split, is nonzero. If s is nonzero, then bucket $2^n + s - 1$ is merged into bucket $s - 1$, s is reset to $s - 1$, and bucket $2^n + s - 1$ is no longer used. If s is zero, then bucket $2^n - 1$ is merged into bucket $2^{n-1} - 1$, s is reset to $2^{n-1} - 1$, bucket $2^n - 1$ is no longer used, and n is reset to $n - 1$.

2.132. $s(\tau) = 1 + \tau/2$ and $u(\tau) = \tau$ [Knut73b, p. 518].

2.133. Calculate the expected number of records as a function of x and z and also as a function of x and α and then solve for z. Therefore $2 \cdot x \cdot (z/2) + (1-x) \cdot z = \alpha \cdot (2 \cdot x + 1 - x)$.

2.134. The probability of encountering a split group is x with an expected search length of $s(\alpha \cdot (1+x)/2)$, while for an unsplit group it is $1-x$ with an expected search length of $s(\alpha \cdot (1+x))$. Therefore $S(\alpha,x) = x \cdot s(\alpha \cdot (1+x)/2) + (1-x) \cdot s(\alpha \cdot (1+x))$, which reduces to $1 + \alpha \cdot (2 + x - x^2)/4$.

2.135. $U(\alpha,x) = x \cdot u(\alpha \cdot (1+x)/2) + (1-x) \cdot u(\alpha \cdot (1+x))$, which reduces to $\alpha \cdot (2 + x - x^2)/2$.

2.136. They arise when the expected number of records in all of the buckets is the same—that is, when $x = 0$ or $x = 1$. $S(\alpha,0) = 1 + \alpha/2$ and $U(\alpha,0) = \alpha$.

2.137. When $x = \frac{1}{2}$, $S(\alpha,\frac{1}{2}) = 1 + (\alpha/2) \cdot (9/8)$ and $U(\alpha,\frac{1}{2}) = (\alpha/2) \cdot (9/8)$.

2.138. $\bar{S}(\alpha) = \int_0^1 S(\alpha,x)\,dx = 1 + (\alpha/2) \cdot (13/12)$ and $\bar{U}(\alpha) = \int_0^1 U(\alpha,x)\,dx = (\alpha/2) \cdot (13/12)$.

2.139. $A(\alpha,x) = \alpha \cdot (1+x)/\alpha = 1+x$ and $\bar{A}(\alpha,x) = \int_0^1 A(\alpha,x)\,dx = 3/2$.

2.142. See [Rama84].

2.143. See [Rama84].

2.144. See [Rama84].

2.145. This should be apparent by noting that the overflow files are accessed with the same hashing function, albeit at a lower level. Thus a bucket in the overflow file corresponds to 'brother' primary buckets.

2.146 Use induction on s.

2.150. See the Peano-Hilbert order discussed in Section 1.3 and shown in Figure 1.11d. It has the property that every element is a 4-adjacent neighbor of the previous element in the sequence. For more details, see the solution to Exercise 2.122.

2.151.

Reversed bit interleaving applied to the result of $f(z) = z$ div 12.5

Name	x	y		CODE(x)	CODE(x)/64	CODE(y)
Chicago	2	3	44	0.687500	28	0.437500
Mobile	4	0	1	0.015625	2	0.031250
Toronto	4	6	11	0.171875	7	0.109375
Buffalo	6	5	39	0.609375	27	0.421875
Denver	0	3	40	0.625000	20	0.312500
Omaha	2	2	12	0.187500	12	0.187500
Atlanta	6	1	37	0.578125	26	0.406250
Miami	7	0	21	0.328125	42	0.656250

2.152. No. Since the hash function is of the form $h(\kappa) = \kappa/2^n$, reversed bit interleaving will have an effect analogous to that in which all records in a given bucket agree in the least significant digits. This is not quite true due to the nonuniformity of the relative load of the buckets.

2.154. The last d buckets should be merged and their contents stored in bucket $s-1$.

2.155. a is already an integer, and thus they are equivalent.

2.156. Mullin [Mull85] gives the following procedure:

recursive integer procedure PHYSICAL(L,D,ORIGIN);
/* Given a spiral hashing implementation with a growth factor D and a physical bucket
   addressing system starting at ORIGIN, return the physical bucket address corresponding to logical bucket address L. */
begin
   value integer L,D,ORIGIN;
   integer LOW,HIGH;
   if L<D **then return**(L);
   HIGH ← (L+1) **div** D;
   LOW ← L **div** D;
   return(**if** LOW<HIGH **then** PHYSICAL(LOW,D,ORIGIN)
          /* A reused address */
          else L-LOW+ORIGIN);
end;

2.157. $\log_d t$.

2.159. Larson [Lars88] suggests the use of a table of segments. Each segment contains a fixed number of buckets. As segments become full, new ones are allocated. Once all of the buckets in a particular segment have been split, the segment can be reused. Of course, this requires a directory whose size is fixed.

2.162. $c = (2 - \sqrt{2})/(3 - 2\sqrt{2}) \approx 3.414$, $b = c \cdot (c-1) \approx 8.243$, $a = 2-c \approx 1.414$.

2.163. Yes. A bucket split will now result in $d-1$, d, or $d+1$ new buckets, whereas previously d new buckets were always created.

2.164. A second degree polynomial can be written as $(a \cdot x + b) \cdot x + c$, which requires four floating point operations, whereas $a + b/(c - x)$ requires only three.

2.165. $p(y) = \log_2(y+dy) - \log_2 y = \log_2(1+dy/y) \approx dy/(y \cdot \ln 2)$. This makes use of the fact that $\log_2 x = \ln x/\ln 2$ and $\ln(1+x) \approx x$ for small x.

2.166. From the assumption about the expected value, there exists a constant c_1 such that $\tau(y) = c_1/(y \cdot \ln 2)$. The average storage utilization factor (i.e., overall value) is α, and solving the equation $\int_1^2 (c_1/(y \cdot \ln 2)) \cdot dy = \alpha$ yields $c_1 = \alpha$.

2.167. From the assumption there exist a pair of constants c_2 and c_3 such that $q(y) = c_2 \cdot \tau(y) = c_2 \cdot \alpha/(y \cdot \ln 2) = c_3/y$. The value of c_3 is obtained by noting that the probability of landing on a bucket address in $[y, y+dy]$ is $q(y) \cdot dy$ and the probability of landing on some bucket in $[1,2]$ is 1. Solving the equation $\int_1^2 (c_3/y) \cdot dy = 1$ yields $c_3 = 1/\ln 2$.

2.168. From Exercise 2.132, the expected number of key comparisons for a successful search for a bucket at address y with a storage utilization factor of $\tau(y)$ is $1+\tau(y)/2$. The

expected cost of a successful search is then $\int_1^2 (1+\tau(y)/2) \cdot q(y) \cdot dy = 1 + \alpha/(4 \cdot (\ln 2)^2) = 1 + (\alpha/2) \cdot 1.041$.

2.169. From Exercise 3.132 the expected number of key comparisons for an unsuccessful search for a bucket at address y with a storage utilization factor of $\tau(y)$ is $\tau(y)$. The expected cost of an successful search is then $\int_1^2 \tau(y) \cdot q(y) \cdot dy = \alpha/(2 \cdot (\ln 2)^2) = \alpha \cdot 1.041$.

2.170. This situation arises with a probability of $1/\alpha$—that is, for every $1/\alpha$ of the record insertions. The expected number of records in the first bucket is $\tau(1) = \alpha/\ln 2$, and thus the expected number of extra hashing operations is $\tau(1)/\alpha = 1/\ln 2 = 1.443$.

2.171. Instances of $\ln 2$ are replaced by $\ln d$.

2.172. See [Chu88b].

2.173. Using Cartesian coordinates, the arc length for the function $y = f(x)$ is $\int \sqrt{1+(f'(x))^2} \cdot dx$. $f'(x)$ can be rewritten as dy/dx. Making the substitutions $x = \rho\cos\theta$, $y = \rho\sin\theta$, and $\rho = e^{k\cdot\theta}$ leads to the integral $\sqrt{1+f^2} \cdot \int e^{k\cdot\theta} \cdot d\theta$. The value of this integral is $(\sqrt{1+k^2}/k) \cdot e^{k\cdot\theta}$, which is $\rho \cdot \sqrt{1+k^2}/f$.

2.175. See [Regn85].

2.177. Linear hashing has an implicit directory with one directory element per grid block and grows by one. A grid file directory grows by the insertion of a $(k-1)$-dimensional cross-section, while an EXCELL directory may double in size.

2.178. The reason is that buckets are not necessarily full when they are split by linear hashing. Also, linear hashing requires overflow buckets and makes use of a storage utilization factor in deciding when to split a bucket.

2.179. As long as the grid directory does not grow too large (i.e., there are not too many clusters of size larger than the bucket capacity), EXCELL seems to be the choice due to its simplicity and performance guarantees.

2.180. It belongs at depth 3 since it provides for a very gentle growth of the number of buckets by successive subdivisions along the individual bits. In this respect it is similar to EXCELL, with the exception that one bucket overflow does not require doubling the number of directory elements; at most two buckets must be added by a split operation (equivalent to a grid refinement operation in EXCELL).

2.181. It is difficult to fit it into this taxonomy because it does not decompose the space into regions that are rectangular parallelepipeds.

2.182. It should be placed alongside the PR k-d tree because it is a PR k-d tree with a truncated path to each node. This path bypasses the tests when one son is empty.

2.183. At depth 3, EXCELL is now type E_1, the grid file is type D_1, and the pyramid is type E_k. At depth 4, the PR k-d tree is a type E_1 son of EXCELL, the PR quadtree is a type E_k son of the pyramid, the point quadtree is a type E_k son of the grid file, and the k-d tree is a type E_1 son of the grid file. At depth 5, the adaptive k-d tree is a type E_1 son of the k-d tree. How do the MX quadtree and linear hashing with reversed bit interleaving fit into the taxonomy?

2.185. A solution that proceeds by finding the closest pair of points in sequence need not be optimal, as can be seen by considering the four points $(0,2)$, $(1,0)$, $(3,0)$, and $(4,2)$. The closest pair is $(1,0)$ and $(3,0)$. This means that the remaining pair is $(0,2)$ and $(4,2)$, which has a cost of 6. On the other hand, taking the pairs $(0,2)$ and $(1,0)$ followed by the pair $(3,0)$ and $(4,2)$ leads to a cost of $2 \cdot \sqrt{5}$, which, of course, is smaller. This is termed the greedy-method heuristic. The best known solution to the Euclidean match-

ing problem using it is $O(N^{3/2} \cdot \log_2 N)$ [Bent80e]. Although the greedy-method heuristic is not optimal, Reingold and Tarjan [Rein81] have shown that the result of its use is never worse than $4/3 \cdot N^{\log_2 1.5}$. For other recent literature on this topic, see the survey of Avis [Avis83] and Tarjan [Tarj84a]. For approximate solutions based on space-filling curves (see Section 1.3), see [Iri81, Bart83].

Recently Vaidya [Vaid88] has developed an algorithm for finding the smallest Euclidean matching (i.e., for finding an exact solution) that runs in $O(N^{2.5} \cdot \log_2^4 N)$ time. Previously the best upper bound for solving this problem was $O(N^3)$ [Tarj84a, Lawl76].

2.187. Lee [Lee83] suggests a transformation of the problem into an instance of the maximum clique problem (see Section 3.3 and the solution to Exercise 3.79).

CHAPTER 3

3.1. The line segments are not permitted to overlap.

3.2. No. For example, consider the segment tree of Figure 3.3 without line segment C (i.e., for segments A, B, D, E, F, and G). Line segments A and E overlap, yet no node in the segment tree contains both of them.

3.3. The alternative solution requires that the list be traversed when attempting to remove the line segment. This could lead to an extra factor of N in the cost of deletion.

3.4. Multiple intersections are reported for line segments that are totally contained within other line segments. Removing duplicates requires sorting a set that may have more than N elements, and the algorithm may take more than $O(N \cdot \log_2 N)$ time.

3.5. Search for P starting at the root. Descend to the son whose interval contains P. Report all intervals associated with the nonleaf nodes on the path to the appropriate leaf node. This takes $O(\log_2 N + F)$ time, where F is the number of intervals that contain P. The $\log_2 N$ term results from the depth of the tree.

3.6. $O(N)$ space is used since only the number of intervals need be stored at each nonleaf node of the segment tree (instead of the identities of the intervals). Descending the tree takes $O(\log_2 N)$ time.

3.10. The segment tree is good for indicating all the one-dimensional intervals that contain a given point. It is not suitable for indicating which intervals lie within a given interval; a range tree is more appropriate. However, without additional structuring, many intervals that do not satisfy the query will be examined.

3.11. The segment tree is good for indicating all the one-dimensional intervals that contain a given point. One possible solution is to search for the endpoints of the given interval and take an intersection of the result. This takes more than $O(\log_2 N + F)$ time. Can you find a better solution?

3.13. Each line segment can be marked in at most $2 \cdot \lceil \log_2 N \rceil$ nodes of the segment tree. There are N line segments that are tested for intersection with these nodes.

3.14. Yes. However, now the intervals represented by the nonleaf nodes are not of uniform size, but once we know the maximum number of intervals there is no problem. The segment tree of Figure 3.3 would have its external nodes marked as in Figure 3.4 with the following differences. Node 10 would be marked with {B} instead of {A,C}, and node 11 would be marked with {B} instead of being unmarked. The only changes in the marking of the nonleaf nodes are that the left son of the right son of the root is marked with {A,C}

instead of being unmarked, and the left son of the left son of the right son of the root is now unmarked instead of being marked with {A,C}.

3.15. All leaf, and some nonleaf, nodes in the tertiary structure have nonempty secondary structures. The tertiary structure is a binary tree. A nonleaf node with an empty secondary structure must have two active sons. The maximum number of such nonleaf nodes is one less than the total number of leaf nodes, all of which have a nonempty secondary structure. This result can also be obtained by viewing the tertiary structure as a variant of an extended binary tree.

3.16. Search for P starting at the root. For each nonleaf node, say I, compare P with the value stored at I, say V_I. If P is less than V_I, report all the intervals stored at I whose left endpoints are less than P. This takes time proportional to the number of intervals that contain P. Next, descend to the left son and repeat. If P is larger than V_I, report all the intervals stored at I whose right endpoints are greater than P. Next, descend to the right son and repeat. This takes $O(\log_2 N + F)$ time, where F is the number of intervals that contain P. The $\log_2 N$ term results from the depth of the tree.

3.17. No. The problem is that the intervals stored with a nonleaf node of the interval tree do not span the entire interval associated with the node.

3.18. Assume that the line segment $[l:r)$ is being processed. The point query returns all line segments $[a:b)$ such that $a < l \le b$, and the range query returns all line segments $[c:d)$ such that $l \le c < r$. Clearly these two sets are disjoint.

3.21. If the task is to be achieved in $O(\log_2 N + F)$ time, the interval tree needs modification, such as the addition of some auxiliary structures analogous to the secondary and tertiary structures. The problem is that currently the interval tree does not facilitate pruning. In particular, at each level of the tree, a good part of the secondary structure may have to be searched without finding any intervals that satisfy the query.

3.22. See the solution to Exercise 3.21.

3.24. Draw the intervals, and the result will be apparent.

3.28. See [Tarj83].

3.29. See [McCr85].

3.30. Perform the semi-infinite range query $([-\infty:P),(P:\infty])$. It takes $O(\log_2 M + F)$ time, where F is the number of intersecting intervals found.

3.31. See [McCr85].

3.32. Perform the semi-infinite range query $([-\infty:a),(b:\infty])$ in search of the points (x,y).

3.33. Perform the semi-infinite range query $((a:\infty],[-\infty:b))$ in search of the points (x,y). This requires the use of an inverse priority search tree for the range of y. Since $x < b$, this can be simplified to $((a:b],[-\infty:b))$

3.34. Perform the semi-infinite range query $([-\infty:b),(a:\infty])$ in search of the points (y,x). Since $a < y$, this can be simplified to $((a:b],(a:\infty])$.

3.36. Use a plane-sweep method [Sham76]. Sort the endpoints of the line segments, and then sweep a vertical line through the set. If some of the lines are vertical, rotate the set slightly. The key is that if there are no intersections, the relative ordering of the line segments will be the same through the entire sweep. Use a balanced binary tree to record the segments that intersect the sweep line. A line segment is inserted into (deleted from) the tree each time a left (right) endpoint is encountered. An intersection has occurred if upon deletion the relative ordering between the line segment and its top and bottom neighbors has changed.

3.37. Use a one-dimensional range tree at each nonleaf node of the segment tree. The range tree is sorted by the x coordinate values of the vertical line segments associated with it.

The one-dimensional range tree for m items uses $O(m)$ space. At each level of the segment tree, $O(\log_2 N + F)$ nodes may be examined. There are $\log_2 N$ levels in the primary segment tree and the result follows.

3.38. Overmars [Over85] suggests decomposing this problem into two cases:

1. R contains an element of L. Build a two-dimensional range tree that contains the left endpoint of each element of L and perform a range query with R.

2. An element of L intersects a boundary of R. Treat the horizontal and vertical boundaries of R separately. For the horizontal boundaries, project all the line segments on a vertical line and build a segment tree for the projections. Let V denote the projections of the line segments. Find all elements of V that intersect either of the two horizontal boundaries using the result of Exercise 3.37. The vertical boundaries are handled in the same way, with the exception that we use the projections of the line segments on a horizontal line.

The storage and execution time requirements follow from previous analyses of these problems. Reporting some intersections more than once is avoided by checking for the possibility of case 2 while performing case 1. A positive answer means that the reporting of the intersection is delayed until it is detected by case 2. This will increase F, the number of intersections, by at most a constant multiplicative factor, and thus the order of execution time is not affected.

3.39. Assume that the balanced binary search tree contains nodes corresponding to the top and bottom boundaries of all active rectangles (i.e., one node per boundary) and that bottom boundaries are smaller in magnitude than top boundaries. A type bit indicates if the node serves as a bottom or top boundary. There is at least one pair of intersecting rectangles if upon inserting a rectangle, say R with bottom and top boundaries B and T, respectively, in the tree one of the following conditions holds:

1. There exists a node L such that B and T are in different subtrees of L.

2. There exists a node L such that L corresponds to a bottom boundary, and one of B and T is inserted as a right son of L.

3. There exists a node L such that L corresponds to a top boundary, and one of B and T is inserted as a left son of L.

3.40. The algorithm proceeds as long as the boundaries in the tree are nonintersecting. Thus it can be used to detect the occurrence of an intersection, but it cannot be used to maintain a set of boundaries that are intersecting. For example, assuming that rectangles are specified by the pairs of coordinate values (x,y) of their lower left and upper right corners, consider the three rectangles $(1,1)$ and $(10,10)$; $(3,7)$ and $(9,9)$; and $(5,3)$ and $(7,5)$. Assuming a horizontal scan from left to right, the intersection of the rectangle specified by $(5,3)$ and $(7,5)$ with either of rectangles $(1,1)$ and $(10,10)$ or $(3,7)$ and $(9,9)$ is not detected.

3.41. Use a plane-sweep method [Bent79d]. Sort the left and right boundaries of the rectangles. Sweep a vertical scan line through them. Let T be the balanced binary search tree that represents the bottom and top boundaries of the active rectangles, and link them in ascending order. Each time a rectangle, with bottom and top boundaries b and t, respectively, becomes active (inactive), enter (remove) b and t in (from) T and output the line segments whose entries in T lie between b and t. The output step visits only the nodes in the range since T is linked in ascending order. The time and space requirements follow.

3.42. Sort the rectangles by their left and right endpoints as well as by the x coordinate value of their centroid. Sweep a vertical line through them. Each time a left (right) endpoint is encountered, the corresponding boundary is inserted into (deleted from) the segment tree. Each time a centroid point is encountered, say corresponding to rectangle R, the segment tree is searched for all segments that overlap R's y coordinate value. The rectangles corresponding to these segments either totally enclose R or intersect R [Bent80f].

3.43. See [Vais80].

3.44. The primary segment tree (containing the projections of the rectangles on the x-axis) uses $O(N \cdot \log_2 N)$ storage as there are $O(N \cdot \log_2 N)$ possible segments. Each of these segments can appear in as many as $O(\log_2 N)$ positions in the secondary segment trees [Edel81b, Edel82].

3.45. Use doubly linked lists. Each rectangle can appear in $O(\log_2 N)$ nonleaf nodes in the primary segment tree. Each of these nonleaf nodes is the root of a secondary segment tree. Insertion in each of relevant nodes in the secondary segment tree takes $O(\log_2 N)$ time.

3.46. The insertion of each rectangle takes $O(\log_2^2 N)$ time. There are N rectangles.

3.47. At each level of the primary segment tree we perform a one-dimensional stabbing query on a segment tree. This takes $O(\log_2 N + F)$ time. There are $\log_2 N$ levels in the primary segment tree, and the result follows.

3.48. $O(N \cdot \log_2^k N)$ storage and $O(\log_2^k N + F)$ time for N points and F rectangles containing them.

3.49. Yes. Use the layered tree approach of Vaishnavi and Wood [Vais82] that makes use of additional pointers.

3.50. There are three possible cases:

1. R contains an element of V. Build a two-dimensional range tree that contains the lower leftmost corner of each element of V, and perform a range query with R.
2. R is contained in some element of V. Build a two-dimensional segment tree for V, and perform a two-dimensional stabbing query for the lower leftmost corner of R.
3. A side of R intersects a side of an element of V. Use the result of Exercise 3.37 to solve two problems. The first stores the line segments corresponding to the vertical sides of V in a segment tree and finds the elements of V that intersect either of the two horizontal sides of R. The second stores the line segments corresponding to the horizontal sides of V in a segment tree and finds the elements of V that intersect either of the two vertical sides of R.

The storage and execution time requirements follow from previous analyses of these problems.

3.51. When performing cases 1 and 2 check for the possibility of case 3. A positive answer means that the reporting of the intersection is delayed until it is detected by case 3. This will increase F, the number of intersections, by at most a constant multiplicative factor, and thus the order of execution time is not affected.

3.55. Project the rectangles on the x axis, and store these intervals in a segment tree, say T. Let I be a nonleaf node in T and let R_I denote the rectangles whose horizontal sides are associated with I. For each I, build an interval tree for the projections of R_I on the y axis. The primary segment tree uses $O(N \cdot \log_2 N)$ storage, as there are $O(N \cdot \log_2 N)$ possible segments. Each of these segments appears in one node in the secondary interval tree [Edel81b, Edel82].

3.56. Use doubly linked lists. Each rectangle can appear in $O(\log_2 N)$ nonleaf nodes in the primary segment tree. Each of these nonleaf nodes is the root of a secondary interval tree.

Insertion in each of the relevant nodes in the secondary interval tree takes $O(\log_2 N)$ time since this many nodes may have to be examined.

3.57. The insertion of each rectangle takes $O(\log_2^2 N)$ time. There are N rectangles.

3.58. At each level of the primary segment tree, we perform a one-dimensional stabbing query on an interval tree. This takes $O(\log_2 N + F)$ time. There are $\log_2 N$ levels in the primary segment tree and the result follows.

3.59. See the solution to Exercise 3.50.

3.67. Use a segment tree with a plane sweep once the endpoints of the lines have been sorted [Bent77a]. Fredman and Weide [Fred78] have shown that it is $\Omega(N \cdot \log_2 N)$.

3.68. 453.

3.69. These intervals are contained in rectangles A and C, but the corresponding horizontal intervals do not overlap. Thus these nodes are not marked for A and C at the same time.

3.70. We need only to record whether a node is covered by an interval (and how many times). The identity of the covering interval need not be recorded.

3.71. At each insertion and deletion, you must update the length of the overlap with the vertical scan line. This is done by recomputing the LEN fields of all nodes encountered during the insertion process with a COUNT field value of 0. It must also be recomputed for all nodes encountered during the deletion process with a COUNT field value that became 0 or are ancestors of nodes with a COUNT field value that became 0. This is an $O(\log_2 N)$ process.

3.72. The procedure is similar to that used for computing the area. The difference is that we must also take into account the contributions of the horizontal boundaries. In this case we must keep track of the number of disjoint segments in the segment tree. Each active disjoint segment $[y_b : y_t]$ at x_i contributes $2 \cdot (x_i - x_{i-1})$ to the perimeter unless there exists another segment $[y_a : y_b]$ or $[y_t : y_c]$. Besides keeping track of the lengths of the vertical segments in the interval corresponding to a node, the node also keeps track of twice the number of disjoint segments in its interval. In addition, each node contains two flags that indicate whether each of the endpoints of its corresponding interval is a bottom or top extreme of a segment in the segment tree. The space and time requirements are the same as for the computation of area. For more details, see [Bent77a, vanL81].

3.73. See [Lee83].

3.75. At each insertion and deletion, you must update the area of the overlap with the scan plane. This is done by recomputing it for all nodes encountered during the insertion process that are currently unmarked. It must also be done for those nodes encountered during the deletion process that are no longer marked or are ancestors of nodes that are no longer marked. This is an $O(N)$ process.

3.77. See [Lee83].

3.79. Lee [Lee83] suggests that each point be treated as the center of a rectangle of size R. Now compute the maximum clique (i.e., the identity of its members). Any point in the intersection of the maximum clique can be used as the center of R.

3.80. The solution is analogous to that of Exercise 3.79, except that in the plane sweep the total weights of the covering rectangles are recorded instead of their cardinality.

3.81. Use induction on the number of horizontal and vertical rectangles.

3.82. (1) Each top and bottom boundary goes through at most one cell in each slab. Each left and right boundary is totally contained in one slab. (2) Each cell can intersect at most $2 \cdot \sqrt{N}$ left and right boundaries of rectangles because of the way the slabs are defined. Each cell can intersect at most two top and bottom boundaries of V-rectangles and at most $\sqrt{N} + 1$ top and bottom boundaries of H-rectangles because of the way the cells are defined. (3) If the boundary of a rectangle intersects the cell, the rectangle is either a v-rectangle or an H-rectangle with respect to the slab containing the cell. In the former case, the top and bottom boundaries of the rectangle are both cell boundaries, so the rectangle's intersection with the cell extends at least as far as the bottom and top boundaries of the cell (i.e., it is a vertical rectangle). In the latter case, the rectangle extends at least as far as the slab boundary in the left and right directions (i.e., it is a horizontal rectangle).

3.84. We need only to record whether a node is covered by an interval (and how many times). The identity of the covering interval need not be recorded.

3.87. Storing a $(d-1)$-dimensional rectangle in a $(d-1)$-dimensional quadtree of side length N uses $O(N^{d-2})$ space and, thus, each insertion and deletion is an $O(N^{d-2})$ process.

3.90. An $O(N^2)$ time solution to this problem can be based on computing an arrangement of the lines forming boundaries of the triangles. An *arrangement* formed by a set of lines is the set of all finite or infinite polygonal regions (i.e., cells) determined by the lines. The arrangement formed by N lines in the plane can be computed in $O(N^2)$ time [Edel86b]. Once the arrangement has been obtained, we add up the area of all the cells in the arrangement contained in some triangle. It is not clear how to solve this problem in subquadratic time.

3.91. 2^{i+1}.

3.92. A 4×4 area of blocks (i.e., 16 blocks) is the maximum since the rectangle corresponding to the representative point can have a side length that is bounded by four times the length of the block containing the representative point.

3.93. Each point of the PR quadtree corresponds to the center of each black block.

3.94. When a black block has three white brothers, the block can be merged with its brothers to yield a node that is one level higher in the tree.

3.95. The center (c_x, c_y, c_z) is a location parameter, and the radius r is an extension parameter.

3.96. Five parameters are necessary: two for the centroid, two for the perpendicular extents, and one for the rotation from the horizontal line.

3.97. Representation 2 is similar to representation 3. It does not suffer from a large, unpopulated embedding space as does representation 1.

3.98. Use Figure 3.11 as an illustration. It is a rectangular region whose upper-left corner coincides with the figure and whose lower-right corner is at (P,P) [McCr80].

3.99. Representation 3 is a clockwise rotation by 45° of representation 1 subject to a scale factor of $\sqrt{2}$.

3.101. A four-dimensional conelike region with the line at its tip and in the c_x-c_y plane.

3.102. A four-dimensional conelike region with the circle at its tip and in the c_x-c_y plane.

3.103. Three-dimensional conelike regions with the (a) point, (b) line, (c) circle, and (d) rectangle at its tip and in the c_x-c_y plane.

3.104. (a) A cone-shaped region whose tip is at C and which opens in the direction of smaller radius values. (b) A cone-shaped region whose tip is at C and which opens in the direction of larger radius values.

3.105. Kurland and Bier [Kurl88] suggest using the center of mass and the point farthest from the center of mass. If there is more than one such furthest point, the representative point is not unique.

3.108. The following proof is due to Sequin [Oust84]. Use induction. Insert the rectangles one at a time in order from right to left. When there is one rectangle, there are four space tiles. Each additional rectangle, say R, causes the creation of at most three new space tiles as follows. The top and bottom edges of R can each cause a space tile to be split, thereby creating one new space tile apiece. Only one new space tile will be created to the left of R since we are inserting them in right-to-left order and there can be no existing rectangle to the left of R at the time of its insertion. No additional space tile is created to the right of R. Note that the rectangles are inserted in a particular order to obtain the upper bound; however, the final configuration is independent of the order of insertion.

3.109. At least two of the rectangles have colinear edges.

3.110. Suppose that the search starts at one of the rightmost rectangles. First, move up or down until locating a tile whose vertical range covers the point. Next, move left or right until finding a horizontal range that contains the point. This may require several iterations due to vertical misalignment resulting from horizontal motion during the search [Oust84].

3.111. Locate a rectangle that intersects a corner of the window—say, the lower left corner. Now use the links to traverse the set of rectangles with the window's boundaries serving to indicate the direction in which the traversal should proceed. Initially up links are followed until encountering a tile outside the window. Next, follow a right link and a down link.

3.112. No. For example, consider rectangles C and D in Figure 3.1.

3.113. Let (K_0, K_1, K_2, K_3) represent a rectangle whose lower left corner is at (K_0, K_1), and whose upper right corner is at (K_2, K_3). Assume that node P is at level j of the k-d tree. Therefore, at P, we discriminate on key $K_{j \bmod 4}(P)$. With P are stored the lower and upper bounds of key $K_{j \bmod 4}$. The lower and upper bounds of the remaining keys are obtained from the three ancestors of P in the k-d tree. Thus only two bound values need to be stored at each node. However, these bound values may not be so useful. For example, when storing rectangles in a 4-d tree, the value of K_0 at the root is an upper bound for the left edges of rectangles in LOSON, which is of little use in cutting off searches.

Rosenberg [Rose85] suggests storing three values at each node, LOMINBOUND, HIMAXBOUND, and OTHERBOUND. LOMINBOUND corresponds to the minimum value of a left or bottom edge in LOSON, while HIMAXBOUND is the maximum value of a right or top edge in HISON. For a node that discriminates on a left or bottom edge, OTHERBOUND is the maximum value of a right or top edge in LOSON, while for a node that discriminates on a right or top edge, it is the minimum value of a left or bottom edge in HISON. At the root we discriminate on the left edges of rectangles. LOMINBOUND is the minimum value of a left edge in LOSON. HIMAXBOUND is the maximum value of a right edge in HISON. OTHERBOUND is the maximum value of a right edge of a rectangle in LOSON. The minimum value of a left edge of a rectangle in HISON is the value of the discriminator key (i.e., K_0).

Searches in LOSON are cut off if the left edge of the search region exceeds OTHERBOUND or if the right edge of the search region is less than LOMINBOUND. Searches in HISON are cut off if the left edge of the search region exceeds HIMAXBOUND or the right edge of the search region is less than K_0. The cutoffs for searches at nodes in the remaining three levels are obtained in a similar manner. Of course, at odd depths of the tree (assuming that the root is at depth 0), the search cutoffs are in terms of the top and bottom edges of the search region.

3.117. Traversing the k-d tree is an $O(N)$ process. Every node must be intersected with the remaining nodes in the tree. Pruning at every right subtree means that the number of comparison operations made is $O(N \cdot \log_2 N)$ since this is the total path length, and for a node at depth L, at most L right subtrees will be examined.

3.119. If the maximum value in LOSON(P) is greater than the minimum value in HISON(P) and the point lies between the maximum and minimum values.

3.140. Consider the four points A = (5,6), B = (6,5), C = (0,4), and D = (4,0). The closest point to A is B, the closest point to B is A, the closest point to C is A, and the closest point to D is B. The result is that the rectangles formed by A and C, and B and D intersect.

3.147. See [Shaf86a].

3.156. See [Shaf86a].

3.160. For each rectangle intersection, find the pixel that contains the lower left corner of the rectangle formed by the intersection. If this pixel is in the current node, report the intersection; otherwise do not report it. It should be clear that each intersection is reported exactly once.

3.161. A node in a B-tree of order $2 \cdot K + 1$ has K records and $K + 1$ sons.

3.162. $\lceil \log_m(N) \rceil$.

3.163. $\lceil N/m \rceil + \lceil N/m^2 \rceil + \cdots + 1$.

3.169. For a set of $M + 1$ items there are 2^{M+1} subsets. Of these subsets we exclude the empty set and the set of M items leaving $2^{M+1} - 2$ subsets. Removing duplicate partitions yields $2^M - 1$ partitions.

3.170. Each rectangle may have to be tested against every other rectangle.

3.181. Each rectangle may have to be tested against every other rectangle.

CHAPTER 4

4.2. At each level of the tree we must examine n points to determine the points on the curve that are at a maximum distance from the line joining the curve's endpoints. The tree has $\log_2 n$ levels.

4.4. At each level of the tree we must process one-half of as many rectangles as were processed on the previous level. Initially we process $n+1$ pairs of points to yield n rectangles. The result follows since we have a geometric series with a ratio of $1:2$.

4.5. In the top-down method the enclosing rectangles are formed by using points on the curve, whereas in the bottom-up method, all rectangles at levels other than the deepest are based on the strips. In other words, in the bottom-up method, the width of the final rectangle is not necessarily the sum of the maximum distances to the curve from the line joining the endpoints of the curve.

4.7. Constructing the rectangular strip takes $O(N)$ time for N points since the perpendicular distance of each point from the line joining the curve's endpoints must be calculated. In contrast, the rectangle of minimum bounding area for N points takes $O(N \cdot \log_2 N)$ time as the convex hull must be obtained first.

4.8. See [Free75].

4.9. When all the strip segments in one tree intersect all the strip segments in the other tree, the algorithm will take $O(2^{d_1 + d_2})$ time.

4.10. The situation depicted in Figure 4.5b requires us to descend further in the strip tree since there is no longer a guarantee that the curves will intersect. Of course, many of the strips in the subtrees will be regular.

4.12. See [Ball81].

4.13. Use a tree traversal and check if the point P is inside or outside the strip. Given a strip s of width w, if P is inside s, then w is an upper bound on the distance. Otherwise the distance is bounded by the sum of the distance from P to s and w.

4.14. Represent it as two closed curves. Alternatively draw an imaginary line across the area and order the points so that the region is always to the right of the curve.

4.15. Draw a semi-infinite line starting at the point and count the number of intersections with the boundary. The line is represented by a strip tree of zero width. An odd number means that the point lies inside the area and an even number that it lies outside. The only possible problem is if the line is tangent to the curve corresponding to the area.

4.16. See [Ball81].

4.17. The key is that if the intersection of any strip of the curve, say s_c corresponding to a node T_c, with the strip tree of the area, say T_a, is null, then (1) if any point on s_c is inside T_a, every point in T_c is inside or on the boundary of T_a; and (2) if any point on s_c is outside T_a, every point in T_c is outside T_a. See [Ball81].

4.18. The key is to decompose the problem into two subproblems of intersecting curves with areas. Let T_1 and T_2 represent the strip trees corresponding to the two areas. First, inter- sect the curve corresponding to T_1 with the area corresponding to T_2, and then reverse the roles of the two strip trees. The final result is represented by the union of the previous two steps. See [Ball81].

4.19. Draw a semi-infinite line starting at the point, and count the number of intersections with the boundary. An odd number means that the point lies inside the area and an even number that it lies outside.

4.20. See [Burt77].

4.21. Not when the curve is closed.

4.22. $\int_a^b \sqrt{1 + f'^2(x)} \cdot dx.$

4.23. Use contradiction. The length of the major axis of the ellipse is equal to the length of the corresponding arc that is being approximated. An ellipse, say E, has the property that the sum of the distances from any point on E to the two foci is equal to the length of the major axis. Thus the arc must be internal to the ellipse. The only way in which the arc can lie outside the ellipse is if its length exceeds the length of the major axis, which is a contradiction because the endpoints of the arc are the two foci of the ellipse.

4.24. The strip tree requires six real numbers (w_L, w_R, x_P, y_P, x_Q, and y_Q) and two pointers, while the arc tree requires two real numbers (for t) and two pointers.

4.25. Check if the sum of its distances from the foci of the ellipse is less than or greater than the length of the major axis of the ellipse.

4.26. Check if the approximation can be used instead of the actual curve. This requires the point to be outside the ellipses represented by the approximation. This can be tested by using the result of Exercise 4.25. Traverse the arc tree in a breadth-first manner. When- ever the point is internal (external) to a node's ellipse, the sons of the node must (not) be tested. A conventional point-inclusion test can be used once it has been determined that the approximation is sufficient.

4.27. The two ellipses must intersect, and the two foci of each ellipse must be external to the other ellipse.

4.28. See [Günt87].

4.29. Yes, in principle, since an area is a closed curve. However, if the curves do not intersect, their areas can still overlap as one area can be totally contained in the other. This can be determined by a point inclusion test.

4.30. See [Günt87]. The common edges contribute to the output only if their orientation is identical when the curves of the areas are traversed in the same order (e.g., clockwise).

4.32. The line quadtree is nothing but a region quadtree with additional information stored at the nonleaf nodes.

4.36. The SE quadrant of the line quadtree requires one node, whereas in the revised line quadtree this quadrant requires four leaf nodes since the northern boundaries of the NW and NE subquadrants differ.

4.38. See Section 3.2.1.1 of [Same90b].

4.39. The maximum degree of a vertex.

4.40. The closer the vertex lies to a quadrant boundary line, the greater the value of D_3. See the discussion in the beginning of Section 4.2.3.2.

4.41. It ensures that the decomposition stops as soon as possible. An alternative formulation is that if a leaf node contains a vertex, say V, then at least one of its brothers must contain a vertex or a q-edge that is a segment of an edge not incident at V. For example, it precludes the further subdivision of the node containing D in Figure 4.12.

4.42. Condition 2′ does not imply condition 1 due to the possible presence of isolated vertices. Conditions 1, 2′, and 4 are insufficient because polygonal maps exist that would require a PM_1 quadtree of infinite depth to satisfy condition 2′. For example, consider vertex E in Figure 4.12. We observe that the node containing vertex E does not satisfy condition 2′ because of the two q-edges incident at it. Assume that the x and y coordinates of E cannot be expressed (without error) as a rational number whose denominator is a power of two (e.g., let both coordinates be one-third). This means that E can never lie on the boundary between two quadrants. Thus, by virtue of the continuity of the q-edges, no matter how many times we subdivide the quadrant containing vertex E, there will always exist a pair of (possibly infinitesimally small) q-edges incident at E that will occupy the same quadtree leaf.

4.43. Recall the definition of D_3 in terms of $d_{min.ee}$, the minimum separation between two non-intersecting q-edges (i.e., portions of edges bounded by either a vertex or the boundary of a PM_1 quadtree leaf).

4.44. PM_INSERT requires only that the DICTIONARY field be set immediately after the call to CLIP_LINES in PM_INSERT and that DICTIONARY(P) be left unmodified in SPLIT_PM_NODE. The revised PM_DELETE is considerably simpler, as shown below. Note that the modified procedures work for all three variants of the PM quadtree (i.e., for PM_2 and PM_3 as discussed in Sections 4.2.3.2 and 4.2.3.3, respectively).

```
recursive procedure PM_DELETE(P,R);
/* Delete the list of edges pointed at by P in the PM (i.e., PM₁, PM₂, and PM₃) quadtree
   rooted at R. It is assumed that the DICTIONARY field of all gray nodes indicates the
   edges in the subtrees below. PM_CHECK is generic. It is replaced by its appropriate
   analog for the PM₁, PM₂, and PM₃ quadtrees. */
begin
  value pointer edgelist P;
  value pointer node R;
  pointer edgelist L;
  quadrant I;
  L ← CLIP_LINES(P,SQUARE(R));
  if empty(L) then return; /* None of the edges is in the quadrant */
  DICTIONARY(R) ← SET_DIFFERENCE(DICTIONARY(R),L);
  if GRAY(R) then
    begin
```

```
            if PM_CHECK(DICTIONARY(R),SQUARE(R)) then PM_MERGE(R)
            else
              begin
                for I in {'NW', 'NE', 'SW', 'SE'} do PM_DELETE(L,SON(R,I));
              end;
          end;
      end;


recursive procedure PM_MERGE(P)
/* Merge the four sons of the quadtree rooted at node P.  The storage taken up by the four
   sons is reclaimed by use of returntoavail.  This process is recursive in the case of a PM₁
   quadtree. */
begin
  value pointer node P;
  quadrant I;
  for I in {'NW', 'NE', 'SW', 'SE'} do
    begin
      if GRAY(SON(P,I)) then PM_MERGE(SON(P,I))
      else
        begin
          returntoavail(SON(P,I));
          SON(P,I) ← NIL;
        end;
    end;
end;
```

4.45. An upper bound when leaf and gray nodes are counted is $\Sigma_{i=0}^{n} (n-i) \cdot m_i$. This is the same as the total path length of the tree (ignoring nonleaf nodes) if there is only one edge stored with each leaf node. A lower bound can be estimated by assuming that for each gray node, at most three of its sons are intersected by a given edge. Actually a better estimate can be achieved by noting that if three sons are intersected at one level, then only one son is intersected at the next level. See the discussion of space requirements in Section 1.5 and the analysis of the dynamic insertion of an edge in a PM₁ quadtree in this section.

4.46. If all four sons of a node are gray, then at least one son contains a vertex, say V, and an edge that does not intersect V.

4.47. A subtree containing two edges cannot be merged until it is large enough to include their common vertex without including any other vertices or nonsharing edges.

4.50. Merging is possible when the number of vertices is 1 and the crossing count is 0 or when the number of vertices is 0 and the crossing count is 1.

4.55. Compute the slopes of the two edges as ratios, say a/b and c/d, and then determine if $a \cdot d = b \cdot c$ as well as whether the edges overlap.

4.57. See [Same86b].

4.58. See [Same86b].

4.59. The interaction of conditions 3 and 4 causes the impossibility, as can be seen by considering a subset of a $2^d \times 2^d$ grid as shown below. Let A be at $(0,0)$, B be at $(0,2^{d-1})$, and C be at $(1,2^{d-1})$. Since both edges AB and AC intersect the upper border of the cell containing A (i.e., B' and C', respectively), both will exist in the cell immediately above A, which contradicts condition 3. Thus we have to increase the resolution of the grid.

However, as we increase the resolution, the size of the cell containing A shrinks and the intercepts of AB and AC with the upper border of that cell become even closer, thereby forcing a further increase in resolution. This increase in resolution can continue indefinitely without ever satisfying condition 3 since a segment of the upper border of a cell is always smaller than the entire upper border of the cell.

4.60. The maximum degree of a vertex.

4.61. Replacement of condition 3 by 3′ means that we no longer need to be concerned with $d_{min.ee}$ because if the edges, say A and B, do not intersect, then one of the edges, say A, has a vertex, say V, such that $d_{min.ev}$ is smaller between V and B than $d_{min.ee}$ between A and B.

4.62. $D_1 > D_2$ when the polygonal map contains isolated edges (i.e., edges with both vertices having degree 1). If the isolated edges are short, then $d_{min.vv}$ is small. If the isolated edges are farther apart than the maximum of their individual lengths, then $d_{min.ev}$ would be larger than $d_{min.vv}$ and, thus, $D_1 > D_2$.

4.63. Because otherwise we will fail to detect the situation that the shared vertex is outside the square and that at least one of the nonshared vertices is in the square.

4.64. For a PM$_2$ quadtree, each son that is gray contains either a vertex and an edge that does not intersect it or a pair of edges that do not intersect. Thus merging is impossible.

4.65. No, because when using PM2_CHECK there is no limit on the size of the square in which the common vertex can lie.

4.68. Lemma 4.1 of Section 4.2.3.1 is applicable if you can show that condition 3′ makes no difference in the derivation of DMAX—that is, $2 \cdot d + 1$.

4.69. If it coincided with two q-edges, then it would have to contain two vertices and thereby violate condition 1 of the PM$_1$ (as well as PM$_2$ and PM$_3$) quadtree definition.

4.70. Since a vertex node in a PM$_3$ quadtree can contain edges that do not intersect the vertex, more vertex nodes appear at shallower levels. The result follows as the total number of vertex nodes is the same for all three variants of the PM quadtree, and thus fewer vertex nodes will appear in the deeper levels.

4.71. For a PM$_3$ quadtree each son that is gray contains two vertices; merging is impossible.

4.72. See Exercise 4.66.

4.73. Isolated vertices are treated as edges of zero length. Technically other edges can share these vertices in the sense that the vertex can serve as their endpoint. Of course, in such a case, the vertex is no longer isolated. If this is undesirable, procedures should be modified accordingly.

4.75. We use contradiction. Let x be the property that the number of line segments in a node is bounded from above by the splitting threshold plus the depth of the node. Assume the existence of a node, say P, at depth k in a tree built with splitting threshold m that contains n line segments where $n > k + m$ (i.e., the existence of P contradicts property x). Also assume that of the nodes that violate property x, node P is the closest to the root. We have two cases: $k = 0$ (i.e., P is a root node) or $k > 0$. If $k = 0$, we have a tree of just the one node P, which contains more items than the splitting threshold. Since line segments are inserted one at a time, P must have been created by inserting one line segment into a node, say Q, that previously contained $n-1$ line segments. From $k = 0$ and $n > k + m$ we have $n-1 \geq m$. However, since Q contains $n-1$ line segments and must be at level 0 itself, it follows that upon inserting yet another line segment into a node Q that is already at or over threshold m, only leaf nodes at depth 1 would result. Therefore k could not be zero, and hence P cannot be a root node.

Since P is not a root node, it has a parent node. Using analogous reasoning as above yields the observation that P's parent, say $P\prime$, must be one level closer to the root and contains one less line segment prior to the creation of P. However, since $n > k + m$, it follows that $n - 1 > k - 1 + m$. Thus $P\prime$ will also violate property X and is one level closer to the root of the tree. This contradicts the assumption that P was the node closest to the root of the tree that could violate property X. Therefore there can be no such node P that contradicts property X. Hence, property X is true; that is, for every node, the number of line segments in the node is bounded from above by the sum of the splitting threshold and the depth of the node.

4.76. This is not a problem for the PM_3 quadtree, while the PM_1 and PM_2 quadtrees will not be able to deal with it. The problem is that for the PM_1 and PM_2 quadtrees it may be impossible to achieve a situation where each node contains just one line segment.

4.77. Every line in L passes through one, two, or three quadrants of the quartered block. Let A be a line perpendicular to the set L, and for any point P on A, let $q(P)$ be the number of quadrants intersected by the element of L that is perpendicular to A at P. A can be partitioned into sections depending on the value of $q(P)$. Because of the symmetry of the square block, the total length of the sections with $q(P) = 1$ is equal to the total length of the sections with $q(P) = 3$ independent of the value of θ. The value of $q(P)$ over the remainder of the intersection of A with L is 2. Therefore the average number of quadrants intersected by the block is 2 [Nels86b].

4.78. The expected number of quadrants of occupancy i produced by splitting a node of occupancy c is $\binom{n}{i} \cdot 2^{2-i}$.

4.80. Since each quadrant has a 0.5 probability of intersecting each line segment in the parent node, the average occupancy of the nodes produced is 0.5 times the occupancy of the parent node.

4.81. A node of occupancy $i > c$ must be produced by a split such that all i line segments intersect the same quadrant. Assuming a uniform distribution, the expected number of sons for $i = c + 1$ is $4 \cdot 2^{c+1}$ per split; for $i = c + 2$ the expected number of sons is $4 \cdot 2^{c+1} \cdot 4 \cdot 2^{c+2}$; etc. Thus the expected number of nodes with occupancy greater than c decreases exponentially with $i - c$.

4.85. We may have to split a node quite deeply before no cutpoint exists in the interior of a block. Thus the rule that the blocks are maximal is violated. However, a block would have had to be split this deeply anyway if the cutpoints would be treated as endpoints.

4.86. Cutpoints do not exist. They are merely a notational device to help define the concept of a q-fragment.

4.91. Use the same techniques as discussed in this section. The only difference is that the discussion must be modified in terms of cutpoints and endpoints.

4.92. This can be seen by the following chain of arguments. First, for 'typical data,' the number of nodes in a PM_1 quadtree of a polygonal map is proportional to the number of vertices in the polygonal map since, typically, the vertex nodes are found at the deepest level in the PM_1 quadtree (although there are rare exceptions, as illustrated in Figure 4.20). In the analysis of quadtrees, a good rule of thumb is that the deepest frequently occurring node type will dominate the size measurement. Second, Hunter and Steiglitz [Hunt78, Hunt79a] have shown that the number of nodes in an MX quadtree of a polygon is proportional to the perimeter of the polygon (recall Theorem 1.1 of Section 1.5). Third, we know that polygonal maps are planar maps, which means that the number of edges in each map is proportional to the number of vertices in the map. Combining these three arguments with the fact that the perimeter of a map is equal to the product of the number of edges and the average length of an edge leads to the desired result.

4.96. Each vertex is visible from every other vertex. To obtain a triangulation, simply pick a vertex at random, and draw lines from it to the remaining vertices. This is an $O(v)$ process.

4.97. **Sort the vertices seen so far by their y coordinate values. See [Hert85], as well as [Mehl84], for more details.**

4.99. Use induction on the number of vertices and start with one triangle.

4.100. Use an array of edge-adjacency lists such that there is one edge-adjacency list per vertex:

1. Identify all K-vertices.
2. Initially the set of mutually independent K-vertices, say M, is empty.
3. Pick a K-vertex, say V, that has not been marked as not mutually independent with elements of M and insert it into M. Now, mark all elements of V's edge-adjacency list as not mutually independent with M, and repeat until there are no vertices left. This process is $O(v)$ since we mark all edges and by Euler's formula, given v vertices, the number of edges is $3 \cdot v - 6$. The data structure requires $O(v)$ array entries and $O(v)$ edge-adjacency list elements.

4.101. If the removed K-vertex had degree k, then its neighborhood (i.e., polygon) had k triangles and k sides. The triangulation of a k-sided polygon contains $k-2$ triangles.

4.103. Note that there are no regions to the left (right) of the extreme left (right) endpoints that are introduced by the regularization process.

4.104. Yes. Each vertex formed by the intersection of the new edge with an existing edge already has at least one edge to each of its right and left sides.

4.105. Yes. The intersection of any two y-monotone regions is always y-monotone.

4.106. A polygonal map of m edges has at most $m+1$ vertices. Two of these vertices are at the extreme left and right of the map, and thus no edges are added to them. At most one edge can be added to each of the remaining $m-1$ vertices since they must have at least either one edge to a vertex at their right or one edge to a vertex at their left.

4.107. Use a plane-sweep algorithm (see Section 3.2). First, sort the edges by their x coordinate values. Next, sweep a vertical line through the sorted list of edges. During the sweep, use a balanced binary search tree to represent the active intervals of the sweep line (i.e., crossed by edges), and order it by the y coordinate values.

4.108. For example, the vertex with the larger y coordinate value can be treated as the left vertex. The 'immediately-above' relation must be extended to mean 'immediately-right' in such a case. The general relation 'above' becomes 'right'.

4.109. This is an open question.

4.110. Use contradiction.

4.111. No. Consider the case that regions R_i and R_j in the left and right subtrees, respectively, of s_k do not exist such that $R_i =$ BELOW(e) and $R_j =$ ABOVE(e).

4.112. See Theorem 8 in [Edel86a].

4.113. Edge e is contained in separator s_k if, and only if, s_k lies above region R_i and below region R_j for $i < k \le j$.

4.114. Use the edge-ordering property and contradiction. In other words, assume that the least common ancestor does not contain e.

4.115. $lca(i,j) = j$ and not $(msb(i \oplus j) - 1)$ where $\oplus$ denotes the 'exclusive or' operation [Edel86a].

4.116. $lca(i,j) = rev(x \oplus (x-1))$ and j where $x = rev(i \oplus j)$ [Edel86a].

4.117.   Adopt the convention that each edge contains its left endpoint but not its right endpoint.

4.119. L_2 consists of vertices C, E, F, I, and K; the x-intervals comprising edges CE and IK; and the gaps αC, EF, FI, and Kδ. L_6 consists of vertices B, C, D, G, J, and L; the x-intervals comprising edges αB, BC, DG, and GJ; and the gaps CD, JL, and Lδ. L_4 consists of vertices A, C, D, E, G, I, J, K, L, and M; the x-intervals comprising edges αA, AC, CD, DE, EG, GI, IJ, JK, KL, LM, and Mδ; there are no gaps.

4.120.   If it were common to more than one x-interval, the x-intervals would have to overlap, which is impossible.

4.121.   See [Edel86a]. The inductive hypothesis is $B_v + b_v \leq 4 \cdot A_v$, which holds trivially for the leaf nodes of the gap tree. Letting $l(u)$ and $r(u)$ denote the left and right sons of node u of the gap tree, $B_u = B_{l(u)} + B_{r(u)} + b_u$ and $A_u = A_{l(u)} + A_{r(u)} + a_u$. Moreover, $b_u \leq 2 \cdot a_u + (b_{l(u)} + b_{r(u)})/2$, since each edge in s_u contributes at most two vertices to L_u. Applying the inductive hypothesis to the subtrees using this inequality and the previous two equalities leads to the desired result.

4.123.   For example, there is no need for links between vertices and adjacent x-intervals. Instead the elements of the layered dag can be stored in consecutive memory locations by use of an array.

4.126.   Use a method analogous to that for the PM$_1$ quadtree. The situation arising when q-edges are ordered about a point exterior to their region is handled in the same way as q-edges that are angularly ordered about their point of intersection. It is convenient to store with each dictionary the point about which the ordering is being performed, although this can be avoided by sampling two q-edges from the dictionary.

4.127.   Locate the leaf node containing the point, and then find the closest bordering q-edge with respect to each of the seven classes. The closest q-edge of these seven q-edges borders the region containing the query point.

4.128.   See [Same85i].

4.132.   There is no obvious way to achieve map overlay using these structures. However, in the case of the K-structure, since the triangulation forms a convex map, a plane sweep algorithm can be used to do the overlay in $O(v \log_2 v + s)$ time and $O(v)$ space [Niev82], where s denotes the number of intersections of edges from the first map with edges from the second map, and v denotes the total number of vertices in the two maps. From this result, a new K-structure can be built in $O(v)$ time. Note that the cartographic model of data used in this section will lead to a large number of short line segments, which, in turn, will tend to cause the creation of long, narrow triangles. This would increase the s factor. Performing map overlay for the layered dag is more complex since the map created by a y-monotone subdivision process is not convex. However, the algorithm still has the same execution time behavior and the same space requirement as the K-structure [Mair88] (since their algorithm does not require that the polygon be convex).

4.134.   If we ignore the nodes that do not contain boundary information, then since the vertices have degree 2, we are usually looking at a binary tree. Most of the line segments are short and appear at the bottom level of the tree. The tree is essentially balanced. The point location operation reduces to a search for a q-edge.

4.135.   Since the vertex nodes are all at the bottom level, the cost of insertion is of the same order as that of search (i.e., point location).

4.136.   Use an array of edge-adjacency lists such that there is one edge-adjacency list per vertex. The re-regularization process simply scans the array, and for each vertex whose edge-adjacency list does not contain vertices to the left (right), it adds the edge to the succeeding (preceding) vertex in the sorted list. By Euler's formula, this is an $O(v)$ space and time process

CHAPTER 5

5.1. It should not result in objects that are invalid in a three-dimensional sense (e.g., dangling edges, faces that bound no volumes). It should be complete—that is, it should contain all the information necessary to determine the interior and exterior of an object. It should be unique so that each object is uniquely represented. The domain of the objects that can be represented should be as large as possible. The representation should be concise. It should be closed; the result of any operation should be capable of being used as input to another operation. For a more thorough discussion of these issues, see [Requ80].

5.2. See [Yau83].

5.3. See [Fran85].

5.4. It is not always possible if the views are silhouettes. Even convex objects can cause problems. However, there are no problems if the views are like engineering drawings (e.g., hidden lines and other auxiliary lines are present).

5.7. See [Roge85].

5.9. See [Marg89].

5.10. Silhouettes from two opposite directions convey the same information.

5.11. See [Chie86a].

5.12. See [Veen86, Ahuj89].

5.13. See [Veen86, Ahuj89].

5.14. See [Chie88].

5.15. $h_1 \wedge h_2 \wedge h_3$, $h_1 \vee h_2 \vee h_3$, $(h_1 \wedge h_2) \vee h_3$, and $(h_1 \vee h_2) \wedge h_3$. The first two yield a vertex of a convex object, while the third and fourth yield the vertex of a concave object.

5.16. 12.

5.18. See [Nava87].

5.19. See [Nava87].

5.22. This is not possible when the CSG primitives are approximated in the PM octree. However, it is possible when the CSG tree is specified using halfspaces.

5.26. (a) Use two sets of lists. The first list contains the eight vertices and their coordinate values. The second list contains the faces. Each face is represented by a list of the identifiers corresponding to its constituent vertices. (b) Use three sets of lists. The first list contains the eight vertices and their coordinate values. The second list contains the twelve edges and the identifiers corresponding to their constituent vertices. The third list contains the faces where each face is represented by a list of the identifiers corresponding to its constituent edges.

5.28. Use the orientation flag to indicate which edge is to be followed next. The orientation in which each edge is being traversed can be deduced by examining the vertex identifiers stored with it and comparing them with the present vertex.

5.29. The ordering can be clockwise or counterclockwise. Let f denote the face and e the first edge in the face. For a clockwise ordering, if $f = $ FCW(e), then the next edge is ENCW(e); otherwise, $f = $ FCCW(e) and the next edge is ENCCW(e). For a counterclockwise ordering, if $f = $ FCW(e), then the next edge is EPCW(e); otherwise $f = $ FCCW(e) and the next edge is EPCCW(e).

5.30. The ordering can be clockwise or counterclockwise. Let v denote the vertex and e the first edge incident at v. For a clockwise ordering, if $v = $ VSTART(e), then the next edge is EPCW(e); otherwise $v = $ VEND(e), and the next edge is EPCCW(e). For a counterclockwise ordering, if $v = $ VSTART(e), then the next edge is ENCCW(e); otherwise $v = $ VEND(e), and the next edge is ENCW(e).

5.31. It is very easy to split edges and faces since the lists are doubly linked.

5.32. Restriction 1 is violated by an hourglass object that consists of two pyramids. Restriction 2 is violated by a pyramid whose vertex or edge is adjacent to a flat surface.

5.33. No. For example, consider the hourglass object that consists of two pyramids. This object can be formed by the union of two pyramids each of which is a two-manifold object, yet the result is not a two-manifold object.

5.34. Two in the case of a two-manifold.

5.35. One way is to store with each loop all the faces that are incident at its edges. Another way is just to store the faces that contain all of the edges that comprise the loop. The second alternative is superior since the importance of loop-face relation is that, given a loop, we know which face(s) we are currently processing.

5.36. Two. Consider a cube. The surface of the cube consists of six squares. Assume that one square, say s_o, contains a smaller square, say s_i. Now, the cube contains the faces s_i and $s_o - s_i$. Let loop l be the external loop of face s_i. l is also the internal loop of face $s_o - s_i$.

5.37. See [Tamm84g].

5.38. Choose a projection plane, say x-y, so that the remaining coefficient (i.e., of z) has a maximal absolute value. In this way, the overestimation of the size of the MX octree is minimized.

5.39. The sizes of the objects are systematically overestimated. Also, some numerical problems are possible.

5.40. The proof must demonstrate that the region octree of each face contains every point (x,y,z) on that face. Since a path from the interior to the exterior must intersect a face, the intersection point must be within a black pixel.

5.41. Change usage of 'BLACK' to 'WHITE' and 'WHITE' to 'BLACK' and recode procedure PHASEII.

5.42. Apply labeling techniques to the border that are similar to those used in the algorithm to build a quadtree from a chain code in Section 4.3.1 of [Same90b].

5.43. This will not work if the object is not convex.

5.46. In a DF-expression it takes time to jump from one node to another, as is the case when a subtree is deleted from one of the trees during the overlay process.

5.47. The offsets must be equal to one-half the width of the bintree block being tested.

5.48. Try as an example the halfspace $4x - 2y - 1 \geq 0$ in the unit square. In essence, we are taking the value of the left side of the inequality at two points to get its value at the midpoint of the line joining them. This can be proved more formally.

5.49. Compute the minimum and maximum values of the left side of inequality 5.2 in each of the eight sons of the octree node, say P. These values are contained in 15 points corresponding to vertices of the sons of P. The values of two of the vertices are the same as those of P (at the corners of the father block), and thus we only need to compute the left side of the inequality at 13 points. Note that one of the 13 points corresponds to the vertex in the center of P's block, and it is shared by two of P's sons in the sense that the value of the left side of the inequality at it serves as the minimum value of one son and as the maximum value of the other son. Thus we need 13 addition operations to compute the minimum and maximum values at the sons of an octree node.

5.50. With bintrees, we obtain two nodes with two addition operations. Thus if we were to split a bintree node three times to get the effect of an octree node we would require $2 + 4 + 8 = 14$ addition operations to compute the minimum and maximum values of the left side of inequality 5.2 at all 8 of the sons. Of course, not all of the operations may be necessary because of possible merging. In fact, bintrees and octrees corresponding to a polyhedron have been observed to have an approximately equal amount of nodes [Tamm84f], so that the bintree conversion turns out to be more economical, as well as simpler to implement.

5.51. This is a relatively inefficient process that processes areas with no chance of being in the final bintree. As an example of the use of this technique, consider the conversion of the triangle given in Figure 5.13 with the CSG tree given in Figure 5.14. It is composed of the intersection of the three halfspaces $2x - 1 \geq 0$, $2y - 1 \geq 0$, and $-2x - 2y + 3 \geq 0$ labeled A, B, and C, respectively. Conversion starts with the unit square universe. Recall that we partition the x coordinate before the y coordinate. Processing the halfspaces A, B, and C in sequence forces us to convert the segment of B between $x = 0$ and $x = 0.5$, whereas that region will be white in the resulting bintree.

5.52. Copying is necessary because we store the minimum and maximum values of the active halfspaces in the H_MIN and H_MAX fields of each leaf node of the CSG tree. These values change dynamically as the bintree is constructed and the CSG tree is evaluated. Thus by keeping a copy, we are able to take advantage of recursion implicitly to restore their previous values. Notice that whenever procedure CSG_TRAVERSE has completed processing a level of the bintree (i.e., both sons), the storage that was allocated for the CSG tree at that level and below is released.

5.53. VOXEL_LEVEL. This situation arises when all of the halfspaces are active in a single voxel. In practical cases the CSG tree gets pruned rather quickly at increasing levels of the bintree so that the total amount of storage required is typically two to three times the size of the original CSG tree.

5.54. Use one stack for each halfspace and a list of the active halfspaces for each level of the bintree. Entries are added to these structures whenever procedure HSP_EVAL determines that the hyperplane of inequality 5.2 is intersected by the bintree node currently being processed. They are removed whenever procedure CSG_TRAVERSE has completed processing a bintree at a given level. Notice that using such a storage mechanism means that a new CSG tree node is allocated to replace an existing one, say T, only if pruning has caused at least one of T's sons to change and the result is not a WHITE or BLACK node, which, of course, will be pruned further. For example, using this method there would have been no need to create a copy of the right son of Figure 5.14 (i.e., Figure 5.16) when pruning the CSG tree with respect to the subuniverse spanned by the right son of node 1.

5.55. It arises when all of the halfspaces are active in a single voxel. The amount of storage required is of the order of VOXEL_LEVEL times the number of halfspaces.

5.56. The total number of nodes in a CSG tree is bounded by two times the number of halfspaces. Thus the worst-case storage requirements of the two techniques are of the same order of magnitude.

5.57. See [Same90c].

5.58. The performance of the procedures, as well as Theorem 5.1, remain valid by adding the following rule to the CSG evaluation in procedure PRUNE: If in a bintree node only a halfspace and its complement are active, then the node is BLACK if the root of the active CSG tree is UNION, and WHITE otherwise.

5.59. It is equivalent to a transformation that eliminates the time dimension.

5.60. Given a CSG tree having A OP B as its root, we cannot necessarily distribute the projection operation—that is,

$$\text{PROJECTION}(A \text{ OP } B) \neq \text{PROJECTION}(A) \text{ OP PROJECTION}(B)$$

For example, suppose we are given two nonintersecting objects that are moving at identical speeds in the direction of the x axis. Clearly their swept areas intersect, whereas the objects themselves do not intersect.

5.61. Let a bintree node be implemented as a record of type *node* with three fields: LEFT, RIGHT, and TYP. LEFT and RIGHT correspond to the left and right sons, respectively, of a node, while TYP indicates a node's type—black, white, or gray. Projection is achieved by procedure PROJ, invoked with a pointer to the bintree corresponding to the object having the desired projection and the name of the coordinate (i.e., dimension) that is being eliminated. The output bintree (i.e., corresponding to the projection) is initialized to the white universe. Procedure PROJ traverses the input and output trees in tandem. Two input brother nodes may be either 'side-by-side' in the projected universe (in cases where the division is not with respect to the axis of projection) or 'on top' of each other. In the latter case, the same subtree of the output bintree is processed against both brothers.

```
recursive procedure PROJ(IN,OUT,C,X);
/* Construct a (D-1)-dimensional bintree rooted at OUT corresponding to the projection of
   the D-dimensional bintree rooted at IN such that coordinate X is eliminated. Initially,
   OUT corresponds to a single white node. The node pointed at by IN partitions the
   universe along coordinate C. */
begin
  value pointer node IN,OUT;
  value integer C,X;
  global integer D;
  if TYP(IN) = 'GRAY' then
    begin
      if TYP(OUT) = 'BLACK' then return /* Output is totally covered */
      else if C ≠ X then /* Coordinate C is not eliminated */
        begin /* The two sons are 'side-by-side' in the projected universe */
          if TYP(OUT) = 'WHITE' then
            begin /* Allocate two son nodes */
              LEFT(OUT) ← create(node);
              RIGHT(OUT) ← create(node);
              TYP(LEFT(OUT)) ← TYP(RIGHT(OUT)) ← 'WHITE';
              TYP(OUT) ← 'GRAY';
            end;
          PROJ(LEFT(IN),LEFT(OUT),(C+1) mod D,X);
          PROJ(RIGHT(IN),RIGHT(OUT),(C+1) mod D,X);
          if TYP(LEFT(OUT)) = 'BLACK' and TYP(RIGHT(OUT)) = 'BLACK'
          then begin /* Merge left and right sons */
            TYP(OUT) ← 'BLACK';
            returntoavail(LEFT(OUT));
            returntoavail(RIGHT(OUT));
          end;
        end
    end
```

```
      else /* Eliminate this coordinate by projecting on top of the brother */
        begin
          PROJ(LEFT(IN),OUT,(C+1) mod D,X);
          PROJ(RIGHT(IN),OUT,(C+1) mod D,X);
        end;
    end
  else if TYP(IN) = 'BLACK' then /* Output must be black */
    begin
      if TYP(OUT) = 'GRAY' then
        begin /* Merge left and right sons */
          returntoavail(LEFT(OUT));
          returntoavail(RIGHT(OUT));
        end;
      TYP(OUT) ← 'BLACK';
    end;
  /* Nothing needs to be done for a white input node. */
end;
```

5.63. Consider a union or intersection operation whose operand primitives are not disjoint. Their constituent primitives can not in general be separated so that each one is in only one cell.

5.64. One possibility is simply to invoke De Morgan's law: $A \wedge B = \overline{\overline{A} \vee \overline{B}}$. Alternatively, $A \wedge B = (A \wedge \overline{A}) \vee (A \wedge B) = A \wedge (\overline{A} \vee B) = A \wedge \overline{A \wedge \overline{B}} = A - (A - B)$.

5.66.

```
recursive pointer pm_csg_tree procedure ADD(A,B,L);
/* Return a pointer to the result of adding PM-CSG octree B to PM-CSG octree A
   corresponding to images of side length 2ᴸ. */
begin
  value pointer pm_csg_tree A,B;
  value integer L;
  global pointer pm_csg_tree NASTY_NODE;
  octant I;
  pointer pm_csg_tree P;
  if NODETYPE(A) = 'EMPTY' then return(B)
  else if NODETYPE(B) = 'EMPTY' then return(A)
  else if NODETYPE(A) = 'FULL' or NODETYPE(B) = 'FULL' then
    error('objects interfere')
  else if L = 0 then return(NASTY_NODE) /* At maximum resolution */
  else
    begin
      P ← create(pm_csg_tree);
      /* Create 8 leaf nodes if A or B are leaf nodes and set type: */
      SUBDIVIDE(A,B);
      for I in {'LDB', 'LDF', 'LUB', 'LUF', 'RDB', 'RDF', 'RUB', 'RUF'} do
        SON(P,I) ← ADD(SON(A,I),SON(B,I),L-1);
      return(P);
    end;
end;
```

5.67. Return a pointer to the inverse of B's boundary type. Note that when B is a negative boundary, then the result is a positive boundary since $A - (-B) = B$ as A is full.

5.68.

```
recursive pointer pm_csg_tree procedure SUBTRACT(A,B,L);
/* Return a pointer to the result of subtracting PM-CSG octree B from PM-CSG octree A
   corresponding to images of side length 2ᴸ. */
begin
  value pointer pm_csg_tree A,B;
  value integer L;
  global pointer pm_csg_tree EMPTY_NODE,NASTY_NODE;
  octant I;
  pointer pm_csg_tree P;
  if NODETYPE(A) = 'EMPTY' then return(EMPTY_NODE)
  else if NODETYPE(B) = 'EMPTY' then return(A)
  else if NODETYPE(B) = 'FULL' then return(EMPTY_NODE)
  else if NODETYPE(A) = 'FULL' and NODETYPE(B) = 'BOUNDARY' then
    /* Convert negative (positive) boundary node to a positive (negative) boundary node */
    return(INVERT(B))
  else if L = 0 then return(NASTY_NODE) /* At maximum resolution */
  else
    begin
      P ← create(pm_csg_tree);
      /* Create 8 leaf nodes if A or B are leaf nodes and set type: */
      SUBDIVIDE(A,B);
      for I in {'LDB', 'LDF', 'LUB', 'LUF', 'RDB', 'RDF', 'RUB', 'RUF'} do
        SON(P,I) ← SUBTRACT(SON(A,I),SON(B,I),L-1);
      return(P);
    end;
end;
```

5.69.

```
recursive pointer pm_csg_tree procedure TRAVERSE_DAG_CSG(P,T);
/* Return a pointer to the PM-CSG tree corresponding to DAG-CSG tree P relative to the
   position given by transformation matrix T. DAG_CSG_SON points to the DAG-CSG tree
   definition of a nonprimitive object. */
begin
  value pointer dag_csg_tree P;
  value matrix T;
  global integer MAX_RESOLUTION;
  pointer pm_csg_tree Q;
  if null(P) then return(NIL)
  else if NODETYPE(P) = 'ADD' then
    return(ADD(TRAVERSE_DAG_CSG(SON(P,'LEFT'),T),
               TRAVERSE_DAG_CSG(SON(P,'RIGHT'),T),
               MAX_RESOLUTION))
  else if NODETYPE(P) = 'SUBTRACT' then
    return(SUBTRACT(TRAVERSE_DAG_CSG(SON(P,'LEFT'),T),
                    TRAVERSE_DAG_CSG(SON(P,'RIGHT'),T),
```

```
                        MAX_RESOLUTION))
    else /* Leaf node */
      begin
        T ← NEW_TRANSFORM_MATRIX(P,T);
        if NODETYPE(P) = 'PRIMITIVE' then
          begin
            Q ← create(node);
            NODETYPE(Q) ← 'BOUNDARY';
            PRIMITIVE(Q) ← INSTANTIATE(P,T);
            return(Q);
          end
        else /* Non-primitive object */
          return(TRAVERSE_DAG_CSG(DAG_CSG_SON(P),T));
      end;
  end;
```

5.74. The structure must be expanded. For example, a cell may be full with respect to shape but not necessarily with respect to color.

5.75. Visit the cells crossed by the ray until encountering a nonempty cell. If the cell corresponds to an octree leaf node, find the intersection with the object. Otherwise the cell corresponds to an rcsg node. Since there are several primitive objects in the cell, we must traverse the tree of the cell and determine the nearest intersection point that corresponds to a boundary of the object (i.e., the point must not be in a subtracted object). Some care must be exercised in performing this operation when the PM-RCSG tree has not been regularized.

5.76. Traverse the node's rcsg tree. The type of each nonleaf node indicates how the result of testing P against the leaf nodes is to be interpreted. For each leaf node, determine if the point is in the corresponding object. This can be tested by creating two additional points, say A and B, on the traced ray such that A is ε ($\varepsilon > 0$) closer to the viewpoint and B is ε farther from the viewpoint. If A is outside the object and B is inside the object, then P is inside the object corresponding to the leaf node. The value of ε is chosen so as to avoid problems that may arise due to the absence of regularity [Wyvi86].

5.77. Each introduction of a new vertex causes the addition of two triangles.

5.78. Each introduction of three new vertices causes the addition of between three and six triangles. Three of the triangles are a direct result of the decomposition of the triangle. The remaining three triangles arise when there is no continuity between adjacent triangles.

5.79. See [Faug83].

5.80. No.

5.81. $6/\pi$.

5.88. If only the split step is used, then even though the initial edges are very bad approximations of the surface, they are never removed.

5.89. The split and adjustment steps result in some faces being bases of new tetrahedra.

5.90. It is alleviated, in part, by the application of the adjustment step after each split step.

5.91. Use neighbor-finding techniques similar to those discussed in Chapter 3 of [Same90b] (see [Ponc87b]).

5.94. No.

5.95. We prove that if the prism is not regular, the surface is not convex. If the prism is not regular, there is a line, lying outside the interior of the surface and in the bisecting plane, from a vertex on the surface to another point of intersection of the surface and the bisecting plane. This implies that the surface is not convex.

5.96. Yes.

5.99. Perform an initial step of subdivision into components of genus 0.

5.100.

$$\rho(s,t) = \rho_{11} + (\rho_{12} - \rho_{11}) \cdot s + (\rho_{21} - \rho_{11}) \cdot t + (\rho_{22} - \rho_{21} - \rho_{12} + \rho_{11}) \cdot st$$

$$\theta(s,t) = \theta_1 + (\theta_2 - \theta_1) \cdot s \quad \phi(s,t) = \phi_1 + (\phi_2 - \phi_1) \cdot t.$$

5.101. Each cone would be a collection of spherical patches similar to that used in the sector tree.

5.102. The only difference is that when the origin of the polar sphere is outside the object, each leaf node of a cone tree contains an even number of spherical patches instead of an odd number. Each successive pair of patches defines a region within the object.

APPENDIX: DESCRIPTION OF PSEUDO-CODE LANGUAGE

The algorithms are given using pseudo-code. This pseudo-code is a variant of the ALGOL [Naur60] programming language, which has a data structuring facility that incorporates pointers and record structures. We make heavy use of recursion. This language has similarities to C [Kern78], PASCAL [Jens74], SAIL [Reis76], and ALGOL W [Baue68]. Its basic features are described below. All reserved words are designated in boldface. This also includes the names (i.e., types) of predefined record structures.

A program is defined as a collection of functions and procedures. Functions are distinguished from procedures by the fact that they return values via the use of the **return** construct. Also the function header declaration specifies the types of the data that it returns as its value. In the following the term *procedure* is used to refer to both procedures and functions.

All formal parameters to procedures must be declared along with the manner in which they have been transmitted (**value** or **reference**). All local variables are declared. Global variables are declared and are specified by use of the reserved word **global** before the declaration. Variables and arrays may be initialized to prespecified values by prefacing the declaration with the reserved word **preload** and appending the reserved word **with** and the initialization values to the declaration.

'Short-circuit' evaluation techniques are used for Boolean operators that combine relational expressions. In other words, as soon as any parts of a Boolean **or** (**and**) are true (false), the remaining parts are not tested. This is similar to what is used in LISP [McCa60] but is different from PASCAL, where the order of the evaluation is deemed to be immaterial.

Record structures are available. An instance of a record structure of type **rec** is created by use of the command **create(rec)**. The result of this operation is a pointer to a record structure of the appropriate type. Pointers to record structures are declared by use of the reserved word **pointer**, which is followed by the name of the type of the record structure. Instances of record structures are referred by using functional notation where the field name is in the position of the function and the pointer is its argument. For example, if variable L points to an instance of a record structure of type **list**, then we use 'NEXT(L)' to refer to the NEXT field of this instance. Of course, L must be declared to be a pointer to a record structure of type **list** by using a declaration of the form '**pointer list** L'. Note the use of boldface for the specification of the type of the record structure since we assume that it has been predefined.

The fields of a record structure may be of any type, including an array. For example, suppose that a record of type has a field called ARR, which is a one-dimensional array. Moreover, assume that L has been declared as a pointer to a record of type **rec**. We use ARR(L)[I] to refer to the Ith element of the ARR field of the **rec** record pointed at by L.

The procedures are usually recursive and make heavy use of the 'if-then-else' mechanism. The value of an 'if-then-else' can be a statement or an expression. They are frequently used like a select statement in BLISS [Wulf71] and are similar to a COND in LISP. They are often nested. Observance of the placement of semicolons ensures a proper understanding of their semantics. In other words, they must nest. A procedure is a block of statements separated by semicolons. A block is delimited by **begin** and **end**. An 'if-then-else' constitutes a statement. Blocks must be used after a **then** and an **else** when there is more than one statement in this position.

There is a rich set of types. These types are defined as they are used. In particular, enumerated types in the sense of PASCAL are used heavily. For example, the type **quadrant** is an enumerated type whose values are NW, NE, SW, SE.

The array data type is treated as a special type of a record; however, there are some differences. Although an identifier that has been declared to be a record type is usually only used as a parameter to a function that allocates storage for an instance of the record type or to qualify the declaration of a pointer variable, when an identifier that has been declared to be an array appears by itself (i.e., without a suffix to indicate a particular array element—e.g., ARR instead of ARR[I]), then the identifier is treated as a pointer to an instance of the data type associated with the array declaration. This is useful when it is desired to pass an array as a parameter to a procedure or to return an entire array as the value of a procedure. Thus, in such cases, the array identifier is analogous to a pointer to a record having a type equal to that of the array declaration.

Storage for an array is allocated from a heap rather than a stack. This means that there is a need for some form of garbage collection for array elements that are not pointed at by any of the currently accessible pointers (i.e., pointer variables). If an array is local to a procedure, then its storage is allocated upon entering the block in which the array is declared. If the array is transmitted as a formal 'value' parameter to a procedure, then its storage is allocated upon entry to the procedure, and its elements are set to the value they had in the corresponding array in the calling procedure. If the array is transmitted as a formal 'reference' parameter to a procedure, then the array occupies the same storage in both the calling and called procedures. It is the user's responsibility to make sure that the type declarations in the calling and called procedure match.

Two subtle points about memory management for arrays are worth noting. The first is that while storage for an array is usually deallocated when exiting from a procedure in which it has been declared or transmitted as a 'value' parameter, deallocation should not take place for an array returned as the value of a procedure. The second is that if an array name, say A, appears on the left-hand side of an assignment statement and the right-hand side is an expression whose value is an array of the same type, then A is overwritten and the original instance of the array that was bound to A is inaccessible once the assignment has taken place.

As an example of the first point, let us examine the situation that a procedure returns as its value an array that has been transmitted to it as a 'value' parameter. In such a case, once the called procedure has exited, there are two instances of the array, one of which is the value returned by the procedure which is a (possibly modified) copy of the array that was transmitted as a parameter.

One shortcoming with the array data type is the absence of a true analogy with record structures. The problem is that the process of allocating storage for an array should be decoupled from its declaration (which is more like setting up a template). This is a shortcoming of many implementations, including the one described here. It could be overcome easily by replacing the keyword **array** by the keyword **array_pointer** whenever it is desired only to set up the template for the array rather than also allocating the storage. For example, the declaration '**integer array_pointer** ARR[0:N]' would set up the template for array ARR without actually allocating the space for it, while '**integer array** ARR[0:N]' retains its original meaning of template declaration and storage allocation.

Note that the C language allows for either array declaration with allocation or without (i.e., template declaration). However, in C, for the case of the array template, the actual size of the array cannot be specified. In other words, the template is really a pointer to an element of the type of the members of the array but cannot indicate how many elements are in the array.

REFERENCES

1. [Abda88] S. K. Abdali and D. S. Wise, Experiments with quadtree representation of matrices, *Proceedings of the International Symposium on Symbolic and Algebraic Computation*, Rome, July 1988 (also University of Indiana Computer Science Technical Report No. 241). [matrices] D.2.6.1

2. [Abel84a] D. J. Abel, A B$^+$-tree structure for large quadtrees, *Computer Vision, Graphics, and Image Processing 27*, 1(July 1984), 19–31. [regions] A.2.1 A.2.1.1 A.4.2.3

3. [Abel84b] D. J. Abel, Comments on "detection of connectivity for regions represented by linear quadtrees," *Computers and Mathematics with Applications 10*, 2(1984), 167–170. [regions] A.5.1.3

4. [Abel85] D. J. Abel, Some elemental operations on linear quadtrees for geographic information systems, *Computer Journal 28*, 1(February 1985), 73–77. [regions] D.3.5.2

5. [Abel83] D. J. Abel and J. L. Smith, A data structure and algorithm based on a linear key for a rectangle retrieval problem, *Computer Vision, Graphics, and Image Processing 24*, 1(October 1983), 1–13. [rectangles] D.3.5 D.3.5.1 A.2.1.1

6. [Abel84c] D. J. Abel and J. L. Smith, A simple approach to the nearest-neighbor problem, *Australian Computer Journal 16*, 4(November 1984), 140–146. [points]

7. [Abel84d] D. J. Abel and J. L. Smith, A data structure and query algorithm for a database of areal entities, *Australian Computer Journal 16*, 4(November 1984), 147–154. [points]

8. [Adam49] O. Adams, Latitude developments connected with geodesy and cartography, US Coast and Geodetic Survey Special Publication No. 67, US Government Printing Office, Washington, DC, 1949. [cartography] D.1.4.1

9. [Adel62] G. M. Adel'son-Velskii and Y. M. Landis, An algorithm for the organization of information, *Doklady Akademii Nauk SSSR 146*, (1962), 263–266 (English translation in *Soviet Math. Doklady 3* (1962), 1259–1262). [general] D.2.4.1 D.2.7

Each reference is followed by a key word(s). It is also followed by a list of the sections in which it is referenced. The format is D or A followed by the section number. D corresponds to this book while A corresponds to [Same90b]. D.P and A.P denote the appropriate preface, and L denotes the appendix describing the pseudo code language. All references that are cited in the solutions to exercises are associated with the section in which the exercise is found.

10. [Aho74] A. V. Aho, J. E. Hopcroft, and J. D. Ullman, *The Design and Analysis of Computer Algorithms*, Addison-Wesley, Reading, MA, 1974. [general] D.P D.2.4.1 D.2.7 D.4.2.3.1 D.4.2.3.6 A.P A.4.5

11. [Ahuj83] N. Ahuja, On approaches to polygonal decomposition for hierarchical image representation, *Computer Vision, Graphics, and Image Processing 24*, 2(November 1983), 200–214. [regions] D.1.4.1 D.5.2 A.4.6

12. [Ahuj84a] N. Ahuja, Efficient planar embedding of trees for VLSI layouts, *Proceedings of the Seventh International Conference on Pattern Recognition*, Montreal, August 1984, 460–464. [hardware]

13. [Ahuj84b] N. Ahuja and C. Nash, Octree representations of moving objects, *Computer Vision, Graphics, and Image Processing 26*, 2(May 1984), 207–216. [volumes] A.6.5.3

14. [Ahuj89] N. Ahuja and J. Veenstra, Generating octrees from object silhouettes in orthographic views, *IEEE Transactions on Pattern Analysis and Machine Intelligence 11*, 2(February 1989), 137–149. [volumes] D.5.2 A.4.6

15. [Alan84a] J. Alander, Interval arithmetic methods in the processing of curves and sculptured surfaces, *Proceedings of the Sixth International Symposium on CAD/CAM*, Zagreb, Yugoslavia, 1984. [surfaces] D.5.5.1.3

16. [Alan84b] J. Alander, K. Hyytia, J. Hamalainen, A. Jaatinen, O. Karonen, P. Rekola, and M. Tikkanen, Programmer's manual of interval package IP, Report-HTKK-TKO-B59, Laboratory of Information Processing, Helsinki University of Technology, Espoo, Finland, 1984. [surfaces] D.5.5.1.3

17. [Alex78] N. Alexandridis and A. Klinger, Picture decomposition, tree data-structures, and identifying directional symmetries as node combinations, *Computer Graphics, and Image Processing 8*, 1(August 1978), 43–77. [regions]

18. [Alex80] V. V. Alexandrov and N. D. Grosky, Recursive approach to associative storage and search of information in data bases, *Proceedings of the Finnish-Soviet Symposium on Design and Application of Data Base Systems*, Turku, Finland, 1980, 271–284. [regions] D.1.3 A.1.4

19. [Alex79] V. V. Alexandrov, N. D. Grosky, and A. O. Polyakov, Recursive algorithms of data representation and processing, Academy of Sciences of the USSR, Leningrad Research Center, Leningrad, 1979. [regions] D.1.3 A.1.4

20. [Alte88] M. Altenhofen and R. Diehl, Conversion of boundary representations to bintrees, in *Proceedings of the EUROGRAPHICS'88 Conference*, D. Duce and P. Jancene, eds., North-Holland, Amsterdam, 1988, 117–127. [volumes]

21. [Aman84] J. Amanatides, Ray tracing with cones, *Computer Graphics 18*, 3(July 1984), 129–135 (also *Proceedings of the SIGGRAPH'84 Conference*, Minneapolis, July 1984). [volumes] A.7.2.2 A.7.3

22. [Ande83] D. P. Anderson, Techniques for reducing pen plotting time, *ACM Transactions on Graphics 2*, 3(July 1983), 197–212. [points] D.2.6.2 A.6.2

23. [Andr85] F. P. Andresen, L. S. Davis, R. D. Eastman, and S. Kambhampati, Visual algorithms for autonomous navigation, *Proceedings of the International Conference on Robotics*, St. Louis, March 1985, 856–861. [regions] A.9.2

24. [Ang88] C. H. Ang, H. Samet, and C. A. Shaffer, Fast region expansion for quadtrees, *Proceedings of the Third International Symposium on Spatial Data Handling*, Sydney, Australia, August 1988, 19–37 (also *IEEE Transactions on Pattern Analysis and Machine Intelligence*). [regions] A.6.6

25. [Ansa85] S. Ansaldi, L. De Floriani, and B. Falcidieno, Geometric modeling of solid objects by using a face adjacency graph representation, *Computer Graphics 19*, 3(July

1985), 131–139 (also *Proceedings of the SIGGRAPH'85 Conference*, San Francisco, July 1985). [volumes] D.5.4

26. [Anto86] R. Antony and P. J. Emmerman, Spatial reasoning and knowledge representation, in *Geographic Information Systems in Government*, vol. 2, B. K. Opitz, ed., A. Deepak Publishing, Hampton, VA, 795–813. [regions]

27. [Appe68] A. A. Appel, Some techniques for shading machine renderings of solids, *Proceedings of the Spring Joint Computer Conference 32*, Atlantic City, NJ, April 1968, 37–45. [ray tracing] A.7.2.1

28. [Arna87] B. Arnaldi, T. Priol, and K. Bouatouch, A new space subdivision method for ray tracing CSG modelled scenes, *Visual Computer 3*, 2(August 1987), 98–108. [volumes] A.7.2.5

29. [Artz81] E. Artzy, G. Frieder, and G. T. Herman, The theory, design, implementation, and evaluation of a surface detection algorithm, *Computer Graphics and Image Processing 15*, 1(January 1981), 1–24. [volumes]

30. [Arvo87] J. Arvo and D. Kirk, Fast ray tracing by ray classification, *Computer Graphics 21*, 4(July 1987), 55–64 (also *Proceedings of the SIGGRAPH'87 Conference*, Anaheim, July 1987). [volumes] D.2.1 A.7.3

31. [Athe83] P. R. Atherton, A scan-line hidden surface removal procedure for constructive solid geometry, *Computer Graphics 17*, 3(July 1983), 73–82 (also *Proceedings of the SIGGRAPH'83 Conference*, Boston, July 1983). [volumes] D.5.5

32. [Atki84] H. H. Atkinson, I. Gargantini, and M. V. S. Ramanath, Determination of the 3d border by repeated elimination of internal surfaces, *Computing 32*, 4(October 1984), 279–295. [volumes]

33. [Atki85a] H. H. Atkinson, I. Gargantini, and M. V. S. Ramanath, Improvements to a recent 3d-border algorithm, *Pattern Recognition 18*, 3/4(1985), 215–226. [volumes]

34. [Atki85b] H. H. Atkinson, I. Gargantini, and T. R. S. Walsh, Counting regions, holes, and their nesting level in time proportional to their border, *Computer Vision, Graphics, and Image Processing 29*, 2(February 1985), 196–215. [regions] D.1.5

35. [Avis83] D. Avis, A survey of heuristics for the weighted matching problem, *Networks 13*, 4(Winter 1983), 475–493. [points] D.2.9

36. [Ayal85] D. Ayala, P. Brunet, R. Juan, and I. Navazo, Object representation by means of nonminimal division quadtrees and octrees, *ACM Transactions on Graphics 4*, 1(January 1985), 41–59. [volumes] D.5.3 A.1.3

37. [Aziz88] N. M. Aziz, A hierarchical model for spatial stacking, in *New Trends in Computer Graphics: Proceedings of CG International '88*, N. Magnenat-Thalmann and D. Thalmann, eds., Springer-Verlag, Tokyo, 1988, 267–274. [volumes]

38. [Ball81] D. H. Ballard, Strip trees: A hierarchical representation for curves, *Communications of the ACM 24*, 5(May 1981), 310–321 (see also corrigendum, *Communications of the ACM 25*, 3(March 1982), 213). [lines] D.4 D.4.1 D.5.7

39. [Barn86] J. Barnes and P. Hut, A hierarchical $O(N\log N)$ force-calculation algorithm, *Nature 324*, 4(December 1986), 446–449. [regions]

40. [Barr87] R. Barrera and A. Hinojosa, Compression methods for terrain relief, CINEVESTAV-IPN, Engineering Projects Section, Department of Electrical Engineering, Polytechnic University of Mexico, Mexico City, 1987. [surfaces] D.5.6

41. [Barr84] R. Barrera and A. M. Vazquez, A hierarchical method for representing terrain relief, *Proceedings of the Pecora 9 Symposium on Spatial Information Technologies for Remote Sensing Today and Tomorrow*, Sioux Falls, SD, October 1984, 87–92. [surfaces] D.5.6

42. [Bart83] J. J. Bartholdi III and L. K. Platzman, A fast heuristic based on spacefilling curves for minimum-weight matching in the plane, *Information Processing Letters 17*, 4(November 1983), 177–180. [points] D.2.9

43. [Baue68] H. Bauer, S. Becker, S. Graham, and E. Satterthwaite, ALGOL W (Revised), Computer Science Department Report No. STAN-CS-68–114, Stanford University, Stanford, CA, October 1968. [general] D.P A.P L

44. [Baue85] M. A. Bauer, Set operations in linear quadtrees, *Computer Vision, Graphics, and Image Processing 29*, 2(February 1985), 248–258. [regions]

45. [Baum72] B. G. Baumgart, Winged-edge polyhedron representation, STAN-CS-320, Computer Science Department, Stanford University, Stanford, CA, 1972. [volumes] D.5.4 A.7.1

46. [Baum74] B. G. Baumgart, Geometric modeling for computer vision, Ph.D. dissertation, STAN-CS-463, Computer Science Department, Stanford University, Stanford, CA, 1974. [volumes] D.5.4

47. [Baum75] B. G. Baumgart, A polyhedron representation for computer vision, *Proceedings of the National Computer Conference 44*, Anaheim, CA, May 1975, 589–596. [volumes] D.5.4

48. [Beau89] J. M. Beaulieu and M. Goldberg, Hierarchy in picture segmentation: a stepwise optimization approach, *IEEE Transactions on Pattern Analysis and Machine Intelligence 11*, 2(February 1989), 150–163. [regions]

49. [Beck85] D. A. Beckley, M. W. Evens, and V. K. Raman, Multikey retrieval from k-d trees and quad-trees, *Proceedings of the SIGMOD Conference*, Austin, TX, May 1985, 291–301. [points]

50. [Beer84] M. Beer, Interactive editing of cartographic raster images, *Photogrammetria 39*, (1984), 263–275. [regions]

51. [Bell83] S. B. M. Bell, B. M. Diaz, F. Holroyd, and M. J. Jackson, Spatially referenced methods of processing raster and vector data, *Image and Vision Computing 1*, 4(November 1983), 211–220. [regions] D.1.4.1 A.1.2

52. [Bent80a] S. W. Bent, D. D. Sleator, and R. E. Tarjan, Biased 2–3 trees, *Proceedings of the Twenty-first Annual Symposium on Foundations of Computer Science*, Syracuse, NY, October 1980, 248–254. [general] D.2.8.2.1 D.4.2.3.1

53. [Bent75a] J. L. Bentley, A survey of techniques for fixed radius near neighbor searching, SLAC Report No. 186, Stanford Linear Accelerator Center, Stanford University, Stanford, CA, August 1975. [points] D.2.1

54. [Bent75b] J. L. Bentley, Multidimensional binary search trees used for associative searching, *Communications of the ACM 18*, 9(September 1975), 509–517. [points] D.1.4.1 D.2.3 D.2.4 D.2.4.1 D.2.4.2 D.2.4.3 D.2.7 A.1.3

55. [Bent77a] J. L. Bentley, Algorithms for Klee's rectangle problems, unpublished, Computer Science Department, Carnegie-Mellon University, Pittsburgh, 1977. [rectangles] D.3.2.1 D.3.3

56. [Bent79a] J. L. Bentley, Decomposable searching problems, *Information Processing Letters 8*, 5(June 1979), 244–251. [points] D.2.3 D.2.5

57. [Bent80b] J. L. Bentley, Multi-dimensional divide-and-conquer, *Communications of the ACM 23*, 4(April 1980), 214–229. [points]

58. [Bent82] J. L. Bentley, *Writing Efficient Programs*, Prentice-Hall, Englewood Cliffs, NJ, 1982. [general] D.1.3 A.1.4

59. [Bent79b] J. L. Bentley and J. H. Friedman, Data structures for range searching, *ACM Computing Surveys 11*, 4(December 1979), 397–409. [points] D.P D.2.1 D.2.2 A.1.3

60. [Bent80c] J. L. Bentley, D. Haken, and R. W. Hon, Statistics on VLSI designs, CMU-CS-80-111, Computer Science Department, Carnegie-Mellon University, Pittsburgh, April 1980. [rectangles] D.3.2.4

61. [Bent79c] J. L. Bentley and H. A. Maurer, A note on Euclidean near neighbor searching in the plane, *Information Processing Letters 8*, 3(March 1979), 133–136. [points]

62. [Bent80d] J. L. Bentley and H. A. Maurer, Efficient worst-case data structures for range searching, *Acta Informatica 13*, 2(1980), 155–168. [rectangles] D.2.3 D.2.5

63. [Bent79d] J. L. Bentley and T. A. Ottmann, Algorithms for reporting and counting geometric intersections, *IEEE Transactions on Computers 28*, 9(September 1979), 643–647. [rectangles] D.3.2 D.3.2.4

64. [Bent81] J. L. Bentley and T. Ottmann, The complexity of manipulating hierarchically defined sets of rectangles, CMU-CS-81-109, Computer Science Department, Carnegie-Mellon University, Pittsburgh, April 1981. [rectangles] D.3.2.4

65. [Bent80e] J. L. Bentley and J. Saxe, Decomposable searching problems I: static to dynamic transformations, *Journal of Algorithms 1*, 4(December 1980), 301–358. [points] D.2.9

66. [Bent75c] J. L. Bentley and D. F. Stanat, Analysis of range searches in quad trees, *Information Processing Letters 3*, 6(July 1975), 170–173. [points] D.2.3.3

67. [Bent77b] J. L. Bentley, D. F. Stanat, and E. H. Williams Jr., The complexity of finding fixed-radius near neighbors, *Information Processing Letters 6*, 6(December 1977), 209–212. [points] D.2.2 D.2.3.2 D.2.3.3

68. [Bent80f] J. L. Bentley and D. Wood, An optimal worst-case algorithm for reporting intersections of rectangles, *IEEE Transactions on Computers 29*, 7(July 1980), 571–577. [rectangles] D.3.2.1 D.3.2.4

69. [Bern88] M. Bern, Hidden surface removal for rectangles, *Proceedings of the Fourth Symposium on Computational Geometry*, Urbana-Champaign, IL, June 1988, 183–192. [rectangles]

70. [Bess82] P. W. Besslich, Quadtree construction of binary images by dyadic array transformations, *Proceedings of the IEEE Conference on Pattern Recognition and Image Processing*, Las Vegas, June 1982, 550–554. [regions]

71. [Bhas88] S. K. Bhaskar, A. Rosenfeld, and A. Y. Wu, Parallel processing of regions represented by linear quadtrees, *Computer Vision, Graphics, and Image Processing 42*, 3(June 1988), 371–380. [regions]

72. [Bier87] H. Bieri, Computing the Euler characteristic and related additive functionals of digital objects from their bintree representation, *Computer Vision, Graphics, and Image Processing 40*, 1(October 1987), 115–126. [regions] A.5.3

73. [Bloo87] J. Bloomenthal, Polygonalization of implicit surfaces, Xerox Palo Alto Research Center Technical Report, Palo Alto, CA, May 1987. [surfaces]

74. [Blum67] H. Blum, A transformation for extracting new descriptors of shape, in *Models for the Perception of Speech and Visual Form*, W. Wathen-Dunn, ed., MIT Press, Cambridge, MA, 1967, 362–380. [regions] D.1.2 A.1.3 A.9

75. [Bolo79] A. Bolour, Optimality properties of multiple-key hashing functions, *Journal of the ACM 26*, 2(April 1979), 196–210. [points]

76. [Bonf88] F. Bonfatti and L. Cavazza, SECT: an effective coding technique for polygonal geographic data, *Computers & Graphics 12*, 3/4(1988), 503–513. [regions]

77. [Borg84] G. Borgefors, Distance transformations in arbitrary dimensions, *Computer Vision, Graphics, and Image Processing 27*, 3(September 1984), 321–345. [regions] A.9.1 A.9.2

78. [Bowy81] A. Bowyer, P. J. Willis, and J. R. Woodwark, A multiprocessor architecture for solving spatial problems, *Computer Journal 24*, 4(November 1981), 353–357. [hardware]

79. [Brai80] I. C. Braid, R. C. Hillyard, and I. A. Stroud, Stepwise construction of polyhedra in geometrical modeling, in *Mathematical Models in Computer Graphics and Design*, K. W. Brodlie, ed., Academic Press, New York, 1980, 123–141. [volumes] D.5.4

80. [Bres65] J. E. Bresenham, Algorithm for computer control of a digital plotter, *IBM Systems Journal 4*, 1(1965), 25–30. [lines] A.7.2.3 A.7.2.4

81. [Brig86] S. Bright and S. Laflin, Shading of solid voxel models, *Computer Graphics Forum 5*, 2(June 1986), 131–137. [volumes] A.7.1.4

82. [Brod66] P. Brodatz, *Textures*, Dover, New York, 1966. [general] A.3.2.1.3

83. [Broo74] J. Brooks, R. Muraka, D. Onuoha, F. Rahn, and H. A. Steinberg, An extension of the combinatorial geometry technique for modeling vegetation and terrain features, Mathematical Applications Group Inc., NTIS AD-782–883, June 1974. [volumes] A.7.2.2

84. [Broo83] R. A. Brooks and T. Lozano-Perez, A subdivision algorithm in configuration space for findpath with rotation, *Proceedings of the Eighth International Joint Conference on Artificial Intelligence*, Karlsruhe, West Germany, August 1983, 799–806. [regions] D.1.3 A.1.4

85. [Brow86] R. L. Brown, Multiple storage quad trees: a simpler faster alternative to bisector list quad trees, *IEEE Transactions on Computer-Aided Design 5*, 3(July 1986), 413–419. [rectangles]

86. [Brun87] P. Brunet and D. Ayala, Extended octtree representation of free form surfaces, *Computer-Aided Geometric Design 4*, 1–2(July 1987), 141–154. [surfaces]

87. [Brun89] P. Brunet and I. Navazo, Solid representation and operation using extended octrees, *ACM Transactions on Graphics 8*, 1989. [volumes]

88. [Buch83] W. Bucher and H. Edelsbrunner, On expected and worst-case segment trees, in *Advances in Computing Research*, vol. 1, *Computational Geometry*, F. P. Preparata, ed., JAI Press, Greenwich, CT, 1983, 109–125. [rectangles] D.3.2.1

89. [Burk83] W. A. Burkhard, Interpolation-based index maintenance, *BIT 23*, 3(1983), 274–294. [points] D.2.7 D.2.8.2.1

90. [Burr86] P. A. Burrough, *Principles of Geographical Information Systems for Land Resources Assessment*, Clarendon Press, Oxford, Great Britain, 1986. [general] D.P A.P

91. [Burt80] P. J. Burt, Tree and pyramid structures for coding hexagonally sampled binary images, *Computer Graphics and Image Processing 14*, 3(November 1980), 271–280. [regions] D.1.4.1

92. [Burt81] P. J. Burt, T. H. Hong, and A. Rosenfeld, Segmentation and estimation of image region properties through cooperative hierarchical computation, *IEEE Transactions on Systems, Man, and Cybernetics 11*, 12(December 1981), 802–809. [regions] D.1.3

93. [Burt83] F. W. Burton and J. G. Kollias, Comment on the explicit quadtree as a structure for computer graphics, *Computer Journal 26*, 2(May 1983), 188. [regions] A.2.1.1

94. [Burt84] F. W. Burton, J. G. Kollias, and N. A. Alexandridis, Implementation of the exponential pyramid data structure with application to determination of symmetries in pictures, *Computer Vision, Graphics, and Image Processing 25*, 2(February 1984), 218–225. [regions]

95. [Burt85] F. W. Burton, V. J. Kollias, and J. G. Kollias, Expected and worst-case storage requirements for quadtrees, *Pattern Recognition Letters 3*, 2(March 1985), 131–135. [regions]

96. [Burt86] F. W. Burton, V. J. Kollias, and J. G. Kollias, Real-time raster to quadtree and quadtree to raster conversion algorithms with modest storage requirements, *Angewandte Informatik 28*, 4(April 1986), 169–174. [regions]

97.   [Burt87] F. W. Burton, V. J. Kollias, and J. G. Kollias, A general PASCAL program for map overlay of quadtrees and related problems, *Computer Journal 30*, 4(August 1987), 355–361. [regions]

98.   [Burt77] W. Burton, Representation of many-sided polygons and polygonal lines for rapid processing, *Communications of the ACM 20*, 3(March 1977), 166–171. [lines] D.4.1

99.   [Butz71] A. R. Butz, Alternative algorithm for Hilbert's space-filling curve, *IEEE Transactions on Computers 20*, 4(April 1971), 424–426. [regions] D.1.3 A.1.4

100. [Came84] S. A. Cameron, Modelling solids in motion, Ph.D. dissertation, University of Edinburgh, Edinburgh, Scotland, 1984. [volumes] D.5.5.1.3

101. [Carl87] I. Carlbom, An algorithm for geometric set operations using cellular subdivision techniques, *IEEE Computer Graphics and Applications 7*, 5(May 1987), 44–55. [volumes] D.5.3

102. [Carl85] I. Carlbom, I. Chakravarty, and D. Vanderschel, A hierarchical data structure for representing the spatial decomposition of 3–D objects, *IEEE Computer Graphics and Applications 5*, 4(April 1985), 24–31. [volumes] D.5.3 A.1.3

103. [Carl82] W. E. Carlson, An algorithm and data structure for 3D object synthesis using surface patch intersections, *Computer Graphics 16*, 3(July 1982), 255–264 (also *Proceedings of the SIGGRAPH'82 Conference*, Boston, July 1982). [surfaces] D.5.6 A.7.1.6

104. [Casp88] E. Caspary, Sequential and parallel algorithms for ray tracing complex scenes, Ph.D. dissertation, Electrical and Computer Engineering Department, University of California at Santa Barbara, Santa Barbara, CA, June 1988. [volumes]

105. [Catm75] E. Catmull, Computer display of curved surfaces, *Proceedings of the Conference on Computer Graphics, Pattern Recognition, and Data Structure*, Los Angeles, May 1975, 11–17. [surfaces] A.7.1.6

106. [Chan86] K. C. Chan, I. A. Gargantini, and T. R. Walsh, Double connectivity filling for 3d modeling, Computer Science Report 155, University of Western Ontario, London, Ontario, December 1986. [volumes]

107. [Chan81] J. M. Chang and K. S. Fu, Extended k-d tree database organization: a dynamic multiattribute clustering method, *IEEE Transactions on Software Engineering 7*, 3(May 1981), 284–290. [points]

108. [Chau85] B. B. Chaudhuri, Applications of quadtree, octree, and binary tree decomposition techniques to shape analysis and pattern recognition, *IEEE Transactions on Pattern Analysis and Machine Intelligence 7*, 6(November 1985), 652–661. [regions]

109. [Chaz88] B. Chazelle, A functional approach to data structures and its use in multidimensional searching, *SIAM Journal on Computing 17*, 3(June 1988), 427–462. [rectangles]

110. [Chaz87] B. Chazelle and D. Dobkin, Intersection of convex objects in two and three dimensions, *Journal of the ACM 34*, 1(January 1987), 1–27. [volumes] A.7.3

111. [Chaz86a] B. Chazelle and L. J. Guibas, Fractional cascading: I. A data structuring technique, *Algorithmica 1*, 2(1986), 133–162. [general] D.3.2.2 D.4.3.2

112. [Chaz86b] B. Chazelle and L. J. Guibas, Fractional cascading: II. Applications, *Algorithmica 1*, 2(1986), 163–191. [general] D.3.2.2 D.4.3.2

113. [Chen88a] C. Chen and H. Zou, Linear binary tree, *Proceedings of the Ninth International Conference on Pattern Recognition*, Rome, November 1988, 576–578. [regions]

114. [Chen88b] H. H. Chen and T. S. Huang, A survey of construction and manipulation of octrees, *Computer Vision, Graphics, and Image Processing 43*, 3(September 1988), 409–431. [volumes]

115. [Chen85a] L. S. Chen, G. T. Herman, R. A. Reynolds, and J. K. Udupa, Surface shading in the cuberille environment, *IEEE Computer Graphics and Applications 5*, 12(December 1985), 33–43. [volumes] A.7.1.4

116. [Chen85b] Y. C. Chen, An introduction to hierarchical probe model, Department of Mathematical Sciences, Purdue University Calumet, Hammond, IN, 1985. [regions] D.1.4.2 D.5.8

117. [Chen86] Z. T. Chen and W. R. Tobler, Quadtree representations of digital terrain, *Proceedings of Auto-Carto London*, vol. 1, London, September 1986, 475–484. [surfaces] D.5.6

118. [Ches85] R. Chestek, H. Muller, and D. Chelberg, Knowledge-based terrain analysis, *SPIE 548 Applications of Artificial Intelligence II*, 1985, 46–56. [regions]

119. [Chie84a] C. H. Chien and J. K. Aggarwal, A normalized quadtree representation, *Computer Vision, Graphics, and Image Processing 26*, 3(June 1984), 331–346. [regions] A.5.2

120. [Chie84b] C. H. Chien and J. K. Aggarwal, A volume/surface octree representation, *Proceedings of the Seventh International Conference on Pattern Recognition*, Montreal, August 1984, 817–820. [volumes] D.5.2 A.4.6

121. [Chie85] C. H. Chien and J. K. Aggarwal, Reconstruction and matching of 3–d objects using quadtrees/octrees, *Proceedings of the Third Workshop on Computer Vision: Representation and Control*, Bellaire, MI, October 1985, 49–54. [volumes] D.5.2 A.4.6

122. [Chie86a] C. H. Chien and J. K. Aggarwal, Volume/surface octrees for the representation of three-dimensional objects, *Computer Vision, Graphics, and Image Processing 36*, 1(October 1986), 100–113. [volumes] D.5.2 A.4.6

123. [Chie86b] C. H. Chien and J. K. Aggarwal, Identification of 3–d objects from multiple silhouettes using quadtrees/octrees, *Computer Vision, Graphics, and Image Processing 36*, 2/3(November/December 1986), 256–273. [volumes] D.5.2 A.4.6

124. [Chie86c] C. H. Chien and J. K. Aggarwal, Computation of volume/surface octrees from contours and silhouettes of multiple views, *Proceedings of Computer Vision and Pattern Recognition 86*, Miami Beach, June 1986, 250–255. [volumes] D.5.3 A.7.1.4

125. [Chie87] C. H. Chien and J. K. Aggarwal, Shape recognition from single silhouettes, *Proceedings of the First International Conference on Computer Vision*, London, June 1987, 481–490. [volumes]

126. [Chie88] C. H. Chien, Y. B. Sim, and J. K. Aggarwal, Generation of volume/surface octree from range data, *Proceedings of Computer Vision and Pattern Recognition 88*, Ann Arbor, MI, June 1988, 254–260. [volumes] D.5.2 A.4.6

127. [Chu88a] J. H. Chu, Notes on expected numbers of nodes in a quadtree, Computer Science Department, University of Maryland, College Park, MD, January 1988. [regions] D.1.5 A.1.2

128. [Chu88b] J. H. Chu and G. D. Knott, An analysis of spiral hashing, Computer Science TR-2107, University of Maryland, College Park, MD, September 1988. [points] D.2.8.2.2

129. [Clar76] J. H. Clark, Hierarchical geometric models for visible surface algorithms, *Communications of the ACM 19*, 10(October 1976), 547–554. [surfaces] A.7.2.2

130. [Clay88] R. D. Clay and H. P. Moreton, Efficient adaptive subdivision of Bézier surfaces, in *Proceedings of the EUROGRAPHICS'88 Conference*, D. A. Duce and P. Jancene, eds., North-Holland, Amsterdam, 1988, 357–371. [surfaces]

131. [Clea88] J. G. Cleary and G. Wyvill, Analysis of an algorithm for fast ray tracing using uniform space subdivision, *Visual Computer 4*, 2(July 1988), 65–83. [volumes] A.7.2.5

132. [Clem83] M. Clemmesen, Interval arithmetic implementations using floating point arithmetic, Institute of Datalogy Report 83/9, University of Copenhagen, Copenhagen, 1983. [general] D.5.5.1.3

133. [Cohe80] E. Cohen, T. Lyche, and R. Riesenfeld, Discrete B-splines and subdivision techniques in computer-aided geometric design and computer graphics, *Computer Graphics and Image Processing 14*, 3(October 1980), 87–111. [surfaces] D.4 D.5.6

134. [Cohe79] J. Cohen and T. Hickey, Two algorithms for detecting volumes of convex polyhedra, *Journal of the ACM 26*, 3(July 1979), 401–414. [volumes] D.5.5

135. [Cohe85a] M. F. Cohen and D. P. Greenberg, The hemi-cube, *Computer Graphics 19*, 3(July 1985), 31–40 (also *Proceedings of the SIGGRAPH'85 Conference*, San Francisco, July 1985). [surfaces] A.7.4

136. [Cohe86] M. F. Cohen, D. P. Greenberg, D. S. Immel, and P. J. Brock, An efficient radiosity approach for realistic image synthesis, *IEEE Computer Graphics and Applications 6*, 3(March 1986), 26–35. [surfaces] A.7.4

137. [Cohe85b] Y. Cohen, M. S. Landy, and M. Pavel, Hierarchical coding of binary images, *IEEE Transactions on Pattern Analysis and Machine Intelligence 7*, 3(May 1985), 284–298. [regions] D.1.4.1 A.1.3 A.2.2 A.8

138. [Cole87] A. J. Cole, Compaction techniques for raster scan graphics using space-filling curves, *Computer Journal 30*, 1(February 1987), 87–96. [regions]

139. [Cole82] A. J. Cole and R. Morrison, Triplex: A system for interval arithmetic, *Software Practice and Experience 12*, 4(April 1982), 341–350. [general] D.5.5.1.3

140. [Come79] D. Comer, The ubiquitous B-tree, *ACM Computing Surveys 11*, 2(June 1979), 121–137. [general] D.2.7 D.3.5.3 D.4.2.3.6 A.2.1 A.2.1.1 A.2.1.4 A.4.2.3

141. [Conn84] C. I. Connolly, Cumulative generation of octree models from range data, *Proceedings of the International Conference on Robotics*, Atlanta, March 1984, 25–32. [volumes] D.5.2 A.4.6

142. [Conn85] C. I. Connolly, The determination of next best views, *Proceedings of the International Conference on Robotics*, St. Louis, March 1985, 432–435. [volumes] D.5.2 A.4.6

143. [Cook78] B. G. Cook, The structural and algorithmic basis of a geographic data base, in *Proceedings of the First International Advanced Study Symposium on Topological Data Structures for Geographic Information Systems*, G. Dutton, ed., Harvard Papers on Geographic Information Systems, 1978. [regions] A.2.1.1

144. [Cook84] R. L. Cook, T. Porter, and L. Carpenter, Distributed ray tracing, *Computer Graphics 18*, 3(July 1984), 137–145 (also *Proceedings of the SIGGRAPH'84 Conference*, Minneapolis, July 1984). [ray tracing] A.7.2.1 A.7.2.5

145. [Cook82] R. L. Cook and K. E. Torrance, A reflectance model for computer graphics, *ACM Transactions on Graphics 1*, 1(January 1982), 7–24. [general] A.7.2.1

146. [Cott85] M. S. Cottingham, A compressed data structure for surface representation, *Computer Graphics Forum 4*, 3(September 1985), 217–228. [surfaces]

147. [Coxe86] H. S. M. Coxeter, M. Emmer, R. Penrose, and M. L. Teuber (eds.), *M. C. Escher, art and science: Proceedings of the International Congress on M. C. Escher*, Elsevier North-Holland, New York, 1986. [general] D.1.2 A.1.2

148. [Creu81] E. Creutzburg, Complexities of quadtrees and the structure of pictures, Friedrich-Schiller University Technical Report N/81/74, Jena, East Germany, 1981. [regions]

149. [Crow77] F. C. Crow, Shadow algorithms for computer graphics, *Computer Graphics 11*, 2(Summer 1977), 242–248 (also *Proceedings of the SIGGRAPH'77 Conference*, San Jose, CA, July 1977). [general] A.7.1.4

150. [Cutl86] M. W. Cutlip, Verification of numerically controlled machine tool programs for 2.5–d parts using Z-tree solid modeling techniques, M.Sc. dissertation, School of Engineering and Applied Science, George Washington University, Washington, DC, 1986. [surfaces]

151. [Cyru78] M. Cyrus and J. Beck, Generalized two- and three-dimensional clipping, *Computers & Graphics 3*, 1(1978), 23–28. [general] A.7.2.3

152. [Dado82] N. Dadoun, D. G. Kirkpatrick, and J. P. Walsh, Hierarchical approaches to hidden surface intersection testing, *Proceedings of Graphics Interface '82*, Toronto, May 1982, 49–56. [volumes] A.7.2.2 A.7.3

153. [Dado85] N. Dadoun, D. G. Kirkpatrick, and J. P. Walsh, The geometry of beam tracing, *Proceedings of the Symposium on Computational Geometry*, Baltimore, June 1985, 55–61. [volumes] A.7.2.2 A.7.3

154. [Dand84] S. P. Dandamudi and P. G. Sorenson, Performance of a modified k-tree, Department of Computational Science Report 84–10, University of Saskatchewan, Saskatoon, Canada, 1984. [points]

155. [Dand85] S. P. Dandamudi and P. G. Sorenson, An empirical performance comparison of some variations of the k-d tree and BD tree, *International Journal of Computer and Information Sciences 14*, 3(June 1985), 135–159. [points] D.2.6.2

156. [Dand86] S. P. Dandamudi and P. G. Sorenson, Algorithms for BD trees, *Software— Practice and Experience 16*, 12(December 1986), 1077–1096. [points] D.2.6.2 D.2.8.1

157. [Davi84] E. Davis, Representing and acquiring geographic knowledge, Ph.D. dissertation, Department of Computer Science, Yale University, New Haven, CT, 1984. [artificial intelligence]

158. [Davi80] L. S. Davis and N. Roussopoulos, Approximate pattern matching in a pattern database system, *Information Systems 5*, 2(1980), 107–119. [regions] D.1.3 A.1.4

159. [Davi86] W. A. Davis, Hybrid use of hashing techniques for spatial data, *Proceedings of Auto-Carto London*, vol. 1, London, September 1986, 127–135. [regions]

160. [Davi85] W. A. Davis and X. Wang, A new approach to linear quadtrees, *Proceedings of Graphics Interface '85*, Montreal, May 1985, 195–202. [regions]

161. [DeCo76] F. De Coulon and O. Johnsen, Adaptive block schemes for source coding of black-and-white facsimile, *Electronics Letters 12*, 3(February 5, 1976), 61–62 (also erratum, *Electronics Letters 12*, 6(March 18, 1976), 152). [regions] D.2.6.1 A.2.2

162. [DeFl87] L. De Floriani, Surface representations based on triangular grids, *Visual Computer 3*, 1(February 1987), 27–50. [surfaces] D.5.6

163. [DeFl84] L. De Floriani, B. Falcidieno, G. Nagy, and C. Pienovi, A hierarchical structure for surface approximation, *Computers & Graphics 8*, 2(1984), 183–193. [surfaces] D.5.6

164. [DeFl85] L. De Floriani, B. Falcidieno, G. Nagy, and C. Pienovi, Efficient selection, storage and retrieval of irregularly distributed elevation data, *Computers and Geosciences 11*, 6(1985), 667–673. [surfaces] D.5.6

165. [Dela34] B. Delaunay, Sur la sphere vide, *Izvestiya Akademii Nauk SSSR, VII Seria*, Otdelenie Matematicheskii i Estestvennyka Nauk 7, 6(October 1934), 793–800. [surfaces] D.5.6

166. [DeMi78] R. A. DeMillo, S. C. Eisenstat, and R. J. Lipton, Preserving average proximity in arrays, *Communications of the ACM 21*, 3(March 1978), 228–231. [general] A.3.2.1.2 A.4.2.2

167. [Dew85] P. M. Dew, J. Dodsworth, and D. T. Morris, Systolic array architectures for high performance CAD/CAM workstations, in *Fundamental Algorithms for Computer Graphics*, R. A. Earnshaw, ed., Springer-Verlag, Berlin, 1985, 659–694. [hardware]

168. [Dill87] M. B. Dillencourt and D. Mount, personal communication, 1987. [regions] D.1.2 A.1.3

169. [Dill88] M. B. Dillencourt and H. Samet, Extracting region boundaries from maps stored as linear quadtrees, *Proceedings of the Third International Symposium on Spatial Data Handling*, Sydney, Australia, August 1988, 65–77. [regions] A.4.3.2

170. [Dins85] I. Dinstein, D. W. L. Yen, and M. D. Flickner, Handling memory overflow in connected component labeling applications, *IEEE Transactions on Pattern Analysis and Machine Intelligence 7*, 1(January 1985), 116–121. [regions] A.5.1.1

171. [Dipp84] M. Dippe and J. Swensen, An adaptive subdivision algorithm and parallel architecture for realistic image synthesis, *Computer Graphics 18*, 3(July 1984), 149–158 (also *Proceedings of the SIGGRAPH'84 Conference*, Minneapolis, July 1984) [hardware] A.7.2.5

172. [Dobk83] D. P. Dobkin and D. G. Kirkpatrick, Fast detection of polyhedral intersections, *Theoretical Computer Science 27*, 3(December 1983), 241–253. [volumes] A.7.3

173. [Dobk74] D. Dobkin and R. J. Lipton, Some generalizations of binary search, *Proceedings of the Sixth Annual ACM Symposium on the Theory of Computing*, Seattle, April 1974, 310–316. [points]

174. [Dobk76] D. Dobkin and R. J. Lipton, Multidimensional searching problems, *SIAM Journal on Computing 5*, 2(June 1976), 181–186. [points]

175. [Doct81] L. J. Doctor and J. G. Torborg, Display techniques for octree-encoded objects, *IEEE Computer Graphics and Applications 1*, 1(July 1981), 29–38. [volumes] A.2.1.2 A.7.1.4

176. [Dors84a] L. Dorst and R. P. W. Duin, Spirograph theory: a framework for calculations on digitized straight lines, *IEEE Transactions on Pattern Analysis and Machine Intelligence 6*, 5(September 1984), 632–639. [lines]

177. [Dors84b] L. Dorst and A. W. M. Smeulders, Discrete representation of straight lines, *IEEE Transactions on Pattern Analysis and Machine Intelligence 6*, 4(July 1984), 450–463. [lines]

178. [Dris89] J. R. Driscoll, N. Sarnak, D. D. Sleator, and R. E. Tarjan, Making data structures persistent, *Journal of Computer and System Sciences 38*, 1(February 1989), 86–124. [general] D.3.2.4

179. [Dubi81] T. Dubitzki, A. Wu, and A. Rosenfeld, Parallel region property computation by active quadtree networks, *IEEE Transactions on Pattern Analysis and Machine Intelligence 3*, 6(November 1981), 626–633. [regions]

180. [Duda73] R. O. Duda and P. E. Hart, *Pattern Classification and Scene Analysis*, Wiley Interscience, New York, 1973. [general]

181. [Duff85] T. Duff, Compositing 3–d rendered images, *Computer Graphics 19*, 3(July 1985), 41–44 (also *Proceedings of the SIGGRAPH'85 Conference*, San Francisco, July 1985). [general] A.7.1.6

182. [Dürs88] M. J. Dürst and T. L. Kunii, Integrated polytrees: a generalized model for integrating spatial decomposition and boundary representation, Department of Information Science Technical Report 88–002, University of Tokyo, Tokyo, January 1988. [volumes]

183. [Dutt84] G. Dutton, Geodesic modelling of planetary relief, *Cartographica 21*, 2&3(Summer & Autumn 1984), 188–207. [surfaces] D.1.4.1 D.5.6

184. [Dyer80a] C. R. Dyer, Computing the Euler number of an image from its quadtree, *Computer Graphics and Image Processing 13*, 3(July 1980), 270–276. [regions] A.5.3

185. [Dyer81] C. R. Dyer, A vLSI pyramid machine for hierarchical parallel image process-ing, *Proceedings of the IEEE Conference on Pattern Recognition and Image Processing*, Dallas, August 1981, 381–386. [hardware]

186. [Dyer82] C. R. Dyer, The space efficiency of quadtrees, *Computer Graphics and Image Processing 19*, 4(August 1982), 335–348. [regions] D.1.5 A.1.2 A.6.5.3 A.6.6 A.8.2.2 A.9.3.4

187. [Dyer80b] C. R. Dyer, A. Rosenfeld, and H. Samet, Region representation: boundary codes from quadtrees, *Communications of the ACM 23*, 3(March 1980), 171–179. [regions] A.4.3.2

188. [East70] C. M. Eastman, Representations for space planning, *Communications of the ACM 13*, 4(April 1970), 242–250. [regions] D.1.3 A.1.4

189. [East81] C. M. Eastman, Optimal bucket size for nearest neighbor searching in k-d trees, *Information Processing Letters 12*, 4(August 1981), 165–167. [points]

190. [East79] C. M. Eastman and K. Weiler, Geometric modeling using Euler operators, *Proceedings of the First Conference on Computer Graphics in CAD/CAM Systems*, Cambridge, MA, May 1979, 248–259. [volumes] D.5.4

191. [East82] C. M. Eastman and M. Zemankova, Partially specified nearest neighbor searches using k-d trees, *Information Processing Letters 15*, 2(September 1982), 53–56. [points]

192. [Edah84] M. Edahiro, I. Kokubo, and T. Asano, A new point-location algorithm and its practical efficiency — comparison with existing algorithms, *ACM Transactions on Graphics 3*, 2(April 1984), 86–109. [points]

193. [Edel85a] S. Edelman and E. Shapiro, Quadtrees in concurrent Prolog, *Proceedings of the IEEE International Conference on Parallel Processing*, St. Charles, IL, August 1985, 544–551. [regions]

194. [Edel80a] H. Edelsbrunner, Dynamic rectangle intersection searching, Institute for Infor-mation Processing Report 47, Technical University of Graz, Graz, Austria, February 1980. [rectangles] D.3.2.2 D.4.3.2

195. [Edel80b] H. Edelsbrunner, Dynamic data structures for orthogonal intersection queries, Institute for Information Processing Report 59, Technical University of Graz, Graz, Aus-tria, October 1980. [rectangles]

196. [Edel81a] H. Edelsbrunner, A note on dynamic range searching, *Bulletin of the EATCS*, 15(October 1981), 34–40. [rectangles] D.2.5

197. [Edel82] H. Edelsbrunner, Intersection problems in computational geometry, Institute for Information Processing Report 93, Technical University of Graz, Graz, Austria, June 1982. [rectangles] D.3.2.4

198. [Edel83a] H. Edelsbrunner, A new approach to rectangle intersections: Part I, *Interna-tional Journal of Computer Mathematics 13*, 3–4(1983), 209–219. [rectangles] D.3.2.2 D.4.3.2

199. [Edel83b] H. Edelsbrunner, A new approach to rectangle intersections: Part II, *Interna-tional Journal of Computer Mathematics 13*, 3–4(1983), 221–229. [rectangles] D.3.2.2 D.4.3.2

200. [Edel84] H. Edelsbrunner, Key-problems and key-methods in computational geometry, *Proceedings of the Symposium of Theoretical Aspects of Computer Science*, Paris, 1984, 1–13 (Lecture Notes in Computer Science 166, Springer-Verlag, New York, 1984). [general] D.P D.4 D.4.2.3.6 D.4.3

201. [Edel87] H. Edelsbrunner, *Algorithms in Combinatorial Geometry*, EATCS Monographs on Theoretical Computer Science, Springer-Verlag, Berlin, 1987. [general] D.P D.4.3

202. [Edel88] H. Edelsbrunner (ed.), A bibliography in computational geometry, Department of Computer Science, University of Illinois at Urbana-Champaign, Urbana, IL, 1988. [general] D.P

203. [Edel86a] H. Edelsbrunner, L. J. Guibas, and J. Stolfi, Optimal point location in a monotone subdivision, *SIAM Journal on Computing 15*, 2(May 1986), 317–340. [regions] D.P D.3.2.2 D.4.3 D.4.3.2

204. [Edel81b] H. Edelsbrunner and H. A. Maurer, On the intersection of orthogonal objects, *Information Processing Letters 13*, 4,5(End 1981), 177–181. [rectangles] D.3.2.4

205. [Edel86b] H. Edelsbrunner, J. O'Rourke, and R. Seidel, Constructing arrangements of lines and hyperplanes with applications, *SIAM Journal on Computing 15*, 2(May 1986), 341–363. [rectangles] D.3.3

206. [Edel85b] H. Edelsbrunner and M. H. Overmars, Batched dynamic solutions to decomposable searching problems, *Journal of Algorithms 6*, 4(December 1985), 515–542. [rectangles] D.3.2 D.3.3

207. [Edel83c] H. Edelsbrunner and J. van Leeuwen, Multidimensional data structures and algorithms: a bibliography, Institute for Information Processing Report F104, Technical University of Graz, Graz, Austria, January 1983. [general] D.P

208. [Egen88] M. J. Egenhofer and A. U. Frank, Towards a spatial query language: user interface considerations, *Proceedings of the Fourteenth International Conference on Very Large Data Bases*, F. Bachillon and D. J. DeWitt, eds., Los Angeles, August 1988, 124–133. [general]

209. [Elbe88] G. Elber and M. Shpitalni, Octree creation via C. S. G. definition, *Visual Computer 4*, 2(July 1988), 53–64. [volumes]

210. [Elco87] E. W. Elcock, I. Gargantini, and T. R. Walsh, Triangular decomposition, *Image and Vision Computing 5*, 3(August 1987), 225–231. [regions]

211. [Elme87] G. A. Elmes, Data Structures for quadtree-addressed entities on a spatial relational database, *Proceedings of the International Symposium on Geographic Information Systems*, vol. 2, Arlington, VA, November 1987, 177–179. [regions]

212. [Enbo88] R. J. Enbody and H. C. Du, Dynamic hashing schemes, *ACM Computing Surveys 20*, 2(June 1988), 85–113. [points]

213. [Este83] D. M. Esterling and J. Van Rosedale, An intersection algorithm for moving parts, *Proceedings of the NASA Symposium on Computer-Aided Geometry Modeling*, Hampton, VA, April 1983, 119–123. [surfaces]

214. [Fabb86] F. Fabbrini and C. Montani, Autumnal quadtrees, *Computer Journal 29*, 5(October 1986), 472–474. [regions]

215. [Fadd59] V. N. Faddeeva, *Computational Methods of Linear Algebra*, Dover, New York, 1959. [general] D.2.6.1

216. [Fagi79] R. Fagin, J. Nievergelt, N. Pippenger, and H. R. Strong, Extendible hashing — a fast access method for dynamic files, *ACM Transactions on Database Systems 4*, 3(September 1979), 315–344. [points] D.2.7 D.2.8.1 D.2.8.2.1 D.2.8.2.3 D.2.8.2.4

217. [Falo86] C. Faloutsos, Multiattribute hashing using Gray codes, *Proceedings of the SIGMOD Conference*, Washington, DC, May 1986, 227–238. [points] D.2.7

218. [Falo88] C. Faloutsos, Gray codes for partial match and range queries, *IEEE Transactions on Software Engineering 14*, 10(October 1988), 1381–1393. [points] D.2.7

219. [Falo87] C. Faloutsos, T. Sellis, and N. Roussopoulos, Analysis of object oriented spatial access methods, *Proceedings of the SIGMOD Conference*, San Francisco, May 1987, 426–439. [rectangles] D.3.5.3

220. [Fan88] N. P. Fan and C. C. Li, Computing quadtree medial axis transform by a multi-layered pyramid of LISP-processor arrays, *Proceedings of Computer Vision and Pattern Recognition 88*, Ann Arbor, MI, June 1988, 628–634. [hardware]

221. [Faug84] O. D. Faugeras, M. Hebert, P. Mussi, and J. D. Boissonnat, Polyhedral approximation of 3–d objects without holes, *Computer Vision, Graphics, and Image Processing 25*, 2(February 1984), 169–183. [surfaces] D.4.1 D.5.2 D.5.6 D.5.7 A.4.6

222. [Faug83] O. D. Faugeras and J. Ponce, Prism trees: a hierarchical representation for 3–d objects, *Proceedings of the Eighth International Joint Conference on Artificial Intelligence*, Karlsruhe, West Germany, August 1983, 982–988. [surfaces] D.4.1 D.5.6

223. [Fave84] B. Faverjon, Obstacle avoidance using an octree in the configuration space of a manipulator, *Proceedings of the International Conference on Robotics*, Atlanta, March 1984, 504–512. [volumes] D.1.3 A.1.4

224. [Fave86] B. Faverjon, Object level programming of industrial robots, *Proceedings of the IEEE International Conference on Robotics and Automation*, San Francisco, April 1986, 1406–1412. [volumes]

225. [Feke84] G. Fekete and L. S. Davis, property spheres: A new representation for 3–d object recognition, *Proceedings of the Workshop on Computer Vision: Representation and Control*, Annapolis, MD, April 1984, 192–201 (also University of Maryland Computer Science TR-1355). [surfaces] D.1.4.1 D.5.6

226. [Feyn63] R. P. Feynman, R. B. Leighton, and M. Sands, *The Feynman Lectures on Physics*, Addison-Wesley, Reading, MA, 1963. [general] A.7.1.4

227. [Fink74] R. A. Finkel and J. L. Bentley, Quad trees: a data structure for retrieval on composite keys, *Acta Informatica 4*, 1(1974), 1–9. [points] D.1.2 D.1.3 D.1.4.1 D.2.1 D.2.3 D.2.3.1 D.2.3.2 D.2.3.3 A.1.3 A.1.4

228. [Flaj83] P. Flajolet and C. Puech, Tree structures for partial match retrieval, *Proceedings of the Twenty-fourth Annual IEEE Symposium on the Foundations of Computer Science*, Tucson, November 1983, 282–288. [points] D.2.6.3 D.2.8.1

229. [Fole82] J. D. Foley and A. van Dam, *Fundamentals of Interactive Computer Graphics*, Addison-Wesley, Reading, MA, 1982. [general] D.5.2 A.4.6

230. [Fong84] A. C. Fong, A scheme for reusing label locations in real time component labeling of images, *Proceedings of the Seventh International Conference on Pattern Recognition*, Montreal, August 1984, 243–245. [regions] A.5.1.1

231. [Forr85] A. R. Forrest, Computational geometry in practice, in *Fundamental Algorithms for Computer Graphics*, R. A. Earnshaw, ed., Springer-Verlag, Berlin, 1985, 707–724. [general]

232. [Fran81] A. Frank, Applications of dbms to land information systems, *Proceedings of the Seventh International Conference on Very Large Data Bases*, C. Zaniolo and C. Delobel, eds., Cannes, France, September 1981, 448–453. [general]

233. [Fran83] A. Frank, Problems of realizing LIS: storage methods for space related data: the field tree, Technical Report 71, Institut für Geodasie und Photogrammetrie, ETH, Zurich, Switzerland, June 1983. [rectangles]

234. [Fran84] W. R. Franklin, Adaptive grids for geometric operations, *Cartographica 21*, 2&3(Summer & Autumn 1984), 160–167. [regions] D.2.2 A.1.3

235. [Fran85] W. R. Franklin and V. Akman, Building an octree from a set of parallelepipeds, *IEEE Computer Graphics and Applications 5*, 10(October 1985), 58–64. [volumes] D.5.2 A.4.6

236. [Fran88] W. R. Franklin and V. Akman, An adaptive grid for polyhedral visibility in object space: an implementation, *Computer Journal 31*, 1(February 1988), 56–60. [regions] D.2.2 A.1.3

237. [Fred60] E. Fredkin, Trie memory, *Communications of the ACM 3*, 9(September 1960), 490–499. [general] D.1.2 D.2.1 D.2.6 A.1.3

238. [Fred78] M. L. Fredman and B. Weide, The complexity of computing the measure of $\cup[a_i,b_i]$, *Communications of the ACM 21*, 7(July 1978), 540–544. [general] D.3.3

239. [Free74] H. Freeman, Computer processing of line-drawing images, *ACM Computing Surveys 6*, 1(March 1974), 57–97. [lines] D.P D.4 D.4.4 A.4.3

240. [Free75] H. Freeman and R. Shapira, Determining the minimum area encasing rectangles for an arbitrary closed curve, *Communications of the ACM 18*, 7(July 1975), 409–413. [regions] D.4.1

241. [Free87] M. Freeston, The BANG file: a new kind of grid file, *Proceedings of the SIG-MOD Conference*, San Francisco, May 1987, 260–269. [points] D.2.6.2

242. [Frie75] J. H. Friedman, F. Baskett, and L. J. Shustek, An algorithm for finding nearest neighbors, *IEEE Transactions on Computers 24*, 10(October 1975), 1000–1006. [points] D.2.2

243. [Frie77] J. H. Friedman, J. L. Bentley, and R. A. Finkel, An algorithm for finding best matches in logarithmic expected time, *ACM Transactions on Mathematical Software 3*, 3(September 1977), 209–226. [points] D.1.4.2 D.2.4.1

244. [Fuch83] H. Fuchs, G. D. Abram, and E. D. Grant, Near real-time shaded display of rigid objects, *Computer Graphics 17*, 3(July 1983), 65–72 (also *Proceedings of the SIG-GRAPH'83 Conference*, Boston, July 1983). [volumes] D.1.4.1 A.1.3 A.7.1.5

245. [Fuch80] H. Fuchs, Z. M. Kedem, and B. F. Naylor, On visible surface generation by a priori tree structures, *Computer Graphics 14*, 3(July 1980), 124–133 (also *Proceedings of the SIGGRAPH'80 Conference*, Seattle, July 1980). [volumes] D.1.4.1 D.2.4 D.3.5.3 A.1.3 A.7.1 A.7.1.5 A.7.3

246. [Fuhr88] D. R. Fuhrmann, Quadtree traversal algorithms for pointer-based and depth-first representations, *IEEE Transactions on Pattern Analysis and Machine Intelligence 10*, 6(November 1988), 955–960. [regions]

247. [Fuji85a] A. Fujimoto and K. Iwata, Accelerated ray tracing, *Proceedings of Computer Graphics'85*, Tokyo, 1985, T1–2, 1–26. [volumes]

248. [Fuji86] A. Fujimoto, T. Tanaka, and K. Iwata, ARTS: accelerated ray-tracing system, *IEEE Computer Graphics and Applications 6*, 4(April 1986), 16–26. [volumes] D.5.3 A.7.2.2 A.7.2.3 A.7.2.4

249. [Fuji85b] K. Fujimura and T. L. Kunii, A hierarchical space indexing method, *Proceedings of Computer Graphics'85*, Tokyo, 1985, T1–4, 1–14. [volumes] D.5.3 A.1.3

250. [Fuji89] K. Fujimura and H. Samet, A hierarchical strategy for path planning among moving obstacles, *IEEE Transactions on Robotics and Automation 5*, 1(February 1989), 61–69. [volumes] D.1.3 D.5.3 A.1.4 A.6.6 A.7.2.4

251. [Fuji83a] K. Fujimura, H. Toriya, K. Yamaguchi, and T. L. Kunii, An enhanced oct-tree data structure and operations for solid modeling, *Proceedings of the NASA Symposium on Computer-Aided Geometry Modeling*, Hampton, VA, April 1983, 269–277. [volumes]

252. [Fuji83b] K. Fujimura, H. Toriya, K. Yamaguchi, and T. L. Kunii, Oct-tree algorithms for solid modeling, *Computer Graphics: Theory and Applications*, T. L. Kunii, ed., Springer-Verlag, Tokyo, 1983, 96–110. [volumes] A.6.5.3

253. [Gao87] P. Gao and T. Smith, Space efficient hierarchical structures: relatively addressed compact quadtrees for GIS, *Proceedings of the International Symposium on Geographic Information Systems*, vol. 2, Arlington, VA, November 1987, 405–414. [regions]

254. [Garc87] G. Garcia and J. F. Le Corre, Geometrical transformations on binary images represented by quadtrees, *Proceedings of MARI'87 (Intelligent Networks and Machines)*, Paris, May 1987, 203–210. [regions]

255. [Gare79] M. R. Garey and D. S. Johnson, *Computers and Intractability, A Guide to the Theory of NP-Completeness*, W. H. Freeman and Co., San Francisco, 1979. [general] D.1.2 D.1.3 A.1.3 A.1.4

256. [Garg82a] I. Gargantini, An effective way to represent quadtrees, *Communications of the ACM 25*, 12(December 1982), 905–910. [regions] D.1.5 D.2.6.2 A.2.1.1 A.3.4.2

257. [Garg82b] I. Gargantini, Linear octtrees for fast processing of three dimensional objects, *Computer Graphics and Image Processing 20*, 4(December 1982), 365–374. [volumes] A.2.1.1 A.3.3

258. [Garg82c] I. Gargantini, Detection of connectivity for regions represented by linear quadtrees, *Computers and Mathematics with Applications 8*, 4(1982), 319–327. [regions] D.1.5 A.2.1.1 A.5.1.3

259. [Garg83] I. Gargantini, Translation, rotation, and superposition of linear quadtrees, *International Journal of Man-Machine Studies 18*, 3(March 1983), 253–263. [regions] A.2.1.3 A.6.3 A.6.5.3

260. [Garg86a] I. Gargantini, M. V. S. Ramanath, and T. R. S. Walsh, Linear octtrees: from data acquisition or creation to display, *Proceedings of Computer Graphics '86*, vol. 3, Anaheim, CA, May 1986, 615–621. [volumes]

261. [Garg82d] I. Gargantini and Z. Tabakman, Linear quad- and oct-trees: their use in generating simple algorithms for image processing, *Proceedings of Graphics Interface '82*, Toronto, May 1982, 123–127. [regions]

262. **[Garg86b] I. Gargantini, T. R. Walsh, and O. L. Wu, Viewing transformations of voxel-based objects via linear octrees**, *IEEE Computer Graphics and Applications 6*, 10(October 1986), 12–21. [volumes]

263. [Gast84] P. C. Gaston and T. Lozano-Perez, Tactile recognition and localization using object models: the case of polyhedra on a plane, *IEEE Transactions on Pattern Analysis and Machine Intelligence 6*, 3(May 1984), 257–266. [volumes] D.4.1

264. [Gaut85] N. K. Gautier, S. S. Iyengar, N. B. Lakhani, and M. Manohar, Space and time efficiency of the forest-of-quadtrees representation, *Image and Vision Computing 3*, 2(May 1985), 63–70. [regions]

265. [Gerv86] M. Gervautz, Three improvements of the ray tracing algorithm for CSG trees, *Computers and Graphics 10*, 4(1986), 333–339. [volumes]

266. [Gibs82] L. Gibson and D. Lucas, Vectorization of raster images using hierarchical methods, *Computer Graphics and Image Processing 20*, 1(September 1982), 82–89. [regions] D.1.4.1

267. [Gill81] R. Gillespie and W. A. Davis, Tree data structures for graphics and image processing, *Proceedings of the Seventh Conference of the Canadian Man-Computer Communications Society*, Waterloo, Canada, June 1981, 155–161. [regions] D.5.3 A.7.1.4

268. [Glas84] A. S. Glassner, Space subdivision for fast ray tracing, *IEEE Computer Graphics and Applications 4*, 10(October 1984), 15–22. [volumes] A.7.2.2 A.7.2.3 A.7.2.5

269. [Glas88] A. S. Glassner, Spacetime ray tracing for animation, *IEEE Computer Graphics and Applications 8*, 2(March 1988), 60–70. [volumes] D.5.3

270. [Gold81] L. M. Goldschlager, Short algorithms for space-filling curves, *Software — Practice and Experience 11*, 1(January 1981), 99. [regions] D.1.3 D.2.7 A.1.4

271. [Gold71] R. A. Goldstein and R. Nagel, 3–D visual simulation, *Simulation 16*, 1(January 1971), 25–31. [volumes] A.7.2.5

288. [Günt89] O. Günther, The design of the cell tree: an object-oriented index structure for geometric databases, *Proceedings of the Fifth IEEE International Conference on Data Engineering*, Los Angeles, February 1989, 598–605. [regions]

289. [Günt88] O. Günther and J. Bilmes, The implementation of the cell tree: design alternatives and performance evaluation, Department of Computer Science TRCS88–23, University of California at Santa Barbara, Santa Barbara, CA, October 1988. [regions] D.3.5.3

290. [Güti80] H. Güting and H. P. Kriegel, Multidimensional B-tree: an efficient dynamic file structure for exact match queries, *Proceedings of the Tenth Gesellschaft für Informatik Conference*, R. Wilhelm, ed., Saarbrücken, West Germany, September 1980, 375–388. [points] D.2.8.2.3

291. [Güti81] H. Güting and H. P. Kriegel, Dynamic k-dimensional multiway search under time-varying access frequencies, *Proceedings of the Fifth Gesellschaft für Informatik Conference on Theoretical Computer Science*, P. Deussen, ed., Karlsruhe, West Germany, March 1981, 135–145 (Lecture Notes in Computer Science 104, Springer-Verlag, Berlin, 1981). [points] D.2.8.2.3

292. [Güti84] R. H. Güting, An optimal contour algorithm for iso-oriented rectangles, *Journal of Algorithms 5*, 3(September 1984), 303–326. [rectangles]

293. [Güti87] R. H. Güting and W. Schilling, A practical divide-and-conquer algorithm for the rectangle intersection problem, *Information Sciences 42*, 2(July 1987), 95–112. [rectangles]

294. [Gutt84] A. Guttman, R-trees: a dynamic index structure for spatial searching, *Proceedings of the SIGMOD Conference*, Boston, June 1984, 47–57. [rectangles] D.2.8.1 D.3.5 D.3.5.3

295. [Hach89] N. I. Hachem and P. B. Berra, Key-sequential access methods for very large files derived from linear hashing, *Proceedings of the Fifth IEEE International Conference on Data Engineering*, Los Angeles, February 1989, 305–312. [points]

296. [Hanr86] P. Hanrahan, Using caching and breadth-first search to speed up ray-tracing, *Proceedings of Graphics Interface '86*, Vancouver, May 1986, 56–61. [volumes]

297. [Hara81] R. M. Haralick, Some neighborhood operations, in *Real Time/Parallel Computing Image Analysis*, M. Onoe, K. Preston, and A. Rosenfeld, eds., Plenum Press, New York, 1981. [regions] A.5.1.1

298. [Hara69] F. Harary, *Graph Theory*, Addison-Wesley, Reading, MA, 1969. [general] D.3.3 D.3.5.2 D.4.2.3.3 D.4.3 D.4.3.1 D.4.3.2 A.5.3

299. [Hard84] D. M. Hardas and S. N. Srihari, Progressive refinement of 3–d images using coded binary trees: algorithms and architecture, *IEEE Transactions on Pattern Analysis and Machine Intelligence 6*, 6(November 1984), 748–757. [volumes] A.8.3

300. [Hayw86] V. Hayward, Fast collision detection scheme by recursive decomposition of a manipulator workspace, *Proceedings of the IEEE International Conference on Robotics and Automation*, San Francisco, April 1986, 1044–1049. [volumes]

301. [Hech77] M. S. Hecht, *Flow Analysis of Computer Programs*, Elsevier North-Holland, New York, 1977. [general] A.4.3.2

302. [Heck84] P. S. Heckbert and P. Hanrahan, Beam tracing polygonal objects, *Computer Graphics 18*, 3(July 1984), 119–127 (also *Proceedings of the SIGGRAPH'84 Conference*, Minneapolis, July 1984). [volumes] A.7.2.2 A.7.3

303. [Hend80] P. Henderson, *Functional Programming: Application and Implementation*, Prentice-Hall International, Englewood Cliffs, NJ, 1980. [general] A.7.3

272. [Gome79] D. Gomez and A. Guzman, Digital model for three-dim representation, *Geo-Processing 1*, 1979, 53–70. [surfaces] D.5.6

273. [Good83] M. F. Goodchild and A. W. Grandfield, Optimizing raster sto nation of four alternatives, *Proceedings of Auto-Carto 6*, vol. 1, Ottawa 400–407. [regions] D.1.3 D.2.7 A.1.4

274. [Gora84] C. M. Goral, K. E. Torrance, D. P. Greenberg, and B. Battaile interaction of light between diffuse surfaces, *Computer Graphics 18* 213–222 (also *Proceedings of the SIGGRAPH'84 Conference*, Minneapc [surfaces] A.7.2.1 A.7.4

275. [Gord85] D. Gordon and R. A. Reynolds, Image space shading of thr objects, *Computer Vision, Graphics, and Image Processing 29*, 3(361–376. [volumes] A.7.1.4

276. [Gors88] N. D. Gorsky, On the complexity of the quadtree and 2d-tree r for binary pictures, *Proceedings of the COST-13 Workshop on From the Features*, Bonas, France, August 1988. [regions]

277. [Gour71] H. Gouraud, Continuous shading of curved surfaces, *IEEE Tra Computers 20*, 6(June 1971), 623–629. [general] A.7.1.4

278. [Gouz84] L. Gouzènes, Strategies for solving collision-free trajectories mobile and manipulator robots, *The International Journal of Robotics* 4(Winter 1984), 51–65. [volumes]

279. [Gowd83] I. G. Gowda, D. G. Kirkpatrick, D. T. Lee, A. Naamad, Dynar diagrams, *IEEE Transactions on Information Theory 29*, 5(September 198: [regions]

280. [Gree89] D. Greene, An implementation and performance analysis of spatial methods, *Proceedings of the Fifth IEEE International Conference on Data E* Los Angeles, February 1989, 606–615. [regions]

281. [Gros83] W. I. Grosky and R. Jain, Optimal quadtrees for image segments, *sactions on Pattern Analysis and Machine Intelligence 5*, 1(January 198 [regions] D.1.5 A.1.2 A.4.3.1

282. [Gros81] W. I. Grosky, M. Li, and R. Jain, A bottom-up approach to construc trees from binary arrays, Computer Science Report CSC-81–011, Wayne Sta sity, Detroit, MI, 1981. [regions] A.4.1

283. [Gros89] W. I. Grosky and R. Mehrotra, A pictorial index mechanism for mo matching, *Proceedings of the Fifth IEEE International Conference on Data Eng* Los Angeles, February 1989, 180–187. [general]

284. [Grün77] B. Grünbaum and G. C. Shephard, The eighty-one types of isohedral the plane, *Mathematical Proceedings of the Cambridge Philosophical Society 8.* tember 1977), 177–196. [regions] D.1.4.1

285. [Grün87] B. Grünbaum and G. C. Shephard, *Tilings and Patterns*, W. H. Freei Co., New York, 1987. [regions] D.1.4.1

286. [Guib78] L. J. Guibas and R. Sedgewick, A dichromatic framework for balance *Proceedings of the Nineteenth Annual IEEE Symposium on the Foundations o puter Science*, Ann Arbor, MI, October 1978, 8–21. [general] D.3.2.3

287. [Günt87] O. Günther, Efficient structures for geometric data management, Ph.D. tation, UCB/ERL M87/77, Electronics Research Laboratory, College of Engin University of California at Berkeley, Berkeley, CA, 1987 (Lecture Notes in Cor Science 337, Springer-Verlag, Berlin, 1988). [regions] D.3.5.3 D.4.1

304. [Hend82] T. C. Henderson and E. Triendl, Storing feature descriptions as 2–d trees, *Proceedings of the IEEE Conference on Pattern Recognition and Image Processing 82*, Las Vegas, June 1982, 555–556. [regions]

305. [Herb85] F. Herbert, Solid modeling for architectural design using octpaths, *Computers & Graphics 9*, 2(1985), 107–116. [volumes]

306. [Herm86a] M. Herman, Fast, three-dimensional, collision-free motion planning, *Proceedings of the IEEE International Conference on Robotics and Automation*, San Francisco, April 1986, 1056–1063. [volumes]

307. [Herm86b] M. Herman, Fast path planning in unstructured, dynamic, 3–d worlds, *Proceedings of SPIE—Applications of Artificial Intelligence 3*, Orlando, April 1986, 505–512. [volumes]

308. [Hert83] S. Hertel and K. Mehlhorn, Fast triangulation of the plane with respect to simple polygons, *Information and Control 64*, 1–3(January/February/March 1985), 52–76 (also *Proceedings of the 1983 International FCT Conference*, Borgholm, Sweden, August 1983, 207–218). [regions] D.4.3.1

309. [Hilb91] D. Hilbert, Ueber stetige Abbildung einer Linie auf ein Flächenstück, *Mathematische Annalen 38*, 1891, 459–460. [regions] D.1.3 A.1.4 A.4.1

310. [Hill67] F. S. Hillier and G. J. Lieberman, *Introduction to Operations Research*, Holden-Day, San Francisco, 1967. [general] D.1.2 A.1.3

311. [Hinr85a] K. Hinrichs, The grid file system: implementation and case studies of applications, Ph.D. dissertation, Institut für Informatik, ETH, Zurich, Switzerland, 1985. [rectangles] D.2.8.2.3 D.3.1 D.3.4

312. [Hinr85b] K. Hinrichs, Implementation of the grid file: design concepts and experience, *BIT 25*, 4(1985), 569–592. [rectangles] D.2.8.2.3 D.3.4

313. [Hinr83] K. Hinrichs and J. Nievergelt, The grid file: a data structure designed to support proximity queries on spatial objects, *Proceedings of the WG'83 (International Workshop on Graphtheoretic Concepts in Computer Science)*, M. Nagl and J. Perl, eds., Trauner Verlag, Linz, Austria, 1983, 100–113. [rectangles] D.3.1 D.3.4

314. [Hirs80] D. S. Hirschberg, On the complexity of searching a set of vectors, *SIAM Journal on Computing 9*, 1(February 1980), 126–129. [points]

315. [Hoar72] C. A. R. Hoare, Notes on data structuring, in *Structured Programming*, O. J. Dahl, E. W. Dijkstra, and C. A. R. Hoare, eds., Academic Press, London, 1972, 154. [matrices] D.1.3 A.1.4

316. [Hong85] T. H. Hong and M. Shneier, Describing a robot's workspace using a sequence of views from a moving camera, *IEEE Transactions on Pattern Analysis and Machine Intelligence 7*, 6(November 1985), 721–726. [volumes] D.5.2 A.4.6

317. [Hong87] T. H. Hong and M. Shneier, Rotation and translation of objects represented by octrees, *Proceedings of the IEEE International Conference on Robotics and Automation*, Raleigh, NC, March 1987, 947–950. [volumes]

318. [Horo76] S. L. Horowitz and T. Pavlidis, Picture segmentation by a tree traversal algorithm, *Journal of the ACM 23*, 2(April 1976), 368–388. [regions] D.1.2 A.1.3

319. [Hosh82] M. Hoshi and T. Yuba, A counter example to a monotonicity property of k-d trees, *Information Processing Letters 15*, 4(October 1982), 169–173. [points]

320. [Hout87] P. Houthuys, Box sort, a multidimensional method for rectangular boxes, used for quick range searching, *Visual Computer 3*, 4(December 1987), 236–249. [rectangles]

321. [Huff52] D. A. Huffman, A method for the construction of minimum-redundancy codes, *Proceedings of the IRE 40*, 9(September 1952), 1098–1101. [general] A.8 A.8.3

322. [Hunt78] G. M. Hunter, Efficient computation and data structures for graphics, Ph.D. dissertation, Department of Electrical Engineering and Computer Science, Princeton University, Princeton, NJ, 1978. [regions] D.1.2 D.1.3 D.1.5 D.2.6.1 D.3.5.1.3 D.4.2.1 D.4.2.4 D.5.5.1.2 A.1.2 A.1.3 A.1.4 A.3.2.2 A.4.3.1 A.4.4 A.5.1.2 A.5.2 A.5.3 A.6.3 A.6.3.2 A.6.5.1 A.7.1.1 A.7.1.2 A.9.2

323. [Hunt81] G. M. Hunter, Geometrees for interactive visualization of geology: an evaluation, System Science Department, Schlumberger-Doll Research, Ridgefield, CT, 1981. [volumes] D.2.6.2 D.5.3 A.1.3

324. [Hunt86] G. M. Hunter Three-dimensional frame buffers for interactive analysis of three-dimensional data, *Optical Engineering 25*, 2(February 1986), 292–295. [hardware]

325. [Hunt79a] G. M. Hunter and K. Steiglitz, Operations on images using quad trees, *IEEE Transactions on Pattern Analysis and Machine Intelligence 1*, 2(April 1979), 145–153. [regions] D.1.5 D.2.6.1 D.3.5.1.3 D.4.2.1 D.4.2.4 D.5.5.1.2 A.1.2 A.3.2.2 A.4.3.1 A.4.4 A.5.1.2 A.5.2 A.5.3 A.6.3 A.6.3.2 A.6.5.1 A.7.1.1 A.7.1.2 A.9.2

326. [Hunt79b] G. M. Hunter and K. Steiglitz, Linear transformation of pictures represented by quad trees, *Computer Graphics and Image Processing 10*, 3(July 1979), 289–296. [regions] D.1.3 A.1.4 A.3.2.2 A.4.4 A.6.5.1

327. [Hutf88a] A. Hutflesz, H. W. Six, and P. Widmayer, Globally order preserving multidimensional linear hashing, *Proceedings of the Fourth IEEE International Conference on Data Engineering*, Los Angeles, February 1988, 572–579. [points]

328. [Hutf88b] A. Hutflesz, H. W. Six, and P. Widmayer, The twin grid file: a nearly space optimal index structure, *Proceedings of the International Conference Extending Database Technology*, Venice, Italy, March 1988, 352–363. [points]

329. [Hutf88c] A. Hutflesz, H. W. Six, and P. Widmayer, Twin grid files: space optimizing access schemes, *Proceedings of the SIGMOD Conference*, Chicago, June 1988, 183–190. [points]

330. [Ibbs88] T. J. Ibbs and A. Stevens, Quadtree storage of vector data, *International Journal of Geographical Information Systems 2*, 1(January–March 1988), 43–56. [lines]

331. [Ibra84] H. A. H. Ibrahim, The connected component labeling algorithm on the NON-VON supercomputer, *Proceedings of the Workshop on Computer Vision: Representation and Control*, Annapolis, MD, April 1984, 37–45. [regions]

332. [Ichi81] T. Ichikawa, A pyramidal representation of images and its feature extraction facility, *IEEE Transactions on Pattern Analysis and Machine Intelligence 3*, 3(May 1981), 257–264. [regions]

333. [Imme86] D. S. Immel, M. F. Cohen, and D. P. Greenberg, A radiosity method for non-diffuse environments, *Computer Graphics 20*, 4(August 1986), 133–142 (also *Proceedings of the SIGGRAPH'86 Conference*, Dallas, August 1986). [surfaces] A.7.4

334. [Iri81] M. Iri, K. Murota, and S. Matsui, Linear-time approximation algorithms for finding the minimum-weight perfect matching on a plane, *Information Processing Letters 12*, 4(August 1981), 206–209. [points] D.2.9

335. [Isma80] M. G. B. Ismail and R. Steele, Adaptive pel location coding for bilevel facsimile signals, *Electronics Letters 16*, 10(May 8, 1980), 361–363. [regions] A.8.2.3

336. [Jack80] C. L. Jackins and S. L. Tanimoto, Oct-trees and their use in representing three-dimensional objects, *Computer Graphics and Image Processing 14*, 3(November 1980), 249–270. [volumes] D.1.3 A.1.4 A.6.5.2

337. [Jack83] C. L. Jackins and S. L. Tanimoto, Quad-trees, oct-trees, and k-trees — a generalized approach to recursive decomposition of Euclidean space, *IEEE Transactions on Pattern Analysis and Machine Intelligence 5*, 5(September 1983), 533–539. [regions] D.5.3 A.3.2.3 A.5.1.2 A.5.1.3 A.5.2

338.   [Jans86] F. W. Jansen, Data structures for ray tracing, *Data Structures for Raster Graphics*, F. J. Peters, L. R. A. Kessener, and M. L. P. van Lierop, eds., Springer Verlag, Berlin, 1986, 57–73. [volumes] A.7.2.3

339.   [Jans87a] F. W. Jansen, Solid modelling with faceted primitives, Ph.D. dissertation, Department of Industrial Design, Delft University of Technology, Delft, The Netherlands, September 1987. [volumes] D.5.5

340.   [Jans87b] F. W. Jansen and R. J. Sutherland, Display of solid models with a multiprocessor system, *Proceedings of the EUROGRAPHICS'87 Conference*, G. Marechal, ed., North-Holland, Amsterdam, 1987, 377–387. [hardware] D.5.5

341.   [Jans83] F. W. Jansen and J. J. van Wijk, Fast previewing techniques in raster graphics, in *Proceedings of the EUROGRAPHICS'83 Conference*, P. J. W. ten Hagen, ed., North-Holland, Amsterdam, 1983, 195–202. [volumes] A.7.2.5

342.   [Jare84] G. E. M. Jared and T. Varady, Synthesis of volume modelling and sculptured surfaces in BUILD, *Proceedings of CAD'84*, Brighton, Great Britain, 1984, 481–495. [surfaces]

343.   [Javi76] J. F. Javis, C. N. Judice, and W. H. Ninke, A survey of techniques for the image display of continuous tone images on a bilevel display, *Computer Graphics and Image Processing 5*, 1(March 1976), 13–40. [regions] A.6.3.1

344.   [Jens74] K. Jensen and N. Wirth, *PASCAL User Manual and Report*, Second Edition, Springer-Verlag, New York, 1974. [general] D.P A.P L

345.   [Jone84] L. Jones and S. S. Iyengar, Space and time efficient virtual quadtrees, *IEEE Transactions on Pattern Analysis and Machine Intelligence 6*, 2(March 1984), 244–247. [regions] A.2.1.4

346.   [Josh88] R. C. Joshi, H. Darbari, S. Goel, and S. Sasikumaran, A hierarchical hex-tree representational technique for solid modelling, *Computers & Graphics 12*, 2(1988), 235–238. [volumes]

347.   [Joy86] K. I. Joy and M. N. Bhetanabhotla, Ray tracing parametric surface patches utilizing numerical techniques and ray coherence, *Computer Graphics 20*, 4(August 1986), 279–285 (also *Proceedings of the SIGGRAPH'86 Conference*, Dallas, August 1986). [surfaces]

348.   [Kaji86] J. T. Kajia, The rendering equation, *Computer Graphics 20*, 4(August 1986), 143–150 (also *Proceedings of the SIGGRAPH'86 Conference*, Dallas, August 1986). [general] A.7.2.1

349.   [Kamb86] S. Kambhampati and L. S. Davis, Multiresolution path planning for mobile robots, *IEEE Journal of Robotics and Automation 2*, 3(September 1986), 135–145. [regions]

350.   [Kana85] K. Kanatani, personal communication, 1985. [regions] D.1.4.1

351.   [Kapl85] M. R. Kaplan, Space-tracing: a constant time ray-tracer, SIGGRAPH'85 Tutorial on the Uses of Spatial Coherence in Ray-Tracing, San Francisco, ACM, July 1985. [volumes] A.7.2.2

352.   [Kapl87] M. R. Kaplan, The use of spatial coherence in ray tracing, in *Techniques for Computer Graphics*, D. F. Rogers and R. A. Earnshaw, eds., Springer-Verlag, New York, 1987, 173–193. [volumes] A.7.2.2 A.7.2.3 A.7.2.4

353.   [Karl88] R. G. Karlsson, Greedy matching on a grid, *BIT 28*, 1(1988), 19–26. [points]

354.   [Karo83] O. Karonen, M. Tamminen, P. Kerola, M. Mitjonen, and E. Orivouri, A geometric mine modeling system, *Proceedings of Auto-Carto 6*, vol. 1, Ottawa, October 1983, 374–383. [volumes]

355. [Kasi88] S. Kasif, Optimal parallel algorithms for quadtree problems, *Proceedings of the Fifth Israeli Symposium on Artificial Intelligence, Vision, and Pattern Recognition*, Tel Aviv, Israel, December 1988, 353–363. [regions]

356. [Kata88] J. Katajainen and M. Koppinen, Constructing Delaunay triangulations by merging buckets in quadtree order, *Fundamenta Informaticae 11*, 3(September 1988), 275–288. [regions]

357. [Kauf83] A. Kaufman, D. Forgash, and Y. Ginsburg, Hidden surface removal using a forest of quadtrees, *Proceedings of the First IPA Conference on Image Processing, Computer Graphics, and Pattern Recognition*, A. Kaufman, ed., Information Processing Association of Israel, Jerusalem, 1983, 85–89. [volumes] A.7.1.1

358. [Kawa80a] E. Kawaguchi and T. Endo, On a method of binary picture representation and its application to data compression, *IEEE Transactions on Pattern Analysis and Machine Intelligence 2*, 1(January 1980), 27–35. [regions] D.1.3 D.1.5 D.5.4 A.1.4 A.2.2 A.3.4.4 A.5.1.3

359. [Kawa83] E. Kawaguchi, T. Endo, and J. Matsunaga, Depth-first expression viewed from digital picture processing, *IEEE Transactions on Pattern Analysis and Machine Intelligence 5*, 4(July 1983), 373–384. [regions] D.1.2 A.1.3 A.2.2 A.6.3 A.8

360. [Kawa80b] E. Kawaguchi, T. Endo, and M. Yokota, DF-expression of binary-valued picture and its relation to other pyramidal representations, *Proceedings of the Fifth International Conference on Pattern Recognition*, Miami Beach, December 1980, 822–827. [regions] D.1.2 D.1.3 A.1.3 A.1.4

361. [Kawa88] E. Kawaguchi and R. I. Taniguchi, Coded DF-expression for binary and multi-valued picture, *Proceedings of the Ninth International Conference on Pattern Recognition*, Rome, November 1988, 1159–1163. [regions]

362. [Kede82] G. Kedem, The quad-CIF tree: a data structure for hierarchical on-line algorithms, *Proceedings of the Nineteenth Design Automation Conference*, Las Vegas, June 1982, 352–357. [rectangles] D.3.5 D.3.5.1

363. [Kela84a] A. Kela, Programmers guide to the PADL-2 octree processor output system, Production Automation Project Input/Output Group Memo 15, University of Rochester, Rochester, NY, January 1984. [finite element]

364. [Kela86] A. Kela, R. Perucchio, and H. Voelcker, Toward automatic finite element analysis, *Computers in Mechanical Engineering 5*, 1(July 1986), 57–71. [finite element] D.1.3 D.5.6 A.P A.1.4 A.7.1.6

365. [Kela84b] A. Kela, H. Voelcker, and J. Goldak, Automatic generation of hierarchical, spatially addressable finite-element meshes from CSG representations of solids, *International Conference on Accuracy Estimates and Adaptive Refinements in Finite Element Computations*, Lisbon, Portugal, June 1984, 221–234. [finite element] D.1.3 A.1.4

366. [Kell71] M. D. Kelly, Edge detection in pictures by computer using planning, in *Machine Intelligence 6*, B. Meltzer and D. Michie, eds., American Elsevier, New York, 1971, 397–409. [regions] D.1.3 A.1.4

367. [Kent86] E. W. Kent, M. O. Shneier, and T. H. Hong, Building representations from fusions of multiple views, *Proceedings of the IEEE International Conference on Robotics and Automation*, San Francisco, April 1986, 1634–1639. [volumes]

368. [Kern78] B. W. Kernighan and D. M. Ritchie, *The C Programming Language*, Prentice-Hall, Englewood Cliffs, NJ, 1978. [general] D.P A.P L

369. [Kers79] M. L. Kersten and P. van Emde Boas, Local optimizations of QUAD trees, Technical Report IR-51, Free University of Amsterdam, Amsterdam, The Netherlands, June 1979. [points] D.2.3.1

370. [Kim83] Y. C. Kim and J. K. Aggarwal, Rectangular coding for binary images, *Proceedings of Computer Vision and Pattern Recognition 83*, Washington, DC, June 1983, 108–113. [regions] D.1.2 A.1.3 A.9.3.4

371. [Kim86] Y. C. Kim and J. K. Aggarwal, Rectangular parallelepiped coding: a volumetric representation of three-dimensional objects, *IEEE Journal of Robotics and Automation 2*, 3(September 1986), 127–134. [regions] D.1.2 A.1.3 A.9.3.4

372. [Kirk83] D. Kirkpatrick, Optimal search in planar subdivisions, *SIAM Journal on Computing 12*, 1(February 1983), 28–35. [regions] D.P D.4.3

373. [Kits89] M. Kitsuregwa, L. Harada, and M. Takagi, Join strategies on kd-tree indexed relations, *Proceedings of the Fifth IEEE International Conference on Data Engineering*, Los Angeles, February 1989, 85–93. [points]

374. [Klee77] V. Klee, Can the measure of $\cup[a_i,b_i]$ be computed in less than $O(n\log n)$ steps? *American Mathematical Monthly 84*, 4(April 1977), 284–285. [rectangles] D.3.3

375. [Klei86] A. Kleiner and K. E. Brassel, Hierarchical grid structures for static geographic data bases, *Proceedings of Auto-Carto London*, vol. 1, London, September 1986, 485–496. [regions]

376. [Klin71] A. Klinger, Patterns and search statistics, in *Optimizing Methods in Statistics*, J. S. Rustagi, ed., Academic Press, New York, 1971, 303–337. [regions] D.1.2 D.1.3 A.1.3 A.1.4

377. [Klin76] A. Klinger and C. R. Dyer, Experiments in picture representation using regular decomposition, *Computer Graphics and Image Processing 5*, 1(March 1976), 68–105. [regions] D.1.2 D.1.3 A.1.3 A.1.4 A.2.1.1

378. [Klin79] A. Klinger and M. L. Rhodes, Organization and access of image data by areas, *IEEE Transactions on Pattern Analysis and Machine Intelligence 1*, 1(January 1979), 50–60. [regions] A.2.1.1 A.3.2.2

379. [Knot71] G. D. Knott, Expandable open addressing hash table storage and retrieval, *Proceedings of SIGFIDET Workshop on Data Description, Access, and Control*, San Diego, November 1971, 187–206. [points] D.2.8.1 D.2.8.2.1

380. [Know80] K. Knowlton, Progressive transmission of grey-scale and binary pictures by simple, efficient, and lossless encoding schemes, *Proceedings of the IEEE 68*, 7(July 1980), 885–896. [regions] D.1.4.1 A.1.3 A.8 A.8.1 A.8.3

381. [Knut73a] D. E. Knuth, *The Art of Computer Programming*, vol. 1, *Fundamental Algorithms*, Second Edition, Addison-Wesley, Reading, MA, 1973. [general] D.P D.1.3 D.2.3.1 D.2.8.2.1 D.2.8.2.3 D.4.3.2 A.P A.1.4 A.2.1.4 A.3.2.1.2

382. [Knut73b] D. E. Knuth, *The Art of Computer Programming*, vol. 3, *Sorting and Searching*, Addison-Wesley, Reading, MA, 1973. [general] D.P D.1.2 D.2.1 D.2.2 D.2.3.1 D.2.3.3 D.2.4.1 D.2.4.3 D.2.5 D.2.6.2 D.2.8.2.1 D.2.8.2.2 A.P A.1.3

383. [Knut76] D. E. Knuth, Big Omicron and big omega and big theta, *SIGACT News 8*, 2(April-June 1976), 18–24. [general] D.P A.P

384. [Koba87] H. Kobayashi, T. Nakamura, and Y. Shigei, Parallel processing of an object space for image synthesis, *Visual Computer 3*, 1(February 1987), 13–22. [volumes] A.3.3

385. [Koba88] H. Kobayashi, S. Nishimura, H. Kubota, T. Nakamura, and Y. Shigei, Load balancing strategies for a parallel ray-tracing system based on constant subdivision, *Visual Computer 4*, 4(October 1988), 197–209. [volumes]

386. [Kois88] P. Koistinen, Interval methods for constructive solid geometry: display via block model conversion, Master's Thesis, Laboratory for Information Processing, Helsinki University of Technology, Helsinki, Finland, May 1988. [volumes] D.5.5.1.3

387. [Kois85] P. Koistinen, M. Tamminen, and H. Samet, Viewing solid models by bintree conversion, in *Proceedings of the EUROGRAPHICS'85 Conference*, C. E. Vandoni, ed., North-Holland, Amsterdam, 1985, 147–157. [volumes] A.7.1.4

388. **[Korn87] M. R. Korn and C. R. Dyer, 3–d multiview object representations for model-based object recognition, *Pattern Recognition 20*, 1(1987), 91–103 (also University of Wisconsin Computer Science TR 602). [surfaces]**

389. [Krie84] H. P. Kriegel, Performance comparison of index structures for multikey retrieval, *Proceedings of the SIGMOD Conference*, Boston, June 1984, 186–196. [points] D.2.8.2.3

390. [Krie86] H. P. Kriegel and B. Seeger, Multidimensional order preserving linear hashing with partial expansions, *Proceedings of the International Conference on Database Theory*, Rome, September 1986, 203–220 (Lecture Notes in Computer Science 243, Springer-Verlag, New York, 1986). [points]

391. [Krie87] H. P. Kriegel and B. Seeger, Multidimensional dynamic quantile hashing is very efficient for non-uniform record distributions, *Proceedings of the Third IEEE International Conference on Data Engineering*, Los Angeles, February 1987, 10–17. [points]

392. [Krie88] H. P. Kriegel and B. Seeger, PLOP-hashing: a grid file without directory, *Proceedings of the Fourth IEEE International Conference on Data Engineering*, Los Angeles, February 1988, 369–376. [points]

393. [Kris85] R. Krishnamurthy and K. Y. Whang, Multilevel grid files, IBM T. J. Watson Research Center Report, Yorktown Heights, NY, 1985. [points]

394. **[Kron85] K. Kronlof and M. Tamminen, A viewing pipeline for discrete solid modeling, *Visual Computer 1*, 1(July 1985), 24–36. [volumes]**

395. [Krop86] W. G. Kropatsch, Curve representations in multiple resolutions, *Proceedings of the Eighth International Conference on Pattern Recognition*, Paris, October 1986, 1283–1285. [lines] D.1.3 A.1.4

396. [Kuma86] P. S. Kumar and M. Manohar, On probability of forest of quadtrees reducing to quadtrees, *Information Processing Letters 22*, 3(March 1986), 109–111. [regions]

397. [Kuni86] T. L. Kunii, I. Fujishiro, and X. Mao, G-quadtree: a hierarchical representation of gray-scale digital images, *Visual Computer 2*, 4(August 1986), 219–226. [regions]

398. [Kuni85] T. L. Kunii, T. Satoh, and K. Yamaguchi, Generation of topological boundary representations from octree encoding, *IEEE Computer Graphics and Applications 5*, 3(March 1985), 29–38. [volumes] D.5.4

399. **[Kurl88] D. Kurlander and E. A. Bier, Graphical search and replace, *Computer Graphics 22*, 4(August 1988), 113–120 (also *Proceedings of the SIGGRAPH'88 Conference*, Atlanta, August 1988). [regions] D.3.4**

400. [Kush82] T. Kushner, A. Wu, and A. Rosenfeld, Image processing on ZMOB, *IEEE Transactions on Computers 31*, 10(October 1982), 943–951. [regions]

401. [Lane80] J. M. Lane, L. C. Carpenter, T. Whitted, J. F. Blinn, Scan line methods for displaying parametrically defined surfaces, *Communications of the ACM 23*, 1(January 1980), 23–34. [surfaces] A.7.1.6

402. [Lars80] P.Å. Larson, Linear hashing with partial expansions, *Proceedings of the Sixth International Conference on Very Large Data Bases*, Montreal, October 1980, 224–232. [points] D.2.8.2.1

403. [Lars88] P.Å. Larson, Dynamic hash tables, *Communications of the ACM 31*, 4(April 1988), 446–457. [points] D.2.8.2.1 D.2.8.2.2

404. [Laur85] R. Laurini, Graphical data bases built on Peano space-filling curves, in *Proceedings of the EUROGRAPHICS'85 Conference*, C. E. Vandoni, ed., North-Holland, Amsterdam, 1985, 327–338. [regions] D.1.3 A.1.4

405. [Laur87] R. Laurini, Manipulation of spatial objects by a Peano tuple algebra, Computer Science TR-1893, University of Maryland, College Park, MD, July 1987. [regions]

406. [Laut78] U. Lauther, 4-dimensional binary search trees as a means to speed up associative searches in design rule verification of integrated circuits, *Journal of Design Automation and Fault-Tolerant Computing 2*, 3(July 1978), 241–247. [rectangles] D.3.4

407. [Lauz85] J. P. Lauzon, D. M. Mark, L. Kikuchi, and J. A. Guevara, Two-dimensional run-encoding for quadtree representation, *Computer Vision, Graphics, and Image Processing 30*, 1(April 1985), 56–69. [regions] A.2.1.3 A.3.4.1 A.5.1.3

408. [Lava89] Lavakusha, A. K. Pujari, and P. G. Reddy, Linear octrees by volume intersection, *Computer Vision, Graphics, and Image Processing 45*, 3(March 1989), 371–379. [volumes]

409. [Lawl76] E. Lawler, *Combinatorial Optimization: Networks and Matroids*, Holt, Rinehart and Winston, New York, 1976. [general] D.2.9

410. [Lawl85] E. L. Lawler, J. K. Lenstra, A. H. G. Rinnooy-Kan, and D. B. Shmoys, *The Traveling Salesman Problem*, John Wiley & Sons, New York, 1985. [general] D.1.3 A.1.4

411. [Lea88] D. Lea, Digital and Hilbert k-d trees, *Information Processing Letters 27*, 1(February 1988), 35–41. [points]

412. [Lee83] D. T. Lee, Maximum clique problem of rectangle graphs, in *Advances in Computing Research*, vol. 1, *Computational Geometry*, F. P. Preparata, ed., JAI Press, Greenwich, CT, 1983, 91–107. [rectangles] D.2.9 D.3.3

413. [Lee77a] D. T. Lee and F. P. Preparata, Location of a point in a planar subdivision and its applications, *SIAM Journal on Computing 6*, 3(July 1977), 594–606. [regions] D.4.3 D.4.3.2

414. [Lee82a] D. T. Lee and F. P. Preparata, An improved algorithm for the rectangle enclosure problem, *Journal of Algorithms 3*, 3(September 1982), 218–224. [rectangles] D.3.2.4

415. [Lee80a] D. T. Lee and B. J. Shacter, Two algorithms for constructing a Delaunay triangulation, *International Journal of Computer and Information Sciences 9*, 3(June 1980), 219–242. [regions] D.2.4.3

416. [Lee77b] D. T. Lee and C. K. Wong, Worst-case analysis for region and partial region searches in multidimensional binary search trees and quad trees, *Acta Informatica 9*, 1(1977), 23–29. [points] D.2.3 D.2.3.2 D.2.3.3 D.2.4.3

417. [Lee80b] D. T. Lee and C. K. Wong, Quintary trees: a file structure for multidimensional database systems, *ACM Transactions on Database Systems 5*, 4(September 1980), 339–353. [points]

418. [Lee82b] Y. T. Lee and A. A. G. Requicha, Algorithms for computing the volume and other integral properties of solids. I. Known methods and open issues, *Communications of the ACM 25*, 9(September 1982), 635–641. [volumes] D.5.5

419. [Lee82c] Y. T. Lee and A. A. G. Requicha, Algorithms for computing the volume and other integral properties of solids. II. A family of algorithms based on representation conversion and cellular approximation, *Communications of the ACM 25*, 9(September 1982), 642–650. [volumes] D.5.5 D.5.5.1.1

420. [Lele87] D. A. Lelewer and D. S. Hirschberg, Data compression, *ACM Computing Surveys 19*, 3(September 1987), 261–296. [regions] A.8

421. [Lete83] P. Letelier, Transmission d'images à bas débit pour un système de communication téléphonique adapté aux sourds, Thèse de docteur-ingénieur, Université de Paris-Sud, Paris, September 1983. [regions] D.2.6.1

422. [Li86] H. Li, M. A. Lavin, and R. J. LeMaster, Fast Hough transform: a hierarchical approach, *Computer Vision, Graphics, and Image Processing 36*, 2/3(November / December 1986), 139–161. [regions]

423. [Li82] M. Li, W. I. Grosky, and R. Jain, Normalized quadtrees with respect to translations, *Computer Graphics and Image Processing 20*, 1(September 1982), 72–81. [regions] D.1.5 A.1.2 A.4.3.1 A.9.3.4

424. [Li87a] S. X. Li and M. H. Loew, The quadcode and its arithmetic, *Communications of the ACM 30*, 7(July 1987), 621–626. [regions]

425. [Li87b] S. X. Li and M. H. Loew, Adjacency detection using quadcodes, *Communications of the ACM 30*, 7(July 1987), 627–631. [regions]

426. [Libe86] F. D. Libera and F. Gosen, Using B-trees to solve geographic range queries, *Computer Journal 29*, 2(April 1986), 176–181. [regions]

427. [Ling82] A. Lingas, The power of non-rectilinear holes, *Proceedings of the Ninth International Colloquium on Automata, Languages, and Programming*, Aarhus, Denmark, July 1982, 369–383 (Lecture Notes in Computer Science 140, Springer-Verlag, New York, 1982). [regions] D.1.2 A.1.3

428. [Linn73] J. Linn, General methods for parallel searching, Technical Report 81, Digital Systems Laboratory, Stanford University, Stanford, CA, May 1973. [points] D.2.4.4

429. [Lipt77] R. J. Lipton and R. E. Tarjan, Application of a planar separator theorem, *Proceedings of the Eighteenth Annual IEEE Symposium on the Foundations of Computer Science*, Providence, RI, October 1977, 162–170. [regions] D.4.3

430. [Litt79] J. J. Little and T. K. Peucker, A recursive procedure for finding the intersection of two digital curves, *Computer Graphics and Image Processing 10*, 2(June 1980), 159–171. [lines] D.4.1

431. [Litw80] W. Litwin, Linear hashing: a new tool for file and table addressing, *Proceedings of the Sixth International Conference on Very Large Data Bases*, Montreal, October 1980, 212–223. [points] D.2.7 D.2.8.2.1

432. [Lome89a] D. Lomet and B. Salzberg, A robust multi-attribute search structure, *Proceedings of the Fifth IEEE International Conference on Data Engineering*, Los Angeles, February 1989, 296–304. [points] D.2.6.2

433. [Lome89b] D. Lomet and B. Salzberg, The hB-Tree: a robust multi-attribute indexing method, *ACM Transactions on Database Systems 14*, 1989 (also Northeastern University Technical Report NU-CCS-87-24). [points] D.2.6.2

434. [Loza81] T. Lozano-Perez, Automatic planning of manipulator transfer movements, *IEEE Transactions on Systems, Man, and Cybernetics 11*, 10(October 1981), 681–698. [regions] D.1.3 A.1.4

435. [Luek78] G. Lueker, A data structure for orthogonal range queries, *Proceedings of the Nineteenth Annual IEEE Symposium on the Foundations of Computer Science*, Ann Arbor, MI, October 1978, 28–34. [points] D.2.3

436. [Lum70] V. Y. Lum, Multi-attribute retrieval with combined indexes, *Communications of the ACM 13*, 11(November 1970), 660–665. [points]

437. [Lumi83a] R. Lumia, A new three-dimensional connected components algorithm, *Computer Vision, Graphics, and Image Processing 23*, 2(August 1983), 207–217. [volumes] A.5.1.1 A.5.1.2 A.5.1.3

438. [Lumi86] R. Lumia, Rapid hidden feature elimination using an octree, *Proceedings of the IEEE International Conference on Robotics and Automation*, San Francisco, April 1986, 460–464. [volumes]

439. [Lumi83b] R. Lumia, L. Shapiro, and O. Zuniga, A new connected components algorithm for virtual memory computers, *Computer Vision, Graphics, and Image Processing 22*, 2(May 1983), 287–300. [regions] A.5.1 A.5.1.1 A.5.1.2 A.5.1.3

440. [Mair88] H. G. Mairson and J. Stolfi, Reporting and counting intersections between two sets of line segments, in *Theoretical Foundations of Computer Graphics and CAD*, R. A. Earnshaw, ed., Springer-Verlag, Berlin, 1988, 307–325. [lines] D.4.3.3

441. [Mano88] M. Manohar, P. S. Rao, and S. S. Iyengar, Template quadtrees for representing region and line data present in binary images, NASA Goddard Flight Center, Greenbelt, MD, 1988. [regions] D.4.2.1

442. [Mänt87] M. Mäntylä, *An Introduction to Solid Modeling*, Computer Science Press, Rockville, MD, 1987. [general] D.P D.5.1 D.5.4 A.P

443. [Mänt82] M. Mäntylä and R. Sulonen, GWB: A solid modeler with Euler operators, *IEEE Computer Graphics and Applications 2*, 7(September 1982), 17–31. [volumes] D.5.4

444. [Mänt83] M. Mäntylä and M. Tamminen, Localized set operations for solid modeling, *Computer Graphics 17*, 3(July 1983), 279–288 (also *Proceedings of the SIGGRAPH'83 Conference*, Detroit, July 1983). [volumes]

445. [Mao87] X. Mao, T. L. Kunii, I. Fujishiro, and T. Noma, Hierarchical representations of 2d/3d gray-scale images and 2d/3d two-way conversion, *IEEE Computer Graphics and Applications 7*, 12(December 1987), 37–44. [regions]

446. [Marb84] D. Marble, H. Calkins, and D. Peuquet, eds., *Basic Readings in Geographic Information Systems*, SPAD Systems, Williamsville, NY, 1984, 2:57–78. [general] D.4.4

447. [Marg89] A. Margalit and G. D. Knott, An algorithm for computing the union, intersection or difference of two polygons, *Computers & Graphics 13*, 2(1989), 167–183 (also University of Maryland Computer Science TR-1995). [regions] D.5.2 A.4.6

448. [Mark86a] D. M. Mark, The use of quadtrees in geographic information systems and spatial data handling, *Proceedings of Auto-Carto London*, vol. 1, London, September 1986, 517–526. [regions]

449. [Mark85a] D. M. Mark and D. J. Abel, Linear quadtrees from vector representations of polygons, *IEEE Transactions on Pattern Analysis and Machine Intelligence 7*, 3(May 1985), 344–349. [regions] A.4.3.1

450. [Mark86b] D. M. Mark and J. A. Cebrian, Octtrees: a useful data-structure for the processing of topographic and sub-surface area, *Proceedings of the 1986 ACSM-ASPRS Annual Convention*, vol. 1, *Cartography and Education*, Washington, DC, March 1986, 104–113. [surfaces]

451. [Mark85b] D. M. Mark and J. P. Lauzon, The space efficiency of quadtrees: an empirical examination including the effects of 2–dimensional run-encoding, *Geo-Processing 2*, 1985, 367–383. [regions] A.2.1.3

452. [Mars88] S. C. Marsh, Fine grain parallel architectures and creation of high-quality images, in *Theoretical Foundations of Computer Graphics and CAD*, R. A. Earnshaw, ed., Springer-Verlag, Berlin, 1988, 728–753. [hardware]

453. [Mart79] G. N. N. Martin, Spiral storage: incrementally augmented hash addressed storage, Theory of Computation Report No. 27, Department of Computer Science, University of Warwick, Coventry, Great Britain, March 1979. [points] D.2.8.2.2

454. [Mart82] J. J. Martin, Organization of geographical data with quad trees and least square approximation, *Proceedings of the IEEE Conference on Pattern Recognition and Image Processing*, Las Vegas, June 1982, 458–463. [lines] D.4.2.1

455. [Mart86] M. Martin, D. M. Chiarulli, and S. S. Iyengar, Parallel processing of quadtrees on a horizontally reconfigurable architecture computing system, *Proceedings of the IEEE International Conference on Parallel Processing*, St. Charles, IL, August 1986, 895–902. [regions]

456. [Mart83] W. N. Martin and J. K. Aggarwal, Volumetric descriptions of objects from multiple views, *IEEE Transactions on Pattern Analysis and Machine Intelligence 5*, 2(March 1983), 150–158. [volumes] D.5.2 A.4.6

457. [Maso87] D. C. Mason, Dilation algorithm for a linear quadtree, *Image and Vision Computing 5*, 1(February 1987), 11–20. [regions] A.6.6

458. [Maso88] D. C. Mason and M. J. Callen, Comparison of two dilation algorithms for linear quadtrees, *Image and Vision Computing 6*, 3(August 1988), 169–175. [regions]

459. [Math87] C. Mathieu, C. Puech, and H. Yahia, Average efficiency of data structures for binary image processing, *Information Processing Letters 26*, 2(October 1987), 89–93. [regions]

460. [Mats84] T. Matsuyama, L. V. Hao, and M. Nagao, A file organization for geographic information systems based on spatial proximity, *Computer Vision, Graphics, and Image Processing 26*, 3(June 1984), 303–318. [points] D.2.8.1 D.3

461. [Mazu87] P. Mazumder, Planar decomposition for quadtree data structure, *Computer Vision, Graphics, and Image Processing 38*, 3(June 1987), 258–274. [regions]

462. [Mazu88] P. Mazumder, A new strategy for octtree representation of three-dimensional objects, *Proceedings of Computer Vision and Pattern Recognition 88*, Ann Arbor, MI, June 1988, 270–275. [regions]

463. [McCa60] J. McCarthy, Recursive functions of symbolic expressions, *Communications of the ACM 3*, 4(April 1960), 184–195. [general] L

464. [McCl65] E. J. McCluskey, *Introduction to the Theory of Switching Circuits*, McGraw-Hill, New York, 1965, 60–61. [general] D.1.2 A.1.3

465. [McCr80] E. M. McCreight, Efficient algorithms for enumerating intersecting intervals and rectangles, Xerox Palo Alto Research Center Report CSL-80–09, Palo Alto, CA, June 1980. [rectangles] D.3.2.2 D.3.4

466. [McCr85] E. M. McCreight, Priority search trees, *SIAM Journal on Computing 14*, 2(May 1985), 257–276. [rectangles] D.2.5 D.3.2.3

467. [McKe84] D. M. McKeown Jr. and J. L. Denlinger, Map-guided feature extraction from aerial imagery, *Proceedings of the Workshop on Computer Vision: Representation and Control*, Annapolis, MD, April 1984, 205–213. [regions]

468. [Meag80] D. Meagher, Octree encoding: a new technique for the representation, the manipulation, and display of arbitrary 3–d objects by computer, Electrical and Systems Engineering Technical Report IPL-TR-80–111, Rensselaer Polytechnic Institute, Troy, NY, October 1980. [volumes] D.1.5 D.5.5.1.2 A.1.2

469. [Meag82a] D. Meagher, Geometric modeling using octree encoding, *Computer Graphics and Image Processing 19*, 2(June 1982), 129–147. [volumes] D.1.3 A.1.4 A.5.1.3 A.6.5.2 A.6.5.3 A.7.1.4

470. [Meag82b] D. Meagher, Octree generation, analysis and manipulation, Electrical and Systems Engineering Report IPL-TR-027, Rensselaer Polytechnic Institute, Troy, NY, 1982. [volumes] D.5.1 D.5.5.1.1 D.5.5.1.3

471. [Meag82c] D. Meagher, Efficient synthetic image generation of arbitrary 3–d objects, *Proceedings of the IEEE Conference on Pattern Recognition and Image Processing*, Las Vegas, June 1982, 473–478. [volumes]

472. [Meag82d] D. Meagher, The octree encoding method for efficient solid modeling, Electrical and Systems Engineering Report IPL-TR-032, Rensselaer Polytechnic Institute, Troy, NY, August 1982. [volumes] A.2.1.2

473. [Meag82e] D. Meagher, Computer software for robotic vision, *Proceedings of SPIE— Robotics and Industrial Inspection 360*, San Diego, August 1982, 318–325. [volumes]

474. [Meag84] D. Meagher, The Solids Engine Ⓣ : a processor for interactive solid modeling, *Proceedings of the NICOGRAPH '84 Conference*, Tokyo, November 1984, A-2, 1–11. [volumes] D.5.3 D.5.5 A.7.1.4

475. [Mehl84] K. Mehlhorn, *Multi-dimensional Searching and Computational Geometry*, Springer-Verlag, Berlin, 1984. [general] D.P D.4.3.1

476. [Mei86] G. G. Mei and W. Liu, Parallel processing for quadtree problems, *Proceedings of the IEEE International Conference on Parallel Processing*, St. Charles, IL, August 1986, 452–454. [regions]

477. [Meno87a] S. Menon, P. Gao, and T. R. Smith, Multi-colored quadtrees for GIS: exploiting bit-parallelism for rapid Boolean overlay, *Proceedings of the International Symposium on Geographic Information Systems*, vol. 2, Arlington, VA, November 1987, 371–383. [regions]

478. [Meno87b] S. Menon and T. R. Smith, Multi-component object search using spatial constraint propagation, *Proceedings of the International Symposium on Geographic Information Systems*, vol. 2, Arlington, VA, November 1987, 281–293. [regions]

479. [Merr78] T. H. Merrett, Multidimensional paging for efficient database querying, *Proceedings of the International Conference on Management of Data*, Milan, June 1978, 277–289. [points] D.2.8.2.3

480. [Merr82] T. H. Merrett and E. J. Otoo, Dynamic multipaging: a storage structure for large shared data banks, in *Improving Database Usability and Responsiveness*, P. Scheuermann, ed., Academic Press, New York, 1982, 237–254. [points] D.2.8.2.3

481. [Merr73] R. D. Merrill, Representations of contours and regions for efficient computer search, *Communications of the ACM 16*, 2(February 1973), 69–82. [lines] D.4.4

482. [Mich80] J. Michener, personal communication, 1980. [regions] A.4.3.1

483. [Milf84] D. J. Milford and P. J. Willis, Quad encoded display, *IEE Proceedings 131*, Part E, 3(May 1984), 70–75. [hardware]

484. [Milf81] D. J. Milford, P. J. Willis, and J. R. Woodwark, Exploiting area coherence in raster scan displays, *Proceedings of Electronic Displays 81*, London, 1981, 34–46. [hardware]

485. [Mill85] R. Miller and Q. F. Stout, Pyramid computer algorithms for determining geometric properties of images, *Proceedings of the Symposium on Computational Geometry*, Baltimore, June 1985, 263–269. [regions]

486. [Mins69] M. Minsky and S. Papert, *Perceptrons: An Introduction to Computational Geometry*, MIT Press, Cambridge, MA, 1969. [general] A.5.3

487. [Moba88] B. G. Mobasseri, Soft-linked quadtree: a cascaded ring structure using flexible linkage concept, *Proceedings of Computer Vision and Pattern Recognition 88*, Ann Arbor, MI, June 1988, 622–627. [regions]

488. [Moor79] R. E. Moore, *Methods and Applications of Interval Analysis*, Philadelphia, SIAM, 1979. [general] D.5.5.1.3

489. [Mort85] M. E. Mortenson, *Geometric Modeling*, John Wiley and Sons, New York, 1985. [general] A.7.1.6

490. [Mort66] G. M. Morton, A computer oriented geodetic data base and a new technique in file sequencing, IBM Ltd., Ottawa, Canada, 1966. [regions] D.1.2 D.1.3 D.2.7 A.1.4 A.2.1.1 A.4.1

491. [Mudu84] S. P. Mudur and P. A. Koparkar, Interval methods for processing geometric objects, *IEEE Computer Graphics and Applications 4*, 2(February 1984), 7–17. [surfaces] D.5.5.1.3 D.5.6

492. [Mull85] J. K. Mullin, Spiral storage: efficient dynamic hashing with constant performance, *Computer Journal 28*, 3(August 1985), 330–334. [points] D.2.8.2.2

493. [Mura88] M. Muralikrishna and D. J. DeWitt, Equi-depth histograms for estimating selectivity factors for multi-dimensional queries, *Proceedings of the SIGMOD Conference*, Chicago, June 1988, 28–36. [points]

494. [Nagy79] G. Nagy and S. Wagle, Geographic data processing, *ACM Computing Surveys 11*, 2(June 1979), 139–181. [lines] D.P D.4 D.4.4 A.P

495. [Nair87] K. N. R. Nair and R. Sankar, An approach to geometric modeling of solids bounded by sculptured surfaces, *Computers & Graphics 11*, 2(1987), 113–120. [volumes]

496. [Naka88] Y. Nakamura, S. Abe, Y. Ohsawa, and M. Sakauchi, MD-tree: a balanced hierarchical data structure for multi-dimensional data with highly efficient dynamic characteristics, *Proceedings of the Ninth International Conference on Pattern Recognition*, Rome, November 1988, 375–378. [regions]

497. [Nand86a] S. K. Nandy and L. M. Patnaik, Linear time geometrical design rule checker based on quadtree representation of VLSI mask layouts, *Computer-Aided Design 18*, 7(September 1986), 380–388. [regions]

498. [Nand87] S. K. Nandy and L. M. Patnaik, Algorithm for incremental compaction of geometrical layouts, *Computer-Aided Design 19*, 5(June 1987), 257–265. [regions]

499. [Nand86b] S. K. Nandy and I. V. Ramakrishnan, Dual quadtree representation for VLSI designs, *Proceedings of the Twenty-third Design Automation Conference*, Las Vegas, June 1986, 663–666. [regions]

500. [Naur60] P. Naur, ed., Revised report on the algorithmic language ALGOL 60, *Communications of the ACM 3*, 5(May 1960), 299–314. [general] D.P A.P L

501. [Nava86a] I. Navazo, Contribució a les tècniques de modelat geomètric d'objectes poliédrics usant la codificació amb arbres octals, Ph.D. dissertation, Escola Tècnica Superior d'Enginyers Industrials, Department de Metodes Informatics, Universitat Politèchnica de Barcelona, Barcelona, Spain, January 1986. [volumes] D.5.3 A.1.3

502. [Nava89] I. Navazo, Extended octree representation of general solids with plane faces: model structure and algorithms, *Computers & Graphics 13*, 1 (1989), 5–16. [volumes] D.5.3

503. [Nava86b] I. Navazo, D. Ayala, and P. Brunet, A geometric modeller based on the exact octree representation of polyhedra, *Computer Graphics Forum 5*, 2 (June 1986), 91–104. [volumes] D.5.3 A.7.1.6 A.7.2.2 A.7.4

504. [Nava87] I. Navazo, J. Fontdecaba, and P. Brunet, Extended octrees, between CSG trees and boundary representations, in *Proceedings of the EUROGRAPHICS'87 Conference*, G. Marechal, ed., North-Holland, Amsterdam, 1987, 239–247. [volumes] D.5.3

505. [Nels86a] R. C. Nelson and H. Samet, A consistent hierarchical representation for vector data, *Computer Graphics 20*, 4(August 1986), 197–206 (also *Proceedings of the SIGGRAPH'86 Conference*, Dallas, August 1986). [lines] D.4.2.3 D.4.2.3.4 D.4.2.3.5 D.5.5.2 A.1.3

506. [Nels86b] R. C. Nelson and H. Samet, A population analysis of quadtrees with variable node size Computer Science TR-1740, University of Maryland, College Park, MD, December 1986. [points] D.2.8.1 D.4.2.3.4 D.5.5.2

507. [Nels87] R. C. Nelson and H. Samet, A population analysis for hierarchical data structures, *Proceedings of the SIGMOD Conference*, San Francisco, May 1987, 270–277. [points] D.2.8.1

508. [Nemo86] K. Nemoto and T. Omachi, An adaptive subdivision by sliding boundary surfaces for fast ray tracing, *Proceedings of Graphics Interface '86*, Vancouver, May 1986, 43–48. [surfaces]

509. [Newe75] M. E. Newell, The utilization of procedure models in digital image synthesis, Computer Science Department UTEC-CSc-76–218, University of Utah, Salt Lake City, Summer 1975. [volumes] A.7.2.2

510. [Niev84] J. Nievergelt, H. Hinterberger, and K. C. Sevcik, The grid file: an adaptable, symmetric multikey file structure, *ACM Transactions on Database Systems 9*, 1(March 1984), 38–71. [points] D.2.1 D.2.8.2.3

511. [Niev82] J. Nievergelt and F. P. Preparata, Plane-sweep algorithms for intersecting geometric figures, *Communications of the ACM 25*, 10(October 1982), 739–746. [general] D.4.3.3

512. [Nils69] N. J. Nilsson, A mobile automaton: an application of artificial intelligence techniques, *Proceedings of the First International Joint Conference on Artificial Intelligence*, Washington, DC, May 1969, 509–520. [regions] D.1.3 A.1.4

513. [Nish85] T. Nishita and E. Nakamae, Continuous tone representation of three-dimensional objects taking account of shadows and interreflection, *Computer Graphics 19*, 3(July 1985), 23–30 (also *Proceedings of the SIGGRAPH'85 Conference*, San Francisco, July 1985). [general] A.7.2.1

514. [Nobo88] H. Noborio, S. Fukuda, and S. Arimoto, Construction of the octree approximating three-dimensional objects by using multiple views, *IEEE Transactions on Pattern Analysis and Machine Intelligence 10*, 6(November 1988), 769–782. [volumes] D.5.2 A.4.6

515. [Noro88] V. T. Noronha, A survey of hierarchical partitioning methods for vector images, *Proceedings of the Third International Symposium on Spatial Data Handling*, Sydney, Australia, August 1988, 185–200. [rectangles]

516. [Ohsa83a] Y. Ohsawa and M. Sakauchi, The BD-tree—a new n-dimensional data structure with highly efficient dynamic characteristics, *Information Processing 83*, R. E. A. Mason, ed., North-Holland, Amsterdam, 1983, 539–544. [points] D.2.6.2

517. [Ohsa83b] Y. Ohsawa and M. Sakauchi, Multidimensional data management structure with efficient dynamic characteristics, *Systems, Computers, Controls 14*, 5(1983), 77–87 (translated from *Denshi Tsushin Gakkai Ronbunshi 66–D*, 10(October 1983), 1193–1200. [points] D.2.6.2

518. [Ohya84] T. Ohya, M. Iri, and K. Murota, Improvements of the incremental method for the Voronoi diagram with computational comparison of various algorithms, *Journal of the Operations Research Society of Japan 27*, 4(December 1984), 306–337. [regions]

519. [Okaw88] F. Okawara, K. Shimizu, and Y. Nishitani, Data compression of the region quadtree and algorithms for set operations, Department of Computer Science Report CS-88–6, Gunma University, Gunma, Japan, July 1988 (translated from *Proceedings of the 36th All-Japan Conference on Information Processing*, Information Processing Society of Japan, Tokyo, Japan, March 1988, 73–74). [regions] A.2.1.2

520. [Okin73] N. Okino, Y. Kakazu, and H. Kubo, TIPS-1: Technical information processing system for computer aided design, drawing and manufacturing, in *Computer Languages for Numerical Control*, J. Hatvany, ed., North Holland, Amsterdam, 1973, 141–150. [volumes] D.5.5

521.   [Oliv84a] M. A. Oliver, Two display algorithms for octrees, in *Proceedings of the EUROGRAPHICS'84 Conference*, K. Bo and H. A. Tucker, eds., North-Holland, Amsterdam, 1984, 251–264. [volumes]

522.   [Oliv86] M. A. Oliver, Display algorithms for quadtrees and octtrees and their hardware realisation *Data Structures for Raster Graphics*, F. J. Peters, L. R. A. Kessener, and M. L. P. van Lierop, eds., Springer Verlag, Berlin, 1986, 9–37. [regions]

523.   [Oliv84b] M. A. Oliver, T. R. King, and N. E. Wiseman, Quadtree scan conversion, in *Proceedings of the EUROGRAPHICS'84 Conference*, K. Bo and H. A. Tucker, eds., North-Holland, Amsterdam, 1984, 265–276. [regions] A.4.2.2

524.   [Oliv83a] M. A. Oliver and N. E. Wiseman, Operations on quadtree-encoded images, *Computer Journal 26*, 1(February 1983), 83–91. [regions] A.2.1.1 A.2.2

525.   [Oliv83b] M. A. Oliver and N. E. Wiseman, Operations on quadtree leaves and related image areas, *Computer Journal 26*, 4(November 1983), 375–380. [regions] A.6.4 A.9.3.4

526.   [Olse85] D. R. Olsen, Jr., and C. N. Cooper, Spatial trees: a fast access method for unstructured graphical data, *Proceedings of Graphics Interface '85*, Montreal, May 1985, 69–74. [regions]

527.   [Omol80] J. O. Omolayole and A. Klinger, A hierarchical data structure scheme for storing pictures, in *Pictorial Information Systems*, S. K. Chang and K. S. Fu, eds., Springer-Verlag, Berlin, 1980, 1–38 (Lecture Notes in Computer Science 80). [regions] D.4.2.1

528.   [Ooi87] B. C. Ooi, K. J. McDonell, and R. Sacks-Davis, Spatial k-d tree: an indexing mechanism for spatial database, *Proceedings of the Eleventh International Computer Software and Applications Conference (COMPSAC)*, Tokyo, October 1987, 433–438. [rectangles] D.2.8.1 D.3.4

529.   [Ooi89] B. C. Ooi, R. Sacks-Davis, and K. J. McDonell, Extending a dbms for geographic applications, *Proceedings of the Fifth IEEE International Conference on Data Engineering*, Los Angeles, February 1989, 590–597. [rectangles]

530.   [Oren82] J. A. Orenstein, Multidimensional tries used for associative searching, *Information Processing Letters 14*, 4(June 1982), 150–157. [points] D.2.6.2 D.2.7 D.2.8.1 D.2.8.2.4 A.1.3

531.   [Oren83] J. A. Orenstein, A dynamic hash file for random and sequential accessing, *Proceedings of the Sixth International Conference on Very Large Data Bases*, Florence, October 1983, 132–141. [points] D.2.7 D.2.8.2.1

532.   [Oren86] J. A. Orenstein, Spatial query processing in an object-oriented database system, *Proceedings of the SIGMOD Conference*, Washington, DC, May 1986, 326–336. [points]

533.   [Oren84] J. A. Orenstein and T. H. Merrett, A class of data structures for associative searching, *Proceedings of the Third ACM SIGACT-SIGMOD Symposium on Principles of Database Systems*, Waterloo, April 1984, 181–190. [points] D.1.3 D.2.7 D.2.8.2.1 A.1.4

534.   [ORou81] J. O'Rourke, Dynamically quantized spaces for focusing the Hough Transform, *Proceedings of the Sixth International Joint Conference on Artificial Intelligence*, Vancouver, August 1981, 737–739. [points] D.2.8.1

535.   [ORou88] J. O'Rourke, Computational geometry, in *Annual Reviews in Computer Science 3*, Annual Reviews, Palo Alto, CA, 1988, 389–411. [general] D.P

536.   [ORou84] J. O'Rourke and K. R. Sloan Jr., Dynamic quantization: two adaptive data structures for multidimensional squares, *IEEE Transactions on Pattern Analysis and Machine Intelligence 6*, 3(May 1984), 266–280. [points] D.2.8.1

537. [Oska88] D. N. Oskard, T. H. Hong, and C. A. Shaffer, Spatial mapping system for autonomous underwater vehicles, *SPIE Symposium on Sensor Fusion: Spatial Reasoning and Scene Interpretation 1003*, Cambridge, MA, November 1988, 439–450. [regions]

538. [Osse84] W. Osse and N. Ahuja, Efficient octree representation of moving objects, *Proceedings of the Seventh International Conference on Pattern Recognition*, Montreal, August 1984, 821–823. [volumes] A.6.5.3

539. [Ottm80] T. Ottmann and D. Wood, 1–2 brother trees or AVL trees revisited, *Computer Journal 23*, 3(August 1980), 248–255. [general] D.2.7

540. [Ouks85] M. Ouksel, The interpolation-based grid file, *Proceedings of the Fourth ACM SIGACT-SIGMOD Symposium on Principles of Database Systems*, Portland, OR, March 1985, 20–27. [points]

541. [Ouks83] M. Ouksel and P. Scheuermann, Storage mappings for multidimensional linear dynamic hashing, *Proceedings of the Second ACM SIGACT-SIGMOD Symposium on Principles of Database Systems*, Atlanta, March 1983, 90–105. [points] D.2.7 D.2.8.2.1

542. [Oust84] J. K. Ousterhout, Corner-stitching: a data structuring technique for VLSI layout tools, *IEEE Transactions on Computer-Aided Design 3*, 1(January 1984), 87–100. [rectangles] D.3.1 D.3.4

543. [Over83] M. H. Overmars, *The Design of Dynamic Data Structures*, Lecture Notes in Computer Science 156, Springer-Verlag, New York, 1983. [general] D.P D.2.1

544. [Over85] M. H. Overmars, Range searching in a set of line segments, *Proceedings of the Symposium on Computational Geometry*, Baltimore, June 1985, 177–185. [rectangles] D.3.2.4

545. [Over88a] M. H. Overmars, Geometric data structures for computer graphics: an overview, in *Theoretical Foundations of Computer Graphics and CAD*, R. A. Earnshaw, ed., Springer-Verlag, Berlin, 1988, 21–49. [rectangles] D.P D.2.1 D.2.5 D.2.6.2 D.3.2.4

546. [Over82] M. H. Overmars and J. van Leeuwen, Dynamic multi-dimensional data structures based on quad- and k-d trees, *Acta Informatica 17*, 3(1982), 267–285. [points] D.2.3.1 D.2.3.2 D.2.4.1

547. [Over88b] M. H. Overmars and C. K. Yap, New upper bounds in Klee's measure problem, *Proceedings of the Twenty-ninth Annual IEEE Symposium on the Foundations of Computer Science*, White Plains, NY, October 1988, 550–556. [rectangles] D.3.3

548. [Ozka85] E. A. Ozkarahan and M. Ouksel, Dynamic and order preserving data partitioning for database machines, *Proceedings of the Eleventh International Conference on Very Large Data Bases*, Stockholm, August 1985, 358–368. [points]

549. [Pali86] J. Palimaka, O. Halustchak, and W. Walker, Integration of a spatial and relational database within a geographic information system, *Proceedings of the 1986 ACSM-ASPRS Annual Convention*, vol. 3, *Geographic Information Systems*, Washington, DC, March 1986, 131–140. [regions]

550. [Park71] C. M. Park and A. Rosenfeld, Connectivity and genus in three dimensions, Computer Science TR-156, University of Maryland, College Park, MD, May 1971. [volumes] A.5.1 A.5.1.1

551. [Patr68] E. A. Patrick, D. R. Anderson, and F. K. Bechtel, Mapping multidimensional space to one dimension for computer output display, *IEEE Transactions on Computers 17*, 10(October 1968), 949–953. [points] D.1.3 A.1.4

552. [Pean90] G. Peano, Sur une courbe qui remplit toute une aire plaine, *Mathematische Annalen 36*, 1890, 157–160. [regions] D.1.3 D.2.7 A.1.4

553. [Pete85] F. Peters, An algorithm for transformations of pictures represented by quadtrees, *Computer Vision, Graphics, and Image Processing 32*, 3(December 1985), 397–403. [regions] A.6.5.1

554. [Peuc76] T. Peucker, A theory of the cartographic line, *International Yearbook of Cartography 16*, 1976, 134–143. [lines] D.4.1

555. [Peuc75] T. Peucker and N. Chrisman, Cartographic data structures, *American Cartographer 2*, 1(April 1975), 55–69. [general] D.4.4 D.5.6

556. [Peuq79] D. J. Peuquet, Raster processing: an alternative approach to automated cartographic data handling, *American Cartographer 6*, 2(April 1979), 129–139. [regions] D.4.4

557. [Peuq83] D. J. Peuquet, A hybrid data structure for the storage and manipulation of very large spatial data sets, *Computer Vision, Graphics, and Image Processing 24*, 1(October 1983), 14–27. [regions] D.4.4

558. [Peuq84] D. J. Peuquet, A conceptual framework and comparison of spatial data models, *Cartographica 21*, 4(1984), 66–113. [general] D.P D.1.4.1 A.P

559. [Pfal67] J. L. Pfaltz and A. Rosenfeld, Computer representation of planar regions by their skeletons, *Communications of the ACM 10*, 2(February 1967), 119–122. [regions]

560. [Phon75] B. T. Phong, Illumination for computer generated images, *Communications of the ACM 18*, 6(June 1975), 311–317. [general] A.7.1.4 A.7.2.1

561. [Piet82] M. Pietikainen, A. Rosenfeld, and I. Walter, Split-and-link algorithms for image segmentation, *Pattern Recognition 15*, 4(1982), 287–298. [regions] D.1.3 A.1.4

562. [Ponc85] J. Ponce, Prism trees: an efficient representation for manipulating and displaying polyhedra with many faces, Artificial Intelligence Memo 838, Massachusetts Institute of Technology, Cambridge, MA, April 1985. [surfaces] D.4.1

563. [Ponc87a] J. Ponce and D. Chelberg, Localized intersections computation for solid modelling with straight homogeneous generalized cylinders, *Proceedings of the IEEE International Conference on Robotics and Automation*, Raleigh, NC, March 1987, 1481–1486. [volumes]

564. [Ponc87b] J. Ponce and O. Faugeras, An object centered hierarchical representation for 3d objects: the prism tree, *Computer Vision, Graphics, and Image Processing 38*, 1(April 1987), 1–28. [surfaces] D.4.1 D.5.6 D.5.7

565. [Port84] T. Porter and T. Duff, Compositing digital images, *Computer Graphics 18*, 3(July 1984), 253–259 (also *Proceedings of the SIGGRAPH'84 Conference*, Minneapolis, July 1984). [general] A.7.1.1

566. [Posd82] J. L. Posdamer, Spatial sorting for sampled surface geometries, *Proceedings of SPIE-Biostereometrics'82 361*, San Diego, August 1982. [surfaces] D.5.2 A.4.6 A.7.1.6

567. [Potm87] M. Potmesil, Generating octree models of 3d objects from their silhouettes in a sequence of images, *Computer Vision, Graphics, and Image Processing 40*, 1(October 1987), 1–29. [volumes] D.5.2 A.4.6

568. [Prat78] W. K. Pratt, *Digital Image Processing*, Wiley-Interscience, New York, 1978. [general] D.1.2 A.1.3

569. [Prep83] F. P. Preparata, ed., *Advances in Computing Research*, vol. 1, *Computational Geometry*, JAI Press, Greenwich, CT, 1983. [general] D.P

570. [Prep77] F. P. Preparata and S. J. Hong, Convex hulls of finite sets of points in two and three dimensions, *Communications of the ACM 20*, 2(February 1977), 87–93. [regions] A.7.3

571. [Prep85] F. P. Preparata and M. I. Shamos, *Computational Geometry: An Introduction*, Springer-Verlag, New York, 1985. [general] D.P D.3 D.3.2 D.3.4 D.4.3 D.5.6

572. [Prio88] T. Priol and K. Bouatouch, Experimenting with a parallel ray-tracing algorithm on a hypercube machine, INRIA Report No. 843, IRISA, Campus de Beaulieu, Rennes, France. [volumes]

573. [Puec85] C. Puech and H. Yahia, Quadtrees, octrees, hyperoctrees: a unified analytical approach to tree data structures used in graphics, geometric modeling, and image processing, *Proceedings of the Symposium on Computational Geometry*, Baltimore, June 1985, 272–280. [regions] A.3.2.1.2

574. [Pull87] R. Pulleyblank and J. Kapenga, The feasibility of a VLSI chip for ray tracing bicubic patches, *IEEE Computer Graphics and Applications 7*, 3(March 1987), 33–44. [hardware] A.7.2.5

575. [Quar84] P. Quarendon, A general approach to surface modelling applied to molecular graphics, *Journal of Molecular Graphics 2*, 3(September 1984), 91–95. [surfaces]

576. [Quin82] K. M. Quinlan and J. R. Woodwark, A spatially-segmented solids database — justification and design, *Proceedings of CAD'82 Conference*, Butterworth, Guildford, Great Britain, 1982, 126–132. [volumes] D.5.3 A.1.3

577. [Ragh77] V. V. Raghavan and C. T. Yu, A note on a multidimensional searching problem, *Information Processing Letters 6*, 4(August 1977), 133–135. [points]

578. [Rama82] K. Ramamohanarao and J. W. Lloyd, Dynamic hashing schemes, *Computer Journal 25*, 4(November 1982), 478–485. [points] D.2.8.2.1

579. [Rama84] K. Ramamohanarao and R. Sacks-Davis, Recursive linear hashing, *ACM Transactions on Database Systems 9*, 3(September 1984), 369–391. [points] D.2.8.2.1

580. [Rama85] K. Ramamohanarao and R. Sacks-Davis, Partial match retrieval using recursive linear hashing, *BIT 25*, 3(1985), 477–484. [points] D.2.8.2.1

581. [Rama83] V. Raman and S. S. Iyengar, Properties and applications of forests of quadtrees for pictorial data representation, *BIT 23*, 4(1983), 472–486. [regions] A.2.1.4

582. [Rana81a] S. Ranade, Use of quadtrees for edge enhancement, *IEEE Transactions on Systems, Man, and Cybernetics 11*, 5(May 1981), 370–373. [regions]

583. [Rana80] S. Ranade, A. Rosenfeld, and J. M. S. Prewitt, Use of quadtrees for image segmentation, Computer Science TR-878, University of Maryland, College Park, MD, February 1980. [regions]

584. [Rana82] S. Ranade, A. Rosenfeld, and H. Samet, Shape approximation using quadtrees, *Pattern Recognition 15*, 1(1982), 31–40. [regions] A.8.1 A.8.2.1

585. [Rana81b] S. Ranade and M. Shneier, Using quadtrees to smooth images, *IEEE Transactions on Systems, Man, and Cybernetics 11*, 5(May 1981), 373–376. [regions]

586. [Rats84] H. Ratschek and J. Rokne, *Computer Methods for the Range of Functions*, Ellis Horwood, Chichester, 1984. [general] D.5.5.1.3

587. [Ravi87] S. Ravindran and M. Manohar, An algorithm for converting a forest of quadtrees to a binary array, *Image and Vision Computing 5*, 4(November 1987), 297–300. [regions]

588. [Redd78] D. R. Reddy and S. Rubin, Representation of three-dimensional objects, CMU-CS-78-113, Computer Science Department, Carnegie-Mellon University, Pittsburgh, April 1978. [volumes] D.1.3 A.1.4

589. [Regn85] M. Regnier, Analysis of grid file algorithms, *BIT 25*, 2(1985), 335–357. [points] D.2.8.1 D.2.8.2.3 D.3.4

590. [Rein77] E. M. Reingold, J. Nievergelt, and N. Deo, *Combinatorial Algorithms: Theory and Practice*, Prentice-Hall, Englewood Cliffs, NJ, 1977. [general] D.2.7

591. [Rein81] E. M. Reingold and R. E. Tarjan, On the greedy heuristic for complete matching, *SIAM Journal on Computing 10*, 4(November 1981), 676–681. [points] D.2.9

592. [Reis76] J. F. Reiser (ed.), SAIL, Stanford Artificial Intelligence Laboratory Memo AIM-289, Stanford University, Stanford, CA, August 1976. [general] D.P A.P L

593. [Requ80] A. A. G. Requicha, Representations of rigid solids: theory, methods, and systems, *ACM Computing Surveys 12*, 4(December 1980), 437–464. [volumes] D.P D.3.4 D.5.1 D.5.5 D.5.5.1 A.P A.7.1.4

594. [Requ82] A. A. G. Requicha and H. B. Voelcker, Solid modeling: a historical summary and contemporary assessment, *IEEE Computer Graphics and Applications 2*, 2(March 1982), 9–24. [volumes] D.5.5

595. [Requ83] A. A. G. Requicha and H. B. Voelcker, Solid modeling: current status and research directions, *IEEE Computer Graphics and Applications 3*, 7(October 1983), 25–37. [volumes] D.5.5

596. [Rhei80] W. C. Rheinboldt and C. K. Mesztenyi, On a data structure for adaptive finite element mesh refinements, *ACM Transactions on Mathematical Software 6*, 2(June 1980), 166–187. [finite element] D.1.3 A.1.4

597. [Rise77] E. M. Riseman and M. A. Arbib, Computational techniques in the visual segmentation of static scenes, *Computer Graphics and Image Processing 6*, 3(June 1977), 221–276. [regions] D.1.3 A.1.4

598. [Robi81] J. T. Robinson, The k-d-B-tree: a search structure for large multidimensional dynamic indexes, *Proceedings of the SIGMOD Conference*, Ann Arbor, MI, April 1981, 10–18. [points] D.2.7 D.2.8.1 D.3.5.3

599. [Roge85] D. F. Rogers, *Procedural Elements for Computer Graphics*, McGraw-Hill, New York, 1985. [general] D.4.2.3.1 D.5.2 D.5.6 A.1.3 A.4.5 A.4.6 A.5.1.1 A.6 A.6.4 A.7.1.2 A.7.1.4 A.7.2.3 A.7.2.4

600. [Rons88] C. Ronse, Codage en liste d'arbres quaternaires, *Technique et Science Informatiques 7*, 2(1988), 235–245. [regions]

601. [Rose85] J. B. Rosenberg, Geographical data structures compared: a study of data structures supporting region queries, *IEEE Transactions on Computer-Aided Design 4*, 1(January 1985), 53–67. [rectangles] D.3.4

602. [Rose74] A. Rosenfeld, Digital straight line segments, *IEEE Transactions on Computers 23*, 12(December 1974), 1264–1269. [lines]

603. [Rose83a] A. Rosenfeld, ed., *Multiresolution Image Processing and Analysis*, Springer-Verlag, Berlin, 1983. [general] D.P A.P A.4.2.3

604. [Rose88] A. Rosenfeld, Image analysis and computer vision: 1987, *Computer Vision, Graphics, and Image Processing 42*, 2(May 1988), 234–293. [general] D.P A.P

605. [Rose82a] A. Rosenfeld and A. C. Kak, *Digital Picture Processing*, Second Edition, Academic Press, New York, 1982. [general] D.P D.3.2.1 A.P A.5.2 A.7.4 A.8.1 A.9.1 A.9.3.4

606. [Rose66] A. Rosenfeld and J. L. Pfaltz, Sequential operations in digital image processing, *Journal of the ACM 13*, 4(October 1966), 471–494. [regions] D.1.2 A.1.3 A.5.1 A.5.1.1 A.5.1.2 A.9

607. [Rose82b] A. Rosenfeld, H. Samet, C. Shaffer, and R. E. Webber, Application of hierarchical data structures to geographical information systems, Computer Science TR-1197, University of Maryland, College Park, MD, June 1982. [general] D.1.5 A.1.2 A.3.2.3 A.6.4 A.6.5.2

608. [Rose83b] A. Rosenfeld, H. Samet, C. Shaffer, and R. E. Webber, Application of hierarchical data structures to geographical information systems: phase II, Computer Science TR-1327, University of Maryland, College Park, MD, September 1983. [general] D.2.6.2 A.2.1 A.2.1.1

609. [Ross86] J. R. Rossignac and A. A. G. Requicha, Depth-buffering display techniques for constructive solid geometry, *IEEE Computer Graphics and Applications 6*, 9(September 1986), 29–39. [volumes] D.5.5

610. [Roth82] S. D. Roth, Ray casting for modeling solids, *Computer Graphics and Image Processing 18*, 2(February 1982), 109–144. [volumes] D.5.2 D.5.5 A.4.6 A.7.2.2 A.7.2.5

611. [Rous85] N. Roussopoulos and D. Leifker, Direct spatial search on pictorial databases using packed R-trees, *Proceedings of the SIGMOD Conference*, Austin, TX, May 1985, 17–31. [points] D.2.8.1 D.3.5.3

612. [Rubi80] S. M. Rubin and T. Whitted, A 3-dimensional representation for fast rendering of complex scenes, *Computer Graphics 14*, 3(July 1980), 110–116 (also *Proceedings of the SIGGRAPH'80 Conference*, Seattle, July 1980). [volumes] A.7.2.2

613. [Ruff84] R. Ruff and N. Ahuja, Path planning in a three-dimensional environment, *Proceedings of the Seventh International Conference on Pattern Recognition*, Montreal, August 1984, 188–191. [volumes]

614. [Ruto68] D. Rutovitz, Data structures for operations on digital images, in *Pictorial Pattern Recognition*, G. C. Cheng et al., eds., Thompson Book Co., Washington, DC, 1968, 105–133. [regions] D.1.2 A.1.3 A.2.1.3 A.4.2 A.9

615. [Saal87] A. Saalfeld, Triangulated data structures for map merging and other applications in geographic information systems, *Proceedings of the International Symposium on Geographic Information Systems*, vol. 3, Arlington, VA, November 1987, 3–13. [regions] D.4.3.1 D.5.2 A.4.6

616. [Saka84] M. Sakauchi and Y. Ohsawa, General framework for n-dimensional pattern data management, in *Proceedings of the International Symposium on Image Processing and its Applications*, M. Onoe, ed., Institute of Industrial Science, University of Tokyo, 1984, 306–316. [points]

617. [Salz86] B. Salzberg, Grid file concurrency, *Information Systems 11*, 3(1986), 235–244. [points]

618. [Salz88] B. Salzberg, *File Structures: An Analytic Approach*, Prentice-Hall, Englewood Cliffs, NJ, 1988. [general] D.2.6.2

619. [Same77] H. Samet, Deletion in k-dimensional quadtrees, unpublished manuscript, 1977. [points] D.2.3.2

620. [Same80a] H. Samet, Region representation: quadtrees from boundary codes, *Communications of the ACM 23*, 3(March 1980), 163–170. [regions] A.4.3.1

621. [Same80b] H. Samet, Region representation: quadtrees from binary arrays, *Computer Graphics and Image Processing 13*, 1(May 1980), 88–93. [regions] D.1.2 A.4.1

622. [Same80c] H. Samet, Deletion in two-dimensional quad trees, *Communications of the ACM 23*, 12(December 1980), 703–710. [points] D.2.3.2 A.7.1.5

623. [Same81a] H. Samet, An algorithm for converting rasters to quadtrees, *IEEE Transactions on Pattern Analysis and Machine Intelligence 3*, 1(January 1981), 93–95. [regions] D.1.2 A.4.2.1

624. [Same81b] H. Samet, Connected component labeling using quadtrees, *Journal of the ACM 28*, 3(July 1981), 487–501. [regions] A.5.1.2 A.5.1.3 A.9.2

625. [Same81c] H. Samet, Computing perimeters of images represented by quadtrees, *IEEE Transactions on Pattern Analysis and Machine Intelligence 3*, 6(November 1981), 683–687. [regions] A.5.2 A.9.2 A.9.3.3

626. [Same82a] H. Samet, Neighbor finding techniques for images represented by quadtrees, *Computer Graphics and Image Processing 18*, 1(January 1982), 37–57. [regions] A.3.2.1.1 A.3.2.1.2 A.3.2.3 A.5.1.2

627. [Same82b] H. Samet, Distance transform for images represented by quadtrees, *IEEE Transactions on Pattern Analysis and Machine Intelligence 4*, 3(May 1982), 298–303 (also University of Maryland Computer Science TR-780). [regions] A.9.2

628. [Same83a] H. Samet, A quadtree medial axis transform, *Communications of the ACM 26*, 9(September 1983), 680–693 (also corrigendum, *Communications of the ACM 27*, 2(February 1984), 151). [regions] A.8 A.9.3

629. [Same84a] H. Samet, Algorithms for the conversion of quadtrees to rasters, *Computer Vision, Graphics, and Image Processing 26*, 1(April 1984), 1–16. [regions] A.4.2.2

630. [Same84b] H. Samet, The quadtree and related hierarchical data structures, *ACM Computing Surveys 16*, 2(June 1984), 187–260. [general] D.P A.P

631. [Same85a] H. Samet, A top-down quadtree traversal algorithm, *IEEE Transactions on Pattern Analysis and Machine Intelligence 7*, 1(January 1985), 94–98. [regions] A.3.2.3 A.4.3.1 A.5.1.2 A.5.1.3 A.5.2 A.9.2

632. [Same85b] H. Samet, Reconstruction of quadtrees from quadtree medial axis transforms, *Computer Vision, Graphics, and Image Processing 29*, 3(March 1985), 311–328. [regions] A.9.3.3

633. [Same85c] H. Samet, Data structures for quadtree approximation and compression, *Communications of the ACM 28*, 9(September 1985), 973–993. [regions] A.8 A.8.2.2

634. [Same88a] H. Samet, Hierarchical representations of collections of small rectangles, *ACM Computing Surveys 20*, 4(December 1988), 271–309. [rectangles] D.P D.3.5.1.3

635. [Same89a] H. Samet, Neighbor finding in images represented by octrees, *Computer Vision, Graphics, and Image Processing 46*, 3(June 1989), 367–386. [volumes] A.3.3 A.3.4

636. [Same89b] H. Samet, Implementing ray tracing with octrees and neighbor finding, *Computers & Graphics 13*, 4(1989), 445–460 (also University of Maryland Computer Science TR-2204). [volumes] A.7.2

637. [Same90a] H. Samet, *The Design and Analysis of Spatial Data Structures*, Addison-Wesley, Reading, MA, 1990. [general] A.P A.1

638. [Same90b] H. Samet, *Applications of Spatial Data Structures: Computer Graphics, Image Processing, and GIS*, Addison-Wesley, Reading, MA, 1990. [general] D.P

639. [Same80d] H. Samet and A. Rosenfeld, Quadtree representations of binary images, *Proceedings of the Fifth International Conference on Pattern Recognition*, Miami Beach, December 1980, 815–818. [regions] D.P A.P

640. [Same84c] H. Samet, A. Rosenfeld, C. A. Shaffer, R. C. Nelson, and Y. G. Huang, Application of hierarchical data structures to geographical information systems: phase III, Computer Science TR-1457, University of Maryland, College Park, MD, November 1984. [general] D.1.5 D.4.2.4 A.1.2 A.6.6

641. [Same85d] H. Samet, A. Rosenfeld, C. A. Shaffer, R. C. Nelson, Y. G. Huang, and K. Fujimura, Application of hierarchical data structures to geographic information systems: phase IV, Computer Science TR-1578, University of Maryland, College Park, MD, December 1985. [general] A.4.2.3 A.6.3.3 A.6.5.3

642. [Same83b] H. Samet, A. Rosenfeld, C. A. Shaffer, and R. E. Webber, Quadtree region representation in cartography: experimental results, *IEEE Transactions on Systems, Man, and Cybernetics 13*, 6(November/December 1983), 1148–1154. [general]

643. [Same84d] H. Samet, A. Rosenfeld, C. A. Shaffer, and R. E. Webber, A geographic information system using quadtrees, *Pattern Recognition 17*, 6(November/December 1984), 647–656. [general] D.4.2.4 A.2.1.2 A.3.4.1 A.8.2.1

644. [Same85e] H. Samet and C. A. Shaffer, A model for the analysis of neighbor finding in pointer-based quadtrees, *IEEE Transactions on Pattern Analysis and Machine Intelligence 7*, 6(November 1985), 717–720. [regions] A.3.2.1.2

645. [Same87a] H. Samet, C. A. Shaffer, R. C. Nelson, Y. G. Huang, K. Fujimura, and A. Rosenfeld, Recent developments in linear quadtree-based geographic information systems, *Image and Vision Computing 5*, 3(August 1987), 187–197. [general] D.1.2 D.4.2.4 A.1.3 A.2.1.2 A.3.2.1.3 A.3.4.1 A.8.2.1

646. [Same86a] H. Samet, C. A. Shaffer, and R. E. Webber, The segment quadtree: a linear quadtree-based representation for linear features, in *Data Structures for Raster Graphics*, F. J. Peters, L. R. A. Kessener, and M. L. P. van Lierop, eds., Springer Verlag, Berlin, 1986, 91–123 (also *Proceedings of Computer Vision and Pattern Recognition 85*, San Francisco, June 1985, 385–389). [lines]

647. [Same86b] H. Samet, C. A. Shaffer, and R. E. Webber, Digitizing the plane with cells of non-uniform size, Computer Science TR-1619, University of Maryland, College Park, MD, January 1986. [lines] D.4.2.3.1 A.1.3

648. [Same87b] H. Samet, C. A. Shaffer, and R. E. Webber, Digitizing the plane with cells of non-uniform size, *Information Processing Letters 24*, 6(April 1987), 369–375. [lines] D.4.2.3.1 A.1.3

649. [Same84e] H. Samet and M. Tamminen, Experiences with new image component algorithms, in *Proceedings of the EUROGRAPHICS'84 Conference*, K. Bo and H. A. Tucker, eds., North-Holland, Amsterdam, 1984, 239–249. [volumes]

650. [Same85f] H. Samet and M. Tamminen, Computing geometric properties of images represented by linear quadtrees, *IEEE Transactions on Pattern Analysis and Machine Intelligence 7*, 2(March 1985), 229–240 (also University of Maryland Computer Science TR-1359). [regions] D.3.5.1.3 A.3.4.4 A.5.1.3 A.5.3 A.6.3.3

651. [Same85g] H. Samet and M. Tamminen, Bintrees, CSG trees, and time, *Computer Graphics 19*, 3(July 1985), 121–130 (also *Proceedings of the SIGGRAPH'85 Conference*, San Francisco, July 1985). [volumes] D.1.3 D.5.3 D.5.5 D.5.5.1.3 A.1.4 A.7.2.4

652. [Same90c] H. Samet and M. Tamminen, Approximating CSG trees of moving objects, *Visual Computer 6*, 1990 (also University of Maryland Computer Science TR-1472). [volumes] D.5.3 D.5.5 D.5.5.1.2 D.5.5.1.3

653. [Same86c] H. Samet and M. Tamminen, A general approach to connected component labeling of images, Computer Science TR-1649, University of Maryland, College Park, MD, August 1986 (also *Proceedings of Computer Vision and Pattern Recognition 86*, Miami Beach, June 1986, 312–318). [regions] A.5.1.1 A.5.1.3

654. [Same88b] H. Samet and M. Tamminen, Efficient component labeling of images of arbitrary dimension represented by linear bintrees, *IEEE Transactions on Pattern Analysis and Machine Intelligence 10*, 4(July 1988), 579–586. [volumes] D.1.4.1 D.3.5.1.3 D.5.2 A.1.3 A.3.4.4 A.4.2.3 A.4.6 A.5.1.2 A.5.1.3 A.6.3.3 A.9.2

655. [Same82c] H. Samet and R. E. Webber, On encoding boundaries with quadtrees, Computer Science TR-1162, University of Maryland, College Park, MD, February 1982. [lines] D.4.2.2 A.3.2.3

656. [Same84f] H. Samet and R. E. Webber, On encoding boundaries with quadtrees, *IEEE Transactions on Pattern Analysis and Machine Intelligence 6*, 3(May 1984), 365–369. [lines] D.4.2.2

657. [Same85i] H. Samet and R. E. Webber, Storing a collection of polygons using quadtrees, *ACM Transactions on Graphics 4*, 3(July 1985), 182–222 (also *Proceedings of Computer Vision and Pattern Recognition 83*, Washington, DC, June 1983, 127–132; and University of Maryland Computer Science TR-1372). [lines] D.4.2.3 D.4.3.3 A.1.3 A.7.2.2

658. [Same88c] H. Samet and R. E. Webber, Hierarchical data structures and algorithms for computer graphics. Part I. Fundamentals, *IEEE Computer Graphics and Applications 8*, 3(May 1988), 48–68. [general] D.P A.P A.6.3.3

659. [Same88d] H. Samet and R. E. Webber, Hierarchical data structures and algorithms for computer graphics. Part II. Applications, *IEEE Computer Graphics and Applications 8*, 4(July 1988), 59–75. [general] D.P A.P

660. [Same89c] H. Samet and R. E. Webber, A comparison of the space requirements of multi-dimensional quadtree-based file structures, *Visual Computer 5*, 6(December 1989), 349–359 (also University of Maryland Computer Science TR-1711). [regions] A.2.1.2

661. [Sand86] J. Sandor, Octree data structures and perspective imagery, *Computers & Graphics 9*, 4(1985), 393–405. [volumes]

662. [Sarn86] N. Sarnak and R. E. Tarjan, Planar point location using persistent search trees, *Communications of the ACM 29*, 7(July 1986), 669–679. [regions] D.3.2.4

663. [Saxe79] J. B. Saxe, On the number of range queries in k-space, *Discrete Applied Math 1*, 3(November 1979), 217–225. [points]

664. [Sche87] I. D. Scherson and E. Caspary, Data structures and the time complexity of ray tracing, *Visual Computer 3*, 4(December 1987), 201–213. [volumes] A.7.2.5

665. [Sche88] I. D. Scherson and E. Caspary, Multiprocessing for ray tracing: a hierarchical self-balancing approach, *Visual Computer 4*, 4(October 1988), 188–196. [volumes]

666. [Sche82] P. Scheuermann and M. Ouksel, Multidimensional B-trees for associative searching in database systems, *Information Systems 7*, 2(1982), 123–137. [points] D.2.8.2.3

667. [Schm86] F. J. M. Schmitt, B. A. Barsky, and W. H. Du, An adaptive subdivision method for surface-fitting from sampled data, *Computer Graphics 20*, 4(August 1986), 179–188 (also *Proceedings of the SIGGRAPH'86 Conference*, Dallas, August 1986). [surfaces] D.5.6

668. [Schm85] F. Schmitt and B. Gholzadeh, Adaptive polyhedral approximation of digitized surfaces, *Proceedings of SPIE—Computer Vision for Robots 595*, Cannes, France, December 1985, 101–108. [surfaces]

669. [Schw88] J. T. Schwartz and M. Sharir, A survey of motion planning and related geometric algorithms, *Artificial Intelligence 37*, 1–3(December 1988), 157–169. [regions] D.1.3 A.1.4

670. [Schw85] J. T. Schwartz, M. Sharir, and A. Siegel, An efficient algorithm for finding connected components in a binary image, Robotics Research Technical Report No. 38, New York University, New York, February 1985 (Revised July 1985). [regions] A.5.1.1

671. [Scot85] D. S. Scott and S. S. Iyengar, A new data structure for efficient storing of images, *Pattern Recognition Letters 3*, 3(May 1985), 211–214. [regions] D.1.2 A.1.3 A.9.3.4

672. [Scot86] D. S. Scott and S. S. Iyengar, TID—a translation invariant data structure for storing images, *Communications of the ACM 29*, 5(May 1985), 418–429. [regions] D.1.2 A.1.3 A.9.3.4

673. [Sedg83] R. Sedgewick, *Algorithms*, Addison-Wesley, Reading, MA, 1983. [general] A.5.1.1

674. [Seeg88] B. Seeger and H. P. Kriegel, Techniques for design and implementation of efficient spatial access methods, *Proceedings of the Fourteenth International Conference on Very Large Data Bases*, F. Bachillon and D. J. DeWitt, eds., Los Angeles, August 1988, 360–372. [points]

675. [Sell87] T. Sellis, N. Roussopoulos, and C. Faloutsos, The R$^+$-tree: a dynamic index for multi-dimensional objects, Computer Science TR-1795, University of Maryland, College Park, MD, February 1987. [rectangles] D.3.5.3

676. [Shaf85] C. A. Shaffer, personal communication, 1985. [regions] A.5.2

677. [Shaf86a] C. A. Shaffer, Application of alternative quadtree representations, Ph.D. dissertation, TR-1672, Computer Science Department, University of Maryland, College Park, MD, June 1986. [regions] D.1.2 D.3.5.2 D.5.2 A.4.2.3 A.6.3.3 A.8.2.3 A.9.3.1 A.9.3.4 ·

678. [Shaf86b] C. A. Shaffer, An empirical comparison of vectors, arrays, and quadtrees for representing geographic data, *Proceedings of the International Colloquium on the Construction and Display of Geoscientific Maps Derived from Databases*, Dinkelsbühl, West Germany, December 1986, 99–115. [general]

679. [Shaf88a] C. A. Shaffer, A formula for computing the number of quadtree node fragments created by a shift, *Pattern Recognition Letters 7*, 1(January 1988), 45–49. [regions] A.6.5.3

680. [Shaf87a] C. A. Shaffer and H. Samet, Optimal quadtree construction algorithms, *Computer Vision, Graphics, and Image Processing 37*, 3(March 1987), 402–419. [regions] D.1.2 D.5.2 A.4.2.3 A.6.3.3

681. [Shaf87b] C. A. Shaffer and H. Samet, An in-core hierarchical data structure organization for a geographic database, Computer Science TR 1886, University of Maryland, College Park, MD, July 1987. [regions] A.2.2

682. [Shaf87c] C. A. Shaffer, H. Samet, and R. C. Nelson, QUILT: a geographic information system based on quadtrees, Computer Science TR-1885.1, University of Maryland, College Park, MD, July 1987. [general] D.4.2.4 A.2.1.2 A.3.4.1 A.6.6 A.8.2.1

683. [Shaf88b] C. A. Shaffer and H. Samet, An algorithm to expand regions represented by linear quadtrees, *Image and Vision Computing 6*, 3(August 1988), 162–168. [regions] A.6.6

684. [Shaf88c] C. A. Shaffer and H. Samet, Set operations for unaligned linear quadtrees, Department of Computer Science TR 88–31, Virginia Polytechnic Institute and State University, Blacksburg, VA, September 1988 (also *Computer Vision, Graphics, and Image Processing*). [regions] A.6.3.3 A.6.5.3

685. [Shaf89] C. A. Shaffer and Q. F. Stout, Linear time distance transforms for quadtrees, Department of Computer Science TR 89–7, Virginia Polytechnic Institute and State University, Blacksburg, VA, 1989. [regions] A.9.2

686. [Sham78] M. I. Shamos, Computational geometry, Ph.D. dissertation, Department of Computer Science, Yale University, New Haven, CT, 1978. [general] D.4.3

687. [Sham75] M. I. Shamos and D. Hoey, Closest-point problems, *Proceedings of the Sixteenth Annual IEEE Symposium on the Foundations of Computer Science*, Berkeley, October 1975, 151–162. [points] D.4.3 A.6.3.2

688. [Sham76] M. I. Shamos and D. Hoey, Geometric intersection problems, *Proceedings of the Seventeenth Annual IEEE Symposium on the Foundations of Computer Science*, Houston, October 1976, 208–215. [points] D.3 D.3.2.4

689. [Shan87] M. A. Shand, Algorithms for corner stitched data-structures, *Algorithmica 2*, 1(1987), 61–80. [rectangles] D.3.4

690. [Shne81a] M. Shneier, Path-length distances for quadtrees, *Information Sciences 23*, 1(February 1981), 49–67. [regions] D.3.5.1.3 A.9.2

691. [Shne81b] M. Shneier, Calculations of geometric properties using quadtrees, *Computer Graphics and Image Processing 16*, 3(July 1981), 296–302. [regions] A.5.2 A.6.3.2

692.   [Shne81c] M. Shneier, Two hierarchical linear feature representations: edge pyramids and edge quadtrees, *Computer Graphics and Image Processing 17*, 3(November 1981), 211–224. [lines] D.1.3 D.4.2.1 A.1.4 A.7.1.2

693.   [Shne87] M. O. Shneier, R. Lumia, and M. Herman, Prediction-based vision for robot control, *Computer 20*, 8(August 1987), 46–55. [volumes]

694.   [Shpi87] M. Shpitalni, Relations and transformations between quadtree encoding and switching function representation, *Computer-Aided Design 19*, 5(June 1987), 266–272. [regions]

695.   [Silv81a] C. Silva, Alternative definitions of faces in boundary representation of solid objects, Technical Memorandum 36, Production Automation Project, University of Rochester, NY, 1981. [volumes] D.5.4

696.   [Silv79] Y. V. Silva Filho, Average case analysis of region search in balanced k-d trees, *Information Processing Letters 8*, 5(June 1979), 219–223. [points]

697.   [Silv81b] Y. V. Silva Filho, Optimal choice of discriminators in a balanced k-d binary search tree, *Information Processing Letters 13*, 2(November 1981), 67–70. [points]

698.   [Six88] H. W. Six and P. Widmayer, Spatial searching in geometric databases, *Proceedings of the Fourth IEEE International Conference on Data Engineering*, Los Angeles, February 1988, 496–503. [rectangles]

699.   [Six80] H. W. Six and D. Wood, The rectangle intersection problem revisited, *BIT 20*, 4(1980), 426–433. [rectangles] D.3.2.1

700.   [Six82] H. W. Six and D. Wood, Counting and reporting intersections of d-ranges, *IEEE Transactions on Computers 31*, 3(March 1982), 181–187. [rectangles] D.3.2.1

701.   [Sloa81] K. R. Sloan Jr., Dynamically quantized pyramids, *Proceedings of the Sixth International Joint Conference on Artificial Intelligence*, Vancouver, August 1981, 734–736. [points] D.2.8.1

702.   [Sloa79] K. R. Sloan Jr. and S. L. Tanimoto, Progressive refinement of raster images, *IEEE Transactions on Computers 28*, 11(November 1979), 871–874. [regions] A.8.3

703.   [Smit87] T. Smith, D. Peuquet, S. Menon, and P. Agarwal, A knowledge-based geographical information system, *International Journal of Geographical Information Systems 1*, 2(April-June 1987), 149–172. [regions]

704.   [Snyd87] J. M. Snyder and A. H. Barr, Ray tracing complex models containing surface tessellations, *Computer Graphics 21*, 4(July 1987), 119–128 (also *Proceedings of the SIGGRAPH'87 Conference*, Anaheim, July 1987). [volumes]

705.   [Sobh86] C. Sobhanpanah and I. O. Angell, Polygonal mesh and quad-tree display algorithms for nonconvex crystal structures, *Computers & Graphics 10*, 4(1986), 341–349. [regions]

706.   [Soln77] N. Solntseff and D. Wood, Pyramids: A data type for matrix representation in PASCAL, *BIT 17*, 3(1977), 344–350. [matrices]

707.   [Somm29] D. M. Y. Sommerville, *An Introduction to the Geometry of N Dimensions*, Methuen, London, 1929. [general]

708.   [Soto78] D. L. G. Sotomayor, Tessellation of triangles of variable precision as an economical representation for DTM's, *Proceedings of the Digital Terrain Models (DTM) Symposium*, St. Louis, May 1978, 506–515. [surfaces] D.5.6

709.   [Spee85] L. R. Speer, T. D. DeRose, and B. A. Barsky, A theoretical and empirical analysis of coherent ray tracing, in *Computer-Generated Images—The State of the Art*, N. Magnenat-Thalmann and D Thalmann, eds., Springer-Verlag, Tokyo, 1985, 11–25 (also *Proceedings of Graphics Interface '85*, Montreal, May 1985, 1–8). [volumes] A.7.3

710. [Sper85] G. Sperling, M. Landy, Y. Cohen, and M. Pavel, Intelligible encoding of ASL image sequences at extremely low information rates, *Computer Vision, Graphics, and Image Processing 31*, 3(September 1985), 335–391. [regions]

711. [Srih81] S. N. Srihari, Representation of three-dimensional digital images, *ACM Computing Surveys 13*, 1(December 1981), 399–424. [volumes] D.P A.P

712. [Sriv87] S. K. Srivastava and N. Ahuja, An algorithm for generating octrees from object silhouettes in perspective views, *Proceedings of the IEEE Computer Society Workshop on Computer Vision*, Miami Beach, November 1987, 363–365. [volumes] D.5.2 A.4.6

713. [Sten86] J. R. Stenstrom and C. I. Connolly, Building wire frames from multiple range views, *Proceedings of the IEEE International Conference on Robotics and Automation*, San Francisco, April 1986, 615–620. [volumes]

714. [Ston86] M. Stonebraker, T. Sellis, and E. Hanson, An analysis of rule indexing implementations in data base systems, *Proceedings of the First International Conference on Expert Database Systems*, Charleston, SC, April 1986, 353–364. [rectangles] D.3.5.3

715. [Stra69] V. Strassen, Gaussian elimination is not optimal, *Numerische Mathematik 13*, 4(August 1969), 354–356. [matrices] D.2.6.1

716. [Suth74] I. E. Sutherland, R. F. Sproull, and R. A. Schumacker, A characterization of ten hidden-surface algorithms, *ACM Computing Surveys 6*, 1(March 1974), 1–55. [surfaces] D.1.2 D.2.1 A.1.2 A.7 A.7.1

717. [Tamm81a] M. Tamminen, The EXCELL method for efficient geometric access to data, *Acta Polytechnica Scandinavica*, Mathematics and Computer Science Series No. 34, Helsinki, Finland, 1981. [regions] D.2.8.2.3 D.2.8.2.4 D.4.2.3.4 D.5.3 A.1.3

718. [Tamm81b] M. Tamminen, Order preserving extendible hashing and bucket tries, *BIT 21*, 4(1981), 419–435. [points] D.2.7

719. [Tamm82a] M. Tamminen, The extendible cell method for closest point problems, *BIT 22*, 1(1982), 27–41. [points]

720. [Tamm82b] M. Tamminen, Efficient spatial access to a data base, *Proceedings of the SIGMOD Conference*, Orlando, June 1982, 47–57. [lines] D.5.3

721. [Tamm82c] M. Tamminen and R. Sulonen, The EXCELL method for efficient geometric access to data, *Proceedings of the Nineteenth Design Automation Conference*, Las Vegas, June 1982, 345–351. [general]

722. [Tamm82d] M. Tamminen, Hidden lines using the EXCELL method, *Computer Graphics Forum 1*, 3(September 1982), 96–105. [lines]

723. [Tamm83] M. Tamminen, Performance analysis of cell based geometric file organizations, *Computer Vision, Graphics, and Image Processing 24*, 2(November 1983), 168–181. [regions] D.2.8.1

724. [Tamm84a] M. Tamminen, Comment on quad- and octtrees, *Communications of the ACM 27*, 3(March 1984), 248–249. [regions] D.1.4.1 A.1.3 A.2.1.2

725. [Tamm84b] M. Tamminen, Efficient geometric access to a multirepresentation geodatabase, *Geo-Processing 2*, 1984, 177–196. [lines] D.2.8.2.1

726. [Tamm84c] M. Tamminen, Encoding pixel trees, *Computer Vision, Graphics, and Image Processing 28*, 1(October 1984), 44–57. [regions] D.5.4 A.2.2

727. [Tamm84d] M. Tamminen, Metric data structures — an overview, Report-HTKK-TKO-A25, Helsinki University of Technology, Espoo, Finland, 1984. [points]

728. [Tamm85a] M. Tamminen, On search by address computation, *BIT 25*, 1(1985), 135–147. [points] D.2.6.2

729. [Tamm85b] M. Tamminen and F. W. Jansen, An integrity filter for recursive subdivision meshes, *Computers & Graphics 9*, 4(1985), 351–363. [surfaces] A.7.1.6

730.   [Tamm84e] M. Tamminen, O. Karonen, and M. Mäntylä, Ray-casting and block model conversion using a spatial index, *Computer-Aided Design 16*, 4(July 1984), 203–208. [volumes] A.7.2.2 A.7.2.3

731.   [Tamm84f] M. Tamminen, P. Koistinen, J. Hamalainen, O. Karonen, P. Korhonen, R. Raunio, and P. Rekola, Bintree: a dimension independent image processing system, Report-HTKK-TKO-C9, Helsinki University of Technology, Espoo, Finland, 1984. [volumes] D.5.5.1.1

732.   [Tamm84g] M. Tamminen and H. Samet, Efficient octree conversion by connectivity labeling, *Computer Graphics 18*, 3(July 1984), 43–51 (also *Proceedings of the SIG-GRAPH'84 Conference*, Minneapolis, July 1984). [volumes] D.5.4

733.   [Tang88] Z. Tang and S. Lu, A new algorithm for converting boundary representation to octree, in *Proceedings of the EUROGRAPHICS'88 Conference*, D. Duce and P. Jancene, eds., North-Holland, Amsterdam, 1988, 105–116. [volumes]

734.   [Tani76] S. Tanimoto, Pictorial feature distortion in a pyramid, *Computer Graphics and Image Processing 5*, 3(September 1976), 333–352. [regions] D.1.3 A.1.4

735.   [Tani80] S. Tanimoto and A. Klinger (eds.), *Structured Computer Vision*, Academic Press, New York, 1980. [general] D.P A.P

736.   [Tani75] S. Tanimoto and T. Pavlidis, A hierarchical data structure for picture process-ing, *Computer Graphics and Image Processing 4*, 2(June 1975), 104–119. [regions] D.1.3 D.2.8.1 A.1.4 A.8.3

737.   [Tani79] S. L. Tanimoto, Image transmission with gross information first, *Computer Graphics and Image Processing 9*, 1(January 1979), 72–76. [regions] A.8.3

738.   [Tarj75] R. E. Tarjan, Efficiency of a good but not linear set union algorithm, *Journal of the ACM 22*, 2(April 1975), 215–225. [general] A.5.1.1

739.   [Tarj83] R. E. Tarjan, Updating a balanced search tree in $O(1)$ rotations, *Information Processing Letters 16*, 5(June 1983), 253–257. [general] D.3.2.3

740.   [Tarj84a] R. E. Tarjan, *Data Structures and Network Algorithms*, SIAM, Philadelphia, 1984. [general] D.2.9

741.   [Tarj84b] R. E. Tarjan and J. van Leeuwen, Worst-case analysis of set union algorithms, *Journal of the ACM 31*, 2(April 1984), 245–281. [general] A.5.1.1

742.   [Thib87] W. C. Thibault and B. F. Naylor, Set operations on polyhedra using binary space partitioning trees, *Computer Graphics 21*, 4(July 1987), 153–162 (also *Proceed-ings of the SIGGRAPH'87 Conference*, Anaheim, July 1987). [volumes]

743.   [Thom83] A. L. Thomas, Geometric modeling and display primitives towards special-ized hardware, *Computer Graphics 17*, 3(July 1983), 299–310 (also *Proceedings of the SIGGRAPH'83 Conference*, Detroit, July 1983). [hardware] D.5.5

744.   [Tikk83] M. Tikkanen, M. Mäntylä, and M. Tamminen, GWB/DMS: a geometric data manager, in *Proceedings of the EUROGRAPHICS'83 Conference*, P. J. W. ten Hagen, ed., North-Holland, Amsterdam, 1983, 99–111. [volumes]

745.   [Tilo81] R. B. Tilove, Exploiting spatial and structural locality in geometric modeling, TM-38, Production Automation project, University of Rochester, NY, 1981. [volumes] D.5.5.1.2

746.   [Tilo84] R. B. Tilove, A null-object detection algorithm for constructive solid geometry, *Communications of the ACM 27*, 7(July 1984), 684–694. [volumes] D.5.5.1.2 D.5.5.2

747.   [Tobl86] W. Tobler and Z. T. Chen, A quadtree for global information storage, *Geo-graphical Analysis 18*, 4(October 1986), 360–371. [surfaces] D.1.4.1

748.   [Torr67] K. E. Torrance and E. M. Sparrow, Theory for off-specular reflection from roughened surfaces, *Journal of the Optical Society of America 57*, (September 1967), 1105–1114. [general] A.7.2.1

749. [Tous80] G. T. Toussaint, Pattern recognition and geometrical complexity, *Proceedings of the Fifth International Conference on Pattern Recognition*, Miami Beach, December 1980, 1324–1346. [points] D.P D.4 D.4.2.3.6 D.4.3

750. [Tous82] G. T. Toussaint and D. Avis, On a convex hull algorithm for polygons and its application to triangulation problems, *Pattern Recognition 15*, 1(1982), 23–29. [regions]

751. [Trop81] H. Tropf and H. Herzog, Multidimensional range search in dynamically balanced trees, *Angewandte Informatik 23*, 2(February 1981), 71–77. [points] D.2.7

752. [Tuck84a] L. W. Tucker, Control strategy for an expert vision system using quadtree refinement, *Proceedings of the Workshop on Computer Vision: Representation and Control*, Annapolis, MD, April 1984, 214–218. [regions] D.1.3 A.1.4

753. [Tuck84b] L. W. Tucker, Computer vision using quadtree refinement, Ph.D. dissertation, Department of Electrical Engineering and Computer Science, Polytechnic Institute of New York, Brooklyn, May 1984. [regions] A.3.2.3

754. [Uhr72] L. Uhr, Layered "recognition cone" networks that preprocess, classify, and describe, *IEEE Transactions on Computers 21*, 7(July 1972), 758–768. [regions] D.1.3 A.1.4

755. [Ullm82] J. D. Ullman, *Principles of Database Systems*, Second Edition, Computer Science Press, Rockville, MD, 1982. [general] D.3.1

756. [Unni88] A. Unnikrishnan, P. Shankar, and Y. V. Venkatesh, Threaded linear hierarchical quadtrees for computation of geometric properties of binary images, *IEEE Transactions on Software Engineering 14*, 5(May 1988), 659–665. [regions]

757. [Unni84] A. Unnikrishnan and Y. V. Venkatesh, On the conversion of raster to linear quadtrees, Department of Electrical Engineering, Indian Institute of Science, Bangalore, India, May 1984. [regions] A.4.2.1

758. [Unni87a] A. Unnikrishnan, Y. V. Venkatesh, and P. Shankar, Connected component labelling using quadtrees — a bottom-up approach, *Computer Journal 30*, 2(April 1987), 176–182. [regions]

759. [Unni87b] A. Unnikrishnan, Y. V. Venkatesh, and P. Shankar, Distribution of black nodes at various levels in a linear quadtree, *Pattern Recognition Letters 6*, 5(December 1987), 341–342. [regions]

760. [Vaid88] P. M. Vaidya, Geometry helps in matching, *Proceedings of the Twentieth Annual ACM Symposium on the Theory of Computing*, Chicago, May 1988, 422–425. [points] D.2.9

761. [Vais84] V. K. Vaishnavi, Multidimensional height-balanced trees, *IEEE Transactions on Computers 33*, 4(April 1984), 334–343. [points] D.2.4.1

762. [Vais80] V. Vaishnavi and D. Wood, Data structures for the rectangle containment and enclosure problems, *Computer Graphics and Image Processing 13*, 4(August 1980), 372–384. [rectangles] D.3.2.4

763. [Vais82] V. Vaishnavi and D. Wood, Rectilinear line segment intersection, layered segment trees and dynamization, *Journal of Algorithms 3*, 2(June 1982), 160–176. [rectangles] D.3.2.4

764. [Vand84] D. J. Vanderschel, Divided leaf octal trees, Research Note, Schlumberger-Doll Research, Ridgefield, CT, March 1984. [volumes] D.5.3 A.1.3

765. [vanL81] J. van Leeuwen and D. Wood, The measure problem for rectangular ranges in d-space, *Journal of Algorithms 2*, 3(September 1981), 282–300. [rectangles] D.3.3

766. [vanL86a] M. L. P. van Lierop, Geometrical transformations on pictures represented by leafcodes, *Computer Vision, Graphics, and Image Processing 33*, 1(January 1986), 81–98. [regions] A.6.3.3 A.6.5.2

767. [vanL86b] M. L. P. van Lierop, Intermediate data structures for display algorithms, *Data Structures for Raster Graphics*, F. J. Peters, L. R. A. Kessener, and M. L. P. van Lierop, eds., Springer Verlag, Berlin, 1986, 39–55. [regions]

768. [Vara84] T. Varady and M. J. Pratt, Design techniques for the definition of solid objects with free-form geometry, *Computer Aided Geometric Design 1* (1984), 207–225. [surfaces]

769. [Veen85] J. Veenstra and N. Ahuja, Octree generation from silhouette views of an object, *Proceedings of the International Conference on Robotics*, St. Louis, March 1985, 843–848. [volumes] D.5.2 A.4.6

770. [Veen86] J. Veenstra and N. Ahuja, Efficient octree generation from silhouettes, *Proceedings of Computer Vision and Pattern Recognition 86*, Miami Beach, June 1986, 537–542. [volumes] D.5.2 A.4.6

771. [Veen88] J. Veenstra and N. Ahuja, Line drawings of octree-represented objects, *ACM Transactions on Graphics 7*, 1(January 1988), 61–75. [volumes] D.5.4

772. [Voel77] H. B. Voelcker and A. A. G. Requicha, Geometric modeling of mechanical parts and processes, *IEEE Computer 10*, 12(December 1977), 48–57. [volumes] D.3.4 D.5.5

773. [VonH88] B. Von Herzen, Applications of surface networks to sampling problems in computer graphics, Ph.D. dissertation, Technical Report Caltech-CS-TR-88–15, Computer Science Department, California Institute of Technology, Pasadena, CA, 1988. [surfaces] D.5.6 D.5.8 A.7.1.6

774. [VonH87] B. Von Herzen and A. H. Barr, Accurate triangulations of deformed, intersecting surfaces, *Computer Graphics 21*, 4(July 1987), 103–110 (also *Proceedings of the SIGGRAPH'87 Conference*, Anaheim, July 1987). [surfaces] D.5.6 D.5.8 A.7.1.6

775. [Walk88] M. Walker, R. S. Lo, and S. F. Cheng, Hidden line detection in polytree representations, *Computers & Graphics 12*, 1(1988), 65–69. [volumes]

776. [Wall84] A. F. Wallis and J. R. Woodwark, Creating large solid models for NC toolpath verification, *Proceedings of CAD'84 Conference*, Butterworth, Guildford, Great Britain, 1984, 455–460. [volumes] D.5.5

777. [Wals85] T. R. Walsh, On the size of quadtrees generalized to d-dimensional binary pictures, *Computers and Mathematics with Applications 11*, 11(November 1985), 1089–1097. [volumes] D.1.5 A.1.2

778. [Wals88] T. R. Walsh, Efficient axis-translation of binary digital pictures by blocks in linear quadtree representation, *Computer Vision, Graphics, and Image Processing 41*, 3(March 1988), 282–292. [volumes] A.6.5.3

779. [Ward88] G. J. Ward, F. M. Rubinstein, and R. D. Clear, A ray tracing solution for diffuse interreflection, *Computer Graphics 22*, 4(August 1988), 85–92 (also *Proceedings of the SIGGRAPH'88 Conference*, Atlanta, August 1988). [volumes]

780. [Warn68] J. E. Warnock, A hidden line algorithm for halftone picture representation, Computer Science Department TR 4–5, University of Utah, Salt Lake City, May 1968. [regions] D.1.3 A.1.4 A.7.1 A.7.1.2

781. [Warn69a] J. E. Warnock, The hidden line problem and the use of halftone displays, in *Pertinent Concepts in Computer Graphics—Proceedings of the Second University of Illinois Conference on Computer Graphics*, M. Faiman and J. Nievergelt, eds., University of Illinois Press, Urbana, IL, March 1969, 154–163. [regions] A.7.1

782. [Warn69b] J. E. Warnock, A hidden surface algorithm for computer generated half tone pictures, Computer Science Department TR 4–15, University of Utah, Salt Lake City, June 1969. [regions] D.1.3 D.4.2.1 A.1.4 A.7.1.2

783. [Wats84] D. F. Watson, and G. M. Philip, Systematic triangulations, *Computer Vision, Graphics, and Image Processing 26*, 2(May 1984), 217–223. [regions] D.4.3.1 D.5.2 A.4.6

784. [Webb84] R. E. Webber, Analysis of quadtree algorithms, Ph.D. dissertation, TR-1376, Computer Science Department, University of Maryland, College Park, MD, March 1984. [lines] D.4.2.3 A.3.3.4 A.4.3.1 A.4.3.2 A.5.1.2

785. [Webb85] R. E. Webber, personal communication, 1985. [regions] A.3.2.1.2

786. **[Webb89] R. E. Webber and M. B. Dillencourt, Compressing quadtrees via common subtree merging, *Pattern Recognition Letters 9*, 3(April 1989), 193–200 (also University of Maryland Computer Science TR-2137). [regions]**

787. [Webe78] W. Weber, Three types of map data structures, their ANDs and NOTs, and a possible OR, in *Proceedings of the First International Advanced Study Symposium on Topological Data Structures for Geographic Information Systems*, G. Dutton, ed., Harvard Papers on Geographic Information Systems, 1978. [regions] A.2.1.1

788. [Wegh84] H. Weghorst, G. Hooper, and D. P. Greenberg, Improved computational methods for ray tracing, *ACM Transactions on Graphics 3*, 1(January 1984), 547–554 [volumes] A.7.2.1 A.7.2.2

789. [Weid78] B. W. Weide, Statistical methods in algorithm design and analysis, CMU-CS-78-142, Computer Science Department, Carnegie-Mellon University, Pittsburgh, August 1978. [general] D.3.2.2 D.3.2.4

790. [Weil85] K. Weiler, Edge-based data structures for solid modeling in a curved-surface environment, *IEEE Computer Graphics and Applications 5*, 1(January 1985), 21–40. [volumes] D.5.4

791. [Weil86] K. Weiler, Topological structures for geometric modeling, Ph.D. dissertation, Department of Computer and Systems Engineering, Rensselaer Polytechnic Institute, Troy, NY, August 1986. [volumes] D.5.4

792. [Weil77] K. Weiler and P. Atherton, Hidden surface removal using polygon area sorting, *Computer Graphics 11*, 2(Summer 1977), 214–222 (also *Proceedings of the SIGGRAPH'77 Conference*, San Jose, CA, July 1977). [volumes] A.7.1 A.7.1.3 A.7.3

793. [Weng87] J. Weng and N. Ahuja, Octrees of objects in arbitrary motion: representation and efficiency, *Computer Vision, Graphics, and Image Processing 39*, 2(August 1987), 167–185. [volumes] D.5.5.1.3 A.6.5.1

794. [Wern87] K. H. Werner, S. Yie, F. M. Ottliczky, H. B. Prince, and H. Diebel, ME CAD geometry construction, dimensioning, hatching, and part structuring, *Hewlett-Packard Journal 38*, 5(May 1987), 16–29. [points]

795. [Whit82] M. White, N-trees: large ordered indexes for multi-dimensional space, US Bureau of the Census, Statistical Research Division, Washington, DC, 1982. [points] D.1.3 D.2.7 A.1.4

796. [Whit80] T. Whitted, An improved illumination model for shaded display. *Communications of the ACM 23*, 6(June 1980), 343–349. [surfaces] A.7.2 A.7.2.1 A.7.2.2 A.7.2.5 A.7.3

797. [Will78] D. E. Willard, Balanced forests of k–d* trees as a dynamic data structure, Aiken Computation Lab TR-23–78, Harvard University, Cambridge, 1978. [points] D.2.4.1

798. [Will82] D. E. Willard, Polygon retrieval, *SIAM Journal on Computing 11*, 1(February 1982), 149–165. [points] D.2.3 D.2.3.3

799. [Will85a] D. E. Willard, New data structures for orthogonal range queries, *SIAM Journal on Computing 14*, 1(February 1985), 232–253. [points]

800. [Will85b] P. Willis and D. Milford, Browsing high definition colour pictures, *Computer Graphics Forum 4*, 3(September 1985), 203–208. [hardware]

801. [Wise84] D. S. Wise, Representing matrices as quadtrees for parallel processors (extended abstract), *ACM SIGSAM Bulletin 18*, 3(August 1984), 24–25. [matrices]

802. [Wise85] D. S. Wise, Representing matrices as quadtrees for parallel processors, *Information Processing Letters 20*, 4(May 1985), 195–199. [matrices] D.2.6.1

803. [Wise86] D. S. Wise, Parallel decomposition of matrix inversion using quadtrees, *Proceedings of the IEEE International Conference on Parallel Processing*, St. Charles, IL, August 1986, 92–99. [matrices]

804. [Wise87a] D. S. Wise, Matrix algebra and applicative programming, in *Functional Programming Languages and Computer Architecture Theoretical Aspects of Computer Science*, G. Kahn, ed., Portland, OR, 1987, 134–153 (Lecture Notes in Computer Science 274, Springer-Verlag, Berlin, 1987). [matrices] D.2.6.1

805. [Wise87b] D. S. Wise and J. Franco, Costs of quadtree representation of non-dense matrices, Technical Report No. 229, Computer Science Department, University of Indiana, Bloomington, Indiana, October 1987. [matrices] D.2.6.1

806. [Witt83] I. H. Witten and B. Wyvill, On the generation and use of space-filling curves, *Software—Practice and Experience 13*, 6(June 1983), 519–525. [regions] D.1.3 D.2.7 A.1.4

807. [Wong85] E. K. Wong and K. S. Fu, A hierarchical-orthogonal-space approach to collision-free path planning, *IEEE Journal of Robotics and Automation 2*, 1(March 1986), 42–53. [volumes]

808. [Woo85] T. C. Woo, A combinatorial analysis of boundary data structure schemata, *IEEE Computer Graphics and Applications 5*, 3(March 1985), 19–27. [volumes] D.5.4

809. [Wood82a] J. R. Woodwark, The explicit quad tree as a structure for computer graphics, *Computer Journal 25*, 2(May 1982), 235–238. [regions] A.2.1.1

810. [Wood84] J. R. Woodwark, Compressed quad trees, *Computer Journal 27*, 3(August 1984), 225–229. [regions]

811. [Wood86] J. R. Woodwark, Generating wireframes from set-theoretic solid models by spatial division, *Computer-Aided Design 18*, 6(July/August 1986), 307–315. [volumes] D.5.5

812. [Wood80] J. R. Woodwark and K. M. Quinlan, The derivation of graphics from volume models by recursive subdivision of the object space, *Proceedings Computer Graphics 80 Conference*, Online Publishers, London, 1980, 335–343. [volumes] D.5.5 D.5.5.1.2

813. [Wood82b] J. R. Woodwark and K. M. Quinlan, Reducing the effect of complexity on volume model evaluation, *Computer-aided Design 14*, 2(March 1982), 89–95. [volumes] D.5.5 D.5.5.1.2

814. [Wu82] A. Y. Wu, T. H. Hong, and A. Rosenfeld, Threshold selection using quadtrees, *IEEE Transactions on Pattern Analysis and Machine Intelligence 4*, 1(January 1982), 90–94. [regions]

815. [Wulf71] W. A. Wulf, D. B. Russell, and A. N. Habermann, BLISS: a language for systems programming, *Communications of the ACM 14*, 12(December 1971), 780–790. [general] L

816. [Wyvi85] G. Wyvill and T. L. Kunii, A functional model for constructive solid geometry, *Visual Computer 1*, 1(July 1985), 3–14. [volumes] D.5.3 D.5.5 D.5.5.2 A.7.2.2 A.7.2.3 A.7.2.4

817. [Wyvi86] G. Wyvill, T. L. Kunii, and Y. Shirai, Space division for ray tracing in CSG, *IEEE Computer Graphics and Applications 6*, 4(April 1986), 28–34. [volumes] D.5.5.2 A.7.2.2

818. [Yahi86] H. Yahia, Analyse des structures de donné arborescentes représentant des images, Thèse de docteur de troisième cycle, Université de Paris-Sud, Paris, December 1986. [regions]

819. [Yama84] K. Yamaguchi, T. L. Kunii, K. Fujimura, and H. Toriya, Octree-related data structures and algorithms, *IEEE Computer Graphics and Applications 4*, 1(January 1984), 53–59. [volumes] D.1.4.1 D.5.2 A.4.6 A.6.5.3 A.7.1.4

820. [Yau84] M. Yau, Generating quadtrees of cross-sections from octrees, *Computer Vision, Graphics, and Image Processing 27*, 2(August 1984), 211–238. [volumes] A.7.1.4

821. [Yau83] M. Yau and S. N. Srihari, A hierarchical data structure for multidimensional digital images, *Communications of the ACM 26*, 7(July 1983), 504–515. [volumes] D.1.3 D.5.2 D.5.3 A.1.4 A.2.1.2 A.4.2.3 A.4.6

822. [Yerr83] M. A. Yerry and M. S. Shephard, A modified quadtree approach to finite element mesh generation, *IEEE Computer Graphics and Applications 3*, 1(January/February 1983), 39–46. [finite element] D.1.3 A.1.4

823. [Ziav88] S. G. Ziavras and N. A. Alexandridis, Improved algorithms for translation of pictures represented by leaf codes, *Image and Vision Computing 6*, 1(February 1988), 13–20. [regions]

NAME AND
CREDIT INDEX

SUBJECT INDEX

All italicized page numbers denote the presence of a definition.

Continued from p. iv

Figures 3.1 through 3.6, 3.10 through 3.16, 3.19, and 3.23 through 3.29 are from H. Samet, Hierarchical representations of collections of small rectangles, *ACM Computing Surveys 20*, 4 (December 1988), 271–309. Reprinted by permission of ACM.

Figures 4.12, 4.16, 4.20 throuh 4.22, and 4.37 are from H. Samet and R. E. Webber, Storing a collection of polygons using quadtrees, *ACM Transactions on Graphics 4*, 3 (July 1985), 182–222. Reprinted by permission of ACM.

Figures 4.17 and 4.18 are from H. Samet, C. A. Shaffer, and R. E. Webber, Digitizing the plane with cells of non-uniform size, *Information Processing Letters 24*, 6 (April 1987), 369–375. Reprinted by permission of Elsevier Science Publishers.

Figures 4.23 through 4.27, 4.31, 4.33, and 4.35 are from R. C. Nelson and H. Samet, A consistent hierarchical representation for vector data, *Computer Graphics 20*, 4 (August 1986), 197–206. Reprinted by permission of ACM.

Figures 5.1 and 5.24 are from H. Samet and R. E. Webber, Hierarchical data structures and algorithms for computer graphics. Part II. Applications, *IEEE Computer Graphics and Applications 8*, 4 (July 1988), 59–75. © IEEE 1988. Reprinted by permission of IEEE.

Figures 5.11 and 5.13 through 5.17 are from H. Samet and M. Tamminen, Bintrees, CSG trees, and time, *Computer Graphics 19*, 3 (July 1985), 121–130. Reprinted by permission of ACM.